New Directions in
Semantics

Cognitive Science Series

Collections

1. Reasoning and Discourse Processes   *T. Myers, K. Brown and B. McGonigle (eds), 1986*
2. New Directions in Semantics   *E. LePore (ed.), 1987*

Monographs

Agreement and Anaphora   *P. Bosch, 1983*

New Directions in Semantics

edited by

ERNEST LEPORE
Rutgers University
New Brunswick
New Jersey, USA

1987

ACADEMIC PRESS
Harcourt Brace Jovanovich, Publishers
London   Orlando   New York   San Diego   Austin
Boston   Sydney   Tokyo   Toronto

ACADEMIC PRESS INC. (LONDON) LTD
24/28 Oval Road
London NW1

United States Edition published by
ACADEMIC PRESS INC.
Orlando, Florida 32887

British Library Cataloguing in Publication Data

New directions in semantics.—(Cognitive
science series)
1. Semantics
I. LePore, Ernest   II. Series
412   P325

ISBN 0-12-444040-1
ISBN 0-12-444041-X (Pbk)

Printed in Great Britain by
St Edmundsbury Press, Bury St Edmunds, Suffolk

Contributors

Richard Grandy *Department of Philosophy, Rice University, PO Box 1892, Houston, Texas 77251, USA*

Anil Gupta *Department of Philosophy, University of Illinois, PO Box 4348, Chicago, IL 60680, USA*

Gilbert Harman *Department of Philosophy, Princeton University, Princeton, New Jersey 08854, USA*

James Higginbotham *Department of Linguistics and Philosophy, Massachusetts Institute of Technology, Cambridge, Massachusetts 02139, USA*

Jaakko Hintikka *Department of Philosophy, Florida State University, Tallahassee, FL 32306, USA*

Asa Kasher *Department of Philosophy, Tel-Aviv University, Tel-Aviv 69978, Israel*

Jerrold J Katz *Ph.D. Programs in Philosophy and Linguistics, Graduate School University Center, CUNY, New York, NY 10031, USA*

Barry Loewer *Department of Philosophy, University of South Carolina, Columbia, SC 29228, USA*

Ernest LePore *Department of Philosophy, Faculty of Arts and Sciences, Rutgers University, Davison Hall, Douglass Campus, New Brunswick, New Jersey 08903, USA*

William G Lycan *Department of Philosophy, University of North Carolina, Chapel Hill, North Carolina 27514, USA*

Robert May *Program in Cognitive Science, School of Social Science, University of California, Irvine, California, USA*

Francis Jeffrey Pelletier *Department of Computing Science, Faculty of Science, 3–38 Assiniboia Hall, University of Alberta, Edmonton, Canada*

Barry Richards *University of Edinburgh, Centre for Cognitive Science, 2 Buccleuch Place, Edinburgh, EH8 9LW, Scotland*

Stephen Schiffer *Department of Philosophy, University of Arizona, Tucson, Arizona 85721, USA*

Lenhart K Schubert *Department of Computing Science, Faculty of Science, 3–38 Assiniboia Hall, University of Alberta, Edmonton, Canada*

For Donald and Marcia

Contents

Editors' Foreword

Cognitive science is the field of study marked off by the common concerns of artificial intelligence, linguistics, philosophy and psychology. The depth and richness of these mutual concerns suggests that certain issues may be essentially interdisciplinary. Nowhere is this clearer than at the intersection of cognition and language, where recent attempts to construct suitable formal theories have had to bring together different theoretical paradigms. The effect has been that the problems in one discipline have become those of another.

Cognitive science embraces a wide variety of topics, including parsing, discourse analysis, problem solving, language acquisition, concept formation, mental representation, semantics, cognitive modelling and visual processing. An interdisciplinary approach to these issues is committed to integrating, or perhaps synthesizing, relevant specialist theories with a view to revealing new horizons. The *Cognitive Science Series* aims to provide both a stimulus and a forum for relevant research. The intention is to encourage work which is either explicitly interdisciplinary or offers results likely to be of interdisciplinary interest. Since cognitive science is at an early stage of development, it is important to maintain the broadest possible perspective and hence, contributions to any aspect of the subject are invited.

Collections

To facilitate the growth of this multi-faceted subject the Series will include a 'Sub-series' of collections devoted to issues of topical interest. Since these issues typically involve a wide spectrum of expertise, it is felt that volumes of selected papers may be particularly appropriate and useful. The Series will seek to publish such collections on a regular basis and would welcome proposals from prospective editors.

Monographs

As cognitive science matures, there will be an ever increasing need to meet the special concerns of the community. At the moment these concerns have yet to take a definite shape, and it is hoped that the Series will in the meantime provide a focus for enquiry. Speculative monographs would be entirely appropriate, as would more empirical studies. In general the objective is to canvas broadly to allow the field to impose its character on the Series, thereby contributing to its definition.

ACKNOWLEDGEMENTS

On Semantics (Chapter 1) first appeared in *Linguistics Inquiry* 16:4 (1985) and is reprinted with permission of MIT Press. The publishers wish to thank the Estate of Edith Wharton for permission to reproduce material which appears in Chapter 9. Tenses, Temporal Quantifiers and Semantic Innocence (Chapter 11) first appeared in E. LePore (Ed), *Truth and Interpretation*. Oxford: Basil Blackwell (1986) and is reprinted with kind permission.

Introduction: New Directions in Semantics

E. LEPORE

Rutgers University
New Brunswick
New Jersey, USA

Recently, the field of semantic research has been characterized by the appearance of numerous new theoretical proposals. Each of these follows a different approach, but most have not been shown to be superior to, in competition with, or even distinct from the others. The problem here is that all of us who are professionally involved with the study of language are frequently faced with choices about what to read, what to teach, how to do research, and of course what to believe—choices which cannot be made intelligently without a clear understanding of the relationships, antagonistic or otherwise, between the various semantic theories. As a result, our choices are less informed, and probably more negative, than they used to be.

Given this situation, a systematic investigation of the interrelationships of the current semantic proposals seems clearly in order. To this end, I have divided the contemporary semantic scene into several somewhat rough and ready divisions, and have asked contributors, while acting as either spokesperson or critic, to answer as many of the following questions as possible: (1) What are the primary data for the semantic approach(es) your contribution investigates? To what extent and in what way do you think semantic accounts should involve describing, predicting or explaining this data? Is there only one correct semantic interpretation for each set of data? If so, what criteria do you use to decide among competing analyses? Do you distinguish between semantic competence and semantic performance? (2) Does the approach (or approaches) you consider involve statements cast in some formal language? If so, is this formalism empirically significant? If not, is the approach in principle empirically unformalizable? (3) Which aspects of the approach are empirically falisifiable? What sort of empirical evidence is relevant? What would it take to increase the falsifiability of your approach? (4) Which of the claims made by the approach(es) you consider do you find the most significant and distinctive? What are the problem areas? Where does further research seem necessary? (5) How would you characterize the relationship of the approach(es) you most fully investigate to others? Which aspects make it (i) competitive with, (ii) superior to, (iii) inferior to, or (iv) combinable with these other approaches? It was my hope that each (or most of the) contributions would focus on one of a few prominent approaches to semantics for natural language, but would include as much discussion as possible of the nature of its disagreements and points of contact with others. I believe that a careful reading of the articles which follow will bear out that this goal has been successfully met in this volume. This sort of comparative evaluation of semantic theories should channel research in fruitful directions and increase collaboration between scholars in philosophy, psychology, linguistics, computer science and cognitive science. I believe that the articles which follow are a step toward that goal. Informed choices are not based solely on presentations of problems and proposed solutions for them, but instead on critical evaluations of these proposals as well. Many of the articles which follow are intended to serve this purpose alone. The reader cannot complain at a lack of critical commentary.

I wish to thank Academic Press for their patience and help in putting this volume together. I also would like to thank Barry Richards and Francesca Bertelli for their help. Loretta Mazlen Mandel, who continues to be the best of all imaginable assistants, I cannot thank enough.

Ernest LePore
Rutgers University

1

On Semantics

James Higginbotham

Department of Linguistics and Philosophy
Massachusetts Institute of Technology

In this article I will formulate and partly develop one conception of semantic inquiry in generative linguistics. In conjunction with specific applications, I will address questions about domains of investigation, the data in those domains that ought to be accounted for, and their characteristic forms of explanation. Much of the semantic discussion will require syntactic assumptions that are not defended here. However, I believe that these assumptions are not the only ones out of which the general point of view would emerge.

DATA AND EXPLANATIONS

If it is an aim of linguistic theory to characterize those systems of human linguistic knowledge that result from native endowment and the ambient environment, then semantic theory, as a chapter of linguistics, will be concerned with those aspects of meaning that emerge in the course of normal maturation of the faculty for language. These aspects will be independent of context; that is, they will be determined by the design features of human language, and not by the way language is put to use. Perhaps nothing at all that people say has its meaning wholly independently of context. It does not follow that semantic theory has little to say, or that

1

NEW DIRECTIONS IN SEMANTICS

ISBN 0-12-444040-1
0-12-444041-X (Pbk)

it is in any way intrinsically incomplete. On the contrary, it is only through the context-independent features of meaning that we know what aspects of a context to take as relevant in the first place to the interpretation of the utterances around us.

Theoretical questions arise in linguistics whenever we find a realm where we know far more than we are taught. By this standard, as Hornstein (1984) emphasizes, the semantics of complex expressions raises questions of the same type as those that occur in phonology and in syntax. Very likely the same considerations apply also to lexical semantics, in the sense that the appearance of a word in a restricted number of settings suffices to determine its position in the language as a whole. My first concern here will be to make some of these questions of semantics explicit.

In much the same way as the data for syntax include observations about sentencehood and those of morphology include the pronunciation and significantly recurring features of complex words, the data for semantics certainly include observations about the meanings of sentences. These are obvious facts about what things mean, known to native speakers, that an adequate semantic theory must have among its consequences. As Donald Davidson especially has emphasized, the *disquotational* truths—that is, statements like (1)—are already a rich source of material (Davidson, 1978, 1984):

(1) *John saw Mary* means that John saw Mary.

They set a fundamental semantic problem, namely that of showing how a string of words under a grammatical description constitutes a sentence with a definite meaning. Of course, Davidson ultimately believes that statements like (1) are best replaced for theoretical purposes by what we might call *directives* for theory construction, and specifically for the construction of a theory of truth. The directive corresponding to (1) would be (2):

(2) Make your theory such that it is provable that:
     John saw Mary is true if and only if John saw Mary.

I will follow Davidson in this view. However, I will freely use simple statements like (1) in discussion. Application of the theory to (1) itself, and particularly to the question of the semantic status of the *that*-clause, might proceed as in Higginbotham (1984a).

Directives like (2) are assumed for expressions of other categories than that of declarative sentences, with the notions appropriate for those categories used in place of that of truth. It will be part of semantic theory, for example, to show both that the expression *Mary's mother* refers to Mary's mother (if it refers to anything) and how the individual words, and their specific mode of combination, bring this about. The theory of the context-independent aspects of truth and reference, flowing from the interpretation of the combinatorial devices of language, forms a significant chapter of semantics. The categories of expressions that have meaning are not limited to the single category of sentences.

In generative syntax, as formulated in Chomsky (1957), one addresses the problem of explicitly defining, for given natural languages *L,* the notion 'sentence of *L.*' The native speaker of *L* knows what the sentences of *L* are; the linguist, if successful, reveals something of the nature of the native speaker's knowledge, by constructing a *grammar* of *L.* Of the first significance in this enterprise is that a datum to the effect that something is *not* a sentence constrains grammar equally with a datum to the effect that something *is* a sentence. Similarly, I think, the data of semantics should be seen in both their positive and their negative aspects: for any given expression, that it *does* mean *X,* or *can* mean *X,* and that it *does not* mean *Y,* or *cannot* mean *Y,* are facts to be deduced in semantic theory. A standard picture of a language as a syntax and semantics, for example as outlined in Lewis (1975), contains both of these aspects. Sentences or their structural descriptions are paired with meanings, or with ranges of meaning, so that what is excluded from the range of meaning of a sentence comprises those things that it does not mean (Lewis, 1975, p. 3). However, I think that something is missing from Lewis's picture, which I will endeavor to bring out by example.

Consider the facts in (3):

(3 a) *The men told the women to vote for each other* can mean that the men told each of women to vote for the other woman.

  (b) *The men told the women to vote for each other* cannot mean that each of the men told the women to vote for the other man.

  (c) *The men told the women to vote for each other* cannot mean that each of the men told the women he would vote for the other man.

(3a–c) should all be deduced in semantic theory. Let us consider how these deductions might be carried out.

In the syntactic framework assumed here, roughly following the lines of Chomsky (1981), linguistic objects are represented at the four distinct levels of *D-Structure, S-Structure, Phonetic Form* (PF), and *Logical Form* (LF). Whatever the nature of LF, it is supposed that all grammatically determined information that is relevant to interpretation is to be found there. The levels of S-Structure and LF, where understood elements are explicitly represented, will chiefly occupy us (for the following discussion, we need not distinguish S-Structure from LF). The S-Structure representation of the sentence in question is as shown in (4):

(4)   [[the men] told [the women][PRO to vote for [each other]]]

If in this structure we assign antecedence as in (5) (following the method of Higginbotham (1983a)),

(5)   [[the men] told [the women][PRO to vote for [each other]]]

then it is up to semantic theory to show that (5) means that the men told each of the women to vote for the other woman. Demonstration of this proposition falls naturally into two parts: first, the account of the structures (6),

(6)   NP told NP [(that) S][1]

and second, the account of the anaphoric relations shown (see below, and Higginbotham (1984a), for a sketch). The datum (3a) will then follow.

How is (3b) to be deduced? Our account proceeds in this way. First, the structure (7) is ungrammatical in English:

(7)   [[the men] told [the women][PRO to vote for [each other]]]

The anaphor, a direct object of the lower clause, does not have its antecedent within that clause. But (7) is the structure that would have to be assigned to the sentence, were it to mean that each of the men told the women to vote for the other man. Therefore, (3b) follows.

Semantic theory applies to (7) exactly as it applies to (5). In a language with 'long-distance' reciprocals, there would be a *grammatical* structure like (7), expressing precisely the meaning that the English sentence would be able to express if (7) were not ungrammatical. Similarly, in a language for which the understood subject PRO of the embedded clause could be related to the subject NP *the men,* as in (8) (ungrammatical in English),

(8)   [[the men] told [the women][PRO to vote for [each other]]]

the word-for-word translation of *The men told the women to vote for each other* could mean that each man told the women he would vote for the other man, which the English sentence cannot; the ungrammaticality of (8) is the basis for (3c).

Here, then, is what I think is missing from Lewis's picture. In that picture, sentences have various ranges of meaning, and some are meaningless, but nonsentences do not have any meanings. However, the last statement is false to natural languages: nonsentences must have definite meanings, as full-blooded as those of ordinary sentences, if the source of their intuitive uninterpretability (or merely partial interpretability) is just the violation of a rule of formal grammar.

In Higginbotham (1984a) I suggested that it was a misperception of the relation between syntax and semantics to suppose that syntax is simply the theory of well-formedness, and semantics, taking the results of syntax as given, the theory of the meanings of well-formed expressions. That expressions that are well-formed can have definite interpretations was illustrated by the example (9), cited in Davidson:

(9)   The child seems sleeping.

This and similar examples already suffice to show that a theory of meaning that limits itself to the well-formed expressions cannot be correct. However, the thesis just advanced about (3) has still stronger implications.

If we enlarge the realm of semantic inquiry beyond the piecemeal discussion of individual languages, to raise the epistemological question of the acquisition of language by human children under normal conditions, then we shall, I believe, be led to construct semantic theory for human language in such a way that a variety of expressions that do not, by ordinary standards, 'mean anything' are seen to have fixed interpretations, deducible from general principles that connect form and meaning. The reasons for this are twofold. First, there is the variety of meaning that results in different languages from replacing words one-to-one with their translations; and second, the most fundamental principles of semantics are so remote from the data available to the child (situations of utterance, the behavior of other speakers, etc.) that it is quite plausible to suppose that these principles vary minimally or not at all from language to language, the differences that show up being attributable to local syntactic conditions.

Our discussion of (3c) already illustrates the point. The Italian sentence (10)

(10)   Gli uomini dissero alle donne   di votare gli uni   per gli altri.
        the men   told   (to) the women to vote .the one (man) for the other

does indeed mean that each of the men told the women that he would vote for the other man (thanks to Alessandra Giorgi for the example, and for discussion). The reason is that the understood subject PRO in the Italian sentence can be controlled by the matrix subject *gli uomini* (as is clear from other examples). Thus, antecedence is assigned as in (11), where locality conditions are observed:

(11)   [[gli uomini] . . . [PRO . . . [gli uni per gli altri]]

English disallows the comparable assignment.

Long-distance reciprocals are not clearly attested in natural languages, to my knowledge.[2] But long-distance reflexives are, as in Icelandic (Thráinsson (1979)). The analogue of (12) in Icelandic is fully grammatical and means that John wishes that Mary would visit him, John:

(12)   John wishes Mary would visit himself.

Now, do children learning Icelandic grasp a rule of interpretation that English-speaking children do not? This seems implausible. We can suppose instead that Icelandic children learn about the lexical items of Icelandic exactly what English-speaking children learn about their respective English translations, the sole difference between them being that English-speaking children assume a condition that implies that reflexive forms have local antecedents, and Icelandic children (because translations of (12) and the like occur as part of their linguistic experience) do not. The principles that distinguish English from Icelandic in this regard are then syntactic, not semantic.

Generalizing, it is suggested that data of the form shown in (13) are to be deduced from the properties of LF as shown in (14),

(13) S can mean that p.
(14)   There is an LF-representation Σ for S such that Σ means that p.

and that data of the form shown (15) are to be explained by formal arguments of the structure (16):

(15) S cannot mean that p.
(16)   Every derivation assigning an LF-representation Σ to S such that Σ means that p is ungrammatical.

Furthermore, where there is no failure on the part of the vocabulary of S to mean that p, there will actually be an ungrammatical derivation with a Σ that means that p. In the cases discussed in this article, Σ itself will be ungrammatical.

The representations Σ may be ungrammatical in some or all grammars. For the explanation to be satisfactory, the basis for the ungrammaticality of the Σ either must be universal, and so supplied by the language learner, or, if particular, must be traceable to the conditions of experience in the languages in question.

The burden for the articulation of semantic theory is thus shifted to LF. Modulo the shift, explanations of data such as (13) in the manner of (14) are of course commonplace in linguistic theory; they are characteristic of the postulation of *structural ambiguities,* which are visible especially when S can mean either *p* or *q,* and *p* and *q* are conspicuously different (very often, the exact working-out of the semantics may be waived, since it is obvious that it will require no special additions to what must be done already for unambiguous sentences). Part of my point, then, is that structural ambiguities are involved in data of the kind in (15) as well as in data of the kind in (13).

Chomsky (1984) has emphasized that, in his view, the *objects* of linguistic theory are best taken to be the grammatical structures, not their spoken forms, noting that this conception is something of a departure from the expressed point of view in Chomsky (1957), cited earlier. For this reason, to speak of 'structurally ambiguous sentences' can be misleading, as though the grammar were merely a device for classifying sentences; it would be better to talk of homonymous syntactic structures. No one supposes that English [pʰēšənts] is a word with two interpretations, one for a trait of behavior and one for persons treated by physicians. If we used the word *sentence* in the way that we customarily use *word,* then we should say of the classic examples, such as *Flying planes can be dangerous,* not that they are single sentences that are ambiguous, but rather that they constitute two sentences that happen to sound alike.

I have spoken of what seems to be an omission from the discussion of Lewis (1975). I am not certain that it affects one philosophical thesis that he formulates there, concerning the conditions under which languages belong to certain human populations. Lewis speaks of sentences as 'strings of signs or marks,' suggesting that only what is heard belongs to the language (on this view, the silent PRO of (4), for example, would have no place). He also expresses the view that the grammar for a given *L* is indeterminate, except insofar as it is tested by its consequences for the class of sentence-and-meaning pairs. Since this view directly contradicts the idea that the grammatical structures are the object of theory, it seems that the omission is a matter of principle.

On the conception advanced here, the central statements of semantic theory must have the character of empirical laws. Under the conditions of my experience, the reciprocal sentence in (3) came to have within its range of meaning that the men told each of the women to vote for the other women; and anyone who had had my experience would be able to mean that by it too. Inversely, if I had had experience comparable to that of the typical Italian child, except with English words instead of their Italian translations, then it would have meant that each of the men told the women he would vote for the other man, which it cannot now do. The generalizations about meaning that flow from the nature of the faculty for language, maturing under normal conditions, must be capable of supporting counterfactual statements in this way.

The theorems of semantic theory are mediated by the notion of a *grammar*, within which they have a mathematically determinate character. In my grammar G, reciprocal expressions must have local antecedents; and if that were not the case, then I would not have *that* grammar. Still, the inquiry does not lose its empirical status. It is an empirical fact that *my* grammar is G, and if my experience had been different it would not have been G, but something else; likewise, anyone with my experience would have had G. Support for empirical counterfactuals does not lag under this conception; at the same time, grammars are to be considered as formal systems, individuated by their syntax and semantics.[3]

Quine (1972) observed that linguistic theory seemed to take as objects of inquiry, not only the expressions classified as sentences or other parts of speech, but also the grammatical constructs that were posited in the course of effecting the classification. Whether the point of view that Quine discerned is justified will depend, I think on the outcome of comparative studies and the theory of the acquisition of language, of which the small story I have told about the examples in (3) is a modest instance.

VALUES

Semantic theory proceeds from assumptions both about the nature of syntactic structures and about the nature of semantic values. On the syntactic side, I will suppose that the objects having values are the points or nodes on *phrase markers*, where a phrase marker is a structure of points, each of which bears a syntactic or lexical label, having the usual hierarchical and linear relations between them.[4] Each point p of a phrase marker Q determines a *sub-phrase marker P* of Q, obtained by taking as the elements of P exactly those points in Q that are dominated by p (including p itself). I recognize also linguistic *relations* between points in phrase markers, of which two that are prominent in recent linguistics are *antecedence*, responsible for semantic relations of anaphora, and *predication*. These relations, like the labels of the points themselves, are purely *formal*. Semantic values are of the usual sort: the values of singular terms are things, the values of predicative expressions are the various things they denote, and so forth. The primitive predicate v of the theory has five places. It is

$$v(x,P,Q,C,f)$$

and is read

> x is a value of the phrase marker P, considered as a sub-phrase marker of the phrase marker Q, in context C, under assignment f.

My reasons for the double relativity of values, to phrase markers and to phrase markers that contain them, are illustrated with reference both to extensional examples and to examples of classical referential opacity, in Higginbotham (1984a). *Assignments* are assignments of values to anaphoric elements, as will be seen in section 5. Contexts, or contextual circumstances, are whatever they are, or may be, insofar as they interact systematically with linguistic structure. In this section, whose main purpose is to clarify the framework, I consider only applications for which the relativization of the values of points in P to the parameters Q, C, and f is not needed.

Consider (17):

(17)   John saw Mary.

We want to be able to conclude that (17) is well-formed, and that it is true if and only if John saw Mary. The S-Structure phrase marker for (17) is assumed to be (18), where +**p** denotes the past-tense formative and Infl is the 'inflectional' element that expresses the presence or absence of tense in a clausal structure. Infl is taken to be the head of a point labeled Infl' that immediately dominates Infl and VP:

(18)

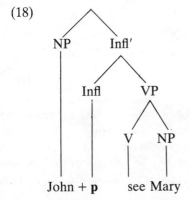

The descriptive task of syntactic theory is not confined to showing that (17) is well-formed as inserted within the phrase marker (18); it also includes the task of showing that (18) is unique and that lexical information, together with other grammatical principles, suffices strictly to determine it. Similarly, on the side of the semantics, it must be demonstrable that the interpretation of the structure (18) is fixed, insofar as determined by the rules of grammar.

Each word that assigns thematic roles to arguments has associated with it, as part of its lexical entry, appropriate information about the number and nature of these arguments. Following Stowell (1981), I will call this information the *thematic grid* of the word. The lexical entry for the verb *see* will include its pronunciation, part of speech, and thematic grid (shown in angled brackets), as in (19):

(19)   *see*, +V −N, $\langle 1,2,E \rangle$

The position 1 will be the thematic position ultimately filled by *John*, and 2 the position filled by *Mary*. Specific information about thematic roles associated with these positions is needed, for instance to ensure that the subject position will be filled by the agent *John*, and not by *Mary*; we must explain that (17) cannot mean that Mary saw John. The position *E* corresponds to the 'hidden' argument place for events, originally suggested by Donald Davidson in (1966). There seem to be strong arguments in favor of, and little to be said against, extending Davidson's idea to verbs other than verbs of change or action. Under this extension, statives will also have *E*-positions. The bundle of objects answering to these positions might well be called 'situations,' following Barwise and Perry (1983).

Besides being a lexical entry, (19) is also to be construed as the label of a terminal point of (18). Since the lexicon already contains the information that *see* is a verb, the point immediately dominating it is redundant. That part of (18) consisting of

V
|
see

comprises just a single point, namely

(*see*, +V −N, $\langle 1,2,E \rangle$).

The same redundancy of labeling affects all the pairs in (18) consisting of a point with a categorial label immediately dominating a point whose label is a terminal string. For graphic ease, I will continue to give diagrams of phrase markers as in (18); but these are to be interpreted as just indicated. The phrase marker shown in (18) then has seven points (not eleven), of which four are terminal.[5]

Like other predicative expressions, the verb *see*, or more precisely the lexical entry (19), is true of some things and false of others. The *values* of a predicate *F*, the things *x* such that $v(x,F)$, are those of which it is true. The values of (19) are at the same time the values of the point *p* of the phrase marker (18) that bears (19) as its label: they are those ordered triples $\langle a,b,e \rangle$ such that *e* is an event of *a*'s seeing *b*; *p* together with its label is itself a phrase marker. Letting *s* range over finite sequences of things, the statement (20) gives the values of p:

(20) $v(s, p) \leftrightarrow (\exists x)(\exists y)(\exists e)(s = \langle x,y,e \rangle \ \& \ see(x,y,e))$

The thematic roles in positions 1 and 2 of entry (19) are, and must be, assigned to arguments. In VP and S, this happens under the configuration of *government*. For our purposes, the head of a phrase may be taken as governing just its sister constituents.[6]

Consider now the object NP *Mary* of (17). Taking the word *Mary* as a simple NP for the sake of this discussion, its lexical entry would be as in (21):

(21)   *Mary*, $-V + N$

The entry (21) is the label of a sister point q of the point p, and the values of q are given by (22):

(22) $v(x,q) \leftrightarrow x = Mary$

The values of the phrase marker P constituting the VP of (18) are given in terms of the values of its parts and their specific mode of organization. Phrase markers are referred to by the labels of their roots, whenever this is possible without ambiguity. With this notation, and understanding that the only values in question are ordered pairs of things, the statement of values for P is (23):

(23) $v(\langle x,e \rangle, VP) \leftrightarrow (\exists y) \ v(\langle x,y,e \rangle, V) \ \& \ v(y,q)$

Therefore, we have (24):

(24) $v(\langle x,e \rangle, VP) \leftrightarrow see(x, Mary, e)$

The statement (24) is a consequence of general principles, applying to structures VP = V $-$ NP, where NP is a certain argument of V. Similarly, general principles apply to predications S = NP $-$ Infl'. An assertion as in (25) will be the ultimate outcome:

(25)   S is true $\leftrightarrow (\exists e)$ see (John, Mary, e)

The assignment of thematic roles in (18) corresponds to the semantic closure of the point S, seen in (25). The position marked by E in (19) ends up bound by an existential quantifier; one way of executing the binding is suggested below. There are several alternatives for tenses, which are tacitly ignored here, since choice among them depends on a far richer array of data than will come under our purview.

The elementary example just discussed should bring out two points about the notion of values used here. First, the semantics is not translational, although, if carried through properly, it will often result in translation. The values of the points in (18) are persons, pairs of persons, events or situations, and truth-values—these are not notations in a formal system, or representations of any sort. Of course, in assuming that the linguistic level LF is the level for which values are defined, and in particular in assuming that S-Structure does not critically differ from LF for simple cases like (25), one ventures a hypothesis about levels of representation. In some proposals, levels other than LF are targeted for semantic interpretation, either because LF-structures are not final or because a rather different framework was chosen from the beginning. Whatever the choice, semantics in the sense understood here, if it is to explain the data of section 1 and others of a similar nature, will involve a conception of values that is not simply translational.[7]

Second, semantic values are not values-in-a-model for the syntax; so the semantics is not model-theoretic either. It could not be, if what is to be explained are facts involving notions like '____is true,' '____refers to a,' '____means that p.' These notions do not express relations between syntactic structures and set-theoretic objects M.[8] Of course, neither of these points is to be construed as an argument against translational or model-theoretic approaches, or on behalf of a proprietary use of the term *semantics*.

Even if values are not relative to models, they are relative to grammars; the very same phrase marker might mean one thing in one grammar, and something quite different in another. In practice, this situation is certainly realized at the level of words; for instance, there are many speakers of English whose adjective *livid* means the same as *flushed*, and many others for whom it connotes pallor. What affects words affects sentences; thus, these speakers mean different things by *He was livid with rage*. Similarly, speakers of English whose dialects show negative concord will mean by *I never said nothing* that they never said anything, and speakers of other dialects will be constrained to mean that they were always talking.[9]

Taking grammars to contain both syntactic and semantic components, we can give a general picture, in fact a modification of the one suggested by Lewis, of the objects of study. If S is a collection of syntactic systems, say a family of sets of phrase markers, we were interested in distinguishing the subcollection S_{human} consisting of those systems s in S that human beings acquire under normal conditions. Suppose that a *grammar* is a pair (s,r), where s is in S, and r assigns values, or conditions on values, to the phrase markers to s, perhaps along the lines of the predictive v used here. Then, if W is the collection of the (s,r), a successful theory will distinguish the part W_{human} of W that comprises those grammars acquired by people, given appropriate experience. Just as there are syntactic systems s that are not instantiated anywhere, so there are grammars (s,r) with assignments r

independently of whether they are, or could be, the grammars of human beings. Concerning these we might wish to say that, had human beings been constructed differently, they would have been the grammars of human beings; and of course some of them, unknown to us, might actually be among the grammars of some other species. In any case, when we say that a name refers to so-and-so, or that a sentence is true under such-and-such conditions, there is a tacit relativization to systems (s,r), whose nature we are trying to discover.[10]

The relation r is a counterpart to Lewis's conception of a language. I allow, however, that the domain of r in (s,r) include syntactic objects that are ungrammatical in the system s.

I have illustrated the projection of values through grammatical trees with respect to one, very simple, example. In the next section I will show others, but of course I omit many applications here. Among these, an account of the *types* of semantic projection is particularly important. Consider the NP *Mary's mother*, with the constituent structure shown in (26):

(26) $[_{NP}[_{NP}$ Mary's$][_N$ mother$]]$

Why can (26) not mean that Mary is a mother? The lexical ingredients *Mary* and *mother* are the same in (26) as in the sentence (27):

(27) $[_S[_{NP}$ Mary$][_{VP}$ is a mother$]]$

What we ask for in cases like (26) and (27) is the source of the semantic distinction between different combinations of the same words. The specific case of (26) would fall under the condition proposed in Williams (1980), that the relation between N and its 'subject' NP (as proposed in Chomsky (1972)) is never that of predicate to subject. Again, the explanation of why (26) cannot mean what (27) means will isolate an ungrammatical structure for (26), namely, the one that assigns prediction of *mother* to *Mary*, that would mean what (27) means if it were grammatical.

The general form of the theory given in Montague (1974) incorporated as part of its intrinsic apparatus the idea that a single syntactic category there corresponded only one semantic category. Thus, Montague's theory would have answered our question by observing that, since NP is plainly a category for *terms*, it cannot also be a category for *formulas* (more precisely, the semantic type of NP is restricted to a single point in the type-theoretic hierarchy). Williams (1983) strongly argues that Montague's thesis cannot be sustained, and if Higginbotham (1984b) is on the right track, there are other cases where syntactic categories crisscross with semantic ones. For further remarks, see section 6 below. I turn now to an elaboration of the methods proposed here for other fundamental cases of semantic combination.

POSITIONS OF ARGUMENTS

In section 2 I discussed the projection of values in phrase markers for simple sentences, as controlled by the thematic grids of lexical items and phrasal structures. The proposal was illustrated with reference to transitive verbs like *see* in English, which meet their arguments in a manner determined by phrasal hierarchy.[11] In this section I will consider other varieties of structures, and the nature of thematic information and its projection, arguing that a certain generalization of the θ-Criterion of Chomsky (1981) will play a significant role in the semantics of complex constructions. I will also introduce a more restricted form of expression for some semantic properties that have seemed to call for higher types, or functionals, in natural languages.[12]

The θ-Criterion has two parts:

θ-Criterion
a.   Every argument is assigned one and only one thematic role.
b.   Every thematic role is assigned to one and only one argument.

Most simply, the θ-Criterion suggests a strict correlation between predicates, which assign thematic roles, and arguments, which bear them. The assignments are understood as the filling of *places* in the predicates, so that the notion of a role's being associated with a place comes on top of the more familiar idea of the sheer *number* of places, or adicity, of a predicate. The statements (a) and (b) then embody two notions, that predicates of any number of places have to meet up appropriately with their arguments, and that the arguments have to be spread among the available thematic roles.

The θ-Criterion is to hold both at LF and at S-Structure. In many cases the distinction between these levels is not significant, and we confine our attention to these in this section.

Recent work on the syntax and semantics of morphological processes, including Fabb (1984) and Roeper (1983), seems to show that thematic information in a stem is visible to the syntax for various purposes. One of these is *control*, as in Rita Manzini's example (28), cited by Roeper,

(28)   The boat was sunk [PRO to collect the insurance]

where the subject PRO of the purpose-clause is also the agent alleged to have sunk the boat. The passive form *was sunk*, then, has two thematic positions besides its *E*-position, of which only one belonging to the derived subject is assigned. The position belonging to the agent is absorbed somehow, but may serve as controller for the subordinate clause. These examples seem to show that part (b) of the θ-Criterion is too simple as it stands.

That thematic roles need not be filled by arguments can be supported also by the properties of nominals that undergo no morphological process. The word *dog*, for instance, a simple noun, has an open place in it (and so denotes each of the various dogs). In many languages, nominals can serve as predicates in main clauses. On these grounds alone, we should expect the word *dog* to have a thematic grid as part of its lexical entry, as in (29):

(29) *dog*, $- V + N, \langle 1 \rangle$

But, as noted in section 2, following Williams, head nouns do not take arguments when they form NPs. What happens instead is that the position 1 is accessible to Spec, which acts as a binder of it. There must be some binder, and there cannot be two. We might display the thematic structure of the NP *the dog* as in (30),

(30) $(NP, \langle 1^* \rangle)$

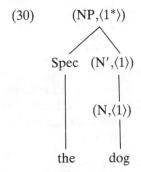

where the asterisk or star indicates that the position open in N′ is not open in NP.

Let the method shown in this example be another way of closing a structure with respect to a θ-role, or as I shall say, *discharging* that θ-role. Then θ-marking is one way of discharging a θ-role; but there is also θ-*binding*, a distinct process. Note that this type of binding must be distinguished from trace-binding. Traces are formatives of the grammar and occupy positions where lexical arguments would go. But a position in a grid is not a formative, being rather part of the entry of the word or phrase whose grid it is. See also Higginbotham (1984b), in connection with certain predicative quantifications in English.

Chomsky (1982) notes that the impossibility of iterating determiners (*every the dog*) may be related to a prohibition against vacuous quantification: in the present terms, one determiner would have to be vacuous, since each is a binder. We can now see this point as an instance of the θ-Criterion, suitably generalized.

Returning now to a point that was left open in the discussion of simple transitive sentences in section 2, we can conjecture that the position E of the thematic grid of the verb is discharged at the point where VP meets Infl. The interpretation is existential generalization over the E-position, as in Davidson (1966); hence, it is a form of θ-binding. This conjecture is natural on several grounds, one being that it fits very well with the semantics of gerunds, if these in fact lack Infl and, as suggested by Williams (1984), have just the structure $[_{NP} NP - (Aux) - VP]$. Gerunds are definite descriptions of events or situations, completed by binding into the position E of VP—an open position, since Infl is absent in this case.[13]

The original statement (b) of the θ-Criterion is now replaced by the more general (31):

(31)   Every thematic position is discharged.

That a thematic role cannot be assigned to more than one argument becomes a special case of (31). Also, in keeping with the intent of (b), no thematic role can be left dangling. Therefore, for those cases where a role can be discharged only by assigning it to an argument, applications of (b) and (31) will coincide.

Part (a) of the θ-Criterion (every argument is assigned one and only one thematic role) is also generalizable. One half of it, expressing the *existence* of a role for A if A is an argument, carries over intact, since an argument of X must be assigned a role that is present in the thematic structure of X. The other half, requiring uniqueness, generalizes to (32):

(32)   If X discharges a thematic role in Y, then it discharges only one.

There are at least three ways the condition (32) could be violated: by simultaneous θ-marking, by simultaneous binding of two positions, and by θ-marking with respect to one and binding with respect to another. In at least the first two cases, it is arguable on the face of it that something of the sort actually occurs; but investigation of the matter would be too lengthy and inconclusive to be included here.[14]

We can now draw a consequence of some significance from the θ-Criterion as understood here, together with the assumption that θ-marking takes place only under government. Let us say that a constituent such that every role in its associated grid is discharged is *saturated*. Consider a binary structure

$$[_X A \ B]$$

where A θ-marks B. Then the thematic grid of the head A is projected to X. Suppose that B is unsaturated, so that it contains an unstarred thematic role in this configuration. Then it will be unable to govern a constituent, and therefore unable to discharge that role. This reasoning applies to any argument. So we may assert (33):

(33)   Every argument is saturated.

Reserving some possible exceptions, I will note that it is an immediate consequence of (33) that functionals are not to be found in the grammars of languages for which it holds; the arguments of a functional must be unsaturated, and this is just what (33) forbids. Similarly, the 'projection rules' of function and argument cannot, on this view, be extended through higher types, as in Montague (1974) or Lewis (1972), among others. I will assume the principle for the duration of this article, mindful that problematic cases, or cases that I have not considered, may force its abandonment.[15]

The notions of θ-marking and θ-binding have their correlatives in standard formalized languages, in the respective forms of structures of functions and arguments, and of quantification. The case is otherwise with *modification*, a unified linguistic phenomenon that does not correspond to any single operation to be found, for example, in quantification theory. Modification of one predicative expression by another can occasionally be taken as expressing *conjunction*: a white wall is a thing that is white (on the outside) and a wall. But this easy treatment is the exception rather than the rule. As everyone knows, a bad violinist is not a thing that is, on the one hand, bad, and, on the other, a violinist. Adjectives like *bad*, the classic *syncategorematic* ones, are the norm.

Nevertheless, I think that we have in the easy routine of conjunction the proper idea of how modification works. The strategy that I will follow can be illustrated with reference to the treatment of certain adverbs suggested in Davidson (1966) (this strategy itself might in turn be motivated by the analogy with adjectives). Davidson was concerned with modifications like the one in (34):

(34)   John walked rapidly.

An important question was how to show the obvious truth of conditionals like (35):

(35)   If John walked rapidly, then John walked.

The answer that Davidson suggested was to take the adverb *rapidly* as predicated of events, with respect to one or another attribute used for classifying them. Thus, (34) would come out as (36) or, more formally, (37),

(36)   There was a walk by John, and it was rapid (for a walk).
(37) $(\exists e)$ walked(John,e) & rapid(e,A)

where *A* is the attribute indicated by the parenthetical in (36). Since *John walked*, in this formalism, is just (38),

(38)   (∃*e*) walked(John,*e*)

the conditional (35) is true, and appropriately obvious. The adverbial modification is interpretable as conjunction when certain unapparent referential places are posited, namely those for *e* and the attribute *A*. I propose to apply a similar strategy to adjectival modification.[16]

Adjectives grade things along dimensions that are partly contextually filled in, but also partly controlled by the syntactic environment. When an adjective combines with an N to form a complex N′, as in *tall man*, *big butterfly*, or *good violinist*, then it is taken as grading with respect to the attribute given in the N. When the adjective is separated syntactically from N, the semantic link is broken also. Thus, in well-known minimal pairs like (39) and (40)

(39)   That is a big butterfly.
(40)   That butterfly is big.

we judge that (39) is true if the object indicated is big for a butterfly, but that (40) is more open-ended; since even big butterflies are not big creatures, (40) can count as false with respect to an object for which (39) counts as true. Now, interpretations of adjective-noun combinations are not always as constrained as the one in (39): a person who says, 'Look at the little butterfly,' or, 'Here comes a big tank,' need not be taken as asserting that the butterfly in question is little even among butterflies, or the tank big even among tanks. Tanks are big things, and butterflies are little things; in these contexts, then, the adjectives might be said to have standard interpretations, and the semantics of the compound to be simple conjunction: the little butterfly is a little thing that is a butterfly, the big tank a big thing that is a tank. Similarly, a rich stockbroker may just be a stockbroker who is a rich person. Since these cases do not raise a distinctive issue of semantic principle, I will not attempt to discriminate them further here.[17]

In strict parallel with Davidson, we can take (39) as shown in (41), and (40) as in (42):

(41)   That is a butterfly, and it is big (for a butterfly).
(42)   That butterfly is big (for an *A*).

Let us consider first how to implement this analysis in more detail, only afterward turning to some potential counterexamples.

Pursuing the idea that modification expresses conjunction, consider how the thematic grids might be assigned and projected in the N′ of (39), namely (43):

(43) $[_{N'}[_A \text{ big}][_N \text{ butterfly}]]$

The word *butterfly* has a single open position, and the adjective must have open positions also, since it occurs as a predicate. The whole N′ has one open position, carried over from the head noun. Therefore, some position in the adjective is *identified* with the nominal position. The thematic structure of (43) is then as represented in (44),

(44) $(N',\langle 1 \rangle)$

$(A,\langle 1 \rangle)$ $(N,\langle 1 \rangle)$

where the connecting line shows identification. On the assumption that the semantics of (44) is given by conjunction, we can compare its structure to that of building up a compound $Fx \ \& \ Gx$ by conjoining Fx and Gy and then identifying y and x.

To this inventory of θ-marking and θ-binding, we add *θ-identification* as a mode of thematic discharge. If this mode is to satisfy the general conditions of the theory, then θ-identification is constrained to take place under government; and so it does, since the configuration of modification, as in (44), is a configuration of government.

We now extend the proposal to take account of the appearance of attributes in the paraphrases (41) and (42). The attribute is an argument of the adjective, so that the head noun in an ordinary adjective-noun construction serves to discharge two thematic positions, one by identification and the other by θ-marking, by the adjective, of the very noun itself. In the usual case of θ-marking, the reference of the θ-marked expression becomes the value of an open position in the θ-marker; but in the case of modification, I suggest, what is θ-marked, the phrase marker with root N, is itself the value. For this reason, this type of θ-marking will be called *autonymous*.

Consider the thematic structure of (43), and its semantics, under the proposal just sketched. For graphic purposes, I mark with an arrow '→' the discharge of a thematic position through autonymous θ-marking, where the tail of the arrow is at the position of the θ-marker and its head abuts the point marked. (43) is then as shown in (45),

(45) $(N',\langle1\rangle)$

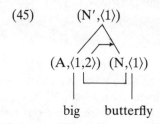

big   butterfly

where what is displayed abbreviates the set of statements (46a–c):

(46) In (43)
   a. the position 1 of N is identified with position 1 of A;
   b. A autonymously θ-marks N, through position 2;
   c. the thematic grid of N is projected to N'.

The following semantics accompanies the syntactic description of (45). For the points A and N we will have (47) and (48), respectively:

(47) $\mathbf{v}(\langle x,y\rangle,A) \leftrightarrow \mathrm{big}(x,y)$
(48) $\mathbf{v}(x,N) \leftrightarrow \mathrm{butterfly}(x)$

To go further we must adopt a notation for the attribute expressed in the phrase marker with root N, assuming that this attribute is distinct from the phrase marker itself. Let ^N refer to the attribute. Then, for (43) as a whole, we will have (49):

(49) $\mathbf{v}(x,N') \leftrightarrow \mathbf{v}(x,N)\ \&\ \mathbf{v}(\langle x,\hat{}N\rangle,A)$

The modified constituent is taken up as a conjunction: (49) says that the big butterflies are the things that are butterflies and big for such.

We have now recognized four species of thematic discharge: the non-modificatory, or *simple*, cases of θ-marking; *autonymous* θ-marking; θ-binding; and θ-identification. All of these are controlled by the configuration of government. In this way, we derive the distinction between (39) and (40), repeated here:

(39) That is a big butterfly.
(40) That butterfly is big.

The attribute chosen in (39) must be that of being a butterfly, since the noun is governed by the adjective; but the choice in (40) is free. I turn now to the application of this apparatus to some widely discussed cases that require a different semantics than the simple examples given so far.

First, consider cases where the adjective cannot be dissociated from the nominal head, as in (50)–(51):

(50)   That is an alleged Communist.
(51)   *That Communist is alleged.

The fact that alleged Communists need not be Communists already shows that the N′ of (50) is not construed by conjoining the head with the adjective. Apart from this, however, it is obvious that the adjective *alleged* is related to the verb *allege* in a way that should be revealed in the theory of its construction. The verb belongs to a class that includes *know* and *suspect*, in both taking S′ complements and admitting adjectival form. An alleged N is a thing that some agency or other has alleged to be an N; similarly if *known* or *suspected* is substituted for *alleged*. in view of the absorption of agency, we may suppose that position 1 of the thematic grid of *allege* is discharged in the course of affixation (for a hypothesis concerning the mechanism of absorption, see Baker (1983)). Then (suppressing the *E*-position, which is not relevant here) the thematic structure of the adjective is (52):

(52) $[_A[_V$ allege, $\langle 1,2 \rangle]$ ed, $\langle 1^*,2 \rangle]$

Similarly, the thematic structure of a single adjective like *batted* would be (53):

(53) $[_A[_V$ bat, $\langle 1,2 \rangle]$ ed, $\langle 1^*,2 \rangle]$

The semantics is given by existential closure of the bound position: *batted* is true of a thing x such that something y bats x.

When the adjective *batted* combines with a noun, as in *batted ball*, then the method of composition is θ-identification, and the semantics is straightforward: a batted ball is a ball that has been batted. This mode of combination also occurs, with some marginality, with *alleged* and *known*, as in *alleged proposition* (meaning 'proposition alleged by Jones'), *known fact*, and the like. The combination seen in (50), however, is different.

Suppose, again without any claim to generality, that alongside the attributes ^N we also recognize, for each object x, the proposition ^N(x), that the object x is N. The N *Communist*, as it occurs in (50), expresses, for each assignment f to the thematic grid $\langle 1 \rangle$ of that word, the proposition that $f(\langle 1 \rangle)$ is a Communist. We can then understand the combinations *alleged N* as cases of θ-marking, as in (54):

(54) $v(x,N') \leftrightarrow$ alleged $(^N(x))$

The phrase *alleged Communist* is then, as desired, a predicate true of the things alleged to be Communists. The ungrammaticality of (51) now follows.

Since θ-marking takes place only under government, position 2 of *alleged* goes undischarged in (51).

But consider the matter more closely. Both (55) and (56) are well-formed:

(55)   Those traits were alleged of Jones.
(56)   His Communism was alleged.

So *alleged* can function as an ordinary predicate after all. What is wrong with (51), it turns out, is that it is a category mistake. The word *alleged*, then, behaves like an ordinary adjective, in that it can both θ-mark a nominal head and occur as a predicate.[18]

We have now considered three types of cases of adjectival modification, namely (i) cases of θ-identification, where the combination indicates conjunction, as in *white wall*, (ii) cases in which identification is combined with θ-marking, as in *big butterfly* (here again the semantics involves conjunction), and (iii) cases in which there is θ-marking but no identification, as in *alleged* (or *known*) *Communist*.[19] In concluding this section, let us briefly examine two more types.

The first is that of the *privative* adjectives, *fake*, *toy*, and others. A fake or toy pistol not only may, but must, fail to be a pistol. However, it *does* have to be a fake or a toy, and it is this fact that, I believe, gives a clue to the basis of the construction.[20] A thing is assessed as a fake or a toy only relative to an attribute, so that, picking *toy* for an example, we will have a binary thematic grid ⟨1,2⟩ and the projection shown in (57):

(57) $(N', \langle 1, 2^* \rangle)$

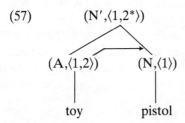

$(A, \langle 1, 2 \rangle)$ $(N, \langle 1 \rangle)$

toy   pistol

In this case the adjective θ-marks the N itself, as in the case of *alleged Communist*. This N serves simply to indicate the attribute, and the grid that is projected is that of *toy*, not of *pistol*. A toy pistol is a thing that is a toy, with respect to the attribute indicated by *pistol*—hence, a toy, in this sense (of course, a thing may also be a toy without being a toy *F*, for any *F*). So the adjective is privative with respect to the head noun, but since, in the semantics, it is as if it were itself the head, this fact does not require changes in the system proposed here.

Structures like (57) are not common and are generally restricted to modifiers that also occur as nouns (e.g. *imitation pistol* but **imitated pistol*).

An exception, pointed out to me by David Lewis, is the word *bogus*, an adjective that behaves semantically like the noun *fake*. In projecting the grid of the modifier, we not only violate the usual conditions on projection, but in a way take an unsaturated constituent, namely the N, as an argument; and the open position 1 in its grid is never discharged. A short diagnosis of this situation is that the N in (57) is mentioned, rather than used: it does not, as it occurs in the N′, denote pistols, but only the attribute that it indicates. Hence, the position 1 need not be discharged, any more than it would in a quotation.[21]

Besides the privative adjectives, certain spatio-temporal modifications, as in *former congressman* and *postman where I live*, call for a distinctive semantic treatment. *Former congressman* designates a person whose congressmanhood is former, and *postman where I live* a person whose postal duties are carried out at the place where I live. It is not difficult in these and similar cases to effect the proper paraphrases, and, if we recognized spatial or temporal positions in the thematic grids of the nouns, we could regard the whole structure as projected by conjunction of its components; a former congressman, for instance, is an x such that x is a congressman at some time t that is former (before now). An alternative method, due to Larson (1983), would locate the spatio-temporal relativity that these modifications exhibit in the circumstances of utterance of the phrases in question, without building positions into their thematic grids. Whichever method is correct, it seems that no questions of semantic principle arise that would show the need for a fundamental change in the methods adopted here.

This discussion of modification may be compared with the account of Montague (1974), following suggestions due to Hans Kamp. In general, the view was that modifiers, whose syntactic function is to produce complex constituents of the same categorial status as the things they modify, should be interpreted as mapping the interpretation of the modified constituent onto the interpretation of the whole, the latter being an element of the same semantic type as its argument. The variety of interpretive procedures given here then gives way to a uniform semantic rule (see also Lewis (1972)). There is no implication that the objects of which the *modified* noun is true are among those of which the noun is true; for instance, there is no implication that the alleged Communists are Communists. How then does one get the obvious fact that big butterflies are butterflies? The answer was that such facts had to be stated outright, by means of semantic postulates.

I remarked above that the view that I would suggest would exemplify one side of a trade-off between a certain generality, purchased in Montague's and Lewis's account by the admission of higher types and functionals, and the positing of a certain internal structure, with truth-functional modes of composition. A simplification that comes from the view suggested here is the absence of semantic postulates. In Montague's theory, all modifications were alike, and so postulates were needed. On the view suggested here, they are distinguished in that some involve θ-marking and identification, others only θ-marking, with further differentiation in the varieties, as we have seen. Each mode of combination, however, has its characteristic semantics, from which there follow the facts that the semantic postulates were used for.

BINDING AND OBVIATION

We have seen that attachment of values to points in phrase markers, in ways that are controlled in part by formal relations such as antecedence or predication, enables us to infer semantic facts about these phrase markers and to take anaphoric relations into account in simple cases. In section 1 I considered certain cases where anaphoric relations are not possible (in English), remarking that the data (namely, that these sentences cannot mean certain things in English) rely crucially for their explanation on the application of the semantics to formally ungrammatical structures. I will now apply this form of explanation to the most basic cases of what I will call the *Disjoint Reference Condition*, following Lasnik (1976). The condition applies between the pronoun and the name in sentences like (58):

(58)   He saw John.

Although there is general agreement about which sentences the Disjoint Reference Condition applies to, there is less than unanimity about what its application determines about their meaning.[22] There are, roughly speaking, two major types of interpretation. The weaker interpretation, represented in Evans (1980), holds that the condition, as applied between two positions *A* and *B*, merely prevents either one from depending on the other for its interpretation; in the case of (58), it prevents *John* from being the antecedent of *he*. The stronger interpretation of Lasnik (1976, 1982) holds that the condition forces *A* and *B* to be 'different' in some sense, or in a relation of *obviation*, to use the traditional term. If the positions *A* and *B* are obviative, then neither is dependent on the other; so the stronger interpretation implies the weaker. However, nondependence does not imply obviation. Clarifying the notion of obviation then becomes an important task.

Let us assume that at least (59) must be explained in semantic theory:

(59)   *He saw John* cannot mean that John saw himself.

Following the strategy of sections 1 and 2, we should look for a structure Σ, such that Σ means that John saw himself, (58) is the sequence of words given in Σ, and Σ is ungrammatical. This structure is (60):

(60)   [[He][saw John]]

Since *he* has been linked to *John,* its value is whatever the value of this antecedent is—that is, John. Therefore:

(61)   (60) is true if and only if saw(John,John).

However, (60) is ungrammatical, since the pronominal *he* has its antecedent in its own c-command domain.

One might try putting the facts about (58) in terms of 'purported' or 'intended' coreference—roughly, as the requirement that a person who says (58) purports or intends that the reference of *he* is not the reference of *John,* or at least does not purport or intend that they are the same. But this thesis is not factually correct in any sense in which its own purport is clear, and even if it were it would not serve as an explanation. It is easy enough to construct cases in which the speaker asserts a sentence S, containing two positions *A* and *B* between which the Disjoint Reference Condition holds, such that the speaker believes, and intends the hearer to believe, that they have the same reference. (62), embedded in the argument (63), is a sentence of this kind:

(62)   *He* put on *John*'s coat.
(63)   He put on John's coat; but only John would do that; so he is John.

(I owe this type of example to Nancy Browman, from her comments on a lecture at New York University, 1979.) In what sense do *he* and *John* not have the same 'intended' reference? Moreover, even supposing that the speaker of (62), as embedded in (63), intends thereby that he or she does not purport the reference of *he* and *John* to be the same, it cannot be that the intentional state explains this aspect of the meaning of (62). That would be getting things backwards. It must be because of the meaning of (63) that the hearer will ascribe the intentional state to the speaker. Thus, an account in terms of associated intentions merely restates the problem.

If (62) cannot be uttered with the intention that *he* should be anaphoric to *John,* that is not because of any failure of the speaker's powers of intention, but because the structure that would realize this meaning is ungrammatical. Now, the weak interpretation of the Disjoint Reference Condition, which states that it amounts just to the prohibition of antecedence, satisfies the requirement that the intentions of speakers be explained by linguistic meaning, and also allows the case (63) freely. The datum is (64):

>   (64)   *He put on John's coat* cannot mean that John is a thing x such that
> x put on x's coat.

This datum follows from the prohibition of antecedence between *he* and
John and is not violated as (62) is used in (63). Indeed, the whole point of
the argument (63) was to demonstrate that the reference of *he* indeed *is*
the reference of *John;* it would defeat the purpose of that argument if its
first premise meant that John put on his own coat.

We have been examining the weak interpretation of the Disjoint Ref-
erence Condition, using the notation suggested in Higginbotham (1983a).
This account of binding incorporated a kind of *transitivity condition* (after
Jackendoff (1972)), in order to prevent the linking shown in (65):

>   (65)   John said [$_S$ he saw him]

The antecedent *John* of both pronouns in (65) is outside the tensed S
containing them; however, the sentence cannot mean that John said that
he, John, saw himself. The transitivity condition was to rule out (65) by
requiring that if X and Y shared an antecedent, and one c-commanded the
other, then one was the antecedent of the other. (65) is then ungrammatical,
since the pronouns share the antecedent *John,* but are not themselves
linked.

However, some examples seem to show that the transitivity condition
should be given up, at least if the advantages of the linking account over
coindexing are to be retained. After enumerating these, I will show how
the introduction of conditions on obviation will both account for some data
that are recalcitrant for the weak interpretation of the Disjoint Reference
Condition and remove the need for a transitivity condition.

Consider (66):

>   (66)   They strike each other as [t intelligent]

The reciprocal phrase must be linked to its c-commanding antecedent *they;*
the trace t must also be linked to *they*. But the reciprocal phrase c-commands
the trace, as is shown by (67):

>   (67)   *It strikes *her* that [*Mary* is intelligent]

The same data appear in other 'raising' constructions. (67) and the like
therefore stand as counterexamples to the transitivity condition.

A major advantage of linking over coindexing is that, in revealing
information about antecedents that the indicial notation suppresses, linking

also expresses information about interpretation that coindexing says nothing about. The following illustrations are due to Finer (1984a) (see also Montalbetti (1984) for examples from Spanish involving conditions on pronouns as variables). The sentence in (68), where the subject pronoun *they* refers, say, to John and Mary, exhibits a three-way ambiguity:

(68)   They told each other they had better leave.

The interpretations are (a) each told the other, 'I had better leave,' (b) each told the other, 'We had better leave,' (c) each told the other, 'You had better leave.' The ambiguity disappears in the control structure (69):

(69)   They told each other to leave.

The only interpretation of (69) is (c).

In (69), a case of object control, the only links possible are as shown in (70):

(70)   They told [each other][PRO to leave]

This linking is also possible in (68), with *they* for PRO, and leads to the same interpretation. But in (68) the embedded pronominal is not controlled, so that the linking shown in (71) is also available:

(71)   They told [each other][they had better leave]

This structure displays an ambiguity that is familiar from examples like (72):

(72)   They said [they would leave]

That is, each said something about himself, or something about the two of them. In either case, the value for the embedded pronominal refers back to the value assigned to the subject, not to the reciprocal.[23]

The sketch of an analysis of the distinction between (68) and (68) is very attractive; but it requires abandoning the transitivity condition, since that condition is violated in (71). Further evidence comes from the behavior of the subject-control verb *promise:*

(73)   They promised each other [(that) they would succeed]
(74)   They promised each other [PRO to succeed]

(74) is unambiguous: each promised the other, 'I will succeed.' However, with some degree of marginality, (73) can be interpreted as meaning that each promised the other, 'You will succeed;' at least, this interpretation

seems to be as acceptable as the sentence (75):

(75)   Mary promised John that he would succeed.

Suppose we give up the transitivity condition, revising the binding conditions (A)–(C) of Chomsky (1981). In the notation of linking, these conditions may be stated as follows:

(A)   An anaphor is locally linked.
(B)   A pronominal is not locally linked.
(C)   An R-expression is not linked.

Or, in the revised version:

(A*)   An anaphor is locally linked (= (A)).
(B*)   A pronominal is locally obviative.
(C*)   An R-expression is obviative.

The relevant notions of locality are perhaps different for different languages, and perhaps also different in (A*) and (B*) for a given language. That the antecedents of anaphors c-command them we take to be a general principle that need not be stated in the condition (A*). Furthermore, as Lasnik (1982) observes, it appears to be a general condition on the interpretation of anaphors that whatever they are linked to *exhausts* their meaning. This fact, together with the condition that elements are interpreted in one and only one way (the condition (R) of Higginbotham (1983a)), suffices to imply that no anaphor can be linked to more than one element. Like anaphoric linking, obviativity universally applies only with respect to c-commanding potential antecedents; hence, (B*) requires obviativity from each local c-commander, and (C*) obviativity from each c-commander. The condition (C*) covers the case of *incomplete descriptions* (sometimes misleadingly confined to those with epithetic status), as in the contrast between (76) and (77):

(76)   When *John* came in, *the man* looked tired.
(77)   **John* thought *the man* was tired.

Completion of this type of account of binding now requires, above all, two sorts of investigations. First, since binding now makes reference both to antecedence and to obviation, we must consider the principles of their interaction. Second, the semantic nature of obviation must be made manifest, insofar as it applies context-independently.

Let us consider more closely how the semantics for pronouns, PRO, and reciprocals will apply to give the proper results for the cases discussed so far. Suppose that pronominal X is linked to antecedent Y in the phrase marker Σ. Then, for a language that distinguishes only singular and plural, the most basic case is the following:[24]

(78)   Include some values of Y among the values of X.

If Y is singular, then it has only one value, and so that thing becomes a value of X—the only value, if X is also singular. If X and Y are both plural, the commonest case seems to be that in which every value of Y is a value of X. Thus, in (79)

(79)   John and Mary told Bill and Susan they should leave.

the interpretation where *they* refers to John and Mary is surely more salient than, say, one where it refers to John and Susan. Finally, suppose that Y is plural and X is singular. Then (78) alone will fail to secure a definite interpretation for X. Some individual elements of the value of Y must be salient, however; we cannot have (80):

(80)   They [waving at a crowd] think he is a nice fellow[25]

Since (78) is the strongest statement that can be made in general about the transference of values from antecedent to pronominal, the relation of antecedence ceases to be universally transitive. The failure of transitivity, however, is located in a particular place, namely the case of singular pronominals (not anaphors) with plural antecedents. I turn now to some elementary considerations on the interpretation of reciprocals and pronouns.

Suppose that R is a reciprocal expression linked to an antecedent Y, where Y is a *plural term*, like *they*, denoting various objects $a, b, \ldots$, all of them among its values. The simplest interpretation of reciprocity is summed up in (81):

(81)   For each a such that $v(a, Y)$, the values of R are those b such that $v(b, Y)$ and $b \neq a$.

On this interpretation, sentences like (82)

(82)   They saw each other.

will be true if each value of *they* saw each of the others.[26]

If P is a plural pronoun with plural antecedent Y, then the values of P are inherited from those of Y. However, there are distinct, salient ways in which this inheritance can take place, as indicated, for instance, by sentences like (72) (repeated here);

(72)   They said they would leave

The interpretive principle (83)

(83)   For each a such that $\mathbf{v}(a,Y)$, $\mathbf{v}(a,P)$.

gives only the interpretation where each of them says, 'We will leave.' The other, *distributed* interpretation arises by a different mechanism. Whatever the mechanism is, I conjecture that it is also responsible for sentences like (84),

(84)   They are cups and saucers.

in the sense in which this sentence is true when the objects in question are divided exhaustively between cups and saucers, and none of them is both a cup and a saucer. But since cases like (84) involve a more extended discussion, I will not pursue this question here.[27]

The rules for inheritance of values provide an account of the difference between (85) and (86), which represent the possible linkings in the sentence (68):

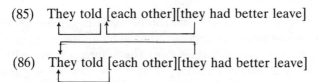

(85)   They told [each other][they had better leave]

(86)   They told [each other][they had better leave]

In the light of these comments on inheritance of values through antecedence, I return to a discussion of obviativity.

As remarked above, if two positions X and Y are obviative, then neither can serve as antecedent of the other. The general notion of obviativity must, however, be stronger than this. A rough description of what is involved might be (87):

(87)   If X and Y are obviative, then they cannot be determined by the structure in which they occur to share a value.

This statement is relatively informal, but I think that it is none the worse for that. (87) will, first of all, do the work that was required of the transitivity condition, now abandoned. In (65) (repeated here)

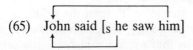

(65)   John said [$_s$ he saw him]

he and *him*-are obviative, by (B*). Nevertheless, they must share a value, namely John, and (87) implies that the structure is ungrammatical.

Lasnik (1982) has pressed the question of examples like (88), as pronounced with ordinary stress on the verb:

(88) *We like me.

(These were first extensively discussed in Postal (1971).) (88) falls under obviativity in the formulation (87), though not under an interpretation that merely prevents antecedence; and, as Lasnik has remarked, the binding condition (B) in Chomsky (1981) fails here as well. It has been noticed that (88) is much more acceptable with contrastive stress on the pronoun *me,* especially if accompanied by ostension, as in (89):

(89) We like *me* [speaker points at self].

Evans (1980) and Roberts (1984) contain other examples of the same type.

What do these exceptions show? The speaker of (89) uses the pronoun *me* as if it were a demonstrative, its interpretation supplied through ostension rather than through its ordinary linguistic meaning. This observation is enough, I think, to remove (89) as a counterexample to (87). At the same time, it is apparent that a full working-out of the import of obviativity would require a comprehensive picture of language use.

As we have been using the term *obviative,* the statement (90) implies (91), but not conversely:

(90) In *John saw him, John* is obviative from *him.*
(91) *John saw him* cannot mean that John saw himself.

Reinhart (1983) argues, however, that the stronger judgment of obviativity (90) might be derived from pragmatic considerations. Briefly, she suggests that the speaker of *John saw him,* in using that form rather than the available form *John saw himself,* invites the hearer to suppose, on the assumption that avoiding or minimizing ambiguity is the norm of speech, that different persons are intended by *John* and *him.* The existence of a contrasting potential utterance, which the speaker did not say, is responsible for our intuitions about these examples, hence for (90).

Arguments of this form have been given by others, as Reinhart notes. Reinhart extends the idea to cases like (92),

(92) *He* thought that I saw *John.*

where the speaker has avoided the bound-anaphora option shown in (93)

(93) John thought that I saw him.

and therefore, it is argued, will be assumed by the hearer to intend obviativity. Although Reinhart's expression of the thesis involves some notions that I find obscure, such as that of 'using a syntactic structure' (Reinhart (1983, 76)), I think that it is clear enough how examples will go.

The most evident difficulty for Reinhart's proposal is that obviativity is found even where there is no contrasting utterance that the speaker could be said to have avoided. Cases of this kind include Lasnik's (88) as well as (94):

(94)   John and Mary saw him.

Since *John and Mary saw himself,* like *We saw myself,* is ungrammatical, the judgment that the value of *him* is obviative from that of *John* cannot be accounted for on the pragmatic basis suggested. Similarly, there is no bound-anaphora option in (95) that has the interpretation that John and Mary told him, John, that she, Mary, should leave:

(95)   They told John that Mary should leave.

A second point, observed in Huang (1982), is that the account predicts that pronominals and reflexives should be in complementary distribution (see Reinhart (1983, 73)); however, this is not the case even in English, as in (96):

(96)   They expect [pictures of them(selves)] to be on sale.

Examples in languages like Icelandic also illustrate this point. Both sentences in (97) are grammatical in Icelandic and can mean that John wishes Mary would visit him, John:

(97)   John wishes that Mary would visit him(self).

Reinhart notes (p. 71) that her grammatical analysis faces problems in that reflexive forms and pronouns (her 'R-pronouns' and 'non-R-pronouns') are sometimes possible in the same contexts. The pragmatic analysis faces similar problems. For these reasons, it seems to me that there is no alternative to regarding the phenomenon of obviativity in terms of formal grammar.[28]

GENERALITY

Consider explicit quantification, as in the S-Structure representation (98), underlying *Every man left:*

(98)

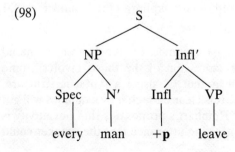

The grammatical relation of the subject NP to Infl' is just as it would be in simple sentences, such as *John left.* The values of Infl' are the various things that left, so that *John left* is true if the value of *John,* namely John, is one of those things. But the quantificational sentence (98) has a different *kind* of truth-condition from that of the simple sentence. In (98) the Infl' is not predicated of some thing called 'every man'; rather, (98) says that every single man is among the values of Infl'. Therefore, if the interpretation of structures S = NP − Infl' is to be predicational in character, then expressions of generality cannot be in their S-Structure positions at LF.

May (1977) has shown that adjunction of quantificational NPs, under the assumptions of trace theory, is a natural way, within a framework of the type assumed here, of representing generality at the level of LF. In the case of (98) his proposed rule of Quantifier Raising (QR) would produce (99):

(99)

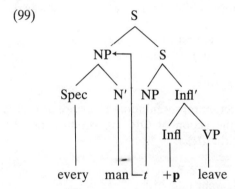

The trace *t* has the adjoined quantifier for its antecedent, as shown by the arrow. With respect to the lower S, *t* behaves like a free variable, so that values of that S are sensitive to assignments of values to *t*. The basic semantic predicate **v** reflects this sensitivity. If Q is the phrase marker whose root is the lower S of (99), then the value of Q is truth for those assignments f such that $f(t)$ left, and falsehood for all others.

The semantics for (99) and similar structures is completed by an appropriate clause for the quantification in the higher S. It is then possible to derive the statement (100) as expressing conditions under which (99) is true:

(100)   (99) is true ↔ [every x: man (x)][$\exists e$] leave(x, e)[29]

In (100) the binding relations between the quantifier *every man* and the subject of the lower clause, and between the binding phrase *every* and the open position in the noun, are not represented abstractly, by means of relations between phrasal points, but rather by the typographical shapes of

certain lexical items, the *variables*. In this respect, the right-hand side of
(100) does not entirely match in form the structure of (99); it is not
homophonic, in the sense of Quine (1968). However, if 'variable' is understood in the precise sense of the variables of quantification theory, there
may be no variables in the most basic parts of natural languages. Variables
x, *y* are a typographical expedient, whose end is disambiguation within the
limitations of customary writing and printing practice. The expedient itself
leads to certain nuisances, for instance in the elaborations that are needed
to take care of alphabetic variance. In quantification theory, there really
are infinitely many sentences *Everything is F*, one for each of the variables
on a denumerable list. But in English, on the view taken here, there is
only one such sentence. Assuming that there are no variables in natural
languages, we are nevertheless free to use them in giving the semantics of
those languages. The departure from homophonicity is just the price we
pay for using a notation that is more familiar to us in a theoretical way than
our mother tongue.[30]

Sentences with *multiple generality*, first satisfactorily treated by Frege,
fall into line as follows. Consider (101), for example:

(101)   A man went into every store.

This sentence has a unique S-Structure representation. But since it contains
two expressions of generality, the action of QR will produce two LF-
representations, namely (102) and (102):

(102)   [[a man][[every store][t went into t']]]

(103)   [[every store][[a man][t went into t']]]

Submitted to interpretation, these expressions differ in truth-conditions in
the standard way: (102) is true provided there is a man such that he went
into every store, and (103) when every store is such that some man or other
went into it. Of more significance than this separation of truth-conditions,
however, is the point that a theory with QR implies that (101) is not one
sentence, but two; it is homonymous between (102) and (103), distinct
grammatical structures that happen to sound alike.

The rationale just given for QR involves three distinct assumptions. The
first is that S = NP − Infl' sentences are interpreted in a uniform way; the
second is that the most elementary cases, such as *John left,* are predicational;
and the third is that in (98) and other quantificational sentences, the

grammatical predicate is not to be construed as predicated of what the subject denotes. The difficulties with granting the first two assumptions while denying the third form a lengthy chapter of the history of logic. Therefore, for any account that incorporates the first assumption (at least for all cases in which the subject is not pleonastic) the question turns on the second assumption alone.

Montague (1970) observed that uniformity of interpretation of basic sentential structures may be maintained, by the device of assimilating names to expressions of generality. The basic idea is that a simple subject like *John* will have for its value, not John himself, but a function that assigns to the interpretation of the VP the value truth if that VP is true of John, and falsehood otherwise. Elementary sentences then are not predicational in the classic sense, and proper names of people then become functionals, since their arguments are functions. Naturally, Montague's suggestion depends on the thesis, which he in fact defended on philosophical grounds, that natural languages are, or are to be translated into, higher-order languages.

The theoretical considerations of section 3 makes Montague's device in principle unavailable to us: since VP is unsaturated, it cannot be an argument of the subject NP.[31] We are led, then, to something like the classical, Fregean view that the forms of quantificational sentences are structurally distinct from those of simple sentences. The assumption common to Montague's approach and the approach taken here is that clausal structures admit a uniform interpretive procedure.

Besides the above abstract considerations, there are a number of linguistic points that support the thesis that LF assigns scope to expressions of generality along the lines of QR. Some of these points turn on the unification of conditions on well-formedness or on interpretation that can be made to follow from the assimilation of cases of overt syntactic movement, on the one hand, and the hypothetical movement into LF, on the other.[32] Further, starting with Chomsky (1976), and pursued in different ways in Higginbotham (1980a, 1983a), Hornstein (1984), and others, LF-movement has been suggested as a mechanism for accounting for the 'crossover' conditions on anaphora, or, as in Hornstein's account, for distinctions among quantifiers.[33]

The strongest theory of the relation between syntactic structure and semantic interpretation is that interpretive principles are universal—that is, that human languages cannot differ in the ways that semantic principles apply to syntactic objects with their specific formal properties. The universality of LF-representations should be seen as a working hypothesis that is advanced about the child's contribution to knowledge of meaning. The differences between languages that do not flow from sheer lexical idio-

syncrasy are then to be seen as differences in the nature of formal grammatical conditions, not semantic rules.

This point of view may be put in terms familiar from Chomsky (1980).
The principles of language variation, or *parameters* in this terminology,
should have the property that the child can find evidence in the linguistic
environment that settles the question of which formal structures are admissible, expressed in terms of the values of these parameters. To speak and
understand the language, the child must know about meaning, including
both the meanings of words and the principles of interpretation of syntactic
structures. Obviously, words must be learned. Suppose that we conjecture
that lexical learning is all that is required to distinguish one language from
another. Then the principles of interpretation of structures cannot differ
from language to language, and the parameters of meaning are confined to
the meanings of words.

If our conjecture is correct, then there are no language-particular rules
of interpretation, apart from the lexicon. In this case, questions of scope,
both within a single language and across languages, will be answered in
just the way the questions raised in earlier sections were answered; in
particular, scopal ambiguity will be structural, and nonambiguity will have
a syntactic explanation. The method of LF-movement is one well-supported
way of formulating a theory with these properties. I will give some illustrations of the method at work, afterwards turning briefly to an alternative
view, due to Cooper (1983).

A point that seems to have exerted some influence on the discussion of
scopal properties of expressions is the observation that straightforward
quantificational ambiguity is not very widespread in English. Studies of
other languages are suggestive also. For instance, Huang (1982) reports
that in Chinese S-Structure c-command determines scope: it is not possible
for *A* to c-command *B* at S-Structure, and for *B* to be taken as having
wider scope than *A*. English then emerges as a marked case, being more
permissive. Even in English, there is a strong inclination to give subjects
wider scope than objects, as in the minimal pair (104)–(105), from Chomsky
(1957):

(104)   Everyone in this room speaks at least two languages.
(105)   At least two languages are spoken by everyone in this room.

It might therefore be thought that to posit distinct grammatical structures
for the sake of disambiguation of quantifiers is a marginal gain for theory.

This line of reasoning, I think, would stand the question of ambiguity on
its head. Seen right side up, the question is not what *allows* ambiguity of
scope, but rather what *prevents* it from occurring everywhere. For example,
a word-for-word rendition of (101) in Chinese is completely unambiguous,

having only the interpretation shown in (102). This consequence of course follows from Huang's syntactic parameter: there is an LF-representation of the Chinese equivalent of (101) as in (103), and it is ungrammatical.

Other conditions that prevent scopal ambiguities are of a syntactic character. For instance, as discussed in Rodman (1976), relative clauses are islands for quantification. The sentence (106).

(106)   There is a man whom every woman loves.

cannot mean that every woman is such that there is a man whom she loves. There is an LF-representation of (106) that does mean this, namely (107), and in virtue of syntactic conditions discussed in May (1977), it is ungrammatical, perhaps universally:

(107)   [[every woman][there is a man whom t loves t']]

Rodman's own method for deriving the nonambiguity of (106) was to introduce a syntactic rule that prevented the generation of the appropriate analysis tree in a Montague grammar. This method differs in the letter, but not in spirit, from that suggested here.

Cooper (1983) presents an interesting alternative picture. On this view, scopal islands and ambiguity are both to be explained by means of rules that associate the right types of interpretations with already given well-formed expressions. Concerning examples like (101), he writes (p. 3):

> There is no reason from a syntactic point of view to give [sentences with multiple generality] more than one syntactic structure. . . . However, it is normally assumed that [they] are semantically ambiguous, depending on which of the quantifiers has wider scope. We will explore the possibility that the semantics can be made to work in an interesting way without introducing an unmotivated syntactic rule, i.e., without creating a syntactic ambiguity corresponding to the semantic ambiguity.

The method that Cooper employs for sentences with multiple generality implies the data about these sentences by assigning to their (unambiguous) structural descriptions distinct courses of computation of their values. A given structural description is associated with an interpretation (an intension) and a pushdown store (the latter possibly empty). The items placed in the store are not phrases of the language, but their interpretations; presumably it is in this sense that the theory does not 'create a syntactic ambiguity.'

However, if cointensive items in the pushdown store are theoretically indistinguishable, then a question arises about the adequacy of the theory. Suppose that there are quantificational expressions, or other expressions that are assigned scope, that are cointensive, but differ in their scopal properties. The theory will then, wrongly, fail to distinguish them. If the natural diagnosis of the distinction between *anything* and *everything* is correct, for example, then in the pair (108)–(109).

(108)   Some people can do anything.
(109)   Some people can do everything.

we should say that the difference between them is just that the scope-bearing elements in (108) are interpreted uniquely with the universal *any* between the subject and the modal, whereas in (109) this is not the case. So if *anything* and *everything* are cointensive, then the account will wrongly assign to (108) an interpretation belonging only to (109), or will fail to assign to (109) an interpretation that it has. Similar examples are given in Lasnik (1972) and in Kroch (1974). The following pair, of a type due to Lasnik, is representative:

(110)   John didn't solve a problem.
(111)   John didn't solve some problem.

(110) is ambiguous, but (111) is not: we cannot have the scopal order *not . . . some*. Both Lasnik and Kroch explain the distinction in terms of a lexical condition, observing that the ambiguity of (110) is correlated with the grammaticality of (112), and the nonambiguity of (111) with the ungrammaticality of (113):

(112)   Not a problem was solved.
(113)   *Not some problem was solved.

On the view taken here (though not in Kroch (1974)), the condition is a filter at LF, ruling out for (111) the structure (114):

(114)   [[not][[some problem][John solved t]]]

But the phrases *some problem* and *a problem*, as they occur, say, in (115),

(115)   John solved $\begin{Bmatrix} a \\ some \end{Bmatrix}$ problem.

seem to be cointensive, each representing existential quantification over problems. Since the information that was used is lost as they are stored, it seems that Cooper's account will produce the wrong results either for (110) or for (111).

It would take us too far afield to speculate here about whether Cooper's view can be maintained in the face of these examples. However, the considerations behind them are, I submit, perfectly general: if there are cointensive items with distinct scopal properties, then either the stores must be augmented with *syntactic* features, in which case there will indeed be syntactic ambiguities in sentences with multiple generality, or else the theory will not be adequate.

In this section, I have not attempted to add to the already considerable arguments in the literature in favor of LF-movement of quantificational expressions, including *wh*-expressions; I do hope, however, to have clarified somewhat the status of the proposal. If Cooper's account cannot ultimately be sustained, then it is not clear to me that there are at present any alternatives that do not end up repeating the contents of the LF-movement theory in other terminology. I hope to discuss this matter elsewhere.

NOTIONAL AND FORMAL CATEGORIES

In the semantics briefly sketched here, the central data about the meanings of sentences have been simple and unexceptionable. But a number of questions of a metaphysical character make themselves felt in applications. The questions that I mean are not those aroused by fictions or by other pretenses of reference that may arise from time to time in speech or thought. Rather, they are manifested in the appearance of *prima facie* dubious objects, of a sort that, as Chomsky (1981) has emphasized, can be marked at least negatively by their nonappearance in the 'fragments' of natural language that are given in most of the literature on formal semantics.

In some cases, I think, the apparently dubious objects turn out not to be dubious except insofar as they are not material, or ordinary. But other cases require further consideration. Although I cannot consider more than a few types here, I will argue, for those examples that I do consider, that what those of the second class may show, in their various ways, is a kind of interaction between syntactic and semantic categories, whose study is potentially of great importance for semantics.

The categories that I call semantic are, in other terms, *notional*, classifying words, phrases, or sentences according to what they express, rather than according to their means of expressing it. Syntactic categories are *formal*, taking into account only part of speech or other grammatical features. The members of these categories overlap to a great extent. In formalized languages, they are either in one-to-one correspondence or at least observe Montague's condition that to a given syntactic category there corresponds only one semantic category. As I have said, even that condition seems to be too strong for natural languages. Nevertheless, that we do not have great difficulties in relating our native speech to the formalized idiom shows the extent of coincidence beetween the formal and the notional.

The notional categories that have been used here are of only three types, namely terms, predicate-expressions (including sentences), and variable-binding operators. The formal categories have been those of X'-theory, namely N, V, A, and P and their various projections, together with Infl and Spec. Inasmuch as elements of the formal categories may be notionally distinct, the grammar does not obey Montague's condition.

The notation in which we have written out the semantics for the examples treated here has been a notation that itself belongs to an outgrowth of our language. It differs somewhat in syntactic form (as in the use of variables) from the structure of the grammars that it is about, but it is not essentially unfamiliar. Metaphysical questions then are transferred to questions about that notation, and particularly about the interpretation of the quantifiers. In the classical setting, these are *objectual*. Nevertheless, other interpretations of expressions of generality are possible; for example, Parsons (1971) has given some reasons why we might regard certain quantifications as substitutional in character.

Plenty of pieces of our language, then, raise metaphysical questions that semantic theory simply transcribes in its own vocabulary. If we ask, for example, whether it is possible to interpret apparent reference to objects of some kind as a mere manner of speaking, the articulation of semantic theory does not have to wait in abeyance on the answer; on the contrary, it may be that the theory, by putting the question in more explicit form, is instrumental in resolving it.

Neither the question of quantifier interpretation, nor that of possible reinterpretation, puts obstacles in the path of semantic investigation. The worrisome cases that will be discussed here are of neither type. In analyzing a few prominent examples, I hope to indicate a method that could be applied to others.

One point of interest to which Chomsky (1981) draws attention is the intuitively different status of NPs like (116) and (117):

(116)   the flaw in the argument
(117)   the coat in the closet

He expresses the difference in terms of the presence or absence of commitment on the part of the user of the expression to an object referred to by the NP (p. 324):

> If I say 'the flaw in the argument is obvious, but it escaped John's attention,' I am not committed to the absurd view that among the things in the world are flaws, one of them in the argument in question. Nevertheless, the NP *the flaw in the argument* behaves in all relevant respects in the manner of the truly referential expression *the coat in the closet*.

Now, what is absurd about the view that there are flaws in arguments? Suppose a particular argument A is flawed. Then there is at least one flaw in it. A flawed F, in general, is in F that, judged by the standards of appraisal that apply to Fs, is not all that an F should be. Thus, *flawed*, like *real*, is a *trouser-word* in the sense of Austin (1962). Still, if an argument is flawed, then it possesses a feature in virtue of which it is not all that an argument should be: an unsupported step, perhaps. This feature is a flaw in the argument—*the* flaw, if there are no others.

Chomsky emphasizes that NPs like (116) have the usual properties of nominals: one can ask *how many* flaws there were in the argument, form statements of identity, and so forth. What room, then, is there for skepticism? Nevertheless, there is an important difference between (116) and (117). It reveals itself in the statement quoted above, in the clause (118):

(118)   '. . . among the things in the world are flaws, one of them in the argument in question.'

Certainly, (118) is a bit of a joke. Why is this? I think that the reasons are not metaphysical, but syntactic, stemming from the separation in (118) of the noun *flaw* from mention of the kind of thing that is said to be flawed. The description *flawed F* is like *bad F*, since a flawed *F* may be a perfect *G*. The noun *flaw*, since it is not interpretable except with reference to a kind of thing and its norms of appraisal, might be expected not to stand on its own. Compare (118) to (119):

(119)   Among the things in the world are bad ones (bad things), some of which are violinists.

(119) seems to be odd in the same way as (118). In particular, one would not assert the existence of bad violinists by using (119).

These examples may be considered in light of the discussion of modification in section 3. It was supposed that the control of thematic discharge by the configuration of government, and in particular the restriction of autonymous θ-marking to this configuration, is what accounts for the semantic distinction between *That is a big butterfly* and *That butterfly is big*. The same hypothesis will acount for a distinction between *He is a bad violinist* and *He is bad, and a violinist*, or between *That is a flaw in the argument* and *That is a flaw, and it is in the argument*. Another point is relevant, however. Terms of appraisal strongly necessitate an attribute, since, intuitively speaking, their interpretation is heterogeneous with respect to the attributive choice, in contrast to the case, say, of *big*, which varies along fewer dimensions. Hence, (118) is odd, since no attribute is available with respect to which the status of anything as a flaw can be determined. In contexts where the attribute is provided for, the noun can stand alone, as in (120):

(120)   The flaw (in your discussion) is in your exposition, not in your argument.

The case we have discussed resolves a worry that may be initially seen as metaphysical in favor of syntactic and semantic analysis. A type distinct from this in structure, but answerable, I believe, by the same general method, is exemplified by (121), discussed in Hornstein (1984):

(121)   That his$_i$ income is falling bothers $[\left\{ \begin{array}{c} \text{the} \\ \text{*every} \end{array} \right\}$ average man$]_i$

As the usual conditions would predict, in this configuration the pronoun can be anaphoric to the definite description, but not to the quantifier: (121) is a 'weak crossover' violation in the sense of Wasow (1972). Exactly the same facts obtain where *average man* is replaced by *tall man* or *man I saw yesterday*. There is a certain *autonomy* to the conditions on anaphora, insofar as they care only for whether the specifier of NP is a determiner like *the* or a quantifier like *every*, and are indifferent to the nature of the noun following. Hornstein expresses his conclusions from this example in metaphysical terms: the distinction between the expressions in (121) is indifferent to *existence*, since 'no one wishes to claim that there are objects that are average men in any meaningful sense.'[34] I will argue that, although Hornstein's point that anaphora are syntactically autonomous is correct and important, the metaphysical conclusions that he draws are not warranted.

First of all, there certainly is a sense in which there are average men. Suppose that we were going to test the truth of (122):

(122)   [The average man]$_i$ is worried that his$_i$ income is falling

We interview a number of men, taking care that we do not count those that are not average on whatever scale is in question: say, net worth. Suppose that by mistake we interview the millionaire Smith, and upon discovering that he as no worries about his falling income, count the result as evidence against (122). Someone who knew about Smith might correct us by saying, 'You shouldn't count Smith. He's not an average man, but a millionaire.'

In the last scenario, the interpretation of *average* was contextual; but that feature raises no metaphysical questions. The more interesting point, and the one that Hornstein presumably had in mind, is that it is only one of the scenarios we can associate with testing the truth of (122); for we might take it in such a way that it is true, not if men who are average are worried about their falling incomes, but only if, *on the average*, men are worried about their falling incomes. In the latter case, Smith counts, millionaire or no. The interpretation of *average* is then analogous to that seen in (123):

(123)   The average temperature here is 78 degrees.

Its meaning is effectively *adverbial*, although it remains formally an adjective. The oddity of (124) supports this diagnosis:

(124) ?The temperature which is average here is 78 degrees.

Again, the word *average* is not unique in showing an adverbial interpretation. Sentences like (125)

(125) Only the exceptional man saves his money.

are ambiguous between (a) only people who are exceptional on some scale of character, such as thriftiness, save their money, and (b) it is only exceptionally the case that one saves one's money. In neither case do we find anything metaphysically suspicious: in both interpretations, the only objects are people.[35]

For a third example, I turn to certain *nominalizations*, noted in Chomsky (1981, 344):

(126) [$_{NP}$ John's lack of [talent]]
(127) [$_{NP}$ John's lack of [interest in mathematics]]

These NPs as wholes, and their internal arguments *talent* and *interest in mathematics*, have abstract values. Depending on context and syntactic configuration, they can pattern with count or with mass nominals (nouns like *truth* have the same property). In a sentence like (128)

(128) John lacks [much interest in mathematics]

it is as if interest in mathematics is a stuff, which John can have more or less of. The stuff plausibly supervenes upon the psychology of persons or other agents: it is because John is little interested in mathematics that he lacks much interest in it. So abstract stuffs are at least a candidate for a reductive program. Semantic theory, at least in its first articulation, need not worry about this; on the other hand, since it seems plausible that the abstract stuffs are supervenient, it may be of interest to carry through the program in part as a reconstruction of the commonsense feel for things.

The nominals (126) and (127), and many other derived forms, have the property that their use implies truth of the sentence corresponding to the nominal. Consider (129):

(129) Mary persuaded me of [John's lack of talent]

(I owe this observation to Steven Abney, to whom I am indebted also for discussion.) What I am persuaded of does not have to be true; but if (129) is true, then John really does lack talent. The reason for this cannot, therefore, be in the verb *persuade*, which is nonfactive both when its object is sentential and when it is an ordinary NP, as in (130)–(131):

(130)   Mary persuaded me [that John lacks talent]
(131)   Mary persuaded me of [something (false)]

Similar contrasts between *that*-clauses and nominals are seen in (132)–(133):

(132)   Mary anticipates [that John lacks interest in mathematics]
(133)   Mary anticipates [John's lack of interest in mathematics]

This property of the abstract nominals seems to follow from the type of analysis suggested in Higginbotham (1983d) for a different type of case, namely the 'naked-infinitive' complements to verbs of perception and causation. Taking full advantage of the E-position, the sentence (134) may be rendered as shown in (135):

(134)   John lacks talent
(135) $(\exists e)$ lack(John,talent,e)

The nominal (126) is then interpreted as the restricted quantification (136),

(136) $[\exists e:$ lack(John,talent,e)$]$

and the sentence (129) as (137):

(137) $[\exists e:$ lack(John,talent,e)$]$ Mary persuaded me of e

If this is correct, then objects of persuasion, anticipation, and the like, include something like situations or facts.[36]

Is there an ontology of facts, or ontological commitment to facts? As given in Quine (1953), the notions of ontology, and of ontological commitment, are relative to the adoption of a *form of language,* or 'canonical notation,' with respect to which they are defined. Ontology, on this view, is the ontology of a theory T in a language L of the appropriate form. Thus, our question about (129) will depend on how (137) is understood relative to the canonical notation. If the account of the factivity of (129) is correct, then that is certainly *some* evidence that we talk about facts or situations, although it does not say more than is needed for the semantic theory about what the nature of these things might be. Similarly, when in section 3 it was suggested that the θ-marking of nominal heads in cases of ordinary modification, such as *big butterfly,* represents the filling of a thematic position in the adjective with an attribute, that is evidence that we in some way talk about attributes in these constructions; but a metaphysical investigation would take much more into account, and would ask more closely what these things are, if anything, that are attributes. What the semantic theory, supposing it is correct, says about these constructions is surely not *irrelevant* to metaphysical questions; but it is not the whole story about them either.

I have considered from the literature three cases of constructions that raise questions about the interaction of formal categories (specifically the category NP) with notional ones, and for each I have attempted an explanation of the judgments cited. The examples were each representative of an unbounded class, so that the explanations had a theoretical character; because of this, I think that further investigation is called for, in English and in other languages. A final example, of what I will call the *semi-productive idioms*, will conclude this discussion.[37]

Consider first the NP *Bill's sake*, say as it appears in (138):

(138)   I did it [for [Bill's sake]]

Everyone will agree that this NP does not refer to a thing. The evidence that this is so is that the construction is *syntactically defective*: we cannot have *every sake (*of Bill*), or even *the sake* in isolation. The predicate *for Bill's sake* applies to actions intended to benefit Bill; but it does not do this by being for a thing that is Bill's sake. Therefore, the semantics must not assign any value to this NP, though it will to the PP of which it is the grammatical object. The semantics is not compositional, and the construction is an idiom, whose properties are given directly in the lexicon.[38]

Syntactic defectiveness is the mark of an idiom; but defectiveness comes in varieties and degrees. In a case like (139),

(139)   I took a look at it.

where we are tempted to view the construction *took a look at* as a verb with approximately the meaning of 'scrutinized', we can see, by varying the construction, that we are in the presence of a process that is linguistically productive, up to a point:

(140)   I took a chance on it/offense at his remarks/etc.
(141)   I took a long, careful look at it.
(142)   The look I took at it was long enough for my purposes.

In (142), in particular, the phrase *take a look* is broken up, with a definite NP subject. However, the construction is not fully productive:

(142)   *Go take the look at it.
(144)   *Which looks did I take at it?
(145)   *A look would be hard to take at it.

Thus, the NP *a look* in (139) behaves in some ways like an argument and in others like a mere fragment of an idiom; and similarly for the phrases *a chance* and *offense* in (140). In this sense, the idiom is semiproductive. These types of examples raise important and rarely considered questions, both about the range of permitted syntactic forms and about the construction of interpretations. Insofar as they are so widespread and the facts about them are clearly known to native speakers, they call, not for abstraction from questions of meaning, but for the elaboration of theory.

CONCLUSIONS

I have argued that semantic theory, conceived as a section of the general project of understanding the nature of human language and the basis for its acquisition, is expressible as a formal system that uses principles connecting form and meaning to deduce, in the first instance, counterparts to ordinary statements about meaning, known to native speakers. It appears that both the nature of the theoretical problem and the kinds of answers that are at present well-supported lead to the conclusion that the basic principles of interpretation of categories or expressions, and of linguistic relations between them, are fixed universally and apply at the level of LF. However, languages differ according to syntactic principles, and these differences are responsible for the differences in interpretation that are observed between expressions in one language and their word-for-word renditions in another. The systems of antecedence and disjoint reference, the properties of the θ-Criterion, generalized to include all cases of thematic discharge, and the representation of generality all support this thesis. Finally, although it is not to be expected that categories of form and categories of meaning will match up in any tidy way, the enormous extent of their interpenetration and the systematic nature of their divergences conspire to suggest that we shall not go wrong in regarding the problems of linguistic theory from both points of view.

ACKNOWLEDGMENTS

The initial impetus for writing down some of the material presented here was an invitation to speak at the University of Massachusetts Conference on Parameters and Language Acquisition. I am grateful to the organizers for inviting me. Besides the specific acknowledgments noted, I should like to express my thanks to the anonymous reviewers, to the students in my spring 1984 classes, to the audience at the Princeton Cognitive Studies Colloquium, and to Noam Chomsky, Howard Lasnik, Daniel Osherson, Scott Weinstein, and Edwin Williams, for their friendly attention no less than for their criticism.

NOTES

[1] The major philosophical questions here, centering around the interpretation of sentential arguments, are not critical for the present discussion.

[2] I am indebted here to discussion with Kenneth Hale. See also Yang (1982) for a descriptive and theoretical discussion of the comparative syntax of reflexives and reciprocals.

[3] Grammatical theory, then, can be both about certain abstract things (the grammars) and of empirical, even psychological, significance. Grammars have empirical as well as abstract descriptions; it is the actual and possible connections between the two that belong to grammatical theory in my sense. The inquiry is psychological, at least if developmental psychology is psychology. (See also Higginbotham (1983c.) Of course, one may also worry about the indirectness of a mode of explanation that proceeds through the construct of a grammar, instead of directly from the experience of persons to what they mean by what they say; but this is an independent question.

[4] Higginbotham (1983b), following ideas due originally to McCawley (1968), gives further details. It may be that the theory can be expressed by a narrower conception of the fundamental syntactic objects, as in Lasnik and Kupin (1977). In general, the theory of grammar may distinguish phrase markers only up to certain equivalences, thereby justifying a more restrictive notation than I will use. For one argument to this effect, see Kupin (1978).

[5] Terminal, that is, as far as phrasal syntax is concerned; morphological structure may further proliferate syntactic trees.

[6] A number of ways of making the notion of government more precise are explored in Chomsky (1981). For a recent discussion, see Saito (1984).

[7] The level of discourse representations in the sense of Kamp (1981), for instance, is a counterpart to LF, since it is with respect to that level that truth and reference are determined, on his view. At another extreme, Barwise and Perry (1983) at least suggest the view that the only level needed is that of expressions themselves (see p. 40 and pp. 133ff.). The approach that individuates linguistic objects as is customary by using structural descriptions (and relations like antecedence) they call 'fine-grained,' and they propose that there is 'no *essential* difference' between this approach and one that recognizes 'an added parameter' that 'reflects ways of uttering the expression' (p. 135). Since I am not aware of any method for getting at the ways that an expression may be uttered that does not go via the attribution of a grammar to the utterer, I am not sure that more than nomenclature is involved here (perhaps Barwise and Perry would grant this, since they write that 'the parameter must in general be a rather abstract feature of the utterance').

[8] See also Davidson (1984, p. 68). Of course, the semantic notions show various kinds of relativity that reflect the contextuality of natural languages, to speaker, time, or place, and in some accounts to possible worlds (Davidson puts the last in the same category with relativity to models or interpretations, but I do not see that they need to be the same).

[9] Examples apart, the relativization is a matter of principle. The grammars of individual speakers are usually taken as the basic unit in linguistics, and I would follow this practice. However, it does not follow that every aspect of a person's grammar can be determined just through the facts about that person; for reasons

given in Burge (1979), the identity of a person's language owes something to its social setting.

[10] The relativization to grammars, rather than to persons (or persons at times) is'the appropriate one for linguistic theory to make, both because we are interested in the grammars that people could have, as well as those that they do have, and because the speech of individual persons shows mixtures of different grammars, given the heterogeneous nature of ordinary experience.

[11] As Richard Larson and Barbara Partee have pointed out to me, the device of projecting thematic grids is a way of incorporating, at least for these examples, a central point of categorial grammars—namely that, semantically, the expression *see Mary* is an intransitive verb, like *walk*.

[12] A *functional* is a function whose argument is itself a function. Chierchia (1983) argues for restrictions on the type-theoretic hierarchies proposed in Montague (1974) and other works.

[13] See also the discussions in Davidson (1980).

[14] Dual θ-marking would occur in verbs that were syntactically intransitive but semantically inherently reflexive, candidates being certain verbs of hygiene in English, such as *wash* and *bathe*. See Bouchard (1982) for a discussion of certain inherently reflexive constructions in French. Dual binding might take place in *comparative* constructions, as in (i).

(i)   [Fewer cups than saucers] are on the table.

where the complex *fewer . . . than* ends up binding the open positions in both nouns. It is not clear to me whether (32) should be modified in light of these examples.

[15] Following Rothstein (1983), for whom this principle figures as a premise. The words *saturated* and *unsaturated* are taken from Frege (who admitted functionals).

[16] Compare also Wallace (1972). Quine (1984) discusses Davidson's proposal both for itself and as an instance of a more general strategy.

[17] I am indebted here to comments by Saul Kripke.

[18] Although I do not discuss Siegel's work directly here, I should like to remark that her (1974) paper has been an important source for me on these questions.

[19] Kamp (1975) calls the adjectives of type (i) *intersective*. He further notes the special properties of the *extensional* adjectives, namely adjectives X for which arguments of the following structure are correct:

(i)   That is an $[_{N'}[_A X][_N F]]$;
      v is an F iff v is a G; therefore,
      That is an $[_{N'}[_A X][_N G]]$

Adjectives of spatial dimension, such as *big*, are presumably extensional. But adjectives of appraisal are not: one could not argue, even if all men were married, that an affectionate man is an affectionate husband (Hide Ishiguro's example). Because of these examples, the attributes indicated by nouns in the examples I attribute to θ-marking cannot be reduced to classes. An anonymous reviewer for *Linguistic Inquiry* remarks that, within the attributive category, there is a further distinction between modifications that make reference just to an attribute that a thing has, and those that make reference to the characteristic activity of a thing having that attribute. Roughly, the distinction is between being an A *for* an F or *among* the Fs and being an A *in the capacity of* an F or *as* an F; for example, between being an affectionate man for a husband and being affectionate as a husband.

[20] I am indebted here to Peter Ludlow.

[21] This type of construction is an example of the need for a relativity of the values of points in phrase markers to the structures they are embedded in, as suggested in Higginbotham (1984a).

[22] See the discussions in Evans (1980), Higginbotham (1980a, 1980b), Engdahl (1981), Lasnik (1982), Reinhart (1983), and Hornstein (1984), among others.

[23] In Higginbotham (1981) I observed distinctions like that between (68) and (69), within an assumed format of coindexing; choice of values was then stipulated as part of interpretation, instead of proceeding from the syntactic structures. Other examples given in that article will also serve to illustrate the points made here.

[24] I do not consider the 'corporate plural' of British English, or other cases where the formal morphology does not match the number of the interpretation.

[25] The restoration of indices, so as to allow multiples like $\{i_1, \ldots, i_n\}$, would not advance the discussion. We would then lose the account of the distinctions, for instance, between (68) and (69), or those in Montalbetti (1984). The question would also arise how these new indices were to be interpreted. The interpretation could not be that the number n gives the intended number of the referent; for it must be possible to wave at a crowd without knowing how many people one is waving at.

[26] More formally, predications $S = NP_{plural} - VP$ will be true only if NP_{plural} has at least two values and, that condition satisfied, if (but not only if) each value a of NP_{plural} is a value of VP. The value of a VP containing anaphoric elements such as *each other* is relative to an assignment f. For any f, the predicate *saw each other* is true of each a such that a is in $f(each\ other)$, and $saw(a,b)$ for each b in $f(each\ other)$ different from a. Because the pronoun is the antecedent of the reciprocal, $f(each\ other)$ must in S be the reference of *they*. This combination of conditions on VP and S then interprets (82).

[27] Schein (1984) discusses related cases.

[28] Given the existence of 'switch-reference' languages, discussed in Finer (1984b), which show overt obviative marking, there is no prospect of avoiding this notion in linguistic theory generally. Besides the examples cited, the free alternation between *her* and *her own* in (i), as well as the occurrence of reciprocals in genitive position, is already sufficient, in my opinion, to show that there is no complementary distribution between pronominals and anaphors in English:

(i)   Mary tied her (own) shoelaces.

The usual arguments against this view, including one due to David Dowty, cited in Reinhart (1983, footnote 15), point to emphatic uses such as (ii), where *her own* has no sentential antecedent:

(ii)   That's her own book.

This observation, employed as evidence against the anaphoric status of *X's own* in English, leaves it quite up in the air why, for instance, (iii) is unambiguous, the sole possible antecedent being the c-commanding NP *Mary's mother*, or why (iv), but not (v), is acceptable without emphatic stress:

(iii)   Mary's mother tied her own shoelaces.
(iv)   Tie your own shoelaces!
(v)   Tie his own shoelaces!

In any case, the evidence from (ii) has little force, since it shows only that the distribution of *X's own*, as used emphatically, is different from that of *X-self*.

[29] More formally, one considers structures as in (i):

(i) $S_0 = [[_{NP} \text{ every } N'] S_1]$

Let the notation '$g \sim_t f$' signify that $g(x) = f(x)$ if $x = t$. Then

(ii) $\mathbf{v}(T, S_0, f) \leftrightarrow [\text{every } g : g \sim_t f \ \& \ \mathbf{v}(g(t), N', g)] \ \mathbf{v}(T, S_1, g)$

The values assigned to the words in (99), and some set-theoretic steps, lead then to (100). As noted in Higginbotham (1984a), other quantifiers are to be treated as *every* is above, including those not expressible by the means available in quantification theory; for example, the clause for *most* would be just like (ii), except for a lexical substitution.

[30] As the letters of written English represent an accommodation to the phonological structure of the spoken language, so the variables of quantification theory represent an accommodation to LF. The customary notation of 'coindexing' should, on this view, be understood as a mere manner of speaking. It represents the importation back into linguistic description of a mode of expression that was created for the formalized languages. At the same time, the notation is clearly not 'variable-free,' in the sense of combinatory logic, for example. Besides myself, Cooper (1983) and Barwise and Perry (1983) carry out a semantic description that depicts anaphoric connections by a family of relations.

[31] Similarly, if the denotation of NP is a functional, it cannot be an argument of VP. Consequently, if the relation of NP to VP is that of function to argument, VP must be regarded after all as saturated. David Lewis has pointed out to me that this last route may be more thoroughly 'Montogovian' than the one that Montague himself took.

[32] For a survey of many of these, together with further arguments and suggestions for the exact shape of LF, see May (1985) and the references cited there, among them especially Huang (1982).

[33] It is sometimes thought that QR and other rules of scope assignment are semantic in character, rather than rules of formal syntax. This misinterpretation surfaces in Rooth (1984, p. 392), where it is conjectured that the reasons for scope assignment in Higginbotham (1983a) are 'interpretive.' In the passage that Rooth cites, however, I refer only to conditions on well-formedness. Rooth also supposes that it was intended that all *and only* operators are subject to scope assignment, a strengthening of the view I advanced that is neither stated nor implied in the material he quotes. Rooth argues very cogently for scope assignment to simple arguments (names) on the basis of distribution of interpretations for words like *only* and *even*; the argument is not unlike that of Reinhart (1983) on sloppy identity. That names may occur in nonargument positions at LF is therefore a feasible view.

[34] Hornstein (1984, p. 58). Although I am not persuaded by Hornstein's skepticism about semantics, I hope that it is clear that the present work is congenial to his view that there is no level of 'semantic representation' between syntax and context-dependent full interpretation. The conditions on meaning that are given by the predicate **v** represent *what* the native speaker knows (in fact, what is known universally without teaching, as a part of Universal Grammar), but, except insofar as they take into account the structure of syntax and the lexicon and are organized in explicit and deductive form, they do not represent *how* the speaker may represent that knowledge to himself. Indeed, the notion of a 'semantic representation' may mislead, since such a representation would be a syntactic object.

Despite his sketicism, much of Hornstein's work seems to me to presuppose semantics, in the sense in which this term is commonly used. For instance, in considering examples such as (i),

(i) *John$_i$ is his$_i$ cook.

he writes (p. 93), 'in [(i)] the indicated interpretation is disallowed.' Elsewhere, he makes it clear that the index i is part of the syntax of (i). So the coindexing—the fact that there are subscripts i in two places in (i)—indicates something about its interpretation. How does it do this? A theory of this matter would be a semantic theory.

[35] I am indebted here to discussion with Isabelle Haïk. Haïk (1983) discusses a number of important examples of related types.

[36] The naked-infinitive complements to perception verbs show referential transparency, as originally noticed by Jon Barwise; but the nominals under discussion here perhaps do not. The full account of these constructions will therefore be more complex than what is given here.

[37] In the following I am particularly indebted to Noam Chomsky.

[38] The NP *X's sake* is also defective, in that it is not a local governing category for pronominals:

(i) John saw *Mary* for *her* sake.
(ii) **John* saw May for *his* sake.

The PP *for X's sake* behaves in this syntactic respect like the purpose-clause *PRO to benefit X*.

REFERENCES

Austin, J. L., *Sense and Sensibilia*. Oxford: Oxford University Press, 1962.

Baker, M., 'Assume GF' and the Order of Morphemes. In I. Haïk and D. Massam (Eds), *MIT Working Papers in Linguistics*, 1983, Vol. 5, pp. 53–101.

Barwise, J. & Perry, J., *Situations and Attitudes*. Cambridge, MA: MIT Press, 1983.

Bouchard, D., *On the Content of Empty Categories*. Doctoral dissertation, Cambridge, MA: MIT, 1982.

Burge, T., Individualism and the Mental. In P. French *et al.* (Eds), *Studies in Metaphysics*, Midwest Studies in Philosophy 4. Minneapolis: University of Minnesota Press, 1979.

Chierchia, G., *The Syntax and Semantics of Infinitives and Gerunds*. Doctoral dissertation, Amherst, MA: University of Massachusetts, 1983.

Chomsky, N., *Syntactic Structures*. The Hague: Mouton, 1957.

Chomsky, N., Remarks on Nominalization. In *Studies on Semantics in Generative Grammar*. The Hague: Mouton, 1972, pp. 11–61.

Chomsky, N., Conditions on Rules of Grammar. In *Essays on Form and Interpretation*. Amsterdam: North-Holland, 1976, pp. 163–210.

Chomsky N., *Rules and Representations*. New York: Columbia University Press, 1980.

Chomsky, N., *Lectures on Government and Binding*. Dordrecht: Foris, 1987.

Chomsky, N., *Some Concepts and Consequences of the Theory of Government and Binding*. Cambridge, MA: MIT Press, 1982.

Chomsky, N., *Knowledge of Language*: *Its Nature, Origins, and Use*. Ms., Cambridge, MA: MIT, 1984.

Cooper, R., *Quantification and Syntactic Theory*. Dordrecht: Reidel, 1983.

Davidson, D., The Logical Form of Action Sentences. In D. Davidson (1980), 1966, pp. 105–122.

Davidson, D., Truth and Meaning. In D. Davidson (1984), 1967, pp. 17–36.

Davidson, D., *Essays on Actions and Events*. Oxford: Clarendon Press, 1980.

Davidson, D., *Inquiries into Truth and Interpretation*. Oxford: Clarendon Press, 1984.

Engdahl, E., *The Syntax and Semantics of Questions in Swedish*. Doctoral dissertation, Amherst, MA: University of Massachusetts, 1981.

Evans, G., Pronouns. *Linguistic Inquiry*, 1980, **11**, 337–362.

Fabb, N. *Syntactic Affixation*. Doctoral dissertation, Cambridge, MA: MIT, 1984.

Finer, D., Linking and Illicit Movement. MS., Madison: University of Wisconsin, 1984a.

Finer, D., *The Formal Grammar of Switch-Reference*. Doctoral dissertation, Amherst, MA: University of Massachusetts, 1984b.

Haïk, I., Syncategorematic Adjectives. MS., Cambridge, MA.: MIT, 1983.

Higginbotham, J., Pronouns and Bound Variables. *Linguistic Inquiry*, 1980a, **22**, 679–708.

Higginbotham, J., Anaphora and GB: Some Preliminary Remarks. In J. Jensen (Ed), *Proceedings of the Tenth Annual Meeting of NELS* (*Cahiers linguistiques d'Ottawa* 9.4). Ontario: Department of Linguistics, University of Ottawa, 1980b, pp. 223–236.

Higginbotham, J., Reciprocal Interpretation. *Journal of Linguistic Research*, 1981, **1**, 97–117.

Higginbotham, J., Logical Form, Binding, and Nominals. *Linguistic Inquiry*, 1983a, **14**, 395–420.

Higginbotham, J., A Note on Phrase Markers. *Revue Québecoise de Linguistique*, 1983b, **13**, 147–166.

Higginbotham, J., Is Grammar Psychological? In L. Cauman *et al.* (Eds), *How Many Questions? Essays in Honor of Sidney Morgenbesser*. Indianapolis: Hackett Publishing Co., 1983c, pp. 170–179.

Higginbotham, J., The Logic of Perceptual Reports: An Extensional Alternative to Situation Semantics. *The Journal of Philosophy* 1983d, **80**, 100–127.

Higginbotham, J., Linguistic Theory and Davidson's Program in Semantics. Cambridge, MA: MIT, unpublished, 1984a.

Higginbotham, J., Indefiniteness and Predication. Cambridge, MA: MIT, unpublished, 1984b.

Hornstein, N., *Logic as Grammar*. Cambridge, MA: MIT Press, 1984.

Huang, C.-T. J., *Logical Form in Chinese and the Theory of Grammar*. Doctoral dissertation. Cambridge, MA: MIT, 1982.

Jackendoff, R., *Semantic Interpretation in Generative Grammar*. Cambridge, MA: MIT Press, 1972.

Kamp, J. A. W., Two Theories About Adjectives. In E. L. Keenan (Ed), *Formal Semantics for Natural Language*. Cambridge: Cambridge University Press, 1975, pp. 123–155.

Kamp, J. A. W., A Theory of Truth and Semantic Representation. In J. Groenendijk *et al.* (Eds), *Formal Methods in the Study of Language*. Amsterdam: Mathematical Centre, 1981.

Kroch, A., *The Semantics of Scope in English*. Doctoral dissertation, Cambridge, MA: MIT, 1974.

Kupin, J., A Motivated Alternative to Phrase Markers. *Linguistic Inquiry*, 1978, **9**, 303–308.

Larson, R., *Restrictive Modification: Relative Clauses and Adverbs*. Philadelphia: University of Pennsylvania, unpublished, 1983.

Lasnik, H., *Analyses of Negation in English*. Cambridge, MA: MIT Press, 1972.

Lasnik, H., Remarks on Coreference. *Linguistic Analysis*, 1976, **2**, 1–22.

Lasnik, H., On Two Recent Treatments of Disjoint Reference. *Journal of Linguistic Research*, 1982, **1**, 48–58.

Lasnik, H. and Kupin, J., A Restrictive Theory of Transformational Grammar. *Theoretical Linguistics*, 1977, **4**, 173–196.

Lewis, D., General Semantics. In D. Davidson and G. Harman (Eds), *Semantics of Natural Language*. Dordrecht: Reidel, 1972, pp. 169–218.

Lewis, D., Languages and Language. In K. Gunderson (Ed), *Language, Mind, and Knowledge*. Minneapolis: University of Minnesota Press, 1975.

McCawley, J., On the Base Component of a Transformational Grammar. *Foundations of Language*, 1968, **4**, 243–269.

May, R., *The Grammar of Quantification*. Doctoral dissertation, Cambridge, MA: MIT, 1977.

May, R., *Logical Form: Its Structure and Derivation*. Cambridge, MA: MIT Press, 1985.

Montague, R., The Proper Treatment of Quantification in Ordinary English. In R. Montague (1974), 1970, pp. 247–270.

Montague, R., *Formal Philosophy*. In R. H. Thomason. New Haven, Connecticut: Yale University Press, 1974.

Montalbetti, M., *After Binding: On the Interpretation of Pronouns*. Doctoral dissertation, Cambridge, MA: MIT, 1984.

Parson, C., A Plea for Substitutional Quantification. *The Journal of Philosophy*, 1971, **68**, 231–237.

Postal, P., *Cross-Over Phenomena*. New York: Holt, Rinehart and Winston, 1971.

Quine, W. V., On What There Is. In *From a Logical Point of View*. New York: Harper and Row, 1953, pp. 1–19.

Quine, W. V., Ontological Relativity. In *Ontological Relativity and Other Essays*. New York: Columbia University Press, 1968, pp. 26–28.

Quine, W. V., Methodological Reflections on Current Linguistic Theory. In D. Davidson and G. Harman (Eds), *Semantics of Natural Language*. Dordrecht: Reidel, 1972, pp. 442–454.

Quine, W. V., Events and Reification. Paper delivered at the Conference on the Philosophy of Donald Davidson. New Brunswick, New Jersey: Rutgers University, 1984.

Reinhart, T., Coreference and Bound Anaphora: A Restatement of the Anaphora Questions. *Linguistics and Philosophy*, 1983, **6**, 47–88.

Roberts, C., Anaphora, Coreference, and the Binding Theory. Amherst: University of Massachusetts, 1984.

Rodman, R., Scope Phenomena, 'Movement Transformations', and Relative Clauses. In B. Partee (Ed), *Montague Grammar*. New York: Academic Press, 1976, pp. 166–176.

Roeper, T., Implicit Thematic Roles in the Lexicon and Syntax. Amherst: University of Massachusetts, 1983.

Rooth, M., How to Get 'Even' with Domain Selection. In C. Jones and P. Sells (Eds), *Proceedings of the Fourteenth Annual Meeting of NELS*. Graduate Linguistic Student Association, Amherst: University of Massachusetts, 1984, pp. 377–401.

Rothsteinb, S., *The Syntactic Forms of Predication*, Doctoral dissertation, Cambridge, MA: MIT, 1983.

Saito, M., On the Definitions of C-Command and Government. In C. Jones and P. Sells (Eds), *Proceedings of the Fourteenth Annual Meeting of NELS*. Graduate Linguistic Student Association. Amherst: University of Massachusetts, 1984, pp. 402–417.

Schein, B., Reference to Events and Quantification. Cambridge, MA: MIT, 1984.

Siegel, M., Capturing the Russian Adjective, In B. Partee (Ed), *Montague Grammar*. New York: Academic Press, 1984, pp. 293–309.

Stowell, T., *Origins of Phrase Structure*. Doctoral dissertation, Cambridge, MA: MIT, 1981.

Thráinsson, H., *On Complementation in Icelandic*. Doctoral dissertation, Cambridge, MA: Harvard University, 1979.

Wallace, J., Positive, Comparative, Superlative. *The Journal of Philosophy*, 1972, **69**, 773–782.

Wasow, T., *Anaphoric Relations in English*. Doctoral dissertation, Cambridge, MA: MIT, 1972.

Williams, E., Predication. *Linguistic Inquiry*, 1980, **11**, 203–238.

Williams, E., Semantic vs. Syntactic Categories. *Linguistics and Philosophy*, 1983, **6**, 423–446.

Williams, E., *There*-Insertion. *Linguistic Inquiry*, 1984, **15**, 131–153.

Yang, D.-W., The Extended Binding Theory of Anaphors. Seoul, Korea: Seoul National University, 1982.

2

(Nonsolipsistic) Conceptual Role Semantics

GILBERT HARMAN

Princeton University

WHAT IS (NONSOLIPSISTIC) CONCEPTUAL ROLE SEMANTICS?

In this paper I will defend what I shall call '(nonsolipsistic) conceptual role semantics'. This approach involves the following four claims:

(1) The meanings of linguistic expressions are determined by the contents of the concepts and thoughts they can be used to express;

(2) the contents of thoughts are determined by their construction out of concepts; and

(3) the contents of concepts are determined by their 'functional role' in a person's psychology, where

(4) functional role is conceived nonsolipsistically as involving relations to things in the world, including things in the past and future.

'Thoughts' here include beliefs, hopes, desires, fears, and other attitudes, in addition to thoughts properly so called. 'Functional role' includes any special roles a concept may play in perception and in inference or reasoning, including practical reasoning that leads to action.

I include the parenthetical modifier '(nonsolipsistic)' in the phrase '(nonsolipsistic) conceptual role semantics' to contrast this approach with that of some recent authors (Field, 1977; Fodor, 1980; Loar, 1981) who

55

think of conceptual role solipsistically as a completely internal matter. I put parentheses around 'nonsolipsistic' because, as I will argue below, the term is redundant: conceptual role must be conceived nonsolipsistically.

Commenting on Harman (1982), Loewer (1982) takes this nonsolipsistic aspect to be an important *revision* in an earlier solipsistic theory. This is not so. Conceptual role semantics derives from nonsolipsistic behaviorism. It was originally and has until recently been a nonsolipsistic theory (e.g., Sellars, 1954; Harman, 1973). This is discussed further below.

(Nonsolipsistic) conceptual role semantics represents one thing that might be meant by the slogan 'meaning is use'. But a proper appreciation of the point requires distinguishing (at least) two uses of symbols, their use in calculation, as in adding a column of figures, and their use in communication, as in telling someone the result.

Two Uses of Symbols: Communication and Calculation

Symbols that are being used in calculation are typically not being used at that time for communication. When you add a column of figures you are not normally communicating anything even to yourself. A similar point holds in reverse. Normally you communicate the results of your calculation to someone else only after you are done calculating. There are, of course, mixed cases. You might go through a calculation on the blackboard, intending your audience to see how things come out.

(Nonsolipsistic) conceptual role semantics may be seen as a version of the theory that meaning is use, where the basic use of symbols is taken to be in calculation, not in communication, and where concepts are treated as symbols in a 'language of thought'. Clearly, the relevant use of such 'symbols', the use of which determines their content, is their use in thought and calculation rather than in communication. If thought is like talking to yourself, it is the sort of talking involved in figuring something out, not the sort of talking involved in communication. Thinking is not communicating with yourself.

However, it would be more accurate to say content is use than to say meaning is use; strictly speaking, thoughts and concepts have content, not meaning.

The Meaning of 'Meaning'

I assume, following Grice (1959), that we can distinguish what he calls natural meaning (smoke means fire) from what he calls nonnatural meaning (the German word 'Feuer' means fire), and we can also distinguish (non-

(margin handwriting) Concepts = symbols in l of thought. Thought is figuring out, not communicating thought to self.

natural) speaker or user meaning (what a speaker or user of certain symbols means) from what certain words, expressions, or other symbols mean.

Grice proposes to analyze expression meaning in terms of speaker meaning; and he proposes, more controversially, to analyze speaker meaning in terms of a speaker's intentions to communicate something. This last proposal appears to overlook the meaningful use of symbols in calculation. You might invent a special notation in order to work out a certain sort of problem. It would be quite proper to say that by a given symbol you meant so-and-so, even though you have no intentions to use these symbols in any sort of communication.

There does seem to be some sort of connection between speaker or user meaning and the speaker's or user's intentions. Suppose you use your special notation to work out a specific problem. You formulate the assumptions of the problem in your notation, do some calculating, and end up with a meaningful result in that notation. It would be correct to say of you that, when you wrote down a particular assumption in your notation, you meant such and such by what you wrote: but it would be incorrect to say of you that, when you wrote the conclusion you reached in your notation, you meant so and so by what you wrote. This seems connected with the fact that, in formulating the assumption as you did in your notation, you intended to express such and such an assumption; whereas, in writing down the conclusion you reached in your notation, your intention was not to express such and such a conclusion but rather to reach whatever conclusion in your notation followed from earlier steps by the rules of your calculus. This suggests that you mean that so and so in using certain symbols if and only if you use those symbols to express the thought that so and so, with the intention of expressing such a thought.

Unexpressed thoughts (beliefs, fears, desires, etc) do not have meaning. We would not ordinarily say that in thinking as you did you meant that so and so. If thoughts are in a language of thought, they are not (normally) also expressed in that language.

I say 'normally' because sometimes one has thoughts in English or some other real language. Indeed, I am inclined to think a language, properly so called, is a symbol system that is used both for communication and thought. If one cannot think in a language, one has not yet mastered it. A symbol system used only for communication, like Morse code, is not a language.

Concepts and other aspects of mental representation have content but not (normally) meaning (unless they are also expression in a language used in communication). We would not normally say that your concept of redness meant anything in the way that the word 'red' in English means something. Nor would we say that you meant anything by that concept on a particular occasion of its exercise.

words have use meaning, not sentences

Thoughts and Concepts

It is sometimes suggested that words have meaning because of the way they are used; the meaning of a word is its use in the language. Ryle (1953, 1961) observes that it would be a mistake to try to extend this idea directly to sentences. There are indefinitely many sentences. Obviously, most of them are never used at all, and most sentences that are used are used only once. Sentences do not normally have regular uses in the way that words do. Sentences have meaning because of the words they contain and the way these words are put together. A use theory of meaning has to suppose it is words and ways of putting words together that have meaning because of their uses, not sentences.

Similarly, it is concepts that have uses or functions or roles in thought, not the possible attitudes in which those concepts occur. There are indefinitely many possible attitudes. Most possible attitudes are never taken by anyone, and most attitudes that are at some point taken by someone are taken by someone only once. Possible beliefs, desires, and other attitudes do not normally have regular uses or functions or roles that make them the possible attitudes they are. Consider, for example, what use or role or function there might be for the possible belief of yours that you have bathed in coca cola. This belief would have a certain content, but no obvious use or role or function. The content of a belief does not derive from its own role or function but rather from the uses of the concepts it exercises.

Loar (1983a) objects to this. He supposes it implies that thoughts literally contain (tokens of) concepts as parts, so that, for example, all conjunctive beliefs share a constituent representing conjunction, and similarly for other concepts. Loar rejects this view, arguing that our ordinary conception of belief and other attitudes does not require it. He agrees we must suppose that all conjunctive beliefs have something in common, and similarly that all negative beliefs have something in common, but this he says is not to suppose that all conjunctive or negative beliefs have a *constituent* in common. He says that conjunctive or negative beliefs might have certain 'second order properties in common' without having any 'first order, structural properties in common'.

I find the issue here quite obscure, like the question of whether the prime factors of a number are constituents of the number or not. All numbers that have three as a prime factor have something in common. Do they have a first order structural property in common or only a second order property? This does not strike me as a well defined issue, and I feel the same way about Loar's issue. Just as it is useful for certain purposes to think of the prime factors of a number as its constituents, it is also useful for certain purposes to think of attitudes as having concepts as constituents. But it is hard to know what is meant by the question whether concepts are literally constituents of thoughts.

It may seem that Loar is thinking along the following lines. A relation of negation might hold between two beliefs without there being anything that determines which belief is the negative one, and similarly for other concepts. In the case of conjunction, let us say that P has the 'relation of conjunction' to Q and R if and only if Q and R together obviously imply and are obviously implied by P. Belief P might have the relation of conjunction in this sense to Q and R without anything distinguishing the case in which P has the structure 'Q and R' from that in which P does not have that structure but instead Q and R have the respective structures, 'P or S' and 'P or not S'. Similarly for other concepts.

This may seem a promising way to understand a denial of the claim that thoughts are constructed out of concepts, until one realizes that what is being imagined is simply that equivalent beliefs cannot be distinguished, so that 'not not P' cannot be distinguished from 'P', 'P and Q' cannot be distinguished from 'neither not P nor not Q', and so on. But is is easy to reject this possibility. If the issue is whether there can be two different but logically equivalent beliefs, the answer is obviously 'Yes'. So this cannot be how Loar intends the issue to be understood.

Loar (1983a) says that the issue is which of the following possibilities is correct: is it (1) that the structures attitudes have helped explain functional relations among attitudes or is it (2) that the functional relations among the attitudes help explain why we assign sentence-like structures to the attitudes? But (1) and (2) are not exclusive alternatives. Any reasonable theory will allow that people often accept conclusions *because* the conclusions are instances of generalizations they accept. This is to allow that beliefs can have the quantified structure of generalizations and that this can explain certain functional relations among beliefs. And any reasonable theory will allow that we determine what structures attitudes have by considering functional relations among attitudes. So any reasonable theory will accept both (1) and (2).

In a reply to this, Loar (1983b) says to consider what it would be like if a conjunctive belief $C(P,Q)$ were internally represented as a single unstructured symbol R that was linked by particular rules to its conjuncts P and Q, so that R obviously implied and was obviously implied by P and Q although one's recognition of the implication did not depend on thinking of R as the conjunction of P and Q. In other words, the reason why one immediately recognized the implication from R to P would in this case be different from the reason why one immediately recognized the implication from U to S, where U was the conjunction of S and T. The fact that R

and U were conjunctions would not be part of the explanation of one's recognition of these implications. And similarly for other logical constants.

But this sort of example is precisely *not* compatible with our ordinary thinking about belief, since (as I have already observed) we do suppose people often recognize implications because of the relevant formal properties; for example, we think people often accept certain conclusions because the conclusions are instances of generalizations they accept, which is to think that beliefs have a certain internal structure. So this example does not support Loar's scepticism.

CONTENT AND INFERENTIAL ROLE

Types of Role

Assuming conceptual role semantics as a basic framework, it is plausible that all concepts have a function in reasoning that is relevant to their content. No doubt, some concepts have the content they have primarily because of a special role they play in perception, color concepts for example. But the content of even these concepts depends to some extent on inferential role. A given color concept is the concept of a normally persisting characteristic of objects in the world, a characteristic that can be used both to keep track of objects and as a sign of other things. For example, greenness is a sign of unripeness in certain fruits. Moreover, there are various internal relations among colors. From the premise that an object is red at a certain place at a certain time one can infer that the object is not also green at that place and time.

In the case of concepts of shape and number, inferential connections play a larger role. Perceptual connections are still relevant; to some extent your concept of a triangle involves your notion of what a triangle looks like and your concept of various natural numbers is connection with your ability to count objects you perceive. But the role these notions play in inference looms larger.

The concept expressed by the word 'because' plays an important role in one's understanding of phenomena and has (I believe) a central role in inference, since inference is often inference to the best explanation. This role makes the concept expressed by 'because' the concept it is, I believe. Is perception relevant at all here? Perhaps. It may be that you sometimes directly perceive causality or certain explanatory relations, and it may be that this helps to determine the content of the concept you express with the word 'because'. Or perhaps not. Maybe the perception of causality and other explanatory relations is always mediated by inference.

Logical words like 'and', 'not', 'every', and 'some' express concepts whose function in inference seems clearly quite important to their content, which is why it seems plausible to say that these words do not mean in intuitionistic logic and quantum logic what they mean in so called classical logic, although even here there may be crucial perceptual functions. It may, for example, be central to your concept of negation that you can sometimes perceive that certain things are not so, as when you perceive that Pierre is not in the cafe, for instance. It may be central to your concept of generality or universal quantification that you can sometimes perceive that everything of a certain sort is so and so, for instance that everyone in the room is wearing a hat.

It is possible that there are certain sorts of theoretical term, like 'quark', that play no role in perception at all, so that the content of the concepts they express is determined entirely by inferential role. (But maybe it is important to the concept of a quark that the concept should play a role in the perception of certain pictures or diagrams!)

Inference and Implication

Logical words have a function in inference and reasoning because certain implications and inconsistencies depend on them. Inference is, of course, a process of thought which typically culminates in a change in view, a change in your beliefs if it is theoretical reasoning, a change in plans and intentions for practical reasoning. (There is also the limiting case in which you make no change.)

There is as yet no substantial theory of inference or reasoning. To be sure, logic is well developed; but logic is not a theory of inference or reasoning. Logic is a theory of implication and inconsistency.

Logic is relevant to reasoning because implication and inconsistency are. Implication and inconsistency are relevant to reasoning because implication is an explanatory relation and because inconsistency is a kind of incoherence, and in reasoning you try among other things to increase the explanatory coherence of your view (Harman, 1986a). Particularly relevant are relations of *immediate* or obvious psychological implication and *immediate* or obvious psychological inconsistency.

These notions, of immediate implication and inconsistency for a person S, might be partly explained as follows. If P and R immediately imply Q for S, then, if S accepts P and R and considers whether Q, S is strongly disposed to accept Q too, unless S comes to reject P or R. If U and V are immediately inconsistent for S, S is strongly disposed not to accept both, so that, if S accepts the one, S is strongly disposed not to accept the other without giving up the first.

I should stress that these dispositions are only dispositions or tendencies, which might be overridden by other factors. Sometimes one has to continue to believe things one knows are inconsistent, because one does not know of any good way to resolve the inconsistency. Furthermore, the conditions I have stated are at best only necessary conditions. For example, as Scott Soames has pointed out to me, U and 'I do not believe U' satisfy the last condition without being inconsistent. Soames has also observed that the principles for implication presuppose there is not a purely probabilistic rule of acceptance for belief. Otherwise one might accept P and Q without accepting their conjunction, which they obviously imply, on the grounds that the conjuncts can have a high probability without the conjunction having such a high probability. I have elsewhere argued against such a purely probabilistic rule (Harman, 1986a).

Now, if logical concepts are entirely fixed by their functions in reasoning, a concept C expresses logical conjunction if it serves to combine two thoughts P and Q to form a third thought $C(P,Q)$, where the role of C can be characterized in terms of the principles of 'conjunction introduction' and 'conjunction elimination'. In other words, P and Q obviously and immediately imply, and are immediate obvious psychological implications of, $C(P,Q)$. Similarly, a concept N expresses logical negation if it applies to a thought P to form a second thought $N(P)$ and the role of N can be characterized as follows: $N(P)$ is obviously inconsistent with P and is immediately implied by anything else that is obviously inconsistent with P and *vice versa*, that is, anything obviously inconsistent with $N(P)$ immediately implies P. (I am indebted to Scott Soames for pointing out that this last clause is needed.) In the same way, concepts express one or another type of logical quantification if their function can be specified by relevant principles of generalization and instantiation. To repeat, this holds only on the assumption that logical concepts are determined entirely by their role in reasoning and that any role in perception they might have is not essential or derives from role in reasoning.

Logical Form

Accounts of the logical forms of sentences of a natural language can shed light on meaning to the extent that they indicate aspects of language on which implications may depend, since this is to indicate something about the inferential role played by the concepts expressed by those aspects of language.

Presumably, such accounts of logical form should be relevant to or perhaps even part of a grammatical analyses of the relevant sentences. Here is an area where there may be useful interaction between what philosophers do and what linguists do. However, as Chomsky (1980) observes, distinctions that are important for linguistics may not coincide with the distinctions that are important for philosophers. Or, to put the point in another way, the factors that determine relations of implication may not all be of the same sort. Some may be aspects of what Chomsky calls 'sentence grammar', others may not. And some aspects of 'sentence grammar' that function syntactically like logical features may not be directly connected with implication. For example, Chomsky suggests that the rules of grammar that determine how quantifiers are understood, which are of course crucial in determining what the logical implications of the sentence are, may be the same as the rules that determine such things as the 'focus' of a sentence, something which seems not to affect the logical implications of a sentence but only its 'conversational implicatures'.

Indeterminacy

There are apparently competing analyses of the logical forms of sentences. Where one analysis sees modal logic or tense logic, another sees reference to possible worlds or times. Where one analysis sees reference to events, another analysis invokes an adverbial logic, and so on. Similarly, there are apparently competing grammatical theories; Montague grammar, Chomsky's current framework in terms of rules of government and binding, and many other variations. What are we to make of all this?

Quine (1960) argues plausibly that, even given all possible evidence about a language, that may not decide between various locally incompatible 'analytical hypotheses', where by 'analytical hypotheses' he means hypotheses about logical or grammatical form of the sort just mentioned. There has been considerable dispute as to exactly how Quine's claim should be interpreted, whether it is true, and what the implications of its truth might be. It has been said (falsely) that all Quine's thesis amounts to is the claim that a theory is underdetermined by the evidence. It has also been said (correctly, I believe) that whatever valid point Quine may be making, it does not involve any significant difference between the 'hard sciences', like physics, and the study of language.

One issue suggested by Quine's argument is this. Suppose you have a theory, of physical reality or of language, which you think is true. Even though you think the theory is true, you can go on to consider what aspects of the theory correspond to reality and what aspects are instead mere

artifacts of the notation in which the theory is presented. A true geographical description of the Earth will mention longitudes as well as cities
and mountains, but longitudes do not have geographical reality in the
way that cities and mountains do. It is true that Greenwich, England, is at
zero degrees longitude, but this truth is an artifact of our way of describing
the Earth, since there are other equally true ways of describing the geo-
graphy of the Earth that would assign Greenwich other longitudes.
Similarly, there are various true physical descriptions of the world, which
assign a given space–time point different coordinates. It may be true that
under a particular description a particular point has the special coordinates
(0,0,0,0) but that is an artifact of the description which, by itself, does not
correspond to anything in reality, and the same is true as regards grammars
and theories of logical form. Even if a given account of grammar or logical
form is true, there is still a question what aspects of the account correspond
to reality and what aspects are merely artifacts of that particular description.
It is quite possible that several different locally incompatible accounts might
all be true, just as several different locally incompatible assignments of
longitudes and latitudes to places on Earth might all be true.

This might be put in another way. Reality is what is invariant among true
complete theories. Geographical reality is what is invariant in different true
complete geographical descriptions of the world. Physical reality is what is
invariant in different true complete physical descriptions of the universe.
What worries Quine is that he has a fairly good sense of physical and
geographical reality but little or no sense of grammatical reality or of the
reality described by accounts of logical form. Indeed, Quine is inclined to
think that there are only two relevant levels of reality here:

(1)   physical reality at the level of neurophysiology, and
(2)   behavioral reality, including dispositions to behave in various ways.

An alternative view is that there are other, functionally defined levels of
reality between the two levels Quine acknowledges. I see no other way to
investigate this issue except by seeing where current investigation of grammar and logical form ultimately leads. Of course, from a heuristic point of
view, it is probably best to suppose that different accounts of grammar and
logical form make conflicting claims about reality unless there is some
reason to think otherwise (Harman 1986c).

The possibility of indeterminacy allows an interpretation of the question
raised by Loar (1983a) and discussed above as to whether thoughts really
contain concepts as parts. Suppose there are many different sets of 'analytical hypotheses' that account for the facts. On one set of hypotheses, Q
would be a simpler belief than P, and P would be the explicit negation of
Q. On a different set of analytical hypotheses things would be reversed and

Q would be the explicit negation of P. Nothing would determine which belief really contained the explicit negation independently of one or another set of hypotheses. If this should prove to be so, which I doubt, it would show that a particular assignment of structure to a given thought was an artifact of a given way of describing thoughts. It would of course also be true that, *relative to a given set of analytical hypotheses*, a given thought would truly consist in a particular structure of concepts.

Meaning and Truth Conditions

Davidson (1967), Lewis (1972), and others have argued that an account of the truth conditions of sentences of a language can serve as an account of the meanings of those sentences. But this seems wrong. Of course, if you know the meaning in your language of the sentence S, and you know what the word 'true' means, then you will also know something of the form 'S is true if and only if . . .', for example '"Snow is white" is true if and only if snow is white' or '"I am sick" is true if and only if the speaker is sick at the time of utterance'. But this is a trivial point about the meaning of 'true', not a deep point about meaning (Harman, 1974).

There are well known difficulties with the view that a theory of truth might provide even part of a theory of meaning (e.g., Foster, 1976). For one thing, how are the truth conditions to be specified? There seem to be two possibilities. The first is that truth conditions are assigned to beliefs by virtue of the theory's implying clauses of the form, 'Belief b is true if and only if C'. Then the problem is that the same theory will also imply indefinitely many results of the form 'C if and only if D', where 'C' and 'D' are not synonymous, so the theory will imply indefinitely many 'incorrect' clauses of the form 'Belief b is true if and only if D'. The problem is, in other words, that specifying truth conditions in this way does not distinguish among beliefs that are equivalent in relation to the principles of the theory.

The other possibility is to allow that equivalent beliefs might have different truth conditions. The trouble with this possibility is that it treats truth conditions as very much like meanings or contents which are no longer specificiable by the usual Tarski-type theories of truth. It is unclear how this appeal to truth conditions might offer any benefit to the theory of content beyond the tautology that a theory of content must include an account of content.

This is not to deny that attempts to develop theories of truth adequate for certain aspects of natural language may well shed light on meaning. Examples might include the truth functional analysis of 'and', 'not', and 'or'; the Frege–Tarski analysis of quantification; Davidson's analysis of action sentences; and the possible worlds account of modality. But in all these cases the analyses help specify implications among sentences. Their bearing on meaning may be due entirely to that apart from anything further necessary to having a theory of truth, although this, of course, allows that there may also be a heuristic point to attempting to develop theories of truth (Harman, 1972, 1974).

Probabilistic Semantics

Field (1977) suggests that inferential role might be captured in terms of a probability distribution. This would yield at best a theory of probabilistic implication or coherence, not a theory of inference in the relevant sense, involving (normally) a certain sort of change in view. Furthermore, people do not and could not operate probabilistically, since keeping track of probabilities involves memory and calculating capacities which are exponentially exploding functions of the number of logically unrelated propositions involved (Harman, 1985, 1986a).

For the most part you have to accept propositions in an all or nothing way. Conservatism is important. You should continue to believe as you do in the absence of any special reason to doubt your views, and in reasoning you should try to minimize change in your initial opinions in attaining other goals of reasoning. Such other goals include explanatory coherence and, of course, practical success in satisfying your needs and desires. But these points are vague and do not take us very far. Furthermore, something ultimately needs to be said about practical reasoning (Harman, 1986a, b).

CONCEPTUAL ROLE AND EXTERNAL WORLD

In the most elementary cases, possession of a concept of something is connected with perceiving that thing and acting appropriately towards it. What one perceives the thing *as* is reflected in the way one acts. For example, an animal perceives something as food if it treats what it perceives as food, for example by eating what it perceives. Of course, there are complications to this simple story and things can go wrong. But this represents the most elementary case and more complex cases must be conceived in terms of it. So for example, we can describe a creature as mistakenly thinking that something is food when it tries to treat it as food. In so describing the animal, we appeal to a conception of what happens in the normal case when nothing goes wrong and there is no mistake.

In Harman (1973) I emphasize how the appeal to a background of normality figures in all identifications of representational states, even those in an artifact such as a radar aimer. A radar aimer interprets data from radar and calculates where to fire guns in order to shoot down enemy planes. We can describe the device as representing the present and future locations of the planes because radar waves reflected from the planes are received and interpreted to form a representation of the future locations of the planes, and that representation is used in the aiming and firing of the guns that shoot down the planes. We can describe the device as representing the locations of planes even if something goes wrong and the guns miss, because we have a conception of the *normal operation* of the radar aimer. We can even treat the device as representing enemy planes when it is being tested in the laboratory, unconnected to radar and guns, since in our testing we envision it *as* connected in the right way. However, given a different conception of normal context, we could not describe the device as representing planes at all.

The moral is that (nonsolipsistic) conceptual role semantics does not involve a 'solipsistic' theory of the content of thoughts. There is no suggestion that content depends only on functional relations among thoughts and concepts, such as the role a particular concept plays in inference. Of primary importance are functional relations to the external world in connection with perception, on the one hand, and action, on the other. The functions of logical concepts can be specified 'solipsistically', in terms of the inner workings of one's conceptual system, without reference to things in the 'external world'. But this is not true for the functions of other concepts.

Concepts include individual concepts and general concepts, where an individual concept functions in certain contexts to pick out a particular object in the external world to which a general concept applies, in the simplest case to enable one to handle the object as a thing of the appropriate sort (cf Strawson, 1974, pp. 42–51). To repeat an earlier example, it is an important function of the concept of food that in certain circumstances one can recognize particular stuff as food, this recognition enabling one to treat that thing appropriately as food by eating it (Dennett, 1969, p. 73). What makes something the concept red is in part the way in which the concept is involved in the perception of red objects in the external world. What makes something the concept of danger is in part the way in which the concept is involved in thoughts that affect action in certain ways.

The Division of Linguistic Labor

The content of certain concepts appears to depend crucially on functional relations between those concepts and certain words in a public language. You might have a concept of an oak tree by virtue of which you have thoughts about oak trees where the crucial functional relation is a relation between your concept and the word 'oak' in English. You might, for example, wonder whether there were any oak trees in your back yard even if you cannot distinguish oak trees from elm trees and do not know any of the distinguishing properties of these two sorts of trees (Putnam, 1975; Kripke, 1972).

(Nonsolipsistic) conceptual role semantics asserts that an account of the content of thoughts is more basic than an account of communicated meaning and the significance of speech acts. In this view, the content of linguistic expressions derives from the contents of thoughts they can be used to express. However, allowance must also be made for cases in which the content of your thoughts depends in part on the content of certain words, such as 'oak' and 'elm'.

Of course, in this case, there are other people who can recognize oaks and distinguish them from elms and who know various distinguishing properties of the trees. These other people may have a concept of an oak tree which has functional roles that are sufficient to make it the concept of an oak tree apart from any relations the concept has with the word 'oak'. It is plausible

(1)   that their concept acquires its content from this aspect of its functional role, i.e. its role apart from its relation to the word 'oak',

(2)   that the word 'oak' as they use it has the meaning it has because of its connection with their concept of an oak tree

(3)   that the word 'oak' as used by a more ignorant person can have the same meaning by virtue of connections between that person's ignorant use of the word and the expert's use, and

(4)   that the content of the more ignorant person's concept of an oak tree derives from its connection to his or her use of the word and its meaning as he or she uses it.

Of course, the content of the more ignorant person's concept of an oak tree is not as rich as, so not the same as, the content of the expert's concept. But the ignorant person's concept is still a concept of an oak tree, by virtue of its connection with the word 'oak'.

(1)–(4) would still allow one to say that the meanings of words derive ultimately from the contents of concepts the words are used to express, where the contents of these concepts do not themselves derive from the meanings of words; however the meanings of a particular person's words may not derive in this way from the contents of that person's concepts.

This suggests an interesting question. Is there any word for which there is a real division of linguistic labor, so that no single person has a corresponding concept whose content is functionally determined apart from its relation to the person's use of that word? It is certainly imaginable that this should be so in connection with some sort of group investigation. Different people might investigate different aspects of a phenomenon which each might identify as 'whatever it is we are all investigating and which has such and such effects when investigated in the way in which I have investigated it'. Even in such a case, the meaning of the word would derive from the role the corresponding concept plays in thought, although different aspects of that role would be fulfilled by different people's instance of the concept.

Twin Earth

Putnam imagines a world, which he calls 'Twin Earth', which is just like Earth except for certain minor differences. There are on Twin Earth duplicates of all the people on Earth and the people on Twin Earth speak the same languages as on Earth, using expressions in the same way, except that, because of the minor differences between Earth and Twin Earth, they sometimes refer to different things by their words. In particular, the main difference between Twin Earth and Earth is that where there is water on Earth there is on Twin Earth a liquid with the same macro properties as water but a different chemical structure, which Putnam calls 'XYZ'.

Now, comparing Earth in 1750 (before the micro-structure of water has been investigated) with Twin Earth at the corresponding time, we find that the English word 'water' means something different in the two places, simply because the word is used on Earth to refer to what is in fact H_2O and is used on Twin Earth to refer to what is in fact XYZ. Similarly, where Earthlings think about H_2O, Twin Earthlings think about XYZ. This difference is not in 1750 reflected in any difference in dispositions to react to various perceptual situations, in any difference in inferences that people in the respective places would make, nor in any differences in the actions which people undertake as the result of thoughts involving the relevant concept.

The difference is also not simply a difference in context of utterance or context of thought. Suppose an Earthling were to travel by spaceship and land on an ocean of XYZ in Twin Earth. Looking around, the Earthling comes to believe there is water all around. This belief is false, since the Earthling's concept of water is a concept of something that is in fact H_2O. The Earthling's concept of water remains a concept of the same thing that is referred to by 'water' on Earth even though the Earthling is now located in a different context. The context of the thoughts of the Earthling and the context of the thoughts of the Twin Earthlings are now the same; but their thoughts are about XYZ where his are still about water. So this difference in the content of the thoughts of Earthlings and Twin Earthlings cannot be simply a difference in the context in which they have their thoughts.

The difference is due rather to the fact that the content of a person's concept is determined by its functional role in some normal context. The normal context for an Earthling's thoughts about what he or she calls 'water' is here on Earth, while the normal context for a Twin Earthling's thoughts about what he or she calls 'water' is on Twin Earth.

The normal context can change. If the traveler from Earth to Twin Earth stays on, after a while the normal context for the concepts he or she uses will be properly taken to be the Twin Earth contexts. Thoughts about what he or she calls 'water' will be properly considered thoughts about XYZ rather than H_2O. There is, of course, a certain amount of arbitrariness in any decision about when this change has occurred. It will sometimes be possible with equal justice to consider a given thought a thought about H_2O or a thought about XYZ.

A similar arbitrariness would arise concerning a person created spontaneously in outer space as the improbable result of random events at the quantum level, supposing the person were saved from space death by a fortuitously passing space ship, and supposing the person spoke something that sounded very much like English. Suppose, indeed, that this person is a duplicate of you and also (of course) of your Twin Earth counterpart. When the person has thoughts that he or she would express using the term 'water', are these thoughts about water (H_2O) or thoughts about XYZ? If we interpret this person's thoughts against a normal background on Earth, we will interpret the relevant thoughts as thoughts about water. If we take the normal background to be Twin Earth, they are thoughts about XYZ. Clearly it is quite arbitrary what we say here.

Qualia

According to (nonsolipsistic) conceptual role semantics, then, the content of a thought is not a matter of the 'intrinsic nature' of either that thought or other mental states and experiences but is rather a matter of how mental states are related to each other, to things in the external world, and to things in a context understood as a normal context. There is a familiar objection (Block & Fodor, 1972; Nagel, 1974) to this which claims that content is not determined always by such functions or relations. In this view the intrinsic qualities or 'qualia' of certain experiences are sometimes relevant. It is said that your concept of red involves your notion of what it is like to see something red, where what it is like to see something red is not just a matter of the functional or relational characteristics of the relevant experience but of its intrinsic character as well.

One argument for this is that it is possible to imagine a person whose spectrum was inverted with respect to yours, so that the quality of experience you have in seeing something red is the quality this other person has in seeing something green, the quality of experience you have in seeing something blue is the quality this other person has in seeing something orange, and similarly for other colors, although in all relevant respects your color experiences function similarly, so that each of you is just as good as the other in applying the public color words to colored objects. According to this argument, the two of you would have different concepts which you would express using the word 'red', although it might be difficult or even impossible to discover this difference, since it is not a functional difference.

I speak of an 'argument' here, although (as Lewis (1980) observes in a similar context), the 'argument' really comes down simply to denying the functionalist account of the content of concepts and thoughts, without actually offering any reason for that denial. This makes the 'argument' difficult to answer. All one can do is look more closely at a functionalist account of the content of color concepts in order to bring out the way in which, according to functionalism, this content does not depend on the intrinsic character of experiences of color.

How could you imagine someone whose spectrum was inverted with respect to yours? One way would be to imagine this happening to yourself. Suppose there were color-inverting contact lenses. You put on a pair of lenses and the colors things seem to have are reversed. The sky now looks orange rather than blue, ripe apples look green, unripe apples look red, and so on. Suppose you keep these lenses on and adapt your behavior. You learn to say 'green' rather than 'red' when you see something that looks the way red things used to look; you learn to treat what you used to consider a green appearance of apples as a sign of ripeness, and so on. The years pass and your adaption becomes habitual. Would not this be an intelligible case in which someone, the imagined future you, has a notion of what it is like to have the experience of seeing something to which the term 'red' applies, where the notion functions in exactly the way in which your notion of what such an experience is like functions, although your notions are different? The functionalist must deny this and say that the imagined you associates the same concept with the word 'red' as the actual you does now and indeed sees the world as you now do.

Consider an analogous case. There actually exist lenses that are spatially inverting. With these lenses on, things that are up look down and vice versa. At first it is very difficult to get around if you are wearing such lenses, since things are not where they seem to be. But after a while you begin to adapt. If you want to grab something that looks high, you reach low, and vice versa. If you want to look directly at something that appears in the bottom of your visual field you raise your head, and so on. Eventually, such adaption becomes more or less habitual.

Now functionalism implies that if you become perfectly adapted to such space inverting lenses, then your experience will be the same as that of someone who is not wearing the inverting lenses (who has adapted to not wearing them if necessary), because now the normal context in relation to which your concepts function will have become a context in which you are wearing the inverting lenses. And in fact, people who have worn such lenses do say that, as they adapt to the lenses, the world tends to look right side up again (Taylor, 1962; Pitcher, 1971; Thomas, 1978).

Similarly, functionalism implies that if you become perfectly adapted to color inverting lenses, the world will come to look to you as it looked before in the sense that given such perfect adaption the normal context in which your color concepts function will be a context in which you are wearing the color inverting lenses. According to functionalism, the way things look to you is a relational characteristic of your experience, not part of its intrinsic character.

In order to get a feel for this aspect of (nonsolipsistic) conceptual role semantics, it may be useful to consider certain further cases. Consider Inverted Earth, a world just like ours, with duplicates of us, with the sole difference that there the actual colors of objects are the opposite of what they are here. The sky is orange, ripe apples are green, etc. The inhabitants of Inverted Earth speak something that sounds like English, except that they say the sky is 'blue', they call ripe apples 'red', and so on. Question: what color does their sky look to them? Answer: it looks orange. The concept they express with the word 'blue' plays a relevantly special role in the normal perception of things that are actually orange.

Suppose there is a distinctive physical basis for each different color experience. Suppose also that the physical basis for the experience of red is the same for all normal people not adapted to color inverting lenses, and similarly for the other colors. According to (nonsolipsistic) conceptual role semantics this fact is irrelevant. The person who has perfectly adapted to color inverting lenses will be different from everyone else as regards the physical basis of his or her experience of red, but that will not affect the quality of his or her experience.

Consider someone on Inverted Earth who perfectly adapts to color inverting lenses. Looking at the sky of Inverted Earth, this person has an experience of color whose physical basis is the same as that of a normal person on Earth looking at Earth's sky. But the sky looks orange to the person on Inverted Earth and blue to normal people on Earth. What makes an experience the experience of something's looking the color it looks is not its intrinsic character and/or physical basis but rather its functional characteristics within an assumed normal context.

Consider a brain spontaneously created in space as the improbable result of random events at the quantum level. The physical events in the brain happen to be the same as those in you on Earth looking at the sky on a clear day and also the same as those in a person adapted to color inverting spectacles looking at the sky of Inverted Earth. What is it like for the brain? Is it having an experience of orange or of blue? According to (nonsolipsistic) conceptual role semantics, there is no nonarbitrary way to answer this question; it depends on what is taken as the normal context for assessing the functional *role* of events in that brain. If the normal context is taken to be the normal context for perception of color on Earth, the brain is having an experience of blue. If the normal context is taken to be the normal context for a wearer of inverted spectacles on Inverted Earth, the brain is having an experience of orange.

Inner and Outer Aspects of Conceptual Role

It is sometimes suggested that we need to distinguish inner and outer aspects of conceptual role, counting only the inner solipsistically specifiable side as conceptual role proper, taking the outer aspects to be part of context (Field, 1977; Loar, 1981). The suggestion is that a theory of the content of attitudes must have two parts: (1) a theory of conceptual role proper, solipsistically conceived, and (2) a theory of context that would indicate how content is a function of inner conceptual role and outer context.

But this distinction is unmotivated and the suggestion is unworkable. The distinction is unmotivated because there is no natural border between inner and outer. Should the inner realm be taken to include everything in the local environment that can be perceived, or should it stop at the skin, the nerve ends, the central nervous system, the brain, the central part of the brain, or what? The suggestion is unworkable because, for most concepts, inner conceptual role can only be specified in terms of conceptual role in a wider sense, namely the function a concept has in certain contexts in relation to things in the so called 'external world' (Harman, 1983, pp. 62–65).

To be sure, there are cases of illusion in which one mistakes something else for food. From a solipsistic point of view, these cases may be quite similar to veridical cases, but clearly the cases of mistake are not cases that bring out the relevant function of the concept of food. They are cases of *mis*functioning. We can see these as cases of mistake precisely because the function of concept of food is specified with reference to real and not just apparent food.

Mental states and processes are functional states and processes, that is, they are complex relational or dispositional states and processes, and it is useful to consider simpler dispositions, like fragility or solubility. Water solubility cannot be identified with possession of a particular molecular structure, because (a) different sorts of molecular structure underlie the water solubility of different substances and, more importantly, (b) attributions of water solubility are relative to a choice of background or *normal* context. Rate of dissolving is affected by such things as the presence or absence of electrical, magnetic, or gravitational fields, the amount of vibration, varying degrees of atmospheric pressure, the purity and temperature of the water, and so forth. Whether it is proper to say a given substance is water soluble will depend on what the normal set of conditions for mixing the substance with water is taken to be. A substance is soluble in water if it would dissolve at a fast enough rate if mixed with water in a certain way under certain conditions. Solubility is a relational state of a substance, relating it to potential external things—water and various conditions of mixture and the process of dissolving under those conditions.

Notice that we cannot say that for a substance to be water soluble is for it to be such that, if it receives certain 'stimuli', at its surface, it reacts in a certain way. We must also mention water and various external conditions. There is a moral here for Quine's (1960) account of language in terms of 'stimulus meaning' and of the related later attempts I have been discussing to develop a purely solipsistic notion of conceptual role.

We are led to attribute beliefs, desires, and so on to a creature only because the creature is able to attain what we take to be its goals by being able to detect aspects of its environment. In the first instance, we study its capacity for mental representation by discovering which aspects of the environment it is sensitive to. Only after that can we investigate the sorts of mistakes it is capable of that might lead to inappropriate behavior. This gives us further evidence about the content of its concepts. But we could never even guess at this without considering how the creature's mental states are connected with things in the outside world.

But the point is not merely one of evidence, since concepts have the content they have because of the way they function in the *normal case* in relation to an external world. If there were no external constraints, we could conceive of anything as instantiating any system of purely solipsistic 'functional' relations and *processes*. We could think of a pane of glass or a pencil point as instantiating Albert Einstein or George Miller, solipsistically conceived. But that does not count. Concepts really must be capable of functioning appropriately. No one has ever described a way of explaining what beliefs, desires, and other mental states are except in terms of actual or possible relations to things in the external world (Dennett, 1969, pp. 72–82; Harman, 1973, pp. 62–65; Bennett, 1976, pp. 36–110).

The most primitive psychological notions are not *belief* and *desire* but rather *knowledge* and *successful intentional action*. Belief and intention are generalizations of knowledge and success that allow for mistake and failure. We conceive a creature as believing things by conceiving it as at least potentially knowing things, and similarly for intention.

Does this show a theory of truth plays a role in semantics? To be sure, in my view the content of a concept is determined by the way in which the concept functions in paradigm or standard cases in which nothing goes wrong. In such cases, one has true beliefs that lead one to act appropriately in the light of one's needs and other ends. But an account of correct functioning is not itself a full account of the truth of beliefs, since beliefs can be true by accident in cases where there is some misfunctioning. And there are no serious prospects for a theory of content that significantly involves an account of truth conditions.

MEANING AND SPEECH ACTS

It may be an exaggeration to say that all aspects of linguistic meaning derive from the use of language to express concepts with corresponding contents. Certain aspects of meaning seem to derive directly from the use of language in speech-acts and communication. (Nonsolipsistic) conceptual role semantics may therefore have to allow for this, attempting (of course) to treat it as a minor and relatively peripheral phenomenon. On the other hand, it may be that no such concession needs to be made. Here are some tentative and preliminary reflections on some of the issues involved.

Greetings

The cases that may seem clearest here concern expressions which are used primarily in greetings and salutations, words like 'Hello' and 'Goodbye' for example. The meanings of these words do not seem to derive from any use they might have to express single concepts that play a distinctive role in calculation and thought. It is true that you might, on occasion, 'greet' a new idea or precept with the thought, 'Hello! What's this?' But this seems to be a case in which the content of your thought derives from the use of the word 'Hello' to greet people and begin conversations rather than the other way round.

However, it may be that such words can be analyzed as expressing a combination of concepts which individually have contents that are connected with distinctive conceptual roles. For example, perhaps 'Hello' means something like 'I acknowledge your presence', or sometimes maybe 'let us talk', and analogously for 'Good-bye' and other words and phrases of this sort. If so, the issue becomes whether the aspect of meaning expressed by the imperative in 'let us talk' and the performative aspect of the meaning of 'I acknowledge your presence' derive irreducibly from the use of words in speech acts or ultimately derive instead from the use of language to express concepts whose content is determined by their role in calculation and thought. These are complex issues which we must consider in a moment. As for the question whether this is the right way to analyze 'Hello', 'Good-bye', and so on, I am not very sure what to think. The analyses I have suggested seem to leave something out, but this might be accommodated by better analyses.

Words of Politeness

Before turning to imperatives and performatives, we might consider words and phrases which function as forms of deference and politeness, words and phrases like 'please' and 'thank you', for example. The use of such words and phrases seems to presuppose some sort of social interaction, rather than simply expressing concepts with a content determined by the way these concepts function in thought and calculation. It is true that you might say 'Please' or 'Thank you' to yourself, in thought, if you were speaking to yourself as an instructor or coach might. But this seems a very special case, which itself presupposes the social use of these expressions.

Again, in this case, it might be argued that in this use 'Please' means the same as some longer expression, like 'if you please', i.e., 'if it pleases you to do so', and 'Thank you' means something like 'I hereby thank you'. If so, the issue would become whether the meaning of the term 'you' derives entirely from its use to express concepts whose content is determined by their distinctive function in calculation or thought, an issue we need to discuss. There is, of course, also again here the question whether the performative element, in 'I hereby thank you', carries a meaning which at least in part is irreducibly connected with speech acts, another issue we will be coming to in a moment. As for the question whether such polite phrases can always be analyzed in this sort of way, I am not sure what to say.

'You'

What about the meaning of the word 'you'? It is plausible that this word means something like 'the person(s) I am now addressing' and each of the words in this phrase is plausibly held to have a meaning that depends on the concept the word is used to express, where the concept in question has the content it has by virtue of the way it functions in thought and calculation. So, even though the word 'you' has the distinctive function in speech acts and communication of designating the intended audience, this function can plausibly be explained in terms of the functional roles in thought of the concepts the word is used to express.

Imperative and Interrogative Mood

The use of the imperative mood in English seems to carry a certain meaning, connected with the giving of directions of some sort. This does not by itself imply this meaning does not derive from the content of certain concepts with a distinctive use in thought and calculation. Indeed, something in your thoughts functions to distinguish your beliefs from your plans and intentions, which are directions of a sort. So, there is a sense in which the upshot of practical reasoning is a modification of certain directions one intends to follow. Perhaps the imperative mood serves to express the concept which functions in thought to thus distinguish practical or directing thoughts from theoretical thoughts.

Similar remarks apply to the interrogative mood. Indeed, questions are not unlike requests for information, so that the interrogative mood is plausibly analyzed in terms of the imperative mood. In any event, questions obviously have a function in thinking. You pose a problem to yourself and work out the answer, perhaps by posing various subquestions and answering them.

Performatives

Consider next explicit performatives, like 'I promise to be there' and 'I hereby apologize for my rude behavior'. It seems part of the meaning of such sentences that they are used not to describe the speaker as promising or apologizing but actually to do the promising or apologizing. Furthermore, it is plausible that promising or apologizing to yourself is not a typical or normal case of promising or apologizing and is rather the sort of case which is to be understood in relation to more typical or normal cases in which you promise someone else something or apologize to another person.

On the other hand, each of the words in a sentence like 'I promise to be there' has a meaning which expresses a concept whose content is arguably determined by its functional role in calculation and thought. And it is possible that the meaning of the whole sentence, including whatever gives the sentence its performative function of being appropriate for actually promising, arises from the meaning of the words used in a regular way. Given what the words in the sentence mean and given the way these words are put together, it may be predictable that the sentence has a performative use (Bach, 1975).

Suppose we adopted the convention that promises have to be made in some special way, for example by writing down the content of the promise in purple chalk on a special promise board that is not used for any other purpose. The convention would be that nothing else is to count as a promise. In such a case, the words, 'I promise to be there' could not be used to promise you will be there. Would this be a way to pry off the performative meaning of 'I promise' from that aspect of its meaning that derives from its use to express concepts whose content is determined by their functional role in thought? Not obviously. For one thing, this might change the concept of promising in a significant way. The word 'promise' might not mean what it means when a promise can be made by saying 'I promise'. It could be argued that if 'I promise' means what it ordinarily means, then it follows from the concepts expressed by the words 'I promise' that these words can be used to promise.

Alternatively, it might be said that, even if the word 'promise' would retain (enough of) its usual meaning when promising was restricted by such a convention, the example is like one in which a special convention is adopted that an utterance of the sentence 'The sky is blue' is not to be interpreted as an assertion that the sky is blue but rather as a question asking whether it rained last week. This would not show that there is any aspect of the meaning of an ordinary assertion of the sentence 'The sky is blue', as we use it now without such a bizarre convention, which does not derive from the way the words in the sentence are used to express concepts that have the content they have because of their functional role in thought.

Conversational Implicature

Grice (1961, 1975) argues that the implications of an utterance do not always correspond directly to the meanings of the linguistic expressions used, even in quite ordinary cases. He suggests in particular that what seem to be aspects of meaning may be due to 'conventional implicature', i.e., to conclusions the audience is intended to reach by reflecting on the speaker's reasons for saying what is said, assuming the speaker is trying to be helpful. For example, if you use 'either . . . or', as in 'Albert is in either Boston or New York', you normally imply you do not know which. This does not have to be taken as showing something special about the meaning of 'either . . . or', a difference in the meaning of this ordinary expression as compared with what the logician takes it to mean. Instead we can suppose this implication is due to the natural assumption that normally, if you know which city Albert is in, you will say which it is. To take another example, the apparent difference in meaning between 'Mary closed the door and turned on the light' and 'Mary turned on the light and closed the door' does not have to be explained by supposing that the English word 'and' sometimes means 'and then'. The suggestion is that the difference can be explained by supposing that a helpful speaker will normally relate events in an orderly way, so that a hearer is normally justified in supposing that the order in which the speaker relates to events is to be understood as the order in which they occurred. Similarly, Grice suggests that certain aspects of presupposition might be explained by considering the normal expectations of speakers and hearers.

However, some of these phenomena can occur in thinking to oneself, where they are presumably not due to conversational implicature. Calculation and reasoning often involve various presuppositions. One will normally want descriptions used in reasoning to relate events in an orderly way, so the same phenomenon with the word 'and' may occur. On the other hand, it is doubtful that use of an 'either . . . or' proposition in thought normally carries the implication that one does not know which alternative is the case; so *this* phenomenon may really occur only at the level of conversation.

Figurative Language

Metaphor and simile occur in thinking. I am inclined to think irony does not. I am not sure about hyperbole.

CONCLUSION

To summarize there are two uses of symbols, in communication and speech acts and in calculation and thought. (Nonsolipsistic) conceptual role semantics takes the second use to be the basic one. The ultimate source of meaning or content is the functional role symbols play in thought.

The content of a concept depends on its role in inference and sometimes in perception. Particularly important for inference are a term's implications. Implication is relevant to inference and therefore to meaning, because implication is explanatory and inference aims at explanatory coherence. Accounts of truth conditions can shed light on meaning to the extent that they bring out implications; it is doubtful whether such accounts have any further bearing on meaning, although they may have heuristic value for studies of logical form. Probabilistic semantics does not provide an adequate conceptual role semantics, because people do not and cannot make much use of probabilistic reasoning.

Allowance must be made for various connections between concepts and the external world. Some concepts have the content they have because of the words they are associated with, although (according to conceptual role semantics) this content ultimately always derives from someone's use of concepts. The content of concepts is often relative to a choice of a normal context of functioning. This is true of color concepts, despite the unargued view of some philosophers that these concepts depend on the intrinsic character of experience.

Finally, it is not clear whether any aspects of meaning derive directly from the use of language in speech acts in a way not reducible to the expression of concepts whose content is independently determined. In any event, many phenomena often taken to be particularly connected with speech acts and conversation also occur in calculation and thought.

REFERENCES

Bach, K., Performatives Are Statements, Too. *Philosophical Studies*, 1975, **28**, 229–236.

Bennett, J., *Linguistic Behaviour*. Cambridge: Cambridge University Press, 1976.

Block, N. & Fodor, J. A., What Psychological States Are Not. *Philosophical Review*, 1972, **81**, 159–181.

Chomsky, N., *Reflections on Language*. New York: Columbia University Press, 1980.

Davidson, D., Truth and Meaning. *Synthese*, 1967, **17**, 304–323.

Dennett, D. C., *Content and Consciousness*. London: Routledge and Kegan Paul, 1969.

Field, H., Probabilistic Semantics. *Journal of Philosophy*, 1977, **74**, 379–409.

Fodor, J. A., Methodological Solipsism as a Research Strategy in Psychology. *Behavioral and Brain Sciences*, 1980, **3**, 63–73.

Foster, J. A., Meaning and Truth Theory. In G. Evans & J. McDowell (Eds), *Truth and Meaning: Essays in Semantics*. Oxford: Oxford University Press, 1976.

Grice, H. P., Meaning. *Philosophical Review*, 1959, **68**, 377–388.

Grice, H. P., The Causal Theory of Perception. *Proceedings of the Aristotelian Society*, 1961, Suppl. Vol. 35.

Grice, H. P., Logic and Conversation. In D. Davidson & G. Harman (Eds), *The Logic of Grammar*. Encino, CA: Dickenson, 1975.

Harman, G., Logical Form. *Foundations of Language*, 1972, **9**, 38–65.

Harman, G., *Thought*. Princeton, NJ: Princeton University Press, 1973.

Harman, G., Meaning and Semantics. In M. K. Munitz & P. Unger (Eds), *Semantics and Philosophy*. New York: New York University Press, 1974.

Harman, G., Conceptual Role Semantics. *Notre Dame Journal of Formal Logic*, 1982, **28**, 252–256.

Harman, G., Problems with Probabilistic Semantics. In A. Orenstein *et al.* (Eds), *Developments in Semantics*. New York: Haven, 1985.

Harman, G., *Change in View*. Cambridge, MA: MIT Press, 1986a.

Harman, G., Willing and Intending. In R. Grandy & R. Warner (Eds), *Festschrift for H. P. Grice*. Oxford: Oxford University Press, 1986b.

Harman, G., Quine's Grammar. In P. Schillp (Ed). *The Philosophy of W. V. Quine*. La Salle, Illinois: Open Court, 1986c.

Kripke, S., Naming and Necessity. In D. Davidson & G. Harman (Eds), *Semantics of Natural Language*. Dordrecht: Reidel, 1972.

Lewis D., General Semantics. In D. Davidson & G. Harman (Eds), *Semantics of Natural Language*. Dordrecht: Reidel, 1972.

Lewis, D., Mad Pain and Martian Pain. In E. Block (Ed), *Readings in Philosophy of Psychology*. Cambridge, MA: Harvard University Press, 1980.

Loar, B., *Mind and Meaning*. Cambridge: Cambridge University Press, 1981.

Loar, B., Must Beliefs Be Sentences? In P. D. Asquith & T. Nickles (Eds), *PSA 1982*, Vol. 2. East-Lansing, MI: Philosophy of Science Association, 1983a.

Loar, B., Reply to Fodor and Harman. In P. D. Asquith & T. Nickles (Eds), *PSA 1982*, Vol. 2. East-Lansing, MI: Philosophy of Science Association, 1983b.

Loewer, B., The Role of 'Conceptual Role Semantics'. *Notre Dame Journal of Formal Logic*, 1982, **23**, 305–332.

Nagel, T., What Is It Like to Be a Bat? *Philosophical Review*, 1974, **83**, 435–450.

Pitcher, G., *A Theory of Perception*. Princeton, NJ: Princeton University Press, 1971.

Putnam, H., The Meaning of Meaning. In H. Putnam (Ed), *Mind, Language, and Reality: Philosophical Papers*, Vol. 2. Cambridge: Cambridge University Press, 1975.

Quine, W. V., *Word and Object*. Cambridge, MA: MIT Press, 1960.

Ryle, G., Ordinary Language. *Philosophical Review*, 1953, **62**. (Reprinted in Ryle (1971))

Ryle, G., Use, Usage, and Meaning. *Proceedings of the Aristotelian Society*, 1961. Suppl. Vol. 35 (Reprinted in Ryle (1971))

Ryle, G., *Collected Papers*, Vol. II. London: Hutchinson, 1971.

Sellars, W., Some Reflections on Language Games. *Philosophy of Science*, 1954, **21**, 204–228.

Strawson, P. F., *Subject and Predicate in Logic and Grammar*. London: Methuen, 1974.

Taylor, J. G., *The Behavioral Basis of Perception*. New Haven, CT: Yale University Press, 1962.

Thomas, S., *The Formal Mechanics of Mind*. Ithaca, NY: Cornell University Press, 1978.

3

Dual Aspect Semantics

E. LEPORE*
B. LOEWER**

*Department of Philosophy,
Rutgers University,
**Philosophy Department,
University of South Carolina

Frege's notion of sense plays (at least) two roles in his theory of meaning. One role concerns the relations between language and reality: an expression's sense determines its reference. The other role relates a language to the mind of someone who understands it: to understand an expression is to grasp its sense. The dual role of sense is seen clearly in Frege's account of the semantics of identity statements. 'The morning star = the evening star' is true, since the sense of 'the morning star' and the sense of 'the evening star' determine the same reference. The sentence is cognitively significant, since it is possible for someone to know the senses expressed by the expressions 'the morning star' and 'the evening star' yet not know that they determine the same reference.

During the last fifteen years or so there has been a sustained attack on the Fregean conception of sense. An examination of proper names, indexicals, and natural kind terms, has led many philosophers of language and mind to conclude that no single notion of sense can play both roles. Hilary Putnam puts the point by saying that "no theory can make it the case that 'meanings' are in the head and simultaneously make it the case that 'meanings' determine external world reference" (Putnam, MH:12).

83

NEW DIRECTIONS IN SEMANTICS

Of course, for Frege, meanings, i.e., senses, are in the head (in that they are grasped) and determine reference.

A number of philosophers have responded to these arguments by constructing two-tiered or dual-aspect theories of meaning. We will call them DATs (Block, 1985; Field, 1977; Fodor, 1980; Harman, 1973, 1974, 1982; Loar, 1982; Lycan, 1981, 1982a, 1982b, 1984; McGinn, 1982). According to these accounts, a theory of meaning for a language L consists of two distinct components. One component is intended to provide an account of the relations between language and the world: truth, reference, satisfaction, etc. The other is supposed to provide an account of understanding and cognitive significance. In this paper we will examine a particular proposal concerning the appropriate form of a DAT according to which the two components are:

I.   A theory of reference and truth for L, and
II. A characterization of the conceptual roles of sentences and other expressions of L.

We will contrast DATs with an approach which is like Frege's in one important respect: it employs a single notion to serve both the purpose of the theory of reference and the theory of understanding. Its central tenet is that a theory of meaning for L is a certain kind of truth theory for L. Since Donald Davidson is the most prominent and subtle defender of this approach we will call such theories of meaning 'Davidsonian truth theories' (Davidson, 1967, 1973b, 1974; LePore, 1982b, 1983; Loewer, 1982; LePore & Loewer, 1981, 1983). At first it may seem that this approach is contained in a DAT, since the latter has a truth theory as one of its components. But this is not so. We will show that the truth theory component of a DAT is quite different from that of a Davidsonian truth theory. We will argue that, by separating a theory of meaning into a theory of reference and a theory of conceptual role, DATs are unable to serve as theories of interpretation or as accounts of cognitive significance.

The organization of our paper is this: we first examine the problems that motivate the construction of DATs. Then we discuss the form of a DAT, focusing primarily on a proposal due to Colin McGinn (1982). We then develop a Davidsonian theory of meaning showing how truth theories serve as theories of interpretation. As such, they provide both an account of truth and reference, on the one hand, and an account of understanding and cognitive significance, on the other. In the next section we show that DATs do not make adequate theories of interpretation. We also challenge their adequacy as theories of meaning for languages of thought. Finally, we return to the problems motivating DATs and discuss the extent to which they can be accommodated within a Davidsonian framework.

MOTIVATION FOR DAT

Hilary Putnam asks us to imagine two planets, Earth and Twin-Earth, and
two of their residents, say, Arabella and twin-Arabella. Twin-Earth is
almost a physical replica of Earth. The only difference is that on Twin-
Earth the clear liquid the twin-people drink, that fills their oceans, and that
they call 'water', is composed not of H_2O molecules but of XYZ molecules
(Putnam, 1975).

According to Putnam, the expression 'water' on Earth refers to the stuff
composed of H_2O and not composed of XYZ. It is exactly the reverse for
the expression 'water' on Twin-Earth. This is so even if no speakers of
English and twin-English know the molecular structures of water and twin-
water or can distinguish between the two. Putnam argues as follows: in
Frege's theory to understand an expression, say, 'water', is to 'grasp' its
sense. Exactly what it is to grasp a sense is not all that clear, but it is to be
in some psychological state or other; perhaps the state of believing that
'water' expresses a certain sense. Since Arabella and twin-Arabella are
physically type identical,[1] they are in type identical psychological states. So
if each understands her word 'water', then each grasps the same sense. But
the references of their words differ. Putnam concludes that if sense is
what is grasped when understanding an expression, then sense does not
determine reference. If sense is what determines reference, then sense is
not what is grasped in understanding.

Putnam's initial reaction to this argument was to distinguish two components of meaning. One he calls 'stereotype'. It is the information which
linguistically competent speakers associate with an expression. The stereotype of 'water' as used both on Earth and on Twin-Earth consists in the
information that water is a clear liquid, that quenches thirst, that fills the
oceans, and so on. To understand 'water' is to know its grammatical role
and its stereotype. This is supposed to be the 'mind' component of meaning
(Putnam, 1975).

The second component of meaning is reference. On Putnam's account
the reference of a natural kind expression like 'water' is determined by
facts which are outside the minds of users of the expression. For example,
'water' refers to whatever stuff is structurally similar to this stuff (pointing
at samples of water). Given that water is H_2O (and that the relevant kind
of structural similarity is sameness of chemical composition), the extension
of 'water' on Earth is H_2O. Analogously, the extension of 'water' on Twin-
Earth is XYZ. On Putnam's theory the stereotype of an expression is the
mind component of sense, its reference is the world component and, as the
Twin-Earth story shows, the first does not determine the second. The

theory of meaning thus divides into two parts: a theory of understanding (and cognitive significance) and a theory of reference (and truth).

Putnam's argument for the bifurcation of meaning depends on accepting his view that 'water' on Earth refers to H_2O, while 'water' on Twin-Earth refers to XYZ. This is a claim which can be (and has been) disputed (Zemach, 1976). But even if Putnam is mistaken about the semantics of natural kind terms, there are other examples that lead to dual component views.

Imagine that Arabella and twin-Arabella each utters 'I am 30 years old'. Once again they are in identical psychological states, but the references of their utterances of 'I' differ, and even the truth values of their utterances can differ. They are physical replicas, but Arabella came into existence only a few minutes ago. Arabella's and twin-Arabella's understandings of 'I' are the same, although their references and the truth values of their utterances differ. This shows that if the sense of 'I' is what is grasped by a person who understands 'I' then that sense does not by itself determine reference. On the other hand, if sense determines reference then Arabella and twin-Arabella do not grasp the same sense. David Kaplan, among others (Kaplan, Ms; cf also Perry, 1978, 1979; White, 1983), distinguishes the character of an expression from its content in a context. The character of an expression is a function from contexts of utterances to contents, e.g., the character of 'I', according to Kaplan, maps a context of utterance onto the utterer. It is the character of 'I am 30 years old' that is grasped by someone who understands the sentence. The utterance's content is its truth conditions. When Arabella and twin-Arbarella each utter 'I am 30 years old', what is in their minds may be the same (they have the same understanding of the sentence) but their utterances have different contents and so may differ in truth value. Kaplan's account, like Putnam's, is a two tiered theory of meaning. But it differs from Putnam's in that stereotype is unlike character in that it does not determine content relative to context, at least as 'context' of utterance is normally construed (see White, 1983).

Our discussion so far seems to show that two expressions can have the same stereotype, or character (or, whatever corresponds to cognitive significance), and yet possess tokens which differ with respect to reference and truth conditions. It has been argued, conversely, that sentences with the same truth conditions can differ with respect to the understanding component of (Kripke, 1979) meaning. According to Kripke proper names designate rigidly (Kripke, 1972). It has been claimed that it follows from this that, for example, the truth conditions of the sentences 'Cicero is bald' and 'Tully is bald' are identical. But what are we to make of Arabella, who understands both sentences and assents to the first and dissents from the second? If understanding a sentence is knowing its truth conditions, then it follows that Arabella is flatly contradicting herself, since she is asserting and denying statements with identical truth conditions. Furthermore, it seems to follow that she has contradictory beliefs; she believes that Cicero is bald and believes that Cicero is not bald. But these are not ordinary contradictions, since no amount of thought on her part would enable her to recognize that she has contradictory beliefs. William Lycan (1982; see also Lycan, 1985, pp. 90–91) reacts to this problem by saying:

> Nothing that [Arabella] carries in her head enables her to tell that . . . 'Cicero' and 'Tully' represent the same person. And, therefore, there is no way for her to deduce from her mental machinery anything she could recognize as a contradiction. The names 'Cicero' and 'Tully' obviously play distinct computational roles for [Arabella] . . . .

Lycan intends this as a solution to the problem as it arises for mental representations. His idea is that there are two distinct ways of semantically individuating Arabella's mental representations; according to truth conditions and according to computational role. According to the way of truth conditions, Arabella believes that Cicero is bald and also believes that Cicero is not bald. But this does not impugn her rationality, since truth conditions are not part of Arabella's 'mental machinery'. According to the way of computational role, the beliefs that Cicero is bald and that Tully is bald are distinct, since her representations 'Cicero is bald' and 'Tully is bald' have different computional roles. When her beliefs are individuated in terms of computational role, Arabella does not have contradictory beliefs.

We could extend Lycan's account (though he does not make this extension) to the semantics of natural languages if we could find something to play the part of computational role for natural language expressions. The simplest suggestion is that the computational role of a person's sentence S at time t is the same as the computational role of the mental representation constituent of the belief expressed by S for P at t. 'Cicero is bald' and 'Tully is bald' have the same truth conditions in English, but they may differ in their computational roles for a particular speaker at t. It is computational role that characterizes one's understanding of an expression. We can see how a person might understand both 'Cicero is bald' and 'Tully is bald', and assert one and deny the other, even though they have the same truth conditions.

As our discussion of Lycan's proposal makes clear, DATs have been proposed for mental representations, a.k.a. languages of thought, as well as for natural languages. Jerry Fodor, the principal proponent of languages of thought, has been developing a theory of mental states and processes he calls the computational theory of mind (CTM). According to CTM, mental states and processes are computations over representations. For example, believing that snow is white is being in a certain computational relation to a representation which means that snow is white. The system of mental representations is like a language in that representations possess both a syntax and a semantics. It is a central tenet of CTM that computations apply to representations in virtue of their syntactic features (Fodor, 1980, p. 226). While Fodor admits that it is not all that clear what count as syntactic features he is clear that semantic properties, e.g., truth and reference, are not syntactic. The mind (and its components) has no way of recognizing the reference or truth conditions of the representations it operates on. Instead, it operates on syntactic features of representations which 'represent' the semantic features. The computational role of a mental representation must depend upon, and only upon, those properties of representations which do not advert to matters outside the agent's head (McGinn, 1982, p. 208).

Fodor claims that a consequence of CTM is a formality condition, which specifies that in CTM psychological states count as different states only if they differ computationally. Applied to belief, this means that beliefs can differ in content only if they contain formally distinct representations. This supervenience principle, that S and S^* are distinct psychological states only if they are distinct computationally, lies at the heart of CTM. Although Fodor endorses the formality condition, he also thinks that cognitive psychology contains true generalizations connecting propositional attitudes with each other, environmental conditions, and behavior. An example of the sort of generalization he has in mind, is: if someone wants to go downtown and believes that the bus provides the only way to get there, then, *cateris paribus,* he will take the bus. As Fodor emphasizes, the specification of propositional contents in these generalizations is essential to their explanatory role. It is a person's belief *that the bus provides the only way to get downtown* that explains his taking the bus. At first, this may seem incompatible with the claim the only formal properties of representations are relevant to the computations which produce behavior. However, there is no incompatibility as long as the contents of attitudes are specified in a way that respects the formality condition. This means that two representations can differ in content only if they differ syntactically. Fodor observes that a characterization of meaning which conforms to the formality condition is *methodologically solipsistic* (Putnam, 1975) in that differences of meaning depend entirely upon internal mental characteristics, e.g., computations over representations.

We have described Fodor's views at some length because we want to show why a DAT theory seems to fit the bill as a theory of meaning for languages of thought. Fodor observes that truth conditional semantics for a language of thought is not methodologically solipsistic. It fails to conform to the formality condition (Fodor, 1982, p. 22). Putnam's Twin-Earth

examples show this. Arabella and twin-Arabella are computationally identical when each is thinking what each would express by uttering 'Water is
wet'. So, each bears the same computational relation to formally identical
representations. But the truth condition of the token representation in
Arabella's mind is that H_2O is wet, while the truth condition of the
representation in twin-Arabella's mind is that XYZ is wet. There is a
difference in truth conditions without a corresponding difference in formal
properties. The characterization of contents in terms of truth conditions
may seem defective from the perspective of CTM in another way as well.
'Water is wet' and 'H_2O is wet' are claimed to have the same truth
conditions, but certainly there is a difference between believing that water
is wet and believing that H_2O is wet. Truth conditions seems to be both
too fine grained (the Twin-Earth problems) and too coarse grained
(Kripke's puzzle (Kripke, 1979)) to specify the contents of mental
representations.

It should be clear why DATs have been proposed as theories of meaning
for languages of thought. The truth conditional component of a DAT
characterizes the relations between representations and the world. But a
second component is needed which characterizes content in a way that
conforms to the formality condition and is fine grained enough to capture
differences in belief like the one mentioned a paragraph back. This second
component is the mind-component aspect.

THE FORM OF DAT

So far, we have discussed some issues which motivate a distinction between
two aspects of meaning. Some philosophers have claimed that the correct
way for a theory of meaning to accommodate the two aspects is by containing two *autonomous* components, a truth conditional component, and
a component accounting for the use or understanding features of meaning.
Colin McGinn (1982, p. 229) explicitly advocates such a view.

> For perspicuity we can separate out the two contributions by taking the meaning
> ascription as equivalent to a conjunction: For S to mean that p is for S to be true iff Q
> for some 'Q' having the same truth conditions as 'p', and for S to have some cognitive
> role φ such that 'p' also has the cognitive role φ. . ... Now to have a complete theory of
> meaning would be to have adequate theories corresponding to each conjunct of this
> schema.

McGinn is not only claiming that an adequate theory of meaning consists
of two separate theories, but is also offering an analysis of 'S means that
p'.

The first component, the truth theory, may seem relatively unproblematic. It is supposed to entail, for each sentence S of language L, an instance of:

(T) S is true in L iff p,

where 'S' is replaced by a structural description of a sentence of L and 'p' is replaced by a meta-language sentence which specifies S's truth conditions. Tarski required that the sentence replacing 'p' be a *translation* of the sentence replacing 'S' (Tarski, 1956). Putnam, Field, Fodor, and McGinn do not have this conception in mind. Fodor says (Fodor, NC:9) that 'a truth condition is an actual or possible state of affairs. If S is the truth condition of (the formula) F, then F is true iff S is actual'. According to McGinn, '. . . a truth theory is a specification of the *facts* stated by sentences of the object language, in the intuitive sense of that recalcitrant notion' (McGinn, 1982, p. 232). As McGinn says 'fact' is a recalcitrant notion. 'State of affairs' is no clearer. However, it is clear that some advocates of DATs would count 'Water is wet' (uttered by an English speaker) as stating the same fact or state of affairs as 'H_2O is wet', and 'Tully is bald' as stating the same fact or state of affairs as 'Cicero is bald'. So, their characterization of an adequate truth theory is different from Tarski's, since two sentences can state the same fact (or state of affairs) without being good translations of each other. Of course, this is not a worry to advocates of DATs, since sameness of meaning requires not only sameness of truth conditions but sameness of cognitive role as well.

The second component of McGinn's DAT is a theory of cognitive role. Other authors use the terms 'conceptual role' (which we prefer) and 'computational role' for similar, though perhaps not identical, notions. While the idea of conceptual role has been around for a while, the form of a theory of conceptual role is much less clear than the form of a truth theory. Sellars speaks of two sentences having the same conceptual role if they are related by inference, both deductive and inductive, to the same sentences in the same ways. Sellars also includes relations between sentences and perception and action, 'language entry and exit rules', in his specification of conceptual role (Sellars, 1956, 1963, 1969). Harman, thinking of the language of thought, characterizes the conceptual role of an expression by its relations to perception, to other expressions, and to behavior (Harman, 1973, 1974, 1982). Both Sellar's and Harman's characterizations suggest that conceptual role theories for a language L will take the form of a theory of inference for L, combined with a causal theory of perceptual inputs and outputs. But neither provide detailed accounts of these theories.

McGinn relies on Hartry Field's account of conceptual role (Field, 1977). Field characterizes conceptual role in terms of a probability function defined over all the sentences of a person's language. It specifies a person's commitments concerning how he will change his degrees of belief when he acquires new information. The probability function, by specifying inductive and deductive relations, characterizes the conceptual roles of expressions. A and B are said to have the same conceptual role iff $P(A/C) = P(B/C)$ for all sentences C in the language. On this account 'Tully is bald' and 'Cicero is bald' may have different conceptual roles for a person, since there may be an S for which $P(\text{'Tully is bald'}/S) \neq P(\text{'Cicero is bald'}/S)$. The conceptual role of a non-sentential expression is specified in terms of the conceptual roles of all the sentences in which it appears. There may be simple characterizations of the conceptual roles of some expressions. For example, the role of negation is specified by the probability laws involving negation.

McGinn claims that two component theories, containing a truth theory and a Fieldian conceptual role theory, can deal with the problems we discussed in the first section (McGinn, 1982, pp. 234–237, 247). Consider Arabella and twin-Arabella. Their languages, English and twin-English, are syntactically identical, and since the twins are physically type identical, the conceptual roles of their expressions are isomorphic. Each one's sentence 'Water is wet' has the same (or isomorphic) conceptual role(s) so their mental states are identical. However, their sentences differ in their truth conditions since *the fact* that makes Arabella's sentence true is H_2O's being wet, while *the fact* that makes twin-Arabella's sentence true is XYZ's being wet. A similar remark can be made concerning indexicals. The sentence 'I am 30 years old' has the same conceptual role for Arabella and twin-Arabella, but tokens of the two differ in their truth conditions. Since it is the conceptual role of an expression (in the language of thought) which determines its role in the production of behavior, Arabella and twin-Arabella will behave identically when each believes what she would express by saying 'I am 30 years old'. But since conceptual role does not determine truth conditions the truth values of their beliefs may differ.[2] The dual component view also seems able to account for sentences which apparently have the same truth conditions but differ in meaning. Thus, 'Cicero is bald' and 'Tully is bald' are supposed to have the same truth condition but a given speaker's probability assignment might contain an S such that $P(\text{'Tully is bald'}/S) \neq P(\text{'Cicero is bald'}/S)$.

There are a number of features of the Field–McGinn characterization of conceptual role that are worth noting.

1. McGinn's account differs from the kinds of accounts suggested by Sellars, Harman, and Block in which conceptual role is characterized in terms of the *causal* relations that hold among representational mental states, perceptions, and behaviors. An individual's probability assignment

does not specify causal relations, but rather his commitments concerning rational change of belief. Only if the probability assignment is reflected in causal relations among belief states, etc, will conceptual role be capable of functioning in psychological explanations.

2. Field's (1978) account of conceptual role obviously involves a great deal of idealization. Gilbert Harman has argued that it is unrealistic to suppose that an individual reasons in terms of probabilities, since this would require keeping track of an enormous amount of information and require an enormous number of computations. Perhaps this objection can be met (Jeffrey, 1983), but a more difficult problem is presented by the evidence which shows that our beliefs do not conform to probability theory. For example, people will often assign a higher probability to a conjunction than to either of its conjuncts and do not typically change beliefs in accordance with conditionalization. So, McGinn's theory of conceptual role might not apply to human thought.

3. Conceptual role is a holistic notion. In characterizing the conceptual role of a sentence one must simultaneously characterize the conceptual roles of all other sentences. Any change in the probability function—even just extending it to a new vocabulary—results in a change in conceptual role for every sentence. Because of this two people will seldom assign the same conceptual role to syntactically identical expressions. Field explicitly offers conceptual role only as an account of intra-individual meaning. He does not think that it makes sense to compare different individual's conceptual roles (Field, 1977). However, McGinn apparently does think that it is meaningful to make inter-personal comparisons of conceptual role. For example, he speaks of Arabella and her twin's mental representations as having the same conceptual roles.

4. Field's characterization of conceptual role is solipsistic, since it is characterized entirely in terms of ingredients within the mind of the individual. It is this feature which suggests to McGinn that conceptual role can provide an account of the aspects of meaning that meets Fodor's methodological solipsism constraint. On some other versions, e.g., Harman's, the characterization of conceptual role also includes relations among sentences, environmental features, and behavior. So, Harman's account of conceptual role, as he insists, is non-solipsistic (Harman, 1986). We can imagine a theory between Field's and Harman's (along this dimension) which includes relations to sensory inputs and behavioral outputs in the characterization of conceptual role. As long as the inputs and outputs are described in ways that do not entail the existence of anything other than the thinker's body, the solipsistic nature of the account is preserved. The difference will be important when we come to evaluate the adequacy of conceptual role theories as semantic theories for languages of thought.

5. It should be clear that Putnam's stereotype and Kaplan's character are quite different from conceptual role (and from each other). The stereotype of 'water' is the information which a typical competent speaker of English associates with 'water', e.g., the water is liquid, necessary for life, fills the oceans, etc. Stereotype differs from conceptual role in a number of ways. (a) Stereotype characterizes cognitive significance, since it specifies the information associated with a term. It is not obvious that the conceptual role of a term or sentence associates with it any information (see fourth section). (b) It is not clear that stereotype is 'in the head' in the way conceptual role is. The expressions used to characterize the information contained in stereotype are themselves subject to Twin-Earth arguments, and this seems to show that stereotype itself is not solipsistic. (c) As we have pointed out, conceptual role is holistic. Stereotype does not appear to be holistic.

There are also important differences between conceptual role and character. (a) Two people can associate the same character with 'I am hungry', even though the sentence has different conceptual roles for each, since the two may differ in their overall probability assignments. So, character can be used to explain the sense in which two people who assert 'I am hungry' share the same belief, while conceptual role cannot. (b) Character determines truth conditions relative to context, but there is no systematic relation between conceptual role, context, and truth conditions. At least, none is built into McGinn's account.

However McGinn might fill in the details of his dual component view, the general picture is clear. On his view the appropriate form for a semantic theory for a language is a conjunction of *two* theories. One characterizing internal mental features of meaning and the other characterizing relations between language and the world. In opposition to the dual component view are semantic theories which provide a *unified* treatment of the mind and world aspects of meaning. Frege's and Davidson's theories are examples. McGinn, of course, thinks that such unified accounts are misguided. He says, 'But it seems that nothing of critical importance would be lost, and some philosophical clarity gained, if we were to replace in our theory of meaning, the ordinary undifferentiated notion of content by the separate and distinct components exhibited by the conjunctive paraphrase' (McGinn, 1982, p. 229). We will argue in the fourth section that, contrary to McGinn's claim, something of critical importance is missed by bifurcating the theory of meaning in the way McGinn proposes. Dual component theories cannot be used as theories of interpretation, and for this reason fail to provide adequate accounts of communication. We will present this argument in the fourth section. First, we want to show how Davidsonian truth theories can be used as theories of interpretation.

TRUTH CONDITIONAL THEORIES OF COMMUNICATION AND UNDERSTANDING

According to DATs, a theory of truth for a language is incomplete qua theory of meaning, because it fails to provide an account of the mental aspects of meaning: language understanding and cognitive significance. The conceptual role component is supposed to do that job. This view of the place of a truth theory in an account of meaning is clearly at variance with Donald Davidson's. Davidson sees a truth theory as capable of providing both an account of language understanding and an account of the relations between language and reality. In this section we will show how it is that knowledge of Davidsonian truth conditions can play a central role in understanding and communication. Our argument is a bit different from the arguments found in Davidson, but we clearly take our cue from his writings.

It is almost a truism (or was a truism until recently) in philosophy of language that to understand a sentence is to know its truth conditions. But if it is a truism, it is an obscure one. We will try to show what truth it contains. Once again, consider Arabella: she utters the words 'Es schneit' within earshot of Barbarella and Cinderella.[3] Barbarella understands German while Cinderella does not. This makes a difference. Barbarella acquires the beliefs that it is snowing and that Arabella believes that it is snowing and perhaps some other beliefs as well. Cinderella does not acquire these beliefs; Arabella's utterances are so many sounds to her. Even if she recognizes them as an assertion, something she is able to do without understanding German, she may acquire only the belief that Arabella's utterance 'Es schneit', whatever it may mean, is true, and perhaps also the belief that Arabella holds her utterance to be true. Still, she does not know what Arabella expresses or believes.

We have argued (LePore, 1982b; Loewer, 1982; LePore & Loewer, 1982) that *a theory of meaning for a language L should include information such that someone who possesses this information is, given his other cognitive capacities, able to understand L.* Understanding a language involves many complex abilities, e.g., to respond appropriately to assertions, orders, questions, and so forth. We will focus on one central ability, the ability to acquire justifiably beliefs about the world, and about what a speaker believes in the presence of that speaker's assertions. Since Cinderella, who does not understand German, can come to know that Arabella's utterance 'Es schneit' is true, we can ask what additional information would enable her to acquire justifiably the beliefs which Barbarella acquires?

A plausible (indeed, we think the inevitable) answer to our question is that if Cinderella knew that 'Es schneit' is true (in German) iff it is snowing, she would be in a position to acquire the target beliefs. Reasoning justifying these beliefs could go as follows:

Paradigm (I):

    1.   Arabella's utterance 'Es schneit' is true.
    2.   'Es schneit' is true iff it is snowing.
So, 3.   It is snowing.

Paradigm (II):

    4.   Arabella believes 'Es schneit' is true.
    5.   Arabella believes 'Es schneit' is true iff it is snowing.
So, 6.   Arabella believes that it is snowing.

Elsewhere we have argued that such reasoning gives substance to the claim that to understand a sentence is to know its truth conditions (LePore, 1982b, 1983; LePore & Loewer, 1981, 1983). However, this claim requires some qualification. We are not saying that a person's understanding of German involves his going through the above inferences, or even that every person who understands German explicitly knows the truth conditions of German sentences. Our claim is that truth conditions explicitly state information which can be used (usually together with other information) to interpret utterances. In this way, a specification of truth conditions for a language can provide an illuminating characterization of language understanding and communication.

    The view that a theory of truth for L can serve as a theory of meaning for L is most prominently associated with Donald Davidson. Our two paradigms exhibit exactly how a theory of truth can play the role of a theory of meaning. But, of course, not just any theory which entails for each indicative sentence S of L a theorem of the form 'S is true iff p' can serve as a theory of interpretation for L. According to Davidson, a theory of interpretation for an individual's language should assign truth conditions to his utterances in a way that results in an attribution of beliefs and preferences to him which are *reasonable* given his situation and behavior. Exactly what we count as reasonable will depend on our theories of belief and desire acquisition and our theories of behaviour, etc (Davidson, 1973b, 1974). We would add that a theory of truth cum theory of intepretation should yield theorems which can be employed in our paradigms. While we have not developed the adequacy conditions on Davidsonian truth theories in detail, what we have said is sufficient to distinguish among truth theories for L. For example, they may serve to eliminate theories which entail

'"Schnee ist weiss" is true if grass is green'. If we use a theory which contains this theorem then we might infer from Arabella uttering 'Schnee ist weiss' that grass is green and that she believes that grass is green. But Arabella might not have this belief. In any case, we would not be justified in believing that she has this belief (or that grass is green) on the basis of the truth of her utterance. It is interesting to see that our constraints also distinguish the truth conditions '"Water is wet" is true iff water is wet' from '"Water is wet" iff H_2O is wet'. The latter, but not the former, license an inference from Arabella who believes that her utterance 'Water is wet' is true to Arabella believes that H_2O is wet. We can imagine circumstances in which this would lead to error, i.e., when Arabella fails to believe that water is H_2O.

Readers familiar with discussions of Davidson's accounts of language will notice that we have emphasized the importance of knowledge of truth conditions, while saying little concerning the nature of the theory which implies instances of (T). Some writers, for example, Harman, claim that whatever a truth theory has to say about meaning is contained in the recursion clauses of the theory which show how truth conditions of complex sentences depend on semantic features of their component expressions (Harman, 1974; cf also Fodor, 1975). Harman argues that such a theory at best characterizes the meanings of logical constants, 'and', 'or', etc, by characterizing their conceptual roles, but that the theory does nothing to specify the meanings of other expressions. It should be clear that we disagree (cf LePore & Loewer, 1981). Truth conditions do specify meanings in that they enable someone who knows the truth conditions of sentences to interpret the speech of another. Of course, the theory is important as well, but not because it characterizes the conceptual roles of the logical connectives. (It is not clear that it does. Cf LePore, 1982a.) Having a truth theory for L is important because it provides a specification of truth conditions for all the (infinitely many) sentences of L in a way that does not presuppose an understanding of L.

We claim that truth theories for natural languages which are theories of interpretation address both aspects which concern DATs. This is clearly seen from our paradigm inference patterns. Someone who knows the truth conditions of the sentences of a language, and knows that this is common knowledge among speakers of the language, is in a position to draw conclusions both about the world and about what other speakers have in mind. On the one hand, truth conditions relate sentences to the world. They specify what must hold for a sentence to be true. On the other hand, they specify what is known by someone who understands a language. Whether they can deal with the specific problems that motivated DATs remains to be seen. We will discuss this matter in the last section.

WHAT'S WRONG WITH DAT

In this section we will compare DATs, focusing mainly on McGinn's version, with Davidsonian truth theories. We will argue for three claims: (1) McGinn's account of 'S means that p' involves necessary conditions for sameness of meaning which are much too restrictive and render it incapable of providing an account of communication. (2) Neither component of a DAT, nor the two together, is a theory of interpretation. (3) The conceptual role component of a DAT does not supply the sort of semantics for the language of thought that is required by (Fodor's version of) cognitive science.

McGinn's (1982, p. 229) analysis of meaning is that:

> for S to mean that p is for S to be true iff Q, for some 'Q' having the same truth conditions as 'p', and for S φ to have some cognitive role φ such that 'p' also has cognitive role φ.

McGinn's analysis specifies that S and S^* have the same meaning only if they have identical conceptual roles. Field explicitly claimed that sameness of conceptual role is a necessary condition for intra-person synonymy but explicitly denies its usefulness in characterizing inter-personal synonymy (Field, 1977). McGinn is unclear on this point, but if his analysis of 'S means that p' is to be used by an interpreter to specify the meanings of a speaker's sentences, then it requires that the conceptual role of the interpreter's sentence 'p' and the conceptual role of S be identical. However, only in science fiction thought experiments are the conceptual roles of Arabella's and Barbarella's sentences the same. As long as there is the slightest difference between Arabella's and Barbarella's probability assignments, no sentence will have the same conceptual role for both. If Arabella assigns a probability of 1, to 'it is raining' while Barbarella assigns it a probability of 0.2, then on McGinn's account their sentences have different meanings. Barbarella would be mistaken if she said that Arabella's sentence 'It is raining' means that it is raining. It is difficult to see how sense can be made of communication on this account of sameness of meaning. If Arabella and Barbarella assign different meanings to 'It is raining' (because they assign different probabilities), then there is nothing in common to be communicated. If they assign the same meaning (and so, have the same probability assignment), then there is no need for communication.

McGinn's account runs into similar difficulties as an account of 'means that' for internal representations. The usual view of advocates of mentalese accounts of belief (e.g., Fodor) is that 'Arabella believes that p' is true iff she bears a certain relation R to a representation S which means that p.

Since it is improbable that any of Barbarella's sentences has the same conceptual role as S, Barbarella's claims concerning what Arabella believes are bound to be incorrect on McGinn's view.

The heart of the problem is that for S to mean that p, S need not have precisely the same conceptual role as 'p' but rather a conceptual role appropriately similar to 'p'. Until the DAT theorist has specified when the conceptual roles of S and 'p' are sufficiently similar to count as their having the same meaning (when they have the same truth condition) he has not adequately characterized 'S means that p'. But this seems to be a hopeless task as long as conceptual role is characterized purely formally, e.g., in terms of probability relations.

Even if McGinn could overcome the difficulties just discussed, we will now show that the two components of McGinn's DAT, neither separately nor together, comprise a theory of interpretation. The adequacy conditions to be met by a DAT truth theory differ significantly from those to be met by a Davidsonian truth theory. McGinn views the truth theory as assigning 'facts' or 'states of affairs' to indicative sentences. This leads him to see a theory which issues in, e.g., '"Water is wet" is true iff H_2O is wet' as adequate since, according to him, 'Water is wet' and 'H_2O is wet' express the same fact. In fact, he says that any statements which are necessarily equivalent (substitutable in all non-psychological contexts) have the same truth conditions. Field's conception of the truth theory component is a bit different. He imagines the theory issuing in theorems like: 'Water is wet' is true iff the stuff denoted by 'water' has the property denoted by 'is wet'. He hopes for a physicalistic theory of the denotation relation. It is clear that McGinn and Field see a truth theory as explicating the relation between language and the world. McGinn thinks that sentences are assigned facts. Field sees expressions as denoting bits of reality.

The first point to notice is that neither McGinn's, nor Field's, truth theories will serve as theories of interpretation (except in very unusual circumstances). We will discuss McGinn's account first. Suppose that Arabella utters 'Water is wet'. If Barbarella knows that 'Water is wet' is true iff H_2O is wet, then she will correctly conclude (following our first paradigm) that H_2O is wet. However, following our second paradigm, she may also conclude that Arabella believes that H_2O is wet, and this might very well be a mistake. The trouble is that even though 'Water is wet' is true iff H_2O is wet, this truth condition does not express the belief Arabella intends to communicate. Field's truth theory is even less adequate as a theory of understanding. If Barbarella knows that 'Water is wet' is true iff the stuff denoted by 'water' has the property denoted by 'is wet', then she will be able to conclude from Arabella's utterance that the stuff denoted by 'water' has the property denoted by 'is wet'. But there is a large gap between this and the conclusion that water is wet. It is certainly the latter, and not the former, that is communicated by Arabella's utterance.

The previous objections show that the truth theory component of a DAT does not provide a full specification of the information which a competent English speaker has, and brings to bear, in interpreting the utterances of others; so, it does not express the information known by a competent speaker. But, of course, Field and McGinn do not advance these theories as theories of understanding. Since the conceptual role component is supposed to characterize the mental aspects of meaning, perhaps it specifies information sufficient to interpret a speaker's utterances. So, we will now examine the conceptual role theory to see whether it will enable one to interpret another's language.[4]

We will first discuss McGinn's and Field's proposal concerning the representation of conceptual role, and then the less precise characterizations given by Sellars and Harman. We will suppose, once again, that Arabella utters 'Es schneit'. We also suppose that Cinderella knows the conceptual roles of all of Arabella's sentences; that is, she knows the conditional probability function $P(A/B)$ defined on all the sentences of Arabella's language. Is this information sufficient to enable her to justifiably infer either that it is snowing or that Arabella believes that it is snowing? The answer is 'No!' Suppose that Cinderella starts by knowing that Arabella believes 'Es schneit' is true (or perhaps that she assigns a probability close to 1 to 'Es schneit'). How can the conceptual role theory support Cinderella's inference to the belief that it is snowing? It may support Barbarella's concluding that Arabella assigns a high probability to 'Es ist kalt', a low probability to 'Das Wetter ist schoen', and so on. She might even be able to predict how Arabella would behave, what sounds she will utter next, etc, but she will not know what Arabella means. In particular, she will not be in any position to infer that it is snowing or that Arabella believes that it is snowing. Unless Barbarella knows that 'Es schneit' is true iff it is snowing, Arabella's assigning a probability of 1 to 'Es schneit' does not count as evidence that it is snowing. Nor does it count as evidence for Arabella believing that it is snowing. Knowledge of Arabella's probability assignments is not sufficient for interpreting her utterances, at least not if that understanding includes the capacity to infer that it is snowing, that Arabella believes that it is snowing, and so on.

One might think that the problem with Field's conceptual role semantics (as a characterization of knowledge sufficient for language understanding) is that it fails to characterize relations between expressions and the world. In contrast, Sellars and Harman sketch a conceptual role theory which includes causal relations between sentences and the world. Harman says:

> There is no suggestion that content depends only on functional relations among thoughts and concepts, such as the role a particular concept plays in inference. Of primary importance are functional relations to the external world in connection with perception, on the one hand, and action on the other.

Harman does not specify the structure of a theory which characterizes conceptual role non-solipsistically. Lycan (1984, Ch. 10) in the course of criticizing Harman's proposal, suggests that such a theory would imply statements like:

(A)   The usual cause of Arabella's uttering 'Es schneit' is her being in belief state K, and the usual cause of her being in belief state K is it's snowing in the vicinity.

If Barbarella knew this, then she would be in a position to infer that it's snowing from Arabella's having uttered 'Es schneit'. This would be a case of inference to the best explanation, rather than an instance of our first paradigm. Truth seems to play no special role. As Lycan is well aware, there are a number of problems with this proposal. It is not plausible for most sentences, especially theoretical ones. The usual cause (if there is such a thing) of my uttering 'There are positively charged electrons' is not my being in a belief state which is itself caused by there being positively charged electons. The latter state of affairs may figure in the causal history of my utterance, but it is only one among many causes and not the 'usual cause'. If we put this objection aside (A) could be used to draw conclusions about the world from Arabella's utterances. But it does not enable one to draw appropriate conclusions about what Arabella believes when she utters, e.g., 'Water is wet'. The problem is that if water's being wet is the cause of her utterance, so is H_2O's being wet. In fact, Lycan's proposal adds nothing more to the theory of interpretation than the truth theory component provides.

We can imagine McGinn replying to our discussion with the suggestion that although neither component of a DAT by itself is a theory of interpretation, the combination is. One might be encouraged to think this since, according to McGinn, the conjunction of the two theories and his definition of meaning (M) yield theorems of the form 'S means that p', for each sentence S of L. Since 'S means that p' entails 'S is true iff p', we could employ these theorems in our two paradigms. But a closer look at McGinn's analysis of 'S means that p' reveals that the two component theories do not entail statements of the form 'S means that p'. Recall McGinn's definition:

(M) S means that p iff S is true iff Q, for some 'Q' having the same truth conditions as 'p', and for S to have some cognitive role @ such that 'p' also has cognitive role @.

The truth theory component may entail, e.g., 'Wasser ist naß' is true iff H_2O is wet. The conceptual role component may entail 'Wasser ist naß' has the same conceptual role as 'Water is wet' (and a different conceptual role from 'H_2O is wet'). But we can put the two components together to explain that 'Wasser ist naß' means that water is wet only if we know that 'Wasser ist naß' means that water is wet. Of course, we knew that if we knew English. But McGinn cannot rely on this since a theory of interpretation is supposed to characterize knowledge sufficient for understanding a language without presupposing the understanding of any language. The difficulty here is the same as we encountered in considering the conceptual role component by itself. Knowing that S has the same conceptual role as 'p' is not sufficient for understanding S (Twin-Earth problems aside) unless one knows what 'p' means. Contrast this with knowing that S is true iff p. Someone might have this knowledge (the knowledge expressed by 'S is true iff p') without knowing what 'p' means. We want theory of interpretation to state information sufficient for interpretation which itself does not depend on understanding the language in which it is formulated. It is this that (M) fails to do. Our conclusion is that the Field–McGinn conceptual role theory is inadequate as a theory of interpretation.

What is the relation between McGinn's two component theory and a Davidsonian truth theory? According to McGinn (1982, p. 240)

> . . . the Davidsonian perspective, while not actually being incorrect—for it is, after all, tacitly a dual component conception—is apt to deceive us about the theoretical resources we need in a full adequate theory of meaning.

McGinn thinks that a Davidsonian theory is 'tacitly a dual component conception', since in a Davidsonian T-sentence 'S is true iff p', 'p' not only specifies a truth condition of S but is also supposed to be a translation of S. If translation is understood as requiring identity (or rather, isomorphism) of conceptual role, then it seems to McGinn that a Davidsonian theory is simply a misleading formulation of a two component theory.

McGinn is correct in thinking that a Davidsonian theory addresses two aspects of meaning. It accounts for language world relations by characterizing truth and reference, and it accounts for mental aspects by characterizing knowledge sufficient for interpreting a language. But we strongly disagree with McGinn's claim that Davidson's theory is tacitly a dual component view presented in a misleading manner. There are significant differences between a Davidsonian theory and McGinn's DAT. First, a Davidsonian theory does not require for the adequacy of its T-sentence theorems that S and 'p' have the same conceptual role. We have already discussed the implausibility of this requirement. Davidson's theory is subject to the much looser constraint that it leads to reasonable attributions of beliefs and other propositional attitudes to speakers. Second, as we have just argued, McGinn's DAT is not a theory of interpretation. Knowledge of it does not enable one to determine what Arabella believes on the basis of her sincere utterances. This is the heart of our objection to McGinn's and other two-component theories. Whatever insight, if any, may be gained from decomposing meaning into two separate features, the resulting characterizations are not suitable as a theory of interpretation. Knowledge sufficient for understanding a language cannot be extracted and separated from knowledge of reference and truth since to understand a sentence is to know what it says about the world.

We have yet to consider the question of whether DATs provide adequate accounts of meaning for mental representations. It is prima facie plausible that DATs are just what is needed for mentalese. Recall that Fodor argues that cognitive science requires a methodologically solipsistic notion of content in its explanations of behavior. It is not unreasonable to look to the conceptual role component of a DAT to characterize this notion of content, while the truth theory component characterizes a broader notion of content involving relations between mental representations and the world. Since mentalese is not a language in which anyone communicates, our arguments that DATs do not provide theories of interpretation may appear irrelevant. In fact, some authors explicitly endorse dual aspect accounts for mentalese, but not for public languages (Lycan, 1985).

In the course of our discussion of Fodor in the first section, we saw that Fodor thinks that cognitive science requires a solipsistic notion of content. That is, a characterization of content which conforms to the formality condition: no difference in content without a difference in formal properties. The Field–McGinn characterization of conceptual role is solipsistic. But, we will argue, it does not yield a specification of content that is methodologically solipsistic, for the simple reason that *it yields no specification of content at all*. We have, in effect, already established this in our discussion of DATs as theories of interpretation. The problem is that a complete specification of the conceptual roles of the sentences S of Arabella's language of thought does not enable us to fill in the blanks in 'If Arabella bears R^* to S, then she believes that ____'. But this is what Fodor requires of a characterization of the contents of mental representations.

It might be thought that the dispute between us and someone who holds that conceptual role provides a solipsistic notion of content is merely a *semantic* quibble about what is to count as content. But it is not, since the operative notion of content is intended (by Fodor, who formulated this problem) to play a particular role in psychological explanations. Consider the following 'psychological' explanation. Arabella jumped because she believed that by jumping she would cause it to rain and she wanted it to rain. The phrases following 'believed that' and 'wanted' express contents. They explain Arabella's action by citing causes (her beliefs and desires) which 'rationalize' it. If we describe the causes of her actions without citing the contents of the propositional attitudes, then the resulting explanation no longer has its 'rationalizing' force. An explanation of Arabella's jumping which employs conceptual role would go something like this. Arabella bears B^* to a mental representation which has conceptual role Q and W^* to a mental representation which has conceptual role V; so, she jumped. Presumably the conceptual roles would be characterized in such a way that jumping normally follows upon bearing these relations to those representations. It is clear that the explanatory force of this explanation, whatever its value, does not rationalize Arabella's behavior. Only an explanation which appeals to content can do that.

DAVIDSONIAN TRUTH THEORIES SOLVE THE PROBLEMS

We have shown that McGinn's two component definition of meaning is inadequate, that his DAT is not suitable for use as a theory of interpretation, and that it fails to yield a solipsistic notion of content for mentalese. Also, we began to show how a Davidsonian truth theory, by providing a unified account of understanding and reference, is suitable for use as a theory of interpretation. Still, we need to inquire into the extent to which Davidsonian theories can cope with the problems which motivated the DAT proposal. So, we will now consider whether a Davidsonian truth theory can be used to interpret sentences containing proper names, indexicals, and natural kind terms. We will conclude with a few remarks on the prospect of obtaining a methodologically solipsistic theory of content.

What T sentences will a Davidsonian truth theory entail for a language with proper names? It is clear that, in contrast to the truth theory component of a DAT, a Davidsonian theory must be able to assign different truth conditions to, e.g., 'Cicero is bald' and 'Tully is bald'. DAT truth theories maintain that these sentences have the same truth conditions, since it is metaphysically necessary that they are equivalent (assuming that names are rigid). If one thinks, as McGinn does, that a truth theory assigns possible states of affairs or facts to indicative sentences, then we can see why DAT truth theories assign the same truth conditions to the two sentences. But it is not necessary to think of truth theories in this way. It is clear that Davidson rejects the reification of truth conditions as states of affairs (Davidson, 1969).

There is no reason why a Davidsonian truth theory cannot contain (1) and (2) without containing (3) and (4) (McDowell, 1980):

1. 'Cicero is bald' is true iff Cicero is bald.
2. 'Tully is bald' is true iff Tully is bald.
3. 'Cicero is bald' is true iff Tully is bald.
4. 'Tully is bald' is true iff Cicero is bald.

Arabella might believe (1) and (2) without believing (3) and (4). In that case it would be a mistake to include (3) and (4) in a theory intended to be employed in interpreting her utterances. If (3) and (4) are included in a truth theory for Arabella's language, then one would be licensed to infer (via paradigm II) that Arabella believes that Tully is bald from the fact that she utters 'Cicero is bald'. Suppose that a truth theory T contains (1) and (2), but not (3) and (4), and that Arabella assents to 'Cicero is bald' and dissents from 'Tully is bald'. We can use T to conclude that Arabella believes that Cicero is bald and believes that Tully is not bald. But there is no contradiction forthcoming unless we have some principle in the theory that permits the substitution of coreferential names in belief contexts. That it leads to attributing contradictory beliefs to Arabella is sufficient reason for rejecting the principle.

Our account of the truth conditions of sentences containing names is compatible with the view that names rigidly designate. If names are rigid designators, then true identity statements composed of names are necessarily true. Suppose that we add to T the 'axiom'—It is necessary that (Cicero = Tully). We can also suppose that Arabella knows that if Tully = Cicero then it is necessary that (Tully = Cicero). Of course, we will not add the axiom that Arabella knows that it is necessary that (Cicero = Tully), since that is false. Even with these additions, we cannot derive from T, and the fact that Arabella assents to 'Cicero is bald' and dissents from 'Tully is bald', that she believes that Cicero is bald and believes that Cicero is not bald. Of course, if one thinks that co-referential rigid designators are substitutible *salva veritatae* in belief contexts, then the consequence will be to saddle Arabella with contradictory beliefs. As we mentioned earlier, that seems to us to be reason to reject substitutivity.

A defender of DATs is likely to respond to our proposal in the following fashion. A Davidsonian truth theory is supposed to be an empirical theory, but what evidence could distinguish between a theory which contains (1) and (2), and a theory which contains (3) and (4)? Our reply, of course, is that the two theories are empirically discriminated in their applications in paradigm II. Assuming that Arabella might believe that Tully is bald without believing that Cicero is bald (and that we can obtain evidence for this), we can distinguish between the two theories. What evidence is relevant to whether Arabella believes that Tully is bald or believes that Tully is not bald? The dual aspect theorist's answer is that conceptual role is relevant. If Arabella bears B^* to an internal representation 'Tully is bald' which has a conceptual role similar to the conceptual role of my sentence 'Tully is bald' then she believes that Tully is bald. But, as we argued previously, identity, or similarity, of conceptual role is too strong a requirement to make us co-believers. Conceptual role seems especially irrelevant when it comes to translating proper names. What does seem relevant is the history of acquisition of a name. Suppose, for example, that I can trace Arabella's current use of 'Cicero' and my current use of 'Cicero' back to a common source, say, we both acquired the name upon hearing it spoken in a history class. Then that would count in favor of my attributing to her the belief that Cicero is bald upon hearing her utter 'Cicero is bald' even if the conceptual role of her sentence is quite different from mine. Of course, considerations governing the interpretation of names are quite complex. Our point is that whatever they are (a) conceptual role is not of great importance, and (b) a Davidsonian truth theorist can (indeed should) avail himself of these considerations in fashioning a truth theory.

Indexicals provide another motivation for DATs. Arabella's and twin-Arabella's understanding of 'I am 30 years old' is the same, but the truth conditions of their utterances of the sentence differ. DATs say that the conceptual roles of the sentences are the same (or isomorphic) while the truth conditions of their utterances differ. As we observed in the second section, a conceptual role theory does not seem to provide an adequate account of our understanding of indexicals. One's understanding of, for example, 'I am now in California', involves knowing how to infer what was said from knowledge of the context in which the sentence is uttered. It is not clear that this can be represented within Field's framework for conceptual role. Be that as it may, we now want to show how truth theories can be modified to interpret sentences with indexicals.

A number of authors have proposed ways of extending truth theories to languages with indexicals (Davidson, 1972; Taylor, 1980). However, no one seems to have addressed the problem of showing how a truth theory for languages with indexicals can be employed to interpret the utterances of a speaker of the language. It may be thought that a truth conditional account will not work for indexicals because 'Arabella is tall' and 'I am tall' uttered by Arabella have the same truth condition, namely, that Arabella is tall. But clearly Arabella's understanding of the two sentences might be different, since she might believe what one expressed and not what the other expressed. DATs deal with this by claiming that there is something other than truth conditions involved in understanding. What we are going to do is to show how a truth conditional account of indexicals can yield an account of understanding according to which Arabella and Barbarella have the same understanding of, e.g., 'I am in California', and yet different information can be communicated by their utterances of the sentence. Our idea builds on Davidson's suggestion that the truth predicate applies to a sentence at a time, for an utterer, at a place (with perhaps further relativizations required).

On our view indexical sentences possess *general truth conditions*. For example, understanding 'I am now reading Russell' includes knowing that the following is common knowledge among speakers of English:

(C) $(x)(t)$ ('I am now reading Russell' is true for x at t iff x is reading Russell at t)

Interpreting a language with indexicals involves introducing a relativized truth predicate. With 'I' and 'now' as the only indexicals in this sentence, the relativized truth predicate is 'true for x at t', where 'x' ranges over utterers and 't' ranges over times. How can knowledge that (C) enable someone to interpret utterances? Suppose that Arabella says to Barbarella 'I am now reading Russell'. Then Barbarella may be able to reason as follows:

(1).   Arabella uttered 'I am now reading Russell' at noon.
So, (2).   'I am now reading Russell' is true for Arabella at noon.
(C) $(x)(t)$ ('I am now reading Russell' is true for x at t iff x is reading Russell at t).
So, (3).   Arabella is reading Russell at noon.

Barbarella is justified, in part, in believing that Arabella is reading Russell at noon on the basis of her hearing Arabella's utterance because she knows that (C). But notice that she *also* makes use of information about the context of utterance. In particular, she uses her belief that Arabella is the utterer and that she made her remark at noon. If Barbarella failed to believe this, she would not be in a position to conclude (3). Exactly what she can conclude depends on what she believes. If she believes that the utterer is the tallest woman in the room and that the time is the same time that Cinderella laughed, then Barbarella could employ (C) to learn from Arabella's remark that the tallest woman in the room was reading Russell at the same time that Cinderella laughed.

Of course, there are ways that any competent interpreter has of identifying an utterer and the time of utterance. For example, if Barbarella hears someone utter 'I am now reading Russell', even if she knew nothing else about the utterer, she would know that the utterer is the utterer of that utterance. She could then use (C) to conclude that the utterer of that utterance of 'I am now reading Russell' is reading Russell.

We can also explain how Barbarella can employ her knowledge that (C) is common knowledge among speakers of English to learn something about what *Arabella* believes when she utters 'I am now reading Russell'. But here the inferences are a bit more delicate. Considering the following reasoning:

(1). Arabella utters 'I am now reading Russell' at noon.

(4). Arabella believes that 'I am now reading Russell' is true for Arabella at noon.

(5). Arabella believes that $(x)(t)$ ('I am reading Russell' is true for x at t iff x is reading Russell at t).

So, (6). Arabella believes that Arabella is reading Russell at noon.

In this bit of reasoning Barbarella employs information concerning Arabella's beliefs about whom she is and about when her utterance occurs. To conclude (6), she uses the information that *Arabella* believes that *Arabella* produced the utterance and that *Arabella* believes that it occurs at noon. If Arabella did not know that she is Arabella or did not know that the time of the utterance is noon, then Barbarella would be mistaken in concluding that (6).

If Barbarella does not know any singular term (or a translation thereof) that she believes Arabella believes refers to herself, then she will be unable to employ the knowledge embodied in the general truth condition (C) to arrive at conclusions about when Arabella believes herself to be reading Russell at noon. Again, there are some ways that any competent speaker of English has of identifying herself and the time of her utterance. Arabella will always know (if she understands English) that 'I' refers to herself. Of course, Barbarella cannot use 'I' to refer to Arabella, but she can express what Arabella believes by ascribing to her the belief that the utterer of that utterance believes of *herself* that she is reading Russell, from which she can conclude that Arabella believes that she (herself) is reading Russell.

Knowledge that (C) together with other information (some available to every competent speaker, some not) enables an interpreter to learn both about the utterer's beliefs and about the world beyond the utterer. Suppose that, as in Perry's story, Hume and Heimson each utter 'I am a Scottish philosopher' (Perry, 1979). Each believes himself to be Hume. If we know all this, we can employ the general truth condition—(x) ('I am a Scottish philosopher' is true for x iff x is a Scottish philosopher)—to conclude from Hume's utterance that Hume is a Scottish philosopher and that he believes himself to be a Scottish philosopher. Since we know that Heimson is deluded, we would not conclude from his utterance that he is a Scottish philosopher. But we can conclude, following the second inference pattern above, that Heimson believes himself to be a Scottish philosopher.

We have indicated how general truth conditions can play a role in a theory of interpretation. To provide an adequate account we would at least have to show how to construct a truth theory for a language with indexicals, which has correct general truth conditions as theorems and we would need to develop a logic in which the inferences to conclusions about the world and the utterer's beliefs can be represented. We leave these tasks to a future paper.

Natural kind terms presented another problem which motivated the development of DATs. Can a truth theory of interpretation be constructed for languages containing natural kind terms? Imagine an English speaking radical interpreter who arrives on Twin-Earth. He notes the patterns of sentences held true (and the degrees to which they are held true) and begins to devise a theory of interpretation. Suppose that he is unaware that the stuff they call 'water' is composed of XYZ molecules. Then he is likely to employ the homophonic truth theory, which contains the clause ' "Water is wet" is true (as uttered by a Twin-Earther) iff water is wet'. When twin-Arabella utters 'This is water', interpreter will conclude that this is water and that twin-Arabella believes that this is water, just as he would conclude if he were interpreting Arabella on Earth. But he will be mistaken. This is not water (since it is composed of XYZ) and twin-Arabella does not believe that it is water (since she has never encountered water). However, these mistakes will pass undetected as long as interpreter does not know the compositions of water and twin-water. Once he discovers that the chemical composition of water is H_2O and the composition of twin-water is XYZ, he will notice that he sometimes incorrectly interprets twin-Arabella. How might he revise his theory in the face of these incorrect interpretations?

He could try ' "Water is wet" is true in twin-English iff XYZ is wet'. This change will lead him to correctly conclude that this is XYZ when he hears twin-Arabella utter 'This is water', but it might also lead him to mistakenly conclude that twin-Arabella believes that this is XYZ. This would be a mistake if twin-Arabella did not know the chemical composition of the stuff she calls 'water'.

The solution is for interpreter to enrich his own language by adding a term 'water[t]' with the stipulation that it rigidly designates XYZ, but has the same conceptual role as Arabella's word 'water'. His truth theory for twin-English should contain the theorem ' "This is water" is true in twin-English iff this is water[t].'

We have shown how understanding of a language which contains names, indexicals, and natural kind terms, can be characterized by the knowledge of a truth theory which satisfies certain constraints. We argued that the DAT account is not successful, since the conceptual role component cannot explain how we acquire information from the utterances of others.

However, it is clear that our Davidsonian account of understanding does not satisfy one of the constraints that the conceptual role component was designed to satisfy; on the Davidsonian account, meaning is not entirely in the head. Arabella and twin-Arabella may be physiologically identical, but the truth theories that describe their understanding of their languages are different, as we saw in interpreting natural kind terms in English and twin-English. We have argued elsewhere (LePore & Loewer, 1986) that this does not show Davidsonian truth theories to be inadequate, but rather that the information that an interpreter can use does not supervene on physiology. The view that it is possible to describe a person's understanding of a language at a level at which understanding supervenes on physiology and which is also able to account for communication is wrong.

CONCLUSION

Dual Aspect theories claim that there are two aspects to meaning: one which relates language to the world and another which relates language to the mind. McGinn goes on to claim that the most perspicacious theory of meaning is one which gives distinct and independent treatments of each aspect: a theory of truth and a theory of conceptual role. We agree that meaning has two aspects but we disagree concerning the appropriate form for a theory of meaning. In this paper we showed that McGinn's dual component theory is incapable of serving as a theory of interpretation and for that reason is not the most perspicacious form for a theory of meaning. McGinn confuses the evidential basis for theory of meaning which may include information about the causal relations between representations and the world and information about conceptual role with a theory of meaning. In contrast, Davidsonian truth theories can accommodate both the aspects while providing a theory of interpretation.

ACKNOWLEDGMENTS

We would like to thank Ned Block, Jerry Fodor, Brian MacLaughlin, Richard Grandy, Gilbert Harman, Bernard Linsky, John McDowell, Colin McGinn, Hilary Putnam, and Stephen Schiffer, for comments on, and discussion of, earlier drafts of this paper. We especially would like to thank John Biro, Donald Davidson, and William Lycan for their help. Earlier drafts of this paper were read at the University of Michigan, Central Michigan University, Rice University, The Pacific APA, 1984, the Florence Center for the Philosophy and History of Science, the University of Urbino, and the City University of New York.

NOTES

[1] Except for XYZ replacing H_2O in twin-Arabella's body, but this, of course, is irrelevant to the argument. Putnam distinguishes 'narrow psychological states' from 'broad psychological states'. Only the former supervene on brain states described in neurophysiological terms. Clearly Putnam supposes that 'grasping a sense' is a narrow psychological state.

[2] McGinn envisions a probability assignment defined over a language which contains indexical sentences. But there are problems in interpreting probabilities of an indexical sentence. One difficulty is accounting for changes in the probability of, e.g., 'The meeting begins now', as time passes. We also note that a probability assignment does not capture the indexicality of indexical sentences, i.e., the way truth value depends on context.

[3] We switch languages here from English to German only emphasize the informational value of T sentences.

[4] It is obvious that the truth theory component of a DAT does not assign content to sentences of mentalese in a way that respects the formality condition. DAT assignments of truth conditions does not respect our ordinary individuation criteria for belief attributions. A representation R might be assigned either the truth condition that water is wet, or equivalently, from the perspective of a DAT, that H_2O is wet. While there may be a 'transparent' sense of belief for which the belief that water is wet is the same as the belief that H_2O is wet, it is clear that this assignment of belief contents is inappropriate for CTM.

REFERENCES

Block, N., Advertisement for a Semantics for Psychology. *Midwest Studies in Philosophy*, 1986, 615–678.

Davidson, D., *Inquiries Into Truth and Interpretation*. Oxford: Oxford University Press, 1984.

Davidson, D., Truth and Meaning. In Davidson (1984), pp. 17–36, 1967.

Davidson, D., On Saying That. In Davidson (1984), pp. 93–108, 1968.

Davidson, D., True to the Facts. In Davidson (1984), pp. 37–54, 1969.

Davidson, D., Radical Interpretation. In Davidson (1984), pp. 125–140, 1973a.

Davidson, D., In Defense of Convention T. In Davidson (1984), pp. 65–76, 1973b.

Davidson, D., Belief and the Basis of Meaning. In Davidson (1984), pp. 141–154, 1974.

Field H., Logic, Meaning and Conceptual Role. *Journal of Philosophy*, 1977, **7**, 379–409.

Field, H., Mental Representation. *Erkenntnis*, 1978, **13**, 9–61.

Fodor, J., *The Language of Thought*. Cambridge: Crowell, 1975.

Fodor, J., Methodological Solipsism Considered as a Research Strategy in Cognitive Psychology. *Behavioral and Brain Sciences*, 1980, **3**, 63–73.

Fodor, J., Cognitive Science and the Twin-Earth Problem. *Notre Dame Journal of Formal Logic*, 1982, **23**.

Fodor, J., Narrow Content. Unpublished manuscript.

Harman, G., *Thought*. Princeton, NJ: Princeton University Press, 1973.

Harman, G., Meaning and Semantics. In M. R. Munitz & P. K. Unger (Eds), *Semantics and Philosophy*. New York: New York University Press, 1974, pp. 1–16.

Harman, G., Conceptual Role Semantics. *Notre Dame Journal of Formal Logic*, 1982, **20**, 242–256.

Harman, G., *Non-Solipsistic Conceptual Role Semantics*, this volume.

Harman, G., *Change in View*. Cambridge, MA: Bradford Books/MIT Press, 1986.

Jeffrey, R., *The First Definneti Lecture*. Unpublished manuscript, 1983.

Kaplan, D., *Demonstratives*. Unpublished manuscript, 1977.

Kripke, S., *Naming and Necessity*. In D. Davidson & G. Harman (Eds), *Semantics of Natural Languages*. Dordrecht: Reidel, 1972, pp. 253–355.

Kripke, S., A Puzzle about Belief. In Margalit (Ed), *Meaning and Use*. Dordrecht: Reidel, 1979, pp. 239–283.

LePore, E., Truth and Inference. *Erkenntnis*, 1982a, **18**, 379–395.

LePore, E., In Defense of Davidson. *Linguistics and Philosophy*, 1982b, **5**, 277–294.

LePore, E., What Theoretical Semantics Cannot Do. *Synthese*, 1983, **54**, 167–187.

LePore, E. & Loewer, B., Translational Semantics. *Synthese*, 1981, **48**, 121–133.

LePore, E. & Loewer, B. Three Trivial Truth Theories. *Canadian Journal of Philosophy*, 1983, 433–447.

LePore, E. & Loewer, B., Solipsistic Semantics, *Midwest Studies in Philosophy*. 1986, 595–614.

Loar, B., *Mind and Meaning*. Cambridge: Cambridge University Press, 1981.

Loewer, B., The Role of Conceptual Role Semantics. *Notre Dame Journal of Formal Logic*, 1982, **23**, 26–39.

Lycan, W., Form. Function and Feel. *Journal of Philosophy*, 1981, **78**.

Lycan, W., Toward a Homuncular Theory of Believing. *Cognition and Brain Theory*, 1982, **4**, 19–31.

Lycan, W., *Logical Form*. Boston, MA: M.I.T. Press, 1984.

Lycan, W., Paradox of Naming. In B. K. Matilal & J. L. Shaw (Eds), *Analytical Philosophy Comparative Perspective*. Dordrecht: Reidel, 1985, pp. 81–102.

McDowell, J., On the Sense and Reference of a Proper Name. In M. Platts (Ed), *Reference, Truth and Reality*. London: Routledge & Kegan Paul, 1980, pp. 111–130.

McGinn, C., The Structure of Content. In A. Woodfield, *Thought and Object*. 1982, pp. 215–271.

Perry, J., Frege on Demonstratives. *Philosophical Review*, 1978, **59**, 474–497.

Perry, J., The Problem of the Essential Indexical. *Nous*, 1979, **12**, 3–21.

Putnam, H., The Meaning of 'Meaning'. *Mind, Language, and Reality: Philosophical Papers*. Cambridge: Cambridge Univeristy Press, vol. 2, 1975, pp. 131–171.

Putnam, H., Meaning Holism. (MH) unpublished manuscript.

Putnam, H., Computations and Interpretations. (CI) unpublished manuscript.

Sellars. W. Empiricism and the Philosophy of Mind. *Minnesota Studies in the Philosophy of Science*. Minnesota: Minnesota Press, 1956, vol. 1.

Sellars, W., Some Reflections on Language Games. *Science, Perception and Reality*, 1963.

Sellars, W., Language as Thought and as Communication. *Philosophy and Phenomenological Research*, 1969, **29**.

Tarski, A., The Concept of Truth in Formalized Languages. *Logic, Semantics, and Metamathematics*. Oxford: Clarendon Press, 1956, pp. 152–278.

Taylor, B., Truth Theories for Indexical Languages. In M. Platts (Ed), *Reference, Truth and Reality*. London: Routledge & Kegan Paul, 1980, pp. 182–198.

White, S., Partial Character and the Language of Thought. *Pacific Philosophical Quarterly*, 1982, **63**, 347–365.

Zemach, E., Putnam and Meaning and Reference. *Journal of Philosophy*, 1976.

4

Extensionalist Semantics and Sententialist Theories of Belief

STEPHEN SCHIFFER

Dept of Philosophy,
University of Arizona

INTRODUCTION

Donald Davidson is the creator of two justly famous theories. The first is about the form that a compositional semantics, or meaning theory, for a particular language should take; and the second is about the logical form of propositional attitude ascriptions. The two theories are very intimately connected, and, I shall argue, problems that infect their intersection make it doubtful that either of them can be true. More than this, I shall argue that the problem for Davidson can be generalized. *Sententialist* theories of propositional attitudes go hand-in-hand with *extensionalist* accounts of compositional semantics. One cannot coherently be a sententialist with respect to the belief-relation unless one supposes that the correct meaning theory, or compositional semantics, for a given natural language is extensionalist; and one who supposes that natural languages have extensionalist meaning theories is constrained to be a sententialist as regards the belief-relation. The primary conclusion of this essay will be that (a) no sententialist account of propositional attitude relations can be correct; but in showing this it will also be shown, I believe, that, relative to a certain assumption, (b) no extensionalist account of compositional semantics can be correct.

113

THREE HYPOTHESES

There are three hypotheses that are very widely accepted among philosophers of language, and they are intimately related.

The first hypothesis is that *every natural language has a correct meaning
theory*. A meaning theory for a language L would be a finitely statable
theory which specifies the meanings of the finitely many words and express-
ion-forming operations in L, and shows how these meanings determine the
meanings of the infinitely many complex expressions in L.

Since the beginning of analytical philosophy of language—that is, since
Frege—it has been more or less taken for granted that natural languages
have compositional meaning theories, theories which construct the meanings of complex expressions out of the meanings of their component parts;
and this is no wonder. For it is the merest platitude that the meaning of a
sentence is determined by its syntax and the meanings of its component
words, and this platitude has been taken strongly to suggest, if not entail,
the widely held hypothesis. And, relatedly, it has often been argued that
the hypothesis that natural languages have compositional meaning theories
is needed to explain our ability to understand novel sentences, sentences
we are encountering for the first time. For in encountering a novel but
understood sentence, one is not being confronted with novel words, but
with familiar words put together, via familiar constructions, in a novel way,
and it may seem obvious that one understands a novel sentence because
one knows the meanings of the words contained in it and, in some sense,
knows a rule of determining the meaning of the sentence on the basis of
its syntax and the meanings of its words. For example, S produces the
sequence of sounds, 'Hey, lady, your kid just bit my dog'. A has an auditory
perception of those sounds and, even though she never encountered that
sequence before, instantaneously knows its meaning, and knows that, in
producing it S said that A's child bit S's dog. A theory of language
understanding, for which it is commonly held that a meaning theory is
essential, would explain how A can go from the auditory perception of
sounds to the knowledge of what they mean and what was said in the
production of them. The rough picture thus suggested of A's understanding
of S's utterance is as follows. A hears the utterance of the sentence, and
because she is somehow related to a correct meaning theory for English
(perhaps she has an internal representation of it) she is somehow able to
ascribe properties to the sentence S uttered that are in some sense constitutive of its meaning. This knowledge of the meaning of the sentence then
interacts with knowledge that A has about the context of utterance, S, and
general psychological, or psychosemantical, truths applicable to speakers

of any language, and this interaction in turn yields the knowledge that S, in uttering the sounds, said that A's child bit S's dog.

But the characterization of a meaning theory that I have given is not ideal: it uses the troublesome notion 'meaning'. It is not merely that the characterization in terms of 'meaning' carries the suggestion, which a theorist may well want to resist, that a meaning theory must issue in theorems of the form 'σ means in L that . . .'. It is also the case that using the notion of meaning to characterize a compositional semantics puts things the wrong way round; for what we should say is that 'meaning' is, as it were, whatever must be ascribed to a sentence in order to explain one's ability to understand utterances of it; to explain, that is, how one can go from an auditory perception of an utterance of the sentence to the knowledge of what was said in that utterance.

In this light one can appreciate Davidson's favored gloss of what a meaning theory for a particular language is: it is a finitely statable theory which 'explicitly states something knowledge of which would suffice for interpreting utterances of speakers of the language to which it applies.' (Davidson, 1984, p. 171.)

What form should a meaning theory for a particular language take? I think it is fair to say that this question was the single most dominant topic in the philosophy of language for at least fifteen years following the appearance of Davidson's 'Truth and Meaning' (in Davidson, 1984). If that question no longer engages philosophers of language in quite the way that it used to, it is not because the question has been answered. Still, the next widely held hypothesis constrains a little the possible answers to the question just posed.

The second widely held hypothesis voices the sentiment of the many for whom 'semantics with no treatment of truth conditions is not semantics' (Lewis, 1972, p. 169) in maintaining that, *whatever form a meaning theory for a natural language L takes, it must at least yield a determination of the truth conditions for utterances in L that can have truth conditions.* After all, it is a fact about the *meaning* of 'I'm thirsty' that an utterance of it would be true just in case the speaker was thirsty, and, furthermore, in order to understand an utterance of the sentence one would have to know that the speaker said that he or she was thirsty, and that, therefore, what was said, and so the utterance of the sentence, is true just in case the speaker was thirsty. In other words: to understand a language is to have the ability to understand utterances in it; and to understand an utterance in the assertive mode is to know that it is true provided that such and such is the case, where what the speaker said in the utterance was precisely that such and such was the case. All this, it is commonly held, does motivate the assumption that a meaning theory for L must also be, in the sense indicated, a truth theory for L. Of course, from the fact (if it is one) that a compositional meaning theory must also be a compositional truth-theoretic semantics—in the sense of being a theory that determines, for each sentence of L that can be used to say something true or false, the condition under which an utterance of that sentence would be true—nothing very specific follows about the form that such a theory would have to take. In particular, this hypothesis by no means endorses Davidson's suggestion that a meaning theory for L should take the form of an extensional, finitely axiomatized theory of truth for L in the style of Tarski, somehow relativized to utterances of sentences.

The third widely held hypothesis is one I shall call *the relational theory of propositional attitudes*. Stated with respect to believing it is, nearly enough, the hypothesis that believing is a relation to things believed, to values of the variable 'y' in the schema 'x believes y', to things having features which determine the intentional and truth-valuational features of beliefs. My present belief that the earth moves is true, this hypothesis has it, just in case what I believe—the referent of the singular term 'that the earth moves' (or is it the singular term 'that'?)—is true. The big question here, which we shall soon be taking up, is, of course: What are these 'things believed', and what are their features that determine the contentful features of beliefs?

Why suppose that the relational theory of propositional attitudes is correct? The classical answer, which derives from Frege, is that the construal of propositional attitude verbs as *relational predicates* is the only feasible construal of them *relative to the assumption that natural languages have compositional truth-theoretic semantics*. For if σ is any well-formed indicative sentence of English, then ⌜believes that σ⌝ is a well-formed predicate phrase. Since there are infinitely many such predicate phrases, no compositional truth-theoretic semantics, being finitely statable, can treat them as semantically primitive. A compositional truth-theoretic semantics must therefore treat 'believes' (or 'believes that') as semantically primitive; and it is arguable that the only tenable way this can be done is to treat 'believes' as a relational predicate true of believers and what they believe.[1]

We garner further support for the relational theory when we notice familiar grammatical and logical facts: quantifier expressions and paradigm singular terms can occur as grammatical complements of 'believes', to form predicate expressions such as 'believes something silly' and 'believes your theory', and inferences such as the following are patently valid:

> Alfred and Donald both believe that snow is white.
> So, there is something which they both believe.

(But can one argue that these familiar facts prove the relational theory of propositional attitudes? That would be precipitate. For one can infer the relational theory from the meaningfulness of quantified sentences such as

[A]   There is something which Alfred believes

only after it has been established that the quantification here ('there is something which') is to be read *objectually* rather than *substitutionally*. On the objectual reading, [A] is true just in case the open sentence 'Alfred believes x' is true of some *object*, and if this is the correct reading, then the relational theory of believing does indeed follow. On the substitutional reading, however, [A] is true just in case some *substitution-instance* of 'Alfred believes that S' (e.g., 'Alfred believes that snow is white') is true, and this does not imply the relational theory, for it is consistent with *any* account of the logical form of the substitution-instances that make the quantification true. The only deep reason for preferring the relational theory of 'believes' is that it is needed to account for the logical form of sentences like 'Alfred believes that snow is white'.)

The first hypothesis gives rise to the question:

What form must a correct theory of meaning for a language take?

and the third hypothesis, we have already noted, gives rise to the question:

What are the relata of the various propositional attitude relations, and what are their intentionality-determining features?

Not surprisingly, the answer one gives to either of these questions constrains the answer one may plausibly give to the other.

EXTENSIONALIST SEMANTICS AND CONTENT-DETERMINING FEATURES

Well, what form should a meaning theory for a particular language take? Since our other concern is the relational theory of propositional attitudes, and since it is doubtful that one can so much as make sense of the claim that propositional attitude predicates are relational other than in terms of their playing a certain role in the determination of the truth conditions of the sentences in which they occur, we may for present purposes take the answer to the question just asked to be constrained by the second widely held assumption; that is, by the assumption that, whatever else a compositional meaning theory will be, it will also be a compositional truth-theoretic semantics.

This understood, we may distinguish two sorts of theories about the form that a meaning theory for a particular language should take. (To keep matters as simple as possible I shall ignore indexicality, ambiguity, and moods other than the indicative.)

A compositional semantics for a language L is *intensionalist* if its theorems somehow correlate each sentence of L with an *intension*—an abstract meaning, a proposition of one kind or another—that determines a truth value for the sentence in the actual world and every other possible world. These entities would be the contents of the sentences mapped onto them. Such an intensionalist theory could directly take the form of a theory which explicitly maps each sentence onto a proposition, or it could take the form of a possible worlds semantics that assigns to each sentence and possible world the condition under which the sentence is true in the possible world, thereby correlating with each sentence as its meaning, or intension, the set of possible worlds in which it is true.

A compositional semantics for a language L is *extensionalist* if its compositional component is a finitely axiomatized truth theory for L. What is meant here is absolute truth, truth in the actual world, rather than truth relative to a model or truth in an arbitrary possible world. The theorems of such a truth theory would not, of course, correlate the sentences of L with anything that could be taken to be the contents of the sentences, but would have the familiar extensionality of, say,

'La neige est blanche' is true in French iff snow is white.

I said that the *compositional component* of an extensionalist meaning theory would be an extensional truth theory for the language because, as is well known (see, for example, Kripke, 1976; Loar, 1976; Foster, 1976; Davidson, 1984), merely to know a correct truth theory for L would not in itself suffice to enable one to interpret speakers of L. For the theorems of such a theory may be true without being *interpretative*; the substituend for 'p' in a given correct instance of the 'T-sentence'

$$\sigma \text{ is true in L iff } p$$

need not be equivalent in meaning to σ, and even if it is there is nothing in the truth theory as such to tell one that that is so.

If a truth theory for a language is to figure into an extensionalist meaning theory for that language, then it must be that if someone knows that theory, and knows that it meets certain further conditions, then he is in a position to understand utterances in the language. And these further conditions, for the extensionalist, must not introduce entities to be contents of sentences. What form, then, should an extensionalist meaning theory for a particular language take? That is, what sort of true theory of a language

L would be at once suitably extensionalist in its avoidance of meanings yet such that knowledge of what that theory states suffices for enabling one to understand utterances in L? Davidson's (1984, p. 172) well-known answer is this:

[MT]   One would have a theory that sufficed for interpreting utterances in L if: (1) one had, and knew what was stated by, a correct, extensional, finitely axiomatized theory of truth for L in the style of Tarski, somehow relativized to utterances of sentences; (2) that theory satisfied such and such empirical constraints (paramount among them being ones determined by evidence concerning pairings of sentences held true with circumstances in which they are held true and by the principle of charity); and (3) one knew that (1) and (2).

In other words, 'someone is in a position to interpret the utterances of speakers of a language L if he has a certain body of knowledge entailed by a theory of truth for L—a theory that meets specified empirical and formal constraints—and he knows that this knowledge is entailed by such a theory.'

In this view, the meaning theory for a language L would not be the truth theory for L; rather, it would be what one knows as characterized in [MT], namely, that such and such a truth theory satisfies such and such constraints.

Whatever else a meaning theory for a language L is, it must also be, we are supposing, a compositional truth-theoretic semantics. In light of this, I think it is safe to say that, while an extensionalist with respect to compositional semantics might well disagree with Davidson over the nature of the empirical constraints alluded to in (2), he would have to agree with the rest of Davidson's characterization. In other words, we may take the following to be definitive of the extensionalist's answer to the question of the form that a meaning theory for a particular language L must take: it must be a correct, extensional truth theory for L that satisfies conditions (themselves entailing no quantification over meanings) such that, if one knows the truth theory and knows that it satisfies those conditions, then that would suffice for interpreting utterances of speakers of L.

There is a curious feature of Davidson's proposal that we should pause to register, although its full import may not be apparent until later. Let M be the correct meaning theory for a natural language L, and let us suppose that M is as Davidson says it would be; i.e., that it satisfies the characterization [MT]. (Davidson, for reasons having to do with indeterminacy, would not say that a language *must* have a *uniquely* correct meaning theory; the assumption of uniqueness is merely a useful expedient in the present context.) What is curious is that:

Davidson evidently does *not*—and certainly *should not*—hold that:

(a)   understanding L requires knowing that M is the case;

while he *does* hold that:

(b)   what makes M a theory of meaning for L is that knowledge that M is the case *would* suffice for understanding L

and that:

(c)   M is entailed by the correct theory of a person's understanding of L.

Davidson (1984, Essay 9) has been fairly careful about avoiding a commitment to (a), and well he should be; for whether or not knowledge of the kind alluded to in [MT] would, if one had it, suffice for understanding a language, it seems very clear that no actual speaker has such propositional knowledge. Consider, in this regard, nine year old Paul: you utter the sounds 'It's raining'; he hears your utterance and knows that you said that it was raining; but it is preposterous to suppose that Paul understands your utterance by virtue of knowing that the fact that your utterance has the truth condition it has is entailed by some correct finitely axiomatized truth theory of English that satisfies the Davidsonian empirical constraints.

That Davidson holds (b) is, of course, obvious, and likewise, I think, as regards his holding (c). For Davidson clearly does hold that the reason for thinking that every natural language has a correct meaning theory is that that assumption is needed to explain language understanding, i.e., one's ability to interpret utterances in a language.

But if M, the correct meaning theory for L, is needed to explain one's understanding of L, though not in the way that the definition of being a meaning theory suggests, then how is it needed to explain the ability to know what is said by utterances in L? Why, in the absence of an answer to this question, should one even suppose that Davidsonian meaning theories are needed to explain language understanding? Matters are exacerbated when one further reflects that (i) we do not really have a complete proposal about the nature of meaning theories for particular languages because we do not really know what a Tarskian truth theory for a *natural* language would look like, nor do we have a very specific proposal about the nature of the empirical constraints alluded to in [MT], and that, consequently, (ii) we really do not know if it is true that, if we had a Davidsonian meaning theory for a language, knowledge of the theory would suffice for interpreting speakers of the language. Let me repeat, however, that these remarks are not intended as objections, but merely to register a certain puzzle, one to which I shall be returning.

It will help later if I am a little more specific about the curious feature in question, and if we notice that it would appear to be an inevitable feature of *any* correct extensionalist meaning theory for a particular language.

Let us say that Φ is a *content-determining feature* of the sentence σ if the knowledge that σ has Φ, together with one's inter-linguistically applicable knowledge, suffices for understanding utterances of σ; suffices, that is, for enabling one to know what a speaker says in uttering σ.[2] Intuitively, to know that σ had Φ would be precisely to know what σ means. Now it follows from Davidson's proposal [MT] that natural language sentences have content-determining features. What is curious is that:

> Whereas, on Davidson's theory [MT], every sentence of a language has a content-determining feature, no one who understands the language knows, for any sentence σ and its content-determining feature Φ, that σ has Φ.

For consider the sentence

[N]   La neige est blanche.

Davidson would hold that [N] has a content-determining feature—a feature such that knowledge that [N] had it would suffice for interpreting an utterance of [N]. For his theory of meaning (together with what we in fact know about the meaning of [N]) commits him to holding that:

> It will suffice for a person to interpret literal utterances of [N] if (refinements aside) he knows that (a) [N] is true iff snow is white, that (b) that fact is entailed by a correct, finitely axiomatized, extensional, Tarski-style truth theory for the language to which [N] belongs, and that (c) that truth theory satisfies . . . empirical constraints (imagine the blank filled by a specification of the empirical constraints forthcoming from Davidson's finished theory).

My point is that, even if this were true (and I doubt, incidentally, that it is), the content-determining feature specified is not one that enters into anyone's propositional knowledge. I hasten to add that I am not denying that Davidsonian content-determining features enter into one's *non-propositional* knowledge, nor that the possession of such features are in some sense 'internally represented'; my point is merely that, if Φ is the Davidsonian content-determining feature of [N], then no one knows that [N] has Φ. Let me sum this up by saying that, if there are Davidsonian content-determining features, then they are not within the ken of plain folk.

At the same time, I think it is clear that it is preposterous to suppose that Davidson's extensionalist program in semantics is correct, except that he has been mistaken about what the content-determining features of utterances are, and that the real content-determining features *are* within the ken of plain folk. In other words, it seems clear that, if there are *extensionalist* content-determining features, then they are not within the ken of plain folk.

So much for curious features later to be exploited.

EXTENSIONALISM AND SENTENTIALISM

Now let us turn to the question raised by the relational theory of propositional attitudes,

> What is believing a relation to—what, that is, are the values of 'y' in 'x believes y'—and what features of those things determine the intentional features of beliefs?

and to how answers to that question are related to extensionalist semantics.

Either belief-objects *are* contents—propositions of one kind or another, abstract, objective, language-independent entities that have essentially the truth conditions they have—or else they are things which *have* content—things, such as sentences, which only contingently have the truth conditions they happen to have.

But the extensionalist with respect to compositional semantics cannot coherently be a propositionalist with respect to propositional attitudes. For to know the meaning of a sentence is to know what would be said by an utterance of it; so if, as the propositionalist claims, *what is said* is a proposition, then the meaning of a sentence must be the proposition it expresses, and thus the correct meaning theory for the language should be intensionalist—i.e., a mapping of its sentences onto those propositions that are the contents of the assertions one would make in uttering the sentences.

The extensionalist must therefore hold that propositional attitudes are relations to things which only contingently have the contents they have. He may therefore be (what I shall call) a *sententialist* with respect to propositional attitudes: he may hold that believing (as well as the other attitudes) is a relation to a sentence or utterance of a language, and that it is the meaning, or content, of that sentence or utterance that determines the contents of the beliefs that are related to it. Mental representations, formulae in the 'brain's language of synaptic interconnections and neural spikes,' (Lewis, 1983) are also things which have only contingently the truth conditions they have; so the extensionalist may, for all we yet know, hold that believing is a relation to a mental representation. And perhaps some other position is in principle available to him as well (see, e.g., Loar, 1981). But I do not think so. I think that there is no hope for the extensionalist if he cannot also be a sentientialist. But I cannot hope to show this here; it would require too long a discussion of the view that believing is a relation to a mental representation, and possibly of other views as well.[3] Thus one conclusion that I shall eventually draw will be qualified. It will not be the conclusion that I would argue for if I had more time and space, that extensionalist semantics cannot be right because the sentientialist theory of propositional attitudes is false; but rather that, on the assumption that the sentientialist theory is the only way of cashing-out the relational theory of propositional attitudes that plausibly coheres with extensionalist semantics, extensionalist semantics cannot be right because the sentientialist theory of propositional attitudes is false.

At the same time, the sentientialist is constrained to be an extensionalist with respect compositional semantics.[4] The motive for the view that believing is a relation, not to things which *are* contents (propositions of one kind or another), but to things which *have* content (sentences or utterances), is the desire to avoid any ontological commitment to contents; so the sentientialist, who takes believing to be a relation to a linguistic entity, to something which has content, will not want self-defeatingly to account for the having of content of linguistic entities in terms of *their* being related to contents, but will construe their having of content in an extensionalist, truth-theoretic way.

So let us suppose that one is an extensionalist as regards compositional semantics. Because one believes that every natural language has a compositional truth-theoretic semantics, one believes that propositional attitude verbs are relational predicates; and because one is an extensionalist one believes that propositional attitudes are not relations to things that are contents, but rather to things that have content—sentences or utterances. It will help to begin with the simplest version of this idea.

BELIEVING AS A RELATION TO SENTENCES

If the sentientialist theory is to be held in a way that is tenable, it must not imply that only speakers of a natural language can have beliefs; room must be left for chimps, dogs, very young children, and feral human adults to have them, too. What we might call the classic sentientialist position would take believing to be a relation between a believer and some sentence-type, a relation that obtains by virtue of the meaning or content of the sentence in the language to which it belongs, but not a relation which requires the believer to understand the sentence. This theorist would represent the logical form of

[a]   Henri believes that love is cruel

as

[b]   B(Henri, 'love is cruel').

That is, it would represent [a] as saying that Henri stands in the belief-relation to the English sentence 'love is cruel'. This would not in any way imply that Henri speaks English; for there are any number of relations that one can stand in to a sentence without understanding it, and the idea now is that the belief-relation is one of them. Perhaps, to paraphrase a remark of Davidson's (Davidson, 1984, p. 167), in uttering [a] it is as though one were saying that Henri is in that state of mind we would be in were we to utter 'love is cruel' assertively and sincerely.

If Henri stands in the belief-relation to 'love is cruel', then that must be because of certain of that sentence's features and not others. Clearly, consisting of three words would be irrelevant, while being true iff love is cruel would be relevant. For the classic sententialist, *what* sentence one believes when one has a belief is determined by the meaning, or content, of that sentence. It is because 'love is cruel' means that love is cruel that Henri stands in the belief-relation to it. It is this fact that makes trouble for the classic theory, as we shall now see.

One well-known problem with the sententialist theory in the simple form that would represent [a] as [b] is this: a sentence can have more than one meaning.

First, a sequence of marks or sounds can be a sentence of more than one language, with a different meaning in each. Davidson (1984, p. 98) gives the example of the sounds 'Empedokles liebt', which in German tell us that he loved, and in English what he did from the top of Mt Etna.

Second, a sequence of marks or sounds can have more than one meaning and truth condition even within a language, as we can see from the sentence 'visiting relatives can be boring'.

The fact that a sentence may have different meanings both within and between languages is a problem for the classic sententialist theory for the following reason. According to that theory in its unqualified form, the truth conditions of a belief are just those of the sentences believed. Thus the belief ascribed in a belief ascription would, unacceptably, have as many truth conditions as the sentence contained in the 'that'-clause. For

example, if there were some language in which 'love is cruel' meant that
kangeroos fly, then [a] would ascribe to Henri a belief that was true iff love
is cruel, and a belief that was true iff kangeroos fly.

There are two ways one might think to repair the classic sentientialist
position in view of the problem of multiplicity of meaning.

(1)   One may entertain the possibility of revising the sentientialist position by taking believing to be a relation between a believer, a sentence,
and *a meaning or interpretation of that sentence*, thus:

[c] $B(x,\sigma,m)$.

This would yield for [a]:

> B(Henri, 'love is cruel', the relevant meaning (or interpretation) of 'love
> is cruel').

Now this suggestion is incomplete pending some account of what 'm' in
[c] is to range over, some account, that is to say, of what sorts of things
meanings or interpretations are supposed to be; and herein lies a problem.
If meanings are taken to be *Fregean* meanings—things that *are* contents,
propositions of one kind or another—then there are two problems. First,
as we noted just lately, the traditional motivation for adopting a sentientialist
theory of belief has been to avoid an ontological commitment to meanings;
so this manoeuver is simply unavailable to this sort of theorist. Second,
and more importantly, if propositions are taken to be the values of 'm' in
[c], then the reference to the sentence becomes wholly otiose, and the
theory collapses into a notational variant of the propositional theory of
propositional attitudes. For if believing is a relation to a sentence that
obtains by virtue of the meaning of that sentence, then in believing any
sentence one is believing every sentence with the same meaning. So if the
meaning of a sentence is a proposition, then the three-place theory can
enjoy no advantage over the two-place theory that results from the three-
place theory merely by dropping its superfluous middle term.

But if 'interpretations' are not contents (i.e., propositions), what can
they be? The problem for the sentientialist who eschews meanings—i.e.,
the extensionalist as regards compositional semantics—is not that he cannot
make sense of a sentence having an interpretation, but that he cannot make
sense of this in a way that delivers interpretations *as entities over which he
can quantify*. The extensionalist, roughly speaking, interprets a sentence
by deriving a 'T-sentence' for it from a correct truth theory that meets
relevant empirical conditions. But the T-sentence, of the wholly extensional
form 'σ is true in L iff p' (wherein 'p' is not a quantifiable variable, but
simply holds the place of a sentence whose occurrence is extensional),
correlates the sentence with no meaning, and the T-sentence cannot itself

be construed as the interpretation, as a value of 'm' in [c], for it is a *sentence* and would itself need an interpretation, thereby providing the first step in an infinite regress. So, the extensionalist cannot deliver interpretations as entities over which one can quantify; but such entities are precisely what are needed in order to make sense of [c].

(2) This second suggestion is not so much a revision of the classic sententialist position as a *reading* of it that would hope to be immune to the problem of multiplicity of meaning. In objecting to the representation of [a] as [b] I relied on the possibility that the sentence 'love is cruel' might also be a sentence of some language in which it meant, say, that kangeroos fly. But might it not be protested that that is not the right way to speak? One might object that, if the *marks* 'love is cruel' meant that kangeroos fly in language X, as well as meaning what they do in English, then we should say that there are two distinct, non-identical sentences, both of which are 'realized' or 'manifested' or 'constituted' by those marks. On this construal, [a] would be more illuminatingly represented, not as [b], but as:

B(Henri, the English sentence whose graphemic realization is 'love is cruel').

Even this is just a first approximation, as what is required is a notion of *sentence* such that it is impossible for there to be ambiguous sentences; for unless sentences are individuated by their meanings one has not avoided the problem raised by the possibility of multiple meanings. One problem with such a very fine-grained understanding of 'sentence' is that it is by no means clear that we could find an ontological category of sentences that was distinct from the marks and sounds that manifested them and individuated by their meanings without again reifying 'interpretations' as objects over which we could quantify, in which case we would have again the objection lately levelled against representing the belief-relation in the style of [c]. If meanings were entities, we could take a sentence to be an ordered pair of a sequence of sounds or marks and a meaning. But how could we otherwise get the desired individuation of sentences?

Rather than try to answer this question, I want to turn instead to what I take to be the most promising sententialist theory of propositional attitudes: the theory suggested in Davidson's seminal article 'On Saying That' (Davidson, 1984). But whether or not a theory along Davidsonian lines of the logical form of propositional attitude ascriptions is the most promising, I do believe that the main problem such an approach will be seen to encounter will provide an insuperable problem for any sententialist account of propositional attitude relations. It will reward us, then, to study Davidson's account of saying that, and the theory of propositional attitude relations implicit in it.

DAVIDSON ON SAYING THAT

Davidson does not *explicitly* offer what we are in search of, a relational theory of propositional attitudes that tells us what propositional attitudes are relations to. But in his article 'On Saying That' he does propose such a relational account of one kind of propositional attitude, that ascribed in sentences of the form '*x* said that *p*'; and a partial account of the logical form of all propositional attitude ascriptions is offered that would at least greatly constrain answers to the question we have been concerned with. Actually, one problem that I shall raise is about the way Davidson intends his theory of· saying-that to generalize to believing and the other propositional attitudes. Consequently, my most perspicuous strategy is first to describe Davidson's theory of saying-that, and then to raise problems for it that would challenge the claim that that account provides the basis for a generalization applicable to all propositional attitudes.

The classic sententialist took belief ascriptions to contain (as it were) a two-place predicate 'believes that' and two singular terms, one denoting an alleged believer, the other, the sequence of words following 'that', denoting itself. Switching from believing to another propositional attitude, this theorist would represent the logical form of

[1]   Galileo said that the earth moves

as:

   S(Galileo, 'the earth moves').

In other words, 'said' (or 'said that') in [1] expresses a two-place relation which, if [1] is true, relates Galileo to the sentence-type 'the earth moves'. This relation will obtain by virtue of the meaning of the content-sentence 'the earth moves', but is consistent with Galileo's having been a monolingual speaker of Italian.

Davidson, too, is eager to account for the logical form of [1]; he would like, that is, an account which leads us 'to see the semantic character of the sentence—its truth or falsity—as owed to how it is composed, by a finite number of applications of some of a finite number of devices that suffice for the language as a whole, out of elements drawn from a finite stock (the vocabulary) that suffices for the language as a whole' (Davidson, 1984, p. 94). For if Davidson could not give such an account, then this would call into question his Tarskian program which requires that there be such an account. This is one connection for Davidson between the theory of meaning and saying-that; another, of course, is that the theory of meaning has as its concern language understanding, and that consists precisely in the ability to know what speakers of a language are saying when they utter sentences of the language. Consequently, an account of saying-that must be part of any complete account of language understanding.

But while Davidson shares the need to account truth-theoretically for the logical form of [1], and while he would applaud the classic sententialist's eschewal of propositions as referents of 'that'-clauses, he would still find fault with that theorist's representation of [1] on the following two counts. First, sharing an objection already made, Davidson (1984, pp. 165–6) would object to taking the relatum of the saying-that relation to be a sentence 'both because . . . the reference [to a sentence] would then have to be relativized to a language, since a sentence may have different meanings in different languages; but also . . . because the same sentence may have different truth values in the same language.' Second, Davidson would raise an objection not raised in the last section, one that he would also raise against the Fregean: both the Fregean and the classic sententialist assign to the content-sentence in [1], 'the earth moves', a semantic role that is radically different from its normal one. They construe it (qualifications aside) as the larger part of a *singular term*, 'that the earth moves', which refers in [1] to what Galileo said—to a proposition, for the Fregean, to the sentence 'the earth moves' for the classic sententialist. Here, Davidson is well aware, both theorists are motivated by failures of coextensional substitutions in the content-sentence to preserve truth value. Notwithstanding this, Davidson would prefer a theory in which the content-sentence had only its old familiar semantic properties. At the same time, Davidson recognizes the need for a relational theory of propositional attitude verbs to cohere with his Tarskian conception of a compositional semantics.

Thus Davidson wants a theory of [1] that satisfies the following desiderata.

(a) 'Said' in [1] is represented as a two-place relational predicate.[5]
(b) The relata of that relation have truth values, but are neither propositions nor sentences.
(c) A relatum of that relation *chez* Galileo (i.e., something to which Galileo stands in the saying relation of indirect discourse) is referred to in [1].
(d) The content-sentence 'the earth moves' has in [1] its normal and familiar semantic properties, its normal sense and reference. It is not part of any singular term; the only reference of the 'the earth' is the earth, and the only extension determined for 'the earth moves' is its truth value. Substitutivity *salva veritate* applies as usual.

Davidson's terrifically ingenious solution is well known. What we have in [1] is an instance of parataxis. Semantically speaking, the utterance of [1] is not the utterance of one sentence which contains 'the earth moves' as a part, but rather utterances of two sentences paratactically joined, something best represented as:

Galileo said that. The earth moves.

Here 'the earth moves' is seen not to occur as part of a single sentence which contains the 'said' construction, but as an autonomous utterance with its predictable sense and reference: this utterance is true iff the earth moves. At the same time, the word 'that' in the first utterance occurs as a *demonstrative*, the referent of which is the utterance which follows it, and the first utterance is true just in case Galileo stands in the saying relation of indirect discourse to the referent of 'that', i.e., to the utterance in question of 'the earth moves'. And he will stand in that relation, Davidson tells us— not as part of his account of the logical form of [1], but as an intuitive and informal gloss on it—provided that he himself produced an utterance that matches in content the speaker of [1]'s utterance of 'the earth moves'. This explains why it is the case that, although the occurrence of a content-sentence is autonomous, it is typically not *asserted*: the speaker produces it not to express his own opinion, but so that he will have produced an utterance that itself has a content that can be exploited to reveal the content of some utterance, no doubt in Italian, of Galileo's.

In this way the above desiderata are achieved.

We achieve (a) because 'said' is in effect represented as

[2] $S(x, u)$.

i.e., as a two-place relation between a speaker x and any *actual* utterance u that matches some utterance of x's in content.[6]

We achieve (b) because these utterances have truth values.

We achieve (c) because 'that' in [1] is a singular term which refers to an utterance—namely, the utterance of the sentence following it—to which Galileo stands in the saying-that relation.

And we achieve (d) because the 'analysis accounts for the usual failure of substitutivity in attributions of attitude without invoking any non-standard semantics, for the reference of the 'that' changes with any change in the following utterance.'[7]

Davidson is aware that his theory must be importantly revised in order to account for quantifications into 'that'-clauses; because as his theory now stands it has no way of making sense of an utterance such as:

Someone is such that Galileo said that she baked terrific lasagna.

Nor, relatedly, can it account for the ambiguity, induced by possibilities pertaining to Galileo's knowledge or ignorance of who bakes terrific lasagna, of

> Galileo said that his mother baked terrific lasagna.

The problems raised by these '*de re*' issues are formidable, and I am aware of no very plausible solution available to Davidson. But this is not a problem that I want now to press.

Another problem with Davidson's theory of saying-that with which I will not be concerned, but do feel compelled just to mention (partly because, to my amazement, I have never seen it raised before), is this: it is by no means clear what the application of Davidson's theory to *French* would be. For it is essential to at least the initial *plausibility* of Davidson's theory *as applied to English* that the word 'that' does have a use as a free-standing demonstrative; otherwise the suggestion that 'that' in [1] ('Galileo said that the earth moves') is a demonstrative would be worse than bizarre. But now consider the French translation of [1]:

[1'] Galilei a dit que la terre bouge.

The word 'que' in French has no use as a demonstrative. So what could possibly be the application of Davidson's theory to [1']?

At all events, it is three other problems that I want now to raise for Davidson's theory of saying-that, and for the extension of it to belief ascriptions.

THREE PROBLEMS

I will now describe three problems for Davidson's theory, each of which seems to require, at best, that the theory be revised in some important way. In each case I will mention a possible or mandatory revision, but will not dwell on them or draw dire conclusions until the end, when the conclusion reached will have application to any sententialist position.

First Problem

Davidson intends his account of the logical form of [1] to be the basis for a general account of the logical form of propositional attitude ascriptions, and his account of saying-that would be of only marginal interest if this were not the case. How, then, does Davidson intend his theory to be extended to the other attitudes, and to believing in particular?

Consider this utterance:

[3]   Galileo believed that the earth moves.

Davidson has made it clear that he intends the analysis of the logical form of [3] to have this much in common with that of [1] (see, e.g., Davidson, 1984, Essay 11):

(i)   The logical form of [3] is that of two utterances paratactically joined, and thus best represented as:

Galileo believed that. The earth moves.

(ii)   As in [1], 'that' in [3] is a demonstrative, its referent the utterance following it of 'the earth moves'.

(iii)   Thus 'believes' is a two-place relational predicate, and the range of the belief-relation—i.e., the values of 'y' in the schema 'x believes y'— includes actual utterances.

But now we come to an important *dissimilarity*, and with it the first problem. For whereas the saying-relation of [1] could plausibly be represented as [2], i.e., as a relation to *actual utterances*, the believing-relation of [3] cannot be correctly represented as a two-place relation

$$B(x,u)$$

which relates a believer x to an *actual utterance u*. The representation of the saying-that relation as [2] is plausible, because if

Galileo said something

is true, then there can be no barrier to inferring

$(Eu)S(Galileo, u)$,

for there is always Galileo's own utterance to be an utterance to which he stands in the saying-relation as portrayed in [2]. But if

Galileo believed something

is true, then there *is* a barrier to inferring

$(Eu)B(Galileo, u)$;

namely, there may not be any actual utterance that gives the content of Galileo's belief (cf Loar, 1976, p. 148). He may never have expressed his belief, and it may be that no one ever produced an utterance that conveys the content of his belief. Believing can be represented as a relation to actual utterances only if one could be assured that for every belief there was some actual utterance that gave the content of that belief, but of course one cannot be so assured.

Well, what now *is* available to Davidson to be the relata of the belief-relation, i.e., the values of '*y*' in '*x* believes *y*'? There would appear to be just this possibility: *utterance-kinds*, or possible utterances (I think that for our purposes we can take these as coming to the same thing). This revision would not be subject to the same difficulty because kinds can be uninstantiated.

But if Davidson is constrained to say that believing is a relation to an utterance-kind, then this will have for him the following problematic features.

(1)   Davidson's theory of propositional attitudes is driven by his need to find a theory of them that coheres with his account of the form that a meaning theory for a particular language should take. Now the hallmark of his famous Tarskian proposal about the form that a meaning theory should take is that it is *extensional*; not for Davidson is a compositional semantics the theorems of which relate sentences to intensions, but rather one which issues in the well-understood extensionality of

'Snow is white' is true iff snow is white.

Now the problem with the only apparent extension of Davidson's account of saying-that to believing is just this: *How is one to square a quantification over utterance-kinds with this extensionalist program?* On the face of it, utterance-kinds are universals, and if one has them one has properties, propositions and the lot, and no need to worry then about achieving an extensionalist semantics. (Utterance-kinds cannot be construed as sets, for then all beliefs whose contents had never been expressed would have, unacceptably, the same object, viz, the empty set.)

(2)   If Davidson is constrained to say that believing is a relation to an utterance-kind, then an utterance-kind, and not an actual utterance, should be represented as the relatum of the belief-relation that is referred to in [3], 'Galileo believed that the earth moves'. Davidson, in other words, has misrepresented his position on the logical form of [3], if he is constrained to say that believing is a relation to utterance-kinds. The logical form of [3] should not be represented as

B(Galileo, that),

where 'that' refers to the actual utterance in question of 'the earth moves', but should be represented as, say,[8]

B(Galileo, the utterance-kind to which that belongs).

In still other words, the skit involved in the utterance of [3] should be caricatured thus:

[4]   The earth moves.
      Galileo believed that kind of utterance.

(3)   Unfortunately, one cannot just say that believing is a relation to an utterance-kind; one has to say what *sort* of utterance-kind. The issue here can be illuminated by noticing the glaring inadequacy of [4]: the utterance of 'the earth moves' will be of *many* kinds. Which one, then, is being referred to in [3]? Until this is answered we know neither what believing is a relation to nor, consequently, the logical form of [3]. Presumably, the kinds would have to be individuated by the *contents* of the utterances they subsume. Perhaps, then, a better version of the skit involved in the utterance of [3] would be:

The earth moves.
Galileo believed the utterance-kind to which an utterance belongs just in case it has the same content as my last utterance.

But even this will not do as it stands. One reason (another comes later) is that we really have not been told what is being referred to in [3] as the relatum of the belief-relation *chez* Galileo until we have been given an account of what the content-determining features of an utterance are. This is not the tired old objection that Davidson's account of saying-that relies on an unexplicated notion of sameness of content. *That* objection is a bad one; for Davidson's account of the logical form of saying-that sentences relies on no such notion. On Davidson's theory, 'says' of indirect discourse is a *semantically primitive* predicate that relates a person to an actual utterance, and it is further consistent with his theory to hold that the relation expressed is not strictly definable; talk of 'sameness of content' is merely intended as an informal gloss on conceptual connections that the saying-that relation bears to other of our semantic concepts, '"an expository and heuristic device": an aid in instructing novices in the use of the saying primitive.'[9] But the point that I am making is that the role of 'content' in Davidson's theory cannot be comfortably trivialized in this way *on the revision being entertained*. On the required revision, 'that' may still be seen as referring to an actual utterance, but now it will no longer enjoy a primary occurrence. Its occurrence will be ensconced in an implicit occurrence of the singular term 'the kind of utterances having the same content as that', and my point is that we will not know the *reference* of that singular term until we know what notion of content is here intended.

But is there really a problem here? Is not the needed sense of 'sameness of content' already available in Davidson's theory of the form that a meaning theory for a particular language should take? We are shortly to see that the answer to this question is: No.

Second Problem

The objection here, which I owe to Brian Loar (in conversation), is that Davidson's theory of saying-that is in conflict with a certain correct principle about the function of singular terms in content-sentences. Before this principle can be stated, we need to say that:

> An occurrence of a singular term in a sentence is a *primary* occurrence iff that occurrence is not properly contained within the occurrence of some other singular term.

Thus, the occurrence of 'that car' in

> That car is blue

is primary, whereas in

> George's car is blue

only 'George's car' has a primary occurrence; 'George' has a secondary occurrence.

Now we can state the principle alluded to, which is this:

[P]   If the occurrence of the singular term t in ⌜So and so said that . . . t . . .⌝ is primary and refers to x, then that sentence is true only if so and so also referred to x.

Thus, suppose I say,

> Ralph said that she drove that car,

myself referring to a certain woman and a certain car. Then my utterance is true only if Ralph also referred to that woman and that car. The reason for the restriction to primary references is this. Consider my utterance of

> Ralph said that she drove George's car,

where I again refer to a certain woman and a certain car. In order for my last utterance to be true Ralph must have referred somehow to George's car, but he need not have referred to George, for he need not have referred to the car as George's car. Perhaps the utterance of Ralph's that makes us samesayers is his utterance of 'She drove that car'.

We can see the problem for Davidson in all this if we now consider:

[5]   Laplace said that Galileo said that the earth moves.

It follows from Davidson's theory that the second occurrence of 'that' in [5] is the primary occurrence of a singular term the referent of which is the utterance following it of 'the earth moves'. Whence we have the following argument in refutation of Davidson:

(1) [P].

(2) If Davidson's theory is correct, the second occurrence of 'that' in [5] is a primary occurrence, the referent of which is the occurrence in [5] of 'the earth moves'.

(3) But [5] can be true even though Laplace did not refer to that utterance.

(4) Ergo, Davidson's theory is not correct.

This argument is valid, and the only premiss Davidson could conceivably challenge is (1). But how is the strategy of denying [P] to be pursued? Davidson cannot with any degree of plausibility simply claim that the uses of 'that' in question constitute the sole exception to [P]. He must either (a) discredit the principle independently of its present application, or else (b) give a *principled* explanation of why the occurrences of 'that' in question constitute an exception to [P]. But I am doubtful that either of thes strategies can be pursued succesfully. It seems to me that the more promising way out for Davidson would be to revise his theory just enough to bring it in line with [P]. The needed revision turns out to be the one he is already committed to if his paratactic theory is to accommodate belief-ascriptions. The idea is to construe 'that' as really having a secondary occurrence in the implicit singular term 'the kind of utterances having the same content as that'. This would plainly square [5] with [P], but it would also, alas, encounter the difficulties we have just finished rehearsing in the first problem.

Third Problem

This, I think, is the really urgent problem; succinctly put, the objection is this:

Davidson's representation of

[a]   Sam PAs that flounders snore.

as

[b]   Sam PAs that. Flounders snore.

cannot be right, for: (1) one cannot know the *assertion made*, the truth stated, by [a] without knowing *what* Sam PAs, the *content* of his PA;

but (2) one can know the assertion made by [b] without knowing what Sam PAs, the content of his PA.

Now (1) seems correct. If in uttering 'Sam said that flounders snore' you assert truly that Sam said that flounders snore, and if I know what truth you asserted in your utterance, then I know that Sam said that flounders snore. And if I know this, then I certainly know the content of Sam's statement. I know that what Sam said is about flounders and snoring; and I know, especially, that what he said is true just in case flounders snore. Davidson, if he acknowledges (2), is evidently constrained to maintain either that I can know the truth you asserted without knowing that Sam said that flounders snore, or that knowing that does not carry with it any knowledge whatever of the content of Sam's statement. But what basis can he have for pursuing either of these disjuncts other than the need to be consistent with his theory?

But (2) is just as certainly correct, and to see this very clearly, let us start with the following dialogue:

> Pierre: La neige est blanche.
> Donald: Tarski said that.

The relevant point about this is that it is a consequence of Davidson's theory that one can know what Donald asserted without knowing the content of Pierre's utterance, and thus without knowing the content of Tarski's saying. For one can know that some utterance of Tarski's had the same content as Pierre's utterance without knowing the content of either utterance.

With this in mind, let us now consider the Davidsonian representation of

[6] Sam said that flounders snore,

which, of course, is:

[7] Sam said that. Flounders snore.

Here the only *assertion* made is made by the first utterance, 'Sam said that'. What this asserts, according to Davidson, is that some utterance of Sam's has the same content as the foregoing utterance of 'Flounders snore'. But this, as (2) correctly notes, can be known without knowing the content of either utterance. So, on Davidson's account, one can know the assertion made by [6], namely, the assertion made by the first utterance in [7], without knowing the content of what Sam said. To be sure, one who knows English and is witness to the whole of [7] will know the content of Sam's statement because he knows the meaning of 'flounders snore'; but that hardly controverts (2). For if *all that one knew* was what was *asserted* by the first utterance of [7], then one would not know what Sam said.

Here is what I take to be another, but non-epistemic, way of making essentially the same objection (to forestall a certain reply I have changed the example from saying to believing):

(1)   The sentence

    [i]   Sam believes that flounders snore

    entails

    [ii]   Sam believes something that is true iff flounders snore

in this sense: there is no possible world in which Sam believes that flounders snore but does not believe something that is true iff flounders snore.

(2)   But [ii] would not be entailed by [i] if Davidson's theory were correct. For if that theory were correct, then [i] would be representable as:

Flounders snore.

Sam believes that.

and from this one cannot in any sense infer [ii] without the further, contingent premiss:

That (i.e., the preceding utterance of 'Flounders snore') is true iff flounders snore.

Is there any way that Davidson's theory can be revised to avoid this objection? Perhaps. At least there is a line to be explored, an extension of the revision already seen to be required by the preceding two objections.

On Davidson's original, unrevised theory, [6] got represented as

S(Sam, that),

the reference of 'that' being to the utterance in [6] of 'flounders snore'. Then we noticed that, if Davidson is to avoid the first two of our objections, he would do better to represent [6] as:

[8]   S(Sam, the utterance-kind to which an utterance belongs just in case it has the same content as that),

'that' construed as before, only now having a secondary, rather than a primary, occurrence.

But even [8] will not escape our third objection; for someone could know the assertion made by [8] without knowing the content of the utterance referred to by 'that'. What is needed is to get a specification of the actual content of the content-sentence 'flounders snore' into the reference to the utterance-kind.

Suppose that M. A, strolling with his daughter in the Bois de Boulogne, is confronted by Mme S, who utters the sequence of sounds, 'Monsieur, votre fille a mordu mon singe encore une fois'. To understand her utterance is to know what she said in it. Suppose that one knows that she did say something in producing her utterance. What *more* would one have to know in order to know what she said, and thereby to understand her utterance? Intuitively, one wants to answer: the *content* of her utterance. Earlier, in the third section, I described the compositional semanticist's thought which implies that there is some feature of Mme S's utterance such that, if one knew that the utterance had it, then one would be in a position to interpret Mme S's utterance, that is, to know what she said in producing it. Suppose that utterances have such content-determining features, and that Φ is that feature for the utterance of the content-sentence 'flounders snore'. This, to repeat, would be to say that, if someone were to utter 'Flounders snore' assertively, then one would be in a position to interpret that utterance— i.e., to know what the utterer said—if one knew that that utterance had Φ. Then one could entertain avoiding our third objection by revising Davidson's theory in such a way as to yield this representation of the skit performed in uttering [6]:

[9]   Sam said the kind of utterances that are Φ, like that.
      Flounders snore.

In short, if Davidson is to have a theory of propositional attitude ascriptions that avoids the three objections raised, then he shall have to find content-determining features of utterances and construe propositional attitudes as relations to *utterance-kinds as individuated by those features*, in the way indicated by [9].

There are, I think, several problems with this entertained way out, but here is the most serious of them:

In order for there to be content-determining features that enter into propositional attitude ascriptions in the way indicated in [9], then, obviously, these features would have to be within the ken of ordinary people; but the only content-determining features that are even *prima facie* available do not enter into anyone's propositional knowledge.

This objection brings us back to Davidson's theory of the nature of meaning theories for particular languages, and to the curious feature of the theory noted in the third section: that, whereas, on Davidson's theory [MT], every sentence of a language has a content-determining feature, no one who understands the language knows, for any sentence σ and its content-determining feature Φ, that σ has Φ. For suppose that Sam utters, assertively and literally, the sentence

[10]   Flounders snore,

and that Carla knows this. Is there any feature Φ of [10] such that, if Carla also knew that [10] had Φ, then she would be able to interpret Sam's utterance, be able, that is, to know that, in uttering [10], Sam said that flounders snore? Now Davidson, we know, does hold that there is such a feature. For his theory of meaning commits him to holding that:

> It will suffice for Carla to interpret Sam's utterance of [10] if (refinements aside) she knows that (a) [10] is true iff flounders snore, that (b) that fact is entailed by a correct, finitely axiomatized, extensional, Tarski-style truth theory for the language to which [10] belongs, and that (c) that truth theory satisfies . . . empirical constraints [imagine the blank filled by a specification of the empirical constraints forthcoming from Davidson's finished theory].

But we have already noticed the main problem with this as regards our present concern. Even if it were true, the content-determining features specified are not ones that enter into anyone's propositional knowledge. As I earlier put it (in the third section), if there are Davidsonian content-determining features, then they are not within the ken of plain folk. This means that we cannot construe propositional attitudes as relations to utterance-kinds as specified by such content-determining features; for that proposal makes sense only if plain people know that these features are features of utterances.

Now the point just made about Davidsonian content-determining features remains true no matter how the above three dots are replaced: the knowledge required by (b) already secures that whatever content-determining features are determined by a specification of empirical constraints will be beyond the ken of plain folk. This means, it was noticed in the third section, that, if there are any extensionalist content-determining features, then they, too, will be beyond the ken of plain people. If there is *any* extensionalist meaning theory for a language L which explicitly states something knowledge of which would suffice for interpreting utterances in L, then no one knows what that theory states.

A LOOK AHEAD

I conclude that there can be no correct sententialist theory of propositional attitudes for at least this reason. Any such theory would require that the values of 'y' in

$$x \text{ PAs } y$$

be utterance-kinds individuated by features that are content-determining, within the ken of plain folk, and consonant with the extensionalist account of compositional semantics. But no such features will ever materialize.

Since there can be no correct sententialist theory of propositional attitudes, I also conclude that there can be no correct extensionalist account of compositional semantics. More accurately, I conclude this on the assumption that the sententialist theory is the only way of cashing-out the relational theory of propositional attitudes that plausibly coheres with extensionalist semantics; but that assumption, though I have made no attempt to prove it here, is one that I am convinced is right.

What, then, are we to conclude? Are we to conclude that natural languages have *intensionalist* compositional semantics, and that propositional attitudes really are relations to propositions after all?

Hardly; for I should maintain that there are good objections to that proposal, too. But if natural languages do not have either extensional or intensional compositional semantics, then what sort of compositional semantics do they have? And if propositional attitudes are neither relations to propositions nor to some sort of linguistic entity, then to what sort of thing are they relations?

None and none. I think that natural languages neither have nor need compositional semantics, finitely statable theories knowledge of which would suffice for interpreting speakers of the language. Since I deny that natural languages have compositional semantics, I have no reason to hold that propositional attitudes are relations, and I do not. All this, however, is another story, for another occasion.[10]

NOTES

[1] The only other proposed accommodation of which I am aware is that of Hintikka and his followers, which construes expressions such as 'Ralph believes that' as logical operators, on analogy with the treatment of modal operators in modal logic (see Hintikka, 1962, 1969). But Hintikka's proposal, as originally presented, entails both that one believes everything entailed by what one believes and that one believes everything if one has any inconsistent beliefs, and it is not certain that his theory can successfully be repaired to avoid these problems. But see Hintikka (1970).

[2] There is plainly much more required for understanding an utterance than knowing the meaning of the sentence uttered. But it is plausible that that is all that must be known as regards the language to which the utterance belongs. The rest

of what we bring to bear in interpretation are truths that apply across languages. Davidson, of course, is not overlooking this platitude when he defines a meaning theory for L as a theory of L knowledge of which suffices for interpreting speakers of L.

[3] But see Schiffer (1987) where I try to show that these alternatives are refuted.

[4] I am assuming that the sententialist shares the standard motivation for holding that 'believes' is a relational predicate: viz, that that is the only tenable way of accommodating it in a compositional semantics. Strictly speaking, however, a theorist can be a sententialist as regards belief while denying that natural languages have compositional semantics (whether such a position could be well motivated is another matter).

[5] This ignores complexities arising from quantification into the position of the content-sentence. The next note introduces a further possible qualification.

[6] Although this is the official position in the text of 'On Saying That', it is evidently denied in a footnote added in 1982. In that note Davidson says the following of his analysis of 'Galileo said that the earth moves':

> Strictly speaking, the verb 'said' is here analysed as a three-place predicate which holds of a speaker (Galileo), an utterance of the speaker ('Eppur si muove'), and an utterance of the attributer (Davidson, 1984, p. 104).

But this seems not to be true. Davidson's account of 'Galileo said that' commits him to holding that (a) 'that' refers to an utterance of 'the earth moves' and that (b) the ascription is true if Galileo uttered some sentence (e.g., 'Eppur si muove') with the same content as the referent of 'that'. Yet this certainly does not entail that 'said' is a three-place relation; one can certainly have a two-place relation that is defined in terms of a three-place relation (e.g., 'x photocopied y'). Clearly, the surface grammar of 'Galileo said that' favors construing 'said' as a two-place relation as there is no grammatical slot for a third singular term (with Davidson I am ignoring implicit temporal references), and parity with 'believes' favors the dyadic construal. But nothing important turns on this issue.

[7] Davidson's (1984, p. 119) point, of course, is that all of the positions in, say,

> Galileo said that. The earth moves.

are extensional, but that substitutions in the second sentence can change the truth value of the first because it will change the reference of 'that'.

[8] 'That' still refers to an actual utterance, but it now no longer refers to that which Galileo believes; rather than having a primary occurrence, 'that' now has a secondary occurrence in another (implicit) singular term which does refer to what Galileo believes—the utterance-kind. Notice, too, how easily the Fregean can accept the paratactic aspect of Davidson's account: he can represent the logical form of [3] as

> B(Galileo, the proposition expressed by that).

[9] McDowell 1980, p. 231. The inner quotation is from Davidson (1984, p. 177).

[10] The story does get told in Schiffer (1987); see also Schiffer (1986a, 1986b, 1986c).

REFERENCES

Davidson, D., *Inquiries Into Truth and Interpretation*. Oxford: Oxford University Press, 1984.

Foster, J., Meaning and Truth Theory. In G. Evans & J. McDowell (Eds), *Truth and Meaning*. Oxford: Oxford University Press, 1976.

Hintikka, J., *Knowledge and Belief*. Ithaca, NY: Cornell Univerisity Press, 1962.

Hintikka, J., *Models for Modalities*. Dordrecht: Reidel, 1969.

Hintikka, J., Knowledge, Belief, and Logical Consequence. *Ajatus*, 1970, **32**, 32–47.

Kripke, S., Is There a Problem about Substitutional Quantification?. In G. Evans & J. McDowell (Eds), *Truth and Meaning*. Oxford: Oxford University Press, 1976.

Lewis, D., General Semantics. In D. Davidson & G. Harman (Eds), *Semantics of Natural Language*. Dordrecht: Reidel, 1972.

Lewis, D., New Work for the Theory of Universals. *Australasian Journal of Philosophy*, 1983, **61**, 343–377.

Loar, B., Two Theories of Meaning. In G. Evans & J. McDowell (Eds), *Truth and Meaning*. Oxford: Oxford University Press, 1976.

Loar, B., *Mind and Meaning*. Cambridge: Cambridge University Press, 1981.

McDowell, J., Quotation and Saying That. In M. Platts (Ed), *Reference, Truth and Reality*. London: Routledge & Kegan Paul, 1980.

Schiffer, S., Compositional Semantics and Language Understanding. In R. Grandy & R. Warner (Eds), *Philosophical Grounds of Rationality: Intentions, Categories, Ends*. Oxford: Oxford University Press, 1986a.

Schiffer, S., The Real Trouble with Propositions. In R. Bogdan (Ed), *Belief: Form, Content, Function*. Oxford: Oxford University Press, 1986b.

Schiffer, S., Kripkenstein Meets the Remnants of Meaning. *Philosophical Studies*, 1986c, **49**, 147–162.

Schiffer, S., *Remnants of Meaning*. Boston, MA: Bradford Books/MIT Press, 1987, forthcoming.

5

Semantic Competence and Truth-Conditions

WILLIAM G. LYCAN

Department of Philosophy,
University of North Carolina

It is commonly held that to understand or know the meaning of a sentence
S is to know *S*'s truth-condition, i.e., to know the circumstances under
which *S* would be true. In previous works I have been concerned to defend
the spirit of this thesis both in general and against one fashionable sort of
objection (Lycan, 1984, 1986), but I have also attacked its letter on the
basis of several queer formal constructions that I called 'funny functors'
(Lycan, 1979; Heidelberger, 1980; van Inwagen, 1981). In the present
paper I shall return to the latter issue, strengthen my attack by introducing
a new hypothetical case, and try to see exactly where the chips fall. Then
I shall address a related issue concerning the truth-conditions of indexical
sentences.

LOGICAL SPACE

It is easy to show that knowing a sentence's truth-value in every possible
state of affairs does not suffice for understanding the sentence, knowing
what it means, or knowing what proposition it expresses; merely consider
a tautology containing a lexical item which you know to be meaningful but

143

Copyright © 1987, by Academic Press Inc. (London) Ltd.
All rights of reproduction in any form reserved.
ISBN 0-12-444040-1
0-12-444041-X (Pbk)

do not understand, such as[1]

(1) If a thing has been zipprodted, that thing has been zipprodted.

But it is also easy to say why you do not understand (1): since you do not understand the verb 'zipprodt', you are unable to grasp (1)'s intension in the normal way, viz, by computing (1)'s truth-condition from the ground up; you grasp the intension only because you see by (1)'s form that (1) is a tautology and must be true regardless of the meanings of its nonlogical terms. Thus we are led to the *modified Intension Thesis*: P knows S's meaning if P knows S's truth-value at any possible world on the basis of being able to compute S's truth-value at that world from S's primitives on up.[2]

In 'Semantic Competence and Funny Functors' (Lycan, 1979) I noted a special sort of counterexample to the modified Intension Thesis, based on operators such as Frege's horizontal and the unconstrained substitutional quantifier which accept arguments of more than one syntactic category as operands. My contention was that such useless but nominally grammatical expressions as '——17' and '$(\exists x)(y)$ Admires xy, Frege' are meaningless and say nothing, even though they have clearly defined truth conditions. But I could think of no general explanation of what it is about such expressions that makes them (as I called it) 'semantically mute' and unintelligible to us despite our knowing their truth-conditions perfectly well. I want now to present a more general and philosophically illuminating counterexample, which does not turn on the eccentricities of any unusual and perhaps negligible construction.

Suppose *per impossibile* that God presents me with a logical spaceship, and offers to accompany me on a tour of all the possible worlds there are. (This is a cross between *Star Trek*, the temptation of Jesus, and Virgil leading Dante through the Inferno.) God also carries a placard with some inscrutable writing on it, and assures me that the writing is a sentence of some supernatural tongue. At each world He tells me the sentence's truth-value at that world. I keep a list of all the truth-values *seriatim*, or remember them. Do I know the sentence's meaning? Do I understand it? Hardly.

This case is itself no counterexample to the modified Intension Thesis, for in it I am not able to compute the sentence's truth-value from the primitives on up. But now we can apply the same principle to a supernatural expression that is a primitive predicate rather than a whole sentence; call the predicate P. God tells me at each world which denizens of that world satisfy P. Now, by applying Mill's methods or by performing some intuitive feat of abstraction to see what all the world-bound extensions have in common, I might then come to know P's meaning, but (it seems to me) I also might well not. And if not, I would not know the meaning of a sentence in which P occurred, despite having the best possible Authority in the matter of truth-conditions.

Let us consider two possible objections. First: If God showed me all the extensions of our mysterious predicate P at all the possible worlds there are, then I can form the union of those extensions and give it a name, say, 'Fred'; and I understand both the new word 'Fred' and expressions of the form '$n \in$ Fred.' Now, I also know that for any name N, $\ulcorner$N is P$\urcorner$ and $\ulcorner$N $\in$ Fred$\urcorner$ are necessarily equivalent. If I understand $\ulcorner$N $\in$ Fred$\urcorner$ and know that $\ulcorner$N is P$\urcorner$ is necessarily equivalent to it (and has no further semantically relevant structure), then surely I understand $\ulcorner$N is P$\urcorner$ (for what is left to understand?), and so must understand P itself after all.

To this I respond by denying the principle that if I understand an expression E_1 and know of a second expression E_2 that it is unstructured and necessarily equivalent to E_1, then I understand E_2. Consider the unstructured sentence '@,' which I stipulate to be true at every world. '@' is now necessarily equivalent to every necessary truth. I understand many necessary truths, but I do not understand '@'; I do not know what it says. Similarly, let '*' be an unstructured predicate that everything satisfies at every world. '*' is equivalent to 'is red or not red', 'is self-identical', 'is not both prime and composite', etc, but (intuitively) synonymous with none of them—why would it be synonymous with any one to the exclusion of the others?

Why do I *not* understand P, or '*'? The rhetorical question parenthesized in our first objection is a good one. I have no very secure answer to it, but what I *seem* to lack is the knowledge of what it is about a thing in virtue of which P or '*' applies to that thing (and of what it is about a world that makes '@' true at that world).[5] The notion of a satisfaction- or truth-maker is ill-defined, but it seems apposite here. I shall be able to say a bit more about what is missing, in reply to the second objection.

Which is:[6] When I acquire my God-given ability to tell at any world which things in that world satisfy P, do I not emulate the celebrated chicken sexer,[7] who by dint of much training and repetition can tell the sex of a baby chick without knowing how he does this? Just as the chicken sexer relies on visual cues to which he will never have conscious access, might I not simply acquire the ability to spot instances of P without knowing what features of these items make them P-satisfiers? We do not accuse the chicken sexer of failing to understand 'male' or 'female' as applied to chicks. Why, then, should we deny that I understand P?

This comparison raises the new question of degrees or *grades* of understanding, which I shall take up in the next section. But there are two more immediate and important replies to be made.

(i) The chicken sexer's subconscious cues are (presumably) neither the genetic and hormonal features of chicks in virtue of which the chicks have the sexes they do, nor the defining features that the chicken sexer may have gleaned from a dictionary or from early exposure to normal English speakers (such as capability of bearing young, and capability of fertilizing a female conspecific). The chicken sexer knows perfectly well what 'male' and 'female' mean, and there is nothing subconscious about this semantic competence; what is subconscious is rather the *evidence* on which his particular judgments are based. The same is not true of my ability to spot instances of P. It is not that I process the evidence of P-hood subconsciously even though I know what P-hood itself is; it is that I do not even subconsciously know what P-hood is at all, though I do know, on the basis of authority, which things have got it.

(ii) Subconsciously or not, the chicken sexer has a *procedure* (perhaps amounting to an algorithm) for judging the sex of a chick, that keys on features of the particular chick being examined. He exercises a discriminative capacity based essentially on this examination. No such thing holds in the case of my sorting of P-instances. Faced with a thing that in fact satisfies P, I have no way of detecting this unless I can recognize this particular individual and remember that God tagged it as falling within the extension of P. My procedure for spotting P-instances works essentially by authority and not, so to speak, from within.

This all sounds—unpleasantly to my ears—like the neo-Verificationism fomented this decade past at Oxford and elsewhere; but happily it is not that. My complaint about P is not that I have no algorithm for recognizing instances of P in this world, subject to the limitations of my geographical situation and representational and reasoning capacity, fc. while God is my guide I am omniscient and epistemically unlimited; nothing is 'verification-transcendent' for me. My complaint is rather that *even though I am omniscient as regards this world and every other*, I have only the evidence of authority and not a recognition-procedure of my own for spotting instances of P. I do not have inner mechanisms of the sort appropriate for genuine understanding.

For the case of primitive predicates, the modified Intension Thesis collapses into Turing-Test-ism regarding semantic competence; the Thesis counts a subject as understanding a primitive predicate so long as the subject can make the appropriate public discriminations, no matter how, even if the discriminations must be made throughout logical space and not only within our own world (which is only to say that counterfactual as well as actual discriminations are required). But Turing-Test-ism is behaviorism in the philosophy of mind. I am a functionalist, not a behaviorist,[8] and so I find the Turing Test overliberal; I trust you are and do too. Just as a hollow anthropoid shell does not have beliefs, desires and sensations merely because some clever MIT students sit at a console and act as puppeteers by remote-control, making the hollow thing behave just as if it had beliefs, desires and sensations, I do not understand predicate P merely because God has tipped me off as to when to bark out ⌐P!¬ in a convincing tone.

I conclude that my counterexample stands, and I think this last point about Turing-Test-ism suggests (though certainly does not establish) a moral: It shifts the focus away from the hyperuncountable crystalline array of possible worlds *per se*, and back to the mechanisms operative within the understanding subject, back into the structure of the speaker's competence. Spitting out the right extensions at the right worlds is important only *qua* manifestation of that competence. And so if the competence can be functionally described in its own right, the allusion to possible worlds may prove expendable in principle.[9]

GRADES OF UNDERSTANDING

We should admit that there is some force to the behaviorist intuition. For one thing, a person who systematically applies P or any other predicate without fault will rightly be credited with having mastered the community's use of that predicate, irrespective of any further semantical shortcomings on that persons's part.[10] For another, there seem to be cases in which computation of a sentence's truth-value 'from the primitives on up' is not after all necessary for what would count as understanding in those cases. It seems to me useful to distinguish at least three different grades of understanding.

I am aware that there is a famous cyclotron at Stanford, and I know what a cyclotron is. Many other people are aware of the same fact, however, without having the faintest idea whether a cyclotron is animal, vegetable or mineral.[11] Do such people understand the word 'cyclotron'? Not fully; and not even in the sense of applying it to the right objects in other possible worlds. Yet there is a minimal sense in which they do understand 'cyclotron'; they get by in ordinary conversation without provoking linguistic indignation—they use 'cyclotron' as a common noun, and know *some* truths incorporating it even though they do not know what a cyclotron is. Let us credit these people with 'proto-understanding'. (If you find yourself wanting to insist that they do not understand 'cyclotron' in any sense at all,[12] and that they are merely cocktail party phonies who *pretend* to understand a word when they really do not, change my term to 'pseudo-understanding'.)

A second, higher grade of understanding is illustrated by a case of Jay Garfield's (1982). Suppose some of our ancestors spoke what he calls 'MegaChinese', a collection of ten thousand unstructured symbols each of which has a truth condition (a distinctive truth-set of worlds). The MegaChinese speakers are 'a taciturn, simple lot' and form a primitive society in which basic needs are met but nothing ever happens of any conceptual complexity or interest. (They are very much like Wittgenstein's builders, whose language consists of simple unstructured commands regarding the deployment of various kinds of construction materials. Brian Loar has imagined a similar community whose members use 'simple signals'.[13]) Now, surely these primitive people understand the symbols of their language, for they grasp both the correct use and the truth conditions of those symbols. Garfield takes this to constitute a counterexample to the converse of the modified Intension Thesis; *computation* of truth condition from the primitives on up is not necessary for understanding.

I find this pretty persuasive, and have just two small points to make in reply. (1) The case is a good deal less straightforward than it might initially appear, in that the *learning* of MegaChinese is mysterious. Our ancestors could not have learned it in the normal Mill's-Methods way, since that way keys on structural elements of sentences and by hypothesis MegaChinese sentences have no structural elements. It seems to me psychologically dubious to suppose that humans might learn each of ten thousand *sentential* items without exploiting any structure internal to those items. (On the other hand, we learn many more than ten thousand primitive predicates without difficulty; and the point is only an empirical one in any case.) (2) Here as in the case of '@', there is no way of saying that a given sentence of MegaChinese means that p rather than that q, where these are logically equivalent but by no means synonymous. So although there surely is a sense in which our primitive people understand sentences of MegaChinese, they do not understand them in the fuller sense of *knowing what they say*.

I conclude that we must distinguish two further grades of understanding. With deliberate tendentiousness, let us call what our ancestors had *behavioral* understanding, and what they did not have *semantical* understanding. Even semantical understanding comes in degrees, n.b., for it is rare that any speaker actually grasps the full extension of a primitive predicate in every detail; even enthusiastic and accomplished birdwatchers may not be fully expert ornithologists. So the distinction between proto- or pseudo-understanding and semantical understanding is not sharp; the two shade off into each other.[14]

Some readers may want to take sides on the question of whether it is behavioral or semantical understanding that is *real* understanding.[15] If I had to choose, I would go for semantical understanding and regard behavioral understanding as a degenerate form, but so far as I can see this is solely a matter of taste and emphasis; there is hardly a further fact of the matter.

INDEXICALS

Herbert Heidelberger[16] has raised a problem concerning our understanding of sentences containing indexicals, and he argues that a purely propositional account of meaning does better at handling this problem than does a truth-conditional account. As an ardent proponent of truth-conditional semantics and at least a temperamental opponent of propositions, I am concerned to rebut Heidelberger's argument and to solve the problem in truth-theoretic terms.

Heidelberger thinks of understanding as the holding of a correct tacit belief as to an expression's meaning; let us fall in with this for purposes of discussion. Thus, let us take (2) to entail the conjunction of (3) and (4), and vice versa.

(2)   Peter believes correctly that 'Je suis paresseux' means 'I am lazy.'
(3)   'Je suis paresseux' means 'I am lazy'.
(4)   Peter understands 'Je suis paresseux'.

Now, the problem is that (3) 'contains what appears to be a puzzling use of the first person pronoun' (p. 23) (3) is certainly not equivalent to

(5)   'Je suis paresseux' means that I am lazy,

for (5), if inscribed by me (WGL) is necessarily equivalent to

(6)   'Je suis paresseux' means that William G. Lycan is lazy,

which is false for most tokens of 'Je suis paresseux'. (If Peter enters a room and finds a token of it written on a blackboard, he will not understand it as saying that William G. Lycan is lazy. For that matter, if *I* enter the room and find the token, I will not understand it in that way either. Both Peter and I will take it instead to say of whoever inscribed the token that he or she is lazy.)

What has truth theory to contribute to this issue? Heidelberger states the truth-condition of 'Je suis paresseux' in this way (p. 29):

(7)   Any occurrence of 'Je suis paresseux' [that expresses a proposition] is true iff its author is lazy.

But suppose Peter (falsely) believes[17]

(8)   'Je suis paresseux' means the author of these words is lazy.

Then surely he will infer (7); but his resulting correct belief of (7) does not suffice for understanding, since by hypothesis he *mis*understands 'Je suis paresseux.' Heidelberger concludes that 'awareness of truth conditions is . . . nowhere near a sufficient condition of understanding' (p. 30).

I have already granted—indeed insisted—that awareness of truth-condition is insufficient for understanding, but I am uncomfortable with Heidelberger's intensifier, 'nowhere near', and I reject the contention that indexicals pose a *special* and intractable problem for the modified Intension Thesis; in what remains of this paper I shall try to refute that contention.

Donald Davidson, the world's most eloquent proponent of truth-theoretic semantics for natural languages, himself pointed out the difficulty that indexical pronouns and other deictic elements create for that program (Davidson, 1971, p. 464). He offered a solution—roughly, to relativize truth to a speaker and a time—but that solution has been found to be unsatisfactory in each of several ways.[18] Heidelberger has presupposed a different solution, in offering (7) as his interpretation of the truth theorist's account of 'Je suis paresseux', and so left it open that yet a third truth-theoretic solution might not succumb to the same objection he put to (7). I have proposed a third solution of my own, in *Logical Form in Natural Language*; so let us see whether it helps. (It does.)

Let us adopt the following strategy in writing T-sentences. Target sentences[19] will be considered true or false only relative to contexts of utterance. I shall suppose that lurking in the background is a valuation function α that assigns denotata to indexical terms in context. Thus, an adequate pragmatics would tell us how α is computed. One rule of a correct pragmatics for French would say that 'Je' denotes in context C whomever is uttering it in C (unless it occurs inside direct quotation).

According to this method, a T-sentence directed upon 'Je suis paresseux' would be

(9) 'Je suis paresseux' is true in C iff α('Je', C) is lazy.

Someone who knew that α('Je', C*) = Jones, where C* is a context in which Peter has come upon a token of 'Je suis paresseux', would be able to go on and derive the 'purer' T-sentence

(10) 'Je suis paresseux' is true in C* [or: Peter's token of 'Je suis paresseux' is true] iff Jones is lazy.

But Peter does not know that.

(9) cannot be substituted into (2) *salva propositione*. But no truth-condition theorist has ever maintained either that a T-sentence could be so substituted into a sentence like (2) or that knowing an extensional T-sentence suffices for understanding or knowing the meaning of the target sentence. (In addition to Heidelberger's objection to the latter thesis, there is the fact that someone might know the truth-values of both sides of a T-sentence and infer the truth-value of the T-sentence itself, without understanding the target sentence.) Indeed, Davidson insists repeatedly

that it is not a T-sentence alone, but the T-sentence along with its derivation and in the context of its whole containing truth theory that gives the meaning of the target sentence upon which it is directed. Accordingly, one must not only know (or believe correctly) that 'Je suis paresseux' is true in C iff α('Je', C) is lazy, but believe it on the basis of at least an implicit Tarskian derivation from the usual sorts of base and recursive clauses; one must begin by knowing that 'paresseux' is satisfied by exactly those things that are lazy, and so on.[20]

It is hard to state a Davidsonian counterpart for (3). He offers no analysis of 'x means y', and can be understood in 'Truth and Meaning' as simply eliminating it rather than trying to explicate it. If pressed, he might try modelling an analysis of 'x means y' on his treatment of indirect quotation (see Davidson, 1968). But a truth-conditional account of 'Je suis paresseux''s meaning would certainly be close to what Peter tacitly knows: that 'Je suis paresseux' is true in C iff α('Je', C) is lazy and that this is because . . . (here follows the derivation). Thus, a Davidsonian counterpart of (2) might well entail a Davidsonian counterpart of (3), and would entail something as near as matters to (4).[21]

Davidsonian's own extension-hugging approach creates many problems. It is hard to see how a truth theorist could succeed in explicating counterfactuals and such without somehow intensionalizing the whole operation, presumably by dint of introducing possible worlds. So let us briefly consider an alternative, model-theoretic attempt (I suppress most of the usual parameters):

(11)   'Je suis paresseux' is true at $\langle C,w \rangle$ iff α('Je', C) is lazy at w.

C is our context of utterance at this world, as before while w is the world relative to which our target sentence is being evaluated. And as before, someone who knew that α('Je', C*) = Jones could derive

(12)   'Je suis paresseux' is true at C* at w (or: Peter's token of 'Je suis paresseux' is true at w) iff Jones is lazy at w.

But Peter does not know that.

One might think that intensionalizing our T-sentences by relativizing truth and satisfaction to worlds would obviate Davidson's motive for requiring knowledge of the T-sentences' derivations, since objections to (7) that are based on the extensionality of the biconditional no longer go through. This is *almost* right. If we substitute (12) into (2), we get

(13)   Peter believes correctly that 'Je suis parasseux' is true in C* at w iff α('Je', C*) is lazy at w.

(13) arguably entails (3) and is entailed jointly by (3) and (4). (13) fails to

entail (4), but not for any reason essentially involving indexicals—only for the anti-behaviorist reason I have defended in the first section. I conclude that there is no *further* problem about indexicals of the sort Heidelberger had in mind.

ACKNOWLEDGEMENTS

I would like to dedicate this paper to the memory of Herbert Heidelberger, whose conversation on this and related topics are greatly appreciated and greatly missed.

NOTES

[1] As I assured readers of 'Semantic Competence and Funny Functors', 'zipprodt' is a perfectly meaningful word of a dialect of American English (for which I am indebted to my cousin, Joan Shepard). I hope that Max Cresswell has forgotten what it means, and that no other philosopher has found out.

[6] 'On the basis of being' here replaces 'and is' in my original formulation (Lycan, 1979), in order to forestall an obvious and uninteresting sort of counterexample.

[3] Max Cresswell has pointed out, quite rightly, that this counterexample does nothing to impugn the bare metaphysical identification of sentence meanings with sets of worlds. That a device A computes a function while a second device B gets the function right in extension just by luck does not entail that A and B compute different functions.

[4] This objection is adapted from some remarks of David Lewis, in correspondence, but he is not responsible for any misuse I may be making of those remarks here.

[5] Paul Ziff (1972, pp. 17–20) explicates linguistic understanding as 'analytical data processing of some sort'. He maintains that 'only that which is composite, complex, and thus capable of analysis, is capable of being understood'. It *seems* to follow from this that what is wrong with our unstructured items P, '$=$' and '*' is just that they are unstructured. But something is wrong here, for there are (lots and lots of) ordinary primitive predicates of English that we do understand despite their lack of semantic structure. For a criticism of Ziff on this point and an illuminating general discussion of understanding *tout court*, see Rosenberg (1981).

[6] This second objection is similarly adapted from some remarks of Murray Kiteley's. I am grateful to Lewis, Kiteley, Max Cresswell and Jay Garfield for helpful discussion of this issue.

[7] I was first introduced to this admirable character by Armstrong (1968), pp. 114–115.

[8] On the difference as it relates to the Turing Test, see Block (1981). For my own version of functionalism, see Lycan (1981a, 1981b); as it applies to the propositional attitudes, see Lycan (1981c).

[9] This is not to say that a creature's functional organization determines the truth conditions of that creature's sentences, which it manifestly does not (see Lycan, 1981c).

[10] He or she might be compared to the actual case of a color-blind person to whom red and green are indistinguishable but who has learned to use the terms

'red' and 'green' appropriately on any normal occasion using various subtle cues. (Wholly blind people, in fact, have been known to pass in restricted contexts for sighted.) Does such a person *understand* 'red' or 'green'? I want to say, yes and no; read on.

There is one difference between our color-blind victim and wielders of predicate P: There are behavioral tests, albeit slightly contrived ones, that would succeed in picking the former out of a crowd. But the color-blindness victim is not thereby revealed to be an externally animated hollow shell; his or her color judgments are the result of autonomous internal processing that largely overlaps a normal person's.

[11] I owe this example to Carl Ginet (1975, pp. 24–25) by way of my colleague George Schlesinger. Ginet is concerned with the connection between understanding and *being confident*.

[12] Stephen Stich (1979) seems to take this hard-hearted line against a helpless puppy, Fido, denying that Fido has the concept of a *bone* in part on the grounds that Fido is ignorant of a bone's role in skeletal structure.

[13] Loar (1976) uses the example to make a more ambitious point against Donald Davidson's theory.

[14] Cf Dennett (1969, p. 183):

> What are the conditions that would suffice to show that a child understood his own statement: 'Daddy is a doctor'? Must the child be able to produce paraphrases, or expand on the subject by saying his father cures sick people? Or is it enough if the child knows that Daddy's being a doctor precludes his being a butcher, a baker, a candlestick maker? Does the child know what a doctor is if he lacks the concept of a fake doctor, a quack, an unlicensed practitioner? Surely the child's understanding of what it is to be a doctor (as well as what it is to be a father, etc.) will grow through the years, and hence his understanding of the sentence 'Daddy is a doctor' will grow.

Jay Rosenberg (1981) offers a general characterization of understanding that explains why there is no fixed cutoff point in a case of this sort.

[15] Loar (1976, p. 145) seems to want to:

> A person may authoritatively be informed as to what a certain sentence of an otherwise unknown language means, without knowing any facts of its structure—in that sense he knows its meaning, and that is how I shall use the notion. Of course, one might want to say that such a person does not *fully* know its meaning; but I would rather say what he does not know are further facts about its semantical structure; facts as to *how* its language assigns it its meaning.

[16] All further page references will be to Heidelberger (1982).

[17] Falsely, because the sentence 'Je suis paresseux' does not mean anything about authorship; it is true, for example, at worlds in which no one has ever written or inscribed anything—indeed, at worlds in which there is no language.

[18] For an excellent discussion see Burge (1974). I criticize Burge's own proposal and put forward a new one (Lycan, 1984, chapter 3).

[19] This is my term for a sentence of the object-language under semantical examination, quoted on the left-hand side of a T-sentence.

[20] An objection similar to the foregoing one could be raised even against this requirement; Someone might know that fact about 'paresseux' indirectly, without actually knowing what 'paresseux' means; cf 'renate' and 'cordate'. One must actually know more about 'paresseux'—its intension in some sense, or perhaps its reference-shifting habits under pressure from nonextensional operators. Davidson sweeps this under the rug, but it is implicit in his view; one would not know all

the truth-conditional properties of 'paresseux' unless one knew its semantical contribution from within (e.g.) counterfactual contexts (likewise for 'renate' and 'cordate').

[21] The discussion so far reminds us of the distinction between behavioral and semantical understanding. If someone knew (3), but knew it only because he had been told it by a reliable informant and did not know what 'Je' or 'suis' or 'paresseux' meant (perhaps he thinks that 'Je' means *lazy*, 'suis' means *I* and 'parasseux' means *am*, French being an OSV language), that person would have behavioral but not semantical understanding. It is semantical understanding that is captured (almost) by Davidson's account.

REFERENCES

Armstrong, D. M., *A Materialist Theory of the Mind*. London: Routledge & Kegan Paul, 1968.

Block, E. Psychologism and Behaviorism. *Philosophical Review*, 1981, **XC**, 5–43.

Burge, T., Demonstrative Constructions, Reference, and Truth. *Journal of Philosophy*, 1974, **LXXXI**, 205–223.

Davidson, D., On Saying That. *Synthese*, 1968, **19**, 130–146.

Davidson, D., Truth and Meaning. In J. Rosenberg & C. Travis (Eds), *Readings in the Philosophy of Language*. Englewood Cliffs, NJ: Prentice-Hall, 1971.

Dennett, D. C., *Content and Consciousness*. London: Routledge & Kegan Paul, 1969.

Garfield, J., Semantic Incompetence and Funny Functors. Unpublished note, 1982.

Ginet, C., *Knowledge, Perception, and Memory*. Dordrecht: Reidel, 1975.

Heidelberger, H., Understanding and Truth Conditions. In P. French, T. E. Uehling & H. Wettstein (Eds), *Midwest Studies in Philosophy V: Studies in Epistemology*. Minneapolis, MN: University of Minnesota Press, 1980, pp. 21–34.

Heidelberger, H., What Is It to Understand a Sentence that Contains an Indexical. *Philosophy and Phenomenological Research*, 1982, **XLIII**, 21–34.

van Inwagen, P., Why I Don't Understand Substitutional Quantification. *Philosophical Studies*, 1981, **39**, 281–285.

Loar, B., Two Theories of Meaning. In G. Evans & J. McDowell (Eds), *Truth and Meaning*. Oxford: Oxford University Press, 1976.

Lycan, W. G., Semantic Competence and Funny Functors, *Monist*, 1979, **62**, 209–222.

Lycan, W. G., Form, Function, and Feel. *Journal of Philosophy*, 1981a, **LXXXVIII**, 24–50.

Lycan, W. G., Psychological Laws. *Philosophical Topics*, 1981b, **12**, 9–38.

Lycan, W. G., Toward a Homuncular Theory of Believing. *Cognition and Brain Theory*, 1981c, **4**, 139–159.

Lycan, W. G., *Logical Form in Natural Language*. Cambridge, MA: Bradford Books/MIT Press, 1984.

Lycan, W. G., Semantics and Methodological Solipsism. In E. LePore (Ed), *Truth and Interpretation*. Oxford: Basil Blackwell, 1986.

Rosenberg, J., On Understanding the Difficulty in Understanding Understanding. In: H. Parret & J. Bouveresse (Eds). *Meaning and Understanding*, Berlin: Walter de Gruyter, 1981.

Stich, S., Do Animals Have Beliefs. *Australasian Journal of Philosophy*, 1979, **57**, 15–28.

Ziff, P., *Understanding Understanding*. Ithaca, NY: Cornell University Press, 1972.

6

Common Sense in Semantics

JERROLD J. KATZ

*Ph.D. Programs in Philosophy and Linguistics, Graduate Center,
The City University of New York*

Q: What is the principal difference between your conception of semantics and other conceptions?

A: On my conception of the subject, semantics is the study of meaning. This may seem an odd characterization—like a historian saying that history is a study of the past. But the conception of semantics as the study of meaning is far from an uninformative truism. In fact, the conception expresses a quite controversial view of semantics which is, moreover, unique among approaches to the subject in the philosophy of language, linguistics, and logic, in taking senses or meanings, *as they present themselves in our ordinary linguistic experience,* to be the proper objects of study in semantics. Other approaches are reductionistic. They seek to reduce the ordinary notions of sense and meaning away, replacing them with something else regarded from the metaphysical perspective of the reductionist as philosophically more respectable or scientifically more tractable. Ever since Russell's attempt to treat meaning as reference, we have had one attempt after another to treat meaning as something else. There have been attempts to reduce it to behavior-controlling stimuli, to images, methods of verification, stereotypes, truth conditions, extensions in possible worlds, use, illocutionary act potential, perlocutionary potential of various sorts, and even physical inscriptions. Indeed, the history of philosophical semantics

157

in this century might well be written as a succession of metaphysically inspired attempts to eliminate the ordinary notion of meaning or sense.

Q: Can you explain what you mean in saying that, on your approach, senses or meanings are taken as they present themselves in our ordinary experience with natural language?

A: There are three aspects of this claim. First, I want to claim that there *is* a particular way in which senses or meanings present themselves to us. Second, knowledge of this way is a matter of common sense. Third, this way constitutes the phenomena that a semantic theory is obligated to save.

Sense and meaning, as ordinarily conceived, present themselves as the aspect of the grammar of expressions and sentences on which their semantic properties and relations depend. It is surely a matter of common sense that a sentence like 'People sometimes procrastinate' is meaningful but a sentence like 'Falsehoods sometimes procrastinate' is not, or that expressions like 'bank', 'ring', and 'visiting relatives' are ambiguous, or that sentences like 'Perhaps it will rain' and 'Maybe there will be rain' are synonymous, or that expressions like 'happy' and 'sad' are antonymous. Moreover, it is also common sense that an expression or sentence of a natural language is meaningful when it has a sense, meaningless when it has none, ambiguous when it has more than one sense, synonymous with another when they have the same sense, and antonymous with another when they have opposite senses. Such facts are as certain as the propositions on G. E. Moore's list in 'A Defense of Common Sense'.

That they are also the phenomena that theories in semantics are obliged to save is shown by the fact that theories which fail to square with them are *ipso facto* rejected. Conformity with these semantic facts has traditionally served as a condition of adequacy for theories of meaning. The standard criticism of Russell's theory of meaning has been that its equation of meaning with reference gets synonymy wrong: it falsely claims that merely coreferential expressions like 'creature with a heart' and 'creature with a kidney' are synonymous. To take another familiar example, the standard criticism of the classical empiricist equation of meaning with mental images is that it falsely claims that expressions like Lewis Carroll's 'slithy toves' are meaningful and ones like 'nevertheless', 'besides', 'implies', 'infinity', 'insofar as', etc, are not. The Russellian equation sacrifices synonymy; the classical empiricist equation sacrifices meaningfulness and meaninglessness.

An adequate theory of meaning, then, has to save the phenomena that common sense recognizes to be semantic facts. It has to correctly represent these phenomena. It cannot ignore them or get them wrong. If a linguistic or philosophical theory of meaning were to say nothing about the facts that pretheoretic intuition recognizes as semantic, it could no more claim to be an account of *meaning* than, say, quantum mechanics or Keynesian economics. If a theory were to address itself to such phenomena, but get them wrong, it could not be a correct account of meaning. Thus, the proper criterion for judging the account of meaning that a theory offers is whether meaning is explained in a way such that, together with appropriate auxiliary assumptions, the explanation implies all and only true predictions about the semantic properties and relations of sentences over the full range of sentences in the language.

Q: I take it then that, as you see it, the primary facts in semantics are facts about the meaningfulness, meaninglessness, ambiguity, synonymy, and other such intuitively discernible properties and relations of sentences. If semantics is the subject that explains what meaning is, it will have to say what meaningfulness is, what meaninglessness is, what multiplicity of meaning is, what sameness of meaning is, what opposition of meaning is, and so on. But how is the 'and so on' to be completed?

A: No theory can, at the outset, specify completely what it is about. This happens late in the course of developing a theory when principles initially adopted to account for the original limited set of phenomena are extended (usually with much revision) to account for a wide range of phenomena outside the original set.

No doubt in semantics the pretheoretically clear cases of semantic properties and relations, meaningfulness, meaninglessness, ambiguity, synonymy, and antonymy, are not exhaustive. Accordingly, the initial task in developing a theory of meaning is to develop a representation scheme for describing the meaning of sentences, and then on the basis of such descriptions to frame necessary and sufficient conditions for meaningfulness, meaninglessness, ambiguity, and the other properties and relations in the set of pretheoretically clear cases. Once substantial progress has been made in accomplishing this initial task, it becomes possible to tackle the question of how to handle properties and relations that pretheoretical intuition does not categorize as semantic or as nonsemantic (either because intuitions are not strong enough or because they conflict). To answer this question, one has to determine whether the principles of semantic structure so far developed for defining properties and relations like meaningfulness, meaninglessness, and ambiguity, and synonymy also enable us to define as yet uncategorized properties and relations. If the principles enable us to define some previously uncategorized property or relation—or do with some straightforward extension—then we can say that it is semantic, too.

Consider an example: let us assume that meaningfulness, ambiguity, and synonymy constitute the clear cases of semantic properties and relations.

We can show that the further property of redundancy exhibited in (1) but not (2)

(1)   naked nude
(2)   naked nudist

is semantic as well. This is shown by the definition (D_1)

(D_1) A modifier-head construction is redundant if, and only if, it is synonymous with the expression that is its head.

which defines redundancy in terms of the acknowledged semantic relation of synonymy. Thus, redundancy belongs to the subject-matter of semantics because it is definable in terms of something that does.

The boundary question for semantics becomes more complicated in connection with the cases that fall outside of semantics. We cannot, of course, conclude that a property or relation is outside the subject-matter of a science just from the fact that it cannot at one particular time be fit into the pattern of definition and explanation. Some crucial principle might not yet have been discovered or might not yet be stated with sufficient generality. But fallibility does not prevent us from being able to argue that a further property or relation is outside the domain of the science. We can argue from what is known about the science at the time that we are unable to define the new property or relation for reasons that have to do with essential aspects of its principles.

For example, even at this early stage in the development of semantics, we can argue that the property of rhyme is nonsemantic. Rhyme involves correspondence of terminal sounds in a pair of expressions, but we have every reason to think that the principles underlying the definitions of meaningfulness, meaninglessness, ambiguity, synonymy and similar properties and relations make no reference to sound patterns. The only consequence of fallibility is that the strength of such negative arguments must depend on the strength of the considerations supporting the principles from which the generalization proceeds.

Q: Do you think that some things are nonsemantic from our common sense standpoint?

A: Yes, but reductionist theorists have tried to make us think common sense is wrong on these points—and unfortunately, with considerable success. For example, I think that we not only exclude phonological properties like rhyme but also syntactic properties like morphological form and, more importantly, properties of the referents of words (e.g., those that appear in stereotypes), psychological associations (e.g., images), and social constraints on use (e.g., emotional values of 'four'-letter words).

Later I will show how common sense reasserts itself against reductionist criticism in providing the plausibility for arguments showing how reductionism goes wrong.

Q: Supposing, then, for present purposes, that we have a reasonably clear idea of the subject-matter of semantics, how, on your view, do we obtain knowledge of the variety of particular facts about meaningfulness, meaninglessness, ambiguity, synonymy, etc, of sentences?

A: Suppose you are asked by a foreigner whom you are helping to learn English whether sentence (3) is meaningful:

(3) Pigs do not fly south in the winter.

or whether (4) is ambiguous

(4) Mary's will can't be broken.

or whether (5) and (6) are synonymous

(5) Give your money to the poor
(6) Give the poor your money

I think you will unhesitatingly say that they are. You will believe, moreover, that in such clear cases you *know* they are on the basis of your grammatical intuitions about them. In other cases, you might hesitate or be unsure of what the right answer is. Your intuition is unclear. But in the clear cases your acquaintance with semantic facts, as with phonological and syntactic facts, is through grammatical intuition.

It is both our initial source and final arbiter in questions of grammatical fact. Indirect evidence, operational tests, behavioral correlates, and the like have to be checked against intuition in order to determine that they are genuinely evidence about, tests for, and correlates of the grammatical structure in question. For example, if an operational test or behavioral correlate for clause boundaries in terms of breath pauses conflicts with our intuitions about clause boundaries, it will be rejected as not testing for or correlating with the proper grammatical structure. Thus, when nonintuitive sources of information about semantic, syntactic, or phonological fact are employed in grammatical argumentation, their employment must be legitimized by ultimately grounding the facts in clear intuitions of fluent speakers. In irreconcilable conflicts with clear intuition, it is always the nonintuitional source of evidence that goes.

Q: I think we have clarified the question of the subject matter of semantics sufficiently to return to the claim that your approach is distinctive in accepting the common-sense notion of meaning as the proper object of study in semantics. Can you now review some of the main reductive attempts and show how common sense 'reasserts itself' against them?

A: If I am correct to think that attempts to replace the notion of meaning with something else are bound to fail because meaning is meaning, and nothing else, then one should be able to find examples, in the case of each such attempt, which exhibit the difference between meaning and what has been introduced to replace it. I shall not try to show that one always does find such counterexamples. My moral will be that, although the reducing theory in these attempts—the theory of reference, associationist psychology, first-order logic, speech act theory, or what have you—may be a truly marvelous theory in all sorts of ways, it is a marvelous theory of something other than meaning.

Let us begin with the attempted behaviorist reduction which claims that meaning is best understood in terms of the notion of behavior-controlling stimuli and with the attempted mentalist reduction which claims that meanings are images or 'pictures in the head'. Since meaning is tied far more tightly to linguistic constructions than their utterances are tied to eliciting stimuli belonging to any well-defined class, the semantic properties and relations of linguistic constructions can be expected to diverge significantly from the significant features of eliciting stimuli. One consequence of this is that, on the behaviorist reduction, the distinction between meaningful and meaningless expressions collapses completely. Nonsense words, as the behaviorist psychologists themselves have shown, are stably elicited by certain well-defined experimental conditions, but meaningful expressions do not have stable or well-defined stimulus conditions (see Chomsky, 1964). The same problem plagues the equation of meaning with images: meaningful words like 'if', 'nonetheless', 'insofar as' come out meaningless because we do not associate a mental picture with them, but nonsense expressions like 'slithy toves' come out meaningful because we do. Another problem is that the amount of imagery connected with a word like 'animal' sharply contrasts with its degree of ambiguity.

Now, neither of these two reductionist attempts is taken very seriously in philosophy nowadays. yet attempts that *are* taken seriously suffer from the same sort of difficulty—failing to save the phenomena of semantics. One of the most widely accepted of the 'serious' reductionist programs is the attempt to equate meaning with use. This program began with a simplistic notion of use which sacrificed a number of semantic phenomena, including synonymy. For obscene words, to take one example, and pejorative terms, to take another, are different in use from their nonobscene and nonpejorative synonyms. The use of words like 'piss' and 'Jew-down' is influenced by a large number of factors, such as culturally associated attitudes, desire to be accepted in society, etc, which do not influence the use of their synonyms 'urine' and 'bargain down' in at all the same ways. The equation of meaning with use also sacrifices the distinction between meaningful and meaningless sentences: sentences that are too long or too syntactically complicated to be used—ones with over two hundred words or ones having ten center-embeddings—will be predicted to be meaningless even though built up from meaningful components by operations (e.g., conjunction) known to preserve meaningfulness. Furthermore, the equation sacrifices the phenomena of ambiguity and antonymy, since almost every word of the language has ironic as well as literal uses. The reduction is thus forced to predict that 'beautiful', 'happy', 'clever', etc, are ambiguous between their sense and the sense of their antonyms.

Alston, in a well-known paper on meaning and use (Alston, 1963), suggests that the equation of meaning with use is basically sound but that use theorists have failed to clarify the notion of use sufficiently and ought to clarify it along Austinian lines. The suggestion to so clarify it has been most systematically developed by Searle (1965). But, as I shall argue now, development of Alston's suggestion does not succeed in removing the difficulties we have found with the unreconstructed notion of use. On the contrary, Searle's speech act theory reveals all the more clearly that such difficulties are inherent in the equation of meaning with use by showing that they are also present in the reconstructed notion of meaning as illocutionary force potential.

Searle's attempt to formulate a systematic theory of meaning as use founders on the same differences between meaning and use that we have found with the simplistic notion of use: cultural, social, psychological, and other factors which contribute nothing to the meanings of words, nonetheless strongly influence the way they are used in speech. These differences show up in Searle's speech act theory as incongruities in that theory's pattern of explanation. Instead of the kind of uniform explanation we find in genuine theories, we find an assortment of observations about various aspects of language and extralinguistic factors of a cultural, social, psychological, etc, nature (see Katz, 1977b).

In Searle's account of syntactic indicators of illocutionary force, one of the rules for using an illocutionary force indicator like 'promise' says that its use involves the undertaking of an obligation. Another rule says that its use involves reference to a future act (relative to the speech point) in which the speaker is the agent. Now two other of Searle's rules, in no relevant way distinguished from these two in his account, say that it must not be obvious that, in the normal course of events, the speaker will perform the act that fulfills the promise, and that the promisee wants the speaker to fulfill the promise. The former pair of rules is about aspects of English verbs and hence about the language, but the latter pair is about extra-linguistic factors, concerning the conditions for something like typical cases of promising. The former rules express components of the grammatical meaning of 'promise' which also play a role in other grammatical phenomena, like the contrast in meaning between 'promise' and 'advise' (no obligation but reference to future act), on the one hand, and between 'promise' and 'thank' (obligation but no reference to future act), on the other. In contrast, the latter rules merely express aspects of the context of use that a speaker normally or usually takes into consideration in using language. Thus, unlike the obligation and future act conditions, the conditions expressed in the latter rules need not be satisfied in straightforward, literal uses of sentences of the form 'I promise to do X'. Oaths and pledges are given even when it is obvious that the speaker will do the act(s) in the normal course of events, e.g., oaths like honest Abe Lincoln's oath to uphold the constitution, or pledges like Romeo and Juliet's or promises where a formal commitment is necessary like some promises to love, honor, and obey. And a promise can be made when the last thing in the world that the promisee wants is to see the promise fulfilled, e.g., a student's promise to turn in his or her three-hundred word paper in time for the instructor to read it during vacation.

Perhaps the clearest instance of a nonsemantic rule in Searle's discussion are his preparatory rules for asserting, viz, that the speaker has reasons for the truth of the assertion and that it not be obvious to both speaker and hearer that the latter already knows the fact(s) is asserted (see Searle, 1969, p. 66). If the former were semantic, there would be no baseless assertions and nobody just shooting off his mouth. If the latter were semantic, there would be no boring relatives who always state the same tired views. If both were, our examination system might be jeopardized.

These considerations, although only some of the cases that can be marshalled to show the basic incongruity in Searle's pattern of explanation, suffice for present purposes to support my claim that Searle's account is a concretion of two distinct things: on the one hand, observations concerning the grammar of syntactic constructions, and on the other, observations concerning extragrammatical (sociological, psychological, etc) aspects of the context of utterance use. Given that my claim is correct, a coherent system of explanation is obtained by eliminating speech act theory in favor of two distinct theories, one dealing with the way in which meaning is determined in the language, and the other dealing with the way in which extragrammatical factors influence a speaker's use of language.

But before we give up on Alston's suggestion that perhaps the simple notion of use can be adequately specified, we have to consider the other principal attempt in contemporary philosophy to explicate it, the explication of the notion of use in terms of Austin's idea of perlocution. This attempt was initiated by Grice who saw how to restrict the notion of perlocution so that its utilization as the basis for an account of meaning does not produce absurd consequences. Since on the unrestricted notion of a perlocutionary act (an act performed *by* uttering something) causal effects of any sort, including breaking the listener's ear drum, count as perlocutionary acts, they become part of meaning. Grice's notion of meaning restricts the totality of causal effects of an utterance to just those that a speaker intends to produce in the listeners in virtue of their recognition of this intention to produce them (see Grice, 1968).

Grice sketched a line of argument to show that this restricted per-locutionary notion is the basic notion of meaning (notions like that of the meaning of a sentence are derivative) and that the principles that underlie the reasoning of speakers and listeners in the performance of these per-locutionary acts enable us to specify the notion of use satisfactorily. I say Grice *sketched* such a line of argument because he never actually argues that his account of utterer's meaning does not itself presuppose the notion of sentence meaning. Without such an argument, the possibility is left open that sentence meaning is only definable in terms of utterer's meaning because the former notion has been assumed in the statement of the principles of intentional reasoning underlying any successful explication of utterer's meaning.

The fact that this possibility is left open is a serious difficulty for an application of Grice's notion of utterer's meaning to suitably specify the concept of use. But worse, Grice's own account of this notion seems to make explicit appeal to the grammatical notion of sentence meaning. This appeal occurs when Grice says that the speaker has a repertoire of semantic procedures for expression types of the language that 'equip' the speaker to use these expression types in any circumstances in which the conditions specified in the procedures are met (see Grice, 1968, pp. 231–234). Grice does not explain his notion of a semantic procedure, but, given the role of the notion in Grice's account, the notion can be nothing but that of the content of the speaker's knowledge of the grammatical meaning of sentences.

Schiffer has tried to supply arguments for the claim that perlocutionary meaning is the basis notion (in Schiffer, 1972, pp. 6–7). He offers two. The first is that what one would 'normally or ordinarily mean by uttering *x*' is a necessary condition for knowing the meaning of the whole utterance type *x* (Schiffer, 1972, p. 5). But, even if this claim were true, it would not establish the priority of the perlocutionary notion of meaning. The problem is the same circular presupposition. What a speaker normally or ordinarily means by uttering an expression may depend on the prior notion of a compositionally fixed, grammatic meaning. Grammatical meaning might be necessary to provide the norm against which the utterance is compared to determine that it has its normal or ordinary meaning.

Schiffer's second argument is that the priority of utterer's meaning follows from the fact that (Schiffer, 1972, p. 7)

. . . it is possible for a person to mean something by uttering x even though x has no meaning.

Schiffer gives the example of someone uttering 'grrr' to inform someone of his or her anger. But the possibility of meaning something by an antecedently meaningless sign-token is not incompatible with the claim that grammatical meaning is prior, any more than the possibility of meaning by a sign-token the opposite of what its sign-type means is incompatible with this claim. If I say 'Snidely is a fine friend', referring to someone who recently betrayed my friendship, the meaning of my sign-token is the meaning of the sign-type 'Snidely is a rotten friend'. The fact that it is possible for an utterance of 'fine' in the proper tone of voice or occurring in the proper circumstances (i.e., where everyone knows of the betrayal) to mean the opposite of what 'fine' means in the language does not at all show that the meaning of 'rotten' which the utterance of 'fine' bears on such occasions is not an antecedent part of English grammar. Ironic usage shows only that speakers, in addition to their knowledge of grammar, must have extragrammatical conventions for hooking up sign-tokens uttered in an ironic tone or in the proper circumstances with the grammatical meaning of its antonym.

Similarly, the fact that, in the example Schiffer gives, it is possible for a sign-token of 'grrr' to have the meaning that the sentence 'I am angry' has in the language need show nothing more than that such conventions also hook up the grammatical meaning of 'I am angry' with such utterances of 'grrr' (by exploiting extragrammatical knowledge that canine grrrs are causally connected with canine anger, perception of onomatopoetic relations, and recognition of the speaker's intent to express such a hook up, in the way the ironic usage exploits knowledge of the betrayal). In order for Schiffer to have shown that meaning is not a contextually prior aspect of the grammar of the language, he would have to have shown—as he clearly has not—that a theory that maintains the priority of grammatical meaning has no way to introduce new meanings for expressions, but must suppose that the perlocutionary meaning of *every* sign-token is associated with its sign-type in the grammar.

Such theories suppose only that every meaning functioning as the per-locutionary meaning of a sign-token is associated with *some* sign-type in the grammar. The point may be made clear if more is said about the conception of language and use underlying these theories. On this conception (Katz, 1977b, pp. 13–22), there are (as suggested in the discussion of Searle's speech act theory) two distinct theories: grammar and pragmatics. Both describe sound/meaning correlations, but the correlations are different. Grammar describes the correlation of sound-types with meanings in the language: the correlation is given by the compositional function that determines the meaning of syntactically complex expressions from the meanings of their parts and syntactic relations. Pragmatics describes the correlation of sound-tokens (specifically, uses of sentences) with their meanings in the context of utterance: the correlation is given by conventions which determine the utterance meaning of a use of a sentence as a function of its grammatical meaning in the language plus extragrammatical information about the context. Such conventions may connect the use of a sentence with a meaning that the sentence type does not have in the language (as in the example of an ironic use of 'Snidely is a fine friend'), but they also may connect a use of a sentence with a meaning that the sentence type does have in the language (as in the case of a mathematics teacher saying in class 'The number two is the only even prime'). Pragmatics, on this view, is about how knowledge of context enables speakers to diverge from the compositional sound/meaning correlation in the language without loss of comprehension. The significant feature of this conception of the relation between language and its use is that, being drawn from a grammatically specified sound/meaning correlation, utterance meaning themselves are not another kind of meaning, but simply grammatical meanings under a different correction.

We may even suppose that Grice's principles are the correct account of the conventions that correlate utterance-tokens with grammatical meanings: speakers use an expression to mean something by uttering it with the intention to produce appropriate comprehension by virtue of the audience's recognition of that intention. These principles, as we have seen above, require a repertory of semantic procedures that connect signs with meanings, that is, with grammatically determined conditions for, *inter alia*, the reference of the signs. The above conception of grammar and pragmatics satisfies this requirement by taking the speaker's knowledge of the grammatical sound/meaning correlation to be this repertoire of semantic procedures. The conception thereby makes it possible to plug a gap in Grice's pragmatic theory. In so doing, however, we adopt just the grammatical/extragrammatical distinction that prevented Searle's systematization of Austin's notion of illocution from saving the simplistic notion of use, thus also preventing Grice's notion of perlocution from saving it.

There is another important tradition of reductionist thinking. It attempts to sophisticate Russell's equation of meaning with reference in much the same way that Searle's and Grice's work attempts to sophisticate the equation of meaning with use. The principal contemporary figure in this tradition is Davidson. He presents a program for replacing the intensionalist paradigm for semantic analysis 's means p' by the extensionalist paradigm ' "s" is true if, and only if, p'.[1] I will show that this program makes the same equation of meaning with reference as Russell's and, hence, sacrifices the same range of semantic phenomena.

As we saw at the outset, Russell's equation sacrifices synonymy: co-referential expressions like 'creature with a heart' and 'creature with a kidney' must be counted as synonymous even though they are not. Davidson's program sacrifices synonymy, too. Coreferential sentences like

(7)   Snow is white
(8)   Grass is green

are counted as the same in meaning since they are the same in truth value.[2] Davidson's program treats (10) as an equally good account of the meaning or logical structure of (7) as (9).

(9)   'Snow is white' is true iff snow is white
(10)   'Snow is white' is true iff grass is green

Moreover, since the truth conditions for every true sentence of English can be given on the basis of any true sentence, and the truth conditions for every false sentence of English can be given on the basis of any false sentence, on Davidson's program there is an optimal semantic analysis of English consisting of an infinite list of biconditionals in which each true sentence is paired with 'Two plus two equals four' and another in which each false sentence is paired with 'Two plus two equals five'. Therefore, Davidson's program implies that English has only two meanings.

Davidson (1971, p. 457) is himself aware of the fact that his program is at this point counterintuitive, but he claims that his 'grotesqueness' is not really a vice of his program. He says,

> ... the grotesqueness of [(10)] is in itself nothing against a theory of which it is a consequence, provided the theory gives the correct results for every sentence ... if [(10)] followed from a characterization of the predicate 'is true' that led to the invariable pairing of truths with truths and falsehoods with falsehoods—then there would not, I think, be anything essential to the idea of meaning that remained to be captured.

There are three things to be said to this. First, Davidson wants to prove that the pairing of truths with truths and falsehoods with falsehoods is all there is to meaning. But when such pairings lead to grotesque consequences, he says, well, so what, pairing truth with truths and falsehoods with falsehoods is all there is to meaning. Davidson is here simply arguing from his own theory. Second, what makes the consequence grotesque is that it flatly contradicts strong pretheoretic intuitions that constitute our firmest hold on the notion of meaning; hence, the theory implying these consequences has to go, not the intuitions. Third, if in the case of less sophisticated equations of meaning with reference, like Russell's, we take such grotesque consequences to refute the attempted reduction, we cannot consistently turn our backs on the guidance of pretheoretic intuitions in essentially the same situation.

Davidson (1971, p. 312) tries to soften the blow of such grotesqueness by saying:

> It may help to reflect that [(10)] is acceptable, if it is, because we are independently sure of the truth of [(7)] and [(8)] but in cases where we are unsure of the truth of a sentence, we can have confidence in a characterization of the truth predicate only if it pairs that sentence with one we have good reason to believe equivalent. It would be ill-advised for someone who had any doubts about the color of snow or grass to accept a theory that yielded [(10)], even if his doubts were of equal degree, unless he thought the color of the one was tied to the color of the other.

But how can reflections about people's degree of confidence in sentences be relevant to the adequacy of Davidson's claims about meaning? The existence of such grotesque consequences depends only on whether biconditionals like (10) are true. Moreover, the particular example does not matter; indefinitely many such biconditionals *are* true—whether we are skeptical or not—and hence indefinitely many grotesque consequences follow—whether we recognize them or not.[3]

Davidson also tries to absolve his theory for blame by separating it from such alledgedly questionable examples. 'It is not easy,' he says, 'to see how [(10)] could be party to (the enterprise of characterizing the truth predicate)' (Davidson, 1971, p. 457). Davidson's claim is that his theory proper ought not to be blamed for such grotesque consequences because it is not itself responsible for asserting that (7) and (8) are equivalent. But is is hard to see why it matters whether such sentences are involved in the enterprise of characterizing the truth predicate in any direct sense. We would not let another theory, say, a theory of color perception, off the hook if, in conjunction with simple truths like grass is green and snow is white, it implies grotesque consequences about vision. Even though theories are not responsible for the auxiliary assumptions used to deduce consequences from them, *good* theories do not have grotesque consequences when conjoined with simple truths. Since the grotesqueness does not derive from the simple truths themselves, and since it has its origin somewhere, we take it that the grotesque consequences must originate in some hidden weakness of the theory. The simple truths merely help to reveal their source.

Although (10) and similar cases may not be directly involved in the enterprise of characterizing the truth predicate, other cases which raise the same problem for Davidson's theory are. Let the sentences $S_1, \ldots, S_n$ be a Davidsonian characterization of the truth predicate for English. Then we obtain essentially the same grotesque consequences from $S_1, \ldots, S_n$ by replacing 's' in the schema T by a name or structural description of a sentence S_i in $S_1, \ldots, S_n$ and replacing 'p' with a different sentence S_j in $S_1, \ldots, S_n$. Since the sentences $S_1, \ldots, S_n$ are the axioms of Davidson's theory, they are presumably all true and nonsynonymous with one another. Hence, the biconditionals resulting from these replacements will express a grotesqueness just as (10) does. But unlike (10) they cannot be disavowable as not party to the enterprise of characterizing the truth predicate.

Closely related to Davidson's reductionism is a family of positions in the Russellian tradition that may be collectively termed 'epistemic role theories'. These include Davidson's own theory of interpretation, Harman's conceptual role theory, Field's probabilistic semantics, and others.[4] Epistemic role theories assimilate meaning to belief systems in a manner that accords complexes of synthetic beliefs the function that analytic beliefs have in classical theories of meaning, in order to eliminate meanings in favor of complexes of beliefs with the same causal role in the speaker's use of language (see Harman, 1973; Field, 1977). Different epistemic role theories choose different complexes of beliefs or handle their causal role in language use in different ways, but all stand or fall on whether their common assimilation of meaning to belief systems sacrifices or saves the semantic phenomena.

That such theories sacrifice semantic phenomena is clear from the case of common and proper nouns. The use of common nouns, on these positions, 'must depend on a background of largely unmentioned and unquestioned true beliefs' (Davidson, 1975, p. 21). For example, the reference of 'the earth' is fixed by such beliefs as: 'this earth of ours is part of the solar system, a system partly identified by the fact that it is a gaggle of large, cool, solid bodies circling around a very large, hot star' (Davidson, 1975, p. 21). But, then, the use of proper nouns is fixed, and according to these positions is fixed in the same way. For example, the reference of a proper noun like 'Hitler' will be fixed by such beliefs as that he was dictator of Nazi Germany, propounded racial doctrines about the superiority of Aryans, carried out the destruction of millions of European Jews, and so on. Given the parallel treatment of common and proper nouns, epistemic role theories have to say that *both* have meaning, just as Russell's equation of meaning with reference has to say that 'creature with a heart' and 'creature with a kidney' have the same meaning.

However, facts about the phenomena of antonymy, synonymy, ambiguity, and redundancy in English show that common nouns have meaning but proper nouns do not. For example, common nouns have antonyms, or expressions with incompatible meaning, but proper nouns do not. The antonym of 'batchelor' is 'spinster' but what is the antonyn of 'Socrates' or an expression incompatible with 'Bertrand Russell'? Mill made virtually this point. Putting his point in the formal mode, we would say that the proper noun 'Dartmouth' has no meaning since it is not incompatible with 'not located at the mouth of the river Dart'. The same semantic asymmetry between common and proper nouns is found in synonymy phenomena: common nouns have synonyms, but proper nouns do not. 'Marijuana' and 'pot' refer to the same substance *because* they have the same meaning; 'Mark Twain' and 'Samuel Clemens' refer to the same literary figure but the explanation cannot be sameness of meaning. Note that it is absurd to say 'Marijuana might not be pot' but not absurd to say 'Mark Twain might not be Samuel Clemens'. Saying the former is like saying that genuine coins might be counterfeit, but one can easily imagine a revisionist literary historian saying the latter.

Nor is the multiple reference of a proper noun a matter of multiple sense. Although it is true to say that the multiple reference of 'bank' is due to its ambiguity, it is absurd to explain the multiple reference of a proper noun like 'Mary Jane' (to a girl, a boat, a pet turtle, etc) in the same way. Finally, nonrestrictive relative clauses on proper nouns do not exhibit semantic redundancy, whereas on common nouns they do. For example, in 'The nightmare, which is a dream, . . .' or 'The king, who is a monarch, . . .' the relative clause is redundant. But in 'Gödel, who discovered the incompleteness of arithmetic, . . .' or 'Aristotle, the most famous student of Plato and teacher of Alexander, . . .' the clause is not redundant. It is amplitive, telling us which Gödel (the mathematician, not the Bauhaus architect) and which Aristotle (the philosopher, not the ship owner).

Thus, given the commitment of epistemic role theories to proper nouns and common nouns *both* having meaning, the theories sacrifice not only the distinction between the meaningful and the meaningless but also the semantic phenomena of antonymy, synonymy, ambiguity, and redundancy, Epistemic role theories may be quite marvelous theories about belief states and their functioning, but they do not concern meaning.

There is another important objection to taking such theories to be theories of meaning. The principal thing about the notion of epistemic role is that it has to do essentially with mental states and processes: Beliefs are themselves mental states and the epistemic role of a complex of beliefs is the causal role it has in thought processes. Thus, suppose that we had a reconstruction of meaning in terms of the notion of epistemic role and suppose even further that, as far as we know, the reconstruction sacrifices no semantic phenomena. Ought we adopt it?

Meaning is, on all sides, regarded as referring to the grammatical features of sentences on which their logical implications depend. Adopting the reconstruction will, accordingly, commit us to characterizing logical implications in terms of cognitive structures assigned to sentences in reconstruction. Since, furthermore, it is an *empirical* question what such cognitive structures are, it will be an empirical question—presumably in psychology—what sentences the reconstruction will say that a given sentence implies. It may turn out that the reconstruction contains no surprises for the logician. 'Henry is a bachelor' implies 'Henry is unmarried', 'Henry is a batchelor' implies 'Henry is a bachelor or Henry is American', and so on. But it may also turn out that the reconstruction contains surprises: 'Henry is English' implies 'Henry is stuffy'. Presumably, the surprises will not really appear in connection with such simple cases. But it *is ex hypothesi* an empirical question, and therefore, in adopting the reconstruction, we commit ourselves to the possibility of arriving at "logical principles" that conflict with laws of logic. About such a commitment, Frege (1964, p. 14, see also pp. 15–16) wrote:

> . . . what if beings were found whose laws of thought flatly contradicted ours and therefore frequently led to contrary results even in practice? The psychological logician could only acknowledge the fact and say simply: those laws hold for them, these laws hold for us. I should say: we have here a hitherto unknown form of madness. Anyone who understands laws of logic to be laws that prescribe the way in which one ought to think— . . . and not natural laws of human beings' taking a thing to be true—will ask, who is right? . . . The psychological logician cannot ask this question; if he did he would be recognizing laws of truth that were not laws of psychology.

Since epistemic role theories allow the possibility for arriving at logical principles that conflict with the laws of logic, epistemic role theories cannot be theories of meaning.

Q: Let me interrupt a moment. Does not this criticism apply as much to your own view of semantics as it does to the epistemic role view? In 'Mentalism in Linguistics' (Katz, 1964a) you also claim that grammatical structure is psychological structure.

A: Just such considerations as Frege's were responsible for changing my view of the ontology of grammatical structure from the psychological position I took in that paper to something like Frege's. The difference between my theory of semantics and epistemic role theories, which allows me but not epistemic role theorists to consider more than one ontological option, is that my theory is a nonreductive explication of the formal grammatical structure underlying semantic properties and relations while their theories are reductive programs proposing to replace meaning with a specifically psychological notion. Thus, they are wedded to psychologism, whereas nothing forces me to interpret the semantic representations that explicate the structure on which properties and relations like mean ingfulness, synonymy, antonymy, ambiguity, etc, depend as representations of mental structure. I am free to interpret them as representations of abstract objects. Very little changes in the formal theory of semantic structure, say, as set out in earlier works like *Semantic Theory* (Katz, 1972), when the theory receives a new interpretation on which it is about sentences in an abstract sense.

Before returning to reductionism in semantics, I want to say a bit about my present view concerning what a theory of semantic structure is a theory of. During most of the time I was developing my conception of intensional semantics, I assumed that a theory of semantic structure is part of a theory of linguistic competence in Chomsky's sense, namely, part of a theory of the ideal speaker–hearer's knowledge of the language. I thought that a theory of semantic structure is properly viewed as a theory of semantic competence, that is, a theory of the ideal speaker–hearer's knowledge of meaning. My present view is that semantics, and the rest of grammar as well, is better thought of as being about a class of abstract objects, sentences, rather than being about human knowledge, however idealized. I now think linguistics is a branch of mathematics, not a branch of psychology (see Katz, 1981).

This, of course, is not to say that there is no such thing as a study of human *knowledge* of grammatical structure. There surely is. Such a study is as legitimate, on my view, as psychological investigations into our knowledge of number. But it is as *il*legitimate, on my view, to treat the study of semantic structure as psychology as it is to treat the study of numerical structure as psychology. A psychological study of the ideal speaker's knowledge of meanings is as distinct from the study of meanings as the study of the ideal arithmetician's knowledge of number is from the study of number. And distinct in the same way: the study of a competence is a study of human *knowledge* while the study of meaning or number is the study of the *object* of such knowledge. Hence, on my present view, semantic theories, and theories of grammar, too, are not required to meet any empirical, 'psychological reality' constraints, reflecting the way in which human knowledge is mentally represented and processed. Rather, a semantic theory of a natural language is required to do no more or less than account for the semantic facts about its sentences—which are meaningful and which meaningless, which ambiguous and how many ways, and so on—in the simplest, most revealing way. There may be more than one such theory, but then, as equally simple, equally revealing, comprehensive accounts of the semantic facts of the language, they will be equivalent and equally correct.[5]

Now, I would like to return to reductionism. There is one more form of reductionism in the Russellian tradition that we need to consider. This form, which I will call 'possible world semantics', equates meaning with extensions in possible worlds. Possible world semantics is a reaction to narrowly truth-theoretic approaches like Davidson's. It prides itself on a more powerful theory of language than is possible within the Davidsonian framework but one that is not so powerful as to embrace meanings in the classical sense. It claims to be able to explain more than Davidsonians can without being subject to Quine's criticisms of classical semantics. But, in fact, it neither avoids Quine's criticisms nor succeeds in explaining enough semantic phenomena.

Possible world semantics is just as vulnerable to Quine's criticisms as classical semantics. The reason, as Quine himself pointed out (Quine, 1953, p. 47), is that the notion of possibility is bound up with that of meaning. The possibility of a world is a matter of the consistency of its description, but consistency is partly a matter of meaning: there are no possible worlds corresponding to the descriptions 'married bachelor', 'mortal who will live forever', and 'genuine coin of the realm which is counterfeit' because the descriptions are semantically inconsistent. Since embracing the notion of possibility is also embracing meaning, possible world semantics like Hintikka can hardly promote their theory as superseding the classical theory of meaning.[6]

In the course of this critical examination of reductionism in semantics, we have seen a pattern emerge: there is an initial suggestion that meaning be reduced to some notion that, on examination, turns out to sacrifice semantic phenomena; one or another revision of the notion is developed, but soon these, too, are shown to sacrifice the same semantic phenomena. We saw this pattern exemplified in the suggestion that meaning is use and Searle's revision of the simplistic notion of use; we saw it exemplified again in the suggestion that meaning is reference and the revisions of Davidson and epistemic role theorists. Now we see it exemplified once more in the revision we are calling possible world semantics. This should not be surprising insofar as all of the reductionist approaches in the Russellian tradition use purely extensional apparatus to handle the phenomena for which classical semantics invokes the concept of meaning. Possible world semantics extends the notion of reference in the Russellian and Davidsonian approaches to reference in all possible worlds, but this extension, since it leaves the essentially referential character of semantic analyses unchanged, must sacrifice the same semantic phenomena as the Russellian and Davidsonian approaches.

The simple equation of meaning with reference leads to the definitions (D_2) and (D_3).

(D_2) An expression or sentence e is meaningful (has a meaning) just in case *e* refers to something in the actual world, i.e., has a nonnull extension.

(**D**$_3$)   An expression or sentence e_1 is synonymous with another e_2 (has the same meaning) just in case e_1 and e_2 refer to the same thing(s) in the actual world, i.e., have the same extension.

These, as we have seen, face counterexamples: 'witch', 'unicorn', 'golden mountain', etc, refer to nothing in the actual world but are meaningful; 'creature with a heart' and 'creature with a kidney' co-refer in the actual world but are different in meaning. Possible world semanticists replace definitions (**D**$_2$) and (**D**$_3$) with (**D**$_4$) and (**D**$_5$):[7]

(**D**$_4$)   An expression or sentence *e* is meaningful (has a meaning) just in case *e* refers to something in at least one possible world, i.e., there is a possible world in which *e* has a nonnull extension.

(**D**$_5$)   An expression or sentence e_1 is synonymous with another e_2 (has the same meaning) just in case e_1 and e_2 refer to the same thing(s) in all possible worlds, i.e., have the same extension in every possible world.

With (**D**$_4$) and (**D**$_5$), the foregoing counterexamples disappear: there are hypothetical circumstances containing unicorns, witches, and golden mountains, and hypothetical circumstances where creatures with hearts have no kidney.

But, although these counterexamples disappear, others just like them remain. To find such counterexamples, we do what critics of simpler referential approaches did, namely, find nonsemantic factors that constrain the extensions of expressions and sentences so that their meanings can vary independently of the extensional structure recognized in referential theories. Critics of the simple referential theory found evolutionary and biological constraints that precluded meaningful expressions like 'unicorn' from having a referent in the actual world and ensured that nonsynonymous expressions like 'creature with a heart' and 'creature with a kidney' are coreferential. What constraints will serve the same critical purpose in the case of the more sophisticated possible world approach?

Part of the notion of possibility, as we observed above, depends on the notion of meaning. But only part. Part of the notion of possibility and necessity depends on extralinguistic matters of logical and mathematical fact. Such fact constrains extension in all possible worlds independent of a wide range of semantic variation. Thus, logical and mathematical fact gives rise to counterexamples that are exactly parallel to those that have been brought against the simpler referential theories. For example, corresponding to the counterexamples to (**D**$_2$), we have expressions like 'the largest natural number', 'a consistent division by zero', and 'a consistent and complete formalization of arithmetic' which are meaningful but have a nonnull extension in every possible world. And, corresponding to the counterexamples to $(\mathbf{D}_3)$, we have sentences like 'One plus one is two' and 'Every even number is the sum of two primes' which are nonsynonymous but have the same extension in very possible world (for further discussion, see Katz & Katz, 1977, pp. 86–96).

Possible world semantics may be thought to fare better than, say, Davidsonian semantics because the former allows more than two meanings in English. But, just as Davidsonian semantics counterintuitively claims that all true sentences have the same meaning and all false sentences have the same meaning, possible world semantics counterintuitively claims that all necessarily true sentences have the same meaning and all necessarily false sentences have the same meaning.

Q: Your mention of Quine raises the question of whether it is legitimate of you to assume a domain of meaning. I can grant you that your arguments go through on this assumption: *if* there is such a thing as meaning, then it is irreducible. But if Quine has shown that there is no such thing as meaning, these various nonintensional approaches are saved. The various equations that you have been criticizing thus no longer need be viewed as reductionist programs, but can now be viewed as proposals concerning how best to handle the logical structure of natural language in the absence of any hope to handle it on the basis of the classical notion of meaning.

A: Your point is exactly right. But it works the other way as well. What makes Wittgensteinian, Davidsonian, and other reductive approaches seem viable in spite of their failure to save semantic phenomena is the belief that Quine has proved that the sacrificed phenomena were not worth saving in the first place. Let us accept the biconditional that these approaches are off the hook if, and only if, it has been shown that there is no such thing as meaning in the classical sense. But the fact is that Quine's arguments against meaning show nothing of this sort.

These arguments, set out in 'Two Dogmas of Empiricism' (Quine, 1953), have a structure that has eluded Quine's friends and foes alike. This structure has to be fully appreciated in order to understand why Quine's criticisms fail.

Grice and Strawson picture Quine's overall argument as a *non sequitur*, generalizing from some failures to draw the analytic-synthetic distinction to the sweeping conclusion that no distinction exists (Grice & Strawson, 1956). Thus, on their view, even if each of Quine's specific criticisms were cogent, there would be no grounds to conclude:

That there is such a distinction to be drawn at all is an unempirical dogma of empiricists, a metaphysical article of faith. (Quine, 1953, p. 37)

But Grice and Strawson fail to appreciate that the cases Quine examines are, in an appropriate sense, exhaustive. Quine's overall argument considers *all* the places where it would be reasonable to expect clarification of the notion of meaning. Hence, if Quine's specific criticisms in each place were cogent, he would have shown that there can be no clarification of this notion in any place where one might reasonably expect it.

There are three such places: definition, logic, and linguistics. In the area of definition, there are three forms of definition to consider, lexical definition (paraphrase), explication, and abbreviational stipulation. Quine quite easily shows that a clarification of meaning cannot come in any of these forms. In the area of logic, he shows, convincingly, that the application of postulational or rule methods to the problem of clarifying meaning—as exemplified in Carnap's use of meaning postulates or semantical rules—can only specify which sentences of a language are analytic and which pairs synonymous, but cannot explain what analyticity or synonymy is (Quine, 1953, pp. 32–37). Finally, in linguistics Quine shows, again convincingly, that attempts to clarify semantic notions by providing substitution criteria for identifying their extensions leads to vicious circularity.

If Quine could in this way establish that neither definition, nor logic, nor linguistics offers hope of clarifying meaning, he could conclude that there is no place from which such clarification will be forthcoming. The problem with Quine's argument, then, is not that it is a bad induction. It is a deductive argument from an exhaustive enumeration of cases. The problem is rather that what is shown in connection with one of the cases does not rule out clarification of meaning in that area. Quine shows that no clarification is possible in the areas of definition and logic, but what he says about linguistics does not rule out clarification there. Failure to provide substitution criteria for analyticity and synonymy does not rule out their clarification.

It is easy to see why Quine thought that it does. He says (Quine, 1953, p. 56):

So-called substitution criteria, or conditions of interchangeability, have in one form or another played central roles in modern grammar. For the synonymy problem of semantics such an approach seems more obvious still.

Modern grammar meant, at the time this was written, the taxonomic theory expounded in the works of Bloomfield, Bloch, and Trager, etc (these are the 'modern grammarians' to whom Quine himself refers (see Quine, 1953, pp. 50 and 52)). Quine thus thought that failure to provide substitution criteria rules out the possibility of clarifying semantic notions in linguistics because the scientific orthodoxy of the time, taxonomic theory, said that such criteria are the only way to clarify notions. However, since the Chomskian revolution, generative theory has introduced a new way of clarifying linguistic notions. Quine's grounds for taking substitution criteria as the proper standard for clarifying linguistic notions are thus undercut and his argument to rule out clarification of semantic notions collapses.

Philosophical faith in the power of Quine's arguments against meaning rests on a failure to appreciate this consequence of the Chomskian revolution. Taxonomic theorists insisted that substitution criteria are the only legitimate means of clarifying linguistic notions because they held a physicalist conception of language which required all such notions to be built up from distributional regularities in a corpus of utterances. The Chomskian revolution replaced this conception with a psychological conception from which no such requirement follows. Instead of viewing grammars as data-cataloguing devices, as the taxonomists had, Chomskian linguists viewed grammars as scientific theories of the ideal speaker's knowledge of the language. This view allows the clarification of a linguistic notion to be a matter of its connections with other notions in a predictively powerful theory of sentence structure. Hence, instead of requiring that a linguistic notion be built up from the empirical base, it can, as it were, be dropped down from above (see Chomsky, 1975, pp. 31–33).

There is, then, the option of explaining meaning, synonymy, and analyticity on the model of Chomsky's explanation of syntactic notions like 'well-formed'. We can construct an abstract system of semantic representations that formally describes the meaning of sentences, characterize semantic notions like meaningfulness, synonymy, and analyticity in terms of such formal representations, and then justify both the representational system and the definitions indirectly on the basis of how well they predict and explain judgments of fluent speakers about such semantic properties and relations of sentences. Quine's criticisms do not apply to this way of clarifying semantic notions: such theoretical clarification of semantic notions can be no more circular than the clarification of syntactic notions like 'well-formedness' on which it is modeled. Indeed, if there were an *a priori* argument establishing the vicious circularity of semantics, there would also be an argument establishing the vicious circularity of syntax, and further one establishing the vicious circularity of logic and mathematics (the notions of 'is logically equivalent to' and 'is numerically identical with' would fare no better than 'is the same in meaning as' judged by the standard of substitution criteria). Quine's demonstration of circularity is best viewed as a *reductio ad absurdum* of his claim that substitution criteria are a proper standard of clarification.

Q: Could not Quine bring in his thesis of the indeterminacy of translation to replace this earlier criticism of meaning?

A: No. Quine's defense of this thesis depends on the criticism of
meaning in 'Two Dogmas of Empiricism'. Recall the point in *Word and
Object* where Quine tries to respond to the objection that indeterminancy
may be nothing over and above ordinary inductive risk (Quine, 1960, p.
75). Quine's response is that to suppose that truth in translation is no worse
off than truth in physics 'misjudges the parallel'. We suppose that, in
semantics, there is a language-independent semantic reality that constitutes
the meanings that sentences and their translations express, just as in physics
there is a theory-independent physical reality. We misjudge the parallel
because there is no semantic reality for hypothesis of translation to be true
or false of, no 'free-floating, linguistically neutral meaning', as Quine puts
it (Quine, 1960, p. 76). There are, according to Quine, no meanings
over and above the sentences of a language or languages for translation
hypotheses to be right or wrong about:

> . . . radical translation tries our meanings: really sets them over against their verbal
> embodiments, or, more typically, finds nothing there. (Quine, 1960, p. 76)

Quine *says* that there is no 'linguistically neutral meaning' but what
reasons does he have for saying this? The only reasons he has given is, first,
those in 'Two Dogmas of Empiricism' with which we have already dealt,
and second, ones that depend on the same taxonomic picture of language
as the argument concerning the circularity of attempts to clarify meaning
on the basis of substitution tests. Quine claims that translation hypotheses
like:

  (i)   'gavagai' translates as 'rabbit'
  (ii) 'gavagai' translates as 'rabbit stage'
  (iii) 'gavagai' translates as 'undetached rabbit part'

can accommodate equally well any evidence from the speech dispositions
of native informants (Quine, 1960, pp. 72–86). But this is so only as long
as what Quine allows as evidence are just judgments about extensional
relations, expressed, typically, in assenting and dissenting behavior to
queries about this application of an English term to a present gavagai. It
seems clear no equal accommodation claim strong enough to support
indeterminacy can be made (even granting compensatory adjustments in
the translation hypotheses for other expressions) if we are allowed to
consider evidence in the form of judgments about intensional relations. If
we can ask a bilingual informant questions such as 'Is "gavagai" *synonymous
with* "rabbit"?' or 'Does "gavagai" *bear the same meaning relation to*
"rabbit" that "finger" bears to "hand" or "branch" bears to "tree"?' or 'Is

the expression "kicking a gavagai" *closer in meaning to* "kicking John in the head" or "kicking John's head",' then there is no reason to think we will be unable to rule out translation hypotheses because they accommodate the available evidence less well than others. Extension of semantic skepticism to intersubject agreement, the treatment of other expressions, or any combination of such factors can be met with compensatory refinement of the eliciting conditions, augmentation of the informant pool, increase in the variety of the questions, construction of a theory which reveals underlying principles (explains deviant judgments, etc), and so on. Nothing in this interplay between criticism and construction, which is familiar in all sciences, suggests more than mere evidential underdetermination of semantic hypotheses.

Quine would of course take the introduction of evidence from judgments about intensional relations to beg the question. He would claim that such evidence illegitimately presupposes that field linguist and informant understand notions like 'synonymy', 'bears the same meaning relation', and 'is closer in meaning than' in the same way. Quine would also claim that introducing such evidence illegitimately presupposes that these notions can be made sufficiently clear.

Such presuppositions are indeed made but there is nothing illegitimate in making them. These presuppositions seem circular to Quine because the taxonomic theory of grammar demands that all linguistic notions be built up from the data without appealing to notions that have not already received physicalistic certification. But, independently of a taxonomic bias, there is nothing illegitimate about presupposing common understanding of semantic notions or the possibility of explicating them. One pursues theory construction in science on the basis of such presuppositions. One takes the attitude that such a course is the best way to determine whether or not they are true. If the presuppositions are false, attempts at such theory construction will come to naught; if they are true, the attempts will eventually be successful and we will learn in this way that the presuppositions are true. Since in sciences generally, we permit theory construction to test the faith we put in the existence of a subject-matter, why not in semantics, too?

Given that reductive approaches get off the hook in connection with their failure to save semantic phenomena if, and only if, Quine's skeptical arguments show that there is no such thing as meaning in the classical sense,[8] we may conclude, having removed these skeptical arguments, that such approaches are inadequate. Without skepticism about meaning, the failure of purported reductions of meaning to account for meaningfulness, ambiguity, synonymy, etc, has to be viewed in the same way that we would view the failure of a purported reduction of lightning to account for flashes, lightning ignitions, ball lightning, etc. The fact that they get semantic properties and relations wrong has to be taken as showing that they offer the wrong explanation of what meaning is.

Q: This may be a good point to turn to your conception of a semantic theory. Could you start by saying why you think your approach will offer the right explanation of meaning?

A: The principal reason for thinking so is that my approach is non-reductive. It does not assume that meaning is something else and then characterize the task for semantics as that of showing how the meaning can be reduced to it. Instead, my approach assumes the viability of the common sense notion of meaning and characterizes the task for semantics as that of constructing a theory of this notion that saves *all* the semantic phenomena with which common sense acquaints us. Thus, my approach starts with no preconceptions about the nature of meaning: it goes on the more modest assumption that the nature of meaning may not be known until we have proceeded quite far in developing such a semantic theory and that our knowledge of its nature will be in terms of what a sophisticated semantic theory of this kind says it is. Another reason for confidence in this approach is that the semantic theory thus far developed sheds light on a number of heretofore recalcitrant problems in the philosophy of logic and language.

A semantic theory is a metatheory. It is a metatheory for theories about the semantic side of the correlation of sentences and senses in natural languages, that is, for the *semantic components* of grammars. A semantic theory has two parts, first, *a notation scheme* for formally representing the senses of sentences in natural languages, and second, *a complete set of definitions* for the semantic properties and relations of natural language. The notation scheme provides a set of *semantic representations* which are employed in semantic components to describe the senses of sentences. The definitions explain semantic properties and relations of sentences in terms of the senses of sentences: hence, the definitions are stated in the form of configurations of symbols in semantic representations. Such configurations constitute generalizations to the effect that the semantic structure they define *is* the grammatical basis for a sentence having the semantic property or relation. Accordingly, the assignment of semantic representations to sentences in a grammar automatically makes a set of predictions about the semantic properties and relations of the sentences. In this way, the success and failure of these predictions reflect on the metatheory as well as on the particular grammars that make them. Success confirms the representation of the correlation of sentences and senses in the grammar, the statement of the definition(s) used, and the notation scheme; failure disconfirms at least one of them. Hence, we can say that a semantic theory saves the semantic phenomena of language just in case its definitions characterize the condition for meaningfulness, meaninglessness, ambiguity, synonymy, etc, so that, for any language, there is a set of semantic representations (in the notation of the definitions) whose assignment to its sentences makes all and only true predictions about their semantic properties and relations.

To make these ideas clearer, let us begin with a first approximation to a semantic theory that saves the phenomena in this sense. The minimal condition for a theory to be an *intensional* theory of the logical structure of natural language is that its notation scheme be a notation for senses. In this sense, Frege proposed an intensionalist theory of logical structure in natural language (Frege, 1952a). But the condition can be satisfied by a very restricted theory. Let the vocabulary of the notation scheme be the infinite list of numericals '1', '2' . . . . Each numerical is taken as the designation of a distinct sense. Let the semantic representations in this vocabulary be finite sets of such numericals including the null set. Let the definitions be (D_6)–(D_8):

(D_6) A sentence of constituent is meaningful if, and only if, the grammar assigns it a semantic representation; otherwise, it is meaningless, that is, semantically deviant.

(D_7) A sentence or constituent is ambiguous if, and only if, the grammar assigns it two or more semantic representations.

(D_8) Two sentences or constituents are weakly synonymous if, and only if, the semantic representations assigned to them have a member in common.

(D_8') Two sentences or constituents are strongly synonymous if, and only if, they are assigned the same semantic representations.

Let us imagine a grammar of English which assigns 'creature with a heart' and 'creature with a kidney' the semantic representations $\{17\}$ and $\{27\}$, 'One plus one equals two' and 'Every even number is the sum of two primes' the semantic representations $\{875\}$ and $\{61\}$, 'piss' and 'urine' $\{74\}$ and $\{74\}$, and 'Richard M. Nixon' the null set. Then, the first two expressions are predicted to be meaningful, unambiguous, and nonsynonymous; the first two sentences likewise; the second two expressions are predicted to be meaningful, unambiguous, and synonymous, and the last is predicted to be meaningless.

Since we have already seen that our intuitions about these expressions and sentences are in accord with these predictions, this first approximation to a semantic theory is confirmed. It is to be noted also that, simple as this first approximation is, it is completely successful in the cases where *all* reductionist approaches considered above fail.

It is natural to take this first approximation as a reconstruction within contemporary linguistic theory of Frege's conception of sense. The first approximation formalizes senses and adds explicit definitions of what are plausibly Frege's notions of meaningfulness, ambiguity, and synonymy. Of course, to do full justice to Frege's conception, this first approximation would have to be fleshed out in various ways. The most important would be to add functions from sets of numerals representing the senses of words to sets of numerals representing the senses of syntactically complex expressions and sentences as a reconstruction of Frege's idea that the sense of a sentence is built up from the senses of its syntactic parts.[9] But my interest in Frege's conception of sense is not with it for its own sake but as an illustration of a position that embodies the limitations of the first approximation in a very direct way. Frege's conception of sense is almost universally taken as the very model of a sense theory. I wish to show not only that his conception is only one intensionalist model but that, in embodying the limitations of this first approximation, it is not the best one.

The easiest way to see these limitations with Frege's conception is to contrast Frege's characterization of sense with my characterization. Frege characterizes sense nontheoretically and derivatively in terms of reference: sense, for Frege, is simply the mode of presentation of reference (Frege, 1952a, p. 57). Frege's technical interest in sense is not with it for its own sake, that is, with the construction of a theory of sense, but with sense as a means to attaining the end of a theory of reference. Aside from remarks here and there about compositionality and the like, the only role that sense plays in Frege's theorizing is to save his theory of reference from problems it would otherwise have to face unaided. Thus, Frege's concern with the technical use of *Sinn* is confined to resolving the paradox of identity and explaining the reference of expressions in opaque contexts.

In contrast, my characterization of sense is theoretical and nonderivative. I take senses to be whatever it will be necessary to take them to be to explain the meaningfulness, ambiguity, synonymy, and *all* the other semantic properties and relations. In short, a sense is whatever the semantic theory that best saves the semantic phenomena of language says it is. One clear difference between this characterization and Frege's is that Frege's leads him to claim that proper names are meaningful. Since they present their referent(s) in some one or another specific way—for example, 'Aristotle' might present Aristotle as Plato's most famous pupil or as Alexander the Great's most famous teacher[10]—they have sense. Frege is led to say that two people whose modes of presenting Aristotle differ, at least in this respect, speak different languages (Frege, 1952a, p. 58). My characterization leads me to the opposite conclusion, as my earlier remarks on the contrast between proper and common nouns have shown.

My theoretical characterization requires a putative theory of sense, such as our first approximation, to be extended whenever a semantic property or relation cannot be explained with existing notational and definitional apparatus. In this vein, consider the semantic properties and relations of superordination, analyticity, and analytic entailment, as illustrated, respectively, by:

(11)   dwelling/cottage
(12)   Southpaws are left-handed pitchers
(13) $\dfrac{\text{Freud had a nightmare}}{\text{Freud had a dream}}$.

These semantic properties and relations are basically different from meaningfulness, ambiguity, and synonymy. Superordination, analyticity, and analytic entailment are *nonexpressional* semantic properties and relations in virtue of applying to senses. One can speak of expressions and sentences also as superordinates, analytic, and analytic entailments but not *simpliciter*, only as superordinates on a sense, analytic on a sense, and analytic entailments on a sense. In contrast, the semantic properties and relations we have been considering up to this point are *expressional*. They apply to linguistic constructions. It is absurd to speak of a sense as meaningful or ambiguous. Expressional semantic properties and relations are simply a count of the number of senses correlated with a linguistic construction in the language. The definitions $(\mathbf{D}_6)$, $(\mathbf{D}_7)$, and $(\mathbf{D}_8)$, respectively, say that meaninglessness is a count of zero senses and meaningfulness a count of at least one, ambiguity a count of two or more, and synonymy a count of the same sense more than once.

The problem with the first approximation is that definitions in the case of nonexpressional semantic properties and relations must refer to the separate parts of the structure of senses differentially but its notation scheme, being adapted for a count of whole senses, does not reflect sense structure. To define the superordination relation illustrated in (11), it is necessary to have a notion scheme that reflects the decomposition of the sense of 'cottage' into the two concepts of a dwelling and of a certain kind of dwelling (different from, say, a dormitory or a skyscraper). Without such a decompositional scheme, it is not possible to formulate the defining condition that the sense of the subordinate expression has as a proper part the sense of the superordinate expression. Similarly, the notational and definitional apparatus in our first approximation cannot reveal the details of sense structure necessary to define analyticity and analytic entailment.

Thus, we have to go beyond a notational scheme consisting, in effect, of numericals functioning as bare names for senses taken as unanalyzed wholes. We require a scheme that describes the structure of senses in the decompositional way that chemical diagrams describe the molecular structure of compounds.

In going beyond this first approximation, we are going beyond both Fregean and standard predicate calculi theories of the logical structure of natural languages (for Fregean theories, see Church, 1951). Such theories represent the so-called 'extralogical' vocabulary of a language—the entire stock of its nouns, verbs, adjectives, etc—with such names. That is, their notation schemes for such vocabulary consists exclusively of symbols I will call *designations*: symbols, functioning as individual or predicate constants, that do not represent the internal structure of senses they name because their orthographic form serves only to determine the assignment of symbol tokens to symbol types (see Katz, 1977c).

Frege does not seem to have recognized the need to replace such schemes with ones whose symbols represent sense structure, although, of course, he recognized complex concepts (in his sense), whose component concepts, which he calls 'marks', are contrasted with properties of concepts because marks are properties of the objects falling under them (see Frege, 1952b, pp. 42–55). But a concept is the reference of a linguistic predicate for Frege, not its sense; furthermore, even if one were to read Frege's account of concept-complexity into his notion of sense, the result would be an account of sense-complexity in which the component senses of an expression are restricted to the senses of its syntactically distinguishable subexpressions. (Frege's examples are all of this sort, e.g., Frege, 1952b, pp. 51–52.) Such composition of senses can be handled within the notation scheme of our first approximation by assigning syntactically complex expressions a sequence of sets of numerals whose members are assigned to their syntactic subexpressions. *The significant point is that there is here no general notion of composition, no notion that applies to composition in the senses of primitives like 'cottage', 'southpaw', and 'nightmare'.* A further point is that, even if Frege were supplied with a general notion of sense composition, he would have no place to use it insofar as his notions of logical truth and logical implication rule out definitions using the containment relation for senses generally (see Frege, 1953, pp. 2–5).

Going beyond our first approximation, then, requires at least replacement of a vocabulary of designations by a vocabulary of what I shall call *descriptions*, that is, symbols whose formal structure describes the structure of the objects they symbolize. The special class of descriptions needed for semantic theory is composed of symbols that I have called 'semantic markers' (see Katz, 1972, 1977b). Semantic markers decompose senses into their component concepts and the relations between them. They are called 'semantic markers' because they mark the semantic structure of senses in the manner that phrase markers mark the phrase structure of syntactic constructions.

The formal structure of a semantic marker is a representation of the conceptual structure of a sense under certain conventions. Current theory takes the formal structure of semantic markers to the trees with labeled nodes. The branching reflects the complexity of the conceptual composition, the labels identify the conceptual components, and the assignment of labels to nodes specifies the logical relations that compose the complex sense out of its components. These conventions may be illustrated with the semantic marker (14) taken as the semantic representation of the sense of 'chase'.

(14)

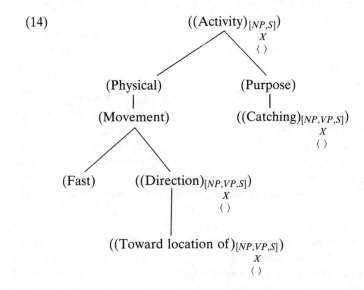

The label on the topmost or root node specifies the category of the concept represented: (14) specifies that the concept of a chase belongs to the category of activity concepts. The labeled branching under the topmost node provides qualifications that distinguish the concept of a chase from other activity concepts. The first subbranch on the left distinguishes it from all concepts of mental activity, such as that of thinking, remembering, planning, and so on. The next longer subbranch on the leftmost full branch adds a further qualification that distinguishes the concept of a chase from that of physical activities not involving change of position like that of doing push ups. The next longer subbranch distinguishes it from concepts of physical movement which have no inherent speed specification like that of walking and from concepts of physical movement which are specified as slow like that of creeping.

The occurrences of the variable 'X' with brackets above and angles below mark positions in a semantic marker at which other semantic markers may be embedded. The notation scheme of semantic markers must provide a set of semantic representations suitable for describing the meaning of every sentence in a language. Since the compositional mechanisms in a language compose the meaning of syntactically complex constructions from the meanings of their parts and since the syntactic mechanisms construct sentences with no limit on their complexity, semantic representations must be built up recursively in a way that reflects the compositional process over the infinite class of sentences. Hence, the notation scheme in semantic theory must contain primitive semantic markers and recursive means of constructing an infinite set of nonprimitive semantic markers out of the primitive semantic markers. One such recursive means is a *projection rule* which substitutes semantic representations for occurrences of variables like those in (14) and a *dictionary* which provides the initial semantic representation for such operations.

The dictionary is a list of morphemes (or syntactic primitives of the language) each of which is paired with a set of semantic representations (describing its senses as a lexical item).[11] The first step in accounting for the compositional meaning of a sentence is to correlate semantic representations from the dictionary with occurrences of morphemes in a syntactic description of the sentence. The next and further steps involve projection rule substitutions of semantic representations for occurrences of categorized variables. The brackets above a categorized variable determine the range of potential values for such substitution. The syntactic symbols in the brackets, called grammatical functions (see Chomsky, 1965, pp. 68–74), specify the semantic representations which may be used in substitutions. The grammatical functions pick out semantic representations in terms of their assignment to constituents with those functions. For example, the function [NP,S] specifies that the variables over which it appears have as values semantic representations that are assigned to subjects of sentences, and [NP,VP,S] specifies that the variables over which it appears have as values semantic representations that are assigned to direct objects of sentences. In the case of:

(15)   The police chased the demonstrators

the projection rule would substitute the semantic representation assigned to 'the police' for the highest variable occurrence in (14) and the semantic representation assigned to 'the demonstrators' for all the other variable occurrences in (14).

The angles below a categorized variable contain a constraint on the substitution of semantic representations. Unlike (15), in the case of:

(16)   Truth chased falsehood

we do not want the semantic representations of the subject and direct object to project. If they do, the sentence (16) will receive a semantic representation, and in accord with $(\mathbf{D}_6)$, it will be marked as fully meaningful in the language. Thus, constraints are required to block the assignment of semantic representations to constituents like (16) that are semantically deviant. Such constraints take the form of conditions on the semantic marker content of semantic representations that are replacements for a variable. For example, the concept of a chase is one in which the agent and the recipient of the action are inherently spatio-temporal particulars, and, hence, when abstractions like truth and falsehood are expressed by the senses of the subject and direct object, there is no sense of the whole sentence deriving from their combination.[12] Accordingly, we want to construct the semantic marker for 'chase' with conditions that restrict substitution to just those semantic representations of subjects and objects that contain the semantic marker '(Physical)'. Such conditions would block substitution of the semantic representations of 'truth' and 'falsehood' in the case of (16), but allow substitution of the semantic representations of 'the police' and 'the demonstrators', since the latter contain the semantic marker '(Physical)' to account, *inter alia*, for the meaningfulness of sentences like 'The fat policeman jumped on and crushed the demonstrator'.

Such conditions on substitution, called *selection restrictions* (see Katz, 1972, pp. 89–98), not only make it possible to distinguish fully meaningful sentences like (15) from deviant sentences like (16), but, in so doing, they provide a general filtering mechanism for blocking semantic combinations that makes it possible to account for the actual degree of ambiguity of sentences under $(\mathbf{D}_6)$–$(\mathbf{D}_8')$. In actuality, the number of senses of morphemes runs, on the average, between five to ten, while the number of senses possible for, say, a twenty-word sentence, runs, on the average, well into the hundreds. Since the actual degree of ambiguity of a sentence is far less than the degree on sheer combinatorial grounds there has to be severe filtering at work in the formation of sentence meanings from the meanings of their parts. To see that selection restrictions meet this need, note that semantic deviance is just the extreme case where the filtering mechanism spares nothing: meaninglessness is just zero degrees of ambiguity. Thus, the same filtering mechanism, operating in less extreme cases spares some combinations and not others, giving rise to senses with degree of ambiguity from 1 to n. Hence, if the dictionary is set up properly, the projection rule will assign sets of semantic representations to sentences in such a way that (D_6)–(D_8') predict the meaningful ones, the meaningless ones, the ambiguous ones, and the synonymous ones.

We come now to the question of how a notation scheme consisting of semantic markers enables us to define the further semantic properties and relations of superordination, analyticity, and analytic entailment. Frege suggests that his rejection of the Kantian notion of analyticity in favor of the broader notion of logical truth is justified by two shortcomings of the Kantian notion of the containment of a predicate concept in the subject concept, namely, the metaphorical character of containment and the restriction of analyticity to subject-predicate sentences (see Frege, 1953, pp. 99–102). These grounds for abandoning Kant's notion have been echoed down to the present. Quine, for example, uses both to motivate his taking analyticity to be, potentially, a class of logical truths (Quine, 1953, p. 21). But neither Frege nor his followers have established that the replacement of the containment notion of analyticity with the notion of truths that follow from laws of logic plus definitions (but no assumptions from special sciences) (see Frege, 1953, pp. 3–4), does not simply replace one form of *a priori* truth by a different one (Katz, 1986a, pp. 52–97).

What they need to show, but have not, is that their notion of logical truth is a better formulation of the *same* notion or replaces an *inadequate* notion. By themselves, the cited shortcomings mean nothing. Instead of taking them as deep difficulties calling for abandonment of the Kantian notion, these shortcomings might just as well be taken as nothing more than temporary features of the sort that one naturally expects in any as yet unexplicated notion.

Therefore, the task for us is to show that both shortcomings are just such temporary features of the Kantian notion and disappear once this notion is explicated within semantic theory, and that the notion of analyticity resulting from such an explication is both a legitimate and distinct form of *a priori* truth. It is clear that the first shortcoming disappears if the second does, since the availability of formal descriptions of sense structure in semantic theory enables us to replace the metaphor of containment with a precise inclusion relation, provided a broad enough one can be stated. Thus, we have to show that descriptions in the form of semantic markers like (14) enable us to construct a definition of analyticity that covers analytic non-subject-predicate sentences as well as analytic subject-predicate sentences.

What are the analytic non-subject-predicate sentences that need to be covered? Frege and his followers stack the deck in favor of their proposal to replace analyticity with logical truth by citing cases of logical truths like

'If John is a bachelor, then John is a bachelor or John is rich'. But, in fact, sentences like:

(17)   John walks with those with whom he strolls

are the intuitively natural counterparts of analytic subject-predicate sentences. This observation puts the question in a new form: How do we formulate a condition (in terms of the formal relations in semantic representations) that captures analytic transitive verb sentences like (17) as well as analytic subject-predicate sentences like (12)?

Once we have an example like (17) in front of us, we can see that the concept of containment in the Kantian notion is not essentially a matter of the subject-predicate form of a sentence like (12). Rather what is essential to the Kantian notion, what makes (17) an intuitively natural counterpart of (12), is that the components of the meaning of an analytic sentence which pick out the object(s) it is about already contain the component of its meaning that expresses the attribution it makes to these object(s). In the case of a subject-predicate sentence, the component of the meaning which picks out the object(s) the sentence is about is the sense of the subject; in the case of a transitive verb sentence, there is more than one component of the meaning which picks out the object(s) the sentence is about, the sense of the subject, direct object, etc. Clearly, the general consideration for analyticity is that at least one of the components of the meaning of the sentence that picks out the object(s) it is about include the component that expresses the property or relation it attributes to them.

Because semantic markers mirror the relations between components of sense structures in formal relations between marker parts, it is a straightforward matter to state such a general condition within semantic theory. Without considering all of the details of this explication, we can convey the basic idea as follows. The concept expressing the attribution of a sentence is represented by a skeletal semantic marker like (14) whose occurrences of categorized variables have not yet been replaced by semantic representations. The components of the meaning of the sentence that pick out the object(s) the sentence is about are represented by the semantic representations that substitute for these occurrences in the projection process. Since both the components picking out the domain of attribution and the components expressing the attribution are formalized in the above tree notion, the formal explication of our general condition for the analyticity of (a sense of) a sentence is that the semantic representation into which such substitutions are made be a subtree of a semantic representation that is substituted into it.[13]

The formalization of the conditions for superordination and analytic entailment are essentially the same. The sense of one expression is superordinate to the sense of another just in case the semantic representation of the latter is a subtree of the semantic representation of the former; and the sense of one sentence analytically entails the sense of another just in case the semantic representation of the latter is a subtree of the semantic representation of the former. To provide an illustration, suppose that the semantic representation for the verb 'follow' is (15): Then (15)

(18)

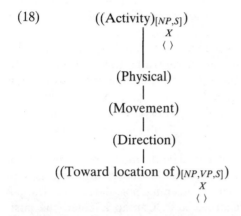

is predicted. correctly, as analytically entailing the sentence:

(19)   The police followed the demonstrators

on the appropriate senses of these sentences.

Having shown how to overcome both of the shortcomings in Kant's notion of analyticity, we must now show that the notion explicated constitutes a *legitimate* form of *a priori* truth and also that it is *distinct* from logical truth and logical implication.

Establishing legitimacy requires showing that the analyticity of a sentence and the analytic entailment of one sentence by another can be determined without knowledge of states of affairs in the world, and further, that the analyticity of a sentence is a sufficient condition for the statement it makes to be true (in all worlds where the object(s) it is about exists) and that the analytic entailment of one sentence by another is a sufficient condition for the entailed sentence to be true whenever the entailing sentence is.

Given how analyticity and analytic entailment have been explicated, determining that a sentence is analytic or that one sentence analytically entails another is entirely a matter of reasoning from intuitive judgments about the semantic properties and relations of their constituents. Since such judgments concern only the structure of senses and the intragrammatical relations between senses and constituents and not relations between language and the world, the determination of analyticity and analytic entailment is *a priori*. Furthermore, since what is determined in determining analyticity is that the conditions expressing what the sentence is about include the condition for the attribution to be true, and since what is determined in determining analytic entailment is that the truth conditions of the entailed sentence are included in the truth conditions of the entailing sentence, analyticity is sufficient for truth (in all worlds where the object(s) the sentence is about exists) and analytic entailment is sufficient for the truth of the entailed sentence in all worlds where the entailing sentence is true.

Establishing distinctness requires showing that there is a genuinely logical difference between analytic truths and logical truths and between analytic entailments and logical entailments. A complete argument for distinctness would first establish the proof-theoretic difference and then exhibit the corresponding model-theoretic difference. The task of exhibiting the model-theoretic difference is beyond the scope of this discussion and will be presented elsewhere.[14]

Frege's notions of logical truth and logical implication provide an account of inferences like (15) to (19) only when the underlying logic is supplemented with an appropriate set of meaning postulates (see Carnap 1956). In order to provide such an account, Carnap adapted the post-ulational treatment of logical implication in predicate calculus to the broader class of implications based on the extra-logical vocabulary by introducing meaning postulates in analogy to logical postulates. Predicate calculi were thus expanded, first, by the addition of an infinite list of designations which serve as individual and predicate constants in the regimentation of sentences from natural languages containing extralogical vocabulary, and second, by the addition of a finite list of new postulates, expressed as formulas of first-order logic but employing such designations. Such postulates restrict the class of admissible models for a calculus in the same way as the logical postulates. An inference like (15) to (19) is accounted for in terms of a meaning postulate like:

$$(20) \quad (x)(y)(C_{x,y} \supset F_{x,y}),$$

where C and F are the designations that regiment 'chase' and 'follow', respectively.

The claim that analytic entailment is a special case of logical implication in Frege's sense can be put as the claim that this meaning postulate account of inferences like (15) to (19) is correct in taking analytic entailments to be continuous with first-order implications generally. But there is the striking discontinuity that a first-order implication has to be justified on the basis of principles of deduction which sanction the step from premiss(es) to conclusion (as one that never leads from truth to falsehood), whereas an analytic entailment requires no such justification. Such a justification is required in the case of logical implications by virtue of the character of the truth conditions associated with the premiss(es) and conclusion of them: the truth conditions of the conclusion are not explicit parts of the truth conditions of the premisses. Thus, the satisfaction of the truth conditions of the conclusion must be shown to obtain whenever the truth conditions of the premiss(es) are satisfied by subsuming the relation between them under a principle, like *modus ponens*, which exhibits the satisfaction of the former as a necessary consequence of the satisfaction of the latter. Analytic entailments, in contrast, require no such justification because the truth conditions of the conclusion *are* an explicit part of the truth conditions of the premiss. Thus, there is no deductive step from premiss to conclusion that makes it necessary to appeal to a principle of logic. Satisfaction of the truth conditions of the premiss is in itself satisfaction of the truth conditions of the conclusion: the latter is not merely a necessary consequence of the former.

This difference can be illustrated using Lewis Carroll's philosophical fable about Achilles and the Tortoise (Carroll, 1936, pp. 1225–1229). The Tortoise's strategy is to challenge Achilles each time he tries to infer a conclusion on the grounds that the principle sanctioning the inference has not yet been written down in Achilles' book of accepted truths. The case in the fable is a Euclidean proof, but we may illustrate the Tortoise's strategy in the case at hand. Let (15) be (A), (20) be (B), and (19) be the elusive conclusion (Z). Achilles reasons that if (A) and (B) are true, then (by *modus ponens*) so is (Z). The Tortoise points out that the principle invoked to sanction the inference has not yet been written down in the book. Achilles dutifully writes it down as (C), thinking that he has done what is required. As Lewis Carroll has Achilles remark at this point, referring to the conclusion,

'You should call it D, not Z. It comes *next* to the other three. If you accept A and B and C, you *must* accept Z.'

But, again, the Tortoise resorts to his strategy. Lewis Carroll has him query, 'And why *must* I?' To which Achilles, not yet realizing his situation, replies,

'Because it follows *logically* from them. If A and B and C are true, Z *must* be true. You don't dispute *that* I imagine?'

"If A and B and C are true, Z *must* be true . . . that's *another* hypothetical, isn't it? And, if I failed to see its truth, I might accept A and B and C, and *still* not accept Z, mightn't I?'

Lewis Carroll concludes this dialogue

'You might', the candid hero admitted; 'though such obtuseness would certainly be phenomenal. Still, the event is *possible*. So, I must ask you to grant one more hypothetical.'

'Very good. I'm willing to grant it, as soon as you've written it down.'

Now, I wish to compare this with a fable of my own. Again, (15) is (A) and (19) is (Z). But in my fable Achilles had once time traveled to the twentieth century where he acquired the rudiments of semantic theory. Reviewing the conditions of the contest proposed by the Tortoise, my Achilles says,

> I'm to force you to accept Z, am I? And your present position is that you accept A. I may write A down in my book. Well, in that case force isn't necessary. For, you see, having written down A, Z, too, is written down! When you asked in our previous contest what else I had written down in my book, all I could reply was, 'Only a few memoranda of the battles in which I have distinguished myself.' But, now, after my visit to the future, I see that I can reply, 'Z'. Surely you won't balk because I've written A and Z in markerese which won't be invented for some two thousand years.

What is the nature of the difference between treating an inference like (15) to (19) as an analytic entailment and treating it as first-order implication in an applied predicate calculus with meaning postulates like (20)? Treating an inference as an analytic entailment explains its validity in terms of the meanings of the sentences: the use of descriptions exhibits the meaning of the premiss and conclusion in fine enough detail to show that the truth conditions of the latter are part of the truth conditions of the former. Treating an inference as a first-order deduction with a meaning postulate as a further premiss makes no claim about a semantic source of its validity. Being constructed with designations, meaning postulates do not describe meaning at all. They state an extensional condition but not one reflecting meaning relations. Such a condition, being a restriction on admissible models, may reflect any relations that hold in all possible worlds, for example, mathematical relations like that between being the number two and being the only even prime or metaphysical relations like being an event and having a cause. The name 'Meaning postulate' is a misnomer! Such statements express a relation between the extensions of the predicate-designations that they contain, but they do not make an explanatory link between the extensional relation and the meaning of the premiss and conclusion. Indeed, such a link is impossible in semantic theories containing a notation scheme with only designations.

In effect, we have just presented one example of how a theory of meaning, because of the greater explanatory power afforded by a notation of descriptions (in the form of semantic markers), can throw light on problems in the philosophy of logic and language. Another problem on which this theory sheds light is the problem of deciding what the categories of our conceptual system are. It has been a persistent complaint about systems of categories like Aristotle's that they retain an arbitrary character as long as there is no rational basis for judging one way of arranging the objects of thought as preferable to others. Kant complained in the *Prolegomena* that in the case of Aristotle's categories

> . . . we are not able to give a reason why each language has just this and no other formal constitution, and still less why any precise number of such formal determinations in general, neither more nor less, can be found in it. . . . This rhapsody must be considered (and commended) as a mere hint for future inquirers, not as an ideal developed according to rule; and hence it has, in the present more advanced state of philosophy, been rejected as quite useless.

Kant's own explanation of why each language has just the formal constitution of the Kantian categories and no other was that these categories are the conceptual means by which our understanding imposes order on the impressions we receive of things in themselves. But this rationale is too deeply embedded in his theory of mind to be an acceptable basis for comparing the ways different philosophical theories arrange the objects of thought. Furthermore, it offers no methodological basis for discovering the categories in natural languages.

Such a basis is available within a semantic theory of the kind we have described (see the discussion in Katz, 1966, pp. 224–239). Recall that a semantic theory is a metatheory consisting of a notation scheme and definitions and that the theories in question are semantic components of grammars (dictionaries, pairings of morphemes of a language with semantic representations of their senses). Lexical semantic representations will have to contain a distinct semantic marker for each component concept into which the sense it represents breaks down. For example, the sense of the noun 'chair' will have to be assigned a semantic representation containing the semantic markers '(Object)', '(Physical)', '(Artifact)', and '(Furniture)', among others. Such marker content is necessary to predict the analyticity of sentences like 'Chairs are physical objects', 'Chairs are artifacts', and 'Chairs are furniture'. Similarly, the dictionary representation for related words like 'table', 'bench', 'stool', etc, will have to contain these same four semantic markers. Further, on the same considerations, the dictionary representation of morphemes like 'truck', 'automobile', 'bus', etc., will contain the semantic markers '(Object)' '(Physical)', '(Artifact)', and '(Vehicle)'. Thus, we find the same pattern, in which the semantic markers '(Object)' and '(Physical)' are found whenever the semantic marker '(Artifact)' occurs, repeated in one dictionary entry after another. This, moreover, is only a small fraction of the cases where such regularities appear: they exist on an enormous scale across the various entries of a dictionary and over the range of dictionaries for all natural languages.

From a methodological viewpoint, such regularities, since they are avoidable without loss in predictive power, constitute redundancy in the formulation of dictionaries. Dictionaries having such redundant semantic markers like '(Object)' and '(Physical)' are stating facts about the occurrence of semantic markers separately for each semantic representation in which '(Artifact)' occurs when these facts could be stated just once. If, furthermore, they are stated just once, then the dictionary rule which states them will capture a generalization about lexical structure that the uneconomical dictionaries fail to capture.

Hence, methodological considerations force us to simplify the formulation of dictionaries by introducing rules that express such generalizations about lexical structure. In previous discussions (Katz, 1966, pp. 230–233; Katz, 1972, pp. 44f, 99), we have, accordingly, expanded semantic theory to contain *redundancy rules*, rules of the form '$(M_i) \rightarrow (M_j)$' which are interpreted to say that if the semantic marker '(M_i)' appears in a semantic representation, then the semantic marker '(M_j)' also appears in it.

Now, putting aside methodological considerations, let us look at the generalizations that redundancy rules express. It is clear that the generalization expressed by the redundancy rule '(Artifact) → (Object)' holds because the concept of an artifact is subordinate to the concept of an object. That is, the concept of an artifact arises from the more abstract concept of an object when this concept is qualified as coming into existence as a product designed to serve a function. Since individual redundancy rules express superordination relations between two concepts, chains of redundancy rules of the form:

$$(21) \quad (M_1) \rightarrow (M_2), (M_2) \rightarrow (M_3), \ldots, (M_{n-1}) \rightarrow (M_n)$$

express a transitive 'less abstract than' relation for concepts. More importantly, if (21) is a maximal chain with respect to a complete set of redundancy rules for semantic theory, then (M_n) is maximally abstract. If, therefore, there are k maximal chains with respect to a complete set of redundancy rules, the set of terminal members of these k chains, viz, $(M_{n_1}), (M_{n_2}), \ldots, (M_{n_k})$, are maximally abstract.

The maximally abstract logical divisions in the sense system of natural language—the concepts represented by the semantic markers (M_{n_1}), $(M_{n_2}), \ldots, (M_{n_k})$—are a plausible explication of the notion 'categories of language'. The explication clearly satisfies our original demand for a nonarbitrary way of arriving at a set of categories that plays no favorites among philosophical theories, for the considerations that motivate the adoption of redundancy rules, apart from the predictive adequacy of the semantic representations, are just a matter of the simplicity of theories.

Consider next the question of how to state the conditions for inferences by substitution into opaque contexts. It is clear that simple referential theories of meaning like Russell's and Davidson's stand no chance of capturing the cases where such inferences go through, namely, cases like the inference from (22) to (23):

(22) Simon believes that his daughter will marry an adult unmarried human male

(23) Simon believes that his daughter will marry a bachelor.

Hence, their supporters have denied the legitimacy of such inferences, usually appealing to Quinian skepticism on meaning to criticize the synonymy relation on which the inferences depend (see Quine, 1960, pp. 141–156, 206–221). This shortcoming of simple referential theories has prompted possible world semanticists to claim that their theory enjoys an advantage because it does not have to flatly claim that there are no valid inferences by substitution into opaque contexts (see Hintikka, 1969). But it is clear that, since coextensitivity in all possible worlds does not adequately reconstruct synonymy, possible world semantics cannot completely capture this class of inferences. Possible world semantics cannot systematically distinguish between cases like the valid inference (22) to (23) and cases like the invalid inference (24) to (25):

(24) Simon believes that Ali has seven wives

(25) Simon believes that Ali has a number of wives equal to the even prime plus the square root of twenty five.

It is thought by those who reject both Quine's criticisms of meaning and the possible worlds semanticist's reconstruction of these inferences that Frege's account of such inference solves all our problems. But this thought is mistaken. The same difficulties we found above with Frege's theory of sense prevent it from providing a satisfactory account of inference by substitution into opaque contexts. I will first explain why this is and then show how semantic theory can provide a satisfactory account.

Frege thought that if he were to make senses the reference of expressions and sentences in opaque contexts, he could characterize both the conditions for inferences by substitution into such contexts and the conditions for inference by substitution into transparent contexts as coreferentiality of the expression or sentence substituted and the expression or sentence substituted for (Frege, 1952a, pp. 64f). In effect, if we substitute an expression or sentence for one that is synonymous with it, then the sentence resulting from the substitution follows validly from the sentence into which the substitution was made. This principle nicely distinguishes cases of valid inference like (22) to (23) from cases of invalid inferences like (24) to (25), and because of the vast improvement that this represents in comparison with previous theories, it has been concluded, erroneously, that Frege's account is adequate in general.

But Frege's principle fails to capture an indefinitely large class of valid inferences that a sense theorist is committed to accepting (see Katz, 1972, pp. 261–292). For example, assuming, it is valid to infer (23) from (22), it must also be valid to infer (27) from (26):

(26)   Simon believes that his daughter will marry a bachelor.
(27)   Simon believes that his daughter will marry someone unmarried.

Yet Frege's principle does not apply to cases where the expression or sentence substituted and the expression or sentence substituted for it are nonsynonymous. Moreover, it is clear that the relations required to handle such cases are superordination and analytic entailment, and, as we have already shown, Frege does not have the apparatus required to handle these relations (see Katz, 1986b).

We have the apparatus and so can formulate the condition for such inferences, but some care is needed in formulating it. If we formulate it in the way Frege formulates his, as a condition on the expression or sentence substituted and the expression or sentence substituted for, we shall run into trouble with 'hyperopaque verbs' (Katz, 1986b, pp. 59–91). Even though the embedded sentence of:

(28)   Simon doubts that his daughter will marry a bachelor

analytically entails the embedded sentence of:

(29)   Simon doubts that his daughter will marry a male

the inference from (28) to (29) is not valid. Simon's suspicions may only concern bigamy.

Hyperopaque verbs have meanings that operate at the verb phrase level in the compositional process whereby the meaning of the full sentence is formed from the meanings of its parts to change the object of the propositional attitude from the proposition expressed by the sentence occurring in the context of the verb. Thus, a Fregean condition for inference by substitution fails in the case of analytically entailed sentences in hyperopaque contexts because the object of the propositional attitude (expressed by the verb creating the context) is determined at a level higher than that at which the condition applies. There is a negative operator in the meaning of the hyperopaque verb 'doubts' that changes the object of doubt from the sense of the sentence substituted to something like the proposition that Simon questions whether his daughter will marry an adult or questions whether his daughter will marry a single person or questions whether his daughter will marry a male. Having neglected the details of the compositional process, Frege formulates his condition for such substitutional inferences as a condition on the pair of the sentence substituted and the sentence it substitutes for. The condition thus applies too early in the compositional process to consider all the semantic relations within the sentences that determine whether one follows validly from the other.

To provide a better account than Frege's, we have to formulate our condition for these inferences at a high enough point in the compositional process to guarantee that the condition will miss no semantic operations on which implications of a sentence depend. The surest way to do this is to formulate the condition to apply to full sentences. This, moreover, has the further advantage that it is now unnecessary to construct a special substitution principle. The definition of analytic entailment, which applies to full sentences, already provides the principle we require. The definition not only handles cases like the inference from (22) to (23) which Frege's principle handles (but the principles of referential theories do not) and cases like the inference from (26) to (27) which Frege's principle does not handle, but, in addition, the definition correctly treats cases of invalid inferences like that from (28) to (29). Because the definition of analytic entailment applies to the semantic representations of full sentences, it applies after all compositional operations have taken place, and, hence, in a case like the invalid inference from (28) to (29), it can take account of the compositional operations which prevent the sentences from meeting the condition for analytic entailment.

The ability of semantic theory to adequately state the conditions for inference by substitution into opaque contexts is not just a matter of following Frege in recognizing sense as well as reference but a matter of going beyond Frege in introducing a notation of descriptions which makes it possible to treat the aspects of sense structure that are involved in all cases of the compositional formulation of sentence meaning (see Katz 1986b).

Q: What you have been saying might be alright in theory, but is there any practical pay-off for the semantic description of natural languages?

A: I will try to show that a decompositional semantic theory of modification in natural languages provides a better descriptive pay-off than nondecompositional semantic theories.[15] The special character of decompositional semantics is that it bases its account of compositional meaning on the structure revealed in analyses of the senses of syntactic simples.

This, I shall argue, enables decompositional semantics to succeed in the description of modification where nondecompositional semantic approaches fail. The reason, as will become clear below, is that exposing the complex sense structure of syntactic simples provides the elements required to state the laws governing the contribution of the meaning of modifiers to the meaning of their heads. Theories which do not take decompositional sense structure into account lack the elements required to state these laws.

Non-decompositional theories base their treatment of the semantics of natural languages on applied predicate logics, so that predicate constants correspond directly to the syntactic simples of a language. On such theories, it is a logical fact that English has one syntactic element 'starve,' denoting the concept of dying from lack of food, but no corresponding syntactic element for the concept of dying from lack of water. In contrast, a decompositional theory claims that the lack of correspondence is a historical accident with no semantic significance. Further, non-decompositional theories cannot properly distinguish between sentences like 'the nurse injected the medicine painstakingly,' and 'the nurse injected the medicine painlessly.' Although the adverbials are syntactically alike, they are quite different semantically: one adverbial refers to the manner in which the injection was administered; the other refers to the sensation that the injection caused in the recipient. In representing the sense of 'inject' as a complex concept of a process whereby an agent forces a liquid into the body of a recipient, a decompositional theory provides formal apparatus to distinguish the way the action of forcing is done from the effects of the forcing on the recipient. Exposing semantic structure thus enables us to describe how sentences take modification in different ways. It also gives a more comprehensive account of compositional structure. The meanings combined to form the meaning of syntactic complexes are now the semantic elements in the decompositional structure of syntactic simples.

The most problematic aspect of current treatments of modification is how the meaning of attributives operate on the meaning of their heads. There is no acceptable solution to this problem within any framework that does not expose decompositional structure. Davidson addresses the problem in 'The logical form of action sentences':

> Susan says, 'I crossed the channel in fifteen hours.' 'Good grief, that was slow.' . . . Now Susan adds, 'But I swam.' 'Good grief, that was fast.' We do not withdraw the claim that it was a slow crossing; this is consistent with its being a fast swimming. Here we have enough to show, I think, that we cannot construe 'It was a slow crossing' as 'It was slow and it was a crossing' since the crossing may also be a swimming and it was not slow, in which case we would have 'It was slow and it was a crossing and it was a swimming and it was not slow.' The problem is not peculiar to talk of actions, however. It appears equally when we try to explain the logical role of the attributive adjectives in 'Grundy

was a short basketball player, but a tall man,' and 'This is a good memento of the murder but a poor steak knife.' The problem of attributives is indeed a problem about logical form, but it may be put to one side here because it is not a problem only when the subject is action. (Davidson, 1967, p. 82)

As Davidson points out, Grundy would be short and tall, and the knife poor and good. Davidson sees no way to handle such attributive modifications in his system, but he recognizes that an account of modification must at some point come to grips with them. He thus shelves the problem of attributives on the grounds that it goes beyond the study of action sentences. But it is hard to see why the fact that the problem is more general than Davidson's chosen topic should be a reason for ignoring it in an explanation of the semantics of action sentences. Examples like 'Grundy shoots baskets well but too poorly to play pro ball' show that the same 'logical inconsistencies' appear in adverbial modification as well. Moreover, why should the generality of the problem be grounds putting it to one side when it threatens to demolish Davidson's theory of action sentences?

Before we look at how a decompositional theory handles the 'attributive paradox' in cases of adjectival modification, we should review the manner in which semantic markers represent complex structures of senses. Semantic markers, like phrase markers, are complex formal symbols whose orthography represents complex grammatical structure under conventions which interpret the representation relation. Semantic markers take the form of tree structures with labelled nodes, like phrase markers, but the branching structure represents sense qualification rather than syntactic subcategorization. A semantic marker of the form (M) represents a complex concept c^* as being built up out of the component concepts $c_1, \ldots, c_n$ and

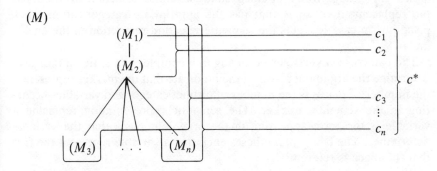

the qualification relations among them. If we were to adopt Aristotle's concept of being human as the sense of the word 'human,' then c^* would be this concept, and the constituent branch structures shown in (M) would represent the concept's internal structure. c_1 would be the concept of a physical object, c_2 the concept of being an animal, and c_3 the concept of being rational. The concept of an animal is formed by qualifying the concept of a physical object, and the concept of a rational animal from qualifying the concept of an animal. The superordinate relations among the concepts $c_1, \ldots, c_n$ and hence, derivatively, between the English words 'physical object,' 'animal,' and 'rational animal' that express them, are given by the branching braced in (M): c_1 is superordinate to c_2, c_2 superordinate to c_3, . . ., c_{n-1}, and c_n; but, for example, $c_3, \ldots, c_{n-1}$, and c_n are not superordinate to one another.[16]

Component semantic markers in a complex semantic representation can be of the form (M), where the *categorized variables* written to the right and slightly below '(M_i)' formally relate the senses of subjects, direct objects, etc, to the sense of a verb, verb phrase, etc, in whose representation '(M_i)' occurs. These variables are substitution symbols to be replaced by semantic representations of subjects, direct objects, etc, in applications of the projection principle. The categorizations appearing in brackets over the variable are syntactic or semantic symbols that pick out semantic representations to replace the variable. For example, if F_i is the grammatical function [NP,S], then semantic representations of the subject of the sentence can replace the categorized variable, and if F_i is the semantic function for the agent concept, then semantic representations of the particular agent concept in the sense of the sentence can replace the categorized variable. The projection principle says that a semantic representation R can replace an occurrence of a categorized variable V only if R has the syntactic or semantic categorization expressed in the function F_i of V. The angles under the categorized variables state semantic selection restrictions: the replacement of an R that has the appropriate categorization takes place just in case R meets the semantic selection restriction in the angles under V.

The categorized variables occurring in a complex semantic marker also determine the argument places of the predicate that the marker represents: the number of places is the number of distinct categorized variables occurring in the semantic marker. The semantic representation replacing a variable is the term appearing in the argument place that the variable determines. The heavy parentheses enclosing a variable represent the fact that the place is referential.

We can now turn to the 'attributive paradox' in the case of adjectival modification. We may work with the example appearing in Davidson's discussion quoted above, namely (30).

(30) This a good memento of the murder but a poor steak knife.

We take the sense structure of 'memento' and 'knife' to be roughly as represented by the semantic markers (31) and (32), respectively.[17]

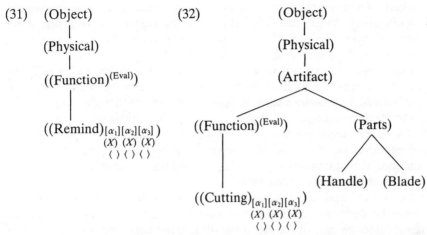

The evaluation is left undetermined by the meaning of 'memento' and 'knife', though it is determined in the case of a noun like 'bonanza.' The evaluation in sentences like 'that's a good knife,' 'that's a bad knife,' etc., is provided by attributive adjectives when their sense combines with the sense of nouns to form the sense of a complex noun phrase. thus, the (Eval) node is left unspecified in the dictionary entry for nouns such as 'knife' and 'memento.' The projection rule introduces the values provided by the adjectives into representations of the decompositional structure of the nouns. The structures of the complex noun phrases of (30), 'good memento' and 'poor knife,' are represented by (31') and (32'), respectively.

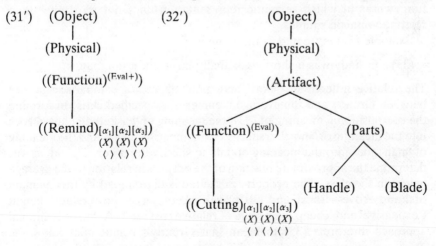

(31′) represents a positive evaluation of the referent of 'this' in (30), saying that it adequately serves to remind. (32′) represents a negative evaluation of the referent of 'this' in (30), saying that it does an inadequate job of cutting. As (31′) and (32′) do not display semantic markers from the same antonymous n-tuple[18] immediately dominated by the same node, their conjunction does not represent an inconsistent sense.

Our treatment explains why concepts devoid of either function or other aspects susceptible to evaluation cannot be combined with evaluative attributives. Expressions such as 'good height' or 'good width' are semantically deviant without a contextually supplied standard of evaluation because the decompositional structures of 'height' and 'width' do not contain an evaluation concept. They become fully meaningful only when a standard of evaluation is supplied, as in 'good height for playing basketball' and 'good height for a coal miner.'

'Memento' and 'knife' have different sense structures since a memento is not be definition an artifact or something having parts. The marker (Eval) forms part of the representation of the decompositional structure of the nouns, figuring as a superscript within the representation of the element specifying the standard of evaluation. Its placement within the (Function) node captures an important fact about the semantic nature of nouns: the senses of 'knife' and 'memento' express evaluations only in terms of knifes and mementos having a function, not in terms of knives or mementos being physical objects or having parts. Thus, 'that's a good knife' means that the knife cuts well, and 'that's a good memento' means that the memento adequately reminds. Hence, there is no inconsistency in (30) because the two adjectives operate on different elements in the sense structure of the nouns. The appearance of inconsistency is an artifact of frameworks in which semantic representation does not go deeper than relating syntactic simples.

Example (33) is treated in the same way.

(33)   Grundy was a short basketball player but a tall man.

The relative adjectives, 'short' and 'tall,' express a comparison in size between Grundy and the average member of a specified class. In forming the compositional meaning of (33), the meaning of 'basketball player' goes into the meaning of 'short' to specify one comparison class, and the meaning of 'man' goes into the meaning of 'tall' to specify the other. The adjectives determine the approximate position of the subjects in relation to the average height in the class. The property measured is determined by the meaning of the adjective—'short' and 'tall' place concepts on a scale of relative height ('expensive' and 'cheap' on a scale of relative cost, etc). A decompositional approach interprets (33) to mean that Grundy's height falls below the height of the average basketball player and exceeds the height of the average man. Since the property of height acquires different evaluations depending on whether it is measured relative to the category of men or to the category of basketball players, the relative nature of the modifiers would be lost, without the decompositional structure of the nouns that provides the contrasting categories.

We have sketched how a decompositional approach treats adjectival modification. My aim is to extend this treatment to adverbial modification. A semantic theory of modification must cover both, since the phenomenon of modification is a uniform one. Indeed, many noun–adjective combinations can be paraphrased with verbs and adverbs. 'This is a good knife,' for example, is synonymous with 'this knife cuts well.'

Q: Would you make the extension to the adverbial case in relation to Davidson's treatment of action sentences?

A: I will consider the treatment of adverbials within two non-decompositional theories, namely, that of Davidson and that of Thomason and Stalnaker.[19] We show that the apparatus in such theories gives rise to problems in the case of adverbial modification similar to those just discussed in connection with adjectival modification. In the final section we show how a decompositional theory can solve these problems for adverbials in the same manner that it solves them for adjectivals.

In 'The logical form of action sentences,' Davidson seeks 'to give an account of the logical or grammatical role of the parts or words of [action] sentences that is consistent with the entailment relations between such sentences and with what is known of the role of those same parts or words in other non-action sentences' (Davidson, 1967, p. 81). The emphasis is on action verbs and their adverbial modifiers. Davidson classifies adverbial modifiers into three categories. The first class contains adverbials which impute intention, such as 'deliberately.' This class of adverbials operates on noun phrases that specify the agent. The second class contains attributive adverbials, like 'slowly,' modify the verb's specification of an action. Davidson dismisses this class from his discussion for the reasons mentioned in the above remarks. The third class includes adverbials denoting time, place, and instrument. Davidson develops a detailed notation to represent the role of this class in the logical form of action sentences.

Davidson begins by looking at nominalizations and pronominalizations of action verbs. How can 'it' be represented in the logical form of 'Jones did it'? In Davidson's example, 'it' represents the buttering of a piece of toast, but in a standard account of such sentences there will be no argument place for the singular term expressing the event of buttering. Davidson's solution is to posit an extra argument place for events. The logical form of every action sentence now contains one more argument place than it might seem to contain. For example, 'kicked' is a three-place predicate with a kicker, a kickee, and a kicking. This notation, as Davidson shows, can capture a number of entailment relations.

But there are some putative entailment relations that the notation does not capture because the notation is based on the standard restriction of logical vocabulary to logical particles. Davidson rejects any liberalization of logical vocabulary that would include elements that emerge on a meaning analysis, such as the factive element in the sense of 'know.' He writes:

> Admittedly there is something arbitrary in how much of logic to pin on logical form. But limits are set if our interest is in giving a coherent and constructive account of meaning: we must uncover enough structure to make it possible to state, for an arbitrary sentence, how its meaning depends on that structure, and we must not attribute more structure than such a theory of meaning can accommodate. (Davidson, 1967, p. 82)

This is a purely theory-internal argument for specifying which elements contribute to the logical form of sentences. The argument suggests that the semantics of natural language be tailored to fit into standard logic. But why should a theory of meaning for natural languages be arbitrarily limited by the structures of an artificial system?[20] The linguistic issue cannot be how much a particular theory can accommodate, but how much there is in the language to be accommodated. If a theory is too weak to accommodate what is in the language, then the theory should be changed. Taken to its logical conclusion, Davidson's style of argument would justify any theory, no matter how weak.

Owing to his theoretical framework, Davidson has to claim that meaning analysis of syntactic simples plays no role in the logical form of sentences. He writes:

> I am not concerned with the meaning analysis of logically simple expressions in so far as this goes beyond the question of logical form. Applied to the case at hand, for example, I am not concerned with the meaning of 'deliberately' as opposed, perhaps, to 'voluntarily'; but I am interested in the logical role of both these words. (Davidson, 1967, p. 81)

The claim is that the logical role of both of these adverbials is solely to denote intention. Other adverbials denoting intention, such as 'maliciously', would presumably share the logical role of 'voluntarily' and 'deliberately'. Thus, the principle entailments Davidson can derive from his representation of the logical form of 'Jones did it maliciously' are ones such that Jones's doing it was intentional. Other entailments, such as that 'maliciously' entails evil intention, cannot be derived.

The exclusion of decompositional analysis from his theory forces Davidson into a contradiction:

we need not view the difference between 'Joe believes that there is life on Mars' and 'Joe knows that there is life on Mars' as a difference in logical form. That the second, but not the first, entails 'there is life on Mars' is plausibly a logical truth; but it is a truth that emerges only when we consider the meaning analysis of 'believes' and 'knows'. (Davidson, 1967, p. 82)

Thus Davidson grants that the meaning difference between the syntactic simples 'believes' and 'knows' determines entailment differences. But this contradicts Davidson's claim that such entailment relations are independent of logical form. Since entailments, on Davidson's account, are supposed to reflect logical form or truth conditions, how can there be entailment differences which correspond to no difference in logical form or truth conditions? How is a logical truth based on 'believes' or 'knows' to be distinguished from ones based on 'is identical with'? (see Katz, 1976).

Davidson's theory claims that each action verb contains an extra argument place filled by the event variable x. Thus (34) has (35) as its logical form.

(34)   Jones buttered the toast in the bathroom with a knife at midnight.
(35) $(\exists x)$(buttered (Jones, toast, x))
       & (in (bathroom, x)) & (with (knife, x))
       & (at (midnight, x))

Davidson can now derive the entailment relations he wants, i.e.: Jones buttered the toast, and Jones buttered the toast with a knife, etc. But the derivation is made possible by introducing an argument place in the representation of action verbs, one which Davidson himself describes as a place 'that they do not appear to [contain]' (Davidson, 1967, p. 92). A decompositional theory, as we will show, can save the appearances. It can say that every action verb contains exactly the number of argument places that it appears to.

For the class of adverbial modifiers that impute intention, such as 'deliberately,' Davidson correctly claims that intentionality 'bears a special relation to the belief and attitudes of the agent . . . but does not mean that the agent is described as performing any further action (Davidson, 1967, pp. 94, 95). As the logical form for sentences with intentionality adverbials Davidson proposes 'It was intentional of x that p' (Davidson, 1967, p. 95). Yet Davidson would give different logical forms for verb structures that contain decompositional intentionality and for synonymous verb structures where intentionality is expressed by a syntactically independent adverbials. If an adverbial denoting intention is in construction with a verb, Davidson would represent intentionality in his account of logical form. If the concept of intention is included in the sense of a verb, then Davidson would not represent intentionality in the logical form. The synonymous sentences

'Jones killed himself intentionally' and 'Jones committed suicide' will be marked nonsynonymous because Davidson's theory gives them nonequivalent logical forms. Again, the view that meaning analysis of syntactic simples does not contribute to logical form turns a historical accident (whether intentionality is expressed in two words or one) into a logical fact.

A corresponding difficulty for Davidson is that sentences like (36) and (37) cannot be marked as inconsistent.

(36)   Grundy is a tall man and a midget.
(37)   Jones sipped his milk in one huge gulp.

A decompositional theory is needed to represent the concept of tallness in the sense of 'tall man' and the concept of shortness in the sense of 'midget' as joint predications. Finally, although Davidson's theory accounts for entailment relations like those from (38) to (39), and (39) to (40), it cannot account for ones like (40) to (41) because the semantic structure of syntactic simples is unavailable.

(38)   Jones sipped a glass of milk before going to bed.
(39)   Jones sipped a glass of milk.
(40)   Jones sipped.
(41)   Jones drank.

A decompositional theory accounts for entailments like (40) to (41) because it can represent the concept of 'drink in small quantities' as part of the sense of 'sip.'

In 'A Semantic Theory of Adverbs' Thomason and Stalnaker attempt to provide the foundations for 'a general semantic theory of adverbs (Thomason & Stalnaker, 1973, p. 196). They discard Davidson's theory as 'explicitly narrow in its scope [because] adverbs such as 'slowly', 'greedily', 'carefully' and 'intentionally' [are] excluded; and we suspect it may prove even more narrow than he anticipated' (Thomason & Stalnaker, 1973, p. 196). The authors feel that Davidson's theory fails to explain the ambiguities in sentences containing adverbials. They see the focus of a general theory of adverbials as representing ambiguities that rise from the scope of adverbials. Rejecting Davidson's use of the logical operator of conjunction to attach adverbials to predicates, they introduce a more powerful device of intensional logic—abstraction—to express scope differences. Using abstraction, they develop two or more formal representations for English sentences that contain both an adverbials and a complex predicate, that is, a predicate containing conjunction, disjunction, quantifers, etc.

Thomason and Stalnaker divide all adverbials into two categories on the basis of scope differences: *sentence modifiers*, whose scope includes the sentence as a whole, and *predicate modifiers*, whose scope includes the predicate only. The authors suggest four tests for assigning adverbials to these categories. An adverbial is a predicate modifier only if it fails all four tests and a sentence modifier if it passes at least one. Most adverbials in English turn out to be sentence modifiers on these tests.

Thomason and Stalnaker discuss the scope of adverbials in sentences containing complex predicates in connection with examples like (42):

(42)   Reluctantly, John bought gas and changed the oil.

They claim that such sentences have two different readings and are therefore ambiguous. On one reading of (42), the scope of the adverbials is distributive over the conjunction, and the sentence can be paraphrased as 'John reluctantly bought gas and John reluctantly changed the oil.' On the second reading, the scope of the adverbial is collective, and the sentence can be explained as 'it was doing both that John disliked—say, because it cost too much—while he was not reluctant to do either separately.'

The authors claim that 'such formal differences of scope frequently correspond to distinctions with which speakers of English are familiar and which are expressed in English in a variety of ways' (Thomason & Stalnaker, 1973, pp. 199–200). This may be so; nonetheless, these two readings do not correspond to two *senses* of (42). 'Reluctantly' specifies a mental disposition of John's, the agent, while he was performing the actions. Whether his disposition was caused by the combination of the two actions or solely by the first (and carried over to the second) or mostly by the first and only slightly by the second is not expressed by the sentence. Moreover, the sentence provides no semantic grounds for speculation about whether John would have been equally reluctant had he only to buy gas or change the oil. These hypothetical conditions merely reflect different situations that can satisfy the truth conditions of the sentence. The apparent ambiguity vanishes when the adverb is properly understood to attribute a mental disposition to the agent in performing the actions.[21]

So evident is it that scope formalism predicts sense ambiguities where none exist that Thomason and Stalnaker themselves admit that their abstraction operator manufactures ambiguities:

> In many cases like these there seems to be no difference in meaning between the two scope readings of a single English sentence, even though the strategy of formalization predicts the existence of two such readings. In such cases, the absence of a difference in meaning may be ascribed to particular semantic properties of the lexical items appearing in the example. (Thomason and Stalnaker, 1973, p. 200)

They seem to regard this situation as acceptable, offering no account of what these mysterious semantic properties are, nor any explanation of why we need such properties when the absence of a difference in meaning is predicted more simply by not assigning multiple scope.

Just as Davidson's use of logic forced him to arbitrarily reject part of a sentence's truth conditions as not pertaining to its meaning, so Thomason and Stalnaker's use of logic forces them to predict ambiguity where sentences are unambiguous. Instead of treating this situation like any other case of false prediction, Thomason and Stalnaker offer *ad hoc* explanations. When predicted ambiguities are not found in natural language, they find no fault with their theory: 'It may happen that one expression of English may be represented by more than one expression of our formalized language. There is much evidence to suggest that the formal operation of abstraction is hardly ever represented explicitly in English, and so is a plentiful source of such ambiguities.' (Thomson and Stalnaker, 1973, p. 212.)

Since Thomason and Stalnaker's formal apparatus is so plentiful a source of ambiguities that are not in English, why is it that they do not drop abstraction in favor of formal apparatus that does not cause trouble? The answer, I believe, is that their approach, like Davidson's, is limited to the apparatus in logic-based theories, and such referential apparatus characteristically transmutes situations in the world that satisfy the truth conditions of a sentence into distinct senses of the sentence. Referential apparatus does not suffice for handling such aspects of sense structure. The phenomenon of multiplicity of sense requires apparatus appropriate for individuating *senses*.

The trouble that Thomason and Stalnaker encounter with their use of abstraction is nothing new. A similar use of quantificational apparatus on the part of McCawley (1968, p. 152ff) caused similar trouble. McCawley claimed that 'John and Harry went to Cleveland' is ambiguous between the senses 'each went separately' and 'they went together'. Harnish has criticized this use of conjunction on the same basis that we have criticized Thomason and Stalnaker's treatment of (42), observing that 'John and Harry went to Cleveland' means nothing more than that John and Harry traversed some distance and arrived in Cleveland (Harnish, 1976). Possibilities like John's reluctance being caused mostly by the buying of gas and only slightly by the changing of oil parallel possibilities like John and Harry travelling together part of the way to Cleveland and separately the other part. Such possibilities cause an ambiguity explosion.

Furthermore, the same mistake of treating sense phenomena with referential apparatus is made in some of Chomsky and Jackendoff's arguments for the Extended Standard Theory. Katz criticizes them as follows:

> The Chomsky–Jackendoff account claims that, in the pair 'Everyone in the room speaks two languages' and 'Two languages are spoken by everyone in the room', the active sentence is two-ways ambiguous: between a sense on which it means that each person speaks the same two languages, and a sense on which it means that each person speaks two but not always the same two. But why not say, instead, between a sense on which it means each person speaks a different two, and one on which it means each person speaks

two but not always a different two? Why not a three-way ambiguity combining these? Why not as many different senses as there are combinations possible for n people and m languages? This will lead to the embarrassing consequence that the sentence 'everyone of the seventeen people in the room speaks twenty-eight languages' is many more ways ambiguous than the sentence 'everyone of the eleven people in the room speaks sixteen languages'—and to the even more embarrassing consequence that the sentence 'Everyone in the room speaks infinitely many languages' is infinitely many ways ambiguous.

Where and how is one to draw the line? The Chomsky–Jackendoff proposal allows only arbitrary decisions. No principle for drawing the line at one point can be given that is not matched by other principles, no better and no worse, for drawing it at the other points. This is because, in fact, there are no different senses to be separated. There is just a range of circumstances under which such sentences would be true; they could, with equal justice, be divided anywhere, so far as matters of grammar are concerned. The object NP of 'Everyone in the room speaks two languages' is not ambiguous because its truth conditions encompass the case of sameness of language and cases of non-sameness, any more that the subject NP of 'A parent can be too protective of his or her children' is ambiguous because its truth conditions encompass over-protective mothers and over-protective fathers. (Katz, 1980, pp. 27, 28)

I conclude that Thomason and Stalnaker, like McCawley, Chomsky, and Jackendoff before them, confuse the sense property of *ambiguity* with the reference property of *vagueness* or *indeterminateness between the different situations that will satisfy a truth condition.* I think that this confusion is due to the fact that their theoretical framework, lacking apparatus appropriate for representing sense structure, forces them to use inappropriate apparatus from the theory of reference.

After the discussion of the ambiguity of adverbials in sentences containing complex predicates, Thomason and Stalnaker proceed to discuss adverbials which modify the sentence as a whole and not just the predicate, such as 'possibly,' 'probably,' and 'unfortunately.' Thus, in (43) the adverb 'necessarily' modifies the proposition expressed by the sentence:

(43)   'Necessarily, nine is an odd number.'

Thomason and Stalnaker observe that 'necessarily' creates an opaque context, as is shown by the argument:

> Necessarily nine is odd.
> Nine is the number of the planets.
> _____
>
> Therefore, necessarily the number of the planets is odd.

This leads them to claim that opacity is a test for classifying adverbs as sentence modifiers: 'Only if an adverb is a sentence modifier, can it give rise to opaque contexts everywhere in a sentence in which it occurs' (Thomason and Stalnaker, 1973, p. 203). The example chosen by the authors to support this test is (44):

(44)   On a number of occasions the President of the United States has died in office.

'On a number of occasions' is said to be a sentence modifier because (44), which is true, yields a false sentence, (45), on substitution:

(45)   On a number of occasions Richard Nixon has died in office.

The example is puzzling for several reasons. Will the same test classify 'on a number of occasions' as a predicate modifier in a sentence where substitution is valid, such as 'On a number of occasions the President has travelled to Europe' (valid substitution: 'On a number of occasions Richard Nixon has travelled to Europe')? Thomason and Stalnaker are unclear on this point. Be this as it may, their test is wrong in that it makes any adverbial that modifies 'The President of the United States has died' a sentence modifier. This has the consequence that the adverbials in sentences like 'The President has died painfully' and 'The President has died in his car' turn out to modify the sentence, when they clearly modify only the predicate. Thus almost all adverbials become sentence modifiers according to this test, and the category becomes proportionately less interesting.

Here, as in the case of the ambiguity of complex predicates, Thomason and Stalnaker's theory predicts distinctions not found in English sentences. There does exist in English a distinction between sentence modifiers and the predicate modifiers. A good example of an adverb truly ambiguous in this respect is pointed out by Thomason and Stalnaker: 'Happily' is ambiguous, having one sense (roughly equivalent to 'fortunately') that is a sentence modifier and another (roughly equivalent to 'gladly') that is a predicate modifier' (Thomason and Stalnaker, 1973, p. 205). However, in order to determine, in cases of true semantic ambiguity, whether an adverb is a sentence adverb, a predicate adverb, or both, one has to examine the meaning of the adverb. Since, like Davidson, Thomason and Stalnaker reject, semantic decomposition, they have no access to the source of adverbial ambiguity.

Not only is the substitution test too strong, in that it declares adverbials such as 'on several occasions' and 'in some restaurants' as sentence modifiers, it is also too weak, as it fails to detect some true sentence modifiers. As Thomason and Stalnaker themselves note, an adverb such as 'actually,' while modifying propositions rather than predicates, is transparent. To account for all other sentence modifiers, the authors suggest three more tests, all yielding the same puzzling results. The second test, for example, says that only sentence modifiers can 'give rise to quantifier scope ambiguities in simple universal or existential sentences.'[22] The test classifies 'frequently' as a sentence modifier on the grounds that 'Frequently someone got drunk', contrasts with 'Someone got drunk frequently' (on one reading of these sentences) (Thomason & Stalnaker, 1973, p. 203–204). According to the authors, 'the semantic difference can be explained only on the assumption that 'frequently' is capable of modifying the sentence 'someone got drunk', and hence is a sentence adverb.[23] By this test, 'quickly' will also be a sentence modifer, for 'Quickly someone volunteers' and 'someone volunteers quickly' contrast in the same way as the 'frequently' sentences. However, 'quickly' must be classified as a predicate modifier because Thomason and Stalnaker cite its antonym, 'slowly', as a clear case of a predicate modifier throughout their article. The tests are therefore not consistent in their predictions. They are too strong in classifying most adverbials as sentence modifiers. Finally, the situation becomes more confusing when Thomason and Stalnaker say they are not even sure the tests are sufficient: 'Though it is strong *prima facie* evidence that an adverb is a predicate modifier if it fails all four tests, we have no conclusive criteria that will prove it is not a sentence modifier' (Thomason and Stalnaker, 1973, p. 206).

Like Davidson's theory, Thomason and Stalnaker's fails to explain anomaly. They admit that their theory cannot rule out such sentences as 'John is slowly tall' or 'John slowly ignored the music'.[24] We observe that the reason for this failure is that the decompositional structure on which the anomaly rests is not accessible. The sense of the constituent modified by a rate adverbial like 'slowly' has to contain a concept of process or action in order for there to be a compositional combination with the sense of such a modifier. This is discussed below.

Thomason and Stalnaker discard some insights of Davidson's. Whereas Davidson carefully distinguishes adverbials modifying the agent's mental state from adverbials modifying the action, Thomason and Stalnaker dismiss this distinction, claiming that the adverbials ambiguously modifies different parts of the complex predicate. Similarly, they discard Davidson's classification of adverbials into time modifiers, place modifiers, and instrument modifiers. Davidson's exclusion of sentence modifiers from his discussion is appropriate, as much modifiers operate on propositions as a whole, and are, therefore, different from adverbials in action sentences. Thus Thomason and Stalnaker's theory, which is an attempt to improve on Davidson's, not only does not do so, but it introduces new problems.

Q: Earlier you showed how a decompositional theory handles attributive adjectives in complex noun phrases and that there are advantages in such a theory over non-decompositional theories. For example, a decompositional theory is not forced to incorrectly predict that (30) is inconsistent.

(30) This is a good memento of the murder but a poor steak knife.

The theory can correctly represent the modified noun phrase because it associates the sense of 'good' and 'poor' with different components in the

internal semantic structure of the noun. Could you now show how to extend
the decompositional treatment to adverbial modification.

A: Explaining modification decompositionally is explaining how the
sense of modifiers fits into the decompositionally exposed structure of the
sense of its head to form a compositional sense for the entire modifier–
head construction. This compositionally emergent sense is a new predicate
whose meaning is more specific than the meaning of the head in virtue of
the contribution of the meaning of the modifier. The compositional meaning
of 'kill with a knife' is a case in point. (46) is a representation of the sense
of the head 'kill' and (47) is a representation of the sense of its modifier
'with a knife.' (48) is a representation of the compositional meaning 'kill
with a knife.'

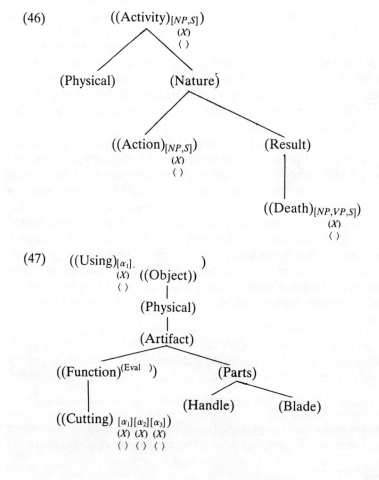

(48)

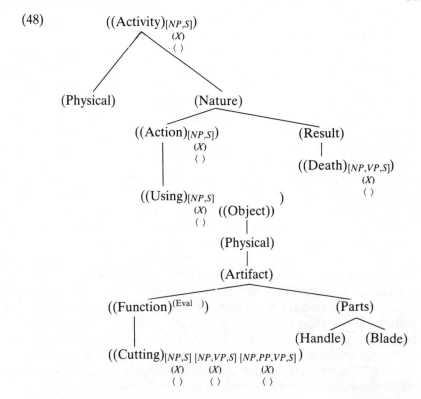

(46) represents the concept of killing as an action of the agent's which results in the recipient's death. (46) will distinguish the sense of 'kill' from that of a verb like 'murder' by the absence of a semantic marker representing the agent's intention to bring about the recipient's death in performing the action (see, Katz, 1977b, pp. 69–77), and distinguish the sense of 'kill' from that of a verb like 'gun down' by the absence of a semantic marker representing the action as firing a gun at the recipient. (47) represents a two-place predicate concept in which the agent of an action is related to the instrument of the action. The agent is left unspecified, but the instrument is specified as a knife. This latter specification is accomplished by having the representation of the noun 'knife', as shown in (32), dominated by a node representing the sense of the preposition 'with.' That the sense of 'with' is the concept of an action performed with an instrument, as represented in (47), can be seen from the fact that expressions of the form 'with NP' are ambiguous: they can mean either by means of NP or accompanied by NP. 'Jones was killed with his dog' can mean either the dog was used to kill Jones or the dog and Jones were killed together. This account of the

sense of 'with' is by no means idiosyncratic. Quirk and Greenbaum classify 'with' in both the instrumental category, as in 'someone had broken the window *with a stone*,' and in the accompaniment category, as in 'I'm so glad you're coming *with us*' (see Quirk & Greenbaum, 1973, pp. 159, 160). All verbs can take the accompaniment modification, and all action verbs can take the instrument modification as well. Therefore, action verbs will often yield ambiguous predicates when modified by expressions of the form 'with NP.' The accompaniment sense of 'with' does not occur in our example, 'kill with a knife', because an expression like 'Jones and his knife were killed together' is anomalous.

The derived semantic representation (48) is formed by the projection principle in application to the representations (46) and (47) for the verb 'kill' and its modifier 'with a knife'. In semantic theory there are three projection operations. One is the *embedding* of a semantic representation into another semantic representation by an operation of substituting the first for an occurrence of a categorized variable in the second. This operation has been discussed sufficiently. The second operation is a *conversion* of a semantic representation into another semantic representation, as for example, in the case of the interaction between the sense of a grammatical particle like negation and the sense of an expression in its scope. The third projection operation, which handles modification, is an *attachment* of the semantic representation of the modifier to the semantic representation of its head. The character of this operation is a consequence of the way in which branching structure in semantic markers represents a complex sense as a superordinate sense qualified successively by concepts that thereby give rise to the subordinate senses making up the complex sense. Such branching structure is what the attachment operation achieves.

Since the attachment that has to be accomplished by explicit compositional steps in cases of multi-word combinations like 'kill by shooting with a gun' is already there, fully accomplished, in the decompositional structure of a single lexical item like 'gun down,' the semantic representation of the item tells us what the result of an attachment operation looks like. Thus, if there were a single lexical item 'knife down' in the way there is a single lexical item 'gun down', the item would have the semantic representation (48). But, due to historical accident, English does not contain a lexical item 'knife down'. The sense is expressed by the multi-word combination 'kill by stabbing with a knife', and hence, it is compositionally formed from the sense of 'kill', 'by stabbing', and 'with a knife'. Accordingly, (48) is the result of an operation of attaching (47) to the node labelled (Action) in (46).

Attachment is brought about by a projection principle with one of two operations, *appending* or *merging*. In appending, the topmost semantic marker of the semantic representation of the modifier is appended to an occurrence of a superordinate semantic marker in the semantic representation of the head. Whether a semantic marker is superordinate to another is also given in the *redundancy rules* of the dictionary (see the account of such rules above). (M_i) is superordinate to (M_j) in case there is a redundancy rule of the form $(M_j) \rightarrow (M_i)$. Appending is formulated in (P'), where (M_m) is the semantic representation of the modifier and (M_h) is the semantic representation of its head:

(P')   If there is a semantic marker (M_i) in (M_h) which is superordinate to the topmost semantic marker in (M_m), viz, (M_j), attach (M_m) to (M_h) by making (M_j) a daughter of (M_i).

Appending occurs when a verb contains a node that can dominate the topmost node of the modifier. All (Action) nodes dominate a (Using) node because the former represent a concept that is superordinate to the concept represented by the latter. The attachment of 'with a knife' to 'kill', forming 'kill with a knife', discussed above, is an example of appending. In contrast, the semantic representation of a state verb like 'believe' contains no (Action) node to which (Using) can be appended because state concepts do not contain action concepts.

In the second attachment operation, merging, the topmost semantic marker of the semantic representation of the modifier is merged with an occurrence of that semantic marker in the semantic representation of the head. Merging is formulated in (P''):

(P'')   If there is a semantic marker (M_i) and (M_h) which is the same as the topmost semantic marker in (M_m), attach (M_m) to (M_h) at this common semantic marker, merging redundant semantic markers.

(P'') operates on the semantic representations of adverbials whose structure is identical to part of the representation of the verbs they modify. The rule merges identical markers, and what is left of the adverbials representation then hangs off the representation of the verb. The semantic representation of the verb must contain a semantic marker that is identical to the topmost node of the semantic representation of the modifier if merging is to occur. When there is no such semantic marker, as in the case of the verb in an expression like 'believe with a knife', the expression will be semantically anomalous. The failure of the projection principle to attach means that no derived semantic representation is assigned to the full expression. This marks 'believe with a knife' as semantically anomalous.

Consider another example: attachment of 'by stabbing' to 'kill', to form 'kill by stabbing', is an instance of merging. (46) represents the meaning of 'kill' and (49) represents the meaning of 'by stabbing'.[25]

(49)

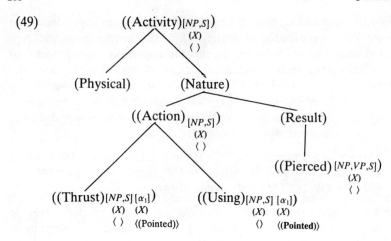

When the projection principle (P″) attaches the semantic representation in (49) to that in (46), the representation of the new predicate, 'kill by stabbing,' is formed, as shown in (50). The identical markers, like (Activity), (Nature), and (Result), have merged. All other semantic markers remain. When dominating nodes merge, their daughter nodes become sisters. For example: (Death) and (Pierced) are now sister nodes dominated by (Result). Unlike the conjunction principle of Davidsonian

(50)

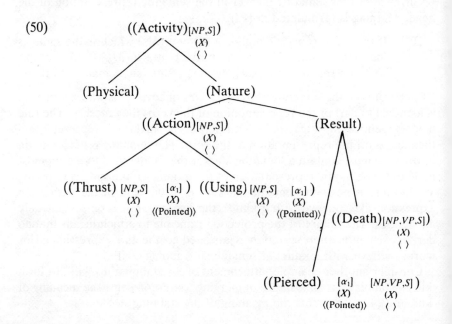

theories, the projection operation here does not require positing an extra argument place representing the event. Thus the only argument places which a decompositional theory has to posit are the standard ones for agent, recipient, and instrument.

Semantic anomaly results when the nodes in the semantic representation of a verb and its adverbial modifier can neither merge nor append. 'Kill by dreaming' is such an anomaly. Since 'dreaming' is a mental activity, its semantic representation cannot merge with the (Activity) node in the semantic representation of 'kill', because the latter contains (Physical) and the representation of 'dream' contains (Mental). There is no possibility of appending either, because the topmost node in the presentation of 'dream' is as high in the superordinate structure as the topmost node in the representation of 'kill'.

We can now show how synonymous expressions can have a single semantic representation regardless of the complexity of their respective syntactic structure. 'Kill by stabbing' is synonymous with 'stab to death'. Both have (50) as their semantic representation. The representation of 'kill by stabbing' results from the merging of (46) and (49). The representation of 'stab to death' results from appending the representation of the modifer 'to death' to the representation of the head, 'stab'. The representation of 'to death' has (Result) as its top node which merges with the (Result) node in the semantic representation of 'stab' (shown in (49)).[26]

Since decompositional theories can identify the same complex structure in the sense of both multi-word combinations and lexical items, the difference between lexical items and multi-word combinations can be treated as a matter of historical accident rather than as a matter of logic. For example, such theories can give the same semantic representation (51) to synonyms like the single lexical item 'strangle'[27] and the multi-word combination 'kill by compressing the throat and causing choking', as shown in (51). Theories like Davidson's, on the other hand, would represent 'strangle' as a single logical element and 'kill by compressing the throat and causing choking' as a conjunction of logical elements, thereby failing to account for the synonymy of the expressions.

The sense of 'strangle' specifies the manner in which the action is performed; that is, this action is performed with a certain amount of strength. This is illustrated in the semantic representation of 'strangle'. As in the case of instrument modification, we posit that the (Manner) node appends to an (Action) node in semantic representations. Thus a decompositional theory predicts that any action can be modified by a manner adverbial. Similarly, the semantic representation of 'kill brutally' is formed by appending (Manner), the topmost node of the semantic representation of 'brutally', to the (Action) node in the semantic representation of 'kill'.

(51)

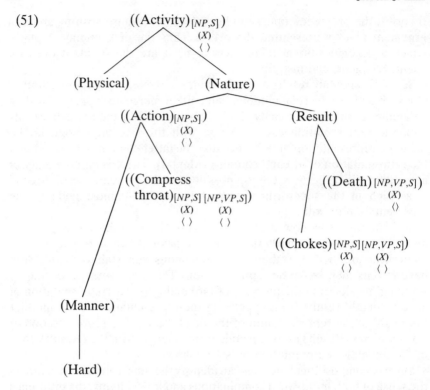

A decompositional theory also captures the semantic property of analyticity in sentences such as (52).

(52)   The man who strangled Bill killed him.

Recall that a sentence is analytic when the sense of one term includes the sense of its main predicate together with the terms occupying the argument places of the main predicate. This is a generalization of the familiar Kantian definition of analyticity as containment of the predicate concept in the subject concept. The generalization is made in order to accommodate analytic transitive sentences like 'Mary marries those whom she weds'. On this informal definition, (52) is marked as analytic because the sense of the 'the man who strangled Bill' in (52) includes the sense of the main predicate 'kill', and its terms—'the man' and 'Bill'.

A decompositional theory formally defines analyticity by means of a subtree relation. In order to specify subtrees, we define the relation of the 'same-rooted subtree of'. It is generally intuitively clear when one structure is a same-rooted subtree of another. For example, in the case of a semantic marker of the form (M), its branches of the form (53), among others, are same-rooted subtrees of the marker, whereas its branches of the form (54) are not.

(M)

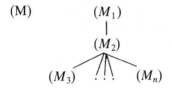

We take (M_i) to be the same-rooted subtree of any semantic marker whose topmost node is (M_i), including the semantic marker (M_i) itself. We do this

(53) $(M_1), (M_1), (M_1)$
          | | |
         (M_2) (M_2) (M_2)
          | |
         (M_3) (M_n)

(54) (M_2)
          |
         (M_3)

to bring sentences like 'A killing is an activity' and 'A knife is an object' under the definition of analyticity.

A simplified version of the definition of analyticity is the following: a sense of a sentence is analytic if and only if the semantic representation of its main predicate is a same-rooted subtree of the semantic representation of one of its terms, T_i, and the representations of the terms occupying the argument places of the main predicate, $T_j, \ldots, T_n$, are same-rooted subtrees of the representation of terms occupying the argument places of T_i. $T_j, \ldots, T_n$ correspond sequentially to the terms of T_j. Somewhat more formally, the definition of analyticity is as follows: A sense is analytic in case its semantic representation is of the form (i):

(i) $P_{T_1,\ldots,T_n}$

and some T_i, $1 \leq i \leq n$, which is of the form (ii),

(ii) $P'_{t_1,\ldots,t_m}$

is such that $P_{x_1,\ldots,x_n}$ is a same-rooted subtree of $P'_{x_1,\ldots,x_m}$ and each of $T_1,$ $\ldots, T_{i-1}, T_{i+1}, \ldots, T_n$ is a same-rooted subtree of the corresponding term in $t_1, \ldots, t_m$. Under this definition, sentence (52) is marked as analytic. The semantic representation of 'kill' is a same-rooted subtree of the semantic representation of 'strangle', and the representation of the terms occupying the argument places of 'kill' are, sequentially, same-rooted subtrees of the representations of the terms in the argument places of 'strangle'. Similarly, 'the man who strangled Bill performed an action' and 'the man who strangled Bill brought about Bill's death' are marked analytic as well, assuming appropriate representations of these sentences.

A second case of sense inclusion, analytic entailment, is illustrated in (55).

(55)   (a)   Jones strangled the bachelor at the stroke of midnight.

       (b)   Jones killed the bachelor.
       (c)   The bachelor is male.

Like analyticity, analytic entailment is defined using the same-rooted subtree relation. A simplified version of the definition of analytic entailment is the following: A sense analytically entails another sense in either of two cases. The first case of entailment is when the semantic representation of a sense, the entailed sense, is a same-rooted subtree of the semantic representation of another sense, the entailing sense, and for each semantic representation of a term in the entailed sense, T_j, there is a semantic representation of a term in the entailing sense, T_i, such that T_j is a same-rooted subtree of T_i. A somewhat more formal definition of this case of analytic entailment is as follows: A sense s^1 analytically entails a sense s^2 in case the semantic representations of s^1 and s^2 are such that the predicate of s^2, $P^2_{x_1,\ldots,x_n}$, is a same-rooted subtree of the predicate of s^1, $P^1_{x_1,\ldots,x_{n+k}}$, and also each of the terms in s^2, $T^2_1, \ldots, T^2_n$, is a same-rooted subtree of one of the terms in s^1, $T^1_1, \ldots, T^1_{n+k}$. The sense of the conclusion (55b) is included in the sense of the premiss (55a). As can be seen from (46) and (51), the semantic representation of (55b) will be a same-rooted subtree of the semantic representation of (55a). Therefore, by the above definition, (55b) is entailed by (55a).

The case of analytic entailment is when the semantic representation of two senses are such that one sense, the entailed sense, is analytic *and* the semantic representation of its including term is a subtree of the semantic representation of one of the terms in the representation of the entailing sense. And more formally: A sense s^1 analytically entails a sense s^2 in case the semantic representations of s^1 and s^2 are such that the latter is analytic (i.e., satisfies the definition given above), and the including term T^2_i is a subtree of some term in $T^1_1, \ldots, T^1_{n+k}$. The sense of (55c) is marked analytic and the semantic representation of its including term, 'bachelor', is a subtree of the semantic representation of 'bachelor' in (55a). Hence, (55a) is marked as analytically entailing (55c).

With the logical vocabulary expanded to include all of the vocabulary of the language,[28] decompositional theories can capture the entailment differences between (56) and (57) without generating the logical contradiction implicit in Davidson's treatment:

(56) Joe believes that there is life on Mars.
(57) Joe knows that there is life on Mars.

(57), but not (56), entails that there is life on Mars because 'knows' is factive, whereas 'believes' is not. Given access to the decompositional structure of the syntactic simple 'know', we can represent factivity in terms of a truth predicate internal to the sense of 'know'. The predicate has its argument place filled with the sense of the complement sentence when the sense of the verb phrase is formed.[29]

Expressions like 'free gift' are semantically redundant. Redundancy is also defined by means of the subtree relation: the sense of a head–modifier combination is redundant if and only if the representation of the sense of the modifier is a subtree of the representation of the sense of the head.[30] Such is the case with 'murder', which has the concept of intention as part of its meaning. Decompositional theories predict that the predicate 'murder intentionally' is redundant, while 'kill intentionally' is not, because the representation of the intention in the representation of the adverbial is already contained in the representation of 'murder' (58).

(58)

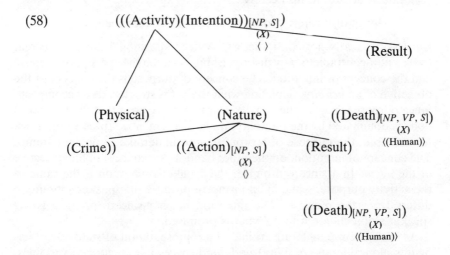

As Davidson points out, intentionality adverbials differ from the adverbials we have been discussing because the former operate on noun phrases that specify the agent. Since we agree with Davidson's distinction, we posit that

(Intention) figures alongside (Activity), thereby sharing its categorized variables, as is shown in the semantic representation of 'murder' (58).

Decompositional theories can also mark contradictory senses, for example, in (59).

(59)   Jones killed Bill unintentionally for money.

Reason adverbials indicate conscious motivation leading an agent to undertake an activity, and therefore their representations have (Intention) as their topmost node. The adverbial 'for money' is an example of a reason adverbial introducing the concept of intention into the meaning of the predicate. The representation of the modifier 'for money' has (Intention) as its topmost node, whereas the representation of the modifier 'unintentionally' is (A/(Intention)). The operator 'A/(M)' represents an exclusive alternation of all the semantic markers in the antonymous n-tuple to which (M) belongs, except for (M) (see Katz, 1972, pp 157–171). A decompositional theory marks a sense as contradictory when its semantic representation contains two members of the same antonymous n-tuple dominated by the same node. Thus (59) is marked as contradictory because it is represented as expressing both intention and lack of intention of the same activity.

The sense of (60) seems to contain the concept of intending, from the semantic structure of 'promise', and the concept of not intending, from the semantic structure of 'insincerely'.

(60)   Jones insincerely promised to pay his college loan.

But (60) is clearly not contradictory. A decompositional theory can treat (60) as non-contradictory by distinguishing between the concept of purpose and the concept of intention. The concept of purpose is the concept of the objective of an *activity*, depicting what the act is structured to accomplish. Since purpose is part of the activity's structure, we posit that the (Purpose) node is dominated by the (Activity) node of a semantic representation (as, for example, the purpose of a promise is to undertake to do something). The concept of intention, on the other hand, is the concept of the objective of the *agent*. In a sincere promise, the speaker's intention is the same as the activity purpose, while in an insincere promise the speaker's intention differs from the purpose. The intention in an insincere promise is the speaker's objective not to do what is promised.

As with intentionality adverbials, the representation of state adverbials figures alongside an (Activity) node and shares its categorized variables. These adverbials describe the state of the agent while performing an action. 'Reluctantly' is a state adverbial, as is shown in the semantic representation of 'kill reluctantly' (61).

(61)

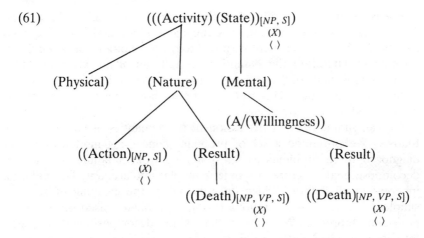

Since the semantic representation of 'reluctantly' figures at the top of the tree structure, it modifies the agent but not the action. Similarly, in (42) the modifier refers to the agent, not to either of the actions.

(42)   Reluctantly, John bought gas and changed the oil.

As noted above, Thomason and Stalnaker's theory predicts that (42) is ambiguous. A decompositional theory can avoid making such predictions by attaching the representation of state modifiers directly to the representation of the agent as in (42).

Finally, a decompositional theory has the apparatus to treat rate adverbials such as 'slowly' in a consistent manner, while Thomason and Stalnaker's treatment leads them to inconsistency, as also noted. 'To kill quickly' is represented in (62).

(62)

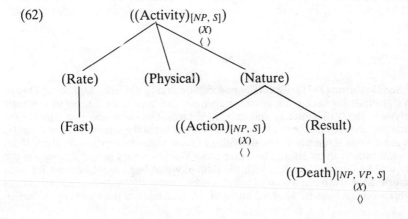

The sense of 'quickly' modifies both the action and the result of the activity. This is clear from the fact that when the agent performs the action quickly but the death of the recipient is slow, the truth conditions of 'kill quickly' are not met. Therefore, the semantic representation of 'quickly' is appended to the topmost node of the semantic representation of 'kill', i.e., it attaches to the (Activity) node. This attachment also shows that every activity can be modified by rate adverbials.

We can summarize our discussion of the semantics of modification as follows: We presented a set of problems concerning modification. We diagnosed these problems as all stemming from a failure to take the decompositional structure of syntactic simples into account. This failure is inherent in all theories which do not analyze the meaning of syntactic simples. We presented solutions to these problems based on a decompositional approach. We showed that taking decompositional structures into account solves all the problems in one stroke. In addition, we showed how our proposal can explain semantic properties and relations of adverbial constructions, such as ambiguity, synonymy, anomaly, analyticity, analytic entailment, redundancy, and contraction. These solutions and explanations provide a strong argument for a decompositional approach to modification.

ACKNOWLEDGEMENTS

This essay was presented in the form of lectures to the students and faculty of the Philosophy Department, University College, London. I wish to thank this audience and, in particular, Gerald Cohen, Colin McGinn, Herbert Heidelberger, Hide Ishiguro and John L. Watling. Thanks also to Mr William Ney for his help preparing the present version of the paper. The section of the present paper which comprises the answer to the last query is adapted from Katz, J. J., Leacock, C., & Ravin, Y., A Decompositional Approach to Modification, In E. LePore & B. McLaughlin (Eds), *Perspectives on Actions and Events*, Oxford: Blackwell, 1985.

NOTES

[1] See Davidson (1971), especially p. 455. Something has to be said about Davidson's grounds for taking the crucial step from the 'means that' form of semantic analysis to the ' "s" is true if, and only if, p' form. Davidson says two things. One is that this step enables us to escape being 'enmeshed in the intension'. Presumably, this is a cryptic reference to the difficulties Quine raises with intensionalism. If so, we shall turn to them later. The other thing Davidson says is that this step is the only way he knows of to deal with the difficulty that 'we cannot account for even as much as the truth conditions of belief sentences and others containing intensional contexts on the basis of what we know of the meanings of the words in the belief'

(pp. 453–455). But Davidson simply says this, giving no argument to back up his claim. In particular, he does not even consider the line of argument in Church, 1954). I should make clear that, in observing that Davidson does not consider the line of response Church introduced, I do not mean to suggest that I think Church's work on the topic is the last word or that it is without problems. I think it is the right line. See Katz, 1972, pp. 27–34 and Katz, 1986b.

Davidson's disciples have done no better than Davidson in motivating this step. Typical is Foster's criticism of the 'means that' form of analysis (see Foster, 1976, p. 6). Foster's first criticism amounts to nothing more than a bare claim to the effect that 'it is hard to envisage an acceptable theory which handles this intensionality'. But since there is no examination of attempts to construct an acceptable theory to back up this claim, the first criticism can be ignored. Foster's second criticism is that use of the form '*s* has the meaning . . .' is circular. He says: '[insight into the nature of meaning] will be diminished if, to gain it, we have to take intensional idiom for granted, for to understand such locutions as "means that" . . . requires an implicit grasp of the very concept of meaning which we hope to explicate'. This criticism is of special interest in connection with our discussion of reductionism in semantics because it quite unabashedly reads reductionism into nonreductionist approaches to explaining what sentences mean. For unless reductionist goals are assumed, there is nothing wrong with presupposing 'an implicit grasp of the very concept . . . we hope to explicate'. No exception is taken to such a presupposition outside of semantics—in, say, syntax, phonology, or logic, no one would think it circular to use the '*x* has the syntax . . .', '*x* has the phonological structure', or '*x* has the logical structure' form of analysis in syntax, phonology, or logic. Only if one supposes in advance that the insight one hopes to gain into the nature of meaning will come by a form of analysis that reduces meaning to something else will it be circular to presuppose an implicit grasp of meaning.

[2] They are clearly different in meaning on the face of it. Note also that they make different semantic contributions to the sentences in which they occur as constituents: compare 'Polar animals are white because snow is white' with 'Polar animals are white because grass is green'.

[3] If they are relevant, we can, of course, exhibit the grotesqueness in cases where everyone is certain by employing arbitrary pairs of simple arithmetic truths in place of (7) and (8).

[4] For further discussion of Davidson, including examples of the kind indicated in the text, see Katz (1975).

[5] A semantic theory of language in general, accordingly, will only have to define the semantic properties and relations in natural languages on the basis of the representational apparatus that enables us to construct semantic theories of every natural language.

[6] Hintikka claims that the '. . . whole concept of meaning (as distinguished from reference) is very unclear and usually hard to fathom'. Well, if so, then the whole concept of possibility is equally unclear and hard to fathom. See Hintikka (1969), pp. 87–88. For further discussion, see footnote 42, p. 107 of Katz (1978).

[7] Whether the definitions are given in this way or in terms of functions from possible worlds on to extensions of expressions and sentences in them does not matter in the present context.

[8] Another form of skepticism about meaning has to be considered, namely, that initiated in Putnam (1970). See my rejoinder in Katz (1977a, 1979, 1986a).

[9] Frege only pays lip service to such compositionality in that he makes no attempt

to go beyond the 'thought-building-block' metaphor and formally specify the function. See Katz (1986b).

[10] This feature of Frege's account of *Sinn* does not remove it as a case of what we have called a first approximation, since whether or not proper nouns have meaning is a question about the grammar of English and other languages rather than a question about the notation scheme or definitions.

[11] Technically, lexical items are given in a notation called 'features'; see Chomsky (1965).

[12] To say that a sentence like (16) has no sense in the language is not to say that it has none in the use of language. Metaphorical uses of semantically deviant sentences to make meaningful statements, on my view, work in a manner similar to that described for conferring meaning on a meaningless expression like 'grrr' (see above).

[13] I have avoided stating the actual definitions because of the considerable complexity of notation and explanation that would be necessary. Earlier statements are found in Katz, 1972, ch. 4; in simplified form in Katz, 1977c, p. 391. See Smith and Katz, to appear, for a full statement.

[14] What is required is a model theory for semantic representations that defines 'admissible model' in such a way that there exist admissible models on which the logical truths are untrue and the logical implications invalidated, while the analytic truths are true on all admissible models and the analytic entailments validated on all admissible models. See Smith and Katz, to appear.

[15] The answer to be presented is taken nearly verbatim from Katz *et al.* (1986).

[16] It should be noted here that Janet Fodor's (1977, p. 150) criticism that semantic marker notation cannot handle superordinate relations is mistaken. She writes:

> What must be faced is that the ultimate components of meaning are atomic in the sense that they are not components themselves decomposible into other smaller components, but are nevertheless internally complex in the sense that they CONTAIN other smaller components. Though the concept of being colored cannot intelligibly be SUBTRACTED from the concept of redness, it is nevertheless contained therein, and this fact must somehow be recorded. This is the way in which decomposition stops short before all significant semantic relations have been captured. At least some relations between concepts must be captured in a different fashion.

Fodor simply fails to see that some primitive semantic markers can have complex branching structure and thereby represent an atomic sense with internal conceptual structure. To take her example, the concept of being red might be represented by the primitive semantic marker:

The sense of the word 'red' is represented by this complex semantic marker. But the symbol '(Red)' does not occur by itself. Thus, according to semantic theory, 'the concept of being colored cannot intelligibly be SUBTRACTED from the concept of redness.' Given that the superordinate concept of being a color is part of the structure of the concept of being red, it is represented as 'contained therein.' Hence, it is simply false to claim that decompositional representation fails to capture superordinate relations.

[17] See Katz (1964) for a more detailed discussion of evaluative modification. We are leaving the selection restrictions blank in almost all the semantic markers in the

text in order for them to be easier to present and read. In certain cases, we provide the semantic marker(s) that a selection restriction requires a semantic representation to contain.

[18] Two semantic markers belong to the same antonymous n-tuple if they have a common base and different superscripts. The base represents concepts in the same domain, and the superscripts indicate incompatible elements within the domain. See Katz, 1972, p. 52, for a detailed analysis.

[19] We have not considered the type of logic-based theory where the treatment of modification would be based on Carnapian meaning postulates (see Carnap, 1957). The reason for narrowing the scope of the present study is that there has been no coherent proposal of this type. We believe that this is not an accident but due to the problem of how to use meaning postulates in compositional constructions. But our reasons for thinking that this type of logic-based theory would not be adequate go beyond the problem just cited. We will ultimately conclude that the logic-based theories considered in this paper fail because they do not countenance enough logically significant structure. It is always an interesting question whether theories which severely restrict themselves in the structure they countenance can account for as much as those which countenance more. Our complaint against Carnapian logic-based theories, however, is the opposite: they countenance too much structure as significant for questions of compositional meaning. For these theories, any and all necessary connections into which expressions enter count as features of their meaning. There is no way to distinguish those deriving from sense from those deriving from mathematics or metaphysics. (See Katz, 1986a for a full statement of this criticism.) Since this is the case, if it turns out that the decompositional theory put forth here deals with the semantics of adverbial modification successfully, we can dismiss Carnapian logic-based theories.

[20] There is, of course, a prepackaged answer to this question, viz, the limitation is not arbitrary because any attempt to go beyond it involves the notion of meaning which Quine has shown to be untenable in 'Two Dogmas of Empiricism' (Quine, 1953). This is perhaps what Davidson has in mind when he motivates his introduction of the paradigm 's is T if and only if p' to replace 's means p' on the grounds that we thereby avoid becoming 'enmeshed in the intensional' (see Davidson, 1971). But there is a rebuttal to this prepackaged answer which is that Quine's argument depends on the erroneous assumption that the tenability of meaning and other linguistic concepts rests on the possibility of providing substitution tests for them. This rebuttal is spelled out above.

[21] Another apparent ambiguity is presented by S. McConnell-Ginet (1982) in an attempt to improve on Thomason and Stalnaker's theory. According to the author, the following sentences differ in cognitive content:

(1) Reluctantly, Joan instructed Mary.
(2) Reluctantly, Mary was instructed by Joan.

'It has often been noted that [(2)] can be interpreted as attributing reluctance to Mary, whereas [(1)] unambiguously attributes reluctance to Joan' (McConnell-Ginet, 1982, p. 145). But 'there is no way to represent the non-synonymy of active and passives with passive-sensitive adverbs if these adverbs are translated as sentence operators of the sort which Thomason and Stalnaker discuss' (McConnell-Ginet, 1982, p. 154).

McConnell-Ginet's claim that the approach of Thomason and Stalnaker cannot handle adverbials in general rests on allegedly ambiguous sentences like (2).

However, these sentences are by no means clearly ambiguous in the language. Mary seems no more reluctant in (2) than she is in (1). Adverbials describing mental states such as 'reluctantly' or 'willingly' seem to modify the state of mind of the agent. Note examples like 'Obediently, Mary was instructed by Joan', which are deviant.

[22] Thomason and Stalnaker (1973, p. 203). The third test relies on the first two. It says (on p. 204) that an adverbial is a sentence modifier if it 'includes within its scope an adverb or adverbial that has already been shown to be a sentence modifier, and if the whole rest of the sentence is within the scope of that sentence modifier.' Our discussion of the first two tests is applicable to this test. The fourth test (on p. 205) classifies an adverbial as a sentence modifier if 'one [can] paraphrase the sentence by deleting the adverb and prefacing the resulting sentence by *It is Q-ly true that*'. The authors claim that the test holds for their paradigm cases. Thus, 'Sam frequently sucks lemons' can be paraphrased as 'It is frequently true that Sam sucks lemons'. This confusion of the sentence type with a statement about the occurrences of its tokens is discussed in note 23.

[23] There is a further problem with classifying 'frequently' as a sentence adverb. 'Frequently' is an adverb representing a parameter of temporal specification. It does not modify the predicate or the sentence as a whole but rather specifies the temporal conditions under which the sentence is true. 'Frequently someone got drunk' means that it was often true that someone got drunk. Because the sentence type itself cannot be either true ot false, 'frequently' expresses the ratio of true to false tokens of the sentence. By accepting 'frequently' as a sentence modifier, Thomason and Stalnaker blur the distinction between terms that refer to tokens and are therefore metalinguistic and terms that are truly linguistic and modify the meaning of sentences they occur in.

[24] These examples are from Thomason & Stalnaker, 1973, p. 218.

[25] The semantic representation of 'by stabbing' is identical to that of 'stab'. This is so because the semantic function of the preposition 'by' is to introduce the concept of activity to the adverbial, if needed. In the case of 'stabbing,' however, the representation of the verb already contains an (Activity) node, which therefore merges with the representation of 'by'.

[26] It might appear that only one operation is necessary for the projection principle, namely the merging operation which merges identical markers in the semantic representations of the head and modifier. However, this reduction of operations would force us to add extra semantic structure to the representations of modifiers. For example, in order to attach a rate modifier, such as 'quickly' (see (62)), to an action verb, we would have to posit an (Activity) node as the topmost node of the semantic representation of the modifier in order to allow merging with the (Activity) node of the semantic representation of the verb. Consequently, the theory would predict ambiguity where none exists because it would require a different semantic representation for the same modifier depending on the type of verb it is attached to. In order to attach 'quickly' to a process verb such as 'die', the topmost node of the semantic representation of 'quickly' would have to be (Process) in order to allow merging with the (Process) node of the semantic representation of the verb. Thus modifiers such as 'quickly' would have at least two semantic representations, hence two senses. Since having only one operation for the projection principle leads to this false prediction, we posit two operations of the projection principle.

[27] By definition, strangling is an act that results in the death of a victim. When the choking does not bring about such death, the act is only an attempted strangling.

28 In the broad sense of 'logical' meaning 'inferential'. See Katz (1986a, pp. 41 f).

29 The structure that fills the argument place as specified by the categorized variable for the complement sentence. The categorization will have the form $[S,S,VP,S]$.

30 Redundancy is sometimes used to emphasize a component of decompositional structure, as in 'free gift'. Redundancy then serves to stress the fact that no charge will be made. This feature of use further demonstrates the existence of the decompositional structure.

REFERENCES

Alston, W. P., Meaning and use. *Philosophical Quarterly*, 1963, **13**, 107–124.

Carnap, R., Meaning postulates. In *Meaning and Necessity* (enlarged edition). Chicago, IL: University of Chicago Press, 1956.

Carroll, L., *The Complete Works of Lewis Carroll* (Modern Library series). New York: Random House, 1936.

Chomsky, N., A review of B. F. Skinner's *Verbal Behavior*. In J. A. Fodor & J. J. Katz, *The Structure of Language: Readings in the Philosophy of Language*. Englewood Cliffs, NJ: Prentice-Hall, 1964.

Chomsky, N., *Aspects of the Theory of Syntax*. Cambridge, MA: MIT Press, 1965.

Chomsky, N., *The Logical Structure of Linguistic Theory*. New York: Plenum, 1975.

Church, A., A formalization of the logic of sense and denotation. In P. Henle, H. M. Kallen & S. K. Langer (Eds), *Structure, Method, and Meaning*. New York: Liberal Arts Press, 1951, pp. 3–24.

Church, A., Intensional isomorphism and identity of belief, *Philosophical Studies*, 1954, **5**, 65–73.

Davidson, D., Truth and meaning. In J. F. Rosenberg & C. Travis (Eds), *Readings in the Philosophy of Language*. Englewood Cliffs, NJ: Prentice-Hall, 1971, pp. 455–480.

Davidson, D., Thought and talk. In S. Guttenplan (Ed), *Mind and Language*. Oxford: Clarendon, 1975.

Davidson, D., The logical form of action sentences. In N. Rescher (Ed), *The Logic of Decision and Action*. Pittsburg: University of Pittsburg Press, 1967 (Reprinted in Davidson, D., *Essays on Action and Events*. New York: Oxford University Press, 1980).

Field, H., Logic, Meaning, and conceptual role. *Journal of Philosophy*, 1977, **74**, 379–408.

Fodor, J. D., Semantics. *Theories of Meaning in Generative Grammar*. New York: Crowell, 1977.

Foster, J. A., Meaning and truth theory. In G. Evans & J. McDowell (Eds), *Truth and Meaning*. Oxford: Clarendon, 1976.

Frege, G., On the sense and reference. In P. Geach & M. Black (Eds), *Translations from the Philosophical Writings of Gottlob Frege*. Oxford: Blackwell, 1952a.

Frege, G., On concept and object. In P. Geach & M. Black (Eds), *Translations from the Philosophical Writings of Gottlob Frege*. Oxford: Blackwell, 1952b.

Frege, G., *The Foundations of Arithmetic*. Oxford: Blackwell, 1953.

Frege, G., *The Basic Laws of Arithmetic* (M. Furth, Ed & transl). Berkeley, CA: University of California Press, 1964.

Grice, H. P. & Strawson, P., In defense of a dogma. *Philosophical Review*, 1956, **65**, 141–158.

Grice, H. P., Utterer's meaning, sentence meaning, and word-meaning. *Foundations of Language*, 1968, **4**, 225–242.

Harman, G., *Thought*. Princeton, NJ: Princeton University Press, 1973.

Harnish, R. M., Logical form and implicature, In T. G. Beaver, J. J. Katz & D. T. Langendoen (Eds), *An Integrated Theory of Linguistic Ability*. New York: Crowell, 1976.

Hintikka, J., *Models for Modalities*, New York: Humanities Press, 1969.

Katz, J. J., Mentalism in linguistics. *Language*, 1964a, **40**, 124–137.

Katz, J. J., Semantic theory and the meaning of good. *The Journal of Philosophy*, 1964, **23**, 1964b, 739–766.

Katz, J. J., *The Philosophy of Language*. New York: Harper & Row, 1966.

Katz, J. J., *Semantic Theory*. New York: Harper & Row, 1972.

Katz, J. J., Logic and language: an examination of recent criticisms of intensionalism. In K Gunderson (Ed), *Language, Mind, and Knowledge (Minnesota Studies in the Philosophy of Science*, vol. 7). Minneapolis, MN: University of Minnesota Press, 1975.

Katz, J. J., The dilemma between Orthodoxy and identity. In A. Kasher (Ed), *Language in Focus*. Dordrecht-Holland: Reidel, 1976, pp. 165–175.

Katz, J. J., A proper theory of names. *Philosophical Studies*, 1977a, **31**, 1–80.

Katz, J. J., *Propositional Structures and Illocutionary Force*. New York: Crowell, 1977b (Paperback reprint, Harvard University Press, 1980).

Katz, J. J., The advantages of semantic theory over predicate calculus in the representation of logical form in natural language. *The Monist*, 1977c, **60**, 380–405.

Katz, J. J., The theory of semantic representation. *Erkenntnis*, 1978, **13**, 63–110.

Katz, J. J., Neoclassical theory of reference. In P. A. French *et al.* (Eds), *Contemporary Perspectives in the Philosophy of Language*. Minneapolis, MN: University of Minnesota Press, 1979, pp. 103–124.

Katz, J. J., *Language and Other Abstract Objects*. Totowa, NJ: Rowman & Littlefield, 1981.

Katz, J. J., Chomsky on Meaning. *Language*, 1980, **56**, 1–41.

Katz, J. J., *Cogitations*. New York: Oxford University Press, 1986a.

Katz, J. J., Why intensionalists ought not to be Fregeans. In E. LePore (Ed) *Truth and Interpretation*. Oxford: Blackwell, 1986b, pp. 59–91

Katz, F. & Katz, J. J., Is necessity the mother of intension? *Philosophical Review*, 1977, **86**, 86–96.

Katz, J. J., Leacock, C., & Ravin, Y., E. LePore & B. McLaughlin (Eds). In *Actions and Events*. Oxford: Blackwell, 1985, pp. 207–234.

McCawley, J., The role of semantics in a grammar. In E. Bach & R. Harms (Eds), *Universals in Linguistic Theory*. New York: Holt, Rinehart, and Winston, 1968.

McConnell-Ginet, S., Adverbs and logical form: A linguistically realistic theory, *Language*, 1982, **58** 144–184,

Putnam, H., Is semantics possible? *Metaphilosophy*, 1970, **1**, 187–201.

Quine, W. V. O., Two dogmas of empiricism. In *From a Logical Point of View*, Cambridge, MA: Harvard University Press, 1953, pp. 20–46.

Quine, W. V. O., *Word and Object*, Cambridge, MA: M.I.T. Press, 1960.

Quirk, R. & Greenbaum, S., *A Concise Grammar of Contemporary English*. New York: Harcourt, Brace Jovanovich, 1973.

Schiffer, S., *Meaning*. London: Oxford University Press, 1972.

Searle, J. R., *Speech Acts*. Cambridge: Cambridge University Press, 1969.

Smith, G. & Katz, J. J., *Supposable Worlds*. Harvard University Press, Cambridge. To appear (former title *Intensionally Admissable Models*).

Thomason, R. H. & Stalnaker, R. C., A semantic theory of adverbs. *Linguistic Theory*, 1973, **4**, 195–220.

7

Game-Theoretical Semantics as a Synthesis of Verificationist and Truth-Conditional Meaning Theories

JAAKKO HINTIKKA

Philosophy Department,
Florida State University,

GAME-THEORETICAL SEMANTICS: THE BASIC IDEAS

Game-theoretical semantics (GTS) is an approach to linguistic, logical and philosophical meaning analysis which I began to develop in the early seventies.[1] Its basic idea is closely related to Wittgenstein's notion of language-game, if Wittgenstein's true intentions are appreciated, in that certain rule-governed human activities in it are thought of as constituting the basic language–world relations.[2] I have taken Wittgenstein more literally than Ludwig did himself and argued that those meaning-constituting language-games are—at least in a number of interesting and important cases—games in the sense of the mathematical theory of games. The concepts of game theory can thus be brought to bear on linguistic and logical semantics.[3]

So far, GTS has been used to analyze a number of specific problems in linguistic semantics and philosophical analysis, including branching quantifiers in natural languages, temporal discourse, the insufficiency of generative grammars as the explanation of the acceptability of English

NEW DIRECTIONS IN SEMANTICS

sentences, the principle of compositionality, negation, the alleged ambiguity of 'is', and a partial reconstruction of Aristotle's theory of categories. However, a different kind of use largely remains to be discussed. GTS is not only an account of the actual semantics of certain formal languages and certain fragments of natural languages. It occupies a pivotal position on the map of different types meaning theories, being—as I shall show below— a synthesis of truth-functional and verificationist approaches to semantics. Largely because of this strategic position of GTS, it also provides a framework for discussing other approaches to semantics and the nature of meaning theory in general. In this essay one such dimension of GTS will be explored.

For the purpose, a brief account of the basic ideas of GTS is needed as a basis of the discussion. Even though many of the most important applications of GTS are to natural languages, it suffices for most of this work to consider GTS as it applied to a formal but applied first-order language.

Such a language L has as its non-logical vocabulary a finite number of predicate symbols, each with a fixed finite number of argument-places, e.g., '$P(x_1, x_2)$', plus a finite number of individual constants.

Since we are dealing with an interpreted language, we are also given a model or M whose domain $D(M)$ of individuals on which the nonlogical symbols of L are evaluated (defined). This means that, if L is extended by adding to it names of members of $D(M)$, every atomic sentence in the extended language is either true or false. The way this truth-value is determined is the usual one. For instance, if 'P' is a two-place predicate symbol and 'a', 'b' names or individual constants and if $v(P)$ and $v(a)$, $v(b)$ are the evaluations of 'P', 'a', and 'b', respectively, then

(T.A) '$P(a, b)$' is true iff $\langle v(a), v(b) \rangle \in v(P)$. Here $v(a)$ is the individual named by 'a' when 'a' is a name.

Likewise

(T =) '$(a = b)$' is true iff $v(a) = v(b)$.

The general truth-conditions which we are dealing with in (T.A) and (T. =) are the same as the truth-clauses for atomic sentences and identities in a usual Tarski-type (recursive) truth-definition.

What the game-theoretical treatment of truth does is to extend the notion of truth to all non-atomic sentences of L. This is done by defining a two-person game. The players may be called Myself and Nature, and the game may be thought of as a zero-sum game. These games will be called *semantical games*. There is such a game connected with each sentence of L (and also with each sentence of any extension $L(l)$ of L obtained by adjoining to L a finite set *l* of names of the members of $D(M)$). The game $G(S)$ associated with a sentence S of L begins with S and proceeds according to certain rules. What these rules are can be appreciated by keeping in mind the intuitive interpretation of G(S) as an attempt on the part of Myself to verify S against the schemes of malicious Nature who is trying to falsify S. This leads naturally to the following game rules:

(G.&) $G(S_1 \,\&\, S_2)$ begins with Nature's choice of S_1 or S_2, say S_i. The rest of the game is $G(S_i)$

(G.v) $G(S_1 \text{ v } S_2)$: Likewise, except that S_i ($i = 1$ or 2) is chosen by Myself.

(G.E) $G((\exists x)S[x])$ begins with a choice by Myself of a member of the domain D(M). If there is no constant 'c' in L such whose value is the chosen individual, a new constant (name) 'c' is adjoined to L as the name of the chosen individual. Then the rest of the game is as in G(S(c)).

(G.U) $G((\forall x)S[x])$ proceeds likewise, except that the initial individual is chosen by nature.

(G.A) If A is an atomic sentence, then Myself wins G(A) on M if A is true in M and Nature loses. If A is false, Nature wins and Myself loses G(A).

(G.) In G(~S), the two players play G(S) with their roles (as defined by these G-rules) exchanged.

Each application of a game rule (except (G.A)) reduces the number of logical constants in the successive sentences the players are considering by at least one. Hence the game will come to an end in a finite number of steps with an atomic sentence. Then (G.A) tells us who won and who lost. Hence the game rules suffice to define the semantical games G(S) completely.

Once the games G(S) have been defined for all sentences S of L (and for all sentences of each extension L(l) of L), the notion of truth can be defined game-theoretically. The basic idea is of course that S is true iff it can in principle be verified. How is this verifiability in principle to be understood? If you are really immersed in the spirit of game theory, the answer is obvious. *The sentence S is true iff Myself (the initial verifier) has a winning strategy in the correlated game* G(S).

By a winning strategy, I mean pretty much what the term says, at least after it has undergone a regimentation and abstraction in general game theory. By a *strategy*, I mean a rule or function which tells a player which move to make in each possible situation that may come up in the course of the game. Once the strategies of all players have been determined, the entire course of the game, and hence also its outcome, is uniquely determined. A *winning* strategies for a given player is one which leads to a win no matter what strategies one's opponents are pursuing.

Thus we can say that S a sentence of L (or L(l)) is true iff there exists a winning strategy for Myself in G(S), and that S is false iff there exists a winning strategy for Nature in G(S).

This completes my précis of GTS. The nature of this approach will become clearer in the course of my discussion.

GTS AS TRUTH-CONDITIONAL SEMANTICS

This game-theoretical truth-definition deserves a few further comments.

(1) The game-theoretical truth-definition and hence the game-theoretical conception of meaning is in a perfectly good sense *truth-conditional*. To understand a sentence S in L is to understand what conditions its truth imposes on the world. Indeed, there is a close relationship between a game-theoretical truth-definition and a Tarski-type one.[4] Both definitions are based on a truth-condition for atomic sentences. Indeed, (T.A) formulated above in a special case is to all practical purposes just a version of Tarski-type truth-conditions for atomic sentences. In both cases, i.e., both in GTS and in the usual truth-definitions, what the rest of the clauses of a truth-definition do is to extend the notion of truth from atomic to non-atomic sentences. Even the different steps in doing so can be made to match one by one. Then each one of the rules for semantical games has precisely one counterpart in a suitable Tarski-type truth-definition, viz, the recursive clause for sentences of the same form.

The most important difference is that a game-theoretical truth-definition operates from outside in, whereas a Tarski-type truth-definition operates from inside out. In other words, Tarski gives rules for as it were building up the truth or falsity of a sentence from those of simpler ones. In contrast, a game-theoretical truth-definition in effect reduces the question of the truth or falsity of a complex sentence to that of certain simpler ones. This difference in tactics has important consequences for the power of the two techniques to handle more complicated cases, as I have shown in detail elsewhere. In particular, the applicability of GTS does not presuppose compositionality, as does the applicability of Tarski-type truth-definitions.[5] However, this difference in the direction in which the two kinds of truth-definitions proceed naturally has absolutely nothing to do with the question whether the resulting concepts of meaning are truth-conditional or not.

(2) At the same time, semantical games are essentially games of attempted verification (on the part of Myself) and falsification (on the part

of Nature). Indeed the game-theoretical truth-definition can be viewed as the abstract true core in the verificationist theory of meaning. The trouble with that theory was that verification and falsification were thought of as concrete mechanical operations which can be performed once and for all in accordance with fixed mechanical rules. What happens in a game-theoretical truth-definition is that the old idea that a sentence S is true if and only if it can be verified is given a new twist. The true abstract core of this idea is reached by interpreting 'S can be verified' as 'Myself [the verifier] has a winning strategy in [the verification game] G(S)'. That this strategy is not a mechanical one ought not to bother anyone. Its non-mechanical character merely means that it is not open to the earlier objections to verificationist (operationalist) theories of meaning.

In this matter, GTS has etymology on its side in all languages in which existence is expressed by speaking of what can be found. Has any Swede ever been bothered by the fact that when he or she speaks of 'what can be found' (*det finns*), there need not be any recipe around for anyone actually to do so? Or, if Swedes are not representative enough a tribe, what can be said of traditional mathematicians who have ever since Cauchy expressed their quantifiers by speaking of what 'we can find' when we are 'given' certain numbers even in cases when there is no algorithm for doing so?[6] There is no reason why any verification theorist of meaning should think of verification as being accomplished in one fell swoop.

GTS VS DUMMETT

Both points (1)–(2) may seem obvious, maybe even trivial. However, taken jointly they have remarkable consequences. One of them is that the contrast between theories of meaning which rely on truth-conditions and theories of meaning which turn on verification and falsification is totally misleading. Yet this contrast is used by several contemporary philosophers. For instance, Michael Dummett (1976) sums up a part of his discussion in a recent paper as follows:

> I have argued that a theory of meaning in terms of truth-conditions cannot give an intelligible account of a speaker's mastery of language; and I have sketched one possible alternative, a generalization of the intuitionist theory of meaning for the language of mathematics, which takes verification and falsification as its central notions in the place of truth and falsity.

The contrast relied on here by Dummett is confounded by the counter-example of GTS. Game-theoretical semantics is the one approach to meaning where there is no contradiction between meaning as being defined by truth-conditions and meaning as defined by the rules for verification and falsification.

It is clear that I share with Dummett a strong emphasis on the actual processes ('games') of verification which connect language with the world. In my most general theoretic stance I am in step with Dummett. What I object to is his claim that, the primacy of verification processes in semantics is incompatible with a truth-conditional approach of semantics.

A closer examination of Dummett's argument betrays the fallacy he is committing. He argues in effect that one's knowledge of truth-conditions cannot be the same as one's mastery of the language in question because truth-conditions cannot always be applied so as to determine the actual truth-value of a sentence. Dummett relies on the idea, which seems eminently acceptable, that 'the ascription of implicit knowledge to someone is meaningful only if he is capable in suitable circumstances of fully manifesting that knowledge'. Hence, it would make no sense (according to Dummett) to ascribe implicit knowledge of meanings to a speaker if that knowledge were knowledge of truth-conditions. For (Dummett avers) knowledge of truth-conditions cannot be fully manifested, as witnessed by various undecidable theories, even in the favorable case of formal theories.

It is becoming patent that Dummett is thinking of truth-conditions as effective once-and-for-all comparisons between a sentence and the world. His argument evaporates if knowledge of truth-conditions is understood as the mastery of certain rule-governed human activities which constitute those truth-conditions. Here game-theoretical semantics offers a clear-cut counterexample. In it, truth-conditions are formulated by reference to certain games. These truth-conditions are therefore understood by a speaker as soon as he or she understands these games. You can give this understanding as radically Wittgensteinian a turn as Dummett might wish, but you cannot escape admitting that a speaker's knowledge of truth-conditions is manifested as completely as any tacit knowledge ever can be manifested in his or her mastery of semantic games. Such a mastery can be complete without its resulting in a decision method for truth or falsity, or even in a definitive decision concerning truth or falsity in the case of particular given theories.

Game-theoretical semantics serves as a counterexample also to other theses of Dummett's. Among them, there are certain comments of his on realism vs idealism in logic. Given the domain D and the evaluation function v, it is completely determined whether or not there exists a winning strategy for Myself or one for Nature in any one given semantical game $G(S)$. For whether there are strategies in $G(S)$ for one of the players which win against any strategy of one's opponent is an objective fact about the world. Hence the assertion that there exists a winning strategy in $G(S)$ likewise states an objective matter of fact which either obtains or does not obtain 'out there' in the world. Since each sentence in L is taken to be an assertion of the existence of a winning strategy for Myself in a game G(S), the theory of meaning resulting from game theoretical semantics is completely objectivistic (realistic). It does not refer to what the utterer of the sentence (or anyone else) knows, believes, or is personally in a position to do.

This point is easily missed. It is in fact easy to fall into a misleading jargon in expounding game-theoretical semantics. It is tempting to say, for instance, that S is true iff Myself 'has' a winning strategy. (Indeed, this formulation was used once above on purpose. It is a safe bet that no suspicions were thereby awakened in the reader's mind.) In reality, Myself need not 'have' this strategy in the sense of possessing any rule for following it. All that S says is that *there exists* in the game G(S) a winning strategy for Myself.

Still less need a speaker who utters S to *know* any winning strategy for Myself in G(S) or even have in his or her mind a plausible candidate for the role. I have argued elsewhere that this is normally not the case—an observation which in fact opens the door for interesting new conceptualizations.[7] Hence game-theoretical semantics, even though it identifies the understanding of a sentence S by a speaker with his or her mastery of the game G(S), does not presuppose that the speaker is in possession of sufficient means of recognizing the truth or falsity of S.

This belies another claim of Dummett's (1976, p. 101). The claim is illustrated by the following quote:

> What is the way out of this impasse? To find this, we must first ask what led us into it. The plain [sic] answer is that our difficulties all arise because of our propensity to assume a realistic interpretation of all sentences of our language, that is, to suppose that the notion of truth applicable to statements made by means of them is such that every statement of this kind is determinately either true or false, independently of our knowledge or means of knowing.

This statement is ambiguous. If 'independently of our means of recognizing its truth-value' means 'independently of the semantical game correlated with it', game-theoretical semanticists could not agree more heartily with Dummett. Yes, we do have to realize that statements are not true or false independently of our means to recognize them as such, as long as these means are codified in the semantical games I have defined. But if this is how Dummett's statement is to be construed, practically none of the consequences he wants to draw from it will actually follow. Our semantics can still be realistic and even the principle of bivalence can be valid, depending on the precise nature of the semantical games in question.

Hence this true interpretation of Dummett's words cannot be what he intended. But if Dummett means 'independently of the state of knowledge and the means of knowledge which characterize an individual speaker', then he is committing a simple fallacy. There is a tacit assumption in

Dummett and in several other recent philosophers which is refuted by game-theoretical semantics. It is that any reliance on the human activities which serve to bridge the gap between language and the world is inevitably a step from realism. There may be just a tad of truth in that assumption, but as it is usually taken, it is not only misleading but mistaken. It is far too often thought that reliance on certain human activities in one's semantics (usually they are activities of verification and falsification) makes one's semantics somehow dependent on the nature of the people carrying out these activities. At the very least, references to such activities is thought to introduce an epistemic element into one's semantics, a dependence on 'our knowledge of our means of knowing', as Dummett puts it.

This is an outright fallacy, however, as the example of game-theoretical semantics shows. Activities of verification and falsification can be studied in terms of their abstract rules, quite as readily the activities of inferring can be studied by references to logical rules of inference, in abstraction from the psychological idiosyncracies of the person who actually happens to be drawing those inferences and in abstraction from whatever knowledge the inferrer may or may not possess. Such an abstract study of verification is in fact precisely what is undertaken in GTS.

The general moral of my story so far can be put as follows: What is overlooked by philosophers like Dummett is the very possibility instantiated by GTS. When they contrast truth-conditions and use, they overlook the possibility that those truth-conditions should be constituted by that use, in the sense that the basic semantic relations which link language and world and which make truth-conditions possible have their mode of existence in the activities of verification and falsification—in the same sense as language-games constitute the truth-conditions of sentences in the language L.

GTS AND THE LAW OF EXCLUDED MIDDLE

Another interesting corollary of the game-theoretical truth-definition is the following: According to the definition, a sentence S is true iff there exists a winning strategy in G(S) for Myself; S is false iff there exists G(S) a winning strategy for Nature. The principle of excluded middle or, strictly speaking, the principle of bivalence hence asserts that one of the two players has a winning strategy. In game-theoretical terms, this is expressed by saying that the game G(S) is *determinate*.

Is this always the case? It can be shown that in the simple sample languages used here as a test case, bivalence does indeed obtain. But it is also known in general that assumptions of determinateness are often extremely strong assumptions.[8] In the case of suitable, fairly simple infinitary games, assumptions of determinacy, known as axioms of determinateness, amount to extremely strong set-theoretical assumptions. In more complicated semantical games, too, determinateness is known to fail. Hence game-theoretical semantics shows that bivalence is an extremely dubious principle in general.

Nevertheless, it is clear that the success or failure of bivalence has nothing to so with the realistic or non-realistic character of one's semantics. Bivalence is a property of the objective bridge connecting sentences with an objective reality and so is its absence. A platonist need not believe in bivalence; rejecting it does not make his position any less realistic.

This refutes another thesis of Dummett's, viz. that realism and bivalence go hand in hand. Dummett's mistake here is again due to his tacit assumption that truth-conditions cannot be mediated by rule-governed human activities.

The reader can perhaps acquire a sense of the situation by noting that at least some of the usual semantical paradoxes can be thought of in game-theoretical terms as involving precisely a failure of bivalence due to infinitely self-repeating loops in a semantical game. For instance, consider the sentence

(4.1)   The sentence (4.1) is false.

Whatever the game rule is that applies here, it clearly involves a way of establishing what the sentence referred to is and then negating it. This leads from (4.1) to (4.2)

(4.2)   The sentence (4.1) is not false.

Now the players have to switch roles and consider the unnegated sentence corresponding to (4.2). But this is (4.1), leading to an infinitely self-repeating loop, i.e., an infinitely long play of a semantical game. There is no natural way of defining winning and losing for such an infinitely long game. Among the available possibilities (not presupposing that the game will come to an end in a finite number of steps) there is the tempting idea that winning and losing in an infinite play are determined on the basis of asking which player (if either) was responsible for pushing the game to infinity.[9] (If the culprit is Myself, the sentence is false. If it is Nature that is to be 'blamed', it is true.) This idea does not yield any decision when applied to the game starting from (4.1), however. Hence (4.1) cannot be considered either true or false.

Applied to

(4.3)   The sentence (4.3) is true

we are naturally led to consider it true. Hence we are naturally led to consider 'This sentence is true' as true but 'This sentence is false' as undetermined, violating bivalence.

This application of game-theoretical ideas may not be very impressive in its own right. However, it illustrates an important general truth. The failure of bivalence here is patently unrelated to the issue of realism as it is usually thought of. It is not the dependence of the truth and falsity on our thinking that makes it impossible to apply these notions to (4.1). This sentence is there objectively, as soon as printer's ink has dried on the copies of this essay, and so is its subject matter. It is the relation of the two (a certain kind of self-referentiality, if you want to put it in that way) that creates the failure of bivalence, not the mind-dependency of the relations of truth and falsity.

VERIFICATION VS PROOF

The mistakes of Dummett's which I have so far diagnosed are compounded by others. I could not agree more with Dummett when he maintains that the alpha and omega of semantics must be the actual processes of verification and the rules governing them. However, I part company with him when it comes to asking what these processes of ascertaining the truth (or falsity) of our propositions really are. It is to me as plain as a pikestaff that those processes are activities of seeking and finding suitable individuals, that is, individuals whose existence will verify the proposition which prompted the quest. At least this is the case for propositions in the notation of an applied first order language or in a language that can be translated into such notation. But Dummett soon slips into thinking that the relevant verification procedures are *formal logical proofs* with the exception of atomic sentences, which are established by observation.[10] I do not see any shred of justification for such an assumption in general semantics. What a verification process aims at is the establishment of truth (material truth); what a logical proof is calculated to accomplish is the establishment of *logical* truth. Now the use of the same word 'truth' here is of course a mere pun. Logical truth is not a species of truth in the sense of truth in some one model or world. Roughly, it may be thought of as truth (material truth) in all possible worlds. From this, it is immediately seen that to ascertain the logical truth of (to give a logical proof for) a proposition S is an entirely different enterprise from making sure that S is (materially) true. Moreover, the notion of logical truth is secondary with respect to (i.e., presupposes) the concept of (ordinary) truth. Hence the procedures (rules of logical inference) which can establish the logical truth of S cannot be the same as the procedures for establishing its truth. Moreover, the latter are more fundamental than the former. Hence the idea that the rules of logical proof will somehow show the way a proposition is verified is simply mistaken.

This conclusion requires several further comments and explanations. Very briefly, the following points have to be registered:

(a) The rules of logical proof are of course not unrelated to the rules of the 'language-games' of verification and falsification. Game-theoretical semantics shows what the relation between the two is.

(b) GTS shows also that, in many relatively simple cases rules of inference just cannot give the meaning of certain types of propositions, for the inescapable reason that there are no complete rules of logical inference for them. Yet the rules for semantical games (the rules for my games of verification and falsification) are immediately obvious for them. A case in point is offered by propositions involving branching (partially ordered) quantifiers.

(c) One can try—more successfully, I believe, than most philosophers have realized—to interpret mathematical truths as material truths in some particular domain. From this it does not follow that we can give complete sets of rules of logical inference for dealing with the resulting kind of mathematical truth.

(d) Sometimes the assumption seems to have been made that the role of the rules of logical inference can be taken to be the same as our game rules, that is, to extend the concepts of truth and falsity from atomic sentences to all other sentences in a given language. This would of course lend rules of logical inference an important role in semantics (truth theory). Unfortunately, that idea simply does not work.

(e) There is little evidence that the logic—in the sense of a set of formal rules of inference—that results from GTS, i.e., results from Dummett's basic idea of basing one's semantics on processes of verification and falsification, should be intuitionistic, even though Dummett argues for the superiority of intuitionistic logic as the true logic of a verificationist meaning theory.

I shall deal with these points one by one.

LOGICAL PROOFS AS FRUSTRATED COUNTERMODEL CONSTRUCTIONS

It is ironic that Dummett (1977) and his ilk should have operated typically with Gentzen-type rules of logical inference. For these rules, sometimes known as sequent calculus rules, are ideally suited for showing that Dummett is wrong and that the rules of logical inference have a role different from what he takes it to be. These rules are not rules defining truth in a model, they are rules for trying to *construct* a model in which certain formulas are true (or, in some cases, false).

For the purpose of seeing this, all that is needed is literally to turn suitable, eminently natural Gentzen-type rules upside down, putting the sequent to be proved on the top and the axioms at the bottom. What do we get? What we obtain, plus minus a few theoretically insignificant notational changes, is a set of rules for Beth's method of so-called semantical *tableau*.[11] And the only overwhelmingly natural way of looking at them is to see them, not as rules of truth, but as rules for trying to construct a model in which certain formulas are true or false, more explicitly speaking, in which the initial left-column sentences are true but the initial right-column sentences are false. The nature of these rules as construction rules is seen most clearly by considering an application of the rule of existential instantiation for the left column. The situation looks as follows:

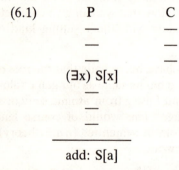

Here 'a' is a new (previously unused) individual constant (dummy name, free individual variable—whatever your favorite term is). Now where did 'a' come from? If we were dealing with the truth of propositions in some given model, the step depicted in (6.1) would be unmotivated, at least if we did not have an effective way of finding instantiations for all true existentially quantified sentences—which we do not in general have. The step (6.1) just does not make any sense conceived of as a rule of truth. (I have argued (Hintikka, 1973) that this problem has vital connections with Kant's philosophy of mathematics; but this is not the place to expound that connection.)

The only reasonable way of looking at the rule (6.1) is to think of it as mandating a construction step. One is in (6.1) not engaged in finding an instantiation for a true existential sentence; one is trying to *construct* a model in which this sentence (suitably reinterpreted, perhaps) would be true. The instantiating term is not the name of an individual *found* to make S[x] true; it is an invented individual *stipulated* to make it true.

All the other rules of inference can be looked upon in the same way, although the brute necessity of doing so is less conspicuous in some of the other cases.

On the basis of this insight, many things fall into place. Since the aim of the construction is to make certain sentences true or false, the failure of all possible ways of doing so will show the falsity of the initial counter-assumption and hence the validity of the initial implication from P to C.

Also, since the ultimate aim of the exercise is to construct a model in which certain formulas are true (or false), it is to be expected that the construction rules are *determined* by the rules governing these concepts. This, indeed is the case. The rules for model construction correspond to, and are closely related to the rules of truth, without yet being identical with each other.

GTS allows a particularly poignant formulation for the relation between the two sets of rules. The rules of attempted construction, i.e., rules of logical proof, can be thought of as rules in certain formal 'games' played with logical formulas. These rules aim at constructing a model in which Myself has a winning strategy in certain semantical games. The rules of these semantical games are in effect the rules of truth. They condition the rules of proof without in any sense being identical with them. Indeed, the difference between the two sorts of games could scarcely be greater. Games of formal logical proof and disproof are indoor games, played with a piece of paper and a pencil; semantical games are outdoor games of seeking and finding played among the objects one's sentences speak of, be they people, physical objects, or what not. It is a rank category mistake to confuse the two, in spite of the close conceptual connection between them. Semantical games are a variant of the games of formal proof as little as football is a variety of chess.

PARTIALLY ORDERED QUANTIFIER PREFIXES AS A COUNTER-EXAMPLE TO DUMMETT

Yet these observations do not close the issue. Since there is a very close connection between the rules of Gentzen-type proof and the rules for my semantical games, at least for first-order languages, what is the harm of thinking about semantical matters in terms of the former, as Dummett does, instead of the latter, as I am urging? None, it might seem. Is it not easy to translate discussions and theses pertaining to semantical games always into the language of Gentzen rules? No, it is not easy in all cases, and in some relatively simple cases it is downright impossible.

A simple example of this kind is offered by languages with partially ordered quantifiers prefixes.[12] Except for such nonlinear quantifier prefixes, the languages are in other respects like applied first-order languages. Logicians have studied such languages in a relatively modest scale since 1960.

Consider a sentence in such a language, say

(7.1) $\quad(\forall x)(\exists y)$
$$\begin{array}{c} (\forall x)(\exists y) \searrow \\ S[x,y,z,u] \\ (\forall z)(\exists u) \nearrow \end{array}$$

where there are no quantifiers in $S[x,y,z,u]$. Now, how is the semantics of (7.1) to be construed? Game-theoretical semantics immediately yields an answer. All we have to do for the purpose is to acknowledge a possibility which any game theorist undoubtedly has so far been missing in my development of GTS: the possibility of imperfect information. A player in a semantical game need not know what has happened at earlier moves of the game. The extent of a player's knowledge of earlier quantifier moves can be indicated by a partial ordering of the quantifiers. At a move addressed to a given quantifier (Q_1x), only such quantifier moves are 'remembered' as were addressed to quantifiers (Q_2x) earlier (higher) in the partial ordering than (Q_1x).

Indeed, this is the natural interpretation of partially ordered quantifier sentences, and it is significant that it was relied on by logicians a decade before GTS was developed in its general form.

But why should not this game-theoretical treatment have a proof-theoretical counterpart, which could be captured by means of suitable Gentzen-type rules of inference? However you prefer to look at the reason, it can be shown that the logic or partially ordered quantifiers cannot be axiomatized. The decision problems for formulas partially ordered quantifier prefixes is of the same order of difficulty as the decision problem for second-order logic, as I have shown (Hintikka, 1974). Since second-order logic is not axiomatizable. there cannot be a complete set of rules of logical inference for formulas with partially ordered quantifier prefixes.

Thus the semantics of partially ordered quantifiers cannot be dealt with by formulating suitable rules of inference (proof) for formulas containing such quantifier structures, for the simple reason that there are no complete sets of such rules.

Ian Hacking (1977) once called a study of meaning based on Gentzen-type rules of inference and the ways they can be varied 'do-it-yourself semantics'. I am afraid that the name is even more appropriate than he intended. The intrinsic limitations of this do-it-yourself approach are nowhere more clearly in evidence than in the semantics of partially ordered quantifiers.

MATHEMATICAL TRUTH

One possible reaction to the failure of a semantics based on inference rules is to restrict the scope of the enterprise. If we cannot characterize truth in general in this way, maybe we can capture mathematical truth by reference to the rules of mathematical proof. There are philosophical precedents for such an idea. It is for instance the view of Ludwig Wittgenstein, who has in fact provided much of Dummett's inspiration.

This is not a place to develop a detailed philosophy of mathematics. For my purposes, which pertain to general semantical theory, it does not matter greatly even if someone can develop an inferential 'do-it-yourself' semantics for mathematical truth.

A few points may nevertheless be in order here. I do not think that an inferential theory of mathematical truth is going to be satisfactory. The usual objection to such a theory is to recall Gödel's incompleteness theorem, which shows that no proof procedure can be adequate to a mathematical theory which includes elementary number theory. In order to get around this objection, an inferential-truth theorist like Dummett is committed to some kind of nonclassical constructivist conception of mathematical truth. This may be a possible and interesting line of thought, but it leaves the classical conception of mathematical truth unexplained, and is unsatisfactory already for that reason. Can one do better here in the teeth of Gödel's incompleteness result?

The most promising line of thought, which I am in the process of developing, is calculated to vindicate the classical conception of mathematical truths as truths about certain structures which mathematicians study.[13] If such a vindication can be accomplished, the semantics of mathematical truth will be a variant of the semantics of ordinary material truth.

By itself, this traditional semantics will not be particularly informative, however, for the main emphasis will be on being able to capture the intended structure (model). How can we do this? How can we eliminate unintended 'nonstandard' models? My main suggestion is to do this by imposing suitable additional restrictions on the models of mathematical axiom systems. It can be shown that by means of suitable restrictions of this sort one can eliminate all 'nonstandard models' of at least some important mathematical theories. This in turn means that mathematical truth, unlike logical truth, can after all be considered as material truth in some particular domain or model.

In such a way, we may seem to vindicate after all the idea that the rules of proof define truth, albeit now only for mathematical truth, not for truth in general. For now the truths of a mathematical theory appear to be precisely the logical consequences of a suitable complete axiom system for it. Hence the logical rules of inference which characterize logical consequence would also seem to characterize mathematical truth. Hence Dummett and his co-workers seem to be partially vindicated after all.

Yet they are not, not even in the limited field of mathematical truth. The statement I just made embodies a fallacy. All that can truly be said here is that *if* there were complete sets of rules characterizing the relation of logical consequence *after* my new restrictions are imposed on the models of one's propositions, they would also characterize the notion of mathematical truth. But the possibility of eliminating nonstandard models and thereby characterizing mathematical truth by means of the (model-theoretical) consequence relation was purchased at the cost of imposing additional restrictions on the models of our propositions.[14] That means making more sentences true in all (remaining) models, i.e., creating more logical truths, i.e., creating more relations of logical consequences. What follows from the well-known incompleteness results is now that the resulting new (model-theoretical) relation of logical consequence cannot any longer be captured by explicit formal rules of inference. In short, mathematical (model-theoretical) completeness was purchased at the cost of deductive incompleteness. (That is why the mathematical completeness, i.e., the elimination of nonstandard models, does not violate Gödel's incompleteness result.) Hence we cannot after all characterize mathematical truth by means of complete sets of inference rules, for the simple reason that there will not be such sets of rules of logical inference any longer.

Hence this attempt to restore the bond between the rules of inference (proof) and the concept of truth fails, for now there are no complete sets of rules of inference to tie the bond to.

TRUTH FOR ATOMIC SENTENCES VS TRUTH FOR COMPLEX SENTENCES

There is another fallacy in this area which is perhaps not entirely easy to pin on any particular logician but which nevertheless seems to have influenced many people's thinking. One question that naturally suggests itself here is: Cannot the rules of proof serve the same purpose as the game rules of GTS and the recursive clauses in Tarski-type true-definitions, viz. to extend the notions of truth and falsity from atomic sentences to all others?

(That Dummett in effect gives an affirmative answer to this question is shown by the quotation given above in note 10.) Indeed, is not that just what Gentzen-type rules of inference in fact do? Look, for instance, at the Gentzen-type rules for (say) conjunction. Do not they simply bring out the fact that a conjunction is true if both of its conjuncts are true and false as soon as either one of its conjuncts is false?

In a reasonable sense, this is true of inference rules for propositional connectives. They can, in fact, be thought of as extending the notions of truth and falsity from atomic propositions to truth-functions of such propositions.

But the same cannot be said of rules of inference for quantifiers. The reason is brought out by what was said in the sixth section above. In using inference rules for quantifiers, we are in effect trying to construct a domain of individuals (with the appropriate properties and relations defined on it) in which certain formulas would be true or false. At any one stage of the procedure, we do not yet have the entire domain of individuals ready to be quantified over. Hence such rules of construction cannot serve to characterize what it means for a quantified proposition to be true in a given ready-made model.

This is reflected by the fact that the actual relation of logical consequence, which is what the rules of inference are calculated to capture, simply is not capable of extending the notions of truth and falsehood from atomic propositions to all the complex (e.g., quantified) ones. In order to see this, let us consider a model M and the diagram (also known as the state-description) $\Delta(M)$ of a model M. (It is the set of all negated or unnegated atomic propositions true in M.) Then it is *not* always the case that a complex sentence S is true in M only if

$$\Delta M \vdash S$$

Indeed, even if we add as an additional premiss some proposition T true in M, we still do not always have the equivalence

$$S \text{ is true in } M \leftrightarrow ((T \cup \Delta(M)) \vdash S)$$

holding for all choices of the proposition S (in the language of M). For if this were the case, we would have

$$(T \cup \Delta M) \vdash S$$

or

$$(T \cup \Delta M) \vdash \sim S$$

for each sentence S in the language of M. A theory for which this holds is referred to (following Abraham Robinson, 1963) as a *model-complete* theory. It is well known that not every theory is model-complete. (Not even all complete theories are model-complete.) This vividly shows how utterly hopeless it is to try to use rules of inference to define the notions of truth and falsity for complex propositions.

Yet this is unmistakenly what, e.g., the Lorenzen school attempts to do.[15] They first introduced certain dialogical games, not to define the notions of truth and falsity, as GTS does, but to capture the rules of logical proof (inference). Then they modified these 'formal dialogues' so that they are based on domains where atomic propositions have a definite truth-value, true or false, while keeping the rules essentially unmodified. What that amounts to is, of course, precisely what I have indicated, viz. to try to use the rules of inference to extend the notion of truth and falsity from atomic propositions to complex ones.

Thus one of the ideas on which the entire approach of Dummett, Lorenzen and their followers seems to be based turns out to be false. In a wider philosophical perspective, I cannot but find this idea—the idea, that is to say, that rules of proof serve to extend the concepts of truth and falsity from observable propositions to all others—is a hopeless one right from the beginning. At a time when virtually all philosophers of science are emphasizing the underdeterminacy of theories by observable propositions, it is an extraordinarily weak argument to assume, as Dummett and Lorenzen are in effect assuming, that our usual truth-conditional notion of truth should be replaced by some verificationist substitute which restores the determinacy of truth by inference—or to assume that the only recourse their semantical opponents have is to assume such a determination for our ordinary notion of truth.

My result here should be complemented by considering possible non-deductive ways of arguing from observable sentences to nonobservable ones. The trouble is that there is no agreement about as to what these ways of argument are. I have proposed (Hintikka, 1984) to conceptualize them as sequences of answers to questions put to nature. If so, it has to be studied whether, and if so in what sense, material truth could be characterized by means of such questioning procedures. The study remains to be carried out, but there does not seem to be any realistic hope of doing that in general.

WHAT IS THE TRUE LOGIC OF A VERIFICATIONIST SEMANTICS?

It was mentioned above that Dummett argues that the true logic ensuing from a verificationist semantics of the kind he propounds is an intuitionist one. The same claim has been made by Lorenzen. Now that we have seen that their main idea, which is to considerable extent shared by GTS, has to be carried out in a way different from the one they rely on, the question arises anew as to what has to be said of their claims to have uncovered the true logic of human reasoning—or at least the true logic on which a satisfactory semantical theory can be based. This in turn leads us to the wider question: What is the true logic of a semantics of the kind Dummett and Wittgenstein favor? Is there in the literature a ready theory waiting for verificationist semanticists? What is the true logic of GTS, anyway? (Is it perhaps the intuitionist logic?)

An interesting answer is in the offing here. According to GTS, the truth of a given sentence S means the existence of a winning strategy for Myself in G(S). Now the existence of such a strategy can be expressed by means of a higher-order sentence which involves quantification over strategies. Such strategies can of course be codified in functions and functionals, wherefore speaking of the existence of a winning strategy can be expressed by quantifying over such functions and functionals. (Notice, for the purpose, that a *winning* strategy is one which wins against *any* strategy of one's opponent.)

Hence part of the force of GTS can be captured by means of a translation of lower-order sentences into higher-order ones.

For instance, if we limit ourselves to the part of strategies that affect quantifiers only, we have the following translations:

(10.1) $(\forall x)(\exists y)\ R(x,y)$

translates into

(10.2) $(\exists f)(\forall x)\ R(x,f(x))$.

Also,

(10.3) $(\forall x)(\exists y)(\forall z)(\exists u)\ R(x,y,z,u)$

translates into

(10.4) $(\exists f)(\exists g)(\forall x)(\forall z)\ R(x,f(x),z,g(x,z))$

while

(10.5) $(\forall x)(\forall z)(\exists y)(\exists u)\ R(x,y,z,u)$

translates as

(10.6) $(\exists f)(\exists g)(\forall x)(\forall z)\ R(x,f(x,z),z,g(x,z))$.

Furthermore

(10.7) $(\exists x)(\forall y)\ R(x,y)$

is obviously its own translation. (Thus the translation does not always take us to higher-order sentences.)

The same translatability applies of course to branching-quantifier sentences. (Cf. the seventh section above.) For instance, we have the following:

$$(10.8) \quad (\exists x)$$
$$R(x,y)$$
$$(\forall y)$$

translates as

$$(10.9) \quad (\exists x)(\forall y) \, R(x,y)$$

while

$$(10.10) \quad (\forall x)(\exists y)$$
$$R(x,y,z)$$
$$(\forall z)$$

translates as

$$(10.11) \quad (\exists f)(\forall x)(\forall z) \, R(x,f(x),z)$$

which happens to be equivalent with

$$(10.12) \quad (\forall x)(\exists y)(\forall z) \, R(x,y,z).$$

In contrast,

$$(10.13) \quad (\forall x)(\exists y)$$
$$R(x,y,z,u)$$
$$(\forall z)(\exists u)$$

translates as

$$(10.14) \quad (\exists f)(\exists g)(\forall x)(\forall z) \, R(x,f(x),z,g(z))$$

which in general does not reduce to a linear first-order form. (It is instructive here to compare (10.13)–(10.14) with (10.3)–(10.4) and (10.5)–(10.6).)

These translations illustrate also a general truth about the translatability from natural languages to a formal language. Several philosophers and linguists have in effect suggested using first-order languages as our 'canonical notation' for the representation of logical form. GTS suggests that there is little reason to think that first-order logic suffices as a representation of the logical structures of all natural-language sentences. The best we can hope translation-wise is a translation of natural-language sentences into *higher-order* logical languages. Of the resulting translations, it has to be studied case by case whether or not they reduce to linear first-order sentences.

GTS AND FUNCTIONAL INTERPRETATIONS

Thus it might seem that there is a simple answer to the title question of the preceding section. The true logic of a verificationist semantics of the kind Dummett's general philosophical position should naturally give rise to seems to be, as closely as we can tell, simply higher-order logic.

And yet it turns out that this is not the definitive answer. For two funny things happens on the way to higher-order logic.

(i)   The semantical game G(S) connected with a sentence S must sometimes be divided into *subgames* (see, e.g., Hintikka, 1983). Consider, for instance, a conditional

(11.1)   If S_1, then S_2.

Here it is natural to think that one first sees if S_1 is true. This corresponds to playing a semantical game starting with S_1, i.e., the game $G(S_1)$. Since it clearly is in the interests of Myself to falsify S_1, this subgame is played with roles reversed, i.e., Nature is trying to verify S_1 and Myself is trying to falsify S_2. Only if Nature wins, i.e., S_1 is verified, do the players move to play the second subgame $G(S_2)$. Now since the truth of the consequent of a conditional is, well, conditional on the truth of its antecedent, it is natural to give the verifier in $G(S_2)$, i.e., Myself, access to the verifier's, i.e., Nature's, strategy in $G(S_1)$.

These informal explanations can be easily converted into an explicit formal game rule. Similar subgame rules are easily formulated for other logical particles.

(ii)   The reason for another important change is seen by taking the game idea seriously. If a player is following a strategy in a semantical game, then this strategy must be codable in an effective (recursive) function. For nonrecursive function cannot give anyone a real instruction as to how to make one's moves in all cases, for there is no method for deciding what the prescription is in all cases.

Hence it seems motivated to restrict the ranges of the higher-order quantifiers used in the game-theoretical translation to recursive functions. (In fact, I am not quite convinced that we *have* to do so, but I will not discuss the question here.)

Only after these two changes does the higher-order translation yield the genuinely characteristic logic of GTS.

At this point, a logician ought to have a *déjà vu* experience. Where have we seen something closely similar? The answer is: in the so-called functional interpretations launched by Gödel in 1958. When I first read Gödel's classical paper (1980, translated into English) 'Über eine bisher noch nicht benützte Erweiterung des finiten Standpunktes' I could not make any heads or tails of his line of thought. Gödel gives there an interpretation of first-order logic and number theory by defining a translation from these theories to a fragment of higher-order logic. The translation rules made no sense to me, however, for *a priori* there could be hundreds of comparable ones, and Gödel himself offers little motivation for the particular rules he presents. It was only years later, when I was already working in the framework of GTS, that the scales fell off and I suddenly saw the truth. Gödel was doing game-theoretical semantics! His rules for translating from first-order languages to higher-order ones are but a codification of one possible set of rules for the game-theoretical semantics for those first-order languages, expressed in the form of higher-order translation rules.

I do not know what line of thought actually guided Gödel's interpretation, but the identity of what he did with what I was led to do is striking. In general, we can say that the true logic of GTS is the logic defined by Gödel-type translations into higher-order languages. Such translations are usually said to define *functional interpretations*. Hence the true logic of GTS is the logic of functional interpretations.

Gödel's actual interpretation is only one case in point, for a number of rules, especially the rule for conditionals, can be formulated in somewhat different ways. The relation between different variant interpretations remains to be studied, even though logicians have paid a fair amount of attention to functional interpretations (a brief bibliography is given in Hintikka, 1983).

It also remains to be investigated what precisely the relation is between functional interpretations and intuitionistic logic. It is known that we do not obtain intuitionistic logic from a Gödelian functional interpretation. But whether this difference is important enough to be used as an argument against intuitionistic logic remains to be discussed.

Thus it is not clear at this time whether Dummett's claim that intuitionistic logic is the true logic of a verificationist semantics is defensible or not.

ACKNOWLEDGEMENTS

The research reported here was made possible by the NSF grants No. BNS-8119033 (Research in Game-Theoretic Semantics) and No. IST-8310936 (Questioning as Knowledge-Seeking Method).

NOTES

[1] Much of the work that has been done on GTS is published or reprinted in Hintikka (1983), Hintikka & Kulas (1985) and Saarinen (1979).

[2] That this is the right way of looking at Wittgenstein's use of the idea of language-game is shown in Hintikka and Hintikka (1986, especially chapter 9).

[3] The most important of these concepts is that of strategy. Its usefulness is partly due to the fact that the strategic angle has frequently been neglected in recent language theory. For examples see Hintikka (1986).

[4] For Tarski-type truth-definitions, see Tarski (1956), Davidson (1967) and Carnap (1947).

[5] For a discussion of the principle of compositionality, see the last chapter of Hintikka (1983).

[6] In fact, GTS can be thought of as a codification of ways of thinking and speaking which mathematicians (and mathematical logicians) have used since time immemorial (or at least since the time of Cauchy) but which they have acknowledged as a conceptual tool only when other ways of treating their subject matter have not done their job. See chapter 1 of Hintikka (1983).

[7] The most important of these is the distinction between *abstract meaning* and *strategic meaning* explained in Hintikka & Kulas (1985).

[8] For a survey of this subject, see Martin & Kechris (1980).

[9] This idea was used in Hintikka & Rantala (1976).

[10] Dummett (1978) expresses this as follows:

> In the mathematical case, that which establishes a statement as true is the production of a deductive argument terminating in that statement as conclusion; in the general case, a statement will, in general, also be established as true by a process of reasoning will not usually be purely deductive in character, and the premisses of the argument will be based on observation; only for a restricted class of statements—the observation statements—will their verification be of a purely observational kind, without the mediation of any chain of reasoning or any other mental, linguistic or symbolic process.

This quotation shows that, even though Dummett acknowledges that the reasoning involved in the establishment of truth is not always purely deductive, it is comparable to deductive reasoning. The reason is that this reasoning is essentially symbolic. Thus, Dummett is completely overlooking the possibility that the processes of truth-establishment should be actual, non-symbolic activities of seeking and finding.

[11] The most readable exposition of the motivation of this technique is still Beth (1955). Of course, the rules of the *tableau* method are the same as the rules of Gentzen-type calculus of sequents, except that they are written out in the reverse direction.

[12] A brief bibliography of the literature on partially ordered quantifier prefixes is given in Hintikka (1983).

[13] See the forthcoming monograph of mine. If my attempt pans out, it means distinguishing sharply between logical 'truth', which amounts to (material) truth in every possible world (model) and mathematical truth, which will be truth in some particular model (structure).

[14] The operative question here is of course: What are these restrictions like? I shall argue that in the classical literature (Hilbert, Poincaré, Dedekind, etc.) contains clues which can be exploited to yield an answer to this crucial question.

[15] For their views, see Lorenzen & Lorenz (1978).

REFERENCES

Beth, E. W., Semantic Entailment and Formal Derivability. *Mededelingen van de Koninklijke Nederlandse Akademie van Wetenschappen Afdeling Letterkunde*, N.R. vol. 18, no. 13, Amsterdam, 1955, pp. 309–342.

Carnap. R., *Meaning and Necessity*. Chicago, IL; University of Chicago Press, 1947.

Davidson, D., Truth and Meaning. *Synthese*, 1967, **17**, 304–323.

Dummett, M., What is a Theory of Meaning (II). In G. Evans & J. McDowell (Eds), *Truth and Meaning: Essays in Semantics*. Oxford: Clarendon Press, 1976, pp. 67–137.

Dummett, M., *Elements of Intuitionism*. Oxford: Clarendon Press, 1977.

Dummett, M., The Philosophical Basics of Intuitionistic Logic. In M. Dummett (Ed.), *Truth and Other Enigmas*. Cambridge, MA: Harvard University Press, 1978, pp. 215–247.

Gödel, K., On a Hitherto Unexploited Extension of the Finitististic Standpoint. *Journal of Philosophical Logic*, 1980, **9**, 133–142.

Hacking, I., Do-it-yourself Semantics for Classical Sequent Calculi including Ramified Type Theory. In R. E. Butts & J. Hintikka (Eds), *Logic, Foundations of Mathematics, and Computability Theory*. Dordrecht: Reidel, 1977, pp. 371–390.

Hintikka, J., *Logic, Language-Games, and Information*. Oxford: Clarendon Press, 1973.

Hintikka, J., Quantifiers vs Quantification Theory. *Linguistic Inquiry*, 1974, **5**, 153–177.

Hintikka, J., *The Game of Language*. Dordrecht: Reidel, 1983.

Hintikka, J., The Logic of Science as Model-Oriented Logic. In P. D. Asquith & P. Kitcher (Eds), *PSA 1984*. East Lansing, MI: PSA, 1984, vol. 1, pp. 177–185.

Hintikka, J., *Tractatus Logico-Mathematicus*. Monograph in progress

Hintikka, J., Logic of Conversation as a Logic of Dialogue. In R. Grandy & R. Warner (Eds), *Philosophical Grounds of Rationality: Intentions, Categories, Ends*. Oxford: Clarendon Press, 1986, pp. 259–276.

Hintikka, M. B. & Hintikka, J., *Investigating Wittgenstein*. Oxford: Blackwell, 1986.

Hintikka, J. & Kulas, J., *Anaphora and Definite Descriptions: Two Applications of Game-Theoretical Semantics*. Dordrecht: Reidel, 1985.

Hintikka, J. & Rantala, V., A New Approach to Infinitary Languages. *Annals of Mathematical Logic*, 1976, **10**, 95–115.

Lorenzen, P. & Lorenz, K. (Eds), *Dialogische Logik*. Darmstadt: Wissenschaftliche Buchgesellschaft, 1978.

Martin, D. A. & Kechris, A. S., Infinite Games and Effective Descriptive Set Theory. In C. A. Rogers *et al.* (Eds), *Analytic Sets*. New York: Academic Press, 1980, pp. 403–470.

Robinson, A., *Introduction to Model Theory and to the Metamathematics of Algebra*. Amsterdam: North-Holland, 1963.

Saarinen, E. (Ed), *Game-Theoretical Semantics*. Dordrecht: Reidel, 1979.

Tarski, A., The Concept of Truth in Formalized Languages. In A. Tarski (Ed.), *Logic, Semantics, Metamathematics*. Oxford: Clarendon Press, 1956.

8

In Defense of Semantic Fields

RICHARD E. GRANDY

Department of Philosophy,
Rice University

There seems to be something to be gained—and nothing worthwhile to be lost—from a less grandiose, more tentative and pragmatic approach to the problem of linguistic fields (Spence, 1961).

The Humboldt–Trier–Weisgerber conception of semantic fields has been criticized repeatedly on the grounds of vagueness and subjectivity, yet even critics seem willing to grant that there is something of semantic and psychological importance underlying the general conception. The theoretical task, therefore, is to try to formulate these ideas more clearly in the hope of dispelling some of the uncertainties and misunderstandings that surround them (Miller & Johnson-Laird, 1976).

Even constancy of literal application is usually relative to a set of labels: what counts as red, for example, will vary somewhat depending upon whether objects are being classified as red or nonred, or as red or orange or yellow or green or blue or violet (Goodman, 1976).

I argue in this essay for an old approach to an old problem. The problem is the theoretical analysis of word meaning, the approach semantic field theory. The problem has not been entirely ignored recently, the work of Katz (1970) and others has continued for the last twenty years and Putnam (1975) and his students have recently taken some interest, but if one surveys the contents of this volume one quickly notes that most of the approaches are primarily, if not exclusively, concerned with sentential matters. I do not wish to argue against those projects, except insofar as the number of people who will work in semantics is finite and if I persuade some to work on an alternative project this will have a negative impact on the others.

259

However, I do want to argue that concentration exclusively on matters concerning literal declarative sentences (truth conditions, implication relations and their ilk) ignores a great deal of potential philosophical interest. I do not know how one would test this claim, but I would conjecture that only a small portion of language use consists of the utterance of[1] literal declarative sentences.

Semantic field theory has been rather widely used by anthropologists and linguists, especially non-Americans, but has received far less theoretical attention than is desirable. Of course for specific practical applications one need not pay attention to foundational niceties, but I hope in this paper to at least somewhat remedy the neglect. My main goal in this paper is to stimulate interest in semantic field theory rather than to persuade readers of my own particular version. Therefore I postpone giving my own definition until the section on contrast sets.

I begin by listing some of the phenomena I regard as important and insufficiently appreciated by semanticists. I will then turn successively to general Quinian arguments that theories of word-meaning are worthless or impossible, to Katzian arguments that the theory is largely extant, to objections to the general notion of a semantic field and to likely objections to my notion of a semantic field. I will conclude by arguing that semantic fields can be used to clarify and amplify some recent work in psychology on classification, prototypes and similarity.

SOME PHENOMENA

As indicated at the outset, there is a great deal of disagreement about the character and size of semantic fields. Writers agree that a semantic field is a collection of related words, but how large a collection and how the items are related is in dispute. By all accounts they are large and complex entities. As a first step toward characterizing semantic fields, I will begin by describing one central and essential ingredient in semantic fields, a *basic contrast set*: Provisionally,[2] a basic contrast set will consist of a linguistic expression L (the covering term) and a set of monolexemic expressions E_1, ..., E_n (the members of the set) such that the extension of each E_i is a subset of the extension of L and the extensions of the E_i are pairwise disjoint.[3]

Most common and interesting examples of contrast sets usually involve simple lexical covering terms and in many cases the union of the extensions of the members exhausts the extension of L. ⟨Parent: mother, father⟩. ⟨Day: Monday, Tuesday, . . . Sunday⟩. ⟨Vegetable: artichoke, . . . zucchini⟩. ⟨Color: red, green, blue, yellow, orange, brown, purple, black, white⟩. Contrast sets of natural kinds are often non-exhaustive and somewhat open-ended, while those for artifacts are usually closed and exhaustive. An expression may occur (with the same sense) within more than one contrast set and contrast sets occur at different levels of generality. 'Dog' will be a member of the contrast set specified by mammal but will also cover a contrast set that includes poodle and dachshund. Although most contrast sets have monolexemic covering terms, some natural ones do not, and indeed some natural ones may have no simpler covering term than the disjunction of the members:

⟨(sibling or spouse of a sibling) of a parent: uncle, aunt⟩

In this section I will argue that part of what speakers know when they know the meaning of a word is the contrast set(s) to which it belongs, that the contrast sets are an essential part of the theoretical description of the meaning, and that this knowledge of contrast sets is evident in semantic memory. In the fourth section I will discuss the role of contrast sets in language learning.

Metaphor

In describing the function of metaphor, as when we can say that someone is a lion/bear/sheep/ostrich, it is often claimed that 'the properties of the objects ordinarily denoted by the metaphorical expression are transferred to the new subject'. And there seems to be something to this, though it is not easy to say what. For not all properties are transferred, in most metaphors the sentence is literally false, probably even semantically deviant. And to say that some properties are transferred is uninformative for the subject already has many properties in common with the denotata of the metaphorical expression. The most promising and constructive suggestion I have seen in this direction is that in metaphor one transfers those general properties that are associated with the metaphorical expression and that the other members of its contrast set lack (Kittay, 1984, 1987).

Thus metaphors, at least good ones, do not simply relate two expressions but also bring into focus a potential relation between two entire contrast sets. This approach accounts for how metaphors can be simultaneously novel and yet rule constrained. In choosing what other contrast set to invoke in the metaphor the author is taking a novel and imaginative step, but for the metaphor to work there must be interesting and significant relations among the two contrast sets that can be worked. The latter is not a matter of creation but discovery.

Questions and Explanation

Analyses of the logic of questions differ in details, but almost all agree that one begins by postulating a set of possible answers (Belnap *et al*, 1976). In most cases a question indicates the relevant response set either by specifying a contrast set ('What color is Susan's car?') or by specifying a member of a contrast set ('Is Susan's car blue?'). A speaker who answered the first by saying 'Chevrolet' or the second by saying, 'No, it's a Chevrolet' would betray a lack of semantic competence.[4] Thus a speaker in answering questions appropriately requires knowledge of the contrast sets available in the language. In addition to the direct applicability to questions, it has recently been suggested (Bromberger, 1966; van Frassen, 1980, pp. 134ff) that explanation is best understood in the framework of a theory of questions and thus semantic fields enter there also.

Conversational Maxims

Paul Grice (1975) has suggested that conversational exchanges are governed by a number of principles of quality and quantity. An obvious quality principle is that one should not say what one knows to be false. Two principles of quantity are that one should make one's conversational contribution informative and that one should be relevant. These two principles together have as a consequence that one ought to provide the right amount of information, neither too much nor too little. Knowledge of the contrast sets available in the language will again be essential to the speaker in complying with the maxims and to the hearer in determining what information is conveyed if the maxims are complied with.

Imagine, for example, the question 'Who is that man?' being answered by 'He is my father's sister's husband'. This answer apparently violates a principle of economy—do not use three words where one ('uncle') would do, so a reasonable conjecture as to the informant's intent, assuming the maxims are being followed, is that he felt it necessary to draw a contrast that is not made by 'uncle'; perhaps he was distinguishing the person in question from another person present who is his mother's brother.

Related Polysemy

The distinction between homonymy and polysemy is clearer in the abstract than in application; but that distinction is easier to draw than that between polysemous words and those that only appear so. That the ursine sense of 'bear' is distinct from the verb form(s) of that string of letters is clear from the fact that the first is a noun. However, whether the verb has more than one meaning is less easy to answer conclusively.

An especially difficult kind of possible polysemy occurs when the one of the alleged senses is contained in the other. These are particularly frequent in everyday biological classifications where often a word can be applied either to both sexes of a species or only to one (man, dog, cow) or is used both for a family and a species within the family (crocodile, cat) but is not infrequent elsewhere in the language (water: ice, water, steam). And in some cases an entire set of terms reappears with a narrower meaning in a second contrast set: ⟨north, east, south, west⟩ and ⟨north, northeast, east, southeast, south, southwest, west, northwest⟩. There is at least some disagreement among linguists whether such items are polysemous or not. I suggest that they are and that one way of distinguishing their meanings is by the different contrast sets that are associated with (part of) the respective meanings.

Semantic Memory

It is easily verified that if one poses to a subject the task of enumerating as many kinds as possible that fall under some common noun within a fixed time the results reveal that memory is, at least partly, organized by contrast sets. For example, a subject instructed to enumerate kinds of animals might produce a response (with . . . indicating longer pauses) such as: 'lion, tiger, leopard, cheetah, panther, cougar, ocelot, lynx, . . ., elephant, rhinoceros, hippopotamus . . .'. The evidence that memory is organized at least partially in terms of contrast sets is quite clear. I will argue in the fourth section that it is essential that it be so organized. (Although it should be noted that it is sometimes difficult to sort out other factors—because most zoos are physically organized in terms of contrast sets the results may reflect association directly and contrast sets only indirectly.)[5]

This in itself is not an argument for contrast sets being of concern to semantic theorists, but it is evidence that contrast sets are psychologically significant. Thus it bolsters the first three arguments above by emphasizing that speakers need to have the relevant information organized in a way that would help with the tasks discussed there. It will also indirectly support the argument to be given in the final section concerning the essential roles contrast sets play in language learning and the nature of categorization.

IS A THEORY OF WORD MEANING POSSIBLE?

Most historians of linguistics agree in tracing the conception of a semantic field back to Saussure (1966, p. 113) and his emphatic holism with regard to meaning.

> . . . to consider a term as simply the union of a certain sound with a certain concept is grossly misleading. To define it in this way would isolate the term from its system; it would mean assuming that one can start from the terms and construct the system by adding them together when, on the contrary, it is from the interdependent whole that one must start and through analysis obtain its elements.

Indeed Saussure seems to be more holistic than Quine and to suggest the irrelevance of extralinguistic factors: 'Language is a system of inter-dependent terms in which the value of each term results *solely* from the simultaneous presence of the others . . .' (emphasis added) (1966, p. 114).

In spite of the strong affinities, I know of no Quine-minded philosophers of language who have seriously considered the theoretical utility of semantic fields. I suspect that this is because there are, *prima facie*, three closely-related Quinian objections to the concept of a contrast set (and by implication to semantic fields). One is that the concept presupposes an analytic/synthetic dichotomy, the second is that the indeterminacy of translation shows the pointlessness of any theory of word meaning. The third, ironically, turns the Saussurean perspective itself against its derivative objecting that one cannot isolate some subset of the language from the remainder.

The characterization of a contrast set does appear as though it pre-supposes something like an analytic/synthetic dichotomy, for we want it not simply to be the case that the elements of the set are disjoint but that they are so as a matter of language.[6] However, my conception of contrast sets differs in two important respects from what would be conveyed by requiring that it be analytic that the items are disjoint.

First, I regard the speaker's knowledge of disjointness to be a matter concerning the expressions of the language, i.e., that the English expressions 'dog' and 'cat' never apply to the same object.[7] Thus it is empirical, language-specific knowledge that is at issue.

Second, the totality of meaning elements and contrast sets may be inconsistent in particular applications. That is, the contrast set might simultaneously:

A. specify that a set exhausts its domain B. assign meanings determining that an object not fall within the extension of any of the member items C. assign a meaning that determines that the object falls within the extension of the covering term. Thus, I claim,[8] the characterization of semantic fields need not presuppose an analytic/synthetic distinction.

With regard to the second Quinian objection, that theories of word-meaning are shown to be impossible by indeterminacy arguments, I should first concede that some of the original motivations and claims for semantic field theory are suspect at best. For Trier (1934) a semantic field consisted of the mapping of one or more lexical fields onto a conceptual field. He also made Whorfish claims about the importance of the lexical field in giving shape to the conceptual field. I advance no such claims here—one may, in some cases where there is a clearly identifiable range of stimuli such as visible radiation, be able to provide comparisons between contrast sets from different languages. But I am extremely dubious about the value of attempting this with abstract or social objects or relations. In short, the presence of contrast sets is of significance for the understanding of a single language and its speakers. Any interlinguistic illumination would be a bonus.

With regard to the third possible objection, that the investigation of contrast sets seeks to artificially isolate a subset of the language, I believe that the objection is unfounded. One ought not to confuse Quine's claims that any sentence of a language is potentially relevant (evidentially) to another with the claim that all such potentialities are equally direct. In any web or network, some points are closer together than others and it is only through a mapping of these relations that any detailed non-metaphorical understanding of the web is to be gained. Members of contrast sets are items which are in very close proximity in the linguistic network and are of primary importance for the various phenomena listed in the first section.

I do not know why the study of semantic fields has been so popular among European linguists while being relatively ignored by American linguists and almost totally ignored by English speaking philosophers. However, in concluding this section, I would like to speculate briefly that the preceding objections may well have mitigated against the serious consideration of the value of semantic fields by philosophers of a Quinian persuasion. On the other hand, those who were inclined to accept an analytic/synthetic distinction and who had an interest in word meaning were likely to be convinced that componential analysis, for example as developed by Katz, would already do the job.

SEMANTIC FIELDS AND COMPONENTIAL ANALYSIS

If one accepts the arguments of the previous sections that theories of word meaning should be taken seriously, or undertaken seriously, then the next issue to consider is adequacy of the componential analysis of word meaning. This is probably the most natural theory and is certainly the best developed (Katz, 1972). *Prima facie* there is a direct opposition between componential analysis, the attempt to identify language independent atoms (semantic markers) that can be combined to produce the meanings of linguistic items, and field theory, the view that meaning depends on relations to other linguistic items and not on internal structure. It may be especially illuminating to analyze the relationship between componential analysis and contrast sets (and, more generally semantic fields) since the *only* explicit discussion I have found in print of this issue is very equivocal. (Lehrer, 1974, pp. 66–72). Her conclusion seems to be that '. . . many of the semantic relationships between words can be deduced from an adequate componential analysis . . .' while '. . . a taxonomy alone is not sufficient for determining the semantic components for words.'

Componential analysis fares well in accounting for containment relations [a cat is an animal] and for pairs of antonyms, where one can postulate that one of the antonyms is simply [-the other].[9] But the approach fares less well when we ask about the larger contrast sets. For example, since (I claim) it is part of the meaning of 'dog' that it contrast with 'cat', an adequate componential analysis will encode that information. We can confine our attention mainly to the level of the most detailed information for the items since 'dog' and 'cat' will share higher markers such as [ANIMATE] and [ANIMAL]. There are four possible approaches to the contrast problem that come readily to mind.

The first is simply to add appropriate markers. Just as one introduces a special distinguishing marker [CANINE] to distinguish dogs from other animals one will include [-FELINE] as a marker. The trouble is that the list does not end there for it will have to include [-BOVINE], [-EQUINE], [-URSINE] and dozens of others. And each of the other entries will have to contain a very similar list. So for a contrast set of n items, there will have to be $n(n - 1)$ entries to represent the information.

A second approach would be to introduce a single item [-OTHER ANIMAL THAN DOG] which would appear in the entry for 'dog', with a similar new item for each other lexical entry. This seems to me to amount to an *ad hoc* backhanded way of admitting the importance of contrast sets. While even Katz now is rather less inclined to press the idea of the semantic components as simple primitive semantic atoms in a chemistry of meaning, the complex and derivative nature of these particular markers seems too far from the spirit of the enterprise to be appealing.

The third approach is to argue that the information is already implicit in the system of markers and that one needs only know how to find it. The idea would be that as a general principle if an item, e.g., 'dog' shares a marker [ANIMAL] with another item 'cat' but they also have different markers, then the two are automatically incompatible. This will not work, however, for the principle does not always hold. In its general sense (i.e., the one in which it includes birds and insects and contrasts with plants) the marker [ANIMAL] is shared by 'bird' and 'insect', but it is also shared by 'herbivore' and 'carnivore' and while 'bird' and 'insect' are incompatible 'bird' and 'carnivore' are not.

The fourth approach would be to add to the componential theory an explicit statement that parellels each of the contrast sets. For example, for each contrast set we would include in the semantic theory the assertions that the extension of each member is included in that of the covering term and that the members are pairwise disjoint. In effect, this amounts to adding postulates that guarantee that the semantic markers have a field structure and that field theory lurks in the theoretical background of a componential analysis. In short, this would be semantic field theory in componential analysis clothing, an approach I would quarrel with only insofar as the garb is unnecessary and misleading.

Thus while we have not given a general argument as to the impossibility of representing the information contained in contrast sets in componential analysis, none of the obvious suggestions seem acceptable.

Even if this problem were to be solved, a more serious one would arise when we went beyond contrast sets to semantic fields. Many contrast sets are internally ordered—⟨days: Monday, . . . Sunday⟩ in a way that the competent speaker knows. In this particular case one might avoid introducing markers mentioning other items at the same level (e.g., [IMMEDIATELY SUCCEEDS WEDNESDAY]) by regarding the order as derivative from numerical order so that 'Monday' would have a marker [FIRST DAY OF WEEK]. For other cases, however, it is very difficult to see how the appropriate markers can be found without embedding reference to other elements of the contrast set within them (e.g., ⟨east, west, north, south⟩ or ⟨port, starboard, fore, aft⟩).

Our conclusions are as follows. Componential analysis emphasizes the atomic view of word meaning whereas consideration of contrast sets points out the relational aspects of word meaning. This is not to deny that componential analysis can have value, especially in discerning the recurrent elements of meaning that appear in various contrast sets. Nonetheless, the main function of contrast sets in elaborating a portion of a speaker's knowledge is at best obliquely served by componential analysis.

INFORMATION, PRAGMATICS AND CONTRAST SETS

In spite of the numerous and disparate phenomena cited earlier which show the presence of semantic fields in the performance of a competent speaker, it may seem that the presence of semantic fields is an accidental feature of natural language, one not worthy of serious theoretical dissection. Or at least not of semantic interest. For most of the phenomena cited might be argued to be either matters of pragmatics or, worse, of psychology.

The most direct way to answer this challenge is to consider the explicitly pragmatic phenomena of Gricean conversational postulates. While Grice formulated these postulates as governing *conversation* I believe that appropriately interpreted they have far wider scope of application. Recall two of the significant and often conflicting maxims:

> Provide sufficient information.
> Be relevant (do not provide unnecessary information.)

The motivation for both principles in plain[10] conversation is evident. And that the principles are much stronger together than separately is of great importance. Sufficient information would be provided, eventually, by a lengthy monologue relating anything of the most remotely possible interest. A selection of relevant information might stop far short of sufficiency.

But similar principles must guide memory. As a guide to action at some time in the future we require sufficient relevant information. If we attempted to recall every detail of every event we saw or heard our memories[11] would be overwhelmed quickly, but if we do not recall enough we act out of unnecessary ignorance. The process of selectively encoding aspects of the world that are considered to be of sufficient importance is a continuing process that is extremely similar in general form to conversation. And for most people the majority of their memory is semantic in character rather than pictorial or auditory.

In short, for our own future benefit it is important that we selectively encode those aspects of our current experience that will be beneficial in guiding our future behavior. And an aspect of our current experience will be relevant and of sufficient interest only if its future occurrences will be sufficiently correlated with phenomena of interest. In short, in coding our current experience for future reference we wish to retain those matters of sufficient salience, significance, and import that they will provide a beneficial guide to future action. But we also wish to use a coding scheme that is efficient, i.e., that incorporates the past experience in a way that is most useful for future applications.

A natural language is a historically evolved coding scheme for representing events, objects and relationships of importance and interest. If one is set a particular coding task where a single level of information is to be represented, perhaps positions on a chess board, then a single level of coding representation can be efficiently designed. However, the demands of understanding, communicating and remembering are quite various. Sometimes we care only that something is an animal, on other occasions we need to know that it is a dog, and on yet others we may need to know whether it is a corgi. Thus the most efficient coding system will have nested sets of distinctions at various levels, i.e., contrast sets.

To this point I have emphasized the utility of contrast sets as coding schemes for current or past experience. But there is a forward looking aspect as well, for we also hope that our coding scheme will provide an appropriate vehicle for predictions of the future. This is a strong constraint on the linguistic evolution of lexical items, which are also, of course, subject to the influence of our interests and many other factors. To give one more precise example, contrast sets (under the name 'families of predicates') played a major role in Carnap's (1950) work on induction and (again not by name) in at least one suggestion for resolving paradoxes of confirmation (cf Grandy, 1967).

CONTRAST SETS REFINED

Contrast Sets Redefined

In the first section, I gave a temporary definition of a simple contrast set in terms of the extensions of the terms. That definition was temporary because unsatisfactory, and unsatisfactory because I want the containment of the elements in the covering term and the disjointness of the elements to be linguistic matters not extensional matters that may merely be accidentally true.

At the very least one would want for a contrast set $\langle L: E_1, \ldots, E_m \rangle$ whose elements are nouns that any speaker competent with respect to those expressions would believe for each i between 1 and m inclusive that 'All E_is are Ls' and for each distinct i and j that 'No E_i is an E_j'. This is undoubtedly too weak; one way of strengthening it would be to replace 'are' with 'must be' in the first test and 'is an' with 'could be' in the second. However, this would still be too weak for it might be that all competent speakers come to these modal conclusions without knowing that others do and thus would not regard the statements as shared beliefs or as linguistic in nature.

Thus for our purposes a better test is that all speakers competent with regard to these expressions[12] would believe that all E_i are Ls and that no E_i is an E_j.

At least five objections will be raised to this criterion for a contrast set:

Objection 1. The phrase 'competent speaker with regard to the elements' introduces a circularity to the definition—one cannot know who is competent with regard to these terms unless one knows what they mean and what the definition is supposed to contribute to (if the claims on behalf of semantic fields are correct).

Response. I chose this phrase rather than the more common 'competent speaker of the language' because I do not think that there are any actual speakers of most languages who are fully competent with regard to all words. There is, of course, some circularity in my approach but I do not think it is vicious. One gradually comes to form hypotheses about who is competent on the basis of the apparent judgments of other speakers. In any event, my phrase only makes more evident a circularity that already lurks in the more common phrase.

Objection 2. The definition requires complex second-order beliefs about the beliefs of competent speakers—many speakers may simply have no such beliefs.

Response. I do not imagine that one must apply the test by direct questioning and elicitation of explicit pre-occurrent beliefs. Observation of reactions to speakers who expressed sentences of the form 'a is an E_i but not an L' would provide considerable information about the beliefs in question.

Objection 3. The test only applies to contrast sets of nouns.

Response. Granted, but the modifications for verbs and adjectives are not difficult to extrapolate. Prepositions are a little more difficult but I think not impossible.

Objection 4. The test only applies in English.

Response. Granted, but the appropriate translation into other languages should not be difficult given the minimal amount of structure (all, is, not, no) involved. One reason for eschewing a modal formulation was to minimize the amount one would need to presuppose that is known about a language in order to formulate a test. I would not be at all confident that a language that lacked analogues of these constructions had contrast sets. It should also be added that in view of the rampant ambiguity in natural languages, and especially as noted hyponomic anomaly in contrast sets, one is going to have to have some considerable knowledge of the language to ensure that speakers have the correct disambiguation of the test sentences in mind.

Objection 5. By your test ⟨kidney or oak: kidney, oak⟩ is a contrast set.

Response. Granted and we had better do something about it. Evidently we must require either that any of the Es can replace any other in all non-anomalous sentences without producing anomaly, or that specific frames such as 'That's not an E_i it's an E_j' are non-anomalous. (I should add that I do not think that one can always clearly distinguish semantic anomaly from other varieties and thus did not specify the character of the anomaly) nor that anomalousness is an all or nothing matter. Elements of a contrast set should clearly pass the test. E.g., no matter exactly how anomalous one thinks 'That's not an oak, it's a kidney' is, it is at least somewhat anomalous unlike 'That's not an oak, it's a pecan'.

Order

One of my main objections against the adequacy of componential analysis as a theory of meaning was that it was at best extremely clumsy in handling orderings among lexical items. Clearly we must incorporate orderings in our semantic fields. Thus the purpose of this subsection is to define 'ordered contrast set'. A suitable phrase is easy to come by: an ordered contrast set is an ordered pair of a contrast set and an ordering of its elements. However, this glib phrase hides a problem for 'ordering' here cannot have its usual set-theoretic meaning of a transitive irreflexive relation. Some orderings of contrast sets, e.g., those of British nobility or of military rank have these properties, but the not uncommon cyclical orderings (as in the days of the week) do not.

Very little work has been done on the appropriate sense of ordering (see Lyons (1977) and Lehrer (1974) for indications of the variety) but I conjecture that the most useful basic notion would be that of a successor function. A successor function will be a one-to-one function on the elements of the contrast set such that there is at least one element which generates the entire set. This last condition means that successive applications of the function produce all members of the set other than the originating one. If these applications also eventually produce the originating element the set is cyclically ordered. I expect that the other significant relations (betweeness and oppositeness, for example) can be defined from the successor function. Thus our final definition of an ordered contrast set is an ordered pair of contrast set and successor function. For example, the ordered contrast set of days of the week would be

⟨⟨days of the week: Sunday, Monday, Tuesday, . . . Saturday⟩, d.a.⟩

where 'd.a.' is the 'day after' function that maps 'Sunday' to 'Monday', 'Monday' to 'Tuesday', . . ., 'Saturday' to 'Sunday'.

Putting the Contrast in the Contrast Set

In the last subsection we defined 'ordered contrast set', which amounts to a contrast set with an ordering tagging along. But this does not do full justice to the orderings. In many cases, such as that considered above of days, it is the ordering that defines the contrast among the members. Similarly, when we consider unordered contrast sets it seems that something is missing. A single covering term can, unambiguously, cover more than one contrast set: 'dog' covers a contrast set that contrasts dogs by sex as well as one that contrasts them by breeds.

This suggests that the contrast sets, as defined previously are too impoverished and that we should *make the specification of the contrast part of the contrast set*. Thus a contrast set should consist not simply of a covering term and a set of members which satisfy the conditions discussed earlier, but should also include a specification of the nature of contrast, whether it is by a seven element cyclic ordering (as in days), a twelve element cyclic ordering (as in months), by sex (as in ⟨stallion, mare⟩ and many other contrast sets), by maturity (as in ⟨horse$_2$, colt⟩ and many other contrast sets), or whatever. In many cases the contrast can be readily described in the language under analysis, but I see no reason to impose this as a requirement. The dissection of contrast sets is the task of the semanticist and should allow the invocation of whatever extra theoretical vocabulary is necessary.

In addition to responding to the sense that contrast sets were too impoverished in the previous definition, this expanded definition also allow field theories to capture the phenomena most significant for componential analysis and most lacking in traditional field theories, the recurrence of certain concepts across the language. Once we have built the contrast in the specification of the contrast sets, we can then, qua field linguists, consider to what extent the same contrasts recur in different sets in a given language, and to the extent that evidence allows, which contrasts recur across various languages.

These questions of recurrence are empirical questions and the definition of contrast set and the field theory I would advocate (in contrast to some earlier versions) is quite neutral as to whether we should expect virtually no overlap between languages or whether we should expect to find exactly 17 contrasts which underly all contrast sets in all languages. Readers who suspect that this indicates a predilection for regarding linguistics as an empirical rather than *a priori* discipline are correct.

WHAT SEMANTIC FIELDS ARE

Although all were inspired by Saussure, the original definitions of semantic field (Bedeutungsfeld) by Ipsen (1924) Porzig (1924) and Trier (1934) were rather at odds with one other. I do not wish to attempt to recapitulate the history here.[13] Rather I want to meet the desiderata expressed in the opening quotes and provide an analysis that is clearer, less grandiose and more pragmatic. It is certainly more tentative. If we are to be more pragmatic and clear, then it is desirable to define semantic fields in such a way that, as much as possible, we avoid appeal to meanings or to any specific conception of meaning. The point is to find a definition that remains relatively close to the phenomena and thus leaves the theoretical ramifications for a later stage. Thus, for a start, a semantic field for me will be a set of linguistic items and must include at least one contrast set. It is true that these are *meaningful* lexical items, but I stress that it is the meaningful lexical items and not their isolated abstract meanings that form the field. I choose the term 'semantic field', rather than 'lexical field' for my concern is with the semantic relations among the expressions.

Converses

Writers concerned with semantic fields (Lehrer, 1974; Lyons, 1977) typically note that some lexical items are converses of each other: husband/wife, buy/sell. No one seems to have noted that these 'converses' are actually instances of different relations. In the relevant sense husband/wife are two place relation such that

x is the husband of y if y is the wife of x

whereas the relationship for buy/sell involves a permutation of the first and third elements rather than first and second:

x buys y from z if z sells y to x

Thus if we are to include information about 'converses' in a semantic field, we should include information about which permutation occurs as well as the pair. Thus, a permutation relation will be an ordered triple consisting of a specification of the permutation, e.g., $P_{i,j}$, which permutes the ith and jth argument places, and two linguistic items that are so related (E.g., $\langle P_{1,3},$ buy, sell $\rangle$).

Semantic Fields, At Last

Other semantic relations deserve consideration and inclusion, but the converse relations are probably the most widely accepted, and I hope that the discussion of them gives some indication of how I would deal with others. Limitations of space prevent me from considering others at this time.[14]

Thus my suggested definition of a semantic field is that it is a set including one or more contrast sets and possibly also including permutation relations such that:

1. at most one covering term does not occur as an element of a contrast set in the semantic field.

2. except for the covering term mentioned in (1) any expression which occurs in a contrast set with an element of the semantic field is also in the field.

3. at least one element of each permutation relation is in some contrast set in the field.

Condition 1 requires the unity of the semantic field, that there is a single general expression that covers all other items. Any other item that occurs as a covering term in one of the contrast sets must be itself a contrasting element in another contrast set if this condition is met. It should be added that this condition is to be understood as requiring that the item occur elsewhere with the same sense since, in many cases as discussed earlier, the covering term will reappear with a narrower sense in its own contrast set.

Condition 2 requires a kind of downward completeness—the contrast set ⟨animal: dog, cat, . . .⟩ qualifies as a semantic field on its own, but if we are to include 'German shepherd' then we must also include all the contrasting terms ('poodle', 'corgi', etc). It should be mentioned that the same covering term may occur with more than one contrast set, e.g., Lehrer's example (1974, p. 31) of two distinct contrast sets covered by the term 'methods of cooking'.

Condition 3 is imposed to ensure that the permutation relations included have some connection to the rest of the field. This clause requires the coherence of the semantic field; for example, it precludes our adding to a contrast set of cooking terms the pair ⟨buy, sell⟩ to form a semantic field.

According to this definition, a semantic field can be as small as a single contrast set or could include a multitude of them together with permutation and other relations and so on. This may seem to be evading a question alluded to earlier as to how large a semantic field is. I see no reason to legislate the matter—a semantic field is a unit of analysis which an investigator chooses to treat in relative isolation from the rest of a language. Depending on the purposes at hand and the degree of isolation this may be a good or bad choice, but whether or not it is depends on these factors and not on absolute size. There is no reason to try to settle on the size of a semantic field any more than there would have been in trying to decide how large a closed system should be in classical mechanics.

Non-Basic Contrast Sets

Thus far I have talked of semantic fields built around basic contrast sets, sets whose monolexemic members contrast as a matter of plain linguistic conditions. But there are also comparable sets whose members are either not monolexemic or which contrast because of contextual factors. (Actually I am using 'context' very broadly because it can include any factor such as shared dialect, shared perceptual orientation, shared family history, shared hobby . . . that enriches the shared assumptions of the participants in the discourse either temporarily or permanently.) In the one case we must relax the condition of monolexemity, in the other the condition that contrast is a matter of semantic bizarreness. I would describe contrast sets whose members are not monolexemic but whose contrasts are otherwise basic as 'derived contrast sets', those whose members contrast only in an appropriate context as 'contextual contrast sets' and those whose contrasts are both derived and contextual in the obvious if awkward resulting jargon. Whether there is any deep philosophical difference that divides these kinds of contrast sets depends on whether there are deep and significant philosophical differences between 'ordinary' and 'contextually bounded' discourse, a matter I shall not pursue in this essay.

Another View of Semantic Fields

The characterization of semantic fields above may make them appear as a heterogeneous jumble, so an alternative view may help defuse this suspicion. We could think as a list of lexical items plus a specification of relations (inclusion, exclusiveness, succession, converse, . . .) among them, imposing some minimum requirements to match those above ensuring coherence and completeness. This equivalent definition would be more perspicuous in some respects, but I prefer not to use it because I think it is heuristically less desirable since it emphasizes less the field aspect.

From this perspective, however, one can see some affinities with the non-statement conceptions of scientific theory espoused by Sneed (1971) and extended by Stegmuller (1976). This should not be surprising if one thinks of theories as tools for structuring information about the world instead of simply providing information.

PROTOTYPES AND SEMANTIC FIELDS

In a series of experiments and papers, Rosch (1973, 1974, 1975a, 1975b, 1978) brought into prominence the role of prototypes in various memory and classification tasks. This conception of categorization was originally proposed for perceptual categories by Wertheimer (1938) and generalized by Attneave (1957), but was only systematically explored in the 1970s, probably under the stimulus of Berlin & Kay (1969).[15] An informal intuitive characterization of a prototype for a category would be an item that would be a 'good example' of the category.

Indeed, one of the experiments consisted of asking subjects to rank various members of various categories in terms of the appropriateness of the use of that member in teaching or explaining the category. The concept, prototype, however, is best seen as a cluster concept, for prototypes are characterized by the repeated occurrence of the same items in different experimental settings. For example, in a reaction time task where subjects are asked to judge whether an object is or is not in a category, prototypes are more quickly classified. Furthermore, being shown either a picture or name of a prototype just before the task (priming) facilitates classification of other items more than priming with non-prototype. When subjects are asked to list items in a category prototypes are more frequently mentioned. Many exaggerated claims have been made (not by Rosch) about the significance of prototypes and of Rosch's work. I do not think, for example (contrary to Lakoff) there is any indication that the phenomena in question show that non-prototypical members of a category are members to a lesser degree or that we require a fuzzy set theory to account for the phenomena. Nor does Rosch's work show that *all* categories have the structure associated with prototypes.

I do think, however, that her work reinforces an intuitively plausible idea about how many of our categories are internally represented for speakers, how these internalizations are acquired and how they are applied in categorization tasks. The intuitive idea is that we learn many words by being shown examples and then generalizing to similar objects. Of course, a defender of an alternative view, perhaps the view that the representation of a mature language speaker consists of a set of features requisite for the category, might grant that an early stage of learning would involve prototypes but would claim that eventually the set of features is abstracted and provides the ultimate form of representation.

The two views suggest different results but I do not here intend to review the experimental evidence concerning this continuing dispute.[16] Instead I want to address a conceptual argument against the prototype based theory. If we state the Naive Prototype Theory of Categories as: 'For many categories C, for any x, x is a member of C just in case it is similar to the prototype p for C.[17] Speakers of a language have internal representations of the prototype and judge membership by similarity'.

There are two obvious objections to this proposal: Similar in what regard?[18] How similar?

I see no way to answer these objections if one persists in formulating the theory in terms of individual categories. I suggest it be replaced by the contrast set with prototype theory: For many contrast sets, speakers competent with regard to the contrast set have internal representations of a particular kind of similarity (associated with the covering term) and prototypes of the members. An object is categorized as E_i just in case it is more similar (in respect L) to the E_i prototype than to any E_j prototype.

For example, an object is classified as red just in case it is more similar in color to the prototypical red than to prototypical green, blue, etc. One would anticipate that a category that was prototypically learned and represented would differ in some important respects from one where the members were independently characterisable in terms of characteristic features. For example in the latter case one would expect that the members could be learned independently and at different times, whereas for a prototypically organized category one would expect the acquisition of all members to (more or less) coincide[19] since it would depend on acquiring the conception of 'similarity-with-respect-to-L'. Colors seem to fit the latter model and ⟨geometric figures: triangle, square, . . .⟩ the former.

On a slightly more abstract level, the prototype theory questions the assumption that a category (one-place predicate) is always definable using only non-relational expressions (one-place predicates). It offers instead an analysis in terms of a two-place relation (similarity-with–regard-to-L) and a prototypical object. This suggests immediately that prototypically-defined contrast sets are only one of three[20] kinds of contrast sets that can be characterized using this apparatus. (Note that what is required for the definitions is the *three* place relation: x is more-similar-with-regard-to-L to y than to z!)

A contrast set is *strongly cohesive* just in case for each i any two members of E_i are more similar-with-respect-to-L to each other than to any member of any E_j.

A contrast set is *prototypical* just in case it is not strongly cohesive and for each i one can find a member (the prototype) of E_i such that any member of E_i is more similar-with-respect-to-L to the prototype P_i of E_i than it is to the prototype P_j of any other E_j.

A contrast set is *weakly cohesive* just in case it is not prototypical and for each i for any member of E_i it is more similar-with-respect-to-L to *some* other member of E_i more than it is any member of any E_j.

The differences among these kinds of contrast sets would lead one to expect differences with regard to how easily they are learned and with regard to the frequency of problematic borderline cases and intersubjective disagreements. (Note that weakly cohesive sets are very sensitive to the speakers having relatively similar overall experiences, not just sharing prototypes.) While I have not yet tested these differences experimentally, I have some considerable confidence the predictions would be borne out.

ACKNOWLEDGEMENTS

I am greatly indebted to Eva Kittay for helpful discussions of the topics of this essay.

NOTES

[1] I will use 'utterance' throughout this paper to include written as well as spoken production of tokens.

[2] I will subsequently (in the fifth section) both modify and clarify the conditions. The current version is far too simple mindedly extensional, for example, but will suffice as a beginning.

[3] That is the extensions of E_i and E_j have no members in common unless $i = j$.

[4] Or some very special knowledge expressed in an oblique way.

[5] See (Gleitman, 1981, pp. 289ff) for references to specific studies.

[6] What would in the old days have been called 'linguistic rules' or 'conventions'— I shall return to the topic of conventionality in the sixth section when we consider categorization and learning.

[7] With the usual qualifications about the attributions being applied to the whole object and at the same time.

[8] This is not a new point; Carnap noted long ago (1936–7, section 8) that a set of meaning postulates may be inconsistent.

[9] But Lehrer (1974, pp. 67–9) also demonstrates that componential analysis has difficulty with gradable antonyms, which are in effect, complex contrast sets.

[10] By 'plain' conversation I mean those occasions on which deceit, humor, cleverness, filling time or many other motivations are absent. I chose this phrase as opposed to 'ordinary' because I do not think such conversations are ordinary. The best example of a plain conversation might be asking directions of a cooperative stranger.

[11] See Miller (1956) and Cherniak (1983).

[12] Probably one should add 'who have been reminded of relevant facts', for I

suspect most English speakers unless suitably prodded would express belief that they and other speakers believe that 'no one's uncle is their brother'. While such a situation may be taboo it is not semantically impossible.

[13] See Lehrer (1974), Lyons (1977), Miller & Johnson-Laird (1976), Ohman (1953) and Spence (1961) for details.

[14] For example, in the middle ages, terms of venery and the associated relations (⟨pride, lion⟩, ⟨flock, sheep⟩, etc) were sufficiently salient that they would demand inclusion in account of a semantics of the language of the period.

[15] Cf also Reed (1972).

[16] Smith & Medin (1981) provide a reasonably broad and balanced summary; Gathercole (1984) provides some very recent evidence for the role of prototypes in the acquisition of comparatives.

[17] Rosch allows, and the evidence seems to require, that for some categories may have more than one prototype, but for simplicity of expression I will ignore that possibility.

[18] See Goodman (1972) for a more detailed statement of the difficulties.

[19] Wittgenstein (1969, p. 21) 'Light dawns gradually over the whole.'

[20] Actually there are more than three—I list the three pure kinds but mixed contrast sets are also possible; defining the four impure kinds is left as an exercise for the reader.

REFERENCES

Attneave, F., Transfer of experience with a class-schema to identification-learning of patterns and shapes. *Journal of Experimental Psychology*, 1957, **54**, 81–88.

Belnap, N. D. & Steel, J. B., *The Logic of Questions and Answers*. New Haven, CT: Yale University Press, 1976.

Berlin, B. & Kay, P., *Basic Color Terms*. Berkeley, CA: Univerisity of California Press, 1969.

Bromberger, S., Why-questions. In R. G. Colodny (Ed), *Mind and Cosmos*. Pittsburgh, PA: University of Pittsburgh Press, 1966.

Carnap, R., Testability and meaning. *Philosophy of Science*, 1936–7, **3**, 419; **4**, 1–40.

Carnap, R., *The Logical Foundations of Probability*. Chicago, IL: University of Chicago Press, 1950.

Cherniak, C., Rationality and the structure of human memory. *Synthese*, 1983, **57**, 163–86.

Dretske, F., Contrastive statements. *Philosophical Review*, 1982, **91**, 411-436.

Gathercole, V. C., Haphazard examples, prototype, theory, and the acquisition of comparatives. *First Language*, 1984, **5**, 169–96.

Gleitman, H., *Psychology*. New York: WW Norton, 1981.

Goodman, N., Seven strictures on similarity. Reprinted in *Problems and Projects*. Indianapolis, IN: Hacket, 1982.

Goodman, N., *Languages of Art*. Indianapolis, IN: Hackett, 1976.

Grandy, R. E., Some comments on confirmation and selective confirmation *Philosophical Studies*, 1967, **18**, 19—24.

Grice, H. P., Logic and conversation. In D. Davidson & G. Harman (Eds), *The Logic of Grammar*. Dickenson, 1975, pp. 64–74.

Ipsen, G., Der alte Orient und die Indogermanen. In *Stand und Aufgaben der Sprachwissenschaft: Festschrift für W. Streitburg*. Heidelberg: C. Winter, 1924.

Kata, J. The semantic component of a linguistic description. In A. Lehner and K. Lehner (Eds), *Theory of Meaning*. Englewood Cliffs, NJ: Prentice-Hall, 1970.

Katz, J., *Semantic Theory*. New York: Harper and Row, 1972.

Kittay, E. & Lehrer, A., Semantic fields and the structure of metaphor. *Studies in Language*, 1981, **5**, 31–63.

Kittay, E., The identification of metaphor. *Synthese*, 1984, **58**, 153–202.

Kittay, E., *The Cognitive Force of Metaphor*. Oxford: Oxford University Press, 1987.

Lehrer, A., *Semantic Fields and Lexical Structure*. Amsterdam: North-Holland, 1974.

Lyons, J., *Semantics*. Cambridge: Cambridge University Press, 1977.

Miller, G. A., The magical number seven, plus or minus two: some limits on our capacity for processing information. *Psychology Review*, 1956, **63**, 81–97.

Miller, G. A. & Johnson-Laird, P. N., *Language and Perception*. Cambridge, MA: Harvard University Press, 1976.

Ohman, S., Theories of the 'linguistic field'. *Word*, 1953, **9**, 123–34

Porzig, W., Wesenhafte Bedeutungsbeziehungen, *Beitrage zur Geschichte der deutschen Sprache und Literatur*, 1934, **58**, 70–97.

Putnam, H., The meaning of 'meaning'. *Minnesota Studies in the Philosophy of Science*, Vol. VII. Minnesota: University of Minnesota Press, 1975.

Reed, S. K., Pattern recognition and categorization. *Cognitive Psychology*, 1972, **3**, 382–407.

Rosch, E., On the internal structure of perceptual and semantic categories. In T. E. Moore (Ed), *Cognitive Development and the Acquisition of Language*. New York: Academic Press, 1973, pp. 111–144.

Rosche, E., Universals and cultural specifics in human categorization. In R. Breslin, W. Lonner & S. Bochner (Eds), *Cross-cultural Perspectives on Learning*. London: Sage Press, 1974.

Rosche, E., Cognitive reference points. *Cognitive Psychology*, 1975a, **7**, 532–547.

Rosch, E., Cognitive representations of semantic categories. *Journal of Experimental Psychology: General*, 1975b, **104**, 192–233.

Rosch, E., Principles of categorization. In E. Rosch & B. B. Lloyd (Eds), *Cognition and Categorization*. Hillsdale, NJ: Erlbaum, 1978.

Saussure, F. de, *Course in General Linguistics*. New York: McGraw Hill, 1966. (Translated from *Cours de Linguistique Generale*, 1915.)

Smith, E. E. and Medin, D. L., *Categories and Concepts*. Cambridge, MA: Harvard University Press, 1981.

Sneed, J., *The Logical Structure of Mathematical Physics*. Dordrecht: Reidel, 1971.

Spence, C. W., Linguistic fields, conceptual systems and the Weltbild (1961). Reprinted in *Essays in Linguistics*. Munich: Wilhelm Fink Verlag, 1976, pp. 72–96.

Stegmuller, W., *The Structure and Dynamics of Theories*. New York: Springer, 1976.

Trier, J., Das sprachliche Feld. *Neue Jahrbucher für Wissenschaft und Jungenbilden*, 1934, **10**, 428–449.

van Fraassen, B., *The Scientific Image*. Oxford: Clarendon Press, 1980.

Wertheimer, M., Numbers and numerical concepts in primitive peoples. In W. D. Ellis (Ed), *A Source Book in Gestalt Psychology*. New York: Harcourt Brace, 1938.

Wittgenstein, L., *On Certainty*. Oxford: Blackwell, 1969.

9

Justification of Speech, Acts and Speech Acts

ASA KASHER

Department of Philosophy,
Tel-Aviv University

'Our language can be seen as an ancient city'—says Wittgenstein in a famous section of his *Philosophical Investigations*—'A maze of little streets and squares, of old and new houses, and of houses with additions from various periods; and this surrounded by a multitude of new boroughs with straight regular streets and uniform houses'.

The salient ingredients of Wittgenstein's parable are, indeed, those picturesque houses and variegated streets which form an intricate as well as intriguing maze. Our starting point is, however, at a different part of Wittgenstein's parable. Rather than depicting language in the form of 'an old town [which] constantly grows through new buildings put up by industrious and enterprising citizens',[1] let us consider language to be represented by a system of boroughs, each standing for a certain type of speech act. Our boroughs enjoy independence in a great measure, on the one hand, but they share common facilities with each other and have to rely for help upon the assertive old city, on the other hand. Should one not be puzzled by the simple observation that whereas every formal act of a citizen comes under the jurisdiction of some borough or other, the underlying system of boroughs is still in want of adequate explanation?

One moral of the old city parable, under this interpretation, seems, then,

NEW DIRECTIONS IN SEMANTICS

clear: the weakest point of semantics is where its methods and systems have to be applied to 'Other Moods', i.e., to non-indicative sentences and non-assertoric speech acts. Even the assertoric force itself is not well understood, though much has been gained by studying forceless sentences (or radicals), that bear truth-values under appropriate conditions.

Some attempts have been made at capturing all speech acts by truth-conditional semantic theories. Without indulging in a full-fledged discussion of ingenious suggestions made to that effect by David Lewis (1972), in his 'General semantics', Donald Davidson (1979), in his 'Moods and per-formances', and others,[2] let me use Wittgenstein's old city parable to point out where such truth-conditional attempts have gone astray. If our undertaking is to provide genuine understanding of a certain borough in operation, we do not render anybody much service by informing him that within the confines of the old city-walls, there is a tiny, mysterious house, carrying the formal shield of the borough on its roof and an inscription of the word 'hereby' on its door, behind which one can find an approximate counterpart to each formal act performed in that borough.[3] To be sure, a complete specification of what is going on within that tiny house would be tantamount to an approximate description of the related borough, but then, why replace the green leas of the borough by a rigid booth, somewhere downtown Assertion?

In order to do full justice to the different boroughs of language, one is tempted to start afresh. Thus, the purpose of the present paper is to make some preliminary steps in a new way. Surely, looking for a new conceptual angle does not necessarily involve ignoring or underrating much that has been done by philosophers and linguists within speech-act theory. However, it still seems to us that the field suffocates with classifications and minute observations, while it is clearly in want of some general conceptual frame-work, pregnant with explanatory power.

One additional remark should be made at the outset. The ultimate theoretical goal of the present efforts is to find the essential semantic or pragmatic ingredients of natural language, if there are any. A full understanding of the concept of natural language would, thus, amount to a demarcation of language, delimiting it within the broader area of human intentional activity.

I

Consider the following simple observation: speech acts are intentional,[4] i.e., performed intentionally. An intentional act, an act performed inten-tionally, is an act performed by an agent who knows what he is doing and does it for a reason. Or, to put it differently, using Miss Anscombe's approach (Anscombe, 1976, Chapter 5), an intentional act is one to which the question 'Why?' is given application in an appropriate sense. The standard answer to such a question characterizes a reason for acting that way.

Consequently, a speech act, *qua* intentional act, is an act performed by an agent, a speaker, who knows what he is doing and does it for a reason. Such reasons for speech acts seem to us to merit some closer attention in a theory of meaning and use for speech acts. Let us see why.

The same intentional act, whether linguistic or not, may be performed for different reasons, at one and the same time. Miss Anscombe's example is a man who is moving his arm in pumping water to replenish a house water-supply to poison the inhabitants (Anscombe, 1976, Chapter 23).

For a linguistic example, consider the reasons Lady Astor had for saying to Winston Churchill: 'Winston, if you were my husband I should flavour your coffee with poison' (to which he answered: 'Madam, if I were your husband, I should drink it.') One may, indeed, assume that Lady Astor had reasons for saying what she said: she wanted Sir Winston to know what she thought and she wanted to insult him. Put differently, the question 'Why?' bears at least two different, genuine answers, when applied to Lady Astor's utterance.

There is a suggestive distinction between Lady Astor's two different reasons for saying what she said: whereas every speaker of a natural language knows that a simple way to let someone know what one thinks is to tell him, only a speaker who has some non-linguistic knowledge about the effects of drinking coffee flavoured with poison would understand that Lady Astor's intention to insult Sir Winston is a reason for her utterance. The general problem is whether a clear distinction can be drawn between linguistic and non-linguistic reasons for utterance, that is to say, between reasons a person *qua* speaker may have for a speech act and reasons by which a person may justify an utterance only if he is willing to hinge on what is part of his knowledge or belief but not part of his knowledge of the language. Of course, this problem of demarcation of linguistic reasons is part of the more general problem of demarcation of language. The common form the latter problem takes in semantics is that of drawing an adequate distinction between analytic and synthetic propositions. A solution of our former problem would be of some interest because it might shed light on an essential ingredient of language by applying to it conceptual frameworks of reasoning theories.

Reasons speakers may have for their speech acts should not be confused with what speakers may actually have in their minds when they perform some speech acts. Wittgenstein (1967) makes a related point by saying that 'the causes of our belief in a proposition are indeed irrelevant to the question what we believe. Not so the grounds, which are grammatically related to the proposition, and tell us what proposition it is.' In other words, what we are here interested in is a certain part of linguistic competence, viz, that related to speakers' reasons and not to any other psychological facet of speakers' linguistic performances. To use another remark of Wittgenstein (1980): '. . . seek your reasons for calling something good or beautiful and then the peculiar grammar of the word . . . in this instance will be evident.'

II

Given any particular speech act, two problems of justification may naturally arise. When a genuine act of assertion, for example, is performed, the speaker may be asked both for grounds of his *belief* that what he has asserted does hold and for the reasons he has had for *saying* what he believes to be the case.

As we all know, having grounds for holding some proposition, is not a sufficient reason for uttering a sentence which expresses it, to the same extent that having reasons for expressing some proposition does not necessarily mean having sufficient grounds for holding that proposition.

The same cleavage of justification takes place when non-assertoric speech acts are performed. Consider, for example, the following anecdote told by Hugh Walpole about Henry James.[5] After two very small and grubby children opened some gate for them, in the fields beyond Rye, 'James smiled beneficently, felt in his deep pocket for coppers, found some and then began an elaborate explanation of what the children were to buy. They were to go to a certain sweet shop because there the sweets were better than any other; they were to see they were not deceived and offered an inferior brand, for those particular sweets had a peculiar taste of nuts and honey, with, he fancied, an especial flavour that was almost the molasses of his own country. If the children took care to visit the right shop and insisted that they should have only that particular sweet called, he fancied, "Honey-nut"—or was it something with "delight" in it? "Rye's Delight" or "Honey Delights" or—But at that moment the children, who had been listening open-mouthed, their eyes fixed on the pennies, of a sudden took fright and turned, running and roaring with terror across the fields.' Thus, excellent grounds one happens to have for an advice, might turn out to form apparently very poor reasons for advising accordingly. We will, therefore, keep apart the discussions of these different kinds of justification.

III

We consider, first, reasons for speech *acts*, rather than reasons for their content or product.

Being interested in a problem of delimiting language, we may ignore differences between reasons for speech acts of distinct types, and look for general principles or forms of justifying acts done with words. We turn, now, to an examination of one general principle and one general form of justification.

An attempt to justify a given speech act might naturally involve showing how that speech act serves the speaker's pursuit of his local ends. Thus, for example, when Juliet asks Romeo 'How cam'st thou hither, tell me, and wherefore?', it is not difficult to justify her question. She herself goes on saying 'The orchard walls are high and hard to climb,/ And the place death, considering who thou art,/ If any of my kinsman find thee here'.[6] Not being able to see how Romeo had entered the orchard, she asked him to tell her 'how?', and since at the time she could not see a reason for Romeo thus endangering his life, she asked him 'wherefore?'. Juliet's reasons for her utterance involve, then, her local ends: to be told something and to express wonder.

However, such relations between a speaker's utterance and his or her local ends do not form the whole story of justification. The crux of the matter is showing that under the circumstances the speech act is the *best* way the speaker could have used for attaining his local ends. Hence, almost nobody would find it hard to understand why another, anecdotal utterance of Henry James seemed unjustified under the circumstances. On one rainy evening James and Edith Wharton arrived at Windsor long after dark and found themselves at a loss to direct their strange driver to the King's Road. When James spied an old man he signalled to him and said, 'In short, my good man, what I want to put to you in a word is this: supposing we have already (as I have reason to think we have) driven past the turn down to the railway station (which in that case, by the way, would probably not have been on our left hand, but on our right), where are we now in relation to' the King's Road? To see why such an utterance could by no means be considered justified under the circumstances, consider the end of the story, as told by Mrs. Wharton:[7] ' "Oh, please", I interrupted, feeling myself utterly unable to sit through another parenthesis, "do ask him where the King's Road is". "Ah—? The King's Road? Just so! Quite right! Can you, as a matter of fact, my good man, tell us where, in relation to our present position, the King's Road exactly *is*?" "Ye're in it", said the aged face at the window.'

When we deem justified speech acts by which speakers serve their local goals to the best of their ability under the circumstances, as contrasted with speech acts by which speakers fail to render themselves such service, what we actually apply to speech acts is a principle of rationality. We may call it the principle of effective linguistic means:

(RL)   Given a desired end, of an appropriate type,[8] one is to choose that speech act which most effectively, and at least cost, attains that end, *ceteris paribus*.

Notice that (RL) is not set just for contexts of utterance, i.e., contexts of issuing speech acts. Although the principle has been formulated as a maxim set for speakers every time they are about to say something and mean it, it applies to hearers as well, every time they hear something being said and are about to try to understand it. Where there is no reason to assume the contrary, we all take our discourse partners to be rational agents. Their ends and beliefs in a context of utterance are assumed to provide complete justification for their linguistic behaviour, unless there is evidence to the contrary. This is the Presumption of Rationality.

The best example of a general application of that principle of effective linguistic means and the accompanying method of rationalization, is Grice's theory of implicature. It can be demonstrated that all Grice's conversational maxims are derivable from the same principle of effective linguistic means. The same holds for other maxims that have been suggested, such as 'Frame whatever you say in the form most suitable for any reply which would be regarded appropriate' (Grice), 'Speak idiomatically, unless there is reason not to' (Searle), and others. Without showing in detail how to derive Grice's super-maxims of Quantity, Quality, Relation and Manner, and other conversational maxims from the principle of effective linguistic means,[9] I would like to make a few general remarks.

IV

First, grounding all conversational maxims on a rationality principle, rather than on Grice's own Cooperative principle, is in one sense a deviation from Grice's programme, but in another sense it seems to advance that programme. Grice (1975, p. 48) himself has been interested in rational justification of his maxims. In his 'Logic and conversation' he says—'I am enough of a rationalist to want to find a basis that underlies these facts, undeniable though they may be; I would like to be able to think of the standard type of conversational practice not merely as something that all or most do *in fact* follow but as something that it is *reasonable* for us to follow, that we *should not* abandon'. It seems to me that a derivation of a conversational maxim from a rationality principle provides the required normative aspect. However, Grice (1975, p. 47) goes on saying about the maxims that he stated them as if '[the] purposes that talk . . . is adapted to serve and is primarily employed to serve . . . were a maximally effective exchange of information . . . or influencing or directing the actions of others'. These being the purposes of talk or talk exchange, Grice (1975, p. 47) sees the latter 'as a special case or variety of purposive, indeed, rational, behaviour'. It is here where, I think, one might find reasons for departing from Grice's programme. Without denying that information exchange is one of the purposes language is employed to serve, it seems to me that granting information exchange the primary linguistic role is a prejudgment of the highly interesting issue of the purposive nature of natural language. If, as many tend to agree, speech acts are governed by constitutive systems of rules; then these systems determine, each for itself, the purposes meant to be served by employing sentences according to their rules. It is of the nature of constitutive systems of rules that they cannot serve 'external' ends, given in advance.[10] Grice's cooperative principle applies to contexts of utterance which have information exchange as a shared, local purpose. The rationality principle of effective linguistic means seems, however, to apply to all contexts of utterance, including those in which information exchange does not play a significant role.

V

Secondly, consider an objection that has been raised to the claim that it is rational for speakers to follow conversational maxims. Elinor Keenan (1976) described a community of Malagasi speakers who make their conversational contributions intentionally uninformative, indefinite, obscure. Does it cast any doubt about the universality of the related conversational maxims? Gerald Gazdar (1979), for example, takes Keenan's findings to 'imply that Grice's maxims are only "reasonable", and "rational" relative to a given culture, community, or state of affairs. They cannot be defended as universal principles of conversation'. Robert Harnish (1976) tried to obviate the difficulty by suggesting that for the maxims to be universal they must be interpreted as conditional and not categorical, applying only when the cooperative principle is in effect.

We would like to suggest another solution to Keenan's problem. We cannot accept Gazdar's cultural relativism of the maxims, because the rationality principle of effective linguistic means, from which they all follow, is not a feature of our culture. Our attitudes, values and purposes may well depend on our culture, but given a desired end, a rational speaker of any cultural denomination is bound to choose that course of actions which most effectively and at least cost attains the given end, *ceteris paribus*.

We cannot accept Harnish's solution to Keenan's problem, because no reference to the cooperative principle has to be made in the derivation of the conversational maxims from the linguistic, rationality principle. Unless the cooperative principle is shown to rest on a *general* rationality principle, the suggested restriction of the conversational maxims is not warranted, and it is clear that the cooperative principle does not follow from any rationality principle which does not rest on the assumption that the point of language is information exchange or the like.

Keenan's interesting observation presents a problem as long as we focus our attention on the wrong part of the picture. Indeed, if the purpose that a speech act of a rational speaker is employed to serve is providing information in a most effective way, then a problem is created by an uninformative rational agent. However, a rational agent opts for a speech act which not only enables him to attain his local ends most effectively, but also does it at least cost, *ceteris paribus*. It is up to the speaker himself, or a community of speakers, to determine what counts as a cost and what may be disregarded. In our culture, or cultures, we do not count the vowels of our speech acts, but we do spare time of utterance, in a way. For Malagasi speakers *commitments* should be spared. Since the more sincerely informative you are, the more commitments you undertake to defend your beliefs, for the Malagasi speakers the less informative they are the better, everything else being equal. Their linguistic behaviour should not, then, be taken to provide a counter-example to neither Grice's maxims nor our principle of effective linguistic means.[11]

Having encountered such a linguistic rationality principle, do we have at our disposal a general principle of justification for speech acts, which is a purely linguistic principle? Actually, this is a double question: First, could that linguistic rationality principle take the form of a justification principle for speech acts; and, secondly, is it a purely linguistic principle?

The obvious answer to the first question is in the affirmative. A speaker well justifies his speech act by showing that by performing it he has tried to attain his local ends in a way which was most effective and at least cost under the circumstances, i.e., given the speaker's state of knowledge, belief and ability.

Notice that the linguistic rationality principle is a source of reasons for speech acts of all kinds. By applying it we see, for instance, the reason why the question 'Have you read the book?' may sometimes be answered by saying 'I saw the movie', and understand similar cases of an apparent flouting of some conversational maxim, one that creates the so-called *dramatic* conversational implicatures. However, reasons for speech acts which involve non-dramatic implicatures are also generated by the linguistic rationality principle. For example, it is clear that an appropriate utterance of the sentence 'I have just seen an interesting painting' conversationally implicates that the speaker holds the belief that not all the paintings are interesting. This is also why we would consider odd an utterance of the sentence 'I met a mortal philosopher', in a common context of utterance.

Now, is the principle of effective linguistic means a purely linguistic principle? Here the interesting answer seems to us to be, in a sense, in the negative. The principle of *effective linguistic means* is just an instance of the much more general principle of *effective means*, whether linguistic or not. The general principle says that:

> Given a desired end, a rational agent is to choose that action, which most effectively, and at least cost, attains that end, *ceteris paribus.*

Thus, reasons speakers have for their speech acts stem from a general rationality principle, as applied to linguistic means, rather than from any purely linguistic or language-specific principle.

VI

One way of defending our claim that a general rationality principle is involved in reasons for speech acts, rather than a purely linguistic one, would be to show that what holds for speech acts, due to the principle of effective linguistic means, is exactly on a par with what holds for acts of another kind, due to a parallel principle of effective means of an appropriate type. We will, now, briefly describe a few examples of such reasoning in art.

Many pieces of art call for explanation in terms of rational activity, intentions and means employed for expressing them. No wonder, for example, that for many years people were trying to find out what is the subject of a certain painting by Titian, the name of which had been unknown for a while. (It is Titian's *Sacred Love and Secular Love*, 1515/6.) To take the trouble to look for the subject in that case does not seem to be significantly different from what happens in the biblical story, in the Book of Daniel, where King Belshazzar asks his conjurers to show him 'the interpretation' of what the fingers of a human hand marked upon the plaster of the wall. In both cases there is an effort to gain understanding by a rational reconstruction of ends and of uses of means. The same presumption operates in both cases.

The title of a painting may be taken to point at an expressive target, while different properties of the painting may be considered contributions to an effort, on the part of the artist, to reach that target by his expressive act. (To be sure, the present claim is not meant to hold throughout the history of art, across periods and genres in general. Francis Bacon (1980), for example, says — '. . . [T]he way I work is totally, now, accidental, and becomes more and more accidental, and does not seem to behave, as it were, unless it is accidental.' But still there have been many periods in art history and many genres, to which the intentionality claim seems to apply.) There is no doubt in an interpreter's mind, that in a painting such as Magritte's *Euclidean Walks* or Picasso's *Guernica* central details require explanation. As far as reasons are involved, for using certain means in performing intentional acts, explanations of speech acts and explanations of certain painting acts are, in many senses, on a par with each other, being similarly related to the same Presumption of Rationality.

It is possible to go through the list of implicature generating devices, both conversational and conventional, and show for each of them a counterpart in art, but instead of doing that we show two simple examples. When we take a painting to be a product of a rational agent, we assume that no *major* detail of it is superfluous. I see no significant difference between this assumption and the one expressed in part of Grice's super-maxim of Quantity. To get an impression of the way this assumption is applied, consider the seeming superfluity of the soldier on the right, in Manet's famous painting *The Execution of Emperor Maximilian*. I leave it for the reader to draw what seems to me a natural implicature.

Notice, finally, that not everything a painting has to tell is straightforwardly detectable. For example, in Carpaccio's painting *St. Augustine in his Study*, St. Augustine's right hand palm is at the focus of perspective. Once this fact has been observed, one becomes inclined to deem it important. Is not that a case of drawing conventional implicatures from a feature of a painting, completely on a par with cases of drawing conventional implicatures from features of speech acts which are, for example, understood to be ironical?

In short, the principle of effective linguistic means should be considered as just an instance of the much more general principle of effective means, rather than as a particular linguistic principle. The general rationality principle applies to activity in the spheres of language to the same extent that it applies to activities in the spheres of art and in other domains.

VII

If justification of a speech act in terms of rationality principles involves considerations which are too general, in the sense of not being particularly linguistic in nature, perhaps we should try to find some particularly linguistic justification principles by examining reasons for speech acts of certain types. Thus, challenged to justify a command a speaker has issued, he might respond by alluding to his responsibility and authority, whether formal or not; and when challenged to justify a question she has posed, a speaker might confess ignorance and curiosity about the subject matter. What is common to such challenges to justify certain speech acts? Do the reasons which may be given in response to such challenges share any interesting property with each other?

There is one simple point we would like to make in answering these two questions. *Given a type of speech acts, as defined by a given constitutive system of rules, a challenge to justify a speech act of that type is linguistically appropriate if and only if it is directly related to any of the rules governing speech acts of that type.* For example, since one of the rules governing requests is that the speaker should believe his addressee to be able to perform the requested action, it would be linguistically appropriate to ask the speaker for the grounds he has for that belief about the addressee's ability. Similarly, since one of the rules governing commands requires that the speaker be in a position of authority over the addressee, there is nothing linguistically inappropriate in the following famous biblical exchange: When Moses and Aaron say to Pharaoh, King of Egypt: 'This is what Jehova the God of Israel has said: "Let my people go, etc." ', the King responds by challenging the order: 'Who is Jehova, so that I should obey his voice to send Israel away?'[12] When any speech act is made, each of the (pragmatical) rules governing it determines a presumption with respect to the context of utterance. Each of these presumptions may be challenged, under appropriate circumstances.

Questions involve an interesting family of such challenges. To see that, consider some cases where an ordinary response to a posed question does not take the form of an answer, but rather that of another question.[13] For example:

A: Who waters these beautiful flowers?
B: Don't you see they are made of plastic?

or

A: Is the new minister reliable?
B: Have you forgotten his earlier career?

or

A: Why are you staring at me like that?
B: Is there any law against it?

The first challenge is related to the rule which requires the presuppositions of a question to hold in a context of utterance for the question to be appropriate for that context. The second challenge involves the rule which requires that the speaker genuinely lacks some information. The third challenge rests on a rule according to which the speaker is required to hold that there is a formal answer to his question.

Notice that not every case of an entirely interrogative discourse involves a question and its challenge. Some interrogative responses are actually conversational *turns*, as is clearly seen in the following simple example of *shirking an answer*:

A: Have you gone through all of Bertrand Russell's books?
B: Have *you*?

And some interrogative responses mark what might be called '*conversational skips*', where the question in response implicates a formal answer or response to the first question. For example:

A; Do you lend biographies?
B: Would you like to read Peter Ustinov's *Dear Me*?

Or, to use a much older and more complicated example:

A: Where is Abel your brother?
B: Am I the guardian of my brother?

Generally speaking, every type of speech act determines a certain gamut of linguistic appropriate challenges, which, in turn, defines a corresponding gamut of linguistically adequate justification. Since these challenges and responses are all induced by the rules that govern our speech acts, one form of presenting a type of speech act is a specification of the correlative reasons, usable in response to linguistically appropriate justification demands. Could such speech act-specific families of reasons provide us with an essential feature of natural language which could be shown to be purely linguistic? Here too the answer seems to be in the negative. When we try to classify those reasons and see what different families of reasons share with each other, we do encounter essential features of language, such as every type of speech act being defined by rules which determine its point, the range of linguistic means usable for its performance, the role played by the speaker, couched in terms of his beliefs, intentions, status and the like, and the characteristic product of standard performance. However, similar features can be found outside the confines of natural language, in each case of an institutional activity governed by a constitutive system of rules, e.g., in formal duelling or ceremonial meetings.

VIII

We turn, now, from justification of speech *acts* to justification of speech *products*, that is to say, from reasons speakers have for *saying* something to grounds they have for *what* they say.

We consider first the case of assertoric speech acts. Whatever one takes to be their product, it is clear that in order to provide a forceful defense of what has been asserted, one has to present genuine grounds for holding it.

Notice that we have not claimed that to justify what has been asserted is to present genuine grounds for holding it *true*. Such a claim would have committed us to the assumption that the concept of *truth* is a basic element of any theory of justification pertaining to what is asserted when assertoric speech acts are felicitously performed. We are reluctant to make that assumption, because it creates a vicious circle of analysis. If one follows, for instance, a correspondence theory of truth and then takes the resulting notion of *truth* to be a basic element of one's theory of *meaning*, then on the one hand one analyses *meaning* in terms of *truth*, but on the other hand one needs some *truth*-independent access to the notion of *meaning* for one's analysis of the correspondence between what is said and what there obtains in reality.[14] This circle of analysis involves the notions of *meaning* and *truth*, but since we would like to analyse *meaning* in terms of *use*, which in turn has *justification* among its essential ingredients, analysis of *justification* in terms of *truth* (and other notions) would involve us in a similar vicious circle. Our intention is to elucidate the notion of *justification* without using any theory of *truth* and then to try analysing the latter by means of a theory of the former.[15]

Upon performing a speech act of assertion, a speaker undertakes a lingual commitment to present on demand grounds he has for holding what has been asserted. This commitment bears direct practicability. Thus, according to Peirce's (1958) view, for example, as expressed in a letter to Lady Welby, '. . . the act of assertion . . . is not a pure act of signification. It is an exhibition of the fact that one subjects oneself to the penalties visited on a liar if the proposition asserted is not true'. To be sure, such penalties are visited not only on liars, but also on speakers who are unreliable, who exaggerate, who jump to conclusions, and similar ones. All these penalties involve some inappropriateness in using language in the assertoric mood without sufficient grounds for holding what has apparently been asserted.

However, these penalties are somewhat indirect facets of the commitment to present on demand grounds for holding what has been asserted. What, then, are the underlying rules of the *practice* of one's presenting grounds for what has been asserted by oneself? In other words, how does one go about a *justification* for holding what one has asserted?

Taking for granted that as part of our knowledge of language we have knowledge of how to justify what we assert and that our knowledge of language provides us with infinitely many different assertions, we have to posit some recursive rules, defining justification of 'molecular' assertions. One justifies a conjunction by justifying each of the conjuncts separately. An existential assertion can be justified by demonstrating an appropriate instance. Perhaps, a conditional assertion of the form 'If P, then Q' is justified on certain grounds just in case it can be shown that any enlargement of these grounds into ones that justify what is asserted in P would turn them also into ones that justify what is asserted in Q.[16]

Such steps of recursive justification carry an intuitionistic air, which actually should come as no surprise: Intuitionism, though developed with respect to mathematical assertions, has taken the concept of *proof*, rather than the concept of *truth*, to play the major role in the practice of mathematical assertion. Of course, proof is just one brand of justification.

We mention in passing that Hintikka's semantical games include similar recursive steps of justification, even though they have been meant to serve a different purpose.[17]

IX

Given a speech act of assertion, assume that we have applied to what has been asserted all the required steps of recursive justification. Here the question arises of how to go about a justification of an 'atomic' assertion.

There is no simple, ready-made solution to the problem of justifying 'atoms' of assertion. To see that, suffices it to compare with each other the standard ways of justifying what is usually asserted when utterances of the following sentences are made in appropriate circumstances.[18]

> I have a headache. He has a headache. She is in pain.
> This is a sheep. This is a chip.
> This is a toy. Here is a catholic church.
> She is writing. She is reading. She is dreaming.
> This opera was composed by Verdi. This adagio is Albinoni's.
> This book was written by Isaiah.
> There is the sepulchre of Jesus Christ.
> Tomorrow, there will be an air-battle over the gulf of Sidra.
> There are genes. There are rules. There are regularities.
> Five plus seven is twelve. Elementary arithmetic is incomplete.
> He is guilty of assassinating Aldo Moro.
> The correspondence theory of truth is wrong.

Such examples suggest that a variety exists of methods that speakers know how to use when required to show why they do hold what they have asserted. Some of these methods are shared by all speakers, under normal contexts of utterance, but some are used only by some of the speakers, under special circumstances, e.g., when certain speakers participate in deliberations of a legal or a scientific nature. Notice to what extent these two methods of deliberation are different from each other: whereas what has been asserted, within some branch of a science, can be justified by being shown to provide the best explanation of some data, much more than that will be required in order to justify the very same assertion in many courts of justice.

Thus, our next problem is to find out whether an interesting generalization can be offered with respect to the existing variety of justification methods. However, before we address ourselves to this problem, we would like to have a glance at non-assertoric speech acts, such as asking, advising or commanding.

Generally speaking, practices of justifying what is said when a non-assertoric speech act of a certain kind is made bear some major points of similarity to practices of justifying what is said when an assertoric speech act is made. First of all, many of the recursive steps which appear when grounds are presented for what has been asserted have formal counterparts when grounds are presented for what has been advised, for example. Indeed, to justify a conjunctive advice *to do this and to do that* (not to be confused with the advice *to do both this and that*) is again to justify each of the conjuncts separately. One may assume that there is a class of recursive step-*forms*, definable without recourse to any type of speech act in particular, that underlie the recursive steps of all justifications of what is said in natural language. Probably, here is where general features of the syntax of natural languages are reflected in the pragmatics of natural language (Kasher, 1981).

Secondly, the non-recursive steps of justifying what is said when a non-assertoric speech act is made also involve varieties of methods of justification, completely on a par with what has just been suggested for the case of assertoric speech acts where what is said is 'atomic'. To grasp this observation, one has just to think about the significantly different ways one has at one's disposal to show that an advise is good or to show that a problem is real.

To a certain extent, such a similarity is natural, because justification always rests on reasons and arguments. Moreover, reasons are factual, and consequently, presenting what one holds to be one's reasons for taking something to obtain, or to be valid, or to be real or what have you, is actually presenting part of what one takes to be the facts. However, as we saw when assertion was under consideration, we all use a variety of ways to form views about the facts. Some facts are observational, some highly theoretical; some are 'brute', others 'institutional'; some facts are internal, some external. For some of these facts we rely mainly on our senses or on introspection, unless there is some reason not to, while for other facts we rely on particular forms of collecting evidence for what happened in the near or distant past or for what goes on in some hidden layer of reality. But the distinctions between different types of speech act do not stem from such differences between methods of justification, but rather from differences between the uses to which those methods are put, i.e., differences between various systems of rules that govern speech acts.

We return, now, to the problem of whether an interesting generalization can be presented, pertaining to the variety of existent methods of justification. We tackle this problem by asking ourselves whether any of the methods of justifying what is said enjoys some priority, from a linguistic point of view. In particular, should any of these methods be taken to constitute part of language itself?

X

In a nutshell, our answer to these questions is that whereas, in a sense, *the recursive steps of justifying what is said are analytic, the 'atomic' steps have an analytic form and a synthetic substance*, so to speak. The substance of each of our methods of justification does not stem from our natural language, but the restrictions imposed on such a game for it to constitute a method of justification, do seem to us to stem from our very concept of natural language.[19] To use one of the most important notions in Chomsky's (1982) view of language, *a concept of justification is part of our 'universal grammar'*.

The simplest case of a similar situation, in semantics, is provided by indexical terms, such as 'she', 'now' or 'here'. Obviously, when we use such an indexical, in an ordinary speech act, we rely on the addressee's ability to determine the intended referent of the indexical term, but the addressee's method of identifying the intended referent of the indexical term is commonly not part of his linguistic competence. Vision is not part of language. Yet, when we closely examine such indexicals and compare them with each other, we realize that the language to which they belong imposes constraints on what may be an intended referent of an indexical term. Speakers' ability to locate intended referents has to conform to these linguistic constraints. Thus, for understanding sentences such as 'she is clever', both an understanding of English and a method for identifying the intended referent of the uttered word 'she' are required. Of course, we have all kinds of ways for identifying, at given contexts of utterance, salient women, different from both the speaker and the addressee(s). The substance of each of these ways is synthetic, involving pieces of, say, cultural or biological information about women, but it is by knowledge of the language that whenever we encounter such a sentence uttered, we supplement our linguistic competence by some method or other of identifying an appropriate referent for each indexical term included in the uttered sentence. The schematic concept of *a method for identifying the intended referent of an utterance of the indexical 'she'* is part of our knowledge of language, whereas the ability to employ certain methods of referent-identification is not part of our knowledge of language, but rather part of our knowledge of language-use.

Our position with respect to methods of justifying what is said is completely on a par with our position with respect to methods of identifying what is indexically referred to. Our concept of language imposes constraints on whatever might count as a method for justifying what is said when speech acts of any type are felicitously performed.

We turn, then, to a brief presentation of some of these constraints. Since what we have at our disposal is a variety of defense practices, we group the constraints under the tentative titles 'defense constraints', 'practice constraints' and 'variety constraints'.

Defense Constraints

[D1]   *Justification is a matter of presenting supportive evidence.*
Indeed, what counts as evidence for what is determined by each method of justifying what is said on its own, on a par with what Wittgenstein (1969, 105) says with respect to justifying belief:

> All testing, all confirmation and disconfirmation of a hypothesis takes place already within a system. And this system is not a more or less arbitrary and doubtful point of departure for all arguments: no, it belongs to the essence of what we call an argument. The system is not so much the point of departure, as the element in which arguments have their life.

None of these systems is wholly determined by natural language itself, but one has not mastered the very use of language if one is not aware of the need to have appropriate evidence in support of what one has said.

If [D1] is indeed a constraint imposed on every method of justifying what has been said by our innate concept of language use, then the latter schematic conception includes also a sub-scheme which is a conception of evidence.

[D2]   *Methods of justification may admit of degrees of justification.*
Some methods of justification will involve the important distinction between
conclusive and inconclusive evidence. The details of such a distinction with
him some method of justification form part of the specification of that
method. However, it seems reasonable to assume that we have a general,
schematic conception of conclusive evidence, which imposes some constraints on whatever might count, within one system of justification or
other, as conclusive evidence. For example, [D2.1] conclusive evidence
does not admit of degrees, and [D2.2] it must be of an extreme, supportive
type.

[D3]   *A justification of what is said has to be surveyable.*
Thus, consider the example of justifying mathematical assertions. Although
in some meta-mathematical sense proofs do not have to be finite, when the
practice is considered of asserting and defending assertions of mathematical
statements proofs are finite (in an appropriate sense). When other types of
assertion are under consideration, e.g., legal or scientific ones, a justification has not only to be finite, but also practically so, i.e., surveyable,
at least relative to the surveyability of the utterance under consideration.[20]

It might be argued that our constraint [D3] is a practice constraint rather
than a defense constraint, but at that early stage of our inquiry into the
nature of the schematic concept of justification, it would not make much
difference to remove a constraint from one list into another.

[D4]   *When a method of justification is attached to a family of speech
acts, some members of the family turn out to be well justified by this method.*
This is perhaps the least evident constraint so far. It amounts to saying
that it would be pointless to participate in a game of justification in which
one can never win. Accordingly, language does not tolerate, so to speak,
forms of extreme scepticism with respect to its own use.

Practice Constraints

[P1]   *Practices of justification are interpersonal.*
To use another of Wittgenstein's remarks: 'If I need a justification for using
a word, it must also be one for someone else'. There are no private practices
of justification and methods applied for gaining it are always interpersonal,
sometimes even social, in a strict sense of the word.[21]

It is important to notice that by thus taking natural language to essentially
involve a community of speakers, of users of the language, one has not
committed oneself to granting communication among members of such a
community the major role in the essence of language. A community of

language users is involved not because they all use the same language for transferring information, but because they all share methods for justifying what is produced in certain ways when their language is used felicitously.

[P2] *A method of justification of what is said specifies norms of admissible 'moves' in its 'game'.*

An explicit justification of what has been said is usually a response to an explicit challenge. When no problem arises in a full-fledged rational reconstruction of a speech act, including its literal product, no challenge is warranted and no act of justification is required.

Hence, a method of justification should define 'opening' positions of the 'game', or in other words, *admissible doubts*, as well as 'end'-positions of various kinds. Most important among the latter is a position which enables the participants in the exchange to recognize that a challenge has been successfully met by reasons and arguments, a justification being thus produced for what was said. 'In certain circumstances, for example, we regard a calculation as sufficiently checked. What gives us right to do so? Experience? May that not have deceived us? Somewhere we must be finished with justification, and then there remains the proposition that *this* is how we calculate' (Wittgenstein, 1969, 212), and that this is how we justify calculations: '. . . justification comes to an end' (Wittgenstein, 1969, 192). End-positions of this type trigger off an assent of a certain type on the part of the challenger and the observers.[22]

There are additional constraints that one can introduce by consideration of the schematic concept of practice, but we will not indulge into that presently.

Variety Constraints

[V1] *A speech act and its context of utterance determine which methods of justification may be applied to what has been said when that speech act was performed at that context of utterance.*

To get an impression of the idea behind this constraint, consider the utterance of a sentence such as 'What this glass contains is water'. The general setting of utterance, including the topic of earlier parts of the conversation, if there were any, will determine whether it would be required to test the liquid in some laboratory, to summon an expert or appropriate witnesses, or just to have a glance at the glass.

Notice that we do not assume that a speech act and a context of utterance fix a *single* method of justification, though on many occasions this happens to be the case. Under some circumstances, different methods which apply to the same, say, assertion belong to a scale of methods, some members of which being improved extensions of other members of it. One's own recollections and historical inquiry are at the cores of two methods of justification belonging to such a scale. However, on some occasions, different methods of justification might form a rivalry of a sort. This is the case, for example, when religious rituals of justifying some assertions are available: 'I believe that every human being has two human parents; but Catholics believe that Jesus only had a human mother. And other people might believe that there are human beings with no parents, and give no credence to all the contrary evidence.' Indeed, Wittgenstein's (1969, 239) example cannot be explained without resort to an underlying variety of methods of justification.

When one method of justification is an improved extension of another, the conception of *conclusive evidence* of the latter system may be defined in deference to the conceptions of *evidence, justification* and *conclusive evidence* of the former system. Therefore, when a given speech act, as performed in a certain context of utterance, is under consideration, though one method of justification may be the most natural one to be applied to what has been said when that speech act was performed, still some other methods of justification may turn out to be somewhat indirectly related to the same case. Hence, though Malcolm (1977) is right in arguing that '[w]*ithin* a language-game there is justification, evidence and proof, mistakes and groundless opinions, good and bad reasoning, correct measurements and incorrect ones', it is not self-evident that what he goes on to say does not lend itself to some misleading interpretation: 'One cannot properly apply these terms to a language-game itself.' This should not be read as implying that language-games of justification are closed systems, strictly unrelated to each other.

[V2]   *No method of justification enjoys an exclusive status.*
The present constraint is not always conspicuously reflected in our practices of justification, where for a long period one method of justification might seem to communities of speakers to be the only appropriate method available. [V2] is rather a constraint which constitutes part of our concept of *method of justification*. What we assume is that nothing in our concept of *method of justification* precludes additional methods of justification from emerging within communities of speakers of a natural language. An obvious result of this assumption is that [V2.1] *the class of methods of justification of what is said is never closed.*

We conclude our preliminary list of constraints by proposing, in a much more tentative way, a constraint which might turn out to be crucial for our understanding of the concept of *truth*:

[V3]   *A family of methods of justification which does not include conflicting members is preferable to a family of such methods which does include conflicting members*, ceteris paribus.

Here methods of justification M_1 and M_2 are *conflicting* if, and only if, there is a possible speech act which under possible circumstances of utterance says p and there is a possible state of information, S, such that according to M_1 S provides conclusive evidence for p, whereas according to M_2 the same S provides conclusive evidence against p.[23]

Constraint [V3] should not be read as assuming any global form of realism, with respect to the truth-value of whatever can be said. On the contrary, this constraint forms part of a general, rather idealistic, conception of truth as what is *conclusively* justified or justified *in the limit* (Putnam, 1981).

ACKNOWLEDGEMENTS

Earlier versions and parts of this paper were presented at several conferences and colloquia at the universities of Gent, Nijmegen, Konstanz, Pavia, Stanford, Trento and Jerusalem. I benefitted from many remarks made on these occasions.

NOTES

[1] These are Ludwig Boltzmann's words, with respect to the growth of science (Boltzmann, 1974). The figure of a city as an organizing principle of a language was used earlier, for example in Urquhart (1652).

[2] For example Cresswell (1973). A critical discussion of some of these approaches is included in Kasher (1974).

[3] According to Davidson's approach such a counterpart actually consists of two old-city devices.

[4] More accurately, *ideal* speech acts are intentional, while some real speech acts might, for example, be just slips of tongue. Since we are interested in linguistic competence and not in any other major aspect of linguistic performance, just ideal speech acts will be presently under consideration.

[5] Quoted from Walpole (1932).

[6] Romeo and Juliet, Act II, scene II, 62ff.

[7] Quoted from Edith Wharton (1934).

[8] For an explanation of what counts here as an appropriate type of an end, see Kasher (1979, p. 40), where we use the term 'literal purposes'.

[9] For our views of the relations between rationality principles and Grice's super-maxims, see Kasher (1979, 1982).

[10] For an analysis of constitutivity in terms of the inexistence of external ends, see N. Kasher (1978).

[11] Geoffrey Leech (1983) includes tact principles in his book which should also be explained in terms of costs, as used in our rationality principle. See Kasher (in press).

[12] *Exodus*, 5:1–2.

[13] For some discussions of related questions, see Driver (1984).

[14] For an elaboration of this and related arguments, see Hilary Putnam (1981).

[15] Many aspects of such an approach have been discussed in Michael Dummett's works (Dummett, 1973, 1978, 1981, 1982).

[16] We follow here Crispin Wright's suggestion (Wright, 1976).

[17] See Hintikka (1978, 1984). For our interpretation of Hintikka's games, see Kasher (1979).

[18] We have grouped the following examples in a way which is also intended to show how different from each other, with respect to ways of justification, might very similar speech acts be.

[19] Here is where one might have introduced the notion of *the pragmatical form* of a method of justification, but at the present stage of our understanding what is involved in methods of justification, the notion of *form* might be misleading.

[20] See Kripke (1982, pp. 105–106). For a discussion of finite representability in pragmatics, see Kasher (1986).

[21] For a detailed interpretation of part of Wittgenstein's *Philosophical Investigations* along such a line, see Kripke (1982). One aspect of our present claim is reflected in Popper's discussion (Popper, 1961) of what he calls 'basic statements': 'Every test of a theory . . . must stop at some basic statement or other which we *decide to accept* . . . (W)e are stopping at statements about whose acceptance or rejection the various investigators are likely to reach agreement'.

[22] From the present point of view, Popper's distinction (1961, pp. 109–111) between a justification and a decision 'reached in accordance with a procedure governed by rules' amounts to nothing more than a distinction between end-points in two different methods of justification.

[23] It would be interesting to compare our discussion of methods of justification with Nozick's discussion of 'Ways and Methods' in Epistemology, in Nozick (1981), but we cannot go into that here.

REFERENCES

Anscombe, G. E. M., *Intention*, 2nd edition. Oxford: Blackwell, 1976.

Bacon, F., *Interviews with Francis Bacon, 1962–1979*, D. Sylvester (Ed). London: Thames and Hudson, 1980, p. 18.

Boltzmann, L., On the development of the methods of theoretical physics in recent times. In B. McGuiness (Ed), *Ludwig Boltzmann: Theoretical Physics and Philosophical Problems*. Dordrecht: Reidel, 1974, p. 77.

Chomsky, N., *Noam Chomsky on the Generative Enterprise*, R. Huybregts & H. van Riemsdijk (Eds). Dordrecht: Foris, 1982.

Cresswell, M. J., *Logics and Languages*. London: Methuen, 1973.

Davidson, D., Moods and performances. In *Meaning and Use*, A. Margalit (Ed). Dordrecht: Reidel, 1979, pp. 9–20.

Driver, J. L., Metaquestions. *Nous*, 1984, **18**, 299–309.

Dummett, M., *Frege, Philosophy of Language*. London: Duckworth, 1973.

Dummett, M., *Truth and Other Enigmas*. London: Duckworth, 1978.

Dummett, M., *The Interpretation of Frege's Philosophy*. London: Duckworth, 1981.

Dummett, M., Realism. *Synthese*, 1982, **52**, 55–112.

Gazdar, G., *Pragmatics*. New York: Academic, 1979, pp. 54–55.

Grice, H. P., *Logic and Conversation, Syntax and Semantic*, volume 3. In P. Cole & J. L. Morgan (Eds), *Speech Acts*. New York: Academic, 1975, p. 48.

Harnish, R., Logical form and implicature. In T. G. Bever, J. J. Katz & D. T. Langendoen (Eds), *An Integrated Theory of Linguistic Ability*. New York: Crowell, 1976, p. 340.

Hintikka, J., In E. Saarinen (Ed), *Game-theoretical Semantics*. Dordrecht: Reidel, 1978.

Hintikka, J., A hundred years later: The rise and fall of Frege's influence in language theory. *Synthese*, 1984, **59**, 27–49.

Kasher, A., Mood implicatures: A logical way of doing generative pragmatics *Theoretical Linguistics*, 1974, **1**, 6–38.

Kasher, A., What is a theory of use? In A. Margalit (Ed), *Meaning and Use*. Dordrecht: Reidel, 1979.

Kasher, A., Minimal speakers, necessary speech acts. In F. Coulmas (Ed), *A Festschrift for Native Speaker*. The Hague: Mouton, 1981, pp. 93–101.

Kasher, A., Gricean inference revisited. *Philosophica*, 1982, **29**, 25–44.

Kasher, A., On the psychological reality of pragmatics. *Journal of Pragmatics*, 1986, **8**, 534–557.

Kasher, A., Politeness and rationality. *Jacob Mey Festschrift*. In press.

Kasher, N., Deontology and Kant. *Revue Internationale de Philosophie*, 1978, **126**, 551–558.

Keenan, E., On the universality of conversational implicatures *Language in Society*, 1976, **5**, 67–80.

Kripke, S. A., *Wittgenstein on Rules and Private Language*. London: Blackwell, 1982, pp. 105–106.

Leech, G., *Principles of Pragmatics*. London: Longman, 1983.

Lewis, D., *Semantics of Natural Language*, D. Davidson & G. Harman (Eds). Dordrecht: Reidel, 1972.

Malcolm, N., The groundlessness of belief. In S. C. Brown (Eds), *Reason and Religion*. Ithaca, NY: Cornell, University Press, 1977, p. 152.

Nozick, R., *Philosophical Explanations*. Cambridge, MA: Harvard University Press, 1981.

Pierce, C. S., *Collected Papers of Charles Sanders Pierce*, volume VIII, A. Burks (Ed). Cambridge, MA: Harvard University Press, 1958, p. 337.

Popper, K. R., *The Logic of Scientific Discovery*. New York: Science Editions, 1961, p. 104.

Urquhart, T., *The Jewel* (1652), D. S. Jack & R. J. Lyall (Eds). Edinburgh: Scottish Academic Press, 1984.

Putnam, H., *Reason, Truth and History*, Cambridge: Cambridge University Press, 1981.

Walpole, H., The Apple Trees (1932). In J. Sutherland (Ed), *The Oxford Book of Literary Anecdotes*. Oxford: Oxford University Press, 1975, pp. 288–289.

Wharton, E., A Backward Glance (1934). In J. Sutherland (Ed), *The Oxford Book of Literary Anecdotes*. Oxford: Oxford University Press, 1975, pp. 283–284.

Wittgenstein, L., *Zettel*, G. E. M. Anscombe & G. H. von Wright (Eds). Oxford: Blackwell, 1967, p. 437.

Wittgenstein, L., *On Certainty*, G. E. M. Anscombe & G. H. von Wright (Eds). Oxford: Blackwell, 1969.

Wittgenstein, L., *Culture and Value*, G. H. Von Wright (Ed). Oxford: Blackwell, 1980, p. 24.

Wright, C., Truth conditions and criteria. *Proceedings of the Aristotelian Society*, 1976, **50**, 236.

10

Logical Form as a Level of Linguistic Representation

ROBERT MAY

School of Social Science,
University of Calilfornia, Irvine

What is the relation of a sentence's *syntactic* form to its *logical* form? This issue has been of central concern in modern inquiry into the semantic properties of natural languages, at least ever since Frege and Russell's disagreement over definite descriptions. Frege was at pains to show how natural language deviated from the logical perfectability of his *Begriffschrift*, holding, for example, that the grammar of natural language did not properly represent the semantic structure of quantified sentences. Russell concurred with this assessment and extended the point to definite descriptions, arguing that their logical form was obfuscated by the grammar even more thoroughly, so as to require their 'elimination' in logical representation. Frege, however, maintained otherwise; descriptions were not so much akin to quantifiers, but rather to arguments, syntactically and semantically comparable, aside from their presuppositions, to proper names. Hence, in this case, for Frege the relation of form and interpretation was rather direct, in that the grammar revealed more or less transparently the logical structure of descriptions, but not so to Russell, who felt that the grammar disguised their true semantic nature.

Since that time it has become a common and traditional supposition in discussions of the relation of linguistic form to its interpretation that the grammar of a natural language, in ultimately mediating between sound and meaning, provides for a mapping from syntactic structures onto logical

305

NEW DIRECTIONS IN SEMANTICS

representations, the latter the objects of formal semantic analysis. As Donald Davidson puts it, 'It would be strange if the structure essential to an account of truth were not effectively tied to the patterns of sound we use to convey truth.' In this paper, I will be introducing a particular approach to this view, in which the role of the grammar in characterizing semantically relevant structural properties of natural languages is explicated in terms of formal levels of grammatical representation, an approach expressed in the earliest discussions of transformational grammar, for example in Chomsky's *Syntactic Structures* (p. 87):

> What we are suggesting is that the notion of 'understanding a sentence' will be explained in part in terms of the notion of 'linguistic level'. To understand a sentence, then, it is first necessary to reconstruct its analysis on each linguistic level; and we can test the adequacy of a given set of abstract linguistic levels by asking whether or not grammars formulated in terms of these levels enable us to provide a satisfactory analysis of the notion of 'understanding'.

What I will propose is that the levels of linguistic representation be articulated so as to include a level of representation, *Logical Form*, (LF), related to (more precisely, derived from) other linguistic levels in specified ways. Logical Form, in the sense to be developed, will then simply be that level of representation which interfaces the theories of linguistic form and interpretation. It represents, in this view, whatever properties of syntactic form are relevant to semantic interpretation; those aspects of semantic structure which are expressed syntactically. Succinctly, the contribution of grammar to meaning.

Two basic questions immediately arise. First, exactly how this semantically relevant level of representation is to be formally defined. Second, how structures at this level are assigned 'meanings'; for our purposes, loosely put, under what conditions a logical representation can be said to truthfully describe, or correspond to, some appropriately individuated aspect of the world, or perhaps more accurately, of our knowledge and belief about the world. Of course, the answers to these questions are intimately intertwined, but conceptually the former, syntactic issue is prior: If there are no representations, then there is nothing to be interpreted, at least in the sense of a formal semantic interpretation. Indeed, the more highly articulated the syntactic properties of logical representations—to us, representations at Logical Form—the more highly determined will be the interpretations such representations receive. Moreover, the more highly determined semantic structure is by syntactic structure, the more 'transparent' the relation of form and interpretation will be. The question then is just how much of the semantic structure of a natural language is manifest in its syntax? In giving an answer to this, we must consider in detail the first issue posed above.

Since the earliest work in generative grammar, an empirical goal has been to provide a class of descriptive levels for grammatical analysis, each constituted by a class of formal representations, well-formed with respect to individually necessary and collectively sufficient conditions on class membership. A *grammar* is understood as a function which specifies for each sentence of a language its formal description at each level of representation. A grammar (strongly) *generates* a class of *structural descriptions*, whose members are sets of representations $\{a_1, \ldots, a_n\}$, where each a_j, $(1 \leqslant j \leqslant n)$, is a representation at level A_j. A 'grammatical' sentence, then, is one that is assigned a structural description each of whose members are well-formed; an ungrammatical sentence one which is assigned a structural description with at least one ill-formed member. A sentence is n-ways grammatically ambiguous if it is assigned n-many distinct well-formed structural descriptions.

Uncovering the properties of any hypothesized level centers around three basic concerns. One has to do with the formal nature of representations at that level, the second with how these representations are derived and the third with constraints on their well-formedness. Though the answers to these questions will be deeply interconnected for any given level, only with respect to specified assumptions as to rules, representations and conditions can levels be initially individuated and their empirical content—what they represent—be ultimately determined.

Let us take an example of the sort of approach I have in mind. D(eep)-Structure is the level of representation projected from lexical properties in accordance with certain conditions determining well-formedness, for example, X̄-theory (Chomsky, 1981). S(urface)-Structure is then that level of representation derived by rules having D-Structure phrase structure representations as their input. From a further assumption, namely that these rules effect a transformational mapping, it follows that S-Structure is a level of *phrase-structure* representation, since transformations map phrase-markers onto phrase-markers. Among the well-formedness conditions applying to S-Structure is Case-theory, in the sense of Chomsky (1980, 1981), Rouveret & Vergnaud (1980) and others, from which it follows that lexical noun phrases may occur only in positions of Case assignment. This differentiates *It is unclear what Bill is doing* from the ungrammatical *It is unclear what Bill to do*; subjects of tensed clauses are assigned nominative Case, but subjects of infinitives are usually assigned no Case at all. Thus the grammar only assigns a well-formed structural description to the former sentence. Representations at S-Structure are, in turn, phonologically interpreted—assigned phonetic values—by rules which are, in part, sensitive to structural properties of this level. To take a well-known example, the possibility of phonologically contracting *want* and *to* to form *wanna*, as in *Who do you wanna visit?* has been argued to depend upon properties of syntactically represented empty categories, and in particular upon the Case properties assigned to these categories at S-Structure (Jaeggli, 1980). In this regard, S-Structure properties in part determine the sound structure assigned to a sentence and S-Structure may be thought of as the contribution of the theory of linguistic form (that is, the syntax) to the theory of linguistic sounds.

In part, then, Universal Grammar (UG) specifies the constitution of the 'core' levels of syntactic representation, now considered to include, in addition to D-Structure and S-Structure, a level of Logical Form. Extending our mode of inquiry to this latter level, we proceed as before by fixing its syntactic properties and the type of interpretations assigned to its representations. As a point of departure, then, let us suppose that representations at LF are derived by rules having S-Structure representations as their input, so that the core levels of representation are as depicted in (1), comprising the syntactic component of what has been called 'sentence grammar':

(1)   D-Structure—S-Structure—Logical Form

D-Structure is projected from the lexicon; it represents syntactically the basic functional and structural properties associated with lexical items. S-Structure is derived by a (possibly null) set of applications of transformational rules, and in turn maps onto LF, the latter level consisting of a class of fully indexed phrase markers. In May (1977) it was proposed that this latter mapping is also transformational. From this it follows that LF is a level of phrase-structure representation as well, consisting of a class of bracketings labeled with linguistic categories, a consequence of the structure-preserving nature of transformational mappings. By hypothesis, S-Structure representations are assigned phonological interpretations, while it is to LF-representations that semantic interpretations are assigned.

To be more specific about the nature of transformational mappings, I will assume, following Chomsky (1981), that there is but one transformational rule, 'Move α': Displace an arbitrary constituent to any other structural position. Among the structures which may be derived is (2), derived by movement of the *wh*-phase to COMP:

(2) $[_{S'}[_{COMP} \text{who}_2] [_S \text{did John see} [_{NP} e_2]]]$

The functioning of 'Move α' will in all cases leave a *trace* (designated by '*e*'), which is a category devoid of lexical content coindexed with, and hence bound to, the moved phrase. Turning to LF, 'Move α' chiefly figures in its derivation in transforming the S-Structure representations of quantified sentences like *John saw everyone* onto LF-representations like (3):

(3) $[_S[_{NP} \text{ everyone}_2] [_S \text{ John saw } [_{NP} e_2]]]$

(3) is derived by (Chomsky)-adjunction of the S-Structure object NP to the S node.[1] This central case of LF-movement, which I will refer to as QR, following the usage of May (1977), derives representations that structurally overlap in certain important ways with *wh*-constructions like (2). In particular, both contain traces coindexed with phrases displaced to positions outside the predicate's argument positions. These positions will be referred to as Ā-positions, as opposed to A-positions (roughly those bearing grammatical relations). Given this, we can recognize both (2) and (3) as containing (logical) variables, which, at a first approximation, are simply those traces contained within A-positions which are Ā-bound (that is, coindexed with phrases in Ā-positions; see Borer (1981), Chomsky (1981)). In turn, the structural properties of (2) and (3) allow us to syntactically characterize certain semantically relevant concepts. Thus *scope* can be defined as follows:[2]

(4) The scope of α is the set of nodes which α c-commands at LF

Thus, in a structure like (5a), ($=$(2)),

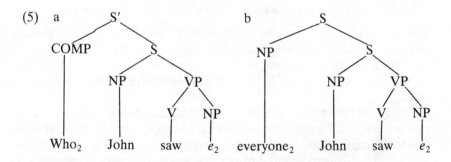

(5) a   ...   b

the *wh*-phrase in COMP has scope over all the nodes it c-commands, that is, S and all the nodes S dominates. This includes the trace of *who*; hence, we may take this variable as a *bound* variable as it lies within the scope of a coindexed *wh*-phrase, interpreted here as a quasi-quantifier.[3] Parallel comments hold for representations in which the binding phrase is a true quantified phrase, as in (5b) ($=$(3)).

The grammar, then, provides for a direct representation of quantificational structure, arguing on syntactic grounds for a particular way of representing natural language quantification, although other types of representation giving rise to the same class of interpretations can be easily imagined. This is afforded to a large extent through the mediation of trace theory. As a result, it becomes possible to explain a range of phenomena by appeal to general principles of syntactic well-formedness which interact to determine the distribution and binding of lexically empty categories, where, in part, this generality is expressed by their holding of LF-representations. To take a simple example, it is a consequence of trace theory of movement rules that 'downgrading' movements are proscribed (Fiengo, 1977; May, 1981). Thus, even though relevant subcategorization restrictions are satisfied, (6) is ill-formed, since the trace is not c-commanded by the *wh*-phrase with which it is coindexed:

(6) $*[_S e_2$ wondered $[_{S'}$ who$_2$ $[_S$ Angleton suspected Philby]]]

Similarly, QR could apply so as to downgrade a phrase:

(7) $*[_S e_2$ believed $[_S$ someone$_2$ $[_S$ Angleton suspected Philby]]]

However, (7) is ill-formed for just the same reason as (6)—the trace is not c-commanded by its antecedent.[4] This allows us to explain why *Someone believed Angleton suspected Philby* may not be construed with the quantifier understood as outside the scope of *believe*; it only has the well-formed logical form in (8):

(8) $[_S$ someone$_2$ $[_S e_2$ believed $[_S$ Angleton suspected Philby]]]

This is an indication of the initial plausibility of proposing that Universal Grammar makes available a class of conditions that determine in part not only the properties of overt movements such as *wh*-movement, but also the properties of 'LF-movements' like QR that also derive structures containing traces.

The extended degree of structural articulation found at LF allows as well for the statement of generalizations not apparently manifest at other syntactic levels. One rather widely discussed case is 'weak crossover' phenomena: the impossibility of construing the pronoun as anaphoric in either *Who did his mother see?* or *His mother saw everything*, although such a construal is possible with a non-quantified antecedent: *His mother saw John*. Given that the relevant representations are as in (9);

(9) a $[_{S'}$ who$_2$ $[_S$ did his mother see e_2]]
    b $[_S$ everyone$_2$ $[_S$ his mother saw e_2]]
    c $[_S$ his mother saw John]

a descriptive generalization is apparently that a trace cannot be the antecedent of a pronoun to its left; see Chomsky (1976), Higginbotham (1980), and, for somewhat different approaches, Reinhart (1983), Koopman & Sportiche (1983) and Safir (1984). In (9a) the trace arises as a result of application of 'Move α' in the mapping from D-Structure to S-Structure;

in (9b), from 'Move α' applying from S-Structure to LF. To (9c) 'Move α' has not applied at all, so, in the relevant respects, its representations at D-Structure, S-Structure and LF are non-distinct. Since the object NP is a full lexical NP, it is not proscribed from being the antecendent of the pronoun by the generalization in question. Notice that the S-Structure representations of (9a)–(9c) would not afford the relevant generalization, since the S-Structure of (9b), like that of (9c), contains not a trace but a lexical object.

Having spelled out to some degree our syntactic assumptions, we now sketch the semantic assumptions underlying our primarily syntactic investigations, so as to be able to isolate those semantic properties that will intersect with the syntax of LF-representations, in particular with our notions of variable and scope. Simplifying from the approach developed in Higginbotham & May (1981a), suppose there is a (non-null)) domain $\mathbf{D}$. A quantifier Q is interpreted by a *quantification* $\mathbf{Q}$ on D, a function from subsets of $\mathbf{D}$ onto $\{1,0\}$, i.e., truth and falsity.[5] *Restricted quantifications* on D, which are typically found in natural languages, differ in that they are functions from the Cartesian product of the power set D on to $\{1, 0\}$. Restricted quantifications of the form

$$\mathbf{Q}(X, Y) = 1 \quad \text{iff } \psi$$
$$= 0 \quad \text{otherwise}$$

where ψ is some function from X and Y onto subsets of D, interpret representations at LF of the form

$$[_\alpha Q - X_i^n [_\beta \dots e_i \dots]]$$

where Q ranges over quantifier elements like *every, some, few, several, so, the, a, no, two*, etc, X^n is an n-level projection of a lexical category and β an open sentence containing e_i free. That β is the maximal domain containing e_i free follows from assuming the coincidence of a quantifier's scope with its c-command domain. A quantification, then, effects a partitioning of the universe, its application to an LF-representation containing a quantifier Q being fixed by simple rule; the value of X is determined on the basis of X^n, that of Y on the basis of β. Supposing that there is an (extensional) category-type correspondence such that both X^n and β denote subsets of the domain, then $\mathbf{Q}$ establishes that relationship that must hold between X and Y, the sets so denoted, for truth to obtain. Multiple quantification sentences, whose syntax we will turn to below, will be treated in the usual way via truth relative to assignment of values to variables.[6]

As an example, consider the sentence *No Russian is a spy*, which has the logical form (10) in the relevant respects:

(10) $[_S[_{NP}$ No $[_{N''}$ Russian$]]_i$ $[_S$ e_i is a spy$]]$

This is interpreted by a quantification in which ψ is an intersective function on subsets of D:

$$\textbf{No}(X, Y) = 1 \quad \text{iff } X \cap Y = \varnothing$$
$$= 0 \quad \text{otherwise}$$

When applied to (10) the value of X will be defined as

$$\{x|\text{ Russian }(x)\}$$

while that of Y will be

$$\{y|\text{ spy }(y)\}.$$

(10) will be true, then, just in case the set of Russians and the set of spies have no members in common, and false otherwise. Similarly, the truth conditions for other quantifiers can be specified. *Every* will be interpreted by the intersective quantification

$$\textbf{Every } (X, Y) = 1 \quad \text{iff } X = X \cap Y$$
$$= 0 \quad \text{otherwise}$$

while *some* will be interpreted by

$$\textbf{Some } (X, Y) = 1 \quad \text{iff } X \cap Y \neq \varnothing$$
$$= 0 \quad \text{otherwise}$$

which is also intersective. Numerals will be interpreted by quantifications of the form

$$\textbf{n}(X, Y) = 1 \quad \text{iff } |X \cap Y| = n$$
$$= 0 \quad \text{otherwise.}$$

This interprets the 'exactly' sense of numerical quantifiers; the 'at least' sense is arrived at by substituting '$\geq$', the 'at most' sense by substituting '$\leq$'. All three quantifications apply equally well (in the absence of any pragmatic constraint), to the LF-representation of *Three professors left*, which will then be true under three related, but distinct, interpretations pertaining to the cardinality of the intersection of the set of individuals who are professors and left. *The* will be interpreted by

$$\textbf{The } (X, Y) = 1 \quad \text{iff } X = X \cap Y = \{a\}, \text{ for } a \in D$$
$$= 0 \quad \text{otherwise}$$

which embeds the existence and uniqueness properties of definite descriptions, found invariantly under alternative scopes:

(11)   The president of every public authority in New York is a crook

Although on the preferred construal of (11) *the* has narrower scope, it can also have broader scope, a construal facilitated by substituting *Robert Moses* for *a crook*. On the former interpretation (11) entails that each authority has one, and only one, president; on the latter it entails that there is exactly one person who is president of all the public authorities. This is as expected, as these properties of interpretation do not accrue to *the* in virtue of its scope. We are thus distinguishing properties of quantifiers traceable to structural sources from those which are lexically inherent, expressed as aspects of quantifications. Indeed, this can be the only source of inherent properties of quantifiers, since syntactic rules, and in particular, transformational mappings, including those onto LF, are context-free, and hence blind to lexical governance. This precludes the possibility of marking quantifiers for specified scopes, although inherent properties may be more consonant with certain scopes. For example, *each* often preferentially takes broad scope. But whatever the source of this preference, we would not want to maintain that it is an obligatorily broad scope quantifier, as it can have narrow scope as well, as in (12), in which it stands inside of the embedded quantifier in logical form:

(12)   Each person in some midwestern city voted for Debs in the '08
       election

Thus the theory sharply distinguishes the general grammatical properties of quantifiers—their scope—from their lexical properties, expressed semantically by quantifications.

The interpretation of quantifiers just sketched constitutes an hypothesis as to the semantic component of our linguistic knowledge of quantification. Now, of course, our syntactic assumptions do not uniquely determine the sort of semantics just outlined; one could imagine other interpretive systems wedded to the structural aspects of Logical Form. But whatever the exact system of semantic interpretation assumed, insofar as it characterizes notions that interact with grammatically determined semantic structure, we will have an argument that linguistic theory should countenance a formal semantic component with those properties. To take an example, the notion of quantification adumbrated above allows us to classify quantifiers as either monotone increasing or decreasing, depending upon whether they warrant upward or downward entailments among pairs like (13a)/(13b) and (13a)/(13c) (Barwise & Cooper, 1981):

(13)   a   Every man left
       b   Every father left
       c   Every man left early

(13a) entails (13b); this is a downward entailment since it runs from a superset, the set of men, to a subset, the set of fathers. On the other hand, the entailment relation between (13a) and (13c) is upward entailing, as it runs from a subset, the set of individuals who left early, to a superset, the set of individuals who left. Thus, we will say that the quantifier *every*, interpreted by the quantification given above, is monotone decreasing for argument X and monotone increasing for Y. (What I am calling 'monotone increasing/decreasing for X', Barwise & Cooper (1981) call persistent/ antipersistent, reserving the term monotone for what I have referred to as monotonicity for Y.) All other quantifiers can be classified by their monotone properties; for example, *no* is monotone decreasing for both X and Y, *some* monotone increasing for both, for example.

Monotone properties of quantifiers afford a number of interesting generalizations with syntactic consequences. To mention one, apparently it is only those quantifiers that are monotone decreasing for Y which can be moved to COMP in S-Structure:[7]

(14)   Only/no/few spies that he trusts would Dulles send inside Russia

This contrasts with quantifiers which minimally differ from those in (14) in being monotone increasing for this argument:

(15)   *Even/all/many spies that he trusts would Dulles send inside Russia Russia

Another very interesting case is discussed in Ladusaw (1981). He argues that a necessary condition on the occurrence of polarity *any* is that it occur within the scope of a monotone decreasing operator. He points to examples like (16), which under the assumptions here have the LF-representations in (17):

(16)   a   No student who ever read anything about phrenology attended Gall's lecture
       b   No student who attended Gall's lecture had ever read anything about phrenology
(17)   a   No student who ever read anything about phrenology$_2$ [e_2 attended Gall's lecture]
       b   No student who attended Gall's lecture$_2$ [e_2 had ever read anything about phrenology]

In deriving (17) it has been assumed that QR applies to the entire restrictive relative clause, and not just its head. This is just as with *wh*-movement; thus *Which book that John likes did he give to Mary to read* contrasts with **Which book did he give that John likes to Mary to read*. Thus, in (17a) the polarity item *anything* is included within that part of the logical form which fixes the value of X in the quantification interpreting *no*, in (17b) that part which fixes the value of Y. Since *no* is monotone decreasing for both arguments, occurrence of polarity items is warranted in either constituent in the LF-representation. On the other hand, both (18a) and (18b) are ungrammatical, since *some* is fully monotone increasing:

(18) a *Some student who ever read anything about phrenology attended Gall's lecture
      b *Some student who attended Gall's lecture had ever read anything about phrenology

In contrast to (16) and (18), Ladusaw points to examples like (19):

(19) a Every student who ever read anything about phrenology attended Gall's lecture
      b *Every student who attended Gall's lecture had ever read anything about phrenology

Since *every* is monotone decreasing for X and increasing for Y, the polarity item can only occur within that part of the LF-representation corresponding to the former argument; thus (19a) is well-formed, but not (19b).

The 'pied-piping' property of QR, whose importance we have just observed in describing the properties of polarity items, has a number of other consequences. For example, VP-deletion is possible, in general, if neither the missing verb nor its antecedent c-commands the other. This will clearly always hold when VP-deletion applies across sentential conjuncts or members of a discourse. But consider (20), the case of antecedent contained deletion discussed in Sag (1976) and elsewhere.

(20) Dulles suspected everyone who Angleton did

This seems to violate the condition, as *suspected* c-commands *did*. But as Sag (1976) and Williams (1977) have argued, the constraints on VP-deletion are properly stated over logical representations, and indeed, the LF-representation of (20) will be consistent with the c-command constraint, as now there is no c-command relation between the verb phrase headed by *suspected* and the missing VP.

(21) [everyone who Angleton did$_2$ [Dulles suspected e_2]]

I will suppose, along with Williams, that VP-deletion involves a reconstruction of the missing VP in the place of the pro-form, respecting certain identity conditions. While matters are in actuality somewhat more complex, for our purposes it will do to simply assume that it is the syntactic VP which is copied; the resulting structure will be as in (22):

(22) [[everyone who Angleton suspected e_2]$_2$ [Dulles suspected e_2]]

This represents just the desired interpretation, namely that Angleton and Philby suspected all the same people. Note that in (22) *who* now properly binds an empty category, presuming that it is normally coindexed with the head of the relative. A comparable substitution of VP in the S-Structure of (20), however, would lead to a reconstructive regress, as substitution of the VP *everyone who Angleton did* would lead to a structure still containing a deleted VP, which itself would have to be reconstructed, and so on. That such a regress is a cause of ungrammaticality can be summized from the deviance of (23), with a non-restrictive relative substituted; compare *Dulles suspected Philby, who Angleton did too*:

(23) *Dulles suspected Philby, who Angleton did

Here, since LF-movement affects only quantified phrases, there is no possibility of deriving the structure which properly permits reconstruction. Needless to say, the contrast of (20) and (23) provides strong evidence for a level of Logical Form, and for movement operations onto that level which single out quantified phrases. This is reinforced by the account of examples like (24):[8]

(24) *Dulles suspected everyone who knew Philby, who Angleton did

It might be thought that substitution of an antecedent VP in a non-restrictive relative would be possible if it were moved as part of another phrase, so as to avoid the regress just described for (23). This is so, but, it turns out, a well-formed LF-representation is still not derivable. Application of QR gives (25a); subsequent substitution of the VP, (25b):

(25) a   [everyone who knew Philby, who Angleton did$_2$ [Dulles sus-
              pected e_2]]
       b   [[everyone who knew Philby, who Angleton suspected e_2]$_2$
              [Dulles suspected e_2]]

The problem with (25b) is that the embedded *wh*-phrase binds no empty category. That is, the two *wh*-phrases will bear distinct indices, but the index of the empty category contained in the reconstructed VP must be that of the higher occurrence of *who*, as only it is coindexed with the phrase which undergoes LF-movement. Thus the ungrammaticality of (24) can be attributed to its LF-representation (25b) containing an operator which binds no variable. Note that the analysis further predicts that *Dulles suspected everyone who knew some agent who Angleton did* is grammatical, but only with an interpretation under which the deleted phrase is understood as the embedded VP, that headed by *knew*.

The grammar, then, provides sufficient structure so that at Logical Form the application of quantifications can be transparently determined. This structure arises from assuming that LF-representations of quantified sentences are derived by transformational mappings, exploiting a notion of logically bound variable which receives grammatical foundation through trace theory. Such mappings, note, do not 'translate' between the *sentences* of some language and those of some other formal representational system; rather, they are mappings wholly within the formal representational system for natural language. Indeed, the assumption that LF is derived in this way adds nothing to linguistic theory which need not otherwise be assumed as provided by UG. Whatever theoretical apparatus is needed to properly characterize the syntactic properties of *wh*-constructions like *Who does Angleton suspect?* will be sufficient, I am arguing, to properly characterize the syntactic properties of the LF-representation of *Angleton suspected everyone*, giving a general theory of the representation of quantificational binding without introducing any special types of rules or principles. This is an important point, and it should be emphasized. Assuming that there is a level of Logical Form derived by 'Move α' does not entail any extension of the formal expressiveness of linguistic theory—that is, there is no extension of the types of grammatical rules or representations which it countenances—although it does extend the range of phenomena which, *prima facie*, fall under its descriptive and explanatory purview. Insofar, then, as this approach can be seen to be empirically motivated, it will represent the best possible circumstance for incorporating a theory of logical representation within the grammar.

We now turn to the logical syntax of multiple quantification. As a point of departure consider the following analysis, that of May (1977), of the class of structures derived by application of QR to (26), an S-Structure containing two quantified phrases:

(26) $[_S[_{NP}$ every spy] $[_{VP}$ suspects $[_{NP}$ some Russian]]]

A single application of QR to either NP in (26) yields the structures in (27):

(27) a $[_S[_{NP}$ every spy]$_2$ $[_S$ e_2 suspects $[_{NP}$ some Russian]]]
      b $[_S[_{NP}$ some Russian]$_3$ $[_S[_{NP}$ every spy] suspects e_3]]

Since QR is a (Chomsky)-adjunction, each of these structures now contains two S nodes to which further application of QR can attach phrases, allowing for the derivation of the distinct structures in (28):[9]

(28) a $[_S[_{NP}$ every spy]$_2$ $[_S$ $[_{NP}$ some Russian]$_3$ $[_S$ e_2 suspects e_3]]]
      b $[_S[_{NP}$ some Russian]$_3$ $[_S$ $[_{NP}$ every spy]$_2$ $[_S$ e_2 suspects e_3]]]

(28a) and (28b) represents the ambiguity of *every spy suspects some Russian* as a matter of quantifier scope. Since in (28a) *every spy* c-commands *some Russian*, but not vice versa, the former has broader scope. The opposite holds in (28b), in which *some Russian* has been adjoined at a higher position from which it has broader scope over *every spy*. Thus, simply given the free application of QR, (and the usual sort of assumptions as to the recursive assignment of truth-conditions), it is possible to represent certain ambiguities of multiple quantification, so that an S-Structure such as (26) will count as grammatically disambiguated with respect to its logical form.

Bear in mind that the issue which concerns us here is to what degree the class of *possible* interpretations which can be assigned to a given syntactic structure is a function of its grammatical properties. This is not to say, however, that every *sentence* of a given form will exhibit every possible interpretation; even less to say a sentence will exhibit every possible interpretation on every use. Which construal or construals will be preferred on a given occasion of use is a matter which goes beyond grammar *per se*, taking into account various properties of discourse, shared knowledge of the interlocutors, plausibility of description, etc.[10] To conflate these matters would be to confuse the grammatical issue—to what degree does a sentence's structure fix its meaning—with an issue ultimately of use. And to do so would undoubtedly not lead to a clear understanding of the content of either topic.

Sentences of mixed universal and existential quantification, such as *Everybody loves somebody*, have the property that one of the inter-pretations represented by their logical forms entails the other, a matter of logic, just as it is a matter of logic that the interpretations represented by the logical forms of *Everyone loves everyone* are equivalent. Regardless of these logical relations, however, both sentences are assigned two struc-turally distinct representations at LF; their equivalence or disequivalence simply amounts to the claim that distinct modes of composition either do or do not lead to identical interpretations. From the logical relations of such sentences, however, another moral can be drawn, namely that there is no need to represent both scope orders, but rather only one, the other to be seen as following in virtue of some logical (or perhaps pragmatic), relation. For instance, with sentences of mixed universal and existential quantifiers, there would be only a representation of the interpretation in which the existential has broader scope, as this entails the other inter-pretation, in which the universal has broader scope. In a sense, this is to take the logical laws of quantification theory as generative, rather than interpretive, as they derive the interpretations not given by the grammar. On this view, however, it would seem that it remains necessary to reserve multiplicity of representation for any sentence whose interpretations are logically independent, as otherwise there would be no way to derive all its interpretations. Just this is found in sentences such as (29), which on one construal is true in case everyone is a lover, on the other just in case everyone is loved:[11]

(29) Nobody loves nobody

Assuming that *no* is logically glossed as the negation of the existential quantifier, the interpretations of these structures can be schematically represented as follows:

(30) a $-\exists x - \exists y\ P(x,y) \leftrightarrow \forall y\ \exists y\ P(x,y)$ (Everyone is a lover)

b $-\exists y - \exists x\ P(x,y) \leftrightarrow \forall x\ \exists x\ P(x,y)$ (Everyone is loved)

But if it is necessary to countenance an ambiguity of representation for *Nobody loves nobody*, as a matter of grammar, it is hard to see how a parallel ambiguity can be disallowed for *Everybody loves somebody*, given that they have identical S-Structure constituencies. One could invoke some sort of semantic or syntactic constraint to obtain this result, but it is unclear how the former would avoid the ill effect of constraining the functioning of grammatical rules not formally but on the basis of a sentence's meaning,[12] while the latter would have to be quite complicated in order to pick out a constant representation under varying surface positions of the particular lexical quantifiers, to which the condition would have to overtly refer. Even if some such approach were feasible, however, it would obscure the possibility of ambiguities of composition accrueing to sentences by virtue of their syntactic construction, and would fail to recognize the role of general syntactic rules and principles in grammatically expressing such ambiguities. But assuredly this is a proposition we wish to entertain, within the context of particular grammatical theories.

For multiple quantification sentences, then, representation at LF disambiguates their interpretations. Ambiguities of multiple quantification, therefore, are syntactic ambiguities, grammatically disambiguated, a 'constructional hononymity'. Such disambiguation as we find at LF, under our syntactic characterization of this level, will clearly be relevant in determining logical consequence in natural language (with respect to a specified semantic interpretation), although since LF does not represent, for instance, contextually assigned values of indexical elements, or the knowledge, beliefs and intentions of the interlocutors, matters which transcend the grammatical, it will only contribute part of the overall characterization of the structure of inference in natural language. (This is not to say that inferences involving non-grammatical factors will not make reference to LF, only to say that they will not be *represented* at this level.) LF will constitute just the grammatical component of this overall system, contributing a notion of consequence following in virtue of syntactic constituency and grammatical form. Note that there can be no *a priori* judgment as to just which inferences fall in this latter class; this is an empirical matter which can be adjudged only with respect to a fixed nexus of assumptions as to the nature of syntax and its relation to semantic interpretation. For instance, it is by no means necessary to hold that ambiguities of multiple quantification are represented at any syntactic level, eschewing the assumption that the representation of quantifier scope involves movement, and maintaining rather that insofar as this is represented, it is within the semantic, not syntactic, component. Part of the appeal of such a view is that it might allow for a seemingly simpler 'surface' syntax; cf Cooper (1983) for an account along these lines.[13] But as pointed out above this may very well be illusory, as assuming movement onto a syntactic level of Logical Form does not extend the formal structure of the theory. Moreover, the motivation for LF does not arise solely from its being disambiguated, to whatever degree, but to a large extent because it extends the empirical domain of syntax so as to afford uniform accounts of a number of generalizations which might otherwise only be describable, in a theory which eschews this assumption, via a disjunction of heterogeneous properties. To take an example, consider certain basic properties of *wh*-questions. As is well-known, the verbs *believe, wonder* and *know* form a paradigm when taking finite complement clauses; *believe* takes only declarative complements, *wonder* interrogative and *know* either. Since *believe* takes only declaratives, *Philby believed who Angleton suspected*, containing an indirect question is ungrammatical, although direct questions with *believe* are possible: *Who did Philby believe that Angleton suspected. Wonder*, on the other hand, requires an interrogative complement. Hence we have *Philby wondered who Angleton suspected* but not *Who did Philby wonder (that) Angleton suspected*. By contrast, *know* takes both types of complements, as witnessed by the grammaticality of the direct question *Who did Philby know that Angleton suspected* as well as the indirect question *Philby knows who Angleton suspected*. Now suppose, as is usual, that predicates subcategorize for declarative or interrogative clauses inclusively. Marking COMP with the feature [±WH] as a convenient method for registering this, the well-formed cases just noted will have the representations in (31) through (33):[14]

(31) Who did Philby believe [$_{S'}$[$_{COMP}$ −WH that] [$_S$ Angleton suspected e]]

(32) Philby wondered [$_{S'}$[$_{COMP}$ +WH who] [$_S$ Angleton suspected e]]

(33) a Who did Philby know [$_{S'}$[$_{COMP}$ −WH that] [$_S$ Angleton suspected e]]

      b Philby knows [$_{S'}$[$_{COMP}$ +WH who] [$_S$ Angleton suspected e]]

As a first approximation, we can account for these observations on the basis of the following principle:

(34) *Wh*-Criterion

    (i)   Every [+WH] COMP must dominate a *wh*-phrase

    (ii) Every *wh*-phrase must be dominated by a [+WH] COMP

(32) and (33b) are consistent with the *Wh*-Criterion, since they contain [+WH] COMPs filled by *wh*-phrases. (31) and (32a) also satisfy this condition, since they contain [−WH] COMPs. If a *wh*-phrase were to move into the complement COMP in either case the resulting structures would be ruled out, since they would contain *wh*-phrases not governed by [+WH]. The effect, then, of the *Wh*-Criterion is to require *wh*-movement whenever there is a [+WH] COMP, since only then can there be the requisite containment in COMP.[15]

The examples discussed so far are neutral as to whether the *Wh*-criterion holds of S-Structure or LF. If it holds of the latter, then not only is movement of the *wh*-phrase obligatory in (32) and (33b), but also in multiple questions like (35).

(35) $[_{S'}$ which spy$_2$ $[_S$ e_2 suspects $[_{NP}$ which Russian$]]]$

Only if the *wh*-phrase not in COMP in S-Structure is moved there in LF will the *Wh*-Criterion be satisfied. This can be accomplished by assuming that LF-movement applies to quantified expressions in general, including the quasi-quantificational *wh*-phrases found in direct and indirect questions, moving them when unmoved at S-Structure into COMP at LF. Then at LF (36) can be derived from (35):

(36) $[_{S'}$ which Russian$_3$ which spy$_2$ $[_S$ e_2 suspects $e_3]]$

As both *wh*-phrases now occur in COMP, the *Wh*-Criterion, now taken as a condition on LF, is satisfied, and (37) can be properly interpreted as a multiple question. If movement is into a COMP to which an interrogative interpretation is not assigned, the result is deviant; thus (37) stands in violation of the *Wh*-Criterion, as there is no [+WH] COMP into which it can move at LF:

(37) *The spy who suspects which Russian is Angleton

The analysis of (36) and (37) assumes that LF-movement of a *wh*-phrase is to COMP, as in S-Structure, and as opposed to movement of other (non-*wh*) quantified phrases, which adjoin to S. This may simply reflect the more general fact, in part formally expressed by the *Wh*-Criterion, that COMP is a selected position, which can be occupied only by phrases satisfying its selectional restrictions, others being excluded.

The role of LF-movements in accounting for properties of *wh*-constructions gains further support from observations of Huang (1982). He notes that in Chinese interrogatives, there is no overt *wh*-movement at S-Structure.[16] Thus we find examples like (38) through (40) which are syntactically identical, aside from choice of matrix verb:

(38) Zhangsan xiang-zhidao [ta muqin kanjian shei]
         wonder   his mother see   who
      "Zhangsan wondered who his mother saw"

(39) Zhangsan xiangxin [ta muqin kanjian shei]
         believe   his mother see   who
      "Who does Zhangsan believe his mother saw?"

(40) Zhangsan zhidao [ta muqin kanjian shei]
         know   his mother see   who
      (i)   "Who does Zhangsan know his mother saw?"
      (ii) "Zhangsan knows who his mother saw"

Huang points out that the interpretations of these examples are identical to their English counterparts. Thus, (38) can only be understood as a direct question, (39) as an indirect question, while (40) is ambiguous between these construals, as indicated by the glosses.

The explanation for this, Huang argues, follows from holding that Chinese differs minimally from English in that unary questions are derived by *wh*-movements confined to the mapping from S-Structure onto LF. What is apparently constant in Chinese and English are the subcategorization properties of the relevant predicates. Thus, 'believe' only takes [−WH] complements, 'wonder' only [+WH] and 'know' either. Given that the *Wh*-Criterion applies at LF, it now follows that the LF representations of the Chinese examples (38) through (40) will be structurally non-distinct from their English counterparts in (31) through (33). That movement is in fact involved here is further evidenced by the fact, observed in Higginbotham (1980), that the pronouns in (38) through (40) cannot be construed as variables bound by *shei*; that is, they display weak crossover effects. As noted above, as a generalization, a variable cannot serve as antecedent of a pronoun to its left. If the derivation of the LF-representations in (38) through (40) involves movement, then the weak crossover effects can be accounted for on exactly the same grounds as their English counterparts. By assuming, then, that *wh*-phrases can—and, in fact, given the *Wh*-Criterion, must—be moved to COMP in LF, the properties of LF afford a general explanation of the apparent universality of *wh*-complementation. Thus, we find identity of interpretation, even though only in English are direct and indirect questions structurally distinguished at S-Structure.

Huang's observations, provide, I believe, a very strong *prima facie* case for the existence of LF movements and, hence, for the level itself. Another example to the same point can be made on the basis of properties of crossing coreference:

(41)   Every pilot who shot at it hit some Mig that chased him

As is well-known, sentences like (41) allow for a construal in which the antecedent of *it* is taken as *some Mig that chased him* simultaneously with *him* being understood as having *every pilot who shot at it* as antecedent. The property of these sentences which interests us here is how this pattern of crossed binding of the pronouns is to be represented at LF. First, however, it is important to take note of some special properties of the anaphoric relation illustrated in (42):

(42)   Every Mig destroyed its target

As many authors have pointed out,[17] the pronoun in (42) is most properly construed as a bound variable; since its antecedent is not referential, anaphora here clearly cannot be explicated through co- or overlapping reference. In our terms, we may represent this construal by (43):

(43) $[_S$ every Mig$_2$ $[_S$ e_2 destroyed its$_2$ target$]]$

The pronoun is (properly) bound by the trace arising from movement of the quantifier phrase. Notice that there is no particular reason to suppose that the pronoun is replaced by a variable at LF, since semantically its interpretation will be wholly determined by the nature of the interpretation of the element which ultimately binds it, here a quantifier.

Now consider a somewhat more complicated example:

(44)   Every pilot hit some Mig that chased him

Like other simple transitive clauses discussed above, (45) exhibits a scope ambiguity; either quantifier may be understood as having broader scope over the other. Interestingly, the construal of the pronoun *him* varies according to the scope relations—*him* can be bound by *every pilot* only if *every pilot* is understood as having broader scope than *some Mig that chased him*. The LF representations derivable from the S-Structure of (44) are those in (45):

(45)   a   [every pilot$_2$ [[some Mig that chased him]$_3$ [e_2 hit e_3]]]
       b   [[some Mig that chased him]$_3$ [every pilot$_2$ [e_2 hit e_3]]]

Consider (45a). Here the pronoun resides within the scope of the c-commanding quantifier phrase *every pilot*, and hence can be construed as a bound variable. In (45b), on the other hand, *him* is not within the scope of *every pilot*; the c-command domain of this latter phrase is solely the most deeply embedded S. When *some* is assigned broader scope, the pronoun is carried along to a position outside the scope of *every*. Hence, in this structure, no bound variable construal of the pronoun is possible.

The relevant property of LF-representations which accounts for the range of interpretations available to (44) can be stated as follows:

(46)   A pronoun is a bound variable only if it is within the scope of a coindexed quantifier phrase

This properly accounts for the availability of a bound construal in (45a), and for its absence in (45b). That this principle holds of LF can be garnered by the availability of a bound variable construal of the pronoun in *Somebody in every city despises it*. If the principle on bound variable anaphora held at S-Structure, we would not expect this to be possible. At LF, however, the embedded quantified phrase must be extracted to a position in which it has broadest scope, a position from which it will c-command, and hence bind, the object pronoun; see May (1977).

Now reconsider the case of crossed binding, the 'Bach–Peters' example in (41), *Every pilot who shot at it hit some Mig that chased him*. Given our assumptions so far, QR can derive two structures from the S-Structure representation of this sentence:

(47)   a   [[every pilot who shot at it]$_2$ [[some Mig that chased him]$_3$ [e_2 hit e_3]]]
        b   [[some Mig that chased him]$_3$ [[every pilot was shot at it]$_2$ [e_2 hit e_3]]]

We are now faced with a problem. In (47a), while *him* can be construed as a bound variable, as it is c-commanded by the *every*-phrase, *it* cannot be construed in this way, since it is not c-commanded by the *some*-phrase. Just the inverse circumstance obtains in (47b); here only *it* can be a bound variable. It would seem, then, that it is not possible to represent the simultaneous binding of the two pronouns.

In Higginbotham & May (1981a, b) it is argued that crossed binding sentences are to be properly analyzed as containing 'binary quantifiers'. The idea developed there is that among the rules applying to LF is *Absorption*, whose effect can be characterized as in (48):

(48)   . . . [NP$_i$ [NP$_j$ . . . → . . . [NP$_i$ NP$_j$]$_{i,j}$ . . .

Structurally, Absorption takes structures in which one NP immediately c-commands another NP and derives structures in which they form something like a conjoined constituent:

(49)

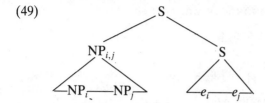

Notice that in the absorbed structure (49), NP_i c-commands NP_j and vice versa. Semantically, such structures are interpreted by binary (actually *n*-ary) quantifications, derived from pairs (*n*-tuples) of unary quantifications, defined as functions from the powerset of the Cartesian product of **D** onto $\{0,1\}$. This is for unrestricted binary quantifiers. Restricted binary quantifiers are functions from $P(D \times D) \times P(D \times D)$. If the binary quantification is made up of 'intersective' quantifiers, that is, those that are defined in terms of intersections of subsets of **D**, then it can be proven that the absorbed and non-absorbed LF-representations lead to equivalent interpretations, with the further proviso that the narrower scope quantifier contains no occurrence of x free. Thus just the same truth conditions will be ascribed to *Everybody loves someone*, regardless of whether it is represented at LF with absorbed quantifiers or not. Where binary quantifiers differ is that they apply to all variable positions simultaneously. So they are particularly suited for the treatment of crossed binding (Bach–Peters) sentences. Both of the representations (47) satisfy the structural description of Absorption, deriving (50)

(50)   a   [[every pilot who shot at it]$_2$ [some Mig that chased him]$_3$]$_{2,3}$
          [e_2 hit e_3]
       b   [[some Mig that chased him]$_3$ [every pilot who shot at it]$_2$]$_{2,3}$
          [e_2 hit e_3]

In both of these structures, the syntactic condition on bound variable anaphora is satisfied, because the *every*-phrase c-commands *him* and the *some*-phrase c-commands *it*. Focusing on (50a) we see that it is interpreted by the binary quantification

$$\textbf{Every, Some } (R, S) = 1 \quad \text{iff } x \in dom\, R \rightarrow (R \cap S)'x \neq \varnothing$$
$$= 0 \quad \text{otherwise.}$$

In the notation of Higginbotham & May (1981a), *dom R* denotes the domain of a relation R on D, and $R'x$ stands for

$$\{y \in D \,|\, \langle x, y \rangle \in R\}.$$

Applying this quantification to (50a), we set R equal to

$\{\langle x, y\rangle|$ x is a pilot who shot at y and y is a Mig that chased x$\}$

and S equal to

$$\{\langle x, y\rangle|\ x\ \text{hit}\ y\}.$$

(50a) is then true iff for any pilot who shot at a Mig that chased him, there is at least one such Mig that he hit, and these truth conditions accord with our intuitive judgment about such sentences, cf Higginbotham & May (1981a) for a detailed formal development of the semantics of binary quantifiers.

From the syntactic side, an important property of this analysis of crossed binding is that it assumes that absorption can apply only to local pairs of quantifiers. Absorption, so to speak, takes two quantifier phrases A and B such that A immediately c-commands B, but not vice-versa, into a structure in which A and B c-command each other. As with *wh*-complementation, the approach assumes that there is LF movement, and moreover, that the relevant properties will also be found where there is overt S-Structure movement. That is, the application of Absorption, it is assumed, is blind to whether quantifier A came to c-command quantifier B via application of overt movements (i.e., those onto S-Structure), covert movements (i.e., those onto LF) or some combination thereof. That this is in fact the case is borne out by the following, all of which exhibit crossed binding:

(51) a Which pilot who shot at it hit which Mig that chased him
      b Which pilot who shot at it some Mig that chased him
      c Which Mig that chased him did every pilot who shot at it hit

Wh-movement has applied in each of these cases, so the initial *wh*-phrase occurs in COMP. In each case, further application of QR gives a representation to which Absorption applies; in (51a) this movement is of another *wh*-phrase, in (51b) and (51c) a quantifier phrase. The contrast between (51b) and (51c) shows that crossed binding is possible regardless of whether the *wh*-phrase in COMP has been moved from subject or object. This is just as we would expect, given the analysis here.

The possibility of crossed binding in these examples contrasts with a similar class of cases, brought out by Jacobson (1977), which differ in that they do not contain quantified phrases. (52) is an example:

(52) His wife saw her husband

Unlike the previous cases, this sentence cannot receive a crossed interpretation: *his* cannot be taken as dependent upon *her husband* simultaneously with *her* being dependent on *his wife*. This is all the more odd, given the possibility of coreference in both *His wife saw John* and *Mary saw her husband.* Higginbotham & May (1981b) argue that the reason for this is that fixing the values of the pronouns in (52) turns on a particular property of reference, namely that it must be fixed in a definite, non-circular fashion. This is not possible for (52); the reference of *his* is given by *her husband*, which in turn contains a pronoun *her*, whose reference is given by *his wife*, which contains *his*, whose reference is given by *her husband*, etc. Thus the 'chain of reference' associated with this sentence is circular and unending, leading to no definite determination of reference at all. If some other phrase is available to which the referential chain can lead that does not contain a pronoun, this sort of vicious circularity is avoided; thus there is no problem interpreting either *His wife, Mary, saw her husband* or *His wife saw Jack, her husband*.

Assuming that there are distinct devices for the establishment of referential, as opposed to bound variable, anaphora, it is possible to account for certain cases which appear to be crossover environments, but in which an anaphoric interpretation can be easily obtained. So consider the difference between the non-restrictive relatives in the (a) examples, and the free relatives in the (b) examples:

(53) a John, who his mother admires, . . .
      b Whoever his mother admires . . .
(54) a Stieglitz, whose picture of O'Keefe he took while she was lying supine, . . .
      b Whoever's picture of O'Keefe he took while she was lying supine, . . .

That an anaphoric interpretation cannot be obtained for the pronouns in the free relatives is not surprising; these are simply cases of crossover. What is surprising is that in the non-restrictive relatives, an anaphoric interpretation *is* possible, since the *wh*-phrase, its trace and the pronoun all stand in the same structural relation as in the free relative. An account is forthcoming once it is recognized that there is an alternative route to anaphora available for the non-restrictive not found with the free relative. Let us suppose that the semantics of this construction require that the reference of the head NP is identical to the individuals who satisfy the relative clause; note that this will be a singleton, as the head is a singular referring expression. Now strictly speaking the pronoun in (53a), for instance, cannot be a bound variable, as this would violate the crossover constraint. This constraint, however, does not bar the pronoun from being referential and from picking up its reference in the manner described above for such pronouns. In particular, there is nothing to stop its picking up the reference of the head of the relative, *John*, which, after all, is an independent referring expression. But then the mechanisms of reference will specify the same value for the pronoun as the mechanisms of quantification, (i.e., assignments of values) specify for the variable the *wh*-phrase binds. These critical properties of reference are not available, however, for free relatives, simply because they are headless. Rather they can avail themselves solely of the mechanisms of quantification and bound variables, which preclude anaphora in the configuration under consideration.

Thus we see from these latter cases, as well as from the distinction in crossed binding sentences between the sensible *Every pilot who shot at it hit some Mig that chased him*, and the non-sensical *His wife saw her husband*, that there is a fundamental distinction between those pronouns which are assigned their values via interpretation of quantification as opposed to the interpretation of reference. Thus the analysis of these cases rests on the assumption, as has all the discussion to this point, that at LF quantified and non-quantified phrases are distinguished, not only in their interpretation, but also in those aspects of their syntax to which the rules of interpretation are sensitive. In this regard the position differs from that found in Montague (1974), for instance, in which quantified and non-quantified phrases are assimilated under a uniform syntactic and semantic treatment. Now insofar as the phenomena we have been discussing turn on distinguishing these types of expressions, it argues against such a conflation of categories, at least from the syntactic perspective. Indeed, given the validity of the analyses, the phenomena we have considered can be employed as a diagnostic of quantificational status. For instance, consider definite phrases, those containing *the*; are they quantified phrases? We have assumed that they are; cf the semantic treatment of definite descriptions above. This is corroborated by their having interacting scope relations, seen in sentences such as *Every man admires the woman he loves*[18] and *The president of every public authority is a crook*, by their allowing VP-deletion in relatives, as seen in *Dulles suspected the agents who Philby did*, by their occurrence in crossed binding sentences such as *The pilot who shot at it hit the Mig that chased him*, and by the differential distribution of *any*, seen in the contrast of *The students who had ever read anything about phrenology attended Gall's lecture* with **The students who attended Gall's lecture had ever read anything about phrenology*. Thus, insofar as the explanation of these phenomena turn on the assumption that there is LF-movement, and insofar as LF-movement is sensitive to whether phrases are quantificational, then it follows that *the*, at least on the uses exemplified in the above examples, is a quantifier, as otherwise we would expect to find quite a different complex of properties. And it is the fact that we do find these contrasting complexes of properties that argues for the fundamental distinction of logical syntax which forms the basic presupposition of our inquiries. In this regard our position agrees with that of the line of thinking from

Frege to Tarski, in which quantified phrases were taken to require treatment quite distinct from that of proper names.

Once we take the distinction in semantic type between quantificational and referential expression as basic, then the syntactic paradigms we find at LF can be seen as consequences of requirements on the mapping of argument structure onto logical form. Following Chomsky (1981), we will suppose that the relation of arguments to their structural manifestations in argument positions of predicates at LF is mediated by the θ-Criterion, which requires that they stand in a one–one correspondence:

(55) θ-Criterion
    (i)   Every θ-role must be assigned to just one argument chain
    (ii) Every argument chain must be assigned just one θ-role

The θ-roles characterize the argument positions of a predicate, specified as part of its lexical structure. Argument positions can differ in the semantic roles which their arguments must fulfil; thus subjects may be agents or themes and objects may be themes, goals, patients, etc (Jackendoff, 1972). Lexical items, such as proper names, can normally stand as arguments bearing θ-roles, and so can certain empty categories, in particular those which are $\bar{A}$-bound and function as variables. An 'argument chain' is any sequence of arguments which bear occurrences of a given index. The structures in (56) are associated with degree 1 chains containing the traces as their members. It is these arguments which bear the θ-roles (here theme) assigned to the subject positions, and not the operators which bind them:

(56)   a   Which agent$_2$ [e_2 is a spy]
       b   Every agent$_2$ [e_2 is a spy]

Given that variables can stand as arguments of predicates, reinforcing the coincidence of the syntactic and semantic notions, we might also hold, inversely, that quantified phrases do not themselves count as arguments, at least with respect to their normal interpretation via quantification theory.[19] Then, we might speculate, on the presumption that the θ-criterion applies just to LF-representations, the fact that movement to $\bar{A}$-positions is usually reserved for phrases that are 'nonreferential' (in some sense), follows, as there is no interpretation available for such phrases in argument positions, since they are not legitimate bearers of θ-roles.[20] The point is more general; no phrase which is functionally an operator can occur in an $\bar{A}$-position at LF, by the θ-criterion, if this line of reasoning is correct. Thus, *wh*-movement is just as well required in relative clauses, as in *wh*-questions.

In effect, then, the θ-criterion makes LF-movement obligatory, although the rule itself would apply optionally. Obtaining this result turns on the assumption that quantified phrases can only be properly interpreted as operators, and are unable to bear semantic roles in argument positions. While to a large extent this assumption is intuitive and uncontroversial, one need not make it. It is not held, for instance, in Montague (1974), who allows quantified phrases, in addition to being interpreted in operator positions, to be interpreted in their surface positions as denoting intensions, functions from possible worlds to famailes of properties of individuals. The utility of this bifurcation is argued to be found in the treatment of *John seeks a unicorn*. Leaving technical details aside, on this view *seek* is a relation between individuals and intensions, functions from possible worlds to denotations. Assuming that *a unicorn* translates as such a function, then the *de dicto* construal is just where this phrase is interpreted as an argument of the predicate. On this interpretation, the truth of *John seeks a unicorn* requires only that John is seeking something with the appropriate properties, properties that in some possible world, distinct from the actual, pick out unicorns in their extension. Thus, *John seeks a unicorn* may be true, on this interpretation, even though John's search is a chimerical one. The *de re* construal, on the other hand, is to be represented by quantifying in, so that its truth requires that there is a unicorn, in the actual world, and John is seeking it. One can construct accounts of this ambiguity, however, which do not turn on assuming that *John seeks a unicorn* has any LF-representation different from that in (57):

(57)   a unicorn$_2$ [John seeks e_2]

Suppose, following Parsons (1980), that the domain of objects is populated by both actual and non-actual objects. Parsons' idea is that any class of what he calls 'nuclear' properties defines a distinct object; on this view, 'being a book about linguistics', just as much characterizes an object as 'being a golden mountain' or 'being a unicorn'. The domain of such objects is then further partitioned by what Parsons calls 'non-nuclear' properties, ot which existence is the central case, so that our quantifiers are existential only insofar as they are restricted to subsets of existent objects. Now if we take verb selection, in the sense of Chomsky (1965), to be sensitive to this partitioning in terms of non-nuclear properties, the difference between an intensional verb like *seek* and an extensional one like *buy* can be reduced to the former ambiguously selecting, for the object NP, either positively or negatively for existence, while the latter only selects positively. Thus, *John seeks a unicorn* will be false if *seek* positively selects, as then the quantifier will range only over that subpart of the domain containing existent objects, but true if it negatively selects, since then the quantifiers will range over the non-existent objects, which includes unicorns. If these conjectures are along the right track, then it means that ambiguities of multiple quantifier scope are of a different sort than the ambiguities of intensional transitive verbs, the former being structural, the latter not.[21]

The θ-Criterion will play other roles in insuring that LF-representations containing $\bar{A}$-binding properly express argument structure. For instance, it will insure that in multiple quantified sentences that each empty category will correspond to a distinct variable. This is because if there is an n-tuple of coindexed empty categories they will form an argument chain which must be assigned only one thematic role. This accounts for the contrast of *John_i admired e_i* with *John_i was admired e_i*. Each of these is associated with the degree 2 chain $\langle John, e_i \rangle$, but it only satisfies the θ-Criterion with respect to the latter structure. This is because in the former the chain is associated with two θ-roles; those of the subject and object positions. But in the latter, passive, sentence, the chain is only associated with a single θ-role, that of the object, as passive subjects, by hypothesis, are dethematized (Chomsky, 1981). Turning to multiple quantification structures, since we are assuming that assignment of indices under movement is free, distinct application of QR can assign the same index, deriving something like (58):

(58) [every professor$_2$ [some student$_2$ [e_2 admires e_2]]]

But this violates the θ-Criterion, the relation between the empty categories being no different than that found in improper movement structures like *Who$_2$ e$_2$ admires e$_2$*. That is, the pair of traces forms a chain, and it is associated with two θ-roles, as above. Only if the empty categories in (58) bear different indices will each trace correspond to a distinct variable, and hence qualify as distinct argument chains with respect to the θ-Criterion. Because the grammar then requires that each LF-movement to an $\bar{A}$-position give rise to a distinct variable, it now follows, for instance, that *Everybody admires everybody* entails, but is not equivalent to *Everybody admires himself*, in which the subject and object positions can be legitimately coindexed, (reflexive pronouns qualifying as independent arguments for the θ-Criterion). For the same reason *Who did he admire* does not ask a reflexive question, to wit, which persons are self-admirers. This would be the interpretation if *he* and the trace of *wh* could be coindexed; but to do so would violate the θ-Criterion, for it would result once again in the illicit coindexing of thematic subject and object positions. Given the θ-Criterion, then, the distinctness of variables in LF-representations is no isolated matter, but rather has as its cause the same principle which accounts for improper movement and strong crossover phenomena.

In beginning this paper, I characterized Logical Form as that level of linguistic representation interfacing the theories of linguistic form and interpretation. I have outlined one way to turn this from an operational to a formal (that is, syntactic) definition, and an examination of some of the basic consequences of the principles and conditions embedded in that definition. I have constructed the assumptions as to the nature of the rules and representations of LF so as to extract the syntactic aspects of semantic interpretation—the 'semantic structure'—and to unify it, in very basic ways, with certain 'overt' aspects of syntactic structure. This reduction has been afforded in part by the hypothesis that the rules mapping onto LF share certain fundamental properties with rules mapping onto S-Structure, in particular *wh*-movement. Thus both are movements to non-argument (Ā) positions and leave empty categories which can be structurally defined as variables, both 'pied-pipe', of importance in the analysis of polarity items and VP-deletion, movement by either can derive structures which accord with the *Wh*-Criterion, give rise to crossover violations, or be input to Absorption, and the output of each obeys general conditions on proper binding and argument structure. Just as *wh*-movement is a well-defined mapping, applying to phrases of a particular type, and giving rise to a specifiable class of S-Structure representations, so too is QR, in giving rise to a definable class of LF-representations. What the commonality of these 'rules' suggests is that the clusters of properties referred to as *wh*-movement and QR are reflections of deeper, more general, properties of grammar; that is, both are just aspects of 'Move α', their divergent properties being attributable to differential principles and conditions on S-Structure and Logical Form. The sorts of discrepancies we do observe between *wh*-movement and QR—in particular in that the range of movement possibilities for LF-movement is broader than for movements onto S-Structure—indicate that movement in LF is, in a sense, less restricted, applying unencumbered by conditions which more severely limit the derivation of *wh*-constructions in S-Structure. LF-movements are subject only to more general conditions on Logical Form, which are applicable as well to structures derived by S-Structure movements. The formal properties, then, of LF-movement can be thought of as the result of factoring out the conditions, universal and particular, holding just of the rules deriving, or the representations at, S-Structure.

What is left are the conditions on Logical Form, specified ultimately by Universal Grammar, which determines the core properties of logical representations, for example, that natural language quantification is represented in operator-variable notation. To a large extent these properties of LF will be invariant from language to language, although one could imagine a range of differences as a function of independently varying properties of the S-Structure input to the rules deriving LF, for instance. Thus we do not want to preclude the possibility that given construction types may give rise to differential classes of interpretations from language to language (although this is not to say that languages will differ in the class of propositions they can express, given the unboundedness of paraphrase). But insofar as the nature of logical representation follows from principles of UG directly, the child will need no evidence from his or her environment to determine its properties; they will be consequences of 'hard-wired' aspects of the language faculty. Indeed, it is difficult to imagine what would be a sufficiently structured environment to provide evidence for a child to 'learn' the various aspects of the syntax of logical form we have been considering thus far. Plausibly, a child learning English might induce the relevant structural properties on the basis of *wh*-constructions, generalizing its formal properties to a class of semantically related elements, and thus inferring that representation involving trace binding extends to the broader class of quantified sentences. The child learning English would be, in this regard, rather fortunate, having evidence available that a child learning Chinese, which does not have overt *wh*-movement, would not. What then would serve as the evidentiary basis for the induction that quantification is represented at LF, in Chinese as well as in English, by variable binding? What this suggests is that the grounding of our knowledge of the logical form of language as represented at Logical Form arises from Universal Grammar, and constitutes, in the final analysis, part of our innately specified knowledge of language.

NOTES

[1] Chomsky-adjunction of a constituent to a node yields structures either of the form '$[_\alpha \beta [_\alpha \ldots]]$' (left Chomsky-adjunction) or '$[_\alpha [_\alpha \ldots]\beta]$' (right Chomsky-adjunction). In what follows the difference between right and left adjunction will turn out to be immaterial, since they manifest the identical hierarchical constituent structures, but the convention will be adhered to of representing QR as affecting a left adjunction.

[2] α c-commands β iff the first branching node dominating α dominates β (and α does not dominate β). This definition is essentially that proposed originally in Reinhart (1976).

[3] Cf Higginbotham & May (1981a) for a formal analysis of the semantics of questions in this framework.

[4] Note that assuming trace theory to apply generally to movement operations rules out the possibility of deriving something like S-Structure from something like LF by 'lowering' quantified phrases, since such movements would give rise to structures containing unbound traces. Thus the approach here is materially distinct from that found in Lakoff (1971), for example.

[5] With the further requirement that such functions assign the same value to $X \subset D$ as to automorphisms of X.

[6] Restricted quantifiers, in the defined sense, can be shown to have a number of properties. For instance, as shown in Higginbotham & May (1981a), they respect only the size of sets, and not the identity of their membership. Also, because such quantifiers encode effectively the same semantic information as the generalized quantifiers of Barwise & Cooper (1981), many of the results obtained there will carry over. Also see van Benthem (1983).

[7] This generalization apparently holds in other languages as well; it also characterizes, for instance, the class of S-Structure preposable phrases in Hungarian, as discussed in Kiss (1981).

[8] This example was brought to my attention by a reviewer.

[9] Actually, there will be derived two equivalence classes of structures.

[10] Linear order has often been claimed to strongly affect preferential order of interpretation. I am doubtful, however, of the overall importance of this factor. In part this is because linear order is easily conflated with topic–comment relations; in most languages the subject precedes the object and corresponds to the discourse topic. And since topics take prominence in discourse, it is not surprising that when they are quantified phrases, they will have preferentially broad scope. Also, examples which purport to show the importance of linear order seem to me less than convincing. For instance, it is often held that in sentences with universal and negative quantifiers, scope is a function of precedence; cf Halvorsen (1983) for a recent discussion. Examples like *No student admires every professor* and *Every professor is admired by no student* are taken to support this contention. But the latter example is considerably less than well-formed, and the former is interpretively suppletive with *No student admires any professor*. And it is rather these latter observations, it seems to me, which are in need of explanation.

[11] These cases were pointed out to me by J. Higginbotham. Notice that such examples have a third interpretation, on which no one is either loved or a lover. This is an independent, or branching, interpretation. Note that this interpretation is also logically independent of either of the dependent interpretations; thus for those who find one or the other of the latter construals difficult to obtain, the argument in the text will still go through substituting the independent interpretation.

[12] A semantically based filter would also be inappropriate here. If the grammar generates a class of representations each expressing, under an interpretation, correct truth-conditions, it would be otiose to filter some just to reconstruct them elsewhere in the system.

[13] See May (forthcoming) for a discussion of Cooper's approach.

[14] I have ignored, for exposition, traces of cyclic movement in the embedded COMPs of the direct questions.

[15] I have left aside the relation of this condition to the application of *wh*-movement in other constructions such as relative clauses and clefts.

[16] We can capture this difference by maintaining that for English, but not Chinese, clause (i) of the *Wh*-Criterion must also be satisfied at S-Structure. There are also languages, such as Polish and Czech, which require that clause (ii) be satisfied at S-Structure, and which consequently allow multiply filled COMPs at this level (Toman, 1981).

[17] For instance, Bach & Partee (1980), Evans (1980), Higginbotham (1980) and Lasnik (1976).

[18] This is pointed out in Heim (1982). There is, however, more here than meets the eye, as only a broad scope interpretation is possible for this sentence if the pronoun is taken non-anaphorically, or a proper name is substituted, as in *Every man admires the woman John loves*.

[19] Note that it is not precluded that types of phrases may cross-classify, as has been argued for indefinite phrases. See Fodor & Sag (1982) for discussion.

[20] Care is needed in clarifying just what is meant by 'non-referential', as it must be taken to denote a type of phrase, and not whether tokens, in fact, make reference to actual objects. Thus, *Pegasus* does not refer in the latter sense, but it is a referential phrase.

[21] Thanks are due to P. Ludlow for discussion of this point.

REFERENCES

Bach, E. & Partee, B., Anaphora and Semantic Structure. In J. Kreiman & N. Odeja (Eds), *Papers from the Parasession on Pronouns and Anaphora*. Chicago, Illinois: University of Chicago, 1980.

Barwise, J. & Cooper, R., Generalized Quantifiers and Natural Language. *Linguistics and Philosophy*, 1981, **4**, 159–219.

Bentham, J. van, Determiners and Logic. *Linguistics and Philosophy*, 1983, **6**, 447–478.

Borer, H., On the Definition of Variables. *Journal of Linguistic Research*, 1983, **1**, 3, 17–40.

Chomsky, N., *Aspects of the Theory of Syntax*. Cambridge, MA: MIT Press, 1965.

Chomsky, N., Conditions of Rules of Grammar. In N. Chomsky, *Essays on Form and Interpretation*. New York: North-Holland, 1976.

Chomsky, N., On Binding. *Linguistic Inquiry*, 1980, **11**, 1–46.

Chomsky, N., *Lectures on Government and Binding*. Dordrecht: Foris Publications, 1981.

Cooper, R., *Quantification and Syntactic Theory*. Dordrecht, Reidel, 1983.

Evans, G., Pronouns. *Linguistic Inquiry*, 1980, **11**, 337–362.

Fiengo, R., On Trace Theory. *Linguistic Inquiry*, 1977, **8**, 35–61.

Fodor, J. D. & Sag, I., Referential and Quantificational Indefinites. *Linguistics and Philosophy*, 1982, **5**, 355–398.

Halvorsen, P.-K., Semantics for Lexical-Functional Grammar. *Linguistic Inquiry*, 1983, **14**, 567–615.

Heim, I., The Semantics of Definite and Indefinite Noun Phrases. Doctoral dissertation, Amherst, MA: University of Massachusetts, 1982.

Higginbotham, J., Pronouns and Bound Variables, *Linguistic Inquiry*. 1980, **11**, 679–708.

Higginbotham, J. & May, R., Questions, Quantifiers and Crossing. *The Linguistic Review*, 1981a, **1**, 41–79.

Higginbotham, J. & May, R., Crossing, Markedness, Pragmatics. In A. Belleti, L. Brandi & L. Rizzi (Eds), *Theory of Markedness in Generative Grammar*. Pisa: Scuola Normale Superiore, 1981b.

Huang, C.-T. J., Move WH in a Language without *Wh*-Movement. *The Linguistic Review*, 1982, **1**, 369–416.

Jacobson, P., The Syntax of Crossing Coreference Sentences. Doctoral dissertation, Berkeley, CA: University of California, 1977. (Distributed by Indiana University Linguistics Club.)

Jackendoff, R., *Semantic Interpretation in Generative Grammar*. Cambridge, MA: MIT Press, 1972.

Jaeggli, O., On Some Phonologically-null Elements in Syntax. Doctoral dissertation, Cambridge, MA: MIT, 1980.

Kiss, K., Structural Relations in Hungarian, a 'Free' Word Order Language. *Linguistic Inquiry*, 1981, **12**, 185–213.

Koopman, H. & Sportiche, D., Variables and the Bijection Principle. *The Linguistic Review*, 1982, **2**, 139–161.

Ladusaw, W., On the Notion *Affective* in the Analysis of Negative-Polarity Items. *Journal of Linguistic Research*, 1981, **1**, 2, 1–16.

Lakoff, G., On Generative Semantics. In D. Steinberg & L. Jakobovits (Eds), *Semantics*. Cambridge: Cambridge University Press, 1971.

Lasnik, H., Remarks on Coreference. *Linguistic Analysis*, 1976, **2**, 1–22.

May, R., The Grammar of Quantification. Doctorial dissertation, Cambridge, MA: MIT, 1977. (Distributed by Indiana University Linguistics Club.)

May, R., Movement and Binding. *Linguistic Inquiry*, 1981, **12**, 215–243.

May, R., Review of R. Cooper *Quantification and Syntactic Theory*. To appear in *Language* (forthcoming).

Montague, R., The Proper Treatment of Quantification in Ordinary English. In R. Thomason (Ed), *Formal Philosophy*: *Selected Papers of Richard Montague*. New haven, CT: Yale University Press, 1974.

Parsons, T., *Nonexistent Objects*. New Haven, CT: Yale University Press, 1980.

Reinhart, T., The Syntactic domain of Anaphora. Doctoral dissertation, Cambridge, MA: MIT, 1976.

Reinhart, T., *Anaphora and Semantic Interpretation*. London: Croon Helm, 1983.

Rouveret, A. & Vergnaud, J.-R., Specifying Reference to the Subject: French Causatives and Conditions on Representations. *Linguistic Inquiry*, 1980, **11**, 97–202.

Safir, K., Multiple Variable Binding. *Linguistic Inquiry*, 1984, **15**, 603–638.

Sag, I., Deletion and Logical Form. Doctoral dissertation, Cambridge, MA: MIT, 1976.

Toman, J., Aspects of Multiple *Wh*-Movement in Polish and Czech. In R. May & J. Koster (Eds), *Levels of Syntactic Representation*. Dordrecht: Foris Publications, 1981.

Williams, E., Discourse and Logical Form. *Linguistic Inquiry*, 1977, **8**, 101–139.

11

Tenses, Temporal Quantifiers and Semantic Innocence

BARRY RICHARDS

Centre for Cognitive Science,
University of Edinburgh

INTRODUCTION

How does temporal reference relate to the semantics of tense and temporal quantification? Broadly speaking, there are two perspectives one can adopt, a Russellian one and a Priorean one. The Russellian view is that temporal reference is an essential feature of the meaning of both tenses and temporal quantifiers. They involve explicit reference to time and this is crucial to understanding their semantic import. In contrast the Priorean view is that temporal reference is irrelevant to the semantics of tenses and temporal quantifiers. While their meaning can be defined over time segments, they invoke no explicit reference to them.

While it is natural to wonder which view does more justice to the facts of language, one may suspect that neither can be uniformly satisfactory. The Russellian account seems more appropriate to tenses while the Priorean account appears better suited to temporal quantifiers. Tensed sentences are typically sensitive to the time of utterance in that they may be true on one occasion and false on another. This shift in truth value can be plausibly traced to a shift in time reference. As the Russellian view would have it, utterances of a tensed sentence involve reference to the time of speech, and thus what is past, present or future is determined relative to that time.

337

NEW DIRECTIONS IN SEMANTICS

ISBN 0-12-444040-1
0-12-444041-X (Pbk)

Since different utterances invoke different speech times, the truth value of
a sentence may vary from time to time. But when sentences are modified
by temporal quantifiers, e.g., *always, twice* or *never*, there seems to be a
certain independence from the time of speech. What is always, twice or
never the case can be judged only from a perspective which surveys the
whole of time rather than being located in it. In the circumstance a Priorean
formulation is perhaps more natural, although not inevitable.

Despite the convenience of eclecticism, there is a disposition to hope
that one of the approaches may emerge as uniformly satisfactory. The form
in which this might arise, i.e., the nature of a generally adequate theory,
has been the subject of considerable speculation, but the results to date
have been less than conclusive. No comprehensively suitable proposal has
yet been identified and hence, it seems not inappropriate to consider
another alternative. We propose to sketch a theory which, though inno-
vative in some technical and philosophical respects, is essentially Russellian
in spirit. Basically we take temporal reference to be the key to a general
explanation of the semantics of both tenses and temporal quantifiers.

Among the more fundamental aspects of the theory is the distinction
between tensed and untensed sentences. When one utters a tensed sentence,
one is understood to refer deictically to the time of utterance and thus to
say something about that time. In contrast an utterance of an untensed
sentence is taken to have no special connection with the time of speech.
No reference to speech time occurs when one utters an untensed sentence,
unless the sentence contains some appropriate adverb, and thus an untensed
utterance does not generally say anything about the occasion of utterance.

Russell is not the only one to regard tensed utterances to be about the
time of speech. Reichenbach has a similar view, although he envisages a
somewhat more elaborate system of reference. He suggests that tensed
assertions involve reference not only to speech time but also to what he
calls event time and reference time. It has been noted that his tripartite
system of temporal reference may make it difficult, if not impossible, to
treat tenses as sentential operators (see Dowty, 1979). Since we intend to
treat tenses in just this way, i.e., as sentential operators, it is worth noting
that nowhere do we resort to Reichenbach's notions of event time and
reference time. Although we often invoke reference to time, we never
appeal to his special concepts of reference time and event time.

While speech time plays an essential role in the analysis of tense, we take
it to be irrelevant to the treatment of temporal quantifiers, i.e., of such
expressions as *always, sometimes* and *never*. This is not to say, however,
that reference to time is generally irrelevant. Temporal quantifiers are
understood to invoke temporal reference just as tenses do, but reference
is not always or even typically to speech time. The interval denoted may

be any one at all, and its role is to restrict the range of quantification. In effect temporal quantifiers range over an interval fixed referentially at the time of utterance. This referential aspect of temporal quantifiers figures significantly in their interaction with temporal connectives, in particular with *when, before* and *after*.

Although we confine our attention to intrasentential phenomena, there is an emerging view that the real test of a temporal theory lies in discourse (see Kamp & Rohrer, 1983). Any truly satisfactory theory must generalize to cover temporal relations among sentences in a discourse. What these relations might be, and how they should be characterized, is not easy to decipher, but it is reasonable to suppose that temporal connectives must be among the more pertinent phenomena. Any approach which is suitable for the treatment of temporal connection might be expected to suggest how discourse itself is to be handled. We would hope that our theory might indicate some of the 'ingredients' of a theory of discourse, although we shall not attempt to elaborate any of them here.

Among our more philosophical concerns will be certain issues revolving around two familiar Davidsonian themes, viz, logical form and semantic innocence. The logical form of tensed sentences has been difficult to characterize, especially in relation to other temporal devices such as adverbs, quantifiers and connectives. We shall argue that if tenses are characterized in a Russellian way, i.e., in the manner we suggest, a fully comprehensive account of temporal phenomena can be constructed. One of the more surprising consequences of the proposal is that semantic innocence may be a misdirected semantic aspiration. Sentences which occur in subordinate position do not generally have the same semantic role which they have as main clauses. This is an important fact of language which can be explained if the role of tenses is appropriately specified.

UNTENSED SENTENCES

Let us start by considering untensed sentences. Linguists may debate whether there are any such sentences, but it cannot be denied that English contains a range of putative candidates, particularly in subordinate position. One might note, for example, the following instances.

(1) It was important that Max exercise regularly.
(2) The doctor recommended that Max run daily.

Prima facie one seems justified in supposing that the two sentences in subordinate position, viz,

(3)   Max exercise regularly.

(4)   Max run daily.

are both untensed. For one thing there is no apparent syntactic marking for tense, and for another this fact seems to be semantically important. Note the following variant of (1) where the subordinate sentence is tensed as past.

(5)   It was important that Max exercised regularly.

Clearly (5) implies that Max did exercise regularly, but no similar implication attaches to (1) which is consistent with the assertion.

(6)   But he never did.

The difference between (1) and (5) is naturally attributed to tense, although it may equally be associated with mood. The subordinate sentence in (5) is in the indicative mood while the subordinate sentence in (1) is in the subjunctive mood. It is interesting to note that the subjunctive mood in English seems to coincide with the absence of tense. In the case of (2) the subordinate sentence can only be read 'subjunctively', and significantly it can never be tensed, as one can see by replacing *run* with *ran*.

(7)   * The doctor recommended that Kim ran.

There is, in effect, no factive reading of *recommended* as there is of *was important*. In the circumstances one is tempted to conjecture that subordinate sentences can be read factively only if they are tensed; when they are untensed, they must be read counterfactually.

It may be suggested that English is perhaps not a sure guide to universal syntax. When (1) and (2) are translated into other languages, the subordinate sentences are typically marked for tense, even though their status is counterfactual. There is a sense, nevertheless, in which such counterfactual sentences are 'semantically' untensed. Later we shall indicate just what sense this is, at which point it may emerge that in English it is not entirely misleading to drop tense.

Since we shall use untensed sentences as a basis for analyzing tensed sentences, we must address the difficult problem of how they are to be semantically characterized, a problem which has worried many philosophers and logicians. It does not seem appropriate to regard untensed sentences as having a truth value, since there is no occasion on which it would be correct to say that they are true or false. Utterances of sentences such as (3) and (4) are not assertions about what is purportedly true and hence, they cannot be rightly seen as bearing truth value. In this respect their status can only be seen as independent of truth. From the perspective of formal semantics this is awkward, for it suggests that the concept of truth cannot be invoked to analyze sentences like (3) and (4). Although truth may yield a natural account of sentences that can bear truth value, there is genuine doubt that it can be applied to other kinds of sentences.

Despite such skepticism, it is arguable that truth can still be invoked to characterize the semantic content of untensed sentences. It is helpful to recall the 'speech act' view of declarative and nondeclarative sentences. According to this theory, both types of sentence express propositions, the only difference being that declaratives assert them and nondeclaratives do not. For example, these two sentences are said to express the same proposition.

(8)   Max exercises regularly.
(9)   Max, exercise regularly!

Significantly the proposition is taken to be the one expressed by the untensed sentence,

(3)   Max exercise regularly.

While (8) is understood to assert this proposition (with respect to the present), (9) is held to command it (with reference to the future).

Bearing in mind the status of (3), viz, that it never bears a truth value relative to an utterance, one might legitimately use truth values to characterize the proposition expressed by (3), provided there is no implication that (3) ever has a truth value simpliciter. Let us suppose then that propositions take the form of functions from moments of time to truth values; that is, let us assume that propositions are distinguished by functions which identify those moments in which the proposition is true. In the case of (3) the proposition expressed picks out those moments of time at which Max has the property of exercising regularly. This is not to say that an utterance of (3) is tantamount to asserting, or even implying, that the given proposition is true at the moment of utterance. Although the proposition may well be true at this particular time, the utterance neither says nor implicates that it is. In effect (3) does not take on truth values relative to utterances. While it expresses a proposition, it does so in what might be called a value-free way; that is, it is of the essence of (3) that it carries no indication (contextual or otherwise) about where, i.e., at which moment, the proposition is to be evaluated, whether at the moment of utterance or somewhere else. This is characteristic of all untensed sentences, which never invoke any moment as a moment of evaluation. Although the propositions expressed are represented as functions from moments to truth values, no moment can have the status of being the intended moment of evaluation.

Evaluation is invoked through the medium of tense, e.g., the present tense, as in (8). To utter (8) is to invoke the time of speech as the intended interval of evaluation; it is tantamount to asserting that the proposition expressed by (3) is true for this particular interval. As a result, (8) is appropriately regarded as bearing a truth value relative to the time of speech. One might say that it is, as it were, value-specific for that interval. This is in marked contrast to (3), no utterance of which identifies any interval as the intended interval of evaluation. What particular interval the truth value of (3) is relative to is not something which an utterance of (3) can raise by itself. Only through tense does this emerge.

If (3) is seen to result from (8) by 'factoring' present tense, it is natural to view the mood of (8) as associated with its tense. Since introducing present tense into (3) must then be sufficient to realize (8), the mood of (8), viz, the indicative mood, seems a parasitic phenomenon; it requires no characterization independent of tense. In effect there is no component of (8), other than the present tense, which corresponds to what has been called the speech act device, here the device associated with assertion. Tense is what makes (8) assertable. Significantly (8) is not taken to express the same proposition as (3). While (8) always asserts something about the time of utterance, viz, that (3) is true there, (3) itself never expresses this proposition. The proposition expressed by (3) is, as it were, value-free while the one expressed by (8) is value-specific.

The contrast between value-specific and value-free propositions will play a central role both in the characterization of tense and in the analysis of sentential subordination. Sentences which occur in subordinate position typically express value-free propositions, as can be seen in the following example.

(10)   It is my wish that God save the Queen.

For me to utter (10) is of course to express a wish relative to the time of utterance, viz, that God save the Queen. However, it is not a wish merely about the present moment, for I plainly intend to invoke's God's good offices for some indefinite period in the future. In fact there is a sense in which my wish might be seen to be omnitemporal; it is a wish that the proposition expressed by the subordinate sentence

(11)   God save the Queen

evaluate to true for any moment of time, at least for all future moments. So understood, the proposition expressed by (11) must be regarded as value-free, i.e., as not involving any moment in particular. How this interpretation can be technically realized will subsequently become clear.

Let us now turn to the task of characterizing the content of sentences that are assumed to be both moodless and tenseless. As we have indicated, albeit obliquely, we propose to treat propositions in general as functions from intervals of time to truth values. Intervals may be of any length as long as they are continuous, with points of time being just minimal intervals. The need for intervals, as well as points, is sometimes justified on metaphysical grounds. It is arguable that some things are true for intervals but not for all points in those intervals, like taking a run which is punctuated with periods of rest. Such considerations, however, do not figure among our reasons for regarding intervals as the fundamental notion. Since tenses and other temporal devices typically involve reference to intervals, it seems appropriate to have them in the theory from the beginning. To be sure, there are other reasons for admitting them but these will become evident in due course.

Much has recently been made of Vendler's classification of verbs according to whether they express activities, accomplishments, achievements or states (see Vendler, 1967). Doubtless there are important semantic differences, of which some may be relevant to formal semantics. One thinks of the adverb *in an hour* which occurs with verbs expressing achievements and accomplishments but not normally with those expressing activities or states (see Dowty, 1979, p. 54). We shall not, however, be concerned with such matters in this paper and thus need not seek to characterize the relevant factors. Moreover, we shall not attempt to account for certain semantic anomalies, e.g., the incommensurability between achievement verbs and durational adverbs.

(12)   * Sandy arrived for 10 minutes.

Some would be disposed to require that a fully adequate semantic theory should explain why (12) is anomalous and the following is not.

(13)   Sandy walked for 10 months.

We shall set such problems aside and treat all verbs as having a common semantic structure. Although this may seem linguistically shortsighted, our general concern is with semantic structure that abstracts from 'lexical' differences.

The envisaged semantic theory will be defined over a quasi-logical language supplemented with certain propositional operators. The syntax of this language is based on a categorial analysis of a fragment of English and is extended to include certain resources from quantified modal logic. The resulting compromise between formality and informality is intended to allow for ease of comprehension while maintaining a certain rigour.

Although we shall focus on those aspects of semantics relating to temporal structures, it will also be necessary to invoke possible worlds. With this in mind we let a model for a our quasi-logical language to be a quintuple (D, W, I, <, f) such that

(14) (i)   D, W and I are nonempty disjoint sets to be understood respectively as the set of possible objects, possible worlds and intervals of moments of time;

(ii) The relation < is the partial ordering of I induced by the 'earlier than' relation defined over moments of time; that is, for intervals i and j, i < j if all the moments in i are earlier than all the moments in j;

(iii) and f is a function that assigns a suitable intension to each nonlogical constant of the language.

Since we do not propose to pin down any particular logic, there is no need here to restrict the definition of a model to any specific temporal structure. Our strategy is to investigate certain issues relating to logical form which do not immediately require a general definition of logical consequence. Once these issues are clarified we can then seek to identify an appropriate model structure. This task we shall leave to another time.

We must, however, specify the range of admissible intensions, for which we invoke two special conditions. The possible extensions of constants will be as usual: the extension of a name will be an individual in D unless the name is a temporal one, in which case its extension will be an interval in I; and the extension of an n-ary relation will be a subset of n-tuples from D^n. The intension denoted by a constant will then be a function with domain (W X I), the cartesian product of W and I, which satisfies the following conditions.

(14) (iv) If b is a name and $f(b)(w,i)$ is an entity of d of D, then for all subintervals j of i $f(b)(w,j)$ is also d.

(v)   If r is an n-ary relation and $f(r)(w,i)$ is a subset of D^n, then for all subintervals j of i $f(r)(w,j)$ includes $f(r)(w,i)$.

The point of (iv) and (v) is basically to ensure that if an atomic sentence is true at a world for an interval it will be true at that world for all subintervals of the given interval.

It will be noted that (iv) and (v) admit the possibility of defining intensions which are partial functions, since there is no requirement that intensions be defined for all intervals. This possibility emerges independently of whether intensions are defined for all moments of time, i.e., for the smallest intervals. With a view to speculating about the general nature of temporal quantification, we shall allow f to assign partial functions; but we shall assume that all such functions are still defined for each moment of time. That is, we shall adopt the following condition on the definition of f.

(14) (vi) If c is a nonlogical constant and i a moment of time in I, $f(c)(w,i)$ must be defined.

Apart from (iv)–(vi) f is free to assign any appropriate intension to a nonlogical constant.

Given the admissibility of partial functions, we must specify their import for the intensions of sentences. Suppose that a sentence (relative to a world) is not true for every subinterval of a given interval. Is it to be taken as false or undefined for that interval? Although it would be convenient (and possible) to adopt the former view, an interesting distinction emerges if the latter is chosen. It will arise from our formalization that the intension of an untensed sentence is usually a partial function but the intension of a tensed sentence (and other types of sentence involving temporal quantification) is always a total function.[1] There is thus a clear semantic difference between tensed and untensed sentences, one that will become more precise below.

The definition of truth will be seen to yield the following homogeneity property for untensed atomic sentences.

(15) An untensed atomic sentence will be true at an index (w,i) only if for all subintervals j of i the sentence is true at (w,j).

It should be stressed that homogeneity is not intended as a general restriction on the truth definition; rather it is a property which characteristically (though not always) emerges from it. With this clarification we specify the initial clauses in the following way, taking A and B to be any sentences of the language, and M any model.

(16) (i) An atomic sentence consisting of an n-ary relation R_n and n terms $a_1, \ldots, a_n$ is true in M at (w,i) if the sequence $f(a_1)(w,i), \ldots, f(a_n)(w,i)$ belongs to $f(R_n)(w,i)$; it is false at (w,i) if the given sequence does not so belong; and otherwise it is undefined.

(ii) (A *and* B) iş true in M at (w,i) if both A and B are true in M at (w,i); it is false at (w,i) if either A or B is false at (w,i); and otherwise it is undefined.

(iii) (A *or* B) is true in M at (w,i) if either A or B is true in M at (w,i); it is false at (w,i) if both A and B are false at (w,i); and otherwise it is undefined.

(iv) *Not* (A) is true in M at (w,i) if A is false in M at (w,i); it is false at (w,i) if A is true at (w,i); and otherwise it is undefined.

Before giving the clauses for the quantifiers, we should note that there is a choice in how to specify the range of quantification. Consider a sentence of the form,

(17)   *Every* x (A).

Given a model, (17) may be treated in at least two different ways. Relative to an index (w,i) it can be interpreted as asserting that every object in the domain of the model has the property A at (w,i). Here the quantifier is understood to range over the whole of the domain. Alternatively, the quantifier can be interpreted as ranging only over those objects in the domain which exist at the index (w,i). In this case (17) will be read as saying that each of the entities in this set has the distinguished property at (w,i). From the point of view of natural language the 'restricted' reading of the quantifier may seem more suitable. Typical quantifier phrases, such as *every swimmer*, seem paradigm instances of restricted quantification. It is arguable, nevertheless, that *every* itself should be treated as an unrestricted quantifier, i.e., as an example of a generalized quantifier. This in effect is how we propose to define it.

Let $A(b/x)$ be the sentence which results from A by replacing all the free occurrences of x by a name b which does not already occur in A. Let M^b be a model which is like M except possibly for what the function f assigns to b. The standard quantifiers *every* and *some* are then defined as follows.

(16)   (v)   *Every* x (A) is true in M at (w,i) if $A(b/x)$ is true at (w,i) for every M^b; it is false at (w,i) if $A(b/x)$ is false at (w,i) for some M^b; and otherwise it is undefined.

      (vi)   *Some* x (A) is true in M at (w,i) if $A(b/x)$ is true at (w,i) for some M^b; it is false at (w,i) if $A(b/x)$ is false at (w,i) for every M^b; and otherwise it is undefined.

It should be noted that quantified sentences may be undefined at an index because they contain a predicate or a name that is undefined at that index.

We can now illustrate how the given semantics may be appropriate for untensed moodless sentences like,

(18)   Hilary swim.

Relative to a model, (18) will express a proposition represented by a possibly partial function. This proposition will be determined by the intensions of *Hilary* and *swim* and will be indifferent as to the intended interval of evaluation. Not only does (18) not contain devices for explicit reference to intervals, but its analysis at the level of logical form does not presuppose any such reference. In effect the proposition is characterized in a value-free way: there is not, nor can there be, an intended interval of evaluation. This is just what distinguishes such an untensed moodless sentence.

TENSED SENTENCES

From the beginning we have supposed that tensed sentences are in a certain sense context sensitive; that is, they express a determinate proposition only relative to an occasion of utterance. Thus the present tense sentence,

    (19)   Hilary swims

does not in itself express any particular proposition; only relative to an utterance does it say anything definite. For such an occasion it says essentially that the proposition expressed by (18) is true at the designated time. On this interpretation the proposition expressed by (18) must be different from the proposition expressed by an utterance of (19). The latter will be about a specific interval of time while the former will not be so.

    The source of difference lies in the deictic nature of tense. Tenses involve deictic reference to speech time, and it is this semantic fact which explains why (18) and (19) diverge in the propositions they can express. Since (19) is tensed, an utterance of it involves reference to the time of utterance and thus says something about it: it says, as we have noted, that the proposition expressed by (18) is true at that interval. Since (18) is not tensed, no utterance of it can invoke reference to the interval of utterance, and for that reason it can only express a proposition different than (19).[2]

    To reflect the referential aspect of tense we shall give the tense operators a complex syntactic structure. The present tense, for example, will be represented as $PRES_{(v,t)}$ with v and t read as deictic parameters ranging over worlds and intervals. These parameters are to be seen as acquiring their values relative to the context of utterance. A certain latitude will be allowed in the possible assignments to t in that they need not be strictly confined to the intervals of utterance. While the value of t must always have a final segment representing the interval of utterance, it may extend back into the past, indeed indefinitely far back. Such an assignment, i.e., where the value of t extends beyond the interval of utterance, is sometimes called the 'extended now'.

    While reference to time seems a natural ingredient of tense, one may wonder about invoking reference to possible worlds. It is not clear that possible worlds have any special relation to tense, that is, one which they do not have to other parts of language. It is arguable, nevertheless, that the value-specific character of tensed utterances involves more than just time. When one utters a tensed sentence, it is not only speech time that is deictically fixed but also the intended 'location', normally the actual world. When one utters (19), for example, one usually intends to say something that is true at the time of speech in the actual world. While reference to the actual world does not obviously arise from tense, it also does not obviously arise from any other device. In the circumstance it is not unreasonable to regard tense as involving deictic reference to worlds. This at least allows a certain economy of analysis and may even lead to an unexpected insight, a matter we shall subsequently consider.

As for the syntactic role of $PRES_{(v,t)}$, we propose to treat it as a sentential operator but, for reasons that will emerge below, do not allow it to iterate without restriction. We let $PRES_{(v,t)}$ apply only to those sentences which later will be defined as context free. Roughly speaking, a context-free sentence will be one that does not contain any occurrences of the deictic parameters, i.e., those ranging over worlds and intervals. On the assumption that A is a context-free sentence, we can specify the semantic content of the present tense operation by extending the truth definition appropriately. Let g_c be a (possibly partial) function which assigns values to the 'deictic' parameters v and t relative to a context c.

(20) $PRES_{(v,t)}A$ is true in a model M at a world-interval index (w,i) if w $= g_c(v)$ and i $= g_c(t)$ and A is true in M at (w,i); it is false in M if either w $\neq g_c(v)$ or i $\neq g_c(t)$ or A is false in M at (w,i); and otherwise it is undefined.

It should be noted that (20) is actually a definition scheme in that it gives rise to different intensions for different assignments to v and t.

By way of example let us consider the logical form of (19). Since (18) is a paradigm instance of a context-free sentence, (19) can be analyzed as follows.

(21) $PRES_{(v,t)}$(Hilary swim)

Relative to an utterance, v and t will acquire specific values, which for convenience may be referred to as V and T. With respect to V and T (19) is construed basically as expressing the proposition that the proposition expressed by (18) is true at (V,T). When formally characterized in terms of (21), this proposition is the intension which takes at most one world-interval pair to true, viz, (V,T). From the definition given in (20), it can be immediately seen that this intension will be true at (V,T) only if the intension denoted by (18) is true at (V,T); otherwise it will be either false or undefined. Since the intension denoted by (21) is, as it were, value specific for (V,T), it captures the special character of an utterance of a tensed sentence.

Some would argue, however, that (20) leads to counterintuitive consequences. Suppose that the two context-free sentences,

(18)   Hilary swim
(22)   Kim walk

are both true in a model at (V,T). Then (20) would imply that

(23) $\text{PRES}_{(V,T)}(\text{Hilary swim})$
(24) $\text{PRES}_{(V,T)}(\text{Kim walk})$

denote the same intension in that model. This may be seen to be awkward since it suggests that cotemporal utterances of

(19)   Hilary swims
(25)   Kim walks

will express the same proposition and hence convey the same information.

Although it is true that the intensions will be the same, there is a clear sense in which the utterances will still convey different information. For the occasion (V,T) (19) will convey the information that the proposition expressed by

(18)   Hilary swim

is true at (V,T), while for the same occasion (25) will intimate that the proposition expressed by

(22)   Kim walk

is true at (V,T). Since the intensions denoted by (18) and (22) will typically differ in a given model, the information content of (19) and (25) will not necessarily be the same for the utterances at (V,T). The difference becomes relevant in statements of propositional attitude. How this difference is to be accommodated technically will be considered in some detail below. For the moment let it suffices to emphasize the main point. Although (19) and (25) may denote the same intension relative to (V,T), they will do so with respect to different intensions, viz, the ones expressed by (18) and (22). These intensions account for the difference in information content between utterances of (19) and (25) and have special relevance in contexts of propositional attitude.

Let us now formalize the notion of a context-free sentence. We first define the concept of a context-sensitive sentence. All tense operators are assumed to have a common form which can be represented as $Q_{(v,t)}$, with Q having PRES, PAST and FUT as substitution instances. Where A and B are sentences,[3]

(26)   A is said to be context-sensitive if it has the form $Q_{(v,t)}B$, where v and t are parameters, or contains a subformula of this form.

We take B to be a subformula of A if it is one of its main clauses, for example if A is of the form B *or* C, but not if it is a subordinate clause of A such as in *Sandy said that B*. Given the definition of a context-sensitive sentence, we shall say that

(27) A is context-free if each occurrence of a tense operation in a subformula is of the form $Q_{(v',t')}$ where v' and t' are variables.

As we have indicated above, (27) will be invoked to restrict the iteration of tenses.

The need to restrict iteration becomes apparent once we define the past and future tenses. Though they have a certain familiar form, the definitions are not entirely standard, mainly because of the role of the deictic parameters. Let A be any context-free sentence; then,

(28) $PAST_{(v,t)}A$ is true in a model M at (w,i) if $w = g_c(v)$, $i = g_c(t)$ and there is an interval $j < i$ such that A is true in M at (w,j); it is false at (w,i) if either $w \neq g_c(t)$ or $i \neq g_c(t)$ or there is no $j < i$ such that A is true at (w,j); (and otherwise it is undefined).

(29) $FUT_{(v,t)}A$ is true in M at (w,i) if $w = g_c(v)$, $i = g_c(t)$ and there is an interval j such that $i < j$ and A is true in M at (w,j); it is false at (w,i) if either $w \neq g_c(v)$ or $i \neq g_c(t)$ or there is no j such that $i < j$ and A is true at (w,j); (and otherwise it is undefined).[4]

Since tense operators are intended to apply only to context-free sentences, the following formula is not syntactically well-formed.

(30) $PAST_{(v,t)}[PAST_{(v,t)}A]$

That (30) is also not semantically coherent can be readily appreciated. According to definition (28), (30) would be true in a model at (w,i) if $w = g_c(v)$, $i = g_c(t)$ and there is a $j < i$ such that $PAST_{(v,t)}A$ is true at (w,j); and this obtains only if $j = g_c(t)$ and there is a $k < j$ such that A is true at (w,k). But obviously no j can satisfy these conditions since it cannot satisfy both $j = g_c(t)$ and $j < g_c(t)$.

Since the parameters v and t obviously occupy referential positions, it is natural to envisage the possibility of binding into these positions. It will be immediately clear that such binding must give rise to context-free sentences. If all the occurrences of v and t give way to variables, the resulting sentence will by definition be context-free, for it will contain no instances of the given parameters. It will, accordingly, be an open formula. With a view to creating a particular kind of context-free sentence we introduce a new operator whose role will be to bind only into those positions where v and t can occur. To this end let v' and t' be variables ranging over worlds and intervals respectively. Where A is any sentence, either context-free or context-sensitive,

(31) $Gv'[A]$ and $Gt'[A]$ are also sentences.

In the first sentence G binds all the free occurrences of v' in A, and in the second it binds all the free occurrences of t'. For sentences of the form Gv'[Gt'[A]] it is convenient to adopt the abbreviation Gv't'[A], which will be used to define the semantics of G. To minimize the complexity of the definition we supplement our quasi-logical language with the following convention: given a world-interval index (w,i), let w* be a name of w and i* a name of i, and let A[w*/v',i*/t'] be the formula which results from A by replacing all free occurrences of v' by w* and all free occurrences of t' by i*. Now for any context-free sentence A, we say that

(32) Gv't[A] is true in a model M at (w,i) if A[w*/v',i*/t'] is true in M at (w,i); it is false at (w,i) if A[w*/v',i*/t'] is false at (w,i); and otherwise it is undefined.

It should be noted here that the intension of Gv't'[A] will typically be a partial function when A does not contain any tense operators.

Let us illustrate the role of G by considering the following instance of tense iteration, where A is assumed to be context-free.

(33) $PAST_{(v,t)}Gv't'[PAST_{(v',t')}A]$

Unlike (30), (33) has a coherent interpretation, since it will express a definite proposition in every model. To be precise, (33) will be true in a model at (w,i) if $w = g_c(v)$, $i = g_c(t)$ and there is a $j < i$ such that $Gv't'[PAST_{(v',t')}A]$ is true at (w,j); and this formula will be true at (w,j) if $PAST_{(w^*,j^*)}A$ is true at (w,j) which obtains if there is a $k < j$ such that A is true at (w,k). If (33) is to be true in a model, there must be distinct intervals i, j and k which satisfy the indicated conditions, one of them being that $k < j < i$. Plainly there are possible models in which these conditions are met. As for the import of (33), it is tempting to think that it may represent the pluperfect, which is sometimes taken to be a tense. Although it may be possible to characterize the pluperfect as a compound of two past tenses, i.e., as given in (33), it can also be analyzed as a compound of past tense and perfective aspect. Below we offer an account of perfective aspect and illustrate the analysis.

To exemplify our approach to tense iteration let us characterize the difference between these two sentences.[5]

(34) A prince was invested who would be king.
(35) A prince was invested who will be king.

Clearly (34) and (35) do not mean the same thing, and this can be traced to the different roles of the future tense in the subordinate clauses. In (35) the future tense is to be evaluated relative to the time of utterance: (35) will be true relative to an occasion of utterance only if there is some future time at which a prince invested in the past will be king. In contrast the future tense of (34) is to be evaluated relative to the past tense in the main clause: (34) will be true relative to an utterance only if there is some time in the past at which a prince was invested such that relative to it there is some future time at which he is king.

To capture the difference in truth conditions we invoke the operator G and render the logical form of (34) as follows.

(36) *Some* x [PAST$_{(v,t)}$[[Prince(x) *and* x be invested] *and* Gv't'[FUT$_{(v',t')}$(x be king)]]]

It can be easily seen that (36) renders the intended sense of (34). Relative to a model and an index (w,i), (36) will be true if there is some b in the model such that

(37) PAST$_{(v,t)}$[[Prince(b) *and* b be invested] *and* Gv't'[FUT$_{(v',t')}$(b be king)]]

is true at (w,i). This will obtain only if $w = g_c(v)$, $i = g_c(t)$ and there is some $j < i$ such that

(38) [[Prince(b) *and* b be invested] *and* Gv't'[FUT$_{(v',t')}$(b be king)]]

is true at (w,j). Obviously this will hold just in case both the conjuncts hold at (w,j), i.e., if and only if these two formulas are true at (w,j)

(39) [Prince(b) *and* b be invested]

(40) Gv't'[FUT$_{(v't')}$(b be king)]

Since (40) will be true at (w,j) only if

(41) FUT$_{(w^*,j^*)}$(b be king)

is true at (w,j), it is plain that the future tense operator is evaluated relative to (w,j). In effect (41) will be true at (w,j) if there is some k such that $j < k$ and

(42) b be king

is true at (w,k). At this point it should be evident that (36) is an appropriate characterization of the logical form of (34), at least as far as the tenses are concerned.

It is easy to see, moreover, how (36) can be adjusted to capture the intended meaning of (35) where both tenses are to be interpreted relative to speech time. Since neither tense has scope over the other, (35) should be analyzed as follows.

(43) *Some* x [PAST$_{(v,t)}$(Prince(x) *and* x be invested) *and* FUT$_{(v,t)}$(x be king)]

Now (43) will be true in a model at an index (w,i) only if there is some b such that

(44) $PAST_{(v,t)}$(Prince(b) *and* b be invested) *and* $FUT_{(v,t)}$(b be king)

is true at (w,i). Since both occurrences of v and t in (44) will be instantiated to the same world and interval, viz, to $g_c(v)$ and $g_c(t)$ respectively, the past and future operators will be evaluated relative to the same world-interval pair. In effect (44) will be true only if there is some interval j earlier than the time of speech such that

(45)   Prince(b) *and* b be invested

is true at (w,j), and also some interval k later than speech time such that

(46)   b be king

is true at (w,k). Plainly these are the truth conditions of the desired reading of (35).

TENSES AND TEMPORAL REFERENCE

Tenses are not the only devices which involve reference to time; other examples are adverbials such as *at* 9.0, *before* 1493, *on* 1*st April* '84, and *yesterday*. We shall treat these adverbials like tenses, i.e., as sentential operators. It has been argued, however, that they function rather differently, finding their proper role only in the context of tense. In effect time adverbs occupy an argument position created by tense and their role is to specify the time of the event (see Tichy, 1980). This would suggest that where there is no tense there can be no time adverbs, a situation which is plainly counterfactual. Note the subordinate clause in the sentence,

(47)   The secretary requests that Sandy phone at 9.0.

Clearly *at* 9.0 is not to be taken as specifying the time of the secretary's requesting. It is rather associated with the untensed verb *phone*, or as we see it, with the untensed sentence *Sandy phone*. How it is so associated remains to be specified.

At 9.0 might be read intuitively as referring to the time at which the proposition expressed by *Sandy phone* is to be considered; it invites one to consider this proposition with respect to the interval 9.0. This idea can be rendered technically by introducing a sentential operator corresponding to *at* 9.0 and defining it as follows. Where A is a context-free sentence,

(48)   AT 9.0 (A) is true in a model M at (w,i) if i = 9.0 and A is true

in M at (w,i); it is false at (w,i) if i ≠ 9.0 or A is false at (w,i); and otherwise it is undefined.

It will be observed that if 9.0 is read 'specifically', i.e., as referring to a definite interval on a definite day, the proposition denoted will be value-specific in respect of time. That is, it can evaluate to true at only one interval, viz, the one referred to by 9.0. This is not to imply that the proposition will also be value-specific with respect to a particular world. There may be many worlds for which the intension evaluates to true.

By way of example let us consider the logical form of the subordinate clause in sentence (47), viz,

(49)   Sandy phone at 9.0.

Its logical structure will be represented by this quasi-logical formula.

(50)   AT 9.0 (Sandy phone).

The proposition expressed by (50), i.e., the intension it denotes, will be taken as the object of the relation *requests*, at least on one natural analysis. It is significant, therefore, that this intension does not necessarily coincide with the one denoted by the formula,

(51)   AT 9.0 (Sandy arrive).

Although both intensions will be value-specific with respect to 9.0, they will not generally be true at the same possible worlds. Hence, the propositions expressed by (47) and

(52)   The secretary suggests that Sandy arrive at 9.0

will be appropriately distinct.[6]

In this connection we should note that (49) and its present-tense 'derivative',

(53)   Sandy phones at 9.0

will be characterized as expressing different propositions.[7] Since the latter involves tense, it will be value-specific for both world and time. This would lead one to ask whether the difference between (49) and (53) will be reflected in a difference between (47) and,

(54)   The secretary requests that Sandy phones at 9.0.

We shall consider the matter below.

There is a certain 'efficiency' in definition (48) in that it allows for an ambiguity in the use of 9.0. It might be used, as we have noted, to refer to a definite time on a definite day; and it might also be used to indicate a definite time simpliciter, i.e., without regard to any particular day. The latter usage will not by itself engender a value-specific proposition; that is, the intension denoted by

(55)   AT 9.0 (A)

may be true at a number of intervals, provided each one has the property of being a '9.0 o'clock' interval. The interpretation of (48) will of course depend upon how 9.0 is used in the definiens, whether with respect to a particular day or not.

Adverbs of temporal reference will generally be treated in a manner similar to *at* 9.0, i.e., in regard to their logical form. For example, the clauses defining *before* 1493 and *on* 1*st April* '84 will be as follows, with A understood as a context-free sentence.

(56)   BEFORE 1493 (A) is true in a model M at (w,i) if i is earlier than 1493 and A is true in M at (w,i); it is false at (w,i) if i is not earlier than 1493 or A is false at (w,i); and otherwise it is undefined.

(57)   ON 1st April '84 (A) is true in M at (w,i) if i is a subinterval of 1st April '84 and A is true in M at (w,i); it is false at (w,i) if either i is not a subinterval of 1st April '84 or A is false at (w,i); and otherwise it is undefined.

It may be helpful to illustrate (56) with respect to a tensed sentence, e.g.,

(58)   Columbus crossed the Atlantic before 1493.

The logical form of (58) must be represented as in (59) since *before* 1493 can apply only to a context-free sentence.

(59) $PAST_{(v,t)}$[BEFORE 1493 (Columbus cross the Atlantic)].

On the given definitions (59) will be true at (w,i) if $w = g_c(v)$, $i = g_c(t)$ and there is a $j < i$ such that

(60)   BEFORE 1493 (Columbus cross the Atlantic)

is true at (w,j); (60) will be true at (w,j) if j is earlier than 1493 and

(61)   Columbus cross the Atlantic

is true at (w,j).

We take this analysis of (58) to reveal in a paradigmatic way the connection between tense and adverbs of temporal reference. Note, in particular, that the analysis invokes no reference to any specific value of j at which (61) is given to be true. The role of *before* 1493 is to indicate that the verifying value of j, whatever it may be, falls before 1493. No further specification is given. Those who would approach (58) from a Reichenbachian perspective would, in contrast, be disposed to look for a precise reference, viz, to the time of the event type distinguished by (61). What they would assume is that (58) invokes a reference to some interval before 1493. This assumption, however, is not immediately obvious. Not only does (58) not contain a suitable referring phrase, it is not easy to add one without anomaly, which can be seen from this sentence.

(62)   * Columbus crossed the Atlantic before 1493 in 1492.

Plainly one of the two adverbs must go, in this case the so-called locating adverb *in* 1492. It seems to have no proper role to play in the analysis of (58). Since our theory implies as much, it does not make use of the Reichenbachian notion of reference time.

It also does not invoke the Reichenbachian concept of event time, as can be seen from the treatment of negative sentences like

(63)   Columbus did not cross the Atlantic before 1492.

Intuitively there is no event which is being referred to here, nor any particular time at which (as opposed to during which) it is alleged not to have occurred. Our theory respects this intuition by rendering the logical form of (63) as follows.

(64)   *Not* [PAST$_{(v,t)}$[BEFORE 1492 (Columbus cross the Atlantic)]]

This formula will be true at (w,i) if

(65)   PAST$_{(v,t)}$[BEFORE 1492 (Columbus cross the Atlantic)]

is false at (w,i). On the assumption that $w = g_c(v)$ and $i = g_c(t)$, (65) is false at (w,i) only if there is no $j < i$ such that

(66)   BEFORE 1492 (Columbus cross the Atlantic)

is true at (w,j). This holds (given the analogue of definition (56)) only if there is no such j earlier than 1492 for which

(61)   Columbus cross the Atlantic

is true, i.e., at (w,j). The import of the analysis can be summarized by the paraphrase,

(67)   Columbus never crossed the Atlantic before 1492.

Some may find this somewhat odd since *not* does not generally mean *never*. Still there seems no denying that (63) and (67) coincide in import.

Let us consider another example, one that happens to invoke the non-specific use of 9.0.

(68)   Mandy did not phone before 9.0 on 1st April '84.

The logical structure of (68) will be represented in the following way.

(69)   *Not* [PAST$_{(v,t)}$[ON 1st April '84 [BEFORE 9.0 (Mandy phone)]]]]

Now (69) will be true at (w,i) if

(70)   PAST$_{(v,t)}$[ON 1st April '84 [BEFORE 9.0 (Mandy phone)]]]

is false at (w,i). On the assumption that w = $g_c(v)$ and i = $g_g(t)$, (70) is false at (w,i) if there is no j < i such that

(71)   ON 1st April '84 [BEFORE 9.0 (Mandy phone)]

is true at (w,j), which itself holds if for no j < i is j a subinterval of 1st April '84 and

(72)   BEFORE 9.0 (Mandy phone)

true at (w,j); and finally this obtains if there is no such j falling before 9.0 such that

(73)   Mandy phone

is true at (w,j). In effect (68) emerges as equivalent to the paraphrase

(74)   Mandy never phoned before 9.0 on 1st April '84.

Though (74) may be linguistically awkward, it does seem to capture the truth conditions of (68). What Mandy never did before a certain date she did not do before that time, and vice versa.

But there are, it must be said, certain problematic cases, in particular negative sentences which contain no time adverbials, as in the following.

(75)   Mandy did not phone.

On the assumption that (75) is similar in structure to (68), its logical form will be

(76)   *Not* [PAST$_{(v,t)}$(Mandy phone)]

and it will thus be equivalent to the paraphrase

(77)   Mandy never phoned.

But (77) is not an obvious paraphrase of (75); at least it is not obvious that (77) and (75) coincide on truth conditions. When one utters (75), one typically intends to say something about some specific time in the past, viz, that Mandy did not phone *then*. No similar specificity seems to be involved in an utterance of (77); one does not purport to assert anything about Mandy's phoning at any particular time in the past. Since there is no explicit reference to past time in (76), it seems insufficient as an analysis of (75), although it may be suitable for (77). To make it adequate for (75) it seems necessary to include some sort of referential parameter.

One natural idea is to interpret such a parameter as identifying a past time at which the event, viz, Mandy's phoning, is purported not to have occurred. This suggestion, which seems similar to Reichenbach's proposal, is not only plausible but predicts that any utterance of (75) 'requires' a certain completion, either by context or explicitly. To express something definite there must be an indication of when the event is claimed to have happened. This could be given by context and thus be implicit in the utterance; it could be understood that the envisaged past time is, say, 9.0 on 1st April '84. On the other hand it could be specified explicitly by continuing the utterance with the phrase *at 9.0 on 1st April '84*. Though somewhat pedantic, the following sentence is complete in the intended sense.

(78)   Mandy did not phone at 9.0 on 1st April '84.

One might be led to conjecture, therefore, that the logical form of (75) is perhaps similar to that of (78), with the 'underlying' structure being something like this.

(79)   *Not* $[PAST_{(v,t)}[AT$ u (Mandy phone)$]]$

Here u is to be taken as an interval parameter which receives its values from context. From an intuitive point of view (79) may be seen to offer an adequate analysis of (75). It may also be seen to 'underlie' (78) whose analysis is arguably as follows.

(80)   *Not* $[PAST_{(v,t)}[AT$ 9.0 $[ON$ 1st April '84 (Mandy phone)$]]]$

Intuition notwithstanding, there are grounds for supposing that (79) cannot constitute the correct analysis of (75), even though the import of uttering (75) may occasionally suggest as much.

Note that (75) can be made explicitly complete (in the intended sense) in ways other than exemplified in (78).

(81)   Mandy did not phone after March '84
(82)   Mandy did not phone before Easter '84
(83)   Mandy did not phone during 1984

Insofar as the intended past interval is concerned, these sentences are entirely explicit and independent of contextual factors. Indeed, if one attempts to add any further specification, e.g., *at 9.0 on 1st April '84*, the effect will be uniformly anomalous. This suggests that (79) cannot generally be the analysis of (75); if it were, it would have to figure in the analyses of (81–(83) in the way exemplified in the putative analysis of (78), i.e., as in

(80). The incompleteness of (75) does not in general arise from a need to specify a particular past time at which Mandy's phoning is supposed not to have happened; it rather arises from the need to indicate an interval during which it supposedly did not happen. Once this is understood, one might reasonably claim that (81)—(83) are equivalent in truth conditions to (84)–(86) respectively.

(84)   Mandy never phoned after March '84
(85)   Mandy never phoned before Easter '84
(86)   Mandy never phoned during 1984.

But what then is the logical form of (75) and how is it related to the logical forms of (81)–(83)?

At this point we would question the 'intuitive' assumption about (75), viz, that it is semantically incomplete. It has been supposed that if (75) is to express a definite proposition it must be supplemented by a reference to some past interval. This can be achieved implicitly at the time of utterance or it can be realized explicitly by adding a suitable referring phrase. But is there always a need for such referential supplementation? Consider the following sentence which is very similar to (75).

(87)   Wittgenstein did not die in Vienna.

What proposition (87) expresses does not depend upon any reference to a past time, either implicit or explicit; there is no need to indicate any specific time in the past in order to fix the proposition expressed by (87). In fact any attempt to add such a reference will give rise to a proposition different from the one expressed by (87) simpliciter. For example no utterance of (87) will be equivalent in import to an utterance of

(88)   Wittgenstein did not die in Vienna at 9.0 on 1st April '49.

To assert that Wittgenstein did not die in Vienna is not to say anything about any specific time in the past. It is rather to say something about the whole of the past, viz, that nowhere in it did Wittgenstein die in Vienna. In effect the truth conditions of (87) coincide with those of

(89)   Wittgenstein never died in Vienna.

Hence the logical form (87) should be represented as follows.

(90)   *Not* [PAST$_{(v,t)}$(Wittgenstein die in Vienna)].

As far as time reference is concerned, there is no further structure to be uncovered.

Since (75) is similar in surface form to (87), it should presumably be

represented as having a similar logical form. That is, the logical structure
of

(75)   Mandy did not phone

should be the following.

(91)   *Not* [PAST$_{(v,t)}$(Mandy phone)].

But as we have noted, this would imply that (75) means

(77)   Mandy never phoned.

Although there may be occasions on which (75) does mean (77), this is not
generally or even typically the case. Usually there is a specific time in the
past which is at issue, one that is implicitly determined by context. It is
thus natural to look for a term in the analysis of (75) whose referent would
be fixed contextually. But this is not the only option, nor one that is easy
to sustain in light of (87). We would conjecture that utterances of (75) are
actually elliptical when they do not coincide in meaning with (77). This is
not to say that (75) is syntactically elliptical; it cannot be because it
sometimes means (77). But when an utterance of (75) is not equivalent to
(77), the utterance is strictly speaking incomplete or, as we would say,
elliptical; it is in need of some further specification which could be given
by a deictic expression. For example an utterance of (75) might be equivalent to,

(92)   Mandy did not phone then

where the deictic *then* is interpreted as referring to a specific past interval.
We might say that this utterance of (75) is 'contextually' elliptical for (92).
The relevant analysis is thus the logical form of (92) which is the following.

(93)   *Not* [PAST$_{(v,t)}$(Mandy phone then)].

Below we shall indicate how temporal adverbs like *then* are to be treated
but in the meantime it is enough to say that the analysis will entail that (92)
is equivalent in truth conditions to

(94)   Mandy never phoned then.

While (94) may be stylistically strange, it nevertheless expresses a coherent
proposition.

　　Having resorted to paraphrases where *not* and *never* seem to have
the same import, we should emphasize that they will not in general be
characterized as meaning the same thing. Before turning to define *never*
and other temporal quantifiers, let us first consider temporal adverbs like
yesterday and *then*. Both of these are paradigmatically contextual in that

their interpretations are given relative to the occasion of utterance. It should be noted, nevertheless, that they acquire these interpretations under somewhat different constraints. In the case of *then* the interpretation may depend partly upon the intentions of the speaker; which time he is talking about is to some degree a matter of which time he intends to talk about. No similar choice is possible with respect to *yesterday*. If a speaker utters a sentence containing *yesterday* on Wednesday, then he must be talking about Tuesday, whatever his intentions at the time of utterance.

There is another difference between *then* and *yesterday* which becomes apparent in the interpretations of these two sentences.

(95) Sammy arrived then.
(96) Sammy arrived yesterday.

The proposition expressed by (95) is that Sammy arrived at a particular time, viz, then; it was at that time that his arriving is claimed to have occurred. In contrast the proposition expressed by (96) is that Sammy arrived sometime during a certain day, viz, yesterday; his arriving is said to have occurred, not at that time, but somewhere in it. To reflect this difference between *then* and *yesterday* at the level of logical form, we shall invoke an ambiguity which is exemplified in the way we indicated the contrast: *then* and *yesterday* may not only be temporal adverbs but also nouns, i.e., referring expressions. From a logical point of view the adverb *then* can be analyzed in terms of the prepositional phrase *at then*, where *then* is the object of the preposition *at*. The adverb *yesterday* may be similarly analyzed, although the choice of preposition is perhaps not uniquely determined. It could be *during* or *within* or *on*. In view of the definition of *on*, which we formulated above, it seems reasonable to render the content of the adverb *yesterday* in terms of the prepositional phrase *on yesterday* where *yesterday* is a noun. Although the chosen analysans is in neither case a linguistic equivalent to its analysandum, i.e., not strictly intersubstitutable salve congruitate, it does nevertheless give a fair rendering of semantic content. As a result we shall represent the logical status of *then* and *yesterday* in terms of their 'prepositional' analyses which will be treated as sentential operators. Let A be any context-free sentence.

(97) AT then (A) is true in a model M at (w,i) if i = then and A is true at (w,i); it is false at (w,i) if i ≠ then or A is false at (w,i); and otherwise it is undefined.

(98) ON yesterday (A) is true in a model M at (w,i) if i is a subinterval of yesterday and A is true in M at (w,i); it is false at (w,i) if i is not a subinterval of yesterday or A is false at (w,i); and otherwise it is undefined.

It should be noted that (97) and (98) are both definition schemas since the occurrences of the nouns *then* and *yesterday* in the definiens admit of alternative interpretations.

With these definitions in hand, we can now consider the logical forms of (95) and (96), which will be represented as follows.

(99) $PAST_{(v,t)}$[AT then (Sammy arrive)]

(100) $PAST_{(v,t)}$[ON yesterday (Sammy arrive)]

For the sake of illustration it will be enough to unpack (100). This formula will be true at (w,i) if $w = g_c(v)$, $i = g_c(t)$ and there is a $j < i$ such that

(101)   ON yesterday (Sammy arrive)

is true at (w,j); this will obtain if j is a subinterval of yesterday and

(102)   Sammy arrive

is true at (w,j). The analysis here is tantamount to taking (95) to be true if Sammy arrived sometime yesterday, i.e., sometime within yesterday.

It should be noted that the definitions of the time adverbs differ in one important respect from the definitions of the tenses: while the latter all involve quantification over intervals, the former do not. It is significant, therefore, that the definitions of the time adverbs allow for partial intensions but those of the tenses do not; they will always be total functions. This suggests a characteristic semantic difference. It is relevant here that perfective aspect also requires a quantificational analysis not unlike tense. Although the interval of quantification is not fixed by speech time, as it is for tense, the nature of the quantification is similar. It is natural to expect then that the definition will admit only total functions.

Before defining perfective aspect, however, we must first distinguish it from tense. Note that perfective sentences can apparently be unmarked for tense. Consider the complement sentence in this example.

(103)   It is important that Ben have finished by the time Hilary comes back.

Here the verb phrase *have finished* cannot properly be construed as involving past tense. If any tense is involved, it must surely be the present tense since the import of (103) can arguably be paraphrased by replacing *have finished* with *finishes*. It is interesting to note, however, that in this position *finishes* does not invoke any reference to speech time, unlike the main verb *is*. Since reference to speech time is taken to be an essential feature of tense, it is reasonable to suspect that the morphology of *finishes* is not a sure guide to its semantic role in complement position. In the circumstance it seems appropriate to envisage a 'tenseless' analysis of *have finished*. We suggest that *have* in conjunction with the morpheme *ed* be understood as marking perfective aspect and be treated as a sentential operator. In our quasi-logical language it will be convenient to represent this operator as HAVE.

Before we define it, it may be helpful to note that perfective aspect is normally taken to have something to do with perspective. It is widely thought that perfective aspect invokes reference to a time from which a certain event is to be viewed. This interval, i.e., the interval of perspective, can be regarded as constituting a time within which the event is supposed to have occurred. When understood in this way, the interval is sometimes called the 'extended-now', which suggests that perfective aspect is essentially related to speech time, viz, in the form of *now*. Although we do not see perfective aspect as having any special relation to speech time and hence to tense, we nevertheless interpret the interval of perspective as comprehending the supposed event.

To render the idea of perspective we introduce the concept of an anchored interval. Where i and j are intervals, we say that

(104)   i is anchored to j if j is a final segment of i.

Intuitively i constitutes a perspective relative to j and is thus a relative notion. Whether this is as it should be will hopefully become clear in the discussion below. Let us now define the operator HAVE for any context-free sentence A.

(105)   HAVE (A) is true in a model M at (w,i) if there is an interval j which is anchored to i such that for some subinterval k of j A is true in M at (w,k); it is false at (w,i) if there is no j anchored to i such that for some subinterval k of j A is true at (w,k); (and otherwise it is undefined).

Since (105) makes no provision for speech time, it effectively distinguishes perfective aspect from tense. To illustrate the definition, it will be useful to consider aspect together with tense, say in the form of the pluperfect.

(106)   Ben had finished before 9.0.

The logical structure of (106) is to be analyzed as follows.

(107) $PAST_{(v,t)}$[BEFORE 9.0 [HAVE (Ben finish)]].

Working through the definitions again, (107) will be true at (w,i), provided $w = g_c(v)$ and $i = g_c(t)$, if there is a $j < i$ such that

(108)   BEFORE 9.0 [HAVE (Ben finish)]

is true at (w,j); (108) will be true at (w,j) if j is earlier than 9.0 and

(109)   HAVE (Ben finish)

is true at (w,j). Now this obtains if there is a k anchored to j such that for some subinterval l of k

(110)   Ben finish

is true at (w,l). What is interesting here is that no unique perspective is identified from which to view the proposition expressed by (110). Only the range of admissible values of k and j is restricted, viz, to those intervals which precede 9.0. Thus the perspective fixed by k and j will be a variable one.[8]

Where the perspective is less variable is in the present perfect, as in this sentence.

(111)   Ben has finished.

The logical rendering of (111) is,

(112) $\text{PRES}_{(v,t)}[\text{HAVE (Ben finish)}]$

which will be true at (w,i), given that $w = g_c(v)$ and $i = g_c(t)$, if

(109)   HAVE (Ben finish)

is true at (w,i). And this holds if there is a j anchored to i such that for some subinterval k of j

(110)   Ben finish

is true at (w,k). Since j is anchored to i, which here is speech time, the interval of perspective, viz, j, has one of its ends fixed. The other end, however, is variable, which reflects a certain indefiniteness in the perspective. This, we would venture, is just as it should be, i.e., as intuition would have it.

TEMPORAL QUANTIFIERS AND CONNECTIVES

Temporal quantifiers, such as *always, never* and *exactly twice*, will be treated in conformity with the 'standard' structure of temporal modifiers; that is, they will be characterized as sentential operators applying only to context-free sentences. With a view to motivating the envisaged analysis, which is similar to that of the tense operators, let us examine the following sentence.

(113)   Scott always dined at home.

It is clear (113) cannot naturally be interpreted as an unrestricted assertion, i.e., as saying that for the whole of time Scott had the property of dining at home. It must rather be understood as a statement restricted to some intended interval; only of this period is it asserted that he had the property.[9] Depending upon context the intended period might be the one in which Scott lived in Edinburgh, or the one in which he lived at Abbotsford, or perhaps some entirely different interval. Which interval is intended on a given occasion of utterance is a pragmatic matter. However, the role it plays in determining the proposition expressed is a semantic matter, i.e., of the semantic structure of (113). Here there is a question. Is the intended interval to be seen as the referent of some deictic expression revealed at the level of logical form? Or is it to be seen as identified in some non-referential way, say by a 'suppressed' *when* clause?

Let us consider a situation which evokes both possibilities. Suppose that one wanted to make an assertion about Scott's dining habits during the period when he lived at Abbotsford. If the context is sufficient to identify this as the intended interval, one might utter (113) with the intention of asserting that Scott always dined at home during that time. If, on the other hand, the relevant interval is not clear from context, one might opt to be more explicit by uttering this sentence.

(114)   When he lived at Abbotsford, Scott always dined at home.

There may be some uncertainty as to whether (114) expresses the same proposition as (113), but there is no doubt that the propositions are closely related, close enough to make them on occasion 'pragmatically' equivalent. What their exact semantic relation is, however, is not uninteresting.

Indeed, since (113) occurs as the main clause of (114), they can only be analyzed together. Thus if (113) is represented as containing a deictic expression at the level of logical form, (114) must be similarly represented. Such an analysis seems very plausible in the case of (113) but it raises an awkward question with respect to (114). The *when* clause in (114) is typically regarded as specifying the interval over which *always* quantifies. If the deictic in the main clause also serves to identify the intended interval, one of them must be semantically redundant. Given that the deictic is part of the logical form of (113), it seems that the *when* clause may be expendable. While such clauses might be useful for emphasis or clarification, they would have no essential semantic role, which seems a rather curious result.

An alternative approach is to start with the analysis of (114) which intuitively requires no deictic reference to specify the interval over which *always* quantifies. The *when* clause seems sufficient for this purpose and hence can be seen to have an essential semantic role, given that there is no deictic with the same role. But this would imply that there is then no deictic in the analysis of (113). As a result there would arise a need to explain how the intended interval is identified in an utterance of (113). It may be ventured that an utterance of (113) is perhaps elliptical for some more explicit utterance, e.g., (114). Although this idea might be worth exploring, it seems a less plausible proposal than the suggestion that (113) involves deictic reference. It is moreover unnecessary to opt for this more heroic alternative, since the 'deictic' account can be developed in a way which reveals that the *when* clause in (114) is not in fact redundant.

Since (113) is taken to involve deictic reference to an interval over which the quantifier *always* ranges, it is natural to locate it as being part of the quantifier itself. Hence *always* will be represented as a complex sentential operator of the form $ALWAYS_r$, where r is a parameter whose values are intervals assigned from context. Since this operator, like all temporal operators, is taken to apply only to context-free sentences, the logical form of (113) is analyzed by the following formula.[10]

(115) $PAST_{(v,t)}[ALWAYS_r(Scott \, dine \, at \, home)]$.

Before we proceed to define $ALWAYS_r$, let us also consider the logical form of (114). As we said above, there is an inclination to feel that the *when* clause serves to fix the interval over which *always* quantifies. Although the intuition is not without substance, it is somewhat misleading since it tends to obscure the fact that the *when* clause has another independent semantic role.

To specify this role it is necessary to 'factor' tense from the sentences conjoined by *when*. In sentences like (114) the tenses of the conjoined sentences are not independent of each other; they are related by what is sometimes called sequence of tense, which is to say that the sentences must be in the same tense. Since the sentences must also be evaluated conjointly, i.e., relative to the same speech time, they are in a sense semantically bound.[11] We can capture this relationship by 'factoring' past tense from the two constituents and representing it as an operator over the resulting compound. To indicate that *when* is a conjunction, the compound will be given in this form.

(116)   Scott dine at home *when* he live at Abbotsford.

The logical form of (114) may now be analyzed in at least two different ways.

(117) $PAST_{(v,t)}[ALWAYS_r(Scott \, dine \, at \, home \, when \, he \, live \, at \, Abbotsford)]$

(118) $PAST_{(v,t)}[ALWAYS_r(Scott \, dine \, at \, home) \, when \, he \, live \, at \, Abbotsford]$

These might naturally be thought to correspond to two different interpretations of (114).

Suppose that Scott had several different periods of residence at Abbotsford but that one wished to say something about just one of these periods. One could utter (114) with the intention of making an assertion about that particular period, in which case it would be asserted that for every subinterval of that period Scott had the property of dining at home. Clearly it is the dispositional property one would have in mind here, since this can be true of Scott even at times when he is not actually in the process of dining at home.[12] The intended reading of (114) may be taken to be characterized by (118), since it would seem natural to interpret *always* as occurring within the scope of *when*.

The other reading of (114) would interpret the scope relation in reverse; in effect it would take (114) to be equivalent to the following paraphrase.

(119)   Whenever Scott lived at Abbotsford, he dined at home.

Usually one would utter (119) with the intention of attributing to Scott the property of dining at home through each of the intervals during which he was resident at Abbotsford. One might also utter (114) with the same intention and thereby express the same proposition. Here the appropriate analysis seems to be (117), since *always* must be taken to have wider scope relative to *when*. Although (117) and (118) seem appropriate analyses of (114) for the given situations, there is a question as to whether they reflect genuinely distinct interpretations of (114). In fact it remains to be seen whether they really capture any reading of (114). Before we can explore these matters, we shall of course have to define ALWAYS$_r$ and *when*.

To this end we invoke the concept of a cover for an interval. The underlying strategy is to partition an interval into its subintervals so as to consider whether some proposition is true in each of them. Each subinterval of such a partition is to be read as determining a potential instance or case of the proposition's being true. With this in mind we define the concept of a cover for an interval as follows.[13]

(120)   A set of intervals P is a cover for an interval i if the elements of P are mutually distinct (non-overlapping) subintervals of i whose 'sum' is identical to i.

The special significance of a cover will not emerge until we consider the treatment of *when*. In the meantime it may be said that *always* is naturally interpreted as quantifying over intervals and hence it is not inappropriate in invoke the concept of a cover. It is with a view to *when*, however, that we define ALWAYS$_r$ in the following way. As usual we assume A to be any context-free sentence.

(121)   ALWAYS$_r$(A) is true in a model M at (w,i) if i = g_c(r) and there is a cover P of g_c(r) such that for each p in P, A is true in M at (w,p); it is false at (w,i) if i ≠ g_c(r) or there is no such cover; (and otherwise it is undefined).

We can illustrate (121) by unpacking (115), which is the analysis of (113).

(115)   PAST$_{(v,t)}$[ALWAYS$_r$(Scott dine at home)].

This formula will be true at (w,i), provided w = g_c(v) and i = g_c(t), if there is a j < i such that

(122)   ALWAYS$_r$(Scott dine at home)

is true at (w,j), which holds if j = g_c(r) and there is a cover P of g_c(r) such that for each p in P

(123)   Scott dine at home

is true at (w,p). Note that if there is a cover for g_c(r) which verifies (123), then (123) will be true for all the points in r (and vice versa). If (123) is true at (w,p), it will (by the homogeneity condition) be true for every subinterval of p, including the singleton points.

As for the connective *when*, there may be a temptation to think that it just means cotemporal with, but it is easy to see that this is not in general the case. Consider these two sentences.

(124)   When Jocelyn received a letter, she wrote a reply.
(125)   When Jocelyn went on holiday, she notified the police.

Clearly (124) will be true if Jocelyn wrote a reply to each letter she received, even though the reply was written sometime after the time of receipt. Since one typically replies only to those letters one has received (although not always so), the event in the *when* clause is ordinarily taken to precede the event in the main clause. In the case of (125), however, there seems to be a perfectly acceptable interpretation where the event in the *when* clause is taken to come after the event in the main clause. If Jocelyn notified the police before she went on holiday, say to protect her house from burglary, (125) is true.

To accommodate these readings, as well as the preferred interpretaion of (114), we shall distinguish two senses of *when*, the case sense and the cotemporal sense. The former is intended to account for both (124) and (125) while the latter is invoked to explain (114). The case sense of *when* is formulated in the following definition, where A and B are any context-free sentences.

(126)   (A *when* B) is true in a model M at (w,i) if there is a unique

subinterval j of i such that B is true at (w,j) and at least one
subinterval k of i such that A is true at (w,k); it is false at (w,i)
if there are no j and k of i which satisfy the indicated conditions;
(and otherwise it is undefined).

The requirement that an interval uniquely satisfy certain conditions is a
relative notion which we define roughly in this way. Assuming an account
of what it is for an interval to satisfy a set of conditions S, we say that

(127)   An interval j uniquely satisfies S with respect to i if j is a
        subinterval of i which satisfies S, and for any subinterval k of i if
        k satisfies S, k is a subinterval of j.

There are at least two features of the case account of *when*, i.e., as defined
in (126), that should be stressed. First the temporal order of subintervals j
and k is undetermined; it does not matter what the order of precedence is,
nor indeed whether they overlap. Second (A *when* B) is not equivalent to
(B *when* A). To see this it is enough to suppose for some interval i that j
uniquely satisfies B with respect to i and that there are two subintervals k
of i which satisfy A. By (126) (A *when* B) is true at i, but (B *when* A) is
not.

The case sense of *when* is actually the more basic one since the cotemporal
sense can be derived from it by adding the requirement that the subinterval
j be a subinterval of k or, as we shall say, that k subsume j. One may
wonder why k should subsume j and not be identical to it, given that the
point is to capture cotemporality. If the relation between j and k were one
of identity, then (A *when* B) would imply (B *when* A), and this seems
almost as counterintuitive on the cotemporal reading as it is on the case
reading. The stipulation that k subsume j blocks this entailment. For the
sake of completeness we give the full definition below.

(128)   (A *when* B) is true in a model M at (w,i) if there is a unique
        subinterval j of i such that B is true at (w,j) and a subinterval k
        of i such that k subsumes j and A is true at (w,k); it is false in M
        at (w,i) if there are no j and k which satisfy the indicated
        conditions; (and otherwise it is undefined).

It is this definition we shall use in considering the two interpretations of
(114), i.e., the readings associated with (117) and (118). To begin with, it
may be helpful to examine (114) without the quantifier *always*, that is, to
consider this sentence first.

(129)   When he lived at Abbotsford, Scott dined at home.

The logical form of (129) is as follows.

(130)   PAST$_{(v,t)}$(Scott dine at home *when* he live at Abbotsford)

Now (130) will be true at (w,i) if w = g_c(v), i = g_c(t) and there is a j < i such that

(116)   Scott dine at home *when* he live at Abbotsford

is true at (w,j). This will hold if there is a unique subinterval k of j such that

(131)   He live at Abbotsford

is true at (w,k), and a subinterval l of j such that l subsumes k and

(123)   Scott dine at home

is true at (w,l). It should be noted that while the value of k may be the whole of the period during which Scott lived at Abbotsford, it need not be so. What matters is that there is some part of that period during which Scott dined at home. If there is such a part, it is (modulo j) an appropriate value of k, and of course also of l.

It should perhaps be mentioned that the definitions of *when*, i.e., both (126) and (128), are best not construed in terms of events, at least not in general. Although there may be a map from intervals to events, the subintervals distinguished in (126) and (128) will typically map to parts of events; and this may lead to some confusion. Since there is no reference to events in the definitions, there is no need to consider parts of events, nor any overlap relations that may be involved.

Let us now turn back to (114), in particular to the reading putatively represented by (118).

(118)   PAST$_{(v,t)}$[ALWAYS$_r$(Scott dine at home) *when* he live at Abbotsford)]

On the familiar pattern, (118) will be true at (w,i) if w = g_c(v), i = g_c(t) and there is a j < i such that

(132)   ALWAYS$_r$(Scott dine at home) *when* he live at Abbotsford

is true at (w,j). Since ALWAYS$_r$ falls within the scope of *when*, (132) will be true at (w,j) if there is a unique subinterval k of j such that

(131)   He live at Abbotsford

is true at (w,k) and there is a subinterval l of j such that l subsumes k and

(122)   ALWAYS$_r$(Scott dine at home)

is true at (w,l). Here the contextually determined referent of r becomes significant; (122) will be true at (w,l) if l = g_c(r) and there is a cover P of

$g_c(r)$ such that for each p in P

(123)   Scott dine at home

is true at (w,p). This is just to say that (123) must be true throughout $g_c(r)$ since there will be an appropriate cover if and only if this is true.

The role of $g_c(r)$ is semantically pivotal since it picks out the interval of temporal quantification. The *when* clause, in contrast, has no semantic status in determining the past interval referred to; this is fixed solely by the reference of r. Nevertheless, the *when* clause helps to identify the object of reference, since (118) will be true only if $g_c(r)$ is an interval for which Scott lived at Abbotsford. If one intends to tell the truth in uttering (118), one must intend to refer to a past interval satisfying this condition. But of course one may not want to tell the truth or may unintentionally say something false.

There is, however, a 'wrinkle' in (118) which deserves comment. Suppose that $g_c(r)$ is only part of some period in which Scott lived at Abbotsford. Suppose that during that subinterval Scott always dined at home but that for some other subinterval of the period he did not do so. Now if one utters (114) intending to refer to the former subinterval, one would be represented by (118) as saying something true. But can (114) be uttered felicitously in such a situation, (118) notwithstanding?

We would say that it can if the context is right. Imagine a situation in which one is in a discussion about Scott's daily habits, say, during the period in which he was writing Waverley. Suppose that one wishes to say of some part of that period that he had the habit of dining at home. If that subinterval is contained as a part of an interval during which Scott resided at Abbotsford, one might locate the intended subinterval for one's audience by uttering (114): the combination of the *when* clause and the context might well serve to identify the relevant subinterval. One's assertion would be restricted, as intended, to just that part of the time during which Scott lived at Abbotsford.

Although it seems possible to use (114) in this way, one will more typically utter it with the intention of referring to the whole of an interval for which Scott lived at Abbotsford. Nevertheless, there is no semantic requirement that one do so. One may refer to just a part of such an interval and may also refer to a more comprehensive interval. Here we turn to the second interpretation of (114), i.e., the one associated with (117).

(117) $PAST_{(v,t)}[ALWAYS_r(Scott$ dine at home *when* he live at Abbotsford)].

As usual (117) will be true at (w,i) if $w = g_c(v)$, $i = g_c(t)$ and there is some $j < i$ such that

(133)   ALWAYS$_r$(Scott dine at home *when* he live at Abbotsford)

is true at (w,j). In contrast. to (132), ALWAYS$_r$ has scope over *when* in
(133). Thus (133) will be true at (w,j) if j = g_c(r) and there is a cover P of
g_c(r) such that for each p in P

(116)   Scott dine at home *when* he live at Abbotsford

is true at (w,p). Here the contextual assignment to r will normally be some
significant stretch of past time in which there may be several distinct periods
of residence at Abbotsford. Given a cover P, (116) will be true at each
(w,p) if there is a unique subinterval k of p such that

(131)   He live at Abbotsford

is true at (w,k) and a subinterval l of p subsuming k such that

(123)   Scott dine at home

is true at (w,l). What this means is that for each interval p of the cover
there must be a unique instance of Scott's living at Abbotsford throughout
which he had the habit of dining at home. If there is a cover of g_c(r) meeting
these conditions, then (117) is true.

It is important to stress that g_c(r) does not necessarily embrace all the
intervals during which Scott was resident at Abbotsford. One might utter
(114), or alternatively,

(119)   Whenever he lived at Abbotsford, Scott dined at home

without intending to make an assertion about all the periods in which Scott
lived at Abbotsford. One might wish to invoke only some particular subset
of these periods. In the event one's assertion would be restricted to this
interval.[14] The restriction here is similar to that noted above in connection
with (118).

We have still to resolve whether (114) really has two distinctions interpretations, one identified by (117) and the other by (118). The issue might
be seen to hinge on the intended value of r, viz, on g_c(r). If one intends to
refer to an interval throughout which Scott lived at Abbotsford, then (118)
seems to give the appropriate reading. On the other hand, if one intends
to refer to an interval which comprehends several distinct instances of
Scott's living at Abbotsford, then (117) seems to be the right rendering.
The fact is, however, that for any particular g_c(r) (118) entails (117).
Although the converse does not hold, it may be argued that (117) uniquely
represents the logical form of (114). No matter what the intended assignment to r, (117) is sufficient to capture the truth conditions. Moreover, it
may be ventured that there is something curious about distinguishing two
senses of (114) simply on the basis of different kinds of assignment to r.

We shall not pursue the issue further, except to say that the correct conclusion remains undecided.

Before we leave the semantics of *when*, it might be useful to examine a sentence where the case reading is appropriate, particularly one that involves *always*.

(134)   When she went away, Jocelyn always phoned the police.

For the purpose of illustration let us restrict our attention to the reading whose logical form is represented in this way.

(135) $PAST_{(v,t)}[ALWAYS_r(Jocelyn$ phone the policy *when* she go away)]

The case interpretation of *when* allows for any ordering between the intervals of Jocelyn's going away and her phoning the police: the former might precede the latter, or succeed it, or overlap it to some degree. With *when* so read, (134) expresses the proposition that for some designated past interval there is at least one case of Jocelyn's phoning the police for each case of her going away. This emerges clearly from the truth conditions of (135), which is true at (w,i) only if there is some $j < i$ such that

(136) $ALWAYS_r(Jocelyn$ phone the police *when* she go away)

is true at (w,j). And (136) is true at (w,j) if $j = g_c(r)$ and there is a cover P of $g_c(r)$ such that for each p in P

(137)   Jocelyn phone the police *when* she go away

is true at (w,p). Here we invoke the case definition of *when*, viz, the one given in (126). According to (126), (137) will be true at (w,p) if there is a unique subinterval k of p such that

(138)   She go away

is true at (w,k) and at least one subinterval l of p such that

(139)   Jocelyn phone the police

is true at (w,l).

Jocelyn might well have had the habit of phoning the police more than once for each occasion of her going away. Perhaps she was never confident whether the initial call was noted and always phoned a second time to be sure. Let us suppose that the following was the case.

(140)   When she went away, Jocelyn always phoned the police exactly twice.

The quantifier *exactly twice* will be treated very similar to *always*; it will be represented as involving a deictic parameter and as quantifying over a cover. The definition goes as follows, with *exacly twice* represented as TWICE!$_r$.

(141)   TWICE!$_r$(A) is true in a model M at (w,i) if i = g_c(r) and there is a cover P of g_c(r) such that for exactly two elements p_1 and p_2 in P A is true at (w,p_1) and (w,p_2) and for any other cover Q of g_c(r) and element q of Q if A is true at (w,q) then q is a subinterval of either p_1 or p_2; it is false at (w,i) if i $\neq$ g_c(r) or there is no cover P satisfying the indicated conditions; (and otherwise it is undefined).

To characterize the logical form (140) one must bear in mind that each of the temporal quantifiers has its own deictic parameter. It is clear, moreover, that the parameters are not to be given the same assignment since there is a significant scope relation; that is, *exactly twice* must be read as occurring within the scope of *always*. In effect the deictic parameter of *exactly twice* must be interpreted relative to the elements over which *always* quantifies.

We have seen an analogous situation with regard to the scoping of tenses, i.e., in respect of tense iteration. To represent such iteration on our approach it is necessary to invoke the quantifier G, and this is just what is required here. The logical form of (140) is thus given by the following formula.[15]

(142)   PAST$_{(v,t)}$[ALWAYS [Gr'[TWICE!$_r$(Jocelyn phone the police) *when* she go away]]]

As usual (142) will be true at (w,i) only if there is a j < i such that

(143)   ALWAYS$_r$[Gr'[TWICE!$_r$(Joscelyn phone the police) *when* she go away]]

is true at (w,j). This will obtain if j = g_c(r) and there is a cover P of g_c(r) such that for each p in P

(144)   Gr'[TWICE!$_r$(Jocelyn phone the police) *when* she go away]

is true at (w,p). Since G has widest scope here, (144) will be true at (w,p) if

(145)   TWICE!$_{p*}$(Jocelyn phone the police) *when* she go away

is true at (w,p), which will hold if there is a unique subinterval k of p such that

(138)   She go away

is true at (w,k), and at least one subinterval l of p such that l = p and there is a cover Q of p for which there are exactly two subintervals m and n of p where

(139)   Jocelyn phone the police

is true at (w,m) and (w,n). What all this amounts to can be summarized as follows: (142) is true at i (modulo w) if there is some past interval j where each case of Jocelyn's going away is matched with exactly two cases of her phoning the police. Clearly this is just what (140) means on one of its interpretations.[16]

Finally we turn to the quantifier *never*. It was noted earlier that sentences involving the connective *not* can sometimes be paraphrased using *never*. In fact there is an inclination to conjecture that they may actually be so close in meaning as to make the difference semantically uninteresting. With a view to pursuing this, let us define *never*. Where A is any context-free sentence,

(146)   NEVER$_r$(A) is true in a model M at (w,i) if i = g$_c$(r) and there is no cover P of g$_c$(r) such that for some p in P A is true in M at (w,p); it is false at (w,i) if i $\neq$ g$_c$(r) or there is a cover P of g$_c$(r) such that for some p in P A is true at (w,p); (and otherwise it is undedefined).

By way of illustration consider the sentence,

(147)   Sally never stayed at the Savoy when she went to London

whose logical form is represented in the following way.

(148)   PAST$_{(v,t)}$[NEVER$_r$(Sally stay at the Savoy *when* she go to London)]

This formula will be true at (w,i) only if there is a j < i such that

(149)   NEVER$_r$(Sally stay at the Savoy *when* she go to London)

is true at (w,j), which will hold if j = g$_c$(r) and there is no cover P of g$_c$(r) such that for some p in P

(150)   Sally stay at the Savoy *when* she go to London

is true at (w,p). On the case reading of *when* this obtains if there is no unique subinterval k of p such that

(151)   She go to London

is true at (w,k), or any subinterval l of p such that

(152)   Sally stay the Savoy

is true at (w,l). In effect (148) will be true only if there are no cases in g$_c$(r) where Sally went to London and stayed at the Savoy.

Although there is undoubtedly a difference between *never* and *not*, it is interesting to consider the sentence which results from (147) by replacing *never* by *not*.

(153)   Sally did not stay at the Savoy *when* she went to London.

Significantly (153) can be used in either of two ways. It can be uttered with the intention of making an assertion about Sally's habit when she went to London, in which case its logical form would be rendered in this way.

(154)   *Not* [PAST$_{(v,t)}$(Sally stay at the Savoy *when* she go to London)]

The import of (154) is equivalent to (148) if the assignment to r is the whole of the past relative to the time of speech. On the other hand, (153) can also be used with the intention of making an assertion about some particular occasion on which Sally went to London. To render the resulting proposition in terms of *not* it is necessary to invoke a 'suppressed' time reference, which (as above) is represented by the time adverbial *at then*. The desired formula is the following

(155)   PAST$_{(v,t)}$[*Not* [AT then (Sally stay at the Savoy)] *when* she go to London)]

In (155) *when* has wider scope relative to both *not* and AT *then*.

An alternative way of characterizing the same proposition can be formulated in terms of NEVER$_r$, viz, in this way.

(156)   PAST$_{(v,t)}$[NEVER$_r$(Sally stay at the Savoy) *when* she go to London]

Here *when* has scope over NEVER$_r$. Given that $g_c(r)$ coincides with some period in which Sally went to London, (156) says that Sally never stayed at the Savoy during that period. This is just what (155) says if the referent of *then* meets the conditions on $g_c(r)$. In fact when the referent of *then* is identical to $g_c(r)$, (155) and (156) are equivalent.

This is not to say of course that one can always substitute *never* for *not salva congruitate*. It does suggest, however, that where propositions are represented in terms of both negation and time reference they can always be recharacterized in terms of NEVER$_r$. This may not be linguistically significant, but it is of some semantic importance.

Although we have only examined one temporal connective, viz, *when*, it should be clear how we would proceed to treat other cases, in particular *before* and *after*. The definition of *after* will be straightforward since it seems to have just one meaning which is strictly temporal in character. In the case of *before*, however, the situation is rather different. While it has a temporal sense which can be defined in the manner of *after*, it seems also to have a modal sense which emerges in this sentence.

(157)   Max stopped the car before he hit the tree.

Since (157) implies that Max did not hit the tree, it is clear that *before* does not have the same existential import that *after* does. That is, the sentence

(158)   Max stopped the car after he hit the tree

can only be interpreted as implying that Max hit the tree. The question then is how to formulate the modal sense of *before*. It is not inconceivable that *before* may only have a modal sense. For those 'special' cases where it has existential import, the reasons may be non-logical: it may be due to lexical features, or contextual factors, or perhaps something entirely different. In any case there is an issue here which we must leave for another time.

OBLIQUE CONTEXTS AND THE SUBJUNCTIVE

Davidson has suggested that the logical form of sentences of indirect discourse, e.g.,

(159)   Galileo said that the earth moves

should be understood in terms of two sentences which are related paratactically, in this case the sentences

(160)   Galileo said that

and

(161)   The earth moves.

The expression *that* in (160) has the status of a demonstrative pronoun which in utterances of (159) is used to refer to the utterance of (161). Since (161) occurs as part of (159) it is not itself asserted. What is asserted is (160), with the utterance of (161) serving to identify what Galileo said. One who utters (161) as part of (159) represents himself as being a samesayer with Galileo. That is, Galileo is given to have uttered some sentence in his language, Italian or Latin, whose purport is the same as one's own utterance of (161).

Let us suppose that sameness of purport consists in expressing the same proposition.[17] The question then is what proposition does (160) attribute to Galileo. On our Russellian theory an utterance of (161), when it stands as an independent sentence, expresses a value-specific proposition, i.e., one which is true at most of the time of utterance. Since the past tense in this context engenders reference to speech time, the utterance amounts to an assertion about that time and must be true of it if it is to be true at all. When (161) stands as part of (159), however, its utterance will have a rather different relation to the time of speech. Plainly there can be no reference to the present speech time if the utterance is to express the same proposition which was expressed by Galileo. Since Galileo will have referred to his speech time, one can be a samesayer with him only if one refers to that time. If one does so refer in uttering (161), it may seem that one would express the same proposition as he did. This must of course be a value-specific proposition, at least according to our theory.

But can such a proposition be a suitable relatum for the relation of saying? To be more precise, can the occurrence of *said* in the utterance of

(160)   Galileo said that

be interpreted as a relation between Galileo and some value-specific proposition? To see that it cannot be one need only consider another contingent sentence, say

(162)   The moon has craters

and suppose that it happens to be uttered with respect to the same speech time as (161). Given that both utterances are true of this time, they will express the same value-specific proposition (modulo a common reference to possible world). In fact there are just two such propositions possible here, one that evaluates to true only for the interval of utterance and the other that evaluates to false for all intervals. If one takes all the utterances uttered simultaneously with Galileo's utterance (regardless of who may have done the uttering), all the true utterances will express one value-specific proposition and all the false ones the another. Hence any relation Galileo sustains to one true utterance he also sustains to the others, and similarly for any false utterance. Clearly value-specific propositions are not appropriate relata for saying, since they cannot discriminate among the different things that may be said. The same is obviously true in the case of all propositional attitudes.

From the viewpoint of our theory it is significant that oblique contexts, such as the one formed by *Galileo said that*, do not allow contained sentences to be asserted. No utterance of (159) can give rise to an assertion of (161). Davidson's analysis of (159) does not explain why this is so. Since he represents (161) as having the status of an independent sentence which is related paratactically to (160), he portrays it as having an occurrence suitable for assertion. The fact that the occurrence is plainly otherwise is a fact that stands against his analysis. If one amends the analysis by supposing that (160) and (161) are connected more than paratactically, it seems possible to explain why (161) is not assertable. On the assumption that (161) occurs as a genuine contained formula in (159), one can say that in such contexts there can be no appropriate reference, i.e., of the sort that occurs when (161) is uttered as a main clause. Assertion requires reference to the actual world and to speech time and thus, it is natural to trace the unassertability of (161) to the impossibility of appropriate reference. Where there can be no reference to both the actual world and time of utterance, there can be no assertion. The point to note is that if there were such reference in uttering (161), it would express a value-specific proposition, which is something we have just seen to be unacceptable in the context.

How then is (161) to be represented when it occurs as part of (159)? The answer is foreshadowed in the treatment of the tense operators. As such operators can apply only to context-free formulas, so (161) will require a context-free rendering when it occurs in an oblique position. Given that the subordinate verb *moves* falls within the scope of the main verb *said*, (161) must be characterized as follows.

(163) $Gv',t'[PRES_{(v',t')}(\text{the earth move})]$

Recall that (163) expresses a value-free proposition which may be true at indices other than the index of utterance. Note moreover that the 'context-free' rendering of (162), viz,

(164) $Gv',t'[PRES_{(v',t')}(\text{the moon have craters})]$

expresses a different value-free proposition. Even if (163) and (164) both happen to be true at the time of utterance, they will not always be true together and hence do not express the same proposition. Since this is the sort of propositional discrimination required for oblique contexts, it is natural to think that value-free propositions are proper objects for the attitudes.

At this point it seems not unreasonable to abandon Davidson's approach to (159). Indeed it now seems right to analyze (159) in the obvious way, with (161) taken as a genuine subordinate clause. While we agree that *said*, or rather *say*, is to be interpreted as a relation, we take *that* to be a propositional operator which creates a name; the result of applying *that* to a formula is a name which refers to the proposition expressed by that formula. Thus the logical form of (159) is represented as follows.

(165) $PAST_{(v,t)}[\text{Galileo say that } [Gv',t'[PRES_{(v',t')}(\text{the earth move})]]]]$

Here *that* applies to the formula (163) to name the value-free proposition expressed by (163). It should be noted that both occurrences of the tense operators apply to context-free formulas, i.e., to formulas which contain no occurrences of the parameters v and t.[18]

On this approach to indirect discourse it emerges that sentences are not semantically innocent, even though their subcomponents may be. An utterance of the sentence,

(161)   The earth moves

will express a different kind of proposition depending upon the linguistic context in which the sentence occurs. It will express a value-specific prop-osition if the sentence stands as a main clause, but when it is embedded in an oblique context, as in (159), it will express a value-free proposition. This would suggest a rather paradoxical situation: it may appear impossible to report what someone said through indirect discourse. The 'feeling' of paradox seems most tangible in this sentence.

(166)   The moon has craters and I said that the moon has craters.

Anyone who utters (166) would seem not to be a samesayer with himself, since his two utterances of

(162)   The moon has craters

will express different propositions.

The paradox, however, is more apparent than real. There is an inclination to suppose that the proposition one expresses in uttering (162) must be what one says. After all there is a long philosophical tradition which would hold just that. Nevertheless, it is still possible to draw a distinction between what one says and the proposition expressed. Since the concept of a proposition is a technical term, it can be defined as one chooses. We choose to define it in a way which implies that it cannot always be identified with what is said. On our analysis one who utters (162) expresses a value-specific proposition whose status is closely related to the truth value of the utterance. If the utterance is true for the index of utterance, it expresses one of the two possible value-specific propositions for that index, viz, the one which is true for that index alone. If the utterance is false, it expresses the universally false value-specific proposition, i.e., the proposition which is false for all indices. The content of one's utterance is plainly not given by either of these propositions.

We take its content to be given by the value-free proposition expressed by the following formula.

(164) $Gv',t'[PRES_{(v',t'))}(\text{the moon have craters})]$

What one says in uttering (162) is distinguished, not by its truth value, but by its content, and this is discriminated by (164). Hence if one wishes to report what one says in such an utterance, one must invoke the value-free proposition expressed by (164). If one wishes to report more, e.g., that what one says is true, one must refer to the index of utterance. This requires an explicit reference, which is not found in (159).

Certain tense phenomena lend support to the view that oblique contexts are not semantically innocent. The 'relational' import of tenses in oblique contexts is not always the same as their import in main clauses. Take this sentence.

(167)   Someone will say that Bush was a great President.

If one were to utter (167) today (17th May 1986), one would naturally intend the complement sentence,

(168)   Bush was a great President

to be understood as saying something about the future relative to some later time in the future. One would at least not wish to be taken as saying something about the past relative to the present time, not unless there were some misapprehension. Note that the future time relative to which (168) is to be interpreted is indeterminate; it is just some time in the future. If one wishes to make the time definite, say 17th May 2000, one could modify (167) as follows.

(169)   Someone will say on 17th May 2000 that Bush was a great President.

It is important to appreciate that the indicated future time cannot be fixed from within the subordinate position itself, i.e., in this way.

(170)   Someone will say that Bush was a great President on 17th May 2000.

In fact there is no way of modifying the contained occurrence of (168) to refer to the time relative to which it is to be considered. When (168) stands as a main clause, however, there is no avoiding such a reference since it must be the time of speech. This strongly suggests that (168) does not occur innocently in (167).

In this connection it may be mentioned that the tenses in (167) should not be seen as iterated. Since the future tense occurs in the main clause and the past tense in the complement clause, the two cannot be rendered at the level of logical form as a 'prenex' prefix to any formula. The relation between the tenses is not really a matter of logical scope but of the linguistic contexts within which the tenses occur. The tense of the subordinate sentence is a significant constituent of the relatum of the main verb and thus, its relation to the tense of the main verb is not strictly a relation of iteration.

We are now able to speculate about what is semantically characteristic of subjunctive sentences, e.g., of occurrences like (168) in (167). Subjunctive sentences may be typically marked for tense (though perhaps not always so), but they are not sensitive to the time of speech, as indicative sentences are. In this respect they may be said to be semantically untensed. Accordingly the logical form of a subjunctive sentence will never have occurrences of both context parameters v and t and hence will always be represented as expressing a value-free proposition.

ACKNOWLEDGEMENTS

For many valuable discussions, suggestions and criticisms I should like to thank the members of the Tense and Discourse Workshop in Edinburgh, in particular Ewan Klein, David McCarty, Marc Moens, Jon Oberlander, Mark Steedman, Lesley Stirling, Jan de Vuyst and Henk Zeevat. I should also like to thank Kit Fine and Dana Scott for a number of useful suggestions. I am particularly grateful to Marc Moens for his generous efforts in helping to improve the final draft. Needless to say, none but myself are responsible for the remaining deficiencies.

NOTES

[1] The semantic theory suggests that tenses and temporal quantifiers should be grouped into one class and time adverbials grouped into another class.

[2] Some have argued that (18) and (19) are not to be seen as differing in this way. The propositions they express do not diverge at the point of utterance, since they always express the same proposition. Where (18) and (19) differ is in respect of a certain conversational convention. There is a general convention that when one utters a tensed sentence, one offers the proposition expressed as being true for the interval of utterance. Thus when one utters (19), one commits oneself by convention to the claim that the proposition expressed by (19) (and also by (18) is true at the time of speech. One does not actually assert this to be so, either by referring to the given time or in any other way. If one did, the proposition expressed by (19) would then be different from the proposition expressed by (18), which it is said not to be. Hence one can only be taken to implicate the intended state of affairs in some indirect sort of way. By eschewing reference to speech time such a view coincides with the Priorian perspective. While it may seem appropriate here to venture a counterargument, we prefer to let the counterargument emerge as a 'byproduct' of developing our Russellian alternative. If this theory is seen to explain a wide variety of complex phenomena, no further argument may be necessary.

[3] It is important to appreciate that the context sensitive parameters, viz, v and t, serve to identify the intended index of evaluation. Their role is actually fixed in the definitions of the tense operators, which follow immediately. While v and t receive their assignments from context, they are not the only parameters that do so. They are, however, the only parameters to be styled as context-sensitive, i.e., according to (26).

[4] It should be noted that for fixed values of v and t (28) and (29) always give rise to intensions which are total functions, hence the reason for the parentheses. This suggests that tenses, and perhaps other devices of temporal quantification, may characteristically determine total functions. In the event it may be possible to distinguish a class of 'temporal' propositions.

[5] For an alternative treatment see Kamp (1971).

[6] Here we see the reason for introducing possible worlds into the model theory.

[7] There is a natural disposition to read (53) either as saying something about the future, viz, about what Sandy will do at 9.0, or as saying something about Sandy's current habits, i.e., his habit of phoning at 9.0. But (53) may also be read as identifying a current event, although perhaps less naturally.

[8] Below we shall consider the interaction of perfective aspect and temporal

quantifiers like *exactly twice*. Tichy (1985) has argued that an interval approach to the semantics of temporal expressions, such as we propose, may not yield a satisfactory characterization.

[9] Plainly it is a dispositional property that is relevant here.

[10] It should be noted that the occurrence of the parameter r in

(i) ALWAYS$_r$(Scott dine at home)

does not make (i) context-sensitive in the technical sense, i.e., according to definition (26).

[11] The following sentence is not really a counterexample.

(i) When he leaves, Max will be happy.

From a semantic point of view the *when* clause is plainly about the future which agrees with the future tense in the main clause. This would be reflected at the level of logical form.

[12] Dispositional properties are typically involved in sentences like (114). In fact the attribution of non-dispositional properties seems to be the special case.

[13] Intuitively the 'sum' of P is given by the idea that if all the elements of P are matched with their place in i, the result is exactly i. It should be noted that a cover may consist of both closed and open intervals; this will be the case for any cover of a real interval.

[14] A more compelling example is perhaps the following.

(i) When he travelled by bus, Franky always took a flask of gin.

Plainly *always* is not naturally read as quantifying over all the cases of Franky's travelling by bus. What he did as a child is irrelevant. But what he did during some interval of his adult life may well be topical, depending upon the context and the intentions of the speaker.

[15] Note that r' is a variable rather than a parameter.

[16] Tichy (1985) has suggested that an interval semantics will find it difficult, if not impossible, to provide an adequate analysis of temporal quantifiers like *exactly twice* while at the same time giving an appropriate rendering of both perfective aspect and adverbials like *yesterday*. It is worth noting, therefore, that the following two sentences seem to be adequately characterized within the present framework.

(i) Jocelyn has visited London exactly twice.
(ii) Jocelyn went to London exactly twice yesterday.

The logical forms of (i) and (ii) are given respectively by these formulas.

(iii) PRES$_{(v,t)}$[HAVE[TWICE! (Jocelyn visit London)]]
(iv) PAST$_{(v,t)}$[TWICE!$_r$[ON yesterday (Jocelyn go to London)]]

To see that (iii) and (iv) result in the intended truth conditions it is essential to appreciate that the value of the parameter is determined contextually in both cases. Its value is $g_c(r)$ and is fixed, as it were, from the beginning, i.e., before the operators are 'peeled off'. In (iv) the intended value of r is yesterday. With the help of lambda abstraction any ambiguity could be removed. Since the verification is straightforward, we shall leave the exercise to the reader.

[17] Although Davidson eschews reference to propositions, it is useful here to set this aside.

[18] See definitions (26) and (27).

REFERENCES

Davidson, D., On Saying That. *Synthese*, 1975, **19**, 130–146.

Dowty, D., *Word, Meaning and Montague Grammar*. Dordrecht: Reidel, 1979.

Heny, F., Tense, Aspect and Time Adverbials II. *Linguistics and Philosophy*, 1982, **5**, 109–154.

Kamp, J. A. W., Formal Properties of "Now". *Theoria*, 1971, **37**, 227–273.

Kamp, H. & Rohrer, C., Tense in Texts. In Baeuerle, Schwarze, and von Stechow (Eds), *Meaning, Use and Interpretation of Language*. Berlin: Walter de Gruyter, 1983, pp. 250–269.

Lewis, D., Adverbs of quantification. In E. L. Keenan (Ed), *Formal Semantics of Natural Language*. Cambridge: Cambridge University Press, 1975, pp. 3–15.

Prior, A. N., *Past, Present and Future*. Oxford: Clarendon, 1967.

Reichenbach, H., *Elements of Symbolic Logic*. New York: The Free Press, 1947 (reprint 1966).

Richards, B., Tense, Aspect and Time Adverbials I. *Linguistics and Philosophy*, 1982, **5**, 59–107.

Russell, B., *The Principles of Mathematics*. Cambridge: Cambridge University Press, 1903.

Taylor, B., Tense and Continuity. *Linguistics and Philosophy*, 1977, **1**, 199–220.

Tichy, P., The Logic of Temporal Discourse. *Linguistics and Philosophy*, 1980, **3**, 343–369.

Tichy, P., Do We Need Interval Semantics? *Linguistics and Philosophy*, 1985, **8**, 263–282.

Vendler, Z., Verbs and Times. In Z. Vendler (Ed) *Linguistics in Philosophy*. Ithaca, NY: Cornell University Press, 1967, pp. 97–121.

12

Problems in the Representation of the Logical Form of Generics, Plurals, and Mass Nouns

LENHART K. SCHUBERT
FRANCIS JEFFRY PELLETIER

Department of Computing Science
University of Alberta

INTRODUCTION

We wish to discuss some problems involved in representing the 'logical form' of sentences whose subjects are generics, (bare) plurals and mass terms. We shall not here have much to say about the syntax of such sentences, except occasionally to refer to such (arguably) syntactic features as [±stative]. We shall also not get embroiled in such issues as exactly what information should be counted as part of the 'logical form' of a sentence in general. We will, for example, remain agnostic on the question of the proper place for (Montague-style) meaning postulates, the proper place for Quantifier Raising, and the proper place for the representation of certain ambiguities involving quantifiers and other logical operations. Instead, our concern is with the final representation of certain natural language sentences, a representation which is immediately correlated with the truth conditions of the original sentence. We take this to be more-or-less first-order quantification theory augmented with certain operators, but feel free to bring in Montagovian intensional logic, expecially when discussing those

385

theorists who make it central in their account. To give a feel for what level our concerns lie at, consider

(1)   (a)   Whales are mammals

Now, there are many 'levels of representation' that different theorists have proposed for such a sentence. Our concern is with such representations as[1]

(1)   (b)   (∀x: whale(x)) mammal(x)
(1)   (c)   **mammal'('whale')**

Or, if one prefers, rather than with these representations, we are concerned with the explicit truth conditions. We merely employ these symbolic forms as a convenient device to exhibit various properties such as scope and the interpretation of English quantifiers. Nothing we say is restricted to those interested in 'logic-like' logical form—the problems we shall discuss are applicable to any theory which claims that there is *some* semantic interpretation to be ascribed to the sorts of English sentences under consideration here.

As we indicated, our concern is with generics, bare plurals and mass terms. Yet, as we shall see, their interactions with quantifiers, time and frequency adverbials, and numerical modifiers are quite complex, interesting in their own right, and can contribute strong reasons for preferring some accounts of the logical form of generics, etc, over others. Our strategy here will be this. First we shall give a list of general problems with generic sentences, a series of problems about which we will have next to nothing to say. Then we will give the 'fundamental intuition' which motivates our thoughts on 'the problem of generics'. After this, we will present 'the simpleminded view'—a view many of us immediately jump to when challenged to account for the fundamental intuition. (No linguist we know of has ever propounded the simpleminded view, although it is unthinkingly expounded by authors of elementary logic textbooks, even sophisticated authors). The simpleminded view *is* simpleminded, and we present a series of (traditional and not-so-traditional) problems for it. We would wish next to move on to 'the sophisticated view', championed in the past 10 years or so by such writers as G. Carlson (1977, 1977a, 1979, 1982, 1985), Chierchia (1982a, 1982b), Farkas & Sugioka (1983), Enç (1981), Hinrichs (1985), and ter Meulen (1985). However, to explain this view adequately, we need first to give some background and so we provide a very general overview to Montague/Gazdar grammars and the associated intensional logic representation of the semantics of natural languages. This section can be skipped by anyone who has even a modicum of acquaintance with these theories. This sophisticated view, however, also suffers from lack of detail and also, importantly, seems unable to correctly capture the facts of cases just slightly more complicated than those that gave us the fundamental intuition. Along the way we consider some more recalcitrant facts about the interaction of generics, plurals and mass terms with certain temporal and adverbial phrases. Finally we shall make a few proposals which appear to be useful in analyzing and giving appropriate logical forms to the type of constructions under consideration.

SOME GENERAL PROBLEMS WITH GENERICS

(A) What *causes* a sentence to be generic?
    (1) Is genericality indicated by some element in surface structure?
    (2) Is genericality carried by a feature on NPs? On VPs? On AUX? Is it some kind of agreement feature? Is it a matter for syntax to decide? Semantics? Pragmatics (whatever that is)?

(B) What is the relation amongst sentences like
    (i)   Snakes are reptiles
    (ii) A snake is a reptile
    (iii) The snake is a reptile
    (iv) Any snake is a reptile

(C) What is the relationship between generic sentences and 'habitual' sentences? Is
    (i)   Sammy smokes cigars
a generic sentence?

(D) Are mathematical (etc) truths generic sentences?

(E) What is the interaction between generics and tenses?
    (i)   Dogs bark (generic?)
    (ii) Dogs barked (non-generic?)

(F) If all babies ever born in Rainbow Lake, Alberta, happened to be right handed, would the generic sentence
    (i)   Babies born in Rainbow Lake, Alberta, are right handed
be true?

(G) Consider the generic sentences
    (i)   Snakes are reptiles
    (ii)   Telephone books are thick books
    (iii) Guppies give live birth
    (iv) Italians are good skiers
    (v)   Frenchmen eat horsemeat
    (vi) Unicorns have one horn

Obviously, we understand the truth of (i)–(vi) as calling for different relative numbers of instances of the subject terms satisfying the predicate term. In (i) it is all; in (ii) most; in (iii) some subset of the females (=less than half); in (iv) some small percentage, but a greater percentage than other countries; in (v), quite possibly a very small percentage—somehow, from the vantage point of North America, the mere fact of its happening at all is striking; and in (vi) no unicorns have one horn.

(H) Is there a 'reading' of these sentences which is generic?
    (i) This car is guaranteed against rust for 5 years
    (ii) Every car in this lot is made in nine different countries

We do not have definitive answers to these questions. Indeed, we shall not discuss these matters directly at all, although partial answers to some of them will be implicit in our discussion of various proposals, including our own tentative proposals in the last section. (This is not to be taken as our thinking these to be unimportant matters. In fact we think them of the utmost importance in the topics, but our interests here are somewhat more specialized.) Our interests instead have to do with the logical form (of the sort described earlier) of certain kinds of sentences—or, more precisely, with the distinction in logical form between two types of sentences containing bare plural and bare mass nouns. It is 'the fundamental intuition' that some of these sentences are gnomic while others are not which motivates our discussion here. Thus, (1a), (Bi), (Ei), (Eii), (Fi), and all the (G) sentences are of direct concern to us; whereas (Bii)–(Biv), (Ci), (Hi), and (Hii) are not. Of course (Bii) and (Biii) *are* generic sentences, as (arguably) is one 'reading' of both (Hi) and (Hii), and many of our comments will bear on such sentences indirectly, providing that one has a way to tell when the subject noun phrases are being 'used generically'.

THE FUNDAMENTAL INTUITION

Intuitively, the subjects of the (a) sentences in (2)–(5) appear to generalize over 'kinds' ('species', 'generic entities', 'types'), while the subjects of the (b) sentences appear to refer to (some) particular 'instance(s)' ('realizations', 'manifestations', 'parts') of those kinds.

(2) (a) Snakes are reptiles
    (b) Snakes are in my garden
(3) (a) Snow is white
    (b) Snow is falling

(4) (a) Dogs are loyal
    (b) Dogs are barking
(5) (a) Children are persons
    (b) Children are present

The logico–linguistic problem is to (i) describe the difference and (ii) find a systematic method of generating the different logical forms (or of giving the different truth conditions).

THE SIMPLEMINDED SOLUTION

At first blush this difference might be supposed to be that the (a)-subjects involve implicit universal quantification while the (b)-subjects involve implicit existential quantification.

(2′) (a) ($\forall$x: snake(x))reptile(x)
     (b) ($\exists$x: snake(x))In(my garden,x)
(3′) (a) ($\forall$x: snow(x))white(x)
     (b) ($\exists$x: snow(x))falling(x)
(4′) (a) ($\forall$x: dog(x))loyal(x)
     (b) ($\exists$x: dog(x))barking(x)
(5′) (a) ($\forall$x: child(x))person(x)
     (b) ($\exists$x: child(x))present(x)

There are a number of difficulties with the simpleminded view. Many of these difficulties have been pointed out by a number of authors, and so we shall only mention them briefly. (Cf, among others, Vendler, 1967; Jackendoff, 1972; Lawler, 1972; Nunberg & Pan, 1975; Dahl, 1975; Lyons, 1977; Carlson, 1977, 1982). For the most part we will concentrate on some issues not usually mentioned.

For one thing, while (3a) and (4a) are intuitively true even in the presence of some dirty snow and some disloyal dogs, (3′a) and (4′a) would be false. Furthermore, when the subject is a mass term, as in (3a), it is not even clear that the quantification makes sense—what *are* the values of x in *snow(x)*? Also, if one were to assume that the (a) sentences are universal and the (b) ones existential, what would we make of certain conjoined predicates, relative clauses, or anaphoric relations like

(6) Snakes, which are reptiles, are in my garden
(7) Snow is white and is falling throughout Alberta
(8) Dogs are noisy animals and are barking outside right now
(9) Although children are not interested in linguistics, *they* are often present at linguistics conferences

Moreover, neither a universal nor an existential 'reading' yields an acceptable interpretation in cases like

    (10)   Water is scarce/abundant
    (11)   Water is a scarce commodity/an abundant liquid
    (12)   Dogs are man's best friend
    (13)   Dinosaurs are extinct

If one were to stipulate a semantic interpretation radically distinct from the universal and existential we again are led to difficulties for sentences with compound predicates such as

    (14)   Water is an abundant liquid and is transparent
    (15)   Water is an abundant, transparent liquid
    (16)   Dogs are loyal and are man's best friend
    (17)   Dinosaurs are extinct but used to live in Alberta
    (18)   Gold is scarce but can be found in my teeth

Furthermore, providing a consistent account of anaphoric relationships would be difficult. (This is not to say it cannot be done. Most theorists would say that terms somehow introduce some 'entities' into the 'model of the world' which has been built up from the preceding discourse; these entities, which can be referred to anaphorically, may be rather indirectly related to the denotations of the terms which introduced them. Nonetheless, the following sentences do pose a challenge for such theories if the theory incorporates the simpleminded view.)

    (19)   Although snow is white, when *it* falls/is falling in the city *it* is dirty
    (20)   Although water is scarce here, *it* is dripping from the faucet
    (21)   Although Italians are good skiers, *they* are doing poorly in the downhill races I am watching on TV

Since the sentences (7)–(8) and (14)–(18) have just one subject, how can that one subject be assigned the distinct interpretations apparently required by the conjuncts comprising the predicate? In the sentences with relative clauses (6) and (8), and in the anaphoric pronoun cases (9) and (19)–(21), how can the anaphoric or relative pronouns be interpreted differently from their antecedents, as they apparently must be by the different predicates?

SOME METHODOLOGICAL REMARKS

It will be noted from the criticisms levelled against the simpleminded view that a certain 'semantic innocence' has been assumed. For instance in sentences like our previous

(6)   Snakes, which are reptiles, are in my garden
(7)   Snow is white and is falling throughout Alberta

it was claimed that whatever semantic contribution *snakes* or *snow* makes, it makes that contribution once and for all in the sentence. For this reason the 'understanding' or 'reading' or denotation of these subjects could not be given twice for the one sentence, as would be intuitively required to account for the two different conjuncts in the predicate.[2]

Although we wish to keep our discussion of the difficulties involved with generic sentences at a very general level so as to show how they impact on any theory which assigns a logical form to such sentences, in order to discuss some recent writers we need to present a specific outlook on the semantics of natural languages. We do not aim here at any comprehensiveness nor at much detail; rather we outline in broad brush strokes the bare essentials needed to understand these recent theories.

The starting point for this conception of semantics is Richard Montague. (See Thomason (1974) for a collection of his papers, with a lengthy introduction. See also Dowty *et al* (1981) for a thorough introduction.) According to this viewpoint, the logical form of a natural language can be represented in a language called Intensional Logic. This language differs from first order logic in a variety of ways, but for our purposes the important differences are these.

(I)   Intensional logic is *typed*. Each expression of the logic is assigned a type which determines (syntactically) the type of predicates which can be asserted of it and the type of arguments it can take. Furthermore this type is correlated with a semantic type which indicates the sort of entity it denotes. Basic terms, for example *a* and *b*, denote basic objects. Basic predicates, for example *F* and *G*, denote sets of the basic objects. Some predicates are not basic in this sense. They might denote sets of the basic predicates, for instance. One might claim that *is a colour* is such a predicate, and that *is white* is a basic predicate. Then a sentence like *white is a colour* might be represented as **colour'(white')**. (The primes indicate that we are talking about the logical translation of the word which is primed.) The syntactic type of **white'** would be written as $\langle e,t \rangle$, indicating that semantically, this predicate maps basic entities into truth values (i.e., its denotation belongs to the class of functions 2^D, where D is the set of basic entities and 2 is the set of truth values $\{0,1\}$). The syntactic type of **colour'** would be written as $\langle\langle e,t \rangle,t \rangle$, indicating that semantically, this predicate maps predicates over basic entities into truth values (i.e., its denotation belongs to the class of functions $2^{(2^D)}$). More generally, syntactic types A, B may be compounded freely to form a new type ⟨A,B⟩, and expressions of this type will denote functions from the type of objects A denotes to the type of objects B denotes.

(II)   Intensional logic is *modalized*. Given an expression α of syntactic type A which denotes a certain type X of object, we can form the expression ˆα of syntactic type ⟨s,A⟩ which denotes that function from possible worlds to the X-type objects in that possible world. Similarly, if β is a function on possible worlds then ˇβ denotes the object which β picks out in the possible world under consideration. For example, **(is a person)**′ might denote a particular set of entities. ˆ**(is a person)**′ then is said to denote the property of being a person—something which tells us, for each possible world, what entities in that world have *is a person* true of them. One of the most important reasons for introducing the operator ˆ is to permit a uniform approach to the semantics of intensional expressions such as *necessarily*, *believes*, *seeks*, and *fake*. The truth value of a sentence of the form *necessarily* Φ in a particular possible world in general depends not only on the truth value of Φ in that world but also on its truth value in other 'accessible' worlds (perhaps all possible worlds). This dependence can be allowed for by ensuring that **necessarily**′ will be applied to the *intension* of the translation of the embedded sentence. Similarly the truth value of *x believes that* Φ depends in general on the intention (not just the extension) of Φ, the truth value of *x seeks y* depends on the intension of *y*, and the truth of *x is a fake P* depends on the intension of *P*. Since intensionality can occur at virtually all syntactic positions, Montague adopts a uniform policy of *always* intensionalizing an argument when applying a logical expression (which translates some English phrase) to it. Where appropriate, extensionality can be recovered, either by ensuring that the translation of the expression applied to the argument will contain an occurrence of the extension operator ˇ which 'cancels' the intension operator prefixed to the argument, or by reliance on *meaning postulates* (see below).

(III)   If Φ is a formula then $(\lambda x)\Phi$ is a predicate of syntactic type ⟨A,t⟩, where A is the type of *x*. Intuitively, Φ should have a free occurrence of *x*, and this 'lambda abstraction' converts the open formula into a predicate; which predicate can then be applied to some term as usual. If Φ were (Fx **&** Gx) then we can form the predicate $(\lambda x)(Fx$ **&** $Gx)$ and apply it to some term of the same type as *x*, say *a*, to get $(\lambda x)(Fx$ **&** $Gx)(a)$ as a formula. A process of 'lambda conversion' alters this to (Fa **&** Ga). Since the language has expressions of all types, lambda abstraction (and conversion) can apply to all expressions. If H and J are predicates of the appropriate type, they can take other predicates as arguments. The formula $[H(P) \rightarrow J(P)]$—where P is a free predicate variable—can be lambda abstracted to form $(\lambda P)[H(P) \rightarrow J(P)]$ and this might be predicated of the property F, which would yield $(\lambda P)[H(P) \to J(P)](F)$. And by lambda conversion this would become $[H(F) \to J(F)]$.

So far we have said little about the relationship between English and this representational language of intensional logic. For example we have not said whether English proper names should be translated as basic terms, or whether English predicates like *is a person* should be translated as basic predicates, etc. Montague in fact had a specific view on this matter, which view is rather complex. Most modern writers in the Montague tradition differ from him on many of these specific recommendations, and so we shall not say much about them. Instead we shall mention a few of the more general aspects of Montague's approach which are relevant to understanding the theories given in the next section, and apart from these, we will let those theories speak for themselves.

It is part of Montague's view that one can determine the semantic representation of any expression by examining the syntactic rule(s) that combine the parts to form that expression (plus the semantic representations of these parts). To determine the semantic representation of, for example, *barking dog*, it is sufficient to use the semantic representations of *barking* and *dog* and to know which syntactic rule allows these terms to be combined in that way. The idea is that every application of that syntactic rule yields the same result (modulo the representations of the parts). More exactly, one says that with each syntactic rule there is exactly one semantic function which takes as arguments the semantic values of the items used in the syntactic rule. According to this view of how one can determine the semantic representation of an expression, the standard method used in first-order logic to generate $(\forall x)(Wx \to Mx)$ as the representation of *all whales are mammals* is incorrect. This standard method somehow first generates $(Wx \to Mx)$ and then attaches $(\forall x)$ to it. But, the syntax of English makes *all whales* a unit and *are mammals* a unit. Thus the representation of the sentence must be some function of the representations of these units. One way to satisfy Montague's requirement, in this instance, would be to translate *all whales* as $(\lambda P)[(\forall x)(\mathbf{whale'}(x) \to P(x))]$ and *are mammals* as $\mathbf{mammal'}$, and to derive the translation of the sentence by applying the former to the latter. (Montague's translation, *à la* his (1973) would be quite similar to this, except that **P** would be prefixed by ˇ, so that application of the translation of *all whales* to the *intension* of the translation of *are mammals* will give $(\forall x)(\mathbf{whales'}(x) \to {}^{\vee}\mathbf{mammal'}(x))$, or $(\forall x)(\mathbf{whale'}(x) \to \mathbf{mammal'}(x))$—see (II) above.) Of course, the translation of *all whales* must in turn be derived from the translation of *all* and the translation of *whales*. These can be taken to be $(\lambda Q)(\lambda P)[(\forall x)(Q(x) \to P(x))]$ and $\mathbf{whale'}$ respectively, so that application of the former to the latter yields the desired translation of *all whales*. (Again, Montague would actually use $(\lambda Q)(\lambda P)[(\forall x)(^{\vee}Q(x) \to {}^{\vee}P(x))]$ and would apply this to the intensionalized argument $^{\wedge}\textbf{whale}'$.)

Montague's translation of *all whales* as a property of properties, $(\lambda P)[(\forall x)(\textbf{whale}'(x) \to {}^{\vee}P(x))]$, may seem bizarre at first sight from the standpoint of classical philosophical logic. But in fact, the translation of all noun phrases as properties of properties allows a uniform and elegant treatment of the truth conditions for English, including intensional constructions, which is one of the strongest selling points of Montague Grammar. Note that the translation of *all whales* can be understood as describing the set of properties that all whales have (i.e., the intersection of the property sets of all individual whales). Similarly, the phrase *some whale* is translated as $(\lambda P)[(\exists x)(\textbf{whale}'(x) \ \& \ {}^{\vee}P(x))]$, i.e., the set of all properties possessed by at least one whale (or, the union of the property sets of individual whales); the phrase *no whale* is translated as $(\lambda P)[(\forall x)(\textbf{whale}'(x) \to \neg {}^{\vee}P(x))]$, i.e., as the complement of the set of properties possessed by whales; and a proper name like *Moby Dick* is translated as $(\lambda P)^{\vee}P(m)$, where m is an individual constant denoting the entity, Moby Dick, so that the name expresses the set of properties that Moby Dick has. Thus, since the subject of a sentence always expresses a property set, the condition necessary for the truth of a sentence is simply that the property expressed by the predicate be an element of the set of properties expressed by the subject. This, of course, is precisely how 'application' of the translation of the subject to the translation of the predicate is interpreted.[3] (We have described the 'PTQ' version of predication (Montague, 1973). In his 'UG' version (Montague, 1970), predicates of English sentences are translated as predicates over property sets, allowing their application to the subject, instead of the other way around.)

Incidentally, we have argued (Schubert & Pelletier, 1982) that it is possible to gain Montague-like uniformity of translation without giving up the notion that proper names denote individuals (in favour of the notion that they denote property sets). We will avail ourselves of some of these devices developed in that paper, including a uniform approach to scope ambiguities (not available within Montague's original framework), in the concluding section.

The particular syntactic theory employed by Montague and by the writers to be discussed below is replaced here by the Generalized Phrase Structure Grammar (GPSG) of Gazdar (see Gazdar, 1982; Gazdar *et al*, 1985). In this theory the syntax is given by a set of context-free rules of the general form

$$A \to B \, C \, D \ldots$$

Along with each rule stated the relevant semantic rule that combines the representations of the right-hand side of the syntactic rule to form the representation of the left-hand side of that rule.[4] In this theory a non-terminal symbol—e.g., the A of the rule stated above—is allowed to be 'complex' by containing 'features'. E.g., the symbol 'NP[+pl]' is interpreted as a Noun Phrase with the feature '+plural'. It is the use of features, and certain principles governing their legitimate places of occurrence, that allows GPSG to capture such aspects of language as 'agreement' and other 'unbounded dependencies' (which aspects had led previous writers to assume that natural languages could not be described by any set of context-free rules). In what follows we will make only the most minimal use of features, but we do wish to emphasize that such use does not violate any of the essential properties of context-free grammars.

The final remark about these Montaguesque grammars has to do with *meaning postulates*. The point of a meaning postulate can best be explained by example. Suppose we are going to translate the two sentences *John is a bachelor* and *John is married*. From the 'purely logical' point of view, their translations into intensional logic could both be true—even if *John* is taken to denote the same entity. This is because there is a model wherein the denotation of *is a bachelor* partially overlaps the denotation of *is married*. But such a model is not relevant to describing English. All the models relevant to English have the two denotations completely disjoint. This fact is stated as a meaning postulate, such as

$$\Box(\forall x)(\textbf{bachelor}'(x) \rightarrow \neg\, \textbf{married}'(x))$$

which is taken to be a way of paring down all the possible models to ones which accurately describe English, at least with respect to the relationship between *bachelor* and *married*. Let us consider a somewhat more interesting case. Suppose we think that *blue* and *fake* belong to the same same syntactic category, namely Adj, and that any Adj can syntactically be combined with a Noun. The relevant semantic rule corresponding to this syntactic combination cannot be one which says that the Adj is true of an object and also the Noun is true of it, for this would give the wrong result for such things as *fake diamond*, even though it would give the correct result for *blue diamond*. Instead we need to say that *fake* denotes some operation, which when applied to a Noun intension, yields some property that does not entail that the Noun is true of the object. But since *blue* and *fake* are in the same syntactic category, it follows that *blue* will have to denote this type of operation also. The relevant rule for these will be, then,

$$N \rightarrow Adj\, N,\ Adj'(^\wedge N')$$

(where the part after the comma is the semantic rule corresponding to the syntactic rule before the comma). Here it is stated that an Adj can combine syntactically with a N to form a (longer) N, and that the semantic representation of this larger N consists of the semantic representation of the Adj (indicated by Adj') applied to the semantic representation of the N (indicated by N'). This would assign *fake diamond* and *blue diamond* the representations, respectively

$$\textbf{fake}'(\hat{\ }\textbf{diamond}')$$

$$\textbf{blue}'(\hat{\ }\textbf{diamond}')$$

But we know that, in English, when *blue diamond* is true of some object, it is both blue and a diamond. But the last formula does not reveal that. Therefore we give a meaning postulate which guarantees this:

if $Q \in \{\textbf{blue}', \ldots\}$ and $P \in \{\textbf{diamond}', \ldots\}$ then

$$\Box(\forall x)[Q(\hat{\ }P)(x) \rightarrow P(x)\&Q(x)]$$

We furthermore know that, in English, when *fake diamond* is true of some object, it is not a diamond; but again our formula does not reveal that, so we give a meaning postulate which guarantees it:

if $Q \in \{\textbf{fake}', \ldots\}$ and $P \in \{\textbf{diamond}', \ldots\}$ then

$$\Box(\forall x)[Q(\hat{\ }P)(x) \rightarrow \neg P(x)]$$

With just this much of an introduction to intensional logic and Montague/Gazdar grammars, we are in a position to state and evaluate

THE SOPHISTICATED VIEW: THREE VERSIONS

General Remarks

Difficulties such as the ones mentioned above have led recent writers on the subject of mass terms and bare plurals to suggest that the (a)-sentences of (2)–(5) uniformly refer to 'kinds' ('substances', 'species', 'generic entities').[5] To avoid making any assumptions about whether a 'kind' is to be identified with the intension of a predicate or with some other, 'more primitive' entity, we use the μ-operator to form a 'kind' (etc) from a predicate: $\mu(\text{snow})$ denotes the kind *snow*, $\mu(\text{dog})$ denotes the kind *dog*, etc.

In the sophisticated view, the semantic representations of (2a)–(5a) might be written schematically as

(2″)   (a)   reptile(μ(snake))

(3″)   (a)   white(μ(snow))

(4″) (a) loyal(μ(dog))
(5″) (a) person(μ(child))

where the predicates may either be simply the lexical translations **reptile′**, ... **person′** (Chierchia) or may be functional transforms of those translations (Carlson; Farkas & Sugioka).[6] The quasi-universal import of the original sentences, that is, the fundamental intuition, would presumably derive from such meaning postulates as the following[7]

(22) For P ∈ {**snake′,snow′,dog′**,child,idea′, ...} and Q ∈ {**reptile′**, **white′,loyal′,person′,expensive′**, ...},

$$\Box[Q(\mu(P)) \rightarrow (Mx: P(x))Q(x)]$$

The fundamental intuition holds that there is a difference in logical form between the (a) and (b) sentences of (2)–(5). In what, then, does this difference consist? The consensus in the literature is that the (b) sentences should still involve the explicit existential quantification. But a point of contention is whether the existential quantifier is supplied by (the translation of) the subject NP itself or by the predicate. Consider for example

(23) Dogs are barking
(24) Snow is falling

Should the subject NPs *dogs* and *snow* be interpreted as equivalent to *some dogs* and *some snow* (thus supplying an existential quantifier directly)? Or should *dogs* here instead be interpreted as μ(dog), and the existential quantifier brought in indirectly by interpretating *are barking* as equivalent to *has a realization/manifestation/instance which is barking*, i.e., $(\lambda y)(\exists x)[R(x,y)$ & barking(x)]? The latter approach can be seen to yield logical form expressions like[8]

(23′) $(\exists x)[R(x,\mu(dog))$ & barking(x)]
(24′) $(\exists x)[R(x,\mu(snow))$ & falling(x)]

where R(x,y) means that *x* is an instance/realization/manifestation/etc of (the kind) *y*.

Krifta (1985), following Kratzer (1980), argues for the direct approach, citing cross-linguistic facts such as that many languages distinguish the (a) and (b) cases via case marking (Finnish), distinct articles (Bairisch), or partitives (French). However, it is difficult to see the relevance of these observations to the point at issue. There seems to be no reason to suppose that the semantic structure of

(25) De l'eau coule du robinet

is phrase-by-phrase identical with that of

(26)   Water is flowing from the faucet

or to that of

(27)   Some water is flowing from the faucet

Nor, it should be added, is there any reason to suppose that the semantic structure of (26) is phrase-by-phrase identical to that of (27). Hence there is no reason to suppose it is the subject NP which supplies the existential quantifier in all three cases.[9] And in any case such an approach seems in principle unable to give an account of conjoined predicates of the form we have considered earlier.

Our sophisticated theorists opt for the indirect approach. This has the advantage that it translates bare NPs (in subject position) uniformly in both the (a) and (b) cases as denoting kinds, rather than treating them as ambiguous: sometimes denoting kinds, and sometimes as introducing an existential quantifier and treating the subject term as a predicate.

As suggested above, there are various flavours of the sophisticated view. In the sections which follow, we shall discuss three of them: G. Carlson's, Chierchia's, and Farkas & Sugioka's (see reference list). Other variants of it can be found in the literature, e.g., Enç (1981), ter Meulen (1985), and Hinrichs (1985), but we leave it as an exercise for the reader to apply the criticisms given here to these others.

Fundamental to all versions of the sophisticated view is that there are three (disjoint) types of entities in reality: *kinds*, *objects*, and *stages*. Objects are the familiar sort of thing . . . 'Jimmy Carter, the chair I now occupy, the world's fattest magician' (Carlson, 1979, p. 53) or 'the Empire State Building, my neighbor, . . . sincerity, the number 3' (Farkas & Sugioka, 1983, p. 226). A *kind* is also an entity (sometimes they are called *substances* or *species* or *generic entities*). They are such items as (the species) *dog* or (the element) *gold* or more complex generic entities like *students standing in line*. As before, we represent these by means of our μ-operator. A stage is a 'space-time slice of individuals'. Not only can objects have stages (such as the various space-time slices of my chair) but also kinds can have stages. (Exactly what is a stage of a kind is disputed by our various sophisticated theorists, and so we shall defer this description to the later sections.)

The sophisticated theory also takes the position that, semantically speaking, some predicates properly (or basically) apply only to kinds, some only to objects, and some only to stages. For example, the predicates *be extinct*, *be common*, *be widespread*, etc, properly apply only to kinds. The predicates *be loyal*, *be white*, *be a mammal*, etc, properly apply only to objects. And the properties *be barking*, *be falling*, *be dripping*, etc, properly apply only to stages. This is claimed to be so in spite of the facts that *be loyal*, for example, syntactically can be correctly predicated of kinds (as in *dogs are loyal*) and that *be barking* can syntactically be correctly predicated of objects (as in *Fido is barking*).

The problem for the sophisticated theories therefore is to show how these syntactically legitimate predications give rise to the appropriate semantic representations, wherein the predicates are applied only to those types of entities of which they 'properly' hold. All of our sophisticated theorists are concerned to give an account which is *explicit*—one is not to 'intuit' the appropriate semantic (intensional logic) representation, but rather one is explicitly to give syntactic rules of formation and pair them with explicit translation rules (into the semantic representation language).

Before we move on to discuss the various individual sophisticated theorists, we might note two very general difficulties for any sophisticated approach.

First, the sophisticated approach posits a rather complex semantic structure for non-stative predicates like *falling* and *barking*, involving a 'realization relation' which has no counterpart in the syntax. This semantic structure is not shared by *falls* and *barks*: the sophisticated approach would treat

(28)   Snow falls
(29)   Dogs bark

as generics and translate them, accordingly, as

(28′)   falls(μ(snows))
(29′)   barks(μ(dog))

where 'falls' and 'barks' are functional transforms of **falls′** and **barks′** *not* involving realization relations. But as we have noted above, the sentences

(23)   Dogs are barking
(24)   Snow is falling

will be translated as

(23′) $(\exists x)[R(x,\mu(dog))$ & barking$(x)]$
(24′) $(\exists x)[R(x,\mu(snow))$ & falling$(x)]$

Secondly, in order to work properly for both cases like

(30)   Snow is falling
(31)   Snowflakes are falling
(32)   Dogs are barking

and synonymous/equivalent cases like

(33)   Some snow is falling
(34)   Some snowflakes are falling
(35)   Some dogs are barking

either the (33)–(35) sentences must somehow suppress the quantification over realizations within the VP, or else the realization relation must be assumed to have a 'bimodal semantics'. The suppression of quantification in the VP might be accomplished by having a syntactic agreement feature in the subject NP and VP which is sensitive to whether the NP is object-level or kind-level. When this feature is positive, the VP translation would lack the quantification over realizations. Alternatively, two rules of VP formation might be postulated, one of which introduces the quantification over realizations of the subject while the other does not. This would give rise to two syntactic analyses, and two different translations, of each sentence, one would be the correct translation if the subject happens to be kind-level, while the other would be the correct translation if the subject happens to be object-level. (This is Carlson's approach.) The 'bimodal semantics' approach assumes that the VP-translation always introduces a quantifier over realizations, but defines the meaning of the realization in two parts, one appropriate to realizations of objects, the other appropriate to realizations of kinds. (This is Chierchia's approach.) We are now in a position to examine the sophisticated theories in more detail.

Version 1: Carlson

Carlson's Position

The founder of the sophisticated view is generally acknowledged to be G. Carlson (see especially his 1977 dissertation). Much of Carlson's discussion is taken up with trying to justify the view that (sometimes, anyway) bare plurals and mass terms are 'name like' or 'referential' or 'denoting'. We shall not consider all his reasons here, but will simply assume it true that there is such a class of sentences, including the sentences we have been calling generic. Briefly, his reasons include the following (besides the failure of quantificational approaches we have already discussed). In sentence pairs like

(36)   Dogs are mammals. They bark.

the pronoun can be replaced by the generic antecedent, without meaning change. This behaviour of generics resembles that of names:

(37)   John walked in. He smiled.

but not that of quantified phrases:

(38)   A man walked in. He smiled.

Also, Carlson (1982, p. 151) claimed that generic terms, like proper names, participate in *de dicto/de re* ambiguities and no others. (While this claim is faulty, the exceptions to it cause no problem for Carlson's theory, as we shall see.) Further, Carlson noted that generics, like proper names, participate in *so-called* constructions such as

(39)   Cardinals are so-called because of their colour

and they can be used to designate the values of a variable, as in

(40)   One of these kinds of mammals barks if and only if either dogs bark or cats bark

As mentioned above, Carlson has three ontologically distinct types of entities: kinds, objects, and stages. An object *realizes* or *manifests* a kind (of which it is an individual). This relation is represented as **R**. Objects have 'spatio-temporal segments', called stages. Such items are John-this-morning and the like. This relation is indicated by **R′**. Kinds also have stages, namely, the stages of the objects which realize that kind. (This is a point of difference with other sophisticated theories, so it is well to mark it.) In Carlson's terminology (although not in Chierchia's), objects and kinds are the two sorts of *individuals*, while stages are temporal manifestations of individuals.

Carlson assumes that certain English VP's, such as *runs into the room, found a match, ate a donut, is available, is present, is running around* (typically inducing an existential reading on a bare plural subject) apply 'basically' to stages/manifestations of individuals (=objects or kinds) only. However, such a stage-level predicate is translated either (on one syntactic analysis) so that it introduces an existentially quantified stage of the subject, or (on another syntactic analysis) so that it is transformed into a 'gnomic' (habitual or generic) predicate. In the former case, the translation is $(\lambda y^o)(\exists x^s)[R'(x^s,y^o)$ **&** $VP'(x^s)]$,[10] while in the latter it is **Gn′**($^\wedge VP'$). Both of these translations are applicable directly to individuals, i.e., objects and kinds, but the former gives an episodic (transitory, time-dependent, non-dispositional) reading, while the latter gives a gnomic reading. This accounts for the differences in

(41)   (a)   John ate a light breakfast back in those days.
       (b)   **Gn′**($^\wedge(^\wedge\lambda x^s)A(x))(j)$—where A translates *ate a light breakfast* (and the adverbial has been ignored)
(42)   (a)   John ate a light breakfast this morning
       (b) $(\exists x^s)[R'(x,j)\&A(x)]$

or in

(43)   Athletes ate a light breakfast back in those days [involves **Gn'**]
(44)   Athletes ate a light breakfast and then went to the game [involves **R'**]

Additional examples of the habitual/episodic distinction are provided by habitual like

(45)   John smokes
(46)   John handles the mail arriving from Antarctica
(47)   John writes books

and episodic ones like

(48)   John is smoking a pipe in Edmonton
(49)   John is writing a book
(50)   John is sorting the mail from Antarctica

Carlson argues for his analysis of habitual sentences in terms of **Gn'** (as in (42)b), and against a quantificational analysis, on the grounds that no one quantifier serves in all cases, and allowing various quantifiers would predict ambiguities where there are none. Indeed, as Lawler (1972) and others had observed before, certain sentences attributing dispositional properties to the subject may be true even if there has *never* been an episode in which the disposition was actualized ((47) can serve as illustration). Carlson notes further that while episodic predications obey certain systematic constraints with respect to place and time of occurrence, habitual predications do not, e.g.,

(51)   John is smoking a pipe in Edmonton

precludes

(52)   John is smoking a cigar in Calgary

and entails

(53)   John is smoking a pipe in Alberta

but no such relations need to hold when *is smoking* is replaced by *smokes*.

This can be accounted for, he says, by assuming that habitual sentences attribute a property to an individual (whose temporal stages need not be spatially localized) while episodic sentences attribute properties to stages of individuals (which are typically quite localized in space and time).[11]

Another group of English VP's, such as *knows how to dance, have ears, is a turtle, can read a newspaper* (typically inducing a quasi-universal reading on a bare plural subject) apply 'basically' to objects only. Such VP's are also translated ambiguously, either without introducing realization or gnomic operators, or with a gnomic operator **Gn**. VP-translations of the former type combine meaningfully with object-level subjects, but not with kind-level subjects (even though such combinations are generated syntactically). Such translations are non-generic. VP-translations of the latter type, i.e., those of the form **Gn(ˆVP′)**, combine meaningfully with kind-level subjects, but not with object-level subjects (though again, such combinations are generated syntactically). Such translations are generic. This accounts for examples like[12]

(54)   (a)   Fido is loyal
      (b) $loyal'(f)$

(55)   (a)   Fido has a tail
      (b) $(\exists x^o)[tail'(x) \ \& \ has'(x)(f)]$

on the one hand, and

(56)   (a)   Dogs are loyal
      (b) $Gn(ˆ(\lambda x^o)loyal'(x))(d)$

(57)   (a)   Dogs have a tail
      (b) $Gn(ˆ(\lambda x^o)(\exists y^o)[tail'(y) \ \& \ has'(y)(x)])(d)$

on the other. In effect, **Gn** in the latter examples 'elevates' the object-level properties *is loyal* and *has a tail* to the kind level, producing the generic reading. Meaning postulates for **Gn′** and **Gn** take care of relating a predication of the form $Gn'(ˆP)(x)$ to stages of x, and a predication of the form $Gn(ˆP)(x)$ to objects realizing (the kind) x.

As in the case of (non-generic and generic) habitual sentences, Carlson argues against a quantificational analysis of generic sentences like (56)–(57) on the grounds that no one quantifier serves in all cases. Equally important, as already stated, is his observation that bare plurals pattern in many respects with names, rather than with quantified NP's.

Some VP's apply to kinds only, e.g., *are rare/common/widespread/ extinct/in short supply/indigenous to, comes in many sizes*, etc. And finally, there are some VP's which apply to both objects and kinds (i.e., to individuals in general), e.g., *is popular, is interesting, is well-known*, etc. Unlike the previously mentioned stage-level and object-level VP's, they apply to objects and kinds 'directly', i.e., without modification by **Gn′** or **Gn**.

The logical form of 'atemporal *when* sentences', such as

(58)   Dogs are fat when they are intelligent

is taken as tantamount to

(58) The kind of dog all of whose realizations are intelligent is (generically) fat

Or to be exact:

(60) $\mathbf{Gn}(\char`^(\lambda x^o)\mathbf{Fat}'(x^o))\ ((\iota y^k)\square(\forall z^o)[R(z^o,y^k)$
$\leftrightarrow R(z^o,\mu(\mathbf{dog}'))\ \&\ \mathbf{Intelligent}'(z^o)])$

The first clause (the **Gn** clause) says 'is generically fat' while the second clause says 'the kind such that necessarily all of its realizations are dog-realizations and are intelligent'. The translation is obtained by regarding *are fat when they are intelligent* as a syntactic constituent (which combines with the subject *dogs*). This VP has the translation

(60′) $(\lambda x^k)[\mathbf{Gn}(\char`^(\lambda x^o)\mathbf{Fat}'(x^o))\ (\iota y^k)\square(\forall z^o)[R(z^o,y^k)$
$\leftrightarrow R(z^o,x^k)\ \&\ \mathbf{Intelligent}'(z^o)])]$

which essentially combines the *fat*-predicate and the *intelligent*-predicate into the kind-level predicate (60′), which can now be applied to $\mu(\mathbf{dog})$ to yield (60).

Carlson's analysis accounts for the synonymy of the above sentence with

(61) Dogs *that are intelligent* are fat

It also accounts for the oddity of

(62) John is fat when he is intelligent

(because there are no objects realizing John), and explains why

(63) Dogs that are intelligent are widespread

is acceptable, while

(64) Dogs are widespread when they are intelligent

is not (because we are applying **Gn** to a predicate which is already kind-level).

Carlson discusses the example

(65) Someone is afraid of ghosts when they are evil

The apparent problem, in view of the preceding analysis, is that the generic to which the when-clause appears to apply is embedded in the object, rather than being in subject position. Thus it would seem that by the time we have combined *afraid of* with *ghosts*, we can no longer 'get at' the generic and combine it with the when-clause. Carlson avails himself of Montague's trick of topicalizing an embedded NP, leaving a co-referential pronoun in the vacated position; i.e., the syntactic analysis uses the 'transformed' version of the sentence

(66)   Ghosts (are such that) someone is afraid of them when they are evil

(where the *them* and *they* are both translated as object-level variables and are co-referential with *ghosts*). Presumably this would also work for

(67)   Mothers of *premature babies* are fortunate when they are normal

(68)   John likes to meet the parents of *girls he dates* when they are pretty

and the like.

Carlson also has an account of 'adverbs of quantification'. For sentences like

(69)   Quadratic equations *usually* have two solutions

(70)   A cat *never* has six legs

(71)   Flags *sometimes* have stripes on them

(72)   Dogs are *always* fat when they are intelligent

he suggests that the adverb acts essentially as a quantifier over object-level realizations of the subject. Thus the above sentences are equivalent to

(73)   Most (realizations of) quadratic equations have two solutions

(74)   No (realizations of) cats have six legs

(75)   Some (realizations of) flags have stripes on them

(76)   All (realizations) of the kind of dogs all of whose realizations are intelligent are fat.

Note that he can, in principle, deal with cases like

(77)   John sometimes likes girls (he meets)

by again using Montague's trick of topicalizing the generic:

(78)   Girls (he meets) (are such that) John sometimes likes them

Technically, Carlson gets the effect of the above paraphrases by regarding the adverbs as VP-adverbs and not Sentence-adverbs. Thus, for example, *usually have two solutions* is rendered as *is a kind most of whose realizations have two solutions*, etc. When there is both a quantificational adverb and an atemporal *when*-clause, he modifies the earlier rule of translation so that instead of applying **Gn** to the main-clause predicate, it applies the adverb's translation. Thus such adverbs, just like **Gn**, are assumed to 'elevate' an object-level predicate to a kind-level predicate; specifically, this can be seen from the translation of

(79)   *always*: $(\lambda P)(\lambda x^k)[(\forall y^o)[R(y^o,x^k) \rightarrow {}^{\vee}P(y^o)]]$

Carlson acknowledges that his analysis of atemporal *when*, atemporal *always*, etc, cannot be extended to the temporal uses of these words, so that a 'schizoid' analysis is required, treating such words as lexically ambiguous.

Finally, we should mention Carlson's tentative proposal with regard to indefinite generics (Carlson 1977). He suggested that a phrase like *a dog*, generically construed, be translated as $(\lambda P)[Gn(P)(d) \vee Gn'(P)(d)]$. When applied as subject to the intension of a predicate like **mammal'** or **bark'**, this yields

$$Gn({}^{\wedge}mammal')(d)$$
$$Gn'({}^{\wedge}bark')(d)$$

respectively, after deletion of the meaningless disjunct in each case. These are, of course, exactly the desired generic translations of

(80)   A dog is a mammal
(81)   A dog barks

respectively. Notice that Carlson's translation of the indefinite generic in effect picks out the *object*-level and *stage*-level properties, which can be ascribed to a kind only after 'elevation' by **Gn** or **Gn'**. As a result, Carlson can explain why

(82)   ?A dog is widespread

is odd: the translation treats *widespread* as object-level, attempting to elevate it to the kind level. Thus (contra Farkas & Sugioka, 1983) (82) is odd for the same reason that a sentence like

(83)   ?Fido is widespread

is odd. Unfortunately, as we shall indicate, this treatment of indefinite generics is unsatisfactory in other respects.

Attractive Features of Carlson's Approach

Carlson's analysis of bare plurals as kind-denoting leads to a rather elegant, uniform account of a remarkably wide range of sentences with bare plural subjects, including both generic and episodic sentences, and sentences involving atemporal *when*. The theory's conformity with Montague grammar (compositionality, intensionality, pairing of syntactic with semantic rules) would allow his analysis to be incorporated into a variety of other theories which require this, and ultimately into a larger grammar of English.

We mentioned above that Carlson believed that bare plurals participate in *de dicto/de re* ambiguities, but do not interact with quantifiers and logical connectives to produce scope ambiguities. However, there *is* such interaction, as illustrated by the following sentences:

(84)   Canadian academics are supported by a single granting agency
(85)   Storks have a favourite nesting area
(86)   Dogs have a tail
(87)   Sheep are black or white
(88)   Whales are mammals or fish

It is an important feature of Carlson's analysis (notwithstanding his inattention to such examples) that it can in principle account for these ambiguities. First, it should be noted that in the most natural syntactic analysis of sentence (84), the NP *a single granting agency* is embedded within the sentence predicate; its (intensionalized) translation will be similarly embedded within the translation of the sentence predicate, and the intension of that translation will in turn be operated upon by **Gn** (given that **supported-by'** is an object-level predicate and that **Canadian-academics'** is a generic subject). Clearly, this yields a narrow-scope reading of *a single granting agency*, wherein the granting agency in question may vary from academic to academic.

But, suppose that we introduce some mechanism such as an alternative syntactic analysis (*à la* Montague's topicalization), or a scoping mechanism (*à la* Cooper, 1983 or Schubert & Pelletier, 1982) to give the equivalent of

(89)   A single granting agency is such that Canadian academics are supported by it

as an analysis of (84), at least at the level of logical form. Then the alternative wide-scope reading becomes available as well.

Much the same can be said about (85) and (86).[13] In (87) and (88) we can invoke conjunction reduction, either at the syntactic level or, more plausibly, at the level of logical form, to obtain the wide-scope *or* readings (again, see Schubert & Pelletier, 1982).

Along the same lines, it is worth noting (for later comparison with Chierchia) that Carlson's analysis yields satisfactory translations of sentences containing bound pronouns such as

(90)   Dogs like themselves
(91)   Dogs make their owners like them

The crucial point is that (just as in sentences (84)–(88)) the predicate is translated in the first place as an *object*-level predicate. In the case of (90), this predicate will say of an object to which it is applied that this object likes itself. Before application to the kind, dogs, this object-level predicate is elevated to a kind-level predicate by application of **Gn** to its intension. Via meaning postulates, this kind-level predicate will now say about certain *objects* realizing the kind—i.e., certain dogs—that they like themselves, and that is intuitively just what is required.[14] The same point applies to (91), irrespective of what particular analysis is adopted for reflexives and other bound pronouns.

Version 2: Chierchia

Distinctive Features of Chierchia's Position

Chierchia (1982) proposes an intensional second-order logic called IL* as a logical form for a grammar of English. The distinctive feature of this logic (which is based on Cocchiarella's (1979) system HST* of 'homogeneously stratified types') is that it allows not only terms denoting individuals, but also arbitrary predicative expressions and intensionalized predicative expressions to occur freely as arguments of predicates. So, for example, if **Fido** and **Mary** are individual constants (and not, *à la* Montague, terms denoting individual concepts), **dog′** and **cat′** are monadic predicates, and **hate′** is a dyadic predicate, then not only formulas like

(92)   hate′(Mary)(Fido)

are well-formed and interpretable, but also formulas like these are:

(93)   hate′(ˆcat′)(Fido)
(94)   hate′(ˆcat′)(ˆdog′)

They are well-formed because predicates are typed only with respect to their adicity, not with respect to the types of their arguments, and accordingly may be applied to arguments of any type. Semantic evaluation relies on a function f which supplies an individual *concept correlate* for any individual or n-adic predicate extension or intension ($n = 0,1,2,...$) to which it is applied. (In the case of individuals, f acts as identity, i.e., individuals are their own concept correlates.) So, for example, given some interpretation, formula (94) will be true at a world-time index i,j just in case the pair of arguments consisting of f[|ˆcat′|(i,j)] (i.e., the concept correlate of the predicate intension which is the value of ˆcat′ at i,j) and Fido (if that is the individual denoted by *Fido* at i,j) renders the semantic function corresponding to **hate′** at i,j true.[15] Thus concept correlates serve as 'surrogates' for more complex objects in the process of semantic evaluation.

In fact, (92)–(94) are precisely how sentences like

(95) Fido hates Mary
(96) Fido hates cats
(97) Dogs hate cats

are translated by Chierchia. The permissive character of predication in IL*
certainly leads to an attractively simple logical form for English. We should
mention, however, that λ-abstracts in IL* behaves less permissibly than λ-
free predicative expressions, in a certain sense. (As we will suggest later on,
this point appears to be problematic for Chierchia's theory.) Specifically,
according to the semantics of λ-abstraction in IL* (1982, pp. 325–326), in
order for a λ-abstract such as $(\lambda x)Fx$ to be true of an argument c, it is
insufficient that the concept correlate of the denotation of c make $F(x)$ true
when used as the value of x; the concept correlate must in addition be
the concept correlate of some entity (individual, predicate, or predicate
intension) *of the type determined by* x. For example, if x is an individual
variable, then $((\lambda x)Fx)(c)$ can be true only if c denotes an individual; if P
is a variable over monadic predicate intensions, then $((\lambda P)F(P))(c)$ can be
true only if c denotes a monadic predicate intensions; and so on. In all
other cases, the result of applying the λ-abstract is falsity.

Chierchia (1982a) extends his theory to deal with bare singulars, i.e.,
mass terms, treating these as kind-denoting just as in the case of bare
plurals. In this combined theory of mass nouns and bare plurals, he modifies
(and formalizes) Carlson's three-tiered ontology of stages, object, and
kinds, but still relies crucially on having a logic like IL* for expressing the
logical form, allowing free application of predicates to intensionalized
predicates.

Chierchia endeavours to simplify the semantic apparatus of Carlson's
theory, in particular by eliminating Carlson's gnomic operator **Gn** for
'elevating' object-level predicates to kind-level predicates. (There is no
need for such 'elevated' predicates because we have the 'concept
correlates'.) Although he does not mention it, he would presumably retain
some operator like Carlson's **Gn'** for 'elevating' stage-level predicates to
object-level predicates, producing the 'habitual' reading of the predicate.

Seeking a further simplification of Carlson's theory, Chierchia collapses
Carlson's realization relations **R'** and **R** (which respectively relate stages to
individuals (in Carlson's sense of individual: a kind or an object) and
objects to kinds) into a single, semantically 'bimodal' relation **Re**. Again,
this is made possible by the fact that wherever an object-denoting expression
is permitted, a kind-denoting expression (i.e., a predicate intension) is
permitted as well. Chierchia modifies Carlson's notion of a stage of a kind
so that stages of any number of objects (but at least one) may be *part of*

it. This not only solves some of the difficulties we will mention below with respect to Carlson's account, but also aligns the account of mass terms with intuitions about the structure of 'quantities of matter'. Quantities of matter are the realizations of kinds such as wine, money, or furniture, and these can intuitively be fused to form larger quantities of the same kind, and can enter into 'part of' relationships.

Attractive Features of Chierchia's Approach

Chierchia's approach has the attractive features mentioned above for Carlson: it gives an elegant and uniform account of a wide range of data including generic and episodic sentences, and it is compositional in nature. In addition, the approach of using IL* appears to lead to a rather robust semantics for natural languages, in which there are no longer rigid type constraints on what may be predicated of what. Furthermore, given that first-order predicates are applicable to intensions of first-order predicates in his approach, he is able to identify kinds simply with predicate intensions. Thus *dogs* (as an NP) translates as $(\lambda P)^\vee P(^\cap dog')$, *wine* (as an NP) translates as $(\lambda P)^\vee(^\cap wine')$, and so on.[16] Another attractive feature of Chierchia's theory (in comparison with Carlson or Montague) is that he needs only one predicate to characterize the meaning of an extensional verb such as *love*, namely **love'**, dispensing with Montague's underlying extensional predicate **love**, (or Carlson's **love$^+$**). (See Chierchia 1982, p. 337.)

Finally, Chierchia's notion of stages, unlike Carlson's, is fully formalized. In particular, Chierchia takes stages to be the (instantaneous) manifestations of objects at particular times, i.e., they are the values of objects at world-time indices. Stages that cut across several objects are obtained as mereological fusions of other stages. Fusion is taken as the join operator of a join semilattice with a partial ordering relation interpreted as 'part of'; this semilattice approach pretty well models the intuitions mentioned in the last subsection about Chierchia's handling of mass terms.

Version 3: Farkas & Sugioka

Distinctive Features of Farkas & Sugioka's Approach

The basic difference of Farkas & Sugioka's approach from that of Carlson's is that (generically construed) predicates applied to generic subjects are assumed to supply a **G** (for 'generally') *quantifier* (which can bind any number of free variables) rather than a **Gn** or a **Gn'** *predicate modifier*. This **G** is called an *unselective quantifier*, which combines with a proposition having at least one free variable. These quantifiers quantify over *cases* (the terminology is from Lewis, 1975) in which the open proposition is true. So a case is an admissible assignment of values for the variables of the open propositions, such that the assignment would make the open proposition true. The quantifier binds *all* the free variables in the proposition. If the subject is a bare plural generic, the predicate also introduces a variable, again to be bound by G, over realizations (using the relation R which is a 'collapsing' of Carlson's R and R' into a single 'bimodal' relation)[17] of a kind. In the translation of the predicate the kind itself is λ-abstracted upon, for binding to the subject. Thus a sentence like

(98)   Dogs hate cats

would be translated as

(99) $(\lambda u^k)(\lambda v^k)[G(\mathbf{hate}'(x^o,y^o))x^o : (\lambda z^o)R(z^o,v^k),y^o : (\lambda z^o,u^k)]$
        $(\mu(\mathbf{dog}))(\mu(\mathbf{cat}))$

which, after two λ-conversions, becomes

(100) $[G(\mathbf{hate}'(x^o,y^o))x^o : (\lambda z^o)R(z^o,\mu(\mathbf{dog})),y^o : (\lambda z^o)R(z^o,\mu(\mathbf{cat}))]$

where, again, the superscripts ^{o} and ^{k} indicate variables of the object-level and kind-level respectively. The last two clauses of (100) tell us 'restrictions' on the type of assignments x^o and y^o can receive—namely that x^o must be a dog-object (a R of $\mathbf{dog}'$) and y^o must be a cat-object (a R of $\mathbf{cat}'$). The sentence (100), as a whole, says 'Generally, for x^o and y^o objects satisfying the appropriate semantic interpretation, x^o hates y^o.' Note that this process of 'restricting' the variables is metalinguistic, and and that the 'object linguistic' formula is just the part $G(\mathbf{hate}'(x^o,y^o))$. The entire 'translation', viz, (99) or (100), is a mixture of object-language and metalanguage expressions. The quantifier G means 'generally' (or 'in a significant number of cases') and is said to be 'inherently vague'.

The main thrust of Farkas & Sugioka's work is to give an account of restrictive *if/when*-clauses. The analysis of a sentence like

(101)   Bears are intelligent when they have blue eyes

amounts to saying that the 'object language part' is *generally, if x has blue eyes then x is intelligent*, the 'metalanguage restriction' is that x must be a realization of a kind, and this 'mixed language predicate' is applied to the kind, bears. Thus we get

(102) $(\lambda y^k)[G(\text{blue-eyed}'(x^o) \rightarrow$
        $\text{intelligent}'(x^o))x^o : (\lambda z^o)R^o(z^o,y^k)](\mu(\text{bear}))$

which, after a λ-conversion, is

(103) $G(\text{blue-eyed}'(x^o) \rightarrow \text{intelligent}'x^o)x^o : (\lambda z^o)R(z^o,\mu(\text{bear}))$

Thus, unlike Carlson who analyzed the *when*-clause as a restriction upon *bears* (forming the kind, bears which have blue eyes, and applying the predicate *are* (*generally*) *intelligent* to this kind), Farkas & Sugioka amalgamate the *when*-clause to the predicate (forming the predicate *if it is blue-eyed then it is intelligent*), and apply this to realizations of the kind, bears.

Farkas & Sugioka (1983, pp. 239ff) replace the material conditional '$\rightarrow$' in sentences like (102) and (103) with a conditional (written 'c') whose truth conditions differ from those of '$\rightarrow$' in that when the antecedent is false, (p c q) is 'not determined' or 'the possibility does not come into consideration'.[18] The problem comes with 'monotone decreasing quantifiers' such as *never*, *seldom*, etc.

(104) Bears are never intelligent if they have blue eyes

(105) $\neg[($blue-eyes$'(x^o) \rightarrow$ intelligent$'(x^o))x^o : (\lambda y^o R(y^o, \text{bears}'))]$

But (105) is true if there is an object realizing *bears* that does not have blue eyes. Surely, though, that is not relevant to the truth or falsity of (105). Thus, say Farkas & Sugioka, the need for the conditional 'c'.

In their discussion of 'non-generic *when*-clauses' (1983, § 4.3), Farkas & Sugioka extend their analysis so that in addition to 'saying something about a kind by saying something which is generally true of objects realizing that kind' (as done with the 'generic *when*-clauses'), it is allowed to 'say something about an object by saying something that is generally true of ilts stages'. For example

(106) John is grouchy when he is hungry

'says something about John by saying something that is generally true of his hungry-stages.' In this discussion, Farkas & Sugioka introduce 'implicit time and place variables' (*t* and *p*) in order to generate the appropriate translation. Thus,

(107) Canaries are popular when they are rare

gives rise to

(108) $G[(\text{rare}'(c) \text{ at } t \text{ in } p) \text{ c } (\text{popular}'(c) \text{ at } t \text{ in } p)]$

which intuitively says 'For times and places, generally speaking, if canaries are rare then and there, they are popular then and there'.

Farkas & Sugioka accommodate frequency adverbs within their framework by the analogue of Carlson's stratagem: when such an adverb is present, it is assumed to take the place of the 'default' quantifier **G**, i.e., such adverbs are treated as unselective quantifiers which bind all variables within their scope. Thus, for example, introduction of *always* into (98) would replace **G** by **always**' in (100), and similarly for (101)–(103) or (107)–(108).

Farkas & Sugioka also have an account of 'indefinite generics' such as the generic reading of

(109) A dog is a mammal

As already noted, part of the problem with indefinite generics is that sentences like

(110) A dog is widespread

seem ill-formed. But if indefinites *can* receive generic interpretations, as in (109), and if generic subjects refer to kinds, why should (110) be bad? We saw that Carlson's solution is to say that when the subject is an indefinite, then the predicate must be a property of objects or stages. Farkas & Sugioka propose to translate (109) as

(111) $G[(\text{mammal}'(x^o))x^o : (\lambda z^o)R(z^o,d)]$,

that is, roughly, as 'Generally, realizations of dogkind are mammals'—the same as the final translation (after λ-conversion) of *dogs are mammals*. Technically this is accomplished by translating *a dog* as a free variable, having a restriction to dogkind-realizations.

Attractive Features of Farkas & Sugioka's Approach
First and foremost should be mentioned the apparent breadth of coverage of a wide range of phenomena: bare plural generics, indefinite generics, 'habitual' sentences, and modification of each of these types by restrictive *if/when*-clauses and by temporal adverbs of quantification. Further, despite the wide range of phenomena apparently covered, the resulting translations are relatively simple and (quite often, anyway) seem to correctly show the relationships between distinct syntactic constructions.

Also, in comparison to Carlson, the ploy of regarding *when*-clauses as part of the sentence matrix (rather than as a restriction on the kind) correctly allows for *when*-clauses that do not have in them a pronoun co-referential with the subject, such as

(112) Bears have thick fur when the climate is cold

Such *when*-clauses do not seem amenable to Carlson's analysis (because *bears such that the climate is cold* does not seem to denote a kind), yet intuitively seem to manifest the same logical form as

(113) Bears have large foreheads when they are intelligent

The analysis of indefinite generics (as in Carlson's analysis) seems to yield the correct result that

(114) A dog is a mammal

and

(115)   Dogs are mammals

will get the same logical representation, and that

(116)   A dog is widespread

is bad for the same reason that

(117)   Fido is widespread.

PROBLEMS WITH THE SOPHISTICATED APPROACH

We have seen how the various versions of the sophisticated theory differ
from one another, but yet how they are fundamentally very similar to each
other. In this section we will mention some difficulties with the sophisticated
theory. Our method will be to first state criticisms which apply to one of
the versions only and then go on to give criticisms that apply to any version
of the sophisticated theory. It is with these criticisms in mind, especially
the general criticisms, that we suggest some possibly fruitful lines of investigation in the section which follows.

Apparent Problems with Carlson's Approach

As we have seen, object-level predicates can be applied meaningfully
to kinds only after they have been elevated to kind-level predicates by
application of **Gn** to their intension. In a grammar conforming with the
rule-to-rule hypothesis, this entails either that the VP-translation must be
made *syntactically* sensitive to whether the subject NP denotes an object
or a kind, or that a syntactic ambiguity must be artificially introduced,
allowing a bifurcation of the VP-translation into object-level or kind-level
predicates. (Carlson chooses the latter option.) Yet English does not make
such a syntactic distinction (and we know of no language that does).[19] As
Enç (1981, p. 225) puts it, the operator **Gn** invoked by Carlson is a
'phantom' operator.

Furthermore, sentences like the following indicate that operators similar
to **Gn** and **Gn'** are necessary to 'elevate' predicates with respect to argument
positions other than the last (i.e., the subject).

(118)   Dogs like people for what they are
(119)   Paranoids never like people for more than a week
(120)   Psychiatrists explain people to themselves

One reading of (118) is roughly equivalent to *Dogs like mankind for what it is*. This can be handled in Carlson's framework by assuming the object position of *like* to permit both sorts of individuals (i.e., objects and kinds). But then the second reading cannot be represented, according to which dogs like (most) individual people for what they are. Or rather, to represent the reading, an operator Gn_2 is needed which 'elevates' a two-place object-level predicate to a kind-level predicate with respect to its *first* (unsaturated) argument position. Similarly (119) shows an ambiguity with respect to the interpretation of the object position (i.e., whether the sentence is about liking people in general or about liking individual people) which again indicates the need for Gn_2. And (120) shows an analogous need for Gn_2', so that the object-controlled reflexive reading can be obtained, without being rendered as *Psychiatrists explain people to people*. In general, it seems that *all* NP positions are potentially subject to this sort of 'elevation', so that the grammar will have to generate 2^n analyses (or employ *ad hoc* agreement features) for any sentence containing n NP's. (While *some* of these alternative analyses are needed to explain the ambiguity of sentences like (118)–(120), many or most will have meaningless logical translations if some of the NP's denote individual objects.)

Carlson thinks of stages of an object as being spatio-temporal segments of that object. Although he does not mention the possibility, it seems plausible to suppose that these segments can be extended in time. But also Carlson thinks of a stage of a kind as being a stage of some object instantiating that kind. Thus a stage of a kind is identical with a stage of some one object. This means that every sentence which uses an episodic kind-level predicate will be incorrectly interpreted. For example,

(121)   Lemurs evolved from tree shrews

will be taken as referring to a (possibly temporally extended) stage of a particular lemur! Similar remarks hold for such sentences as

(122)   Leaves cover the ground

and the like.

Even as just an analysis of progressive VPs, Carlson's theory falls short. For example

(123)   Oil is becoming scarce
(124)   Alligators are becoming extinct

express propositions about kinds, or perhaps about the totality of the current manifestations of those kinds (as allowed by Chierchia's theory), but certainly not about the current manifestations of particular individuals of those kinds.

The treatment of restrictive *when*-clauses, as well as that of frequency (quantificational) adverbs is non-uniform in Carlson. The treatment of 'atemporal *when*' in particular does not extend to cases in which the *when* clause lacks a pronoun coreferential with the subject NP, or to cases that 'shade off' into temporal readings. Similarly, his treatment of frequency adverbs is 'schizoid', depending on a distinction between an atemporal reading that implicitly quantifies over realizations of a generic subject, and a temporal reading which involves no such implicit quantification.

Carlson's proposal for handling indefinite singular generics, described earlier is ingenious but ultimately unworkable. Sentences like the following present apparently insuperable difficulties.

(125)   A bear sometimes has blue eyes
(126)   A house is sometimes built out of bamboo

The trouble with the translation $(\lambda P)[\mathbf{Gn}(P)(b) \vee \mathbf{Gn}'(P)(b)]$ for *a bear* is that it allows a 'generic bear' to have only properties that individual bears can have, and 'sometimes having blue eyes' is not such a property. **sometimes**$'$ already elevates an object-level predicate to the kind level, and so

$$\mathbf{Gn}(\text{˄}\mathbf{sometimes}'(\text{˄}\mathbf{blue\text{-}eyed}'))$$

is meaningless.

There appears to be a slight problem as well in the translation of plural generics as kinds whose realizations are *individual* objects of those kinds. Sentences like

(127)   Swarming killer bees are a serious menace
(128)   Convergent lines share a common point
(129)   Compatible employees make for a productive company
(130)   Opposing viewpoints can lead to a synthesis

suggest that the plural subject nouns *killer bees*, *lines*, *employees*, and *viewpoints* should be interpreted as applicable to *collections* of individuals, rather than single individuals, since a single bee cannot swarm, a single line cannot converge, and so on. Note that this problem is different from the problem in the conception of stages of kinds as stages of individual objects of those kinds. The problem here is not so much in the predicates themselves (which could be 'lowered' to apply to collections of individuals, via suitable meaning postulates); rather, the problem lies in Carlson's *definition* of kinds, e.g., the definition of swarming killer bees as the kind whose realizations are all *individually* swarming killer bees (in a given world). Predicates applicable to collections might be obtained from the singular by application of a 'plur' predicate-modifying operator (cf. the 'two-or-more' operator in Schubert 1982). Thus plur(**bee′**) holds of collections of one or more bees, plur(**line′**) holds of collections one or more lines, and so on. Such an approach would also dovetail with a handling of numeral adjectives as operators which combine with plural noun denotations to form predicates applicable to collections of particular sizes. Note that such a collection appears to be referred to in

(131)   Three men lifted the piano

Moreover, such collections allow the same sorts of generic readings as bare plurals:

(132)   Three men can lift a piano

The subjects in these sentences could be translated as $\mu(\mathbf{three′}(\mathrm{plur}(\mathbf{man′})))$, where **three′** transforms a predicate true of collections of arbitrary size to a predicate true of collections of size 3. This modification in the translation of plural generics would automatically solve the problem with stages of kinds as well: regarded as stages of *collections* of objects of those kinds, they would no longer be confined to single-object stages.

It might be thought that a distinction between singular and plural generics based on plur would resolve the difficulty with indefinite singular generics (114), (116), (125)–(126). However, since *definite* singular generics presumably do not involve a plur operator, yet allow attributions like

(133)   The dog is widespread in urban areas.

the difficulty remains.

Apparent Problems with Chierchia's Approach

Most importantly, Chierchia's elimination of **Gn** also eliminates readings—often the preferred ones—of ambiguous sentences like the following (repeated from above)

(134)   Canadian academics are supported by a single granting agency
(135)   Storks have a favourite nesting area
(136)   Dogs have a tail
(137)   Sheep are black or white
(138)   Whales are mammals or fish

and leads to faulty truth conditions for certain others involving pronouns bound to bare NPs, like the following (again repeated from above)

(139)   Dogs like themselves
(140)   Dogs make their owners like them.

For example, the translation of (136) is

(141)   **has'($\hat{}(\lambda Q)(\exists x)$[tail'(x) & ˘Q(x)])($\hat{}$dog')**

(where Q is a variable over predicate *intensions*); and by an extensionalizing postulate[20] this leads to

(142)   **($\exists x$)[tail'(x) & has'(x)($\hat{}$dog')]**

which is the non-preferred reading that there is a tail such that dogs have it. A similar difficulty would be encountered for sentences like (137), in which only a wide-scope reading of the disjunction would be obtained.

It may be possible to solve this particular problem by modifying the extensionalizing postulate to make it dependent upon whether the subject of the predicate is a kind or an object. However, no such escape seems available in the case of sentences (139) and (140), involving bound pronouns. The translation of (139) is

(143)   **(λx)[(λx_1)][like'($\hat{}(\lambda P)˘P(x_1)$)](x)(x)($\hat{}$dog')**

As noted earlier, the definition of λ-abstraction in IL* ensures that this formula will be false, since x is an individual variable and the denotation of ˆ**dog'**, being a predicate intension, cannot be among the *individuals* in the extension of the λ-abstract. (As we pointed out, a sentence of this form will be false even if the assignment of the concept correlate of the argument as value of x in the embedded open sentence would have made it true.) While it would be possible to reformulate the rule of reflexive translation which gives the above result so that it abstracts a variable over predicate intensions rather than individuals, the resulting translation would, in effect, say that dogs like dogs, rather than themselves. Given the intensional translation of mass terms, the same difficulty is encountered for sentences like

(144)   Damaged skin renews itself

whose translation will be false or, with intensional reflexive variables, equivalent to *damaged skin renews damaged skin.*

Carlson (1982) has offered some objections to the view underlying Chierchia's treatment of generics and mass terms, that kinds are nominalized properties. He points to the contrast between such a and b pairs as

(145)   (a)   Redness is a property
        (b)   Horses are a property
(146)   (a)   The property of being a horse is a very abstract thing
        (b)   Horses are a very abstract thing
(147)   (a)   Being a horse is fun
        (b)   Horses are fun

One may question as well whether Chierchia's formalization of Carlson's stages as *instantaneous* manifestations of objects (or rather as the mereological fusion of instantaneous manifestations of objects) can properly serve the purposes for which Carlson seems to have enlisted this notion. Consider, for example, verbs like *displace, hollow out, envelop, build, fight a war*, and *throw a party*. All of these meet Carlson's main criteria for stage-level predicates: they induce existential readings on bare NP subjects, and they allow progressive forms. Yet it seems inappropriate to regard the following sentences as ascribing properties to instantaneous stages.

(148)   Mammals displaced the remaining dinosaurs
(149)   Water hollowed out the rock
(150)   Ivy gradually enveloped the building
(151)   New settlements were built on the West Bank
(152)   Wars have been fought over worthless land
(153)   Friends threw a party for him
(154)   Termites hollowed out the tree
(155)   Shah Jahan built the Taj Mahal

The following-out or envelopment cannot be ascribed to instantaneous manifestations, but only to (watery or leafy) individuals acting over some extended time period. It is hard to see how *building the Taj Mahal* could be true of anyone's instantaneous stage since the task took at least 14 years, or how *displacing the remaining dinosaurs* could be true of a species' instantaneous stage. These sentences show that the problem arises both for generics (bare plurals and for mass terms) and also for proper nouns. In all these cases, one can reasonably maintain that properties of *temporally extended* stages of kinds are being specified (though not if stages of kinds are stages of single objects of those kinds, as one of Carlson's meaning postulates requires). But treating stages as instantaneous makes this view much less plausible.

Apparent Shortcomings of Farkas & Sugioka's Approach

Surprisingly, Farkas & Sugioka do not attempt a treatment of 'existential readings' of bare NP's. In light of the fact that these were Carlson's motivation for introducing 'stages' in the first place, one wonders whether Farkas & Sugioka's relation **R** really bears any relation to Carlson's.

It should be noted that the approach has not been formalized, e.g., it is unclear when 'at time t and place p' are to be introduced and how they are to be formally interpreted. As remarked above, 'logical translations' for Farkas & Sugioka are a mix of object language and metalanguage formulas (including metalanguage expressions embedded within object language sentences). Interpretation of such translations could turn out to be extremely difficult.

Farkas & Sugioka rely on a conditional which differs from the material conditional in that its value is undefined when the antecedent is false. But intuitively, a statement like

(156)   If a dog is always intelligent when it has purple eyes, and there is a dog with purple eyes on Mars, then there is an intelligent dog on Mars

is true—indeed, necessarily true—rather than meaningless, regardless of whether or not there are any purple-eyed dogs. But if they give up their non-standard conditional, there are serious technical problems for their translations of *when*-sentences.

According to Farkas & Sugioka, the sentence

(157)   Lizards are always pleased if the sun shines

means that all stages of the kind, lizards, are pleased if any stage of the sun shines. Now as this stands, it requires all stages of lizardkind, throughout all time, to be pleased, as long as some stage of the sun does in fact shine. Clearly, it remains to connect up the two parts of the conditional in time and space. As we have seen, a device that they use elsewhere is to append modifiers 'at t in p' (i.e., 'at time t in place p') to clauses in logical translations of generic sentences. With this device, the interpretation of the sentence could be refined to read, 'For all times t and places p, all stages of the kind, lizards, are pleased at t in p if any stage of the sun shines at t in p'. However, this translation *still* requires all stages of lizardkind, throughout all time, to be pleased, though now it requires them to be pleased at any time t and any place p featuring sunshine. But this is absurd, for a given stage of lizardkind is by definition the manifestation of that kind at a particular time, and such a manifestation cannot be pleased at some *other* time t. What seems to be required, to make the correct connection between stages and times, is a relation which expresses that a stage *occupies* a particular time. This would allow the meaning of the sentence to be expressed as 'For all times t and places p, and any stage of lizardkind occupying t, that stage is happy in p if a stage of the sun occupying t shines in p'.

It is not at all obvious, however, how to accommodate such an 'occupies' relation systematically in Farkas & Sugioka's translations. Also, were one to do so, it is not clear that stages would still serve any useful purpose as an ontological category. Why not render the meaning of the sentence simply as 'For all times t and places p, lizardkind (as an individual persisting in time) is happy at t in p, if the sun (as another individual persisting in time) shines at t in p'? The fundamental problem, it seems to us, is that Farkas & Sugioka are trying to represent time relationships by quantifying explicitly over time variables, while adopting Carlson's 'stages' which are expressly designed to allow treatment of times as *indices*. These indices serve as arguments of semantic functions interpreting object language expressions, but cannot be referred to by object language variables. We shall come back to this observation later, when we discuss general shortcomings of the sophisticated approach.

Farkas & Sugioka translate generic sentences with the aid of an unselective quantifier **G** which, they say, is to be understood as 'in a significant number of cases', and which is 'inherently vague'. However, it is surely true that

(158)   In a significant number of cases, leukemia patients are children

yet it is surely false that

(159)   Leukemia patients are children

Similar examples have already been noted by Carlson (1977, p. 40):

(160)   Seeds do not germinate
(161)   Books are paperbacks
(162)   Prime numbers are odd
(163)   Crocodiles die before they attain an age of two weeks

These false sentences become true when prefixed with *In a significant number of cases*. One basic difficulty in finding a workable quantifier lies in the neglect of a contextually determined 'ensemble of cases or situations', a topic to which we will return in our general critique of the sophisticated approach. Another serious obstacle to any quantificational approach is the inherently intensional character of certain habitual and generic statements, as pointed out by Dahl (1975) and Carlson (1982). For example,

(164)   This machine crushes oranges

may be true even if the machine is fresh off the assembly line and is destined never to be used. Its truth comes from its *capability* for crushing oranges, an essentially modal notion. Similarly

(165)   Members of this club help one another in emergencies

may be true, even though no emergencies have yet arisen to put this code of behaviour to the test. Much as in (164), its truth comes more trom the *preparedness* of the agents to act in certain ways, than from their actually doing so.

Finally, the approach of Farkas & Sugioka is unable to handle relative-clause sentences like

(166)   A man who owns a stubborn donkey usually beats it

because indefinite singular NPs are translated as free variables with meta-linguistic auxiliary constraints restricting the free variable. Thus the relative clause *who owns a stubborn donkey* becomes part of a metalinguistic constraint on the variable translating the subject, so that *usually* fails to bind *a stubborn donkey*.

A General Critique of the Sophisticated Approach

In this subsection, we shall adduce some general doubts about the entire sophisticated approach. We intend these criticisms to apply to all the theorists we have considered above, and have in mind that appreciation of these points will lend credence to the proposals sketched in the next section.

In the first place there is the very general question of whether it is indeed appropriate to regard episodic predicates as applying to stages rather than to individuals. Various considerations appear to us to indicate that it is not. First, it seems a little puzzling why there are stage-level predicates at all, if they need to be converted to predicates over individuals (i.e., objects or kinds) in each case and every case in which they are actually applied. Second, the distinction between stage-level and object-level predicates leads to a formally very non-uniform treatment of semantically alike predicates such as those in the following (a) and (b) sentences:

(167)   (a)   John is riding on the bus
        (b)   John is a passenger on the bus
(168)   (a)   John will speak at the conference
        (b)   John will be a speaker at the conference
(169)   (a)   John received a prize
        (b)   John was the recipient of a prize
(170)   (a)   John started the quarrel
        (b)   John was the instigator of the quarrel
(171)   (a)   John was subject to ridicule by Mary
        (b)   John was subjected to ridicule by Mary
(172)   (a)   Their eyes glowed
        (b)   Their eyes were luminous

We do not deny that there are significant semantic differences between some of the (a) and (b) sentences, but we do feel that their truth conditions are equally dependent upon fleeting 'stages' of the subject. Conversely, they can be viewed equally well as attributing properties to *objects* at particular times. Moreover, many predicates can induce quasi-universal readings (suggesting that they apply to objects, according to our sophisticated theorists) as easily as they can induce existential readings (suggesting that they apply to stages).

(173) Poor people live in that part of town
(174) Dollar bills are printed in that building
(175) People devote years to the study of such problems
(176) People are asleep/homeless/away from home/on the beach/on the brink of starvation
(177) People with links to organized crime support his candidacy

(This point did not elude Carlson, who noted that many such examples involve locative adverbials.) Related observations can be made about progressive participles, which according to the sophisticated theory are paradigms of inducing the existential reading. There are a large number of such cases in which a *range* of interpretations seem possible, from the particular to the generic. For example,

(178) Wildlife is being destroyed

might refer to a very limited number of individuals at a particular time (e.g., when the cause is a forest fire), or to a larger number of individuals over an extended period of time (e.g., when the cause is widespread and persistent hunting and poaching), or to wildlife *in general* (e.g., when the cause is man's encroachment on the natural habitats of all wildlife). In general, one can always get at least two 'interpretations' of such sentences as

(179) Leaves are turning yellow
(180) Ducks are flying south
(181) Bats are hunting food
(182) Wolves are howing
(183) Dissidents are being thrown in jail

One reading derives from the 'on the scene reporter', who looks at his surroundings and 'states what he sees'. As the camera pans around him, our reporter says

> Ladies and gentlemen, as you can see,
> leaves are turning yellow and ducks are flying south

Later in the day, our reporter stumbles across a provincial capital, turns on his TV camera, and announces

> Dissidents are being thrown in jail

And still later that night he again scans his surroundings with the camera and announces

> You will note now that bats are hunting food and wolves are howling

again reporting on what activities are before him. This 'on the scene' reporting is perhaps the sophisticated theory's 'realization reading'. But there is a second reading of these sentences provided by 'storytellers' remarking on the 'trends of the times'. Instead of reporting about the scene, our storyteller says:

> It's that time of year, autumn.
> Leaves are turning yellow and ducks are flying south

Our storyteller is not remarking about the current scenery, but rather about current trends pertaining to leaves and ducks *in general*—these are generic sentences. Let's listen to him again:

> Ah, fall! It's election time in Central America:
> dissidents are being thrown in jail
> It's midnight: it's that time when bats are hunting food
> and wolves are howling

If these 'trends of the times' readings are possible for progressive cases—and they surely are—then it is incorrect to posit 'realization readings' as the logical form for *any* of the particular utterances of such sentences. Any 'realization reading' which can come out of them must then be accounted for by some other factor, such as the context of utterance. But then it would *not* be part of the meaning or logical form that they are about realizations rather than about the kinds.

Interpretation of episodic sentences in terms of stages runs into difficulty when the sentence predicates are intensional or involve reference to individuals displaced in time:

(184) Houses are being designed

(185) War heroes are being remembered

(186) Nixon is fading from people's memories

(187) Mozart is gaining new admirers

Clearly, (184) should not be interpreted as saying that a (present) stage of the kind, houses, is being designed, and (185) should not be interpreted as saying that a (present) stage of the kind, war heroes, is being remembered. The analysis of such sentences by Chierchia would have it that we are remembering a current, *instantaneous* stage of the kind, which is surely wrong. In Carlson, the stage might be temporally extended, but this is still wrong, since (185) is not referring to any particular *stages* of war heroes, but rather is referring to *objects*—individual war heroes. Much the same can be said about (186) and (187).

As remarked in previous subsections, there is a more general point to be made about stages. They appear to be both intuitively and technically redundant in a theory that already posits time indices (for semantic evaluation). After all, talk of stages can be replaced by talk of individuals at particular times. Conversely, time is redundant (as a primitive notion) in a system with stages, since simultaneity can be expressed in terms of being part of a common stage, and time-ordering can be recast as stage-ordering.

An important shortcoming of all of the sophisticated accounts of generic sentences is their neglect of what strikes us as one of their most salient features: their explicit or implicit reference to an ensemble of situations or episodes with respect to which the main clause is to be evaluated. Consider, for example, the following sentences

(188) (a)   Robin Hood never misses
        (b)   Robin hood shoots (an arrow) at a target
(189) (a)   A cat always lands on its feet
        (b)   A cat drops to the ground
(190) (a)   A student (always) admires a fair professor
        (b)   A student knows a fair professor (as a student in one of his classes)
(191) (a)   Men (usually) notice pretty women
        (b) Sm^{21} men are near sm pretty women (and not yet aware of them)
(192) (a)   Dogs give live birth
        (b)   Sm dogs give birth

We shall return to these examples (and ones like them) and dwell on them at some length in the next section. For the present, we wish merely to draw attention to the implicit reference in the (a)-sentences to *underlying ensembles of situations or episodes* like those in the (b)-sentences. We will suggest that these situations or episodes are systematically related to the sentences to which they pertain, and that the frequency adverbs in the (a)-sentences are to be interpreted with reference to these underlying ensembles. Nowhere in the sophisticated theory is there to be found an explanation of how this can be. Notice that certain puzzles are immediately clarified by the assumption of such ensembles. For example, we can see why the truth of (189a) does not require cats to be landing all the time, or why it is irrelevant to the truth of (192a) what *fraction* of dogs give live birth.

SOME PROPOSED LINES OF INQUIRY

We have outlined some of the problems besetting any attempt to explicate formally the 'fundamental intuition' about sentences containing bare plurals, mass terms, and related constructions. The three 'sophisticated theories' we have discussed undoubtedly represent major steps forward in our understanding of such constructions. Yet, as we have tried to show, many facets of the problem remain obscure and puzzling.

In this concluding section we discuss two possible lines of further investion, which seem to us to hold some promise. The first is a 'conservative' proposal: essentially, it attempts to find a middle ground between Carlson's and Chierchia's theories which would permit the simplicity of Chierchia's logical-form representations of generic (and related) sentences to be retained, while remedying the defects that seem to result from relinquishing Carlson's operator **Gn**.

The first proposal, however, seems fundamentally limited; the sort of approach indicated may be unable in principle to deal satisfactorily with indefinite singular generics, or with the problem of 'ensembles' underlying generic statements, or to avoid the 'schizoid' view of frequency adverbs as temporal/atemporal. The second, more radical line of inquiry is therefore one which proposes to take such ensembles seriously. In this sense it takes its cue from the Lewis/Farkas & Sugioka view of quantifying adverbs and restrictive clauses, although it seeks to ground 'cases' in something other than sets of free variables. However, here our discussion is even less concrete than in the case of the 'conservative' proposal.

Indirect Semantic Evaluation

The fundamental problem confronted by all theories of generics, as we have seen, is to explicate the truth conditions of sentences which, at least on the surface, appear to predicate the same property (such as the property of being intelligent) of both objects (such as Fido) and of kinds (such as dogs).

The simplest sort of account of this phenomenon would be one like Chierchia's, which takes the logical form of such sentences to be the same, regardless of whether the subject is an object or a kind. Indeed, Carlson's initial Montague-style fragment dealt with generic predications in this straightforward fashion. But, as Carlson noted, such an account misconstrues certain sentences involving bound pronouns, and we have given additional kinds of sentences, involving ambiguities, for which the straightforward account fails.

Is something like Carlson's **Gn**-operator (or Farkas & Sugioka's **G**-quantifier) essential at the level of logical form, then, if we are to make formal sense of generic predictions? We would hope not, since (as we showed) this would have undesirable effects on the formal syntax, introducing otherwise unmotivated syntactic ambiguities or features.

It seems to us that certain avenues remain open for retaining the simplicity of logical form sought by Chierchia, while avoiding the semantic problems such an approach can engender. We briefly sketch two closely-related possibilities. The idea in both is to shift some of the burden of providing correct truth conditions from the rules of translation to the rules of semantic evaluation; or, to put it a little differently, the idea is to 'liberalize' the logical syntax of predication slightly, at the expense of a slight complication in the rules of evaluation (no greater complication than in Chierchia's semantics, however).

In particular, we make the following observations. The standard way to evaluate a predication of the form $\Phi(t)$ is to say that this is true (i.e., $|\Phi(t)| = 1$ under a particular interpretation, for a particular variable assignment function, at a particular index) just in case $|t|$ is in the extension of $|\Phi|$ (under that interpretation, etc). Furthermore, to say $|t|$ is in the extension of $|\Phi|$ is standardly regarded as an alternative way of saying $|\Phi|(|t|) = 1$. There is, however, nothing sacred about either of these conventions. All we require, ultimately, is some formalized way of saying that for $\Phi(t)$ to be true in a state of affairs, whatever t denotes must have whatever property Φ denotes, in that state of affairs. (In fact, there are ways of proceeding, exemplified by the initial formulations of Situation Semantics, which take this statement essentially at face value.)

There is no reason in principle why we could not distinguish several ways of evaluating predications formally, depending on the types of the predicate and argument(s) involved, where these methods do not necessarily depend on checking whether the thing denoted by the argument is an object for which the semantic value of the predicate (when applied to the object) will yield 1.

To carry this proposal out, let us introduce our terminology. We use the term *extension* as the formal equivalent of 'the set of entities that have a particular property at a particular index'. Thus if **intelligent'**$(\mu(\textbf{dog'}))$ is true, we want $\mu(\textbf{dog'})$ to be in the extension of **intelligent'**. In this we proceed as Chierchia (1982) and Cocchiarella (1979). Thus, to say $|\textbf{intelligent'}(\mu(\textbf{dog'}))| = 1$ is the same as saying $|\mu(\textbf{dog'})| \in \text{Ext}(\textbf{intelligent'})$. The concept of 'extension' is distinguished from the concept 'objects for which the semantic value of the predicate (at an index) yields 1'. We may, for example, wish to deny that $\mu(\textbf{dog'})$ is such an object when the predicate is **intelligent'**. This would mean that we do not equate extensions of predicates with the subdomains on which semantic values of those predicates are 1, but rather, we just say that if t denotes a kind, and Φ is an object-level predicate, then the kind $|t|$ is in the extension of Φ (under an interpretation, for a given variable assignment function, at an index) iff $|\Phi|(r) = 1$ (under that interpretation, etc) for 'sufficiently many' realizations r of $|t|$ (under that interpretation, etc), i.e., if sufficiently many realizations of the kind are in the extension of Φ. This means that we do not identify $|\mathbf{intelligent'}(\mu(\mathbf{dog'}))| = 1$ with $|\mathbf{intelligent'}|(|\mu(\mathbf{dog'})|) = 1$. How many realizations are 'sufficiently many' can itself be made a matter of interpretation: we could specify, as part of an interpretation, which sets of realizations of any given kind will make any given (object-level) predicate true of that kind (at a given index). Technically, this requires that we associate with each object-level predicate a function which, given an index and a kind as argument, supplies a class of sets of realizations[22] of that kind as value. The notion of 'sufficiently many' can be 'intensionalized' (by specifying, as part of an interpretation of an object-level predicate, which *mappings from indices* to classes of sets of realizations of a given kind will make the predicate true of the kind at a given index), and can be extended to n-adic predicates which are 'basically' object-level but allow kind-level arguments in any argument position. So we see that the above is a device for evaluating object-level predicates that have been applied to kinds. At the object level, we *do* assume that an object is in the extension of Φ iff $|\Phi|$ yields 1 for that object—this equivalence only breaks down for 'mixed' predications, *as it does in Chierchia's IL**.

The point is that there really *do* seem to be two distinct ways in which a predicate can truthfully be applied to a kind. This is what the problems with Carlson's initial fragment (without **Gn**) and the problems with Chierchia's theory indicate. For example, how is one to account for the ambiguity of

> Storks have a favourite nesting area

and by contrast, the non-ambiguity of

> Dinosaurs became extinct when a big meteor fell to Earth.

In Chierchia's theory there are no resources to distinguish these. Under the present theory, the former is true only 'indirectly', i.e., *has a favourite nesting area* is true of $\mu(\text{storks})$ only in virtue of being true of sufficiently many storks. The ambiguity formally corresponds to the logical forms (with HF(x,y): x has a favourite nesting area y):

$$[(\lambda x)(\exists y)HF(x,y)](\mu(\text{storks})) \text{ vs } (\exists y)\{[(\lambda x)HF(x,y)](\mu(\text{storks}))\}$$

These do not collapse into the same reading precisely because of the 'indirect interpretation' semantics, for which λ-conversion does not apply in general (for reasons we will discuss shortly) when the semantic types of the λ-variable and the argument do not agree. By contrast, the other sentence (using BEM(x,y): x became extinct when meteor y fell to Earth) also will ge these two types of logical forms, but after λ-conversion from *either* of them we will get

$$(\exists y)BEM(\mu(\text{dinosaur}),y)$$

because $|\mu(\text{dinosaurs})|$ has the property $(\lambda x)(\exists y)BEM(x,y)$ 'directly', that is, $|(\lambda x)(\exists y)BEM(x,y)|(|\mu(\text{dinosaur})|) = 1$ or alternatively put, the kind $|\mu(\text{dinosaur})|$ is in the domain of the function denoted by $(\lambda x)(\exists y)BEM(x,y)$. In the case of HF, $|\mu(\text{stork})|$ was *not* in the domain of the function denoted by $(\lambda x)(\exists y)HF(x,y)$. It is the ability to account for such examples, without invocation of **Gn** in the logical form translations, which is the proof of the 'indirect evaluation' pudding.

In the preceding account, a sentence like *Dogs are intelligent* would be translated as **intelligent'(μ(dog'))** and would be evaluated by applying a rule that would yield

$|\textbf{intelligent'}(\boldsymbol{\mu}(\textbf{dog'}))| = 1$ [that is, $|\mu(\textbf{dog'})| \in \text{Ext}(\textbf{intelligent'})$] iff

$|\textbf{intelligent'}|(r) = 1$ for 'sufficiently many' realizations r of $|\mu(\textbf{dog'})|$

The application of the evaluation rule makes it appear as though the syntax allows arbitrary predications without regard to the types of the predicate and its argument, and the semantic evaluation takes care of all such violations. Other sentences, however, explicitly introduce an 'adverb of quantification', as in *Dogs are generally intelligent.* Here the translation and evaluation would be (using **Gn** as the translation of the predicate operator *generally*):

$|\textbf{Gn}(\hat{}\textbf{intelligent'})(\boldsymbol{\mu}(\textbf{dog'}))| = 1$ iff $|\textbf{Gn}(\hat{}\textbf{intelligent'})|(|\mu(\textbf{dog'})|) = 1$

The explicit mention of *generally* explicitly 'elevates' the predicate *intelligent* so that it can be directly applied to $\mu(\textbf{dog'})$, and thus the evaluation is 'direct'. However, the understanding of these two sentences is the same; and so for the latter one, we will require some meaning postulate that will entail that 'sufficiently many' realizations of $\mu(\textbf{dog'})$ are intelligent.

The fact that our two sentences are understood the same way suggests that perhaps we should all along treat them the same. Rather than trying to 'inductively' evaluate them both (by considering only subformulas of the formula under consideration), perhaps we should use a 'non-inductive evaluation' on the former. This slightly tidier way of proceeding is very much in the spirit of Carlson's approach. We allow object-level predicates to be applied to kind-level arguments in the logical syntax, but rather than regarding the resulting expressions as meaningless, we regard them as 'abbreviations', in which a **Gn** operator has been eluded. Or putting it in terms of truth conditions, we say that, where Φ is 'basically' object level and t is kind denoting, $|t|$ is in the extension of Φ (with respect to an interpretation, variable assignment, and index) iff $|\mathbf{Gn}(^\smallfrown\Phi)|(|t|) = 1$ (with $|\ |$ evaluated with respect to that interpretation, etc). This latter condition can be evaluated recursively in the usual manner, since $\mathbf{Gn}(^\smallfrown\Phi)$ is a kind-level predicate. In a similar way, $\mathbf{Gn_2},\mathbf{Gn_3},...$ operators can be invoked in the evaluation of dyadic, triadic, etc, object-level predicates applied directly to a kind, where such application yields an object-level predicate of adicity reduced by 1.[23]

This 'slightly tidier way of proceeding' is technically legitimate. It amounts to claiming that, when faced with the task of evaluating certain sentences, we should instead 'shift our attention' to the evaluation of a different sentence which is not a constituent of the sentence under consideration. To see the legitimacy of this, let us proceed by means of an analogy. Consider the case of a propositional logic in which there is a set of propositional variables $\{P_1,P_2,...\}$, parentheses as usual, and the connectives $\{\neg,\rightarrow,\&,\leftrightarrow\}$. (These connectives are to be considered as primitive and not introduced by means of definitions, although they are to receive their usual interpretation). $\mathbf{I}$ is an interpretation function that assigns to each $\mathbf{P_n}$ some truth value. Now, there are various ways to proceed in giving the recursive definition of truth of a formula (with respect to $\mathbf{I}$). $|\Phi|$ indicates the function which, given $\mathbf{I}$, maps arbitrary formulas Φ into the truth values $\{0,1\}$. A standard way to define this function is

(α)   if Φ is a propositional variable, then $|\Phi| = \mathbf{I}(\Phi)$
(β) $|\neg\Phi| = 1$ **iff** $|\Phi| = 0$
(γ) $|(\Phi\ \&\ \Psi)| = 1$ if $|\Phi| = 1$ and $|\Psi| = 1$
(δ) $|(\Phi \rightarrow \Psi)| = 1$ iff either $|\Phi| = 0$ or $|\Psi| = 1$
(ε) $|(\Phi \leftrightarrow \Psi)| = 1$ if $|\Phi| = |\Psi|$

This might be called 'the inductive interpretation' of the logic. The crucial feature of such an interpretation is that, for complex formulas Φ, one computes whether $|\Phi|=1$ by looking only to the values of the function of sub-formulas of Φ. But (α)–(ε) is not the only possible 'inductive interpretation' that will yield the same results. For example, (ε) could be replaced by

(ε') $|(\Phi \leftrightarrow \Psi)| = 1$ iff both 1) if $|\Phi| = 1$ then $|\Psi| = 1$, and 2) if $|\Psi| = 1$ then $|\Phi| = 1$

More importantly for our purposes, 'inductive interpretations' are not the only viable methods of proceeding. A 'non-inductive interpretation' of some formula Φ would provide a method of evaluating Φ which did not exclusively rely on the interpretations of subformulas of Φ. For example, (ε) might be replaced by

(ε'') $|(\Phi \leftrightarrow \Psi)| = 1$ iff $|((\Phi \rightarrow \Psi) \,\&\, (\Psi \rightarrow \Phi))| = 1$

It is easy to see that (α)–(δ) yields the same results whether joined to (ε) or to (ε''). A 'non-inductive evaluation' (of $\leftrightarrow$ formulas), one might say, is a recursive evaluation which is not an inductive evaluation. Such is our strategy for evaluating formulas like $\Phi(\alpha)$ when Φ is 'basically' an object-level predicate and α denotes a kind. We instead evaluate a different sentence which is not a subformula of the original, namely we evaluate $[\mathbf{Gn}(^\smallfrown\Phi)](\alpha)$.

It is easy to see that the desirable properties of the sophisticated theory are retained on this modified account. The essential observation is that *lambda-conversion fails for object-level lambda expressions applied to kinds.* So for example, expressions like

(193)   (a) (λx°)like$'(x,x)$—the property of an object liking itself
         (b) $(\lambda x^\circ)(\exists y^\circ)[$tail$'(y) \,\&\,$ has$'(x,y)]$—the property of an object having a tail

applied to a kind-level expression such as d (that is, $(\iota x^k)[(\forall y^\circ)\square [R(x,y) \leftrightarrow$ dog$'(y)]]$), *cannot* be converted to

(194)   (a)   like$'(d,d)$
         (b) $(\exists y^\circ)[$tail$'(y) \,\&\,$ has$'(d,y)]$

respectively, since the value of *d* is not in the domain of the functions denoted by those λ-expressions. Rather, the application of such object-level expressions to kind-denoting terms is interpreted using the 'generic evaluation' rule (which introduces $\mathbf{Gn}$) proposed earlier, instead of applying λ-conversion. Consequently, the truth conditions will not be those of (194), but rather, will require that particular dog-realizations like themselves (generally speaking), and have a tail (generally speaking).

We should mention that certain apparent λ-conversion identities, such as

(195) $[(\lambda x^\circ)$intelligent$'(x)](d) =$ intelligent$'(d)$

still hold (necessarily), but this is not so in virtue of λ-conversion, but in virtue of

(196) $\square[(\lambda x^\circ)$intelligent$'(x) =$ intelligent$']$

A caveat about the above proposal is that the suggested generic rule of evaluation for object-level predicates applied to kind denoting terms must be invoked only where the predicate is *exclusively* object level at the argument position in question. For, if the predicate allows both objects and kinds in its extension at some argument position (as many of Carlson's predicates do), sanctioning the generic rule of evaluation at that position would lead to ambiguity when the predicate is applied to a kind-denoting expression.

So, for example, if we want to hold (like Carlson) that *popular*, *well-known*, etc, apply directly to kinds (i.e., the kind is an object for which the semantic value of the predicate applied to it is 1), then a formula like

(197)   popular′(d)

cannot be interpreted as a generalization about the popularity of individual dogs. But then how *do* we express generalizations about popularity (etc) of individuals, such as that *cheerleaders are popular* (*with the boys*)? The answer is that we need to posit a second translation, **popular**$'_2$, which is *strictly* object-level in its extension. Thus

(198)   popular$'_2$(c)

will be the desired generalization about individual cheerleaders. So in general, if a predicate derived from English is thought informally to admit two sorts of interpretations with respect to a kind-denoting argument, one of which allows the property or relation in question to 'trickle down' to realizations while the other does not, then a lexical ambiguity must be stipulated for that predicate.

In summary, the idea in both proposals is to postpone the introduction of 'generalization' operators to the stage of semantic evaluation, rather than making the rules of translation responsible for their introduction. Logical translations which 'mix' object level predicates with kind level arguments are regarded as implicit generalizations. This strategy unburdens the syntax and rules of translation, obviating the need for artificial structural ambiguities, unmotivated syntactic features, and phantom operators in the rules of translation. As can be easily seen, this is quite close to Chierchia's proposal; it just replaces the notion of 'concept correlates', as a basis for evaluating generic predictions, with the notion of 'indirect evaluation', involving evaluation with respect to realizations, as we have outlined above.

Note that it would be wrong to regard this move as merely a notational trick. It does, after all, have the effect of assigning formal truth values to expressions such as **intelligent′(d)**, where *d* denotes dogkind, which were not assigned values on Carlson's account. In other words, a kind really *can* have an object-level property; it does so just in case its realizations 'generally' exhibit the property (at appropriate indices).

Let us preface our grammatical sketch with a word on our ontology. We expressed certain doubts about the need for stages as an ontological category, particularly in a system in which time is already presupposed as a primitive. Hence we take a predication such as **happy′(fido′)** to be about a particular individual at a particular time and not about a stage of an individual. The stative/nonstative distinction plays a significant role in the grammar (phrase structure rules and rules of translation) but not in the model theory.

We begin our grammatical sketch by presenting the translations of four of the sentences we used to illustrate 'the fundamental intuition' in the third section:

(199) (a) Snow is white
     (b) white′(μ(snow′))

(200) (a) Snow is falling
     (b) PROG(fall′(μ(snow′)))

(201) (a) Dogs are loyal
     (b) loyal′(μ(plur(dog′)))

(202) (a) Dogs are barking
     (b) PROG(bark′(μ(plur(dog′))))

The final step in the syntactic analysis of these sentences, and in the calculation of the translations, is determined by the rule pair

(203) S→NP VP, VP′(NP′)

Here the phrase structure rule states that a sentence may be constituted of a noun phrase followed by a verb phrase. (Separate feature agreement and inheritance principles enforce constraints such as person and number concord and inheritance of certain features of the VP by the S.) The accompanying rule of translation states that the VP-translation is to be applied to the NP-translation to obtain the translation of the sentence.

Semantically, **snow′** is to be taken as 'basically' an object-level predicate true of 'snowy objects' (such as quantities of snow, snowflakes, and snowballs), and 'indirectly' (i.e., by the process of indirect evaluation we have sketched) a predicate over kinds, true of kinds of snow (such as powder snow, granular snow, or dirty snow). Similarly **dog′** is basically an object-level predicate, and indirectly, a predicate over kinds.[24] We remain non-committal about the exact interpretation of μ(**snow′**), μ(plur(**dog′**)), etc except to say that μ(P) is some function $f(\hat{}P)$ of the intension of P (possibly the identity, or possibly a function whose range consists of individuals sortally distinct from ordinary individuals). **white′, fall′, loyal′**, and **bark′** are similarly interpreted as basically object-level predicates. In all cases evaluation of predicates and formulas is indexed to worlds and times.

Since we do not evaluate objects at particular times, there is no difficulty for sentences involving temporal displacement, such as

(204)   Mozart is gaining new admirers

If we do not distinguish episodic from characterizing predicates in the model theory, how do we account for the fundamental intuition about the contrast between (199) and (200), or (201) and (202)? The answer is that we take the distinction to be a semantic (rather than model-theoretic) distinction, to be encoded in meaning postulates such as the following,

(205)   For P ∈ {**white′,loyal′,soft′,four-legged′**, . . .}

$$(\forall x^k)\Box[Gn(\hat{} P)(x^k) \leftrightarrow \Box(My^\circ : R(y,x)) P(y)]$$

(206)   For P ∈ {**fall′,bark′**, . . .}

$$(\forall x^k)\Box[Gn(\hat{} P)(x^k) \leftrightarrow (M'y^\circ : R(y,x)) P(y)]$$

where M and M′ encode slightly different notions of 'sufficiently many (much)', perhaps roughly verbalizable as 'most of the relevant' and 'significantly many (much)' respectively. The embedded necessity operator in (205) is intended to capture the gnomic, or lawlike, character of statements like (199a) or (201a).[25] That is, we are saying that if a substance is not white in most cases, it not only is not, but *cannot* be, snow; and if animals of a certain kind are not loyal in most cases, they not only are not, but *cannot* be, dogs. Admittedly (205) is a little too strong for **white′** and **loyal′**.[26] (Certainly we would not assert (205) for *all* stative predicates; for example, *is expensive*, *are cancer patients*, and *prefer vodka to beer* have a contingent character even when applied to kinds, and so fit better with (206)). Nevertheless, we regard the contrast between (205) and (206) as encapsulating, at least in an approximate way, and at least for many kinds of predicates, the 'fundamental intuition'.

Thus it is not an existential/universal distinction which underlies the fundamental intuition in examples of this type, but rather a contingent/ necessary distinction. If snow is white (or solid, or crystalline, or frozen water) then it is necessarily so in the sense that most of its relevant realizations must be white, but if snow is falling (or on the ground, or causing me trouble), it need not be. The existential/universal distinction, on such an account, comes as a 'byproduct': necessary truths (other than logical ones) owe their status to *conventions* (linguistic, scientific, mathematical, or whatever) designed to match our vocabulary to the categorical, statistical and lawlike trends of the world. This makes it likely that they will have near-universal validity for the instances of the categories they talk about. On the other hand, contingent properties are acquired causally, and since causal effects are often localized, the number of objects of a particular kind affected is often limited. This explains why, in some of our earlier examples, such as

(207) Wildlife is being destroyed
(208) Ducks are flying south

and so on, arbitrarily narrow or wide interpretations are possible, depending on how local or global the underlying causes are taken to be.

However, (205) will not serve in all cases of intuitively generic readings. For example,

(209) Athletes ate a light breakfast in those days
(210) People are poor in that part of the world
(211) Canadian scientists are supported by a single granting agency
(212) Frenchmen eat horsemeat

do not attribute essential properties to kinds, yet are generic in content. We will not attempt a detailed analysis, except to suggest that the relevant meaning postulate (except for sentence (212)) may be like (206), with M' replaced by M.

Our verbalizations 'most of the relevant' and 'significantly many (much)' for M and M' were deliberately chosen to allow for content-dependence. Again, we will not pursue this point further. However, we wish to comment that we chose 'most' rather than 'all' in the verbalization of M, because of examples like

(213) Conservatives favour heavy investment in defense

(and many of the others we have considered). Note that there may be no factors dependent on content, or any general knowledge, allowing exclusion of exceptions to (213) as 'irrelevant'. This leaves the problem of explaining why some generic statements, such as

(214) Dogs are mammals
(215) Electrons are negatively charged.

appear to have genuinely universal import. The answer, it seems to us, lies in the availability of a meaning postulate stronger than (205) for predicates denoting natural kinds and certain scientifically formalized properties:

(216) For $P \in \{$**snow′,dog′,mammal′,electron′,negatively-charged′**$\ldots\}$

$$(\forall x^k)\Box[Gn(^\frown P)(x^k) \leftrightarrow \Box(\forall y^\circ : R(y,x)) P(y)]$$

Let us now return to grammar. The tense/aspect operators PAST, PRES, FUTR, PROG (signalled by *be V-ing*), and PERF (signalled by *have V-en*) are to be treated syntactically as VP-operators and semantically as sentence operators, with the rule

(217)   VP → F VP, $(\lambda x)(F(VP'(x)))$, for F ∈ {PRES,...,PERF}

where x is object-level or kind-level (or both) depending on the 'basic' type of VP'. PRES is taken as $(\lambda P)P$, and hence has been omitted in (199)–(201). We cannot here go into tense/aspect semantics, but should mention that we take the above operators as relating their operands not only to the time of speech, but also to a contextually determined reference time.

The translations of the noun phrases in (199)–(202) would come from

(218)   NP → N, $\mu(N')$

which applies to both singular and plural phrases. (The translation of a plural N like *dogs* as plur(**dog'**) would derive from a morphological stage of analysis.)

Before proceeding to further rules, we should comment on the apparent lack of intensionality in the translations seen so far. As already stated, μ is in fact implicitly intensional. In addition, we intend functors we write in upper case (such as the tense/aspect operators) to be potentially intensional as well. Thus PAST(**bark'(fido')**), for example, may actually stand for **past($^\cap$(bark'(fido')))** by setting PAST = (λP)**past($^\cap$P)**; alternatively, we might not introduce the intension operator here at all, but rather arrange for the rules of evaluation to treat upper-case functions as intensional (in the traditional manner of modal logics). Of course, we might adopt Montague's strategy of uniformly intensionalizing operands, but this would somewhat obscure our exposition.

We now illustrate briefly the scoping mechanism from Schubert & Pelletier (1982). A quantified phrase such as *every woman* is analyzed and translated by the rule

(219)   NP → DET[QUANT] N, ⟨DET' N'⟩

neglecting various fine points. The angle brackets indicate that the 'generalized quantifier' they enclose is ambiguously scoped. The translation of a sentence like (220a) is as in (220b).

(220)   (a)   Some man loves every woman
         (b)   love'(⟨every' woman'⟩)(⟨some' man'⟩)
               = love'(⟨∀ woman'⟩)(⟨∃ man'⟩)

The two quantifiers can now be 'raised' to encompass any sentential formula that embeds them, at the same time introducing variables, with possible results

(221)   (a)   (∃x: man(x))(∀y: woman(y)) love(y)(x)
         (b)   (∀y: woman(y))(∃x: man(x)) love(y)(x)

It is this mechanism which allows us to retain the view that names denote individuals, and also to dispense with dual versions of predicates such as **love′** and **love$_*$** (or **love$^+$**), which Montague introduced to distinguish the direct translations of English transitive verbs (whose objects are intensionalized property sets) from extensionalized versions (whose objects are individuals).

The same sort of scoping mechanism is used for coordination. Thus (222a) is translated as (222b):

(222) (a) John will love Mary or hate Bill
        (b) FUTR[⟨v love′(Mary′) hate′(Bill′)⟩(John′)]

The ambiguously scoped conjunction allows the minimal scoping in (223a) or the wider scope in (223b), or the still wider scope in (223c) (with conversion from prefix to infix form):

(223) (a) FUTR[(λx)[love′(Mary′)(x) $\lor$ hate′(Bill′)](John′)]
        (b) FUTR[love′(Mary′)(John′) $\lor$ hate′(Bill′)(John′)]
        (c) FUTR(love′(Mary′)(John′)) $\lor$ FUTR(hate′(Bill′)(John′))

As it turns out, all three 'readings' are equivalent. But if FUTR were **certainly′** (for example), (c) would be distinct from (a) and (b).

The same mechanism can now be deployed for frequency adverbs, regarded syntactically as VP operators and semantically as sentence operators:

(224) VP[+STAT] → ADV[FREQ] VP[−AUX,−STAT], ⟨ADV′ VP′⟩

Let us apply the rule to (226a), with result (226b):

(225) (a) Dogs always bark
        (b) ⟨ALWAYS$_1$ bark′⟩ (μ(plur(dog′)))

The minimal-scope and wide-scope versions are then

(226) (a) (λx)ALWAYS$_2$(bark′(x))(μ(plur(dog′)))
        (b) ALWAYS$_1$(bark′(μ(plur(dog′))))

The first version *cannot* be λ-converted. Rather, by our rule of indirect evaluation, it is equivalent to

$$\text{Gn}(\hat{}(\lambda x)\text{ALWAYS}_1(\text{bark}'(x)))(\mu(\text{plur}(\text{dog}')))$$

and says that *dogs in general bark all the time*.

The alternative translation, (226b), is equivalent to

$$\text{ALWAYS}_1(\text{Gn}(\hat{}\text{bark}')(\mu(\text{plur}(\text{dog}'))))$$

and says in effect that *all the time, sm (significantly many) dogs bark*, via postulate (206).

Note that contexts are easily constructed in which these readings are salient; as far as we can tell, none of the theories we have considered can readily deliver both of them.

There is, however, a third reading not yet accounted for, namely one according to which *all dogs bark*. This corresponds to the 'atemporal' interpretation of *always*, and like Carlson, we find it necessary to treat *always* as ambiguous. Its second translation, ALWAYS_2, is regarded as an unambiguously scoped VP operator (both syntactically and semantically), accommodated by the rule

(227)   VP[+STAT] → ADV[FREQ]   VP(−AUX,+STAT),
        ADV'(VP')

Note that (in contrast with (224)) the VP daughter is here required to be stative. Thus ALWAYS_2 is not directly applicable to the nonstative predicate **bark'**. However, it becomes stative on a 'dispositional' interpretation via the rule

(228)   VP[+STAT] → VP[−STAT], DISP(VP')

where DISP is an intensional operator somewhat analogous to Carlson's **Gn'**, though it operates on an object-level rather than stage-level predicate and its output is still object-level. (To the extent that **Gn'** is not a 'phantom' operator because it finds expression in the aspectual systems of various languages, neither is DISP.)[27]

The new translation of (225)a obtained via (227) and (228) is

(229) $\text{ALWAYS}_2(\text{DISP}(\text{bark'}))(\mu(\text{plur}(\text{dog'})))$

ALWAYS_2 (like **Gn**) is assumed to evaluate its operand to the kind level (i.e., making it applicable directly to kinds and inapplicable to objects). ALWAYS_2 might be taken as equivalent to $(\lambda P)(\lambda x^k)(\forall y^\circ : R(y, x))P(y)$.[28]

Note that VP's admitted by rule (224) can feed into (227), as can VP's admitted by (227) itself. The latter are clearly ruled out by the semantics. The former may occasionally yield comprehensible results (cf Enç, 1981, p. 222).

Restrictive *if/when* clauses can be added to the grammar fragment along the lines suggested by Carlson, i.e., by arranging for the predicate expressed by the subordinate clause to combine with the subject, forming a more restricted kind. As far as the conversion of the (presumed) pronoun in the subordinate clause to a lambda variable is concerned, GPSG already has a suitable mechanism to accomplish this, designed to deal uniformly with reflexives and gaps (Pollard, 1983).

However, it is not clear that the exercise is worth the trouble, since the requisite syntactic and semantic manoeuvers are rather unnatural and intricate, and the results suffer from the same limitations as Carlson's: a 'schizoid' approach to adverbials, and severe difficulties in extending the treatment of atemporal restrictive clauses to temporal ones.

We are also unable at this time to deal with indefinite singular generics, and perhaps most importantly, the prospects for incorporating an intuitively satisfactory theory of 'cases' into the present framework do not seem very bright. That is why we now focus briefly on this topic.

Towards a Theory of Cases

We have already mentioned that we think one of the most salient features of habitual and generic statements to be their reliance on a reference to an 'ensemble of cases' for their semantic evaluation. For example, a habitual sentence with an explicit adverb of quantification like

(230)   John usually beats Marvin at ping pong

does *not* say that most of the time John is beating Marvin at ping pong. Rather, the *usually* gathers a certain class of 'reference situations', namely situations in which John and Marvin play a game of ping pong, and the *usually* is evaluated with respect to this class of situations. Similarly, when the sentence is generic, such as

(231)   Cats always land on their feet

it is *not* evaluated as if it said at all times cats are landing on their feet, but rather a certain class of 'cases' or 'situations' is set up—such as cases where cats drop to the ground—and the sentence is evaluated with respect to those cases.

Thus it is our view that semantic evaluation of habitual and generic statements depends on reference to these 'ensembles of cases', where the ensemble is determined in part or entirely by context, or in part or entirely by restrictive clauses and adverbials. There are two kinds of such reference ensembles, closely paralleling the two kinds of uses of adverbs of quantification: ensembles of (intuitively) *situations* (corresponding to 'temporal' uses of adverbs of quantification) and ensembles of *objects* (corresponding to 'atemporal' uses of adverbs of quantification).[29]

Let us look first at examples involving reference ensembles of situations where these ensembles are determined by same-sentence context. Examples (232)–(247) are examples where the (a)-sentence is the gnomic sentence and the (b)-sentence gives the type of situation which is implicitly referenced by the (a)-sentence

(232)   (a)   Robin Hood never misses
        (b)   Robin Hood shoots (an arrow) at a target

(233) (a) John usually remembers people's names
       (b) John is called upon to remember the names of sm people
            whose names he has been told
(234) (a) Canada Post sometimes loses letters
       (b) Canada Post has sm letters (for the purpose of conveying
            them from senders to addressees)
(235) (a) John usually beats Marvin at ping pong
       (b) John and Marvin play a game of ping pong
(236) (a) John is always teasing Mary
       (b) John is talking with Mary
(237) (a) Tabby always lands on her feet
       (b) Tabby drops to the ground
(238) (a) A cat always lands on its feet
       (b) A cat drops to the ground
(239) (a) Cats usually land on their feet
       (b) Sm cats drop to the ground
(240) (a) Nice guys finish last
       (b) Sm nice guys participate in a competitive event or process
(241) (a) Lumberjacks drink their whiskey straight
       (b) Sm lumberjacks drink sm whiskey
(242) (a) Bullfighters are often injured
       (b) Sm bullfighters participate in a bullfight
(243) (a) Muggers often threaten their victims with a knife
       (b) Sm muggers mug sm people
(244) (a) Hit-and-run drivers are almost always caught
       (b) Sm drivers have hit someone or something, have fled the
            scene, and are still at large
(245) (a) A student (always) admires a fair professor
       (b) A student knows a fair professor (as a student in one of his
            classes)
(246) (a) Men (usually) notice pretty women
       (b) Sm men are near sm pretty women (and not yet aware of
            them)
(247) (a) Dogs give live birth
       (b) Sm dogs give birth

What is striking about those of the above examples which involve indefinite
singulars and bare plurals (i.e., (238)–(247)) is that these singulars and bare
plurals *appear to refer at one level to kinds, and on another level, to
realizations of those kinds in particular situations.* In our (b)-sentences, the
realizations at issue are signalled by the indefinite determiner *sm*. It is the
reference to kinds which gives bare plurals and other generic terms their

name-like character (making them *rigid* designators), while it is their reference to realizations of those kinds in particular situations which gives them their indefinite character (or, we should say, their *non-rigid* referential character; this phrasing allows for definite and indefinite generic terms).

Moreover, this observation is closely related to the 'fundamental intuition' concerning 'quasi-universal' versus existential import of bare plurals and mass terms: in the (b)-sentences corresponding to the (a)-sentences under consideration, the occurrences of *sm* can be deleted, leaving bare plurals with existential import (under episodic readings of the sentences); the realizations these terms refer to are also what the generic terms in the (a)-sentences are 'non-rigidly' referring to (despite their 'quasi-universal' import).

It is this referential connection between generic sentences (at least those of the habitual or dispositional type illustrated above) and the presupposed underlying situations which is in need of formal explication. Of course, the approaches we have surveyed can be viewed as attempts to provide such an explication. In particular, the Lewis/Farkas & Sugioka approach tries to explicate a set of situations as a set of assignments to a tuple of variables, constrained to realizations of corresponding kinds, and the above referential connection is made by way of these variables. However, this view of situations discards much of their content. It says, for example, that (in (246)) a situation is which sm men are near sm pretty women is abstractly just a pair consisting of sm men and sm women. But that is no more accurate than saying that the content of the *(a)-sentence* (i.e., that men usually notice pretty women) just consists of such pairs. Besides, they do not have a mechanism for making an existentially quantified term in a restrictive clause (such as *sm cats* in (239b)) coreferential with a term in another clause (such as the subject in (239a) after pronominalization).

It therefore seems clear that an adequate theory of generic sentences (at least those of the above variety) must take situations seriously, incorporating them into the model-theoretic framework. That is to say, the generic terms in such sentences need to be treated as *indexical* (i.e., as having senses that are context-dependent). There needs to be a notion of 'an ensemble of situations (or a type of situation) referred to' as part of a context. (This point seems closely related to Enç's (1981) claim that nouns are indexical.)

After looking at some examples involving previous-sentence context, we shall attempt to formulate some principles concerning the way in which sentences like those above determine an ensemble of situations referred to. Then, following a brief statement of the relationship between sentences with an implicitly determined reference ensemble and sentences with a reference ensemble determined by an explicit *if/when* restrictive clause, we shall offer some ideas on how the above 'referential connection' might be made.

Having seen examples where a sentence sets up its own reference ensemble of situations, let us turn to examples where the reference ensemble of situations is provided by a preceding sentence. In (248)–(251), the (a)-sentence is the context-setter while the (b)-sentence is the gnomic sentence.

(248) (a) John is an excellent marksman
      (b) He rarely misses
(249) (a) Canada is well-represented at world cup ski races
      (b) Canadians sometimes take the gold
(250) (a) Most monkeys flee when leopards approach
      (b) Baboons form a protective circle with males on the outside
(251) (a) Christmas has become a protracted event
      (b) Stores are decorated for at least six weeks

Note that it is often *presuppositions of the verb phrase*[30] which suggest the reference ensemble, especially in same-sentence-context examples. (See (232)–(235), (237)–(240), (244)–(247).) In addition, 'characterizing properties' of the subject can play a role, as in (232), (238)–(239), (242)–(245), and possibly (246). Presuppositions of the verb phrase may derive from an intrinsically presuppositional verb (as in (232)–(235), (237)–240), (244)–(246)). Alternatively, presuppositions may derive from stress patterns, since stress of a phrase may be used to distinguish what is *not* presupposed in a sentence from what is presupposed. So, for example, when the phrase *in trees* is stressed in

(252) (a) Leopards usually attack monkeys <u>in trees</u>[31]

there seems to be a presupposition that leopards do attack monkeys, while the information that such attacks usually occur in trees is the new, non-presupposed, information. So, because of the relation between pre-supposition and reference ensembles, the reference ensemble in (252a) consists of situations in which sm leopards attack sm monkeys.

Thus we have the following principle. For a sentence containing a quantificational adverbial (at the S or VP level), with a non-presuppositional verb, and with some phrase in the VP stressed,[32] a sentence describing the presupposed type of situation (and hence the type of situation constituting the reference ensemble) can usually be derived by (i) dropping the adverbial, and (ii) 'generalizing' the stressed constituent. (For example, in (252a), *in trees* is generalized to *somewhere*.) So for (252a) we get

(252) (b) (Situations in which) leopards attack monkeys (somewhere)

Similarly, other ways of assigning stress lead to other reference ensembles:

(253) (a) Leopards usually attack monkeys <u>in</u> trees
      (b) (Situations in which) leopards attack monkeys near trees
(254) (a) Leopards usually attack <u>monkeys</u> in trees
      (b) (Situations in which) leopards attack something in trees
(255) (a) Leopards usually <u>attack</u> monkeys in trees
      (b) (Situations in which) leopards are near monkeys in trees

Note that in all cases, the 'generalization' is *entailed* by the ungeneralized version; e.g., attacking monkeys entails (has as prerequisite) being near them.

It is not clear how this sort of way of working out the reference ensemble interacts with presuppositions based on presuppositional verbs (as opposed to presuppositions based on stress patterns). Our impression is that verb presuppositions tend to 'win out' if there is a conflict. So when we say

(256) Little John usually misses the <u>target</u>

this does not seem to say 'In most situations in which Little John misses something, he misses the target.' Rather, it is the presupposition of the verb, viz., *shooting*, which determines the reference ensemble; and the stress on *target* just gets interpreted as implicit denial of an alternative, i.e., he misses the target, but does not miss something else.

It is also not clear what the effect of stressing the subject NP is. We think that when *leopard* is stressed in the leopard sentence, we can get a reading in which *usually* quantifies over situations in which 'something attacks monkeys in trees' (i.e., it is usually leopards that are the culprits, when something attacks monkeys in trees). But in other sentences, this does not work at all:

(257) <u>Lumberjacks</u> usually drink their whiskey straight

does not say that when people drink their whiskey straight, they are usually lumberjacks. Also

(258) <u>Bullfighters</u> are often injured

does not say that when people are injured, they are often bullfighters, etc. Certainly there are many complications to what we have said about stress and VP presupposition as determiners of reference ensembles of situations. But we shall not here pursue this topic further.

We now turn our attention to sentences in which a reference ensemble of situations is determined by a restrictive clause or adverbial. We note that most of the sentences (232)–(248) can be turned into such examples via the pattern of combination:

When/if (b), (a)

or the pattern

(a), when/if (b)

except that generics and indefinites in (a) or (b) need to be replaced by pronouns. Thus we have, for example

When (sm) cats drop to the ground, they always land on their feet

Lizards are pleased when the sun shines

Small fish are widespread when big fish are rare

and so on.

Having seen various examples of reference ensembles of situations induced either by linguistic context or by explicit *if/when* clauses, we are ready for some brief speculation on the formal role of such ensembles. In essence, we would like to be able to 'quantify' over the situations in an ensemble, where (i) the quantification is potentially intensional as well as extensional (i.e., is evaluated with reference to situations in other possible worlds, as well as the current one), and (ii) a 'referential connection' can be made between entities in the situations quantified over and entities referred to in the matrix formula. For example, we would like to say something like the following for the representation of the *when* (*b*), (*a*) pattern for (240):

$$\text{USUALLY(WHEN}(\exists x : R(x, \mu(\text{cats})))\text{drop-to-the-ground}(x))$$
$$(\text{land-on-feet}(x))$$

Note the 'dangling' variable in the matrix formula, which we would like to think of as bound implicitly in the 'quantifier' (viz, USUALLY in combination with its first operand); i.e., as we iterate through situations satisfying the WHEN-clause, we use choices of x which render the restriction true in order to evaluate the matrix formula. This distinction between the scope of a quantifier determining which occurrences of a variable are bound and the use of objects which satisfy one formula to be the objects that are used to give a value to a pronoun (free variable) in another formula, seems closely related to Evans's (1977) distinction between semantic binding (or semantic scope) and anaphoric binding.

Presumably, these are the sorts of intuitions which lay behind Farkas & Sugioka's approach. But notice that the above formula could be true even if *most cats* were too clumsy to land on their feet, as long as it was predominantly the agile ones that were involved in situations in which cats drop to the ground. However, we will not attempt to formalize these ideas. Perhaps a model theory could be provided for the above sort of extension to conventional logics; evidently the notion of what can serve as a 'situation' would need clarification. Perhaps some version of Situation Semantics could serve our purposes. This would be very much in line with current trends in the theory of generics (ter Meulen, 1985; Carlson, 1985).

Besides *if/when* clauses, other sorts of restrictive clauses and adverbials include

(259)   *Around the New Year in Edmonton*, it usually snows
(260)   *In emergency situations*, flight attendants are (usually) effective
(261)   Cats *dropped to the ground* always land on their feet
(262)   Rats *crowded together in a small cage* are usually aggressive

Such examples could apparently be expressed formally in the same sort of way as those involving *if/when* clauses, though the details are far from clear.

As we noted above, we can also have reference ensembles of *objects* (as opposed to situations). This is the reason for using the more general term *cases*, subsuming both situations and objects. Here are some examples involving same-sentence context (plus presuppositions) only, in the determination of the reference ensembles:

(263)   (a)   Dogs are usually intelligent
        (b)   The dogs that have existed, currently exist (and will exist?) over some fairly extensive time span including the present
(264)   (a)   Passengers on the No. 3 line often do not get seats
        (b)   The passengers that have existed (*as* passengers, not as people) and currently exist over some fairly extensive time span including the present
(265)   (a)   Dutchmen are good sailors
        (b)   Dutchmen that have existed, currently (and will exist?) over some fairly extensive time span including the present, who are (or were) *good sailors as Dutchmen go*

(The (a)-sentence then claims these select Dutchmen (in (b)) are good sailors by *international* standards. We take this part of the interpretation as coming from context-dependent interpretation of *good*).[33]

We now move to examples of explicit restrictive clauses and adverbials determining the objects comprising the reference ensemble:

(266)   Dogs with/that have blue eyes are (usually) intelligent
(267)   Dogs are (usually) intelligent if/when they have blue eyes
(268)   Dogs dislike cats when they (the cats) have blue eyes

We would want to represent all such examples in a manner similar to the 'situational' examples (again, in the spirit of Farkas & Sugioka's approach). For example, (268) might be

$$G(\text{WHEN}((\exists x : R(x,\mu(\text{dogs})))\,(\exists y : R(y,\mu(\text{cats})))\,\text{have-blue-eyes}(y)))$$
$$(\text{hate}(y)(x)))$$

where variable bindings are again carried from the 'quantifier' into the matrix formula. The G here is a two-place operator (as opposed to the **Gn** predicate operator) which gathers together those cases described by its first argument for use in evaluating the sentence given as second argument— again, quite similar to Farkas & Sugioka's understanding, but without assuming that the cases are merely assignments of values to free variables.

To adequately convince the committed sophisticated theorist of the viability of our conception of semantics and the interpretation of generics and habituals (of the bare plural type, the bare singular type, the indefinite singular type, proper nouns, adverbs of quantification, restrictive *if/when* clauses, and the like) we ought to give an explicit grammar with explicit formal semantics that uses our reference ensembles. But this is not the place to attempt this; instead we hope that our critiques and suggestions for further work will provide an incentive for continued work in this intriguing and important area of linguistic semantics. A further development of our own account can be found in Schubert & Pelletier (1986).

ACKNOWLEDGEMENTS

The authors wish to thank the members of the Logical Grammar Study Group at the University of Alberta for their comments and suggestions: Matthew Dryer (Linguistics), Brendan Gillon and Bernard Linsky (Philosophy), Sven Hurum (Computing Science). We also gratefully acknowledge the (Canadian) Natural Science and Engineering Research Council for grants A8818 (LKS) and A5525 (FJP) which have partially supported the research reported herein. Thanks also go to Ernie LePore for his encouragement.

NOTES

[1] In (1b) we employ 'restricted quantification' in an obvious manner. The (1b) sentence is to be understood as a notational variant of the unrestricted $(\forall x)(\text{whale}(x) \rightarrow \text{mammal}(x))$; the restricted $(\exists x: \text{dog}(x))\,\text{small}(x)$ as a variant of the unrestricted $(\exists x)\,(\text{dog}(x)\,\&\,\text{small}(x))$. Our use of the restricted notation is to capture the similarity between these quantifiers and the other ones (such as *most*) which do not have an unrestricted variant. *Most cats are small* would be $(Mx: \text{cat}(x))\text{small}(x)$. In general here we follow McCawley (1981). Our choice, in the Montaguesque (1c), of making the subject term denotation be the argument of the verb phrase denotation, or of using the intension operator ˆ, should not be taken as indicating anything important. We are using these as examples only.

[2] The notion of 'semantic innocence' given here is really very weak and innocuous, saying only that the semantic value of one (lexically unambiguous) term is unique.

This conception is not to be confused with a somewhat stronger notion—which in fact we do not believe, but this does not form part of the present paper—to the effect that each (lexically unambiguous) term plays the same semantic role no matter where it occurs. We think, for example, that *wine* is to be interpreted (lexically) as a predicate, and that this is the role it plays in *the contents of this glass are (is) wine*. But in sentences like *wine is a liquid* it plays the role of denoting a kind. For further exposition on how this is possible, and what causes it, see Pelletier & Schubert (1985). Our thanks to Ernie LePore for pointing this out to us.

[3] Formally, the *sets* we have talked about are determined by binary-valued functions, as should be clear from our earlier remarks on *typing*. So, for example, the value of **whale'** at a given index is a function in 2^D. As a function on I, **whale'** thus denotes a function in $(2^D)^I$. In general, Montague represents functions in the Schönfinkel–Church manner, i.e., a two-place function is represented as a one-place function whose values are one-place functions, a three-function is a function whose values are one-place functions whose values in turn are one-place functions, and so on.

[4] In recent writings within GPSG, the two aspects of a phrase structure rule— what symbols are dominated by the left-hand side of the rule, and in what order these symbols occur—are separated. This is called 'the immediate dominance, linear precedence format' (ID/LP), and separate principles are employed in the two subparts of the theory. In the discussion which follows, we do not employ this format, instead retaining the original context-free rule statement which combines these two functions.

[5] Both Carlson and Chierchia (personal communication, 1986) have expressed to us their dissatisfaction with the accounts they had given earlier. Carlson's new account will be given in a book he is currently preparing on the topic, and Chierchia would wish to avail himself of 'property theory' (see Chierchia & Turner, Ms.).

[6] Various technical issues are raised here: not only is Rover loyal but so is μ(dog). Is μ(dog) a dog? Does this give rise to contradiction? Is μ(dog) even of the right type for *loyal* to apply to it? These issues are dealt with quite differently in the different versions of the sophisticated approach, and so cannot be addressed at this point.

[7] We have stated this meaning postulate with the quantifier 'Most'—so if *dogs are loyal* is true then *most dogs are loyal* is true. Recall, however, our earlier discussion of how there seems to be no good measure for the number of instances required to make the generic true. However, if the quantifier is interpreted *comparatively*, so that it merely requires most P's *belonging to a contextually determined reference ensemble* to be Q's, the meaning postulate becomes somewhat plausible. Meaning postulate (205) is a refinement of (22).

[8] Ignoring, once again, the precise meaning of existentially quantifying over 'realizations of snow.' (That is, ignoring the problem of identifying what the values of x in (24') are.)

[9] Besides, French *does* allow one to say

L'eau coule du robinet

[10] The superscripts ^{s}, ^{o} and ^{k} indicate stage level variables, object level variables, and kind level variables respectively.

[11] This point—that episodic sentences seem to have these sorts of entailments while habitual ones do not—seems to us to be a matter of degree and not a matter calling for an ontological dichotomy. For example, a river could be simultaneously

flooding a city in Alberta and *flooding fields in Manitoba*; I could be *building a shopping mall in Edmonton* and *building a high-rise in Winnipeg*, etc. (Here we have cases of the episodic not precluding spatially different episodes). On the other hand it would be difficult to be *native to Edmonton* and also be *native to Calgary*, or not to be *native to Alberta*, even though predicates apply to objects and not their manifestations. (Of course Carlson probably does not consider the present 'entailment test' to be crucial to the episodic/habitual distinction. But these examples show that it seems to carry very little, if any, weight.)

[12] We follow Carlson (1982) in using simplified translations for purposes of exposition. For example, **has'** in (56b) cannot really be the lexical translation of *has* in a Montague (1973) style grammar, since the object of the lexical translation will be a property of properties, $(\lambda P)(\exists y^\circ)$ [tail'(y) **&** ˅P(y)].

[13] The reading of (86) according to which there is a tail such that dogs have it is eliminated on 'pragmatic' grounds.

[14] The predicate in *Human beings are a hazard to themselves* might be taken to be ambiguous between an object-level predicate and a kind-level predicate. Thus one reading would be analogous to that of (90), while the other would be synonymous with *Mankind is a hazard to itself*.

[15] More accurately, since semantic values of dyadic predicates are viewed as elements of $(2^D)^D$ (where D is the domain of individuals), the extension of *hate'* must map the first element of the pair into an element of 2^D which in turn maps the second element, Fido, into the truth value 1.

[16] In a PTQ-style grammar (Montague, 1973), the translation of a sentence such as *dogs are mammals* would be obtained by applying the NP-translation, $(\lambda P^\cdot P(^\cdot$**dog'**$))$, to the intensionalized VP-translation, ˄**mammal'**, yielding **mammal'** $(^\cdot$**dog'**$)$ after 'up-down cancellation'.

[17] One might justifiably wonder what Farkas & Sugioka think a realization of a kind is: an object (as all their examples require) or a stage (as other examples discussed by Carlson and Chierchia would require). Farkas & Sugioka do not say, probably because they do not consider any of the examples that induce 'an existential reading' on the subject.

[18] One must be careful when reading this section of Farkas & Sugioka: when they say 'ordinary *if* clauses', what they mean is 'counterfactual conditional'.

[19] A better case seems to exist for identifying **Gn'** with absence of aspectual particles, or with certain inflections, in Turkish (see Dahl, 1975), Hopi, Chinese, and Slavic languages.

[20] Namely $\square[[\mathbf{R(x)(y)} \ \& \ \mathbf{Qn(x)}] \leftrightarrow {}^\cdot(\lambda z)[\neg \mathbf{Qn(z)} \ \& \ \mathbf{R(z)(y)}]\Delta \mathbf{x}]$, where Qn(x) can be read as 'x is a quantifier' (or 'x is a property of properties') and yΔx can be read as 'y is in the extension of x'. See Chierchia (1982, pp. 337, 345).

[21] *Sm* is the unstressed *some*.

[22] Or an appropriate function from characteristic functions of sets of realizations to truth values.

[23] As a side benefit of doing this, we would be in a better position to characterize the role of **Gn** by means of axioms or meaning postulates uniformly, whereas in the former approach we have to separately state principles governing the two different cases.

[24] For some views on whether **dog'** can also apply to quantities of dog flesh and the like, see Pelletier & Schubert (1985).

[25] Cf Dahl (1975). We take the necessary operator as quantifying metalinguistically over both worlds and times. Thus if snow is white, it always will be.

[26] We are inclined to replace the embedded necessity operator by a weaker one expressing 'in most of the relevant possible worlds'.

[27] It is worth remarking that DISP probably splits into a sense roughly equivalent to *is able* (*or prepared*) *to* and another roughly equivalent to *habitually*. Both interpretations are salient in *John speaks German, John rides a horse*, etc. (Cf Dahl, 1975.)

[28] But something would be lost in the translation, namely its gnomic character, and its residual temporal flavour, as evident in the absence of a reading like (i) or (ii) in sentence (iii)

(i)   All stars visible at this moment twinkle
(ii) In all cases, stars visible at this moment twinkle
(iii) Stars visible at this moment always twinkle.

[29] Some closely related views can be found in McCord (1981) and Aqvist *et al* (1980). In the former, reference situations or objects are encoded into restrictions on variables bound by unselective quantifiers, while in the latter, and explicitly statistical approach is proposed, though without grammatical underpinnings.

[30] Or perhaps it would be better to speak of sentence presupposition.

[31] This example is from McCord (1981). McCord would say that *in trees* is the 'focus' and that the sentence is to be understood as saying that the majority of leopard attacks on monkeys occur in trees. Our account is a little different in that it allows more ways of 'generalizing' to find the reference ensemble than merely the deletion of a conjunct (as McCord's theory has it).

[32] Stress is ambiguous. It seems that if a word or phrase is stressed, then phrases terminating in that word or phrase can also be considered stressed.

[33] It is perhaps worth pointing out that Carlson's (1977, pp. 181–186) 'solution' to 'the Port-Royal Puzzle' does not work. The puzzle is that from *Dutchman are good sailors* we should not be able to derive *Dutchmen are sailors* even though all good sailors are sailors. Clearly *is a good sailor* is logically equivalent to *is a good sailor and is a sailor* (see Carlson's meaning postulate MP14, p. 264). But then by meaning postulate MP12 (p. 184) [Carlson erroneously uses **Gn′** here, but clearly intends **Gn**]:

$$(\forall P)(\forall Q)(\forall x^k)\Box[\mathbf{Gn}(\hat{}(\lambda y)\check{}P(y) \& \check{}Q(y))(x) \leftrightarrow \mathbf{Gn}(P)(x) \& \mathbf{Gn}(Q)(x)]$$

we obtain *Dutchmen are sailors* from *Dutchmen are good sailors*!

REFERENCES

Aqvist, L., Hoepelman, J., & Rohrer, C., Adverbs of Frequency. In C. Rohrer (Ed), *Time, Tense and Quantifiers*. Tübingen: Max Niemeyer, 1980, pp. 1–17.

Carlson, G., *References to Kinds in English*. Ph.D. dissertation, Amherst, MA: University of Massachusetts, 1977. (Available from Indiana University Linguistics Club.)

Carlson, G., A Unified Analysis of the English Bare Plural. *Linguistics and Philosophy*, 1977a, **1**, 413–456.

Carlson, G., Generics and Atemporal *When*. *Linguistics and Philosophy*, 1979, **3**, 49–98.

Carlson, G., Generic Terms and Generic Sentences. *J. Philosophical Logic*, 1982, **11**, 145–181.

Carlson, G., *Exceptions to Generic Generalizations* (Ms). Linguistics, University of Iowa.

Chierchia, G., Nominalization and Montague Grammar: a Semantics without Types for Natural Languages *Linguistics and Philosophy*, 1982, **5**, 303–354.

Chierchia, G., On Plural and Mass Nominals. *Proceedings of the West Coast Conference on Formal Linguistics*, 1982a, **1**, 243–255.

Chierchia, G. & Turner, M., *Semantics and Property Theory* (Ms). Cornell/Essex.

Cocchiarella, N., The Theory of Homogeneous Types as a Second Order Logic. *Notre Dame Journal of Formal Logic*, 1979, **20**, 505–524.

Cooper, R., *Quantification and Syntactic Theory*. Dordrecht: Reidel, 1983.

Dahl, O., On Generics. In E. Keenan (Ed), *Formal Semantics of Natural Language*. Cambridge: Cambridge University Press, 1975, pp. 99–111.

Dowty, D., Wall, R. & Peters, S., *Introduction to Montague Semantics*. Dordrecht: Reidel, 1981.

Enç, M., *Tense Without Scope*. Ph.D. dissertation, Madison, WI: University of Wisconsin, 1981.

Evans, G. Pronouns, Quantifiers and Relative Clauses (I) and Pronouns, Quantifiers and Relative Clauses (II): Appendix. *Canadian Journal of Philosophy*, 1977, **7**, 467–536 and 777–798.

Farkas, D. & Sugioka, Y., Restrictive If/When Clauses. *Linguistics and Philosophy*, 1983, **6**, 225–258.

Gazdar, G., Phrase Structure Grammar. In P. Jacobson & G. Pullum (Eds), *The Nature of Syntactic Representation*. Dordrecht: Reidel, 1982, pp. 131–186.

Gazdar, G., Klein, E., Pullum, G. & Sag, I., *Generalized Phrase Structure Grammar*. Oxford: Blackwell, 1985.

Hinrichs, E., *A Compositional Semantics for Aktionsarten and NP Reference in English*. Ph.D. dissertation, Columbus, OH: Ohio State University, 1985.

Jackendoff, R., *Semantic Interpretation in Generative Grammar*. Cambridge: MIT Press, 1972.

Kratzer, A., Die Analyse des blossen Plurals bei Gregory Carlson. *Ling. Berichte*, 1980, **70**, 47–70.

Krifka, M., Massenterme. In D. Wunderlich & A. von Steckow (Eds), *Handbuch der Semantik*. Berlin: de Gruyter, 1985.

Lawler, J., *Studies in English Generics*. Ph.D. dissertation, Ann Arbor, MI: University of Michigan, 1972.

Lewis, D., Adverbs of Quantification. In E. Keenan (Ed), *Formal Semantics of Natural Languages*. Cambridge: Cambridge University Press, 1975, pp. 3–15.

Lyons, J., *Semantics*, 1. Cambridge: Cambridge University Press, 1977.

McCawley, J., *Everything Linguists have Always Wanted to Know About Logic*. Chicago: Chicago University Press, 1981.

McCord, M., *Focalizers, the Scoping Problem, and Semantic Interpretation Rules in Logic Grammars*. Technical Report, University of Kentucky.

Montague, R. (1970), Universal Grammar. In Thomason (1974), pp. 225–246.

Montague, R. (1973), The Proper Treatment of Quantification in English. In Thomason (1974), pp. 247–270.

Nunberg, G., & Pan, C., Inferring Quantification in Generic Sentences. *Proceedings of the Chicago Linguistic Society*, 1975, **11**, 412–422.

Pelletier, F. J., & Schubert, L. K., Mass Expressions. In D. Gabbay & F. Guenthner (Eds), *Handbook of Philosophical Logic*. Dordrecht: Reidel, 1985.

Pollard, C., *On the Correct Use of Lambda Calculus in Generalized Phrase Structure Grammars* (Ms). Stanford University.

Schubert, L. K., An Approach to the Syntax and Semantics of Affixes 'Conventionalized' Phrase Structure Grammar. In *Proc. of the Fourth CSCSI/SCEIO Conference*. University of Saskatchewan, 1982, pp. 189–195.

Schubert, L. K. & Pelletier, F. J., From English to Logic: Context Free Computation of 'Conventional' Logical Translation. *American Journal of Computational Linguistics*, 1982, 26–44.

Schubert, L. K. & Pelletier, F. J., Generically Speaking. To be presented at a conference on 'Properties' at University of Massachusetts, Amherst, 1986.

ter Meulen, A., Generic Information, Conditional Contexts and Constraints. In E. Trayott, C. Ferguson, J. Reilly & A. ter Meulen (Eds), *On Conditionals*. Cambridge: Cambridge University Press, 1985.

Thomason, R., *Formal Philosophy*. New Haven, CT: Yale University Press, 1974.

Vendler, Z., *Linguistics and Philosophy*. Ithaca, NY: Cornel University Press, 1967.

13

The Meaning Of Truth

ANIL GUPTA

Department of Philosophy,
University of Illinois, Chicago

Any attempt to give a systematic account of the meaning of the word 'true' faces a number of preliminary difficulties. It is a feature of very general words such as 'true', 'exists', and 'necessarily' that not only are the principles underlying their application unknown, but even the logical category to which they belong is disputable, and indeed disputed. With 'true', philosophers have argued whether its logical category is that of predicate, or singular term, or sentence-operator, or prosentence, or some other. Even if we decide that the logical category to which 'true' belongs is predicate, we face further questions concerning the 'objects' of truth. What sorts of things are true? Sentences? Sentence tokens? Thoughts? Propositions? Or something else? And we need to decide whether truth is a simple property of these objects or a relational one. Ideally an account of the concept of truth should begin by answering these difficult formal questions, and then go on to articulate the material principles underlying the concept.[1] Unfortunately, at the present stage of inquiry definitive and workable answers to these questions cannot be given. As the aim of this essay is to develop and defend a proposal concerning the material principles underlying truth let us take a tentative stand on the answer to the formal questions. Let us assume that truth is a one-place predicate of sentences. This choice has the advantage of making our assumptions the same as that of much other work in the theory of truth. Furthermore, it yields clarity.

453

NEW DIRECTIONS IN SEMANTICS

Sentences are clearer and better understood than such entities as propositions. The assumption is also harmless, for much of what is said below can be preserved even if it turns out that the formal questions are to be answered differently.

An account of the meaning of 'true' must accord with and illuminate the ordinary uses of the word. Let us begin by examining some examples of its use. These examples will lead us to a clearer and better formulation of the problem that needs to be solved.

Example 1. We apply the concept of truth to the sentence

(1) Snow is white.

What licenses the application of the concept to (1)? This is a good question of metaphysics and deserves a long and subtle answer. Let us be brief and even naive and say for the present that (1) is true in virtue of a fact about snow: the fact that snow is white.

Example 2. We also apply the concept to the sentence (2).

(2) 'Snow is white' is true.

The question of the truth or falsity of (2) reduces to the truth or falsity of (1). Having decided that (1) is true, we say immediately that (2) is true.

We may say as before that (2) is true in virtue of a fact. But now that fact is about the sentence 'snow is white' and has the concept of truth as a constituent. However, there is also a sense in which (2) is true in virtue of a fact about snow, the fact that snow is white. Let us call the facts of the first sort *semantical facts* and those of the second sort *nonsemantical facts*. For present purposes semantical facts may be taken as those that contain the concept of truth as a constituent. The rest are nonsemantical facts. Facts such as that two plus two is four, that promises ought to be kept, are nonsemantical; whereas facts such as that the sentence 'two plus two is four' is true, that Darwin's theory is true, are semantical. (The reader has a right to be uneasy about the distinction between semantical and nonsemantical facts, and indeed about the notion of fact in general. We will later replace these by more exact notions. The vague and rough notions are useful in the interim.)

Example 3. Suppose we wish to determine whether (3) is true.

(3) Something Leah has said is not true.

Suppose also that Leah has made statements (2), (4) and (5).

(4) Everything Gillian says is true.

(5)   Something Gillian says is not true.

The truth or falsity of (3) depends entirely on the truth or falsity of (2), (4) and (5). (2) depends on (1), and is evaluated true as before. But (4) and (5) cannot both be true. So we evaluate (3) as true. The 'dependence tree' for (3) can be represented in the following way:

$$
\begin{array}{c}
\mathbf{t}(3) \\
\diagup \quad | \quad \diagdown \\
\mathbf{t}(2) \quad ?(4) \quad ?(5) \\
| \\
\mathbf{t}(1)
\end{array}
$$

(The truth values of the sentences are indicated on the left. That the value is The True is indicated by **t**; that the value is The False is indicated by **f**; that the value is unknown is indicated by a question mark.)

Example 4.   Suppose the only statements that Leah has made are (2) and (4), and that Gillian's only statement is (6).

(6)   She [Gillian] has a lamp that once belonged to Carnap.

Now the dependence tree looks like this:

$$
\begin{array}{c}
\mathbf{f}(3) \\
\diagup \quad \diagdown \\
\mathbf{t}(2) \quad \mathbf{t}(4) \\
| \qquad | \\
\mathbf{t}(1) \quad \mathbf{t}(6)
\end{array}
$$

Since (1) and (6) are true, we conclude that (2) and (4) are also true. Hence (3) is false.

These examples show that the truth or falsity of a sentence may depend on the truth or falsity of other sentences. These latter sentences, if they themselves contain the word 'true', may depend on yet other sentences. And this process can continue indefinitely. Sometimes, as in the examples considered above, the process terminates. In such cases the truth or falsity of the initial sentence is seen to depend entirely on the nonsemantical facts, on such facts as that snow is white, that two plus two is four, that (4) and (5) are inconsistent, etc. The concept of truth has this interesting feature: *the truth or falsity of unproblematic sentences is completely determined by the nonsemantical facts.* The principles underlying this determination, however, are not known to us. One task of a theory of truth is to determine, in a principled way, what unproblematic sentences are true and what false, given the nonsemantical facts.

It is well known that for certain sentences not only do the dependence trees fail to terminate, but the nonsemantical facts do not determine the truth or falsity of the sentences in question. Such sentences we will call *pathological*.

Example 5.   Suppose the only statements that Leah has made are (2) and (4) and that Gillian's statements are (6) and (7).

(7)   Nothing that I, Gillian, say is untrue.

Now the truth or falsity of (3) depends upon that of (2) and (4). Since (2) is true, it depends crucially on the truth or falsity of (4). (4), in turn, depends upon (6) and (7). Since (6) is true, the status of (4) depends crucially on (7). For similar reasons the status of (7) depends on (7) itself. We get the following dependence tree.

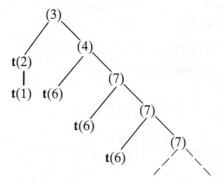

Unlike the earlier examples, now the truth values of some of the sentences in the tree are left undetermined. It is not that there is some fact unknown to us that does determine the truth values of these sentences. Rather it is an objective feature of the concept of truth that under certain conditions the nonsemantical facts leave the truth or falsity of some sentences undetermined. In this example if we suppose that (7) is true, we evaluate (4) as true, (3) as false, and we confirm that (7) is true. So our supposition has a certain stability. But we notice that this supposition is arbitrary. We could equally well have supposed that (7) is false. Now (4) and (7) are evaluated as false and (3) as true. This too has stability. There is no reason to prefer one supposition over the other. Sentences that behave as (7) does in this example (and also (4) and (3)) we will call *divergent*. Though their semantic behavior has a certain stability, no truth value is forced on them in semantic evaluation. In this respect they differ from ordinary nonpathological sen-

tences. They are somewhat puzzling and ill behaved. But worse things are
in store.

Example 6. Suppose that the only statements that Leah has made are,
as before, (2) and (4), but Gillian's statements are (6) and (3). Now the
dependence tree looks like this:

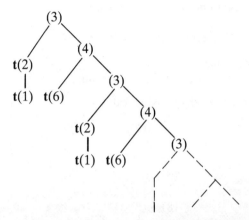

As in Example 5 we have an infinitely descending dependence tree: (3)
depends crucially on (4), and (4) crucially on (3). But in this example a
new element enters the picture. We cannot coherently suppose that (4) is
true. For if (4) is supposed true then (3) is evaluated false. As a result (4)
is evaluated false. On the other hand we cannot suppose that (4) is not true
either. For then (3) is evaluated true and hence so is (4). Now no judgment
is stable: we cannot say that (4) is true, and we cannot say that (4) is not
true. This is very perplexing. Some have taken it to indicate incoherence
in our concept of truth. We will call sentences which behave as (4) and (3)
do in this example *paradoxical.*

These examples illustrate an observation first made by Saul Kripke. He
has pointed out that the status of a sentence, e.g., whether it is paradoxical
or not, may depend on nonsemantical facts. Thus the sentence (3) is
nonpathological and false if the situation is as described in Example 4. It
is paradoxical if the situation is as in Example 6. It is nonparadoxical but
still pathological if the situation is as in Example 5. So, whether a sentence
is paradoxical or not, is not in general determined by the syntactical form
of the sentence alone. Nonsemantical facts may be relevant also. We can,
however, generalize our earlier observation: *If the totality of nonsemantical
facts is given then the status of a sentence—that is, whether the sentence is
paradoxical, or divergent, or nonpathological and true, etc,—is completely*

determined. In particular cases, as the above examples illustrate, we can calculate, and even intuit, the status of a sentence, if the nonsemantical facts are given; but the general principles that govern our calculations and intuitions are not known to us.

Two points are worth noting. First, the paradoxical and the divergent are not the only types of sentences to be found amongst the pathological. There are also sentences of a *mixed character*.

Example 7.   Consider sentences (8) and (9).

(8)   The sentence (8) is true.
(9)   Either (8) is true or (9) is not true.

The dependence tree of (9) is as follows.

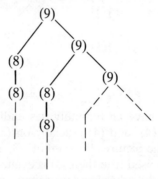

Sentence (8) is divergent. Semantic evaluation leaves its truth value undetermined. Both the values **t** and **f** are possible for it. Neither is ruled out. But sentence (9) is not divergent. The value **f** is not possible for it, for that would imply that (9) is true. Nor is the sentence paradoxical; the value **t** is a possible one for it. Nor is (9) nonpathological, for it is true only if the divergent (8) is true. (9), then, is an example of a pathological sentence of a mixed character.

The second point is this. Although we have fairly good intuitions about the status of simple sentences in simple situations, we should not suppose that we have equally good intuitions in all cases. When the type of 'self-reference' found in an example is complex or unusual we may fail to have clear intuitions. Or if we do, it may happen that our intuitions are a result of inappropriate emphasis on certain features of the example. It is very unlikely that we are wrong on the simple sentences of the sort considered above. The fact that we can use 'true' effectively in ordinary everyday communication entitles us to this much confidence. But it does not entitle us to treat all our intuitions as unrevisable. Detailed reflection on a particular example and the general theory may lead us to change our mind on the status of a sentence. The simple-minded model of revisable theory and unrevisable data is as inappropriate in the theory of truth as elsewhere. An example which may illustrate the foregoing is this.

Example 8.[2]   Suppose Professor X is asked to read a paper on the liar paradox at a certain university. X, for unknown reasons, only says the following two things in his lecture.

(10)   Either The Liar is true or it is not true.
(11)   Everything I [i.e., X] say is true.

On the blackboard we find the name 'The Liar' explained thus.

(The Liar)   The Liar is not true.

What are we to say of (10)? Is it pathological or not? And of (11)? Is it divergent or not?

Consider also this variant of Example 8.

Example 9.   Suppose X at a different lecture says only (12) and (13).

(12)   Either The Truth-Teller is true or it is not true.
(13)   Everything I [i.e., X] say is true.

The blackboard inscription explains 'The Truth-Teller' thus

(The Truth-Teller)   The Truth-Teller is true.

What about (12) and (13)? Are they pathological or not? Also, do (11) and (13) have the same status? We may have intuitions about how these questions are to be answered, but we should recognize that these intuitions are fallible. In fact, different theories of truth give quite different judgments on these sentences, and different speakers have different prereflective intuitions about these sentences.

A great deal of attention has been devoted to finding a way of solving or dissolving the liar paradox. It has often been maintained that there is something wrong with the sentences that exhibit paradoxical behavior, and philosophers and logicians have attempted to isolate what this feature is. A number of different accounts have been offered: sortal incorrectness, presupposition failure, referential opacity, and others. These types of studies have improved our understanding of truth and of paradox, but they have not solved the liar paradox, nor have they removed the mystery that surrounds it. It seems to me that a reason for this failure may be that insufficient attention has been paid to the ordinary, unproblematic uses of the concept of truth. When confronted with some perplexing and extraordinary phenomenon it is tempting to focus one's study on it, and to ignore the ordinary and familiar phenomena that are related to it. However, this may not be the best strategy for achieving an understanding of the puzzling phenomenon. An analogy may help to make the point clear. Imagine that before the development of astronomy the members of a tribe observe a solar eclipse. They are naturally perplexed by this most extraordinary and singular occurrence, and seek an explanation of it. Their first tendency may well be to speculate on the causes of the event. We can imagine the sorts of hypotheses that might be put forward to explain it—the wrath of God, the flight of a dragon, and what not. The proper method for understanding the eclipse, however, is to undertake a patient and systematic study of the ordinary and familiar behavior of the Sun, the Moon, the stars, etc. Only when we see the extraordinary in terms of the patterns exhibited by the ordinary do we come to understand it. The suggestion that I am making is that for a proper understanding of the liar paradox we should try to understand the principles that underlie the ordinary unproblematic uses of the concept of truth.

We may formulate the problem to be solved as follows. We want a theory that given the totality of nonsemantical facts would tell us in a systematic and principled way which sentences are pathological and which nonpathological. Further, it would divide the set of nonpathological sentences into the true and the false, and the set of pathological sentences into the paradoxical, the divergent, etc. A theory which does this for all possible totalities of nonsemantical facts may well claim to have elucidated the material principles underlying truth. For such a theory would tell us for each sentence the conditions under which it is true, false, and pathological.

This formulation of the problem, however, is not completely satisfactory. It uses the vague and unclear notion of 'the totality of nonsemantical facts'. Unless this notion is clarified, we would not know what will count as a solution to our problem and what not. Fortunately, for simple fragments of the language the notion can be made clear and precise. If we confine ourselves to a classical first-order quantificational fragment of our language we can identify the relevant totality of nonsemantical facts with a model for the language.[3] Actually the exact notion of model that we need is slightly different from the standard notion. It is the following.

Let L be a first-order language with a distinctive predicate T (for 'true-in-L'). Let us suppose that L has $\forall$, &, $\sim$, $=$. The other logical connectives, $\exists$, $\vee$, $\supset$, $\equiv$, are defined in the usual way. We suppose for simplicity that L has no function symbols.

Definition 1.　A *model* for a language L is an ordered pair $\langle D, I \rangle$ consisting of a domain D and an interpretation function I such that

(i)　the set of sentences of L is included in D,
(ii)　I assigns to each name a member of D; and to each n-place nonlogical predicate G (thus excluding T and $=$) a function belonging to $\{t, f\}^{D^n}$. $I(G)$ will be called *the extension of G* in the model $\langle D, I \rangle$.[4]

A model for L, then, gives the denotations of all the names, and the extensions of all the predicates except T and $=$, which it treats as logical. We may think of a model as a representation of a possible relevant totality of nonsemantical facts. It encodes enough information to fix the status of all the sentences, including those that contain T. We can now formulate the problem to be solved thus: to determine in a systematic and principled way the sentences of L that are nonpathological and true, nonpathological and false, paradoxical, etc., in an arbitrary model M of L.

A number of ideas have been put forward in the literature that have a bearing on the problem we have formulated.[5] We cannot exposit and evaluate all these ideas in this essay, but the following remarks are offered as a guide to a selected part of the literature. Four sorts of theories may be distinguished.

(1)　*The Levels Theory*. This theory divides the problem of truth into two subproblems. First to give an account of a Tarskian hierarchy of truth predicates for an arbitrary model M, and second, to interpret the occurrences of T in the sentences of L in terms of this hierarchy. So each occurrence of T is thought to have an implicit level, though the level may vary from model to model. This results in the idea that truth is indexical. This theory is interesting but has not been developed in detail. See Burge (1979) and Parsons (1974, 1983) for an exposition and defense of the theory.

(2)　*Three-valued Approaches*. These approaches are built on the remarkable fact that for certain languages that admit truth-value gaps, interpretations for the truth predicate can be found that agree completely with what is *evaluated* as true, false, and gappy in the language. Mathematically this fact amounts to the observation that certain functions of semantical evaluation have fixed points. Fixed point theorems for three-valued languages are proved explicitly in Martin and Woodruff (1975), Kripke (1975), and Kindt (1978). Feferman (1984) traces them back to the work of Fitch, Skolem, Gilmore, Brady and others. (See the bibliography for some of the references.) Kripke (1975) gives an iterative construction of the minimal fixed point and offers a very plausible intuitive account of the construction. Kripke's paper is of fundamental importance. It contains a rich theory of truth, and it develops a number of fruitful techniques. A Kripke-type construction is used by Maddy (1983) to construct a theory of proper classes. Davis (1976), Yablo (1982), and Hawthorn (1983) give a 'downward' or dependence-tree type analysis of Kripke's theory. (See also Hazen, 1981.) For a critical discussion of the first two sorts of theories consult Gupta (1982) and Hawthorn (1983).

(3) *Four-Valued Approaches.* These are similar to the three-valued approaches, but differ in that they admit truth-value 'gluts' as well as truth-value gaps. That is, they countenance not only the possibility that a sentence has neither truth value **t**, **f** but also the possibility that a sentence has both the truth values. Fixed point phenomenon of the sort noted for the three-valued approaches obtains here. For theories of this sort consult Woodruff (1984), Visser (1984), and Dowden (1984). For a philosophical defense of the idea that a paradoxical sentence is both true and false see Priest (1979, 1984). For a criticism of Priest see Chihara (1984).

(4) *The Revision Theories.* These theories will be explained below. They have been developed in Gupta (1981, 1982), Herzberger (1982a, b), and Belnap (1982). Interesting results about them have been obtained by Burgess (1983) and McGee (1983). Hawthorn (1983) has some information on their relationship to the dependence-tree accounts. Hellman (1984) contains a few criticisms of the revision theory as well as the three-valued approaches. The presentation below is much influenced by Nuel Belnap. It incorporates the central idea of Belnap (1982). However, familiarity with this paper, or any of the other papers mentioned above, is not presupposed. The only exception is Kripke (1975), familiarity with which is assumed in a few footnotes and in the last three paragraphs of this paper.

The central idea of the revision theory is that underlying some of our concepts—truth, in particular—there is not a rule of application but rather a rule of revision. If we ignore vagueness, sortal incorrectness, etc, we can say that underlying our use of words such as 'red' is a rule of application that divides objects into two classes: those to which the word applies and those to which it does not apply. And simplifying a great deal we can say that our understanding of 'red' consists in a grasp of such a rule. In contrast, I want to suggest that underlying our use of the word 'true' is a rule of revision, not a rule of application. This rule does not in general divide objects into those to which 'true' applies and those to which it does not apply. It does not in general yield the extension of truth. Rather it enables us to improve on a proposed candidate for the extension of truth. It is the existence and the nature of such a rule, I wish to argue, that explains the characteristic features of the concept of truth.

To see the intuitive motivation of the idea let us think of the problem of truth in this way. Suppose that we are speakers of a first-order language L with a truth predicate T. Suppose also that we are given all the relevant nonsemantical facts—say we are given a model M of L—and we are asked to determine the sentences of L that are true/false in M. How are we to solve this problem? We notice that if we ignore the truth predicate, there is little difficulty in saying what sentences are true and what false. For now we have the denotations/extensions of *all* the constants and we know how to determine the extension of truth if we are given this information. Tarski's definition of 'truth-in-a-model' is essentially a formalization of this knowledge. However, the presence of T in L creates a problem for applying this knowledge (and Tarski's definition) to the case at hand. To apply it we already need to know the extension of truth. But the extension of truth is exactly what we are trying to determine. We are tempted to say that we can determine the extension of truth, if we are already given the extension of truth. However, this claim seems to be trivial. But it is not.

Let us observe that although our intuitive understanding of the rule mentioned above (i.e., the rule that yields the extension of truth given the denotations/extensions of *all* the constants; we will call this the *Tarskian* rule) does not determine the extension of truth for L in M because of the circularity just noted, yet it can be applied to determine what the extension of truth *would be* given an arbitrary, possibly fictitious, extension for T. The central claim we make is that the resulting extension is a better interpretation for truth than the one that we started with, or at least it is as good an interpretation. (Henceforth we take this qualification for granted.) The Tarskian rule cannot be used to determine the extension of truth, but it can be used to improve on a proposed candidate for the extension of truth. The Tarskian rule is fundamental to our understanding of the concept of truth. But it does not yield a rule of application. Rather it yields a rule of revision.

Formally the claim may be put as follows. Let $M(=\langle D, I \rangle)$ be a model of a language L with a truth predicate T. Let $g, g', \ldots$ range over possible interpretations of T, that is, $g, g', \ldots \in \{t, f\}^D$. Now the Tarskian rule does not determine what things are true/false in M, because to apply it we need to have the interpretations of *all* the constants, including T. But suppose we arbitrarily assign to T the interpretation g. This yields a richer model, designated by $M + g$, that interprets all the constants. We can now apply the Tarskian rule to determine the extension of truth in $M + g$. This itself is a possible interpretation of T. The Tarskian rule thus yields an operation τ_M on the possible interpretations of T. τ_M is defined thus:

$$\tau_M(g)(d) = \begin{cases} t & \text{if d is a sentence true in } M + g, \\ f & \text{otherwise.} \end{cases}$$

Our central claim is that τ_M *is a rule of revision*: $\tau_M(g)$ is at least as good a candidate for the extension of truth as g. The main argument for this claim is theoretical. It will be argued that a great many phenomena concerning truth fall into a simple coherent pattern if we see τ_M as a rule of revision. Still, some things can be said to make the idea a little more intuitive than may appear initially.

First, even though there is a problem about determining the extension of truth for L, there is little difficulty in evaluating and criticizing a proposal for the extension of truth. If a person were to claim that the extension of truth is g, then we can rightly say that if the person is correct then the extension of truth is really $\tau_M(g)$. For now the interpretation of all the constants is in accordance with M + g and the Tarskian rule implies that under these conditions the extension of truth is $\tau_M(g)$. A person who takes the extension of truth to be g must on semantical reflection revise his/her estimate to $\tau_M(g)$.

Second, we can intuitively see that $\tau_M(g)$ is a better candidate for the extension of truth than g by looking at some simple examples. Consider, for instance, the following.

Example 10.   Let L' contain one 1-place predicate G and one individual constant a. We suppose that the only other nonlogical constants of L' are the quotational names of the sentences of L'. Let $M'(=\langle D', I'\rangle)$ be a model of L' such that $D' = S \cup \{1\}$ (S is the set of sentences of L'); $I'(a) = 1$; $I'(G)(d) = \mathbf{t}$ iff d = 1, for all $d \in D'$; and the quotational names have their intended interpretation. Finally let g', g'' be two possible interpretations of T in M such that

$$g'(d) = \mathbf{f} \quad \text{for all } d \in D',$$

$$g''(d) = \mathbf{t} \quad \text{for all } d \in D'.$$

Intuitively, g' and g'' are very poor interpretations of T: g' declares everything to be false, and g'' everything true. Consider now $\tau_{M'}(g')$ and $\tau_{M'}(g'')$. Calculation shows that the sentences in (i) and (ii) are true under $\tau_{M'}(g')$ and $\tau_{M'}(g'')$ respectively, and their negations false.

(i) $Ga, \sim(\forall x)Gx, \sim T('Ga'), \sim T('\sim Ga'), (\forall x)\sim Tx, \ldots$
(ii) $Ga, \sim(\forall x)Gx, T('Ga'), T('\sim Ga'), (\forall x)Tx, \ldots$

We notice that whereas g' and g'' are wrong even on sentences without the predicate T, $\tau_{M'}(g')$ and $\tau_{M'}(g'')$ are right on all such sentences. In this respect the latter are better candidates for the extension of truth than the former. It is true that $\tau_{M'}(g')$ and $\tau_{M'}(g'')$ give intuitively wrong truth values to some of the sentences containing T. For example, $\tau_{M'}(g')$ is wrong on $T('Ga')$ and $\tau_{M'}(g'')$ is wrong on $T('\sim Ga')$. So these interpretations are not perfect. But notice that the particular imperfections mentioned can be removed by another application of τ_M.

This example shows that even though successive applications of τ_M may give us better and better candidates for the extension of truth, yet finitely many applications of τ_M may well fail to give us a best candidate. In this example, after n applications of τ_M to g′ we have an extension that gives wrong truth values to some sentences with n iterations of truth. So we need to consider the effects of transfinitely many applications of τ_M. Let us try to define the notion 'the result of α many applications of τ_M', where α is any ordinal. The zero and the successor stages are easy. At the zero stage we begin with some arbitrarily chosen possible extension for T. At a successor stage we improve the result of the previous stage by an application of τ_M. The question is: How to treat the limit stages? It is because reasonable disagreement is possible on how best to answer this question that there is not one but several revision theories. I will not try to decide in this essay what the correct treatment of limit stages is. I will indicate some of the ways this question can be answered, and draw attention to the common strengths of the resulting theories.

When I first thought about this question I came to the conclusion that at a limit stage α we should somehow sum up the effects of the earlier revisions. These revisions divide sentences into three classes:

(a)   *the locally stably true sentences:* these are the sentences that after some ordinal $\beta < \alpha$ always get assigned the value **t** (by revisions before α),

(b)   *the locally stably false sentences:* these are the sentences that after some ordinal $\beta < \alpha$ always get assigned the value **f** (by revisions before α),

(c)   *the locally unstable sentences:* these are the sentences that are not *locally stable*, i.e., they are neither locally stably true nor locally stably false.[6]

The locally stably true sentences are those over which the earlier revisions are giving a stable verdict: by their lights these sentences should be true. Similarly the locally stably false sentences, according to the earlier revisions, should be false. On the locally unstable sentences the earlier revisions are fluctuating. So a natural way to sum up the effects of revisions before a limit ordinal is to declare the locally stably true sentences true, the locally stably false sentences false, and to keep to the initial guess (of stage 0) over the locally unstable sentences.

The treatment of the first two cases can hardly be disputed. The third is problematic. Nuel Belnap has persuaded me that my original way of dealing with the locally unstable sentences is in need of improvement. He has observed that we should separate two components in a revision sequence: the contribution of the revision rule, and the arbitrary and unsystematic element needed to get the revisions going. At the limit stages the revision rule fixes the treatment of the locally stable sentences. But it does not dictate a treatment of the locally unstable sentences. Belnap has proposed that these should be handled in analogy with the zero stage. Just as we make an arbitrary choice at zero, we ought to make an arbitrary choice for the locally unstable sentences. Following Belnap, we define the notion 'the result of α applications of τ_M relative to a choice policy Γ' (abbreviated to $\tau_M^\alpha(\Gamma)$). A *choice policy*[7] Γ (for a model M) is a function that assigns to each nonsuccessor ordinal a member of $\{t, f\}^D$. Here is the fundamental definition.

Definition 2.

  (i)   If $\alpha = 0$ then $\tau_M^\alpha(\Gamma) = \Gamma(0)$.
  (ii) If $\alpha = \beta + 1$ then $\tau_M^\alpha(\Gamma) = \tau_M(\tau_M^\beta(\Gamma))$.
  (iii) If α is limit then

$$\tau_M^\alpha(\Gamma)(d) = \begin{cases} \mathbf{t} & \text{if d is locally stably true at } \alpha, \\ \mathbf{f} & \text{if d is locally stably false at } \alpha, \\ \Gamma(\alpha)(d) & \text{otherwise.} \end{cases}$$

One great advantage of Belnap's scheme is that it yields generality. It provides us with a simple way of representing and studying alternative treatments of limit stages. For instance, my earlier suggestion can be viewed as putting a condition on admissible choice policies. It requires that the choice policies be *constant*: for all nonsuccessor ordinals α, β, the admissible choice policy Γ must be such that $\Gamma(\alpha) = \Gamma(\beta)$. Herzberger treats the limit stages differently. He declares as false anything that is not locally stably true. Let us say that Γ is a *Herzberger choice policy* (**H**-*choice policy*) iff $\Gamma(\alpha)(d) = \mathbf{f}$ at all limit ordinals α and for all objects $d \in D$. In Herzberger's theory, then, the admissible choice policies are the **H**-choice policies. (Actually, Herzberger appears to favor the unique **H**-choice policy that is constant.) Belnap, as already noted, recommends that no restrictive conditions be placed on the choice policies. At limit stages, he suggests, a completely arbitrary choice be made. In effect, then, alternative treatments of limit stages can be viewed as putting alternative conditions on choice policies. (From this point of view, Belnap's theory puts the vacuous condition that is met by all choice policies.)

Certain conditions on choice policies are naturally viewed as representing *ideals* in a revision process. In any revision process we begin with something to revise. It may be a system of beliefs, as in epistemology; or an initial guess as to the value of π, as in mathematics; or, as in the present theory, a hypothetical interpretation of T. In all these cases there is an element of choice and a degree of arbitrariness. Nonetheless it may be a feature of some revision processes that this external contribution is required to conform to certain ideals. For instance, it may be a requirement on the systems of beliefs up for revision in epistemology that they not be closed, but be refutable. In the case of truth, it is a natural requirement that the choices be such that at each stage the sentences that are accorded the value **t** constitute a maximally consistent set. A theory of truth that imposes the ideal of maximal consistency is represented in Belnap's scheme as requiring that the admissible choice policies be *normal*, where a choice policy Γ is normal iff the set of sentences

$$\{A : \tau_M^\alpha(\Gamma)(A) = \mathbf{t}\}$$

is maximally consistent for all nonsuccessor ordinals α. (Note that the maximal consistency of the sentences declared to be **t** by Γ at arbitrary α is neither necessary nor sufficient for the normality of Γ.) There are other natural ideals that yield yet other constraints on choice policies, but ignoring them for the present, we have the following revision theories.

Theory	Condition on choice policies Γ
B	$\Gamma = \Gamma$
C	Γ be a constant choice policy, i.e., for all nonsuccessor ordinals α, β, $\Gamma(\alpha) = \Gamma(\beta)$.
H	Γ be a **H**-choice policy, i.e., for all limit ordinals α, and all $d \in D$, $\Gamma(\alpha)(d) = \mathbf{f}$.
N	Γ be a normal choice policy, i.e., for all nonsuccessor ordinals α, the set $\{A : \tau_M^\alpha(\Gamma)(A) = \mathbf{t}\}$ be maximally consistent.

No matter how we treat the limit stages, the following phenomenon is observed. Under certain conditions, i.e., certain models M, we begin the revision process with some arbitrary extension for T. We apply the Tarskian rule τ_M over and over, treating the limit stages in accordance with some choice policy. We find that after a number of applications, the revision rule τ_M ceases to revise. It declares the resulting extension to be perfect. The revisions stabilize at a fixed point of τ_M, i.e., at an extension g such that $\tau_M(g) = g$. *This happens irrespective of the choices made at the nonsuccessor ordinals.* Furthermore, *all choices bring us to the same fixed point.* In these models the Tarskian rule behaves like an ideal revision rule. Applications of τ_M gradually eliminate all arbitrariness in the initial and subsequent choices and bring us to the perfect interpretation of T. Models in which the revision process behaves in this way I call 'Thomason models'.

Definition 3.   A model M for L is a *Thomason model*[8] iff there is an extension g for T such that for all choice policies Γ there is an ordinal α meeting the condition that

$$\tau_M(g) = g \quad \text{and} \quad \tau_M^\alpha(\Gamma) = g.$$

Thomason models can be roughly characterized as those in which there is no vicious reference.[9] The model M' given in Example 10 illustrates this. Intuitively it is clear that when L' is interpreted in accordance with M' no sentence can be constructed that behaves in the manner of The Liar or The Truth-Teller. Further, it can be shown that M' is Thomasonian.[10,11] In a Thomason model the revision rule yields a definite classical interpretation of the predicate T. In these models the revision rule τ_M has a unique fixed point,[12] and the revisions converge to and stabilize at this fixed point irrespective of the choice policies. So we have the intuitively satisfying result that in a certain class of models, a class that can be roughly characterized as consisting of models that are free of vicious reference, the revision rule yields an ordinary classical interpretation for T. When vicious reference is absent, we do not perceive any difficulty with the Tarski biconditionals. They are consistent. They determine the extension of 'true'. They seem to give a complete account of the concept of truth. In a Thomason model too, since the revision rule interprets T by the unique fixed point of τ_M, the Tarski biconditionals[13] are true, and there is only one possible extension of truth that makes the biconditionals true. If we were concerned only with these special models, we could well have stopped our inquiry by reiterating Tarski's Convention T. But the presence of vicious reference destroys this easy and happy state of affairs.

There are models M in which τ_M has a unique fixed point, and thus there is only one interpretation of T that makes the biconditionals true, but that are not Thomasonian. In these models the revision process does not converge to a fixed point.

Example 11 (a formalization of Example 7). Let the nonlogical resources of L'' consist solely of two names a, b, and the quotational names of the sentences of L''. Let L'' be interpreted via M'' ($=\langle D'', I'' \rangle$) where D'' consists of the sentences of L'' and I'' assigns to the quotational names their intended interpretation and

$$I''(a) = Ta,$$

$$I''(b) = Ta \lor \sim Tb.$$

It can be shown that $\tau_{M''}$ has a unique fixed point. Also, M″ is not Thomasonian (in any sense). If Ta is declared to be false initially, it stays false in all later stages of revision, and Tb oscillates between The True and The False. The revisions do not stabilize.

In M″, according to the revision rule, there is no such thing as *the* extension of truth, even though there is a unique interpretation of T that makes the Tarski biconditionals true. I think that the revision rule gives the right result here. The Tarski biconditionals do not determine the correct interpretation of T. For they imply that Ta is true, and they do this because of a feature that is irrelevant to the status of Ta, namely, that b denotes the sentence $Ta \lor \sim Tb$. If b had denoted $\sim Ta \lor \sim Tb$ then the biconditionals would have implied that Ta is false. But what b denotes is irrelevant to the status of Ta. Tarski biconditionals, if used to interpret truth in models like M″, make the status of many sentences dependent on irrelevant factors. In fact, they violate the *local determinability* of truth. (For a discussion of this property see Gupta (1982, Section III).)

Two components of the behavior of the revision rule in a Thomason model are worth distinguishing: its stability and its convergence. The revision rule is stable in the sense that revisions with respect to all choice policies culminate in fixed points. If this property holds, I say that the model is *stable*.[14] The notion of convergence is not quite so easy to define. We will return to it. Let us note in the meantime that there are stable models that are not Thomasonian. An example is the model M* obtained from M″ by eliminating the constant b from the language.[15] Revisions always result in a fixed point in M*, but they do not converge. Different choices may result in one of two different fixed points. In non-Thomasonian stable models, vicious reference is present, but it is of the sort exemplified by The Truth-Teller. In these models neither the revision process nor the Tarski biconditionals fix a unique extension of T. However, the two agree on what the best candidates for the extension of truth are: they are the fixed points of the revision rule.

A model is stable in virtue of the fact that all vicious reference in it is of the Truth-Teller variety. Presence of the Liar-type reference destroys this stability. Similarly, we expect that if the only vicious reference in a model is of the Liar-type then the revision process will be convergent, though it will fail to be stable. In particular, we expect the revision process to be convergent but not stable in the model M⁺ obtained from M* by changing the denotation of a to $\sim Ta$. Let us define an appropriate notion of convergence. We begin by noticing that in any revision process generated by the rule τ_M and choice policy Γ (M, Γ arbitrary) there are certain interpretations of T that occur over and over again. These are naturally thought of as *the best candidates for the interpretation* (or *extension*) *of truth relative to Γ and M* ($\mathscr{C}_M(\Gamma)$)- [More precisely: g $\in \mathscr{C}_M(\Gamma)$ iff for all ordinals α there is an ordinal $\beta \geqslant \alpha$ such that $\tau_M^\beta(\Gamma) = $ g.] During the initial stages, the revision process may generate interpretations of truth that are eventually discarded. But in all processes there is a stage after which only best candidates appear. The ordinal of the least such stage is the *initial ordinal* for M and Γ. After this stage the revisions do not result in any improvement of the interpretations of truth. The results of revisions are all equally good. We can now define the notion of convergence thus. *The revision process in M is convergent* (We also say: *M is convergent*[16]) iff for all choice policies Γ,Γ' that differ at most at 0

$$\mathscr{C}_M(\Gamma) = \mathscr{C}_M(\Gamma').$$

Notice that the definition cannot be strengthened by removing the restriction 'that differ at most at 0' on Γ,Γ'. If the restriction is removed then only Thomason models turn out to be convergent. The definition given recognizes that in a convergent model the best candidates may differ because of the choices made at later stages.[17] However, for convergent models, the stipulations at stage 0 are irrelevant to the final outcome of revisions. This is not so for models in which Truth-Teller type self-reference is present. Every Thomason model is convergent, but the converse does not hold. It can be shown that $M^\dagger$ is a non-Thomasonian convergent model. Every convergent model that is stable, however, is Thomasonian.[18]

The presence of vicious reference destroys the perfect stability and convergence of the revision process in Thomason models. The Truth-Teller destroys its convergence, and The Liar its stability.

In many models, then, the revision process is neither stable nor convergent in the sense defined. Nonetheless it *is* stable and convergent locally, i.e., on particular sentences. The status of many sentences is completely determined in the revision process. These sentences, possibly after some initial instability, keep the same truth value throughout the revision process and throughout variation of choice policy. They have the same status in all best candidates generated by all choice policies. Let us say that g *is a best candidate for the interpretation* (or *extension*) *of truth in* M (g $\in \mathscr{B}_M$) iff there is a Γ such that g $\in \mathscr{C}_M(\Gamma)$. A sentence A is *stably true in* M iff g(A) = **t**, at all g $\in \mathscr{B}_M$. Similarly, A is *stably false in* M iff g(A) = **f**, at all g $\in \mathscr{B}_M$. We say that A is *stable in* M iff A is either stably true or stably false in M. A is *unstable in* M iff A is not stable in M. We can similarly define relativized versions of these notions. For example, A is *stably true in* M *relative to* Γ iff g(A) = **t**, at all g $\in \mathscr{C}_M(\Gamma)$. Note that in a

Thomason model M, $\mathscr{B}_M$ is a unit set and, therefore, there is a unique best interpretation of truth. Every sentence is either stably true or stably false. None are unstable. For a stable model M, $\mathscr{B}_M$ may fail to be a unit set, though $\mathscr{C}_M(\Gamma)$ is a unit set for all Γ. There may be unstable sentences in these models but they have a special character. They are all *divergent* in the sense that relative to all Γ they are either stably true or stably false. In a non-Thomasonian convergent model neither $\mathscr{B}_M$ nor $\mathscr{C}_M(\Gamma)$ will be a unit set. Here paradoxical sentences will be expressible in the language. We say that A is *paradoxical in* M iff A is unstable in M relative to all Γ. It can be verified that the sentences (3), (4) and (7) are divergent in the situation described in Example 5; as also are (8), (11), and (13) of Examples 7, 8 and 9 respectively. Sentences (3) and (4), it can be shown, are paradoxical in Example 6. There are unstable sentences that are neither paradoxical nor divergent. These are sentences of a *mixed character*. The sentence Tb of Example 11 is one such.[19]

The ordinary unproblematic sentences are stable. The revision process yields a definite verdict on them. As evidence for this, note that the sentences discussed in Examples 1–4 are stable and are granted the intuitively correct truth values by the revision process.[20] Logical laws are stably true.[21] And if the premises of a classically valid argument are stably true then so also is the conclusion. If A is stably true then the Tarski biconditional for A is also stably true. As far as the stable sentences are concerned, then, the theory implies that we may freely use classical reasoning and the Tarski biconditionals. It sanctions our ordinary ways of working with the concept of truth on these sentences.

The pathological sentences are unstable. The revision process does not give a definite verdict on them. They are true on some best candidates and false on others. This accords with the fact that we cannot intuitively assign these sentences a truth value. Of the unstable sentences, the divergent are the least contrary to our preconceptions about truth. It is true that they require an arbitrary stipulation to decide their status. But once such a stipulation is made they pose no threat to our preconceptions on the workings of truth. The paradoxical sentences show up our preconceptions for what they are: hasty generalizations of the laws that hold only for the stable sentences. The Tarski biconditionals are no longer stably true. Any attempt to assign a truth value to the paradoxical sentences has an unstable character. Our very understanding of the concept of truth leads us to revise our judgment to its opposite. And the revision process does not rest there either. It revises the result to give us our previous judgment back again. The cyclical pattern that emerges in ordinary arguments involving the paradoxical is reflected in our theory.

If we view the concept of truth as governed by a rule of revision the existence of the paradoxes seems as natural as the existence of the eclipses. From this viewpoint the paradoxes do not appear ominous, indicative of an incoherence in our conceptual scheme. Rather they appear to be a natural outcome of the revision character of the concept of truth, much as the eclipses are a natural outcome of the motions of the Earth, the Moon, etc. We may continue with our old ways of talking and call the paradoxes 'pathological', but now there should not be any connotation of disease or a suggestion of a need for elimination. If we understand the paradoxes better, we see a need to eliminate not them but only our preconceptions on the workings of our language in general, and the concept of truth in particular. A major source of puzzlement over the paradoxes is the presumption that there is something called *the* extension of truth. The revision account shows us that there isn't, and also *why* there isn't such a thing.

It should be noted that the problem of interpreting a language with a truth predicate is entirely distinct from the problem of constructing 'universal' languages, i.e., languages in which everything meaningful can be expressed. Tarski thought that natural or colloquial languages are universal ('if we can speak meaningfully about anything at all, we can also speak about it in colloquial language' (Tarski, 1956, p. 164)). And he suggested that it is this universality that is the source of the semantic paradoxes. To assess Tarski's suggestion fully, we would need to separate out the various possible meanings of 'universal'—something we will forgo here. However, it is clear that there is a problem of truth and of paradox even if the language in question is not universal. For example, the problem formulated earlier in the paper makes no assumption on the score of universality. So it is not an objection to the theory presented here that it does not enable us to construct universal languages, or even to prove the possibility of such. In fact, as long as the meaningful expressions of a language form a set, there will be concepts that are not expressed in the language. Simple cardinality considerations are sufficient to prove this. Moreover, if (i) all the predicates (other than T) of a language L have a classical interpretation, and if (ii) the language is rich enough in syntactic resources, then semantic concepts such as 'stability' are not expressible in L. This can be shown by the following argument, which is similar to that for Tarski's theorem.

Let us say that a set $U \subseteq D$ is *expressible* in a language L (with a truth predicate) in a model M iff there is a formula with exactly one free variable that defines U in the classical sense in all models M + g, where g is a best candidate for the extension of truth in M. We show that the set of stable sentences is not expressible in L in M when L has sufficiently rich syntactic resources. *Proof*: Suppose, for reductio, that a formula $A(x)$ defines the set of stable sentences in all models M + g, where g is a best candidate. By the condition of syntactic richness on L we get that there is a term t that denotes

(14) $\sim(A(t) \ \& \ T(t))$.

(If there are no terms in the language, something practically equivalent is still obtainable.) Now the assumption that (14) is not stable yields a contradiction. For then $A(t)$ is false in all M + g, g a best candidate. By induction one shows that for all Γ and all α greater than the initial ordinal for Γ

$$\sim(A(t) \ \& \ T(t)) \in \tau_M^\alpha(\Gamma).$$

Hence (14) is stably true, which conflicts with our initial assumption. A simpler argument shows that the assumption that (14) is stable also implies a contradiction.

This argument should not lead us to the precipitous conclusion that no language can contain its own concept of stability, and that stability must belong to the metalanguage, not to the object language itself. All that we can conclude is that some languages—those for which the assumptions used in the argument (viz, (i), (ii), and that stability has a definite extension) hold—do not contain their own notion of stability. The situation here is parallel to that with truth. Tarski's theorem shows analogously that certain languages—those for which the assumptions of Tarski's theorem hold—do not contain their own concept of truth. Once these special assumptions are given up we can understand how a language can contain its own notion of truth and also its own notion of stability.

The parallel between truth and stability is remarkable. Just as we can interpret truth via a rule of revision, we can interpret stability via a rule of revision also. The core intuition here is this: if we have a language with its own truth predicate (T) and its own stability predicate (S) then provided we are given an extension for S, we can determine, using the theory above, what sentences are stable and what are not stable. So, given a model M (a model that inerprets everything except S and T) and given an extension for S, say g, we can determine a new extension for S, $\psi_M(g)$, where

$$\psi_M(g)(d) = \begin{cases} \mathbf{t} & \text{if d is stable in the model M' that is} \\ & \text{just like M except that it assigns to } S \text{ the} \\ & \text{interpretation g,} \\ \\ \mathbf{f} & \text{otherwise.} \end{cases}$$

Note that the model M' interprets everything except T, so we can determine in the usual way the sentences that are stable and those that are not stable. We claim, as before, that ψ_M is a rule or revision: $\psi_M(g)$ is at least as good a candidate for the extension of S as g. We define the notion 'the result of the αth application of ψ_M relative to a choice policy Γ' in the manner of Definition 2. Now the following phenomena are observed for ψ_M. When vicious reference is present for T but absent for S, ψ_M is perfectly stable and convergent! No matter what arbitrary choices we make, ψ_M brings us to a fixed point. And irrespective of the choices, it brings us to the same fixed point. Thus, even if there is no unique best candidate for the extension of T, there can be a unique best candidate for the extension of S. If vicious reference exists for S then this perfect stability and convergence breaks down. Revisions of the extensions of S may fail to settle down, i.e., they may fail to reach fixed points. Or they may reach a fixed point, but different choices may result in different fixed points. The parallel between truth and stability, as I said earlier, is remarkable.

Presumably the same sort of revision account can be given of other semantical concepts such as divergence, paradoxicality, etc. I have not fully investigated this. A revision account can easily be extended to the 'first level' concepts of denotation, satisfaction, etc, and also to the semantical concepts pertaining to nonclassical logics, e.g., many-valued logics. I conclude this paper by remarking on the benefits that are obtained when we apply the revision theory to a Kripkean three-valued approach.

We begin with some conventions and definitions. Let L be a first-order language with a truth predicate and M $(= \langle D, I \rangle)$ be a model of it (Definition 1). Let g, g', g_1, . . . now range over possible three-valued interpretations of T: that is, g, g', g_1, . . . $\in \{\mathbf{t}, \mathbf{f}, \mathbf{n}\}^D$. By M + g we now understand the standard three-valued model of L that interprets all the nonlogical constants in accordance with M and assigns to T the interpretation g. Let $\leq$ be the usual partial ordering of the values $\mathbf{t}, \mathbf{f}, \mathbf{n} : \mathbf{n} \leq \mathbf{t}; \mathbf{n} \leq \mathbf{f}; \mathbf{t}, \mathbf{f}$ incomparable. We say g $\leq$ g' iff for all d $\in$ D, g(d) $\leq$ g'(d). Define a three-valued revision rule κ_M in the usual way using the Strong Kleene scheme.

$$\kappa_M(g)(d) = \begin{cases} \mathbf{t} & \text{if d is a sentence true in M + g} \\ \mathbf{n} & \text{if d is a sentence that is neither true nor} \\ & \text{false in M + g,} \\ \mathbf{f} & \text{otherwise.} \end{cases}$$

κ_M is monotonic, i.e., if g $\leq$ g' then $\kappa_M(g) \leq \kappa_M(g')$. We can define revision sequences $\kappa_M^\alpha(\Gamma)$ generated by a (three-valued) choice policy Γ as before. If $\Gamma(0)$ is *sound*, in the sense that $\Gamma(0) \leq \kappa_M(\Gamma(0))$, then $\Gamma(0)$ alone fixes the revision sequence. The values $\Gamma(\alpha)$, for $\alpha > 0$, are immaterial. For such choice policies we get a monotonically increasing sequence that culminates in a fixed point of κ_M. The Kripkean hierarchy is one such sequence. We get it if $\Gamma(0)$ is the function g_n defined thus: $g_n(d) = \mathbf{n}$, for all $d \in D$. This hierarchy culminates in the least fixed point of κ_M. *Grounded true (false)* sentences are those that are true (false) in the least fixed point of κ_M. If we call a sentence *stably true (false)* whenever it is stably true (false) relative to all choice policies then it is easily seen that grounded truths coincide exactly with the stable truths; and similarly for the grounded falsehoods. However, revision sequences enable us to make distinctions that we cannot make if we confine ourselves to fixed points. A simple example is this. Let L be a Liar-type sentence. Now all the three sentences L, $L \,\&\, {\sim}L$, $L \lor {\sim}L$ are neither-true-nor-false in all the fixed points of κ_M, and hence paradoxical by Kripke's definition. However, by using revision sequences we can distinguish amongst them in a very natural way. L is neither stably true nor stably false relative to any choice policy; $L \,\&\, {\sim}L$ is stably false relative to some choice policies, but never stably true; and similarly $L \lor {\sim}L$ is stably true relative to some choice policies but never stably false. Another benefit that the revision processes bring to the three-valued approach is that they give iterative access to fixed points that we otherwise do not know how to construct. In particular, revision processes yield a natural way of constructing intrinsic fixed points. The construction is due to Visser (1984) and is given in outline below.

Visser's construction rests on two observations. (1) If the choice policy Γ assigns to each limit ordinal the constant function g_n—so that in the revision process the locally unstable sentences at a limit ordinal are declared to have the value $\mathbf{n}$—then $\kappa_M^\alpha(\Gamma)$ is a fixed point for some α. So, if we begin with any interpretation g, sound or unsound, two-valued or three-valued, and apply repeatedly the rule κ_M in the manner stated above then we get a fixed point of κ_M. Following Visser we designate this fixed point by $(g)_\infty$. (2) If g and g' are consistent in the sense that there is a g″ such that $g \leqslant g''$ and $g' \leqslant g''$ then so are $\kappa_M(g)$ and $\kappa_M(g')$. This yields by an easy induction that $(g)_\infty$ and $(g')_\infty$ are consistent also.

Combining (1) and (2) we have the following recipe for constructing intrinsic fixed points. Begin with a starting function that is consistent with all the fixed points; apply the rule κ_M over and over again; declare the locally unstable sentences at limits to be $\mathbf{n}$, and one will end up with an intrinsic fixed point. Illustrations: Consider the starting functions g_n, g_1, g_2.

$$g_1(d) = \begin{cases} \mathbf{t} & \text{if d is Kripke-paradoxical,} \\ \mathbf{n} & \text{otherwise.} \end{cases}$$

$$g_2(d) = \begin{cases} \textbf{t} & \text{if d is true in some fixed point of } \kappa_M \text{ and false in none,} \\ \textbf{f} & \text{if d is false in some fixed point and true in none,} \\ \textbf{n} & \text{otherwise} \end{cases}$$

Each of g_n, g_1, g_2 is easily seen to be consistent with all the fixed points. So repeated applications of κ_M in the manner indicated yield the intrinsic fixed points $(g_n)_\infty$, $(g_1)_\infty$, and $(g_2)_\infty$. In fact, $(g_n)_\infty$ is the least intrinsic fixed point (= the least fixed point); $(g_2)_\infty$ is the largest intrinsic fixed point; $(g_1)_\infty$ falls somewhere in between. So, $(g_n)_\infty \leqslant (g_1)_\infty \leqslant (g_2)_\infty$. None of these relations can be strengthened to an identity.[22]

ACKNOWLEDGEMENTS

This essay is derived from talks that I have given at various universities in Canada and the U.S. over the last two years. The queries and criticisms I received at these talks have helped me to improve and sharpen my ideas. I have benefitted also from informal discussions with many friends, and more recently from the comments of the participants in my seminar on Truth given in Winter 1984 at the University of Illinois, Chicago.

My debts to four philosophers require particular acknowledgment. First, I am highly indebted, as usual, to Nuel Belnap. This paper incorporates the important idea of 'choice policy' due to him, and also many valuable suggestions that he has made in conversations. Second, I have learnt much from discussions with Hans Herzberger, and from reading his important papers Herzberger (1982a, b). Third, I am indebted to Saul Kripke not only for the stimulus of his seminal 'Outline of a theory of truth', but also for enlightening lectures on Truth given in Fall 1982 at Princeton University, and for a number of very helpful conversations. Finally, I want to thank Leah Savion for some very useful discussions. She read the first draft of this essay and helped to improve it.

NOTES

[1] I adopt sometimes the formal mode of speech and speak of the problem of giving the meaning of 'true'; sometimes the material mode, and then I speak of the problem of giving the meaning of truth or of giving an account of the concept of truth. These are *merely* modes of speech. There are not three problems here, only one.

[2] This is a variant of an example constructed by Albert Visser for a different purpose. (See Visser, 1984, p. 207.)

[3] Restriction to classical first-order languages removes little that is of interest to us in our study of the interaction of truth and self-reference. The gain in simplicity and workability is enormous. The theory presented below can be extended to any language for which we have a model-theoretic account, such as many-valued, intuitionistic, and modal languages.

[4] The extension of G is usually thought of as the *set* of n-tuples of objects for which G holds. Since this set and $I(G)$ carry the same information (given the domain D), I call the latter 'the extension of G' also for the sake of convenience.

[5] I do not mean to suggest that the authors of these ideas view the problem of truth in the way I have formulated it, or that they would approve of my formulation.

[6] Note that the notions of local stability, etc., are relativized notions. A sentence that is locally stable at a limit ordinal may become locally unstable at higher limit ordinals.

[7] Choice policies are called 'bootstrapping' policies in Belnap (1982).

[8] Actually, we should distinguish between the different notions of Thomason models obtained in the different revision theories **B**, **C**, **H**, and **N**. The definition given belongs to the theory **B**, and the notion defined is really that of a **B**-Thomason model. We can define analogously **C**-, **H**-, **N**-Thomason models. For example, the notion '**H**-Thomason model' is obtained by replacing the expression 'choice policy' in Definition 3 by '**H**-choice policy'. All the notions defined below admit of this relativity. To keep the discussion from getting labyrinthine I will focus on the theory **B**, and remark on the other theories and notions occasionally. I drop the prefix '**B**-' when I have the theory **B** in mind.

[9] I say 'roughly' because it is not entirely clear where the boundary between the models in which vicious reference is present and those in which it is absent lies. Neither intuition nor theory is a perfect guide here. Different revision theories, though they agree on a large class of models, draw the boundary somewhat differently. Their relationships to each other and to Kripke's theory are indicated in the diagram below.

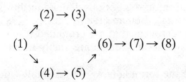

The diagram uses the following abbreviations: (1) M is **B**-Thomasonian; (2) M is **C**-Thomasonian; (3) M is **H**-Thomasonian; (4) M is **N**-Thomasonian; (5) The largest intrinsic fixed point (i.f.p.) of the supervaluational scheme using maximally consistent extensions is classical; (6) The largest i.f.p. of the general supervaluational scheme is classical; (7) The largest i.f.p. of the Strong Kleene scheme is classical; (8) The largest i.f.p. of the Weak Kleene scheme is classical. The arrow indicates implication.

[10] Here and elsewhere I omit proofs. A proof of this particular claim can be found in Gupta (1982, Section II). I hope to supply the missing proofs and much other material in a larger work to be written with Nuel Belnap.

[11] M′ is a particularly simple example of a Thomason model. Revisions in M′ result in a fixed point by stage ω. However in other Thomason models the ordinals by which revisions culminate in a fixed point can be anywhere from 2 to ω_1, assuming a countable language. Note that we can switch the quantifiers 'there is an

ordinal α' and 'for all choice policies Γ' in Definition 3. So it follows that in a Thomason model there is an ordinal by which the revision process is complete, irrespective of the choice policies.

[12] If τ_M has no fixed points then by Definition 3, M cannot be Thomasonian. Further, if g is a fixed point of τ_M then any revision process that begins with g will stabilize immediately and yield g at all stages. It follows that if τ_M does not have a unique fixed point then M cannot be Thomasonian in any of the four senses considered above.

[13] Assuming that the language has names for all its sentences. Henceforth I take this qualification for granted.

[14] The relationships of the various notions of stable model to each other and to the notions of Kripke's theory can be represented using the diagram of note 9. In place of 'M is **X**-Thomasonian' read 'M is **X**-stable' (**X** = **B**, **C**, **H**, **N**), and in place of 'The largest intrinsic fixed point of . . . is classical' read 'All maximal fixed points of . . . are classical'.

[15] M* is not Thomasonian in any of the four theories.

[16] The notion of **C**-convergence is not interesting. Every model turns out to be **C**-convergent. Definition of a proper notion of convergence does not appear to be possible within the theory **C**. This is a defect in my original way of dealing with the limit stages.

We can use the diagram in note 9 again, this time to represent the relationships of the various notions of convergence to each other and to the notions of Kripke's theory. We drop statement (2). Further in place of 'M is **X**-Thomasonian' we read 'M is **X**-convergent' (**X** = **B**, **H**, **N**), and for 'The largest intrinsic fixed point of . . . is classical' we read 'All fixed points of . . . are intrinsic'.

[17] Consider the results of revisions in M^+ for two choice policies, one of which declares all locally unstable sentences to be true and the other declares them to be false. The best candidates for the two choice policies will obviously differ.

[18] The claim holds in all theories except **C**.

[19] For more information on the notions defined in this paragraph consult Gupta (1982), Herzberger (1982a), Belnap (1982), McGee (1983), and Burgess (1983).

[20] Furthermore, the sentences that are grounded true (false) in Kripke's theory by the general supervaluational scheme are stably true (false) in all four revision theories.

[21] As a consequence the formula $(L \vee \sim L)$ is stably true, where L is a Liar-type sentence. This may be thought objectionable by some. But notice that $(L \vee \sim L)$ is equivalent to $\sim(L \& \sim L)$ by DeMorgan's law, and the stable truth of the latter is hardly objectionable. In any case, it is possible to construct revision theories in which $(L \vee \sim L)$ is not stably true.

[22] Visser defines a number of intrinsic fixed points and studies their properties. Two in particular are j and j^B (pp. 203 and 208 of Visser, 1984). These are defined as follows. Let

$$
g_3(d) = \begin{cases}
\mathbf{t} & \text{if d is true in all fixed points } (g)_\infty \text{ obtained} \\
& \text{from classical g,} \\
\\
\mathbf{f} & \text{if d is false in all fixed points } (g)_\infty \text{ obtained} \\
& \text{from classical g,} \\
\\
\mathbf{n} & \text{otherwise.}
\end{cases}
$$

$$g_4(d) = \begin{cases} \mathbf{t} & \text{if d is } \mathbf{B}\text{-stably true (in the two-valued theory),} \\ \mathbf{f} & \text{if d is } \mathbf{B}\text{-stably false (in the two-valued theory),} \\ \mathbf{n} & \text{otherwise.} \end{cases}$$

Then $j = (g_3)_\infty$ and $j^B = (g_4)_\infty$. It is easily seen that j and j^B are intrinsic fixed points, that $j \leqslant j^B$, and that in some models $j = j^B$. Visser asks whether j is always j^B? This question is to be answered negatively. Suppose L has the individual constants a, b, c, and the one-place predicates G and H. Let M ($= \langle D, I \rangle$) be a model for L such that $D = S \cup \{1\}$ and

$I(a) = 1;$ $I(b) = (\forall x)\,(Gx \supset Tx) \vee \sim Tb;$

$I(c) = T(b) \;\&\; (Tc \vee \sim Tc);$

$I(H)(d) = \mathbf{t}$ iff $d = 1;$

$I(G)(d) = \mathbf{t}$ iff $d = Ha$ or $d = T`Ha'$   or   $d = T`T`Ha''$ or $\ldots$

Calculation shows that

$$j(Tc) = \mathbf{n}$$

but

$$j^B(Tc) = \mathbf{t}.$$

REFERENCES

Belnap, N. D., Gupta's rule of revision theory of truth. *Journal of Philosophical Logic*, 1982, **11**, 103–116.

Brady, R. T., The consistency of the axioms of abstraction and extensionality in three-valued logic. *Notre Dame Journal of Formal Logic*, 1971, **12**, 447–453.

Burge, T., Semantical paradox. *The Journal of Philosophy*, 1979, **76**, 169–198. (Also reprinted in Martin (1984).)

Burgess, J. P., The truth is never simple (Ms.). Princeton University, 1983.

Chihara, C. S., Priest, the liar, and Gödel. *Journal of Philosophical Logic*, 1984, **13**, 117–124.

Davis, L., An alternative formulation of Kripke's theory of truth. *Journal of Philosophical Logic*, 1979, **8**, 289–296.

Dowden, B. H., Accepting inconsistencies from the paradoxes. *Journal of Philosophical Logic*, 1984, **13**, 125–130.

Feferman, S., Toward useful type-free theories I. *The Journal of Symbolic Logic*, 1984, **49**, 75–111. (Also reprinted in Martin (1984).)

Fitch, F. B., An extension of basic logic. *The Journal of Symbolic Logic*, 1948, **13**, 95–106.

Fitch, F. B., A consistent combinatory logic with an inverse to equality. *The Journal of Symbolic Logic*, 1980, **45**, 529–543.

Gilmore, P. C., The consistency of partial set theory without extensionality. In *Axiomatic Set Theory* (*Proceedings of Symposia in Pure Mathematics* **13**, Part II). Providence, RI: American Mathematical Society, 1974.

Guenthner, F. & Schmidt S. J. (Eds.), *Formal Semantics and Pragmatics of Natural Languages*. Dordrecht: Reidel, 1978.

Gupta, A., Truth and paradox (abstract). *The Journal of Philosophy*, 1981, **78**, 735–736.

Gupta, A., Truth and paradox. *Journal of Philosophical Logic*, 1982, **11**, 1–60. (Also reprinted in Martin (1984).)

Hawthorn, J., The Liar and Theories of Truth. Doctoral dissertation, McGill University, 1983.

Hazen, A., Davis's formulation of Kripke's theory of truth: a correction. *Journal of Philosophical Logic*, 1981, **10**, 309–311.

Hellman, G., Review of recent work in truth theory. *The Journal of Symbolic Logic*, 1984 (forthcoming). (A review of Martin and Woodruff (1975), Kripke (1975), Gupta (1982), and Herzberger (1982a).)

Herzberger, H. G., Notes on naive semantics. *Journal of Philosophical Logic*, 1982a, **11**, 61–102. (Also reprinted in Martin (1984).)

Herzberger, H. G., Naive semantics and the liar paradox. *The Journal of Philosophy*, 1982b, **79**, 479–497.

Kasher A. (Ed.), *Language in Focus*. Dordrecht: Reidel, 1976.

Kindt, W., The introduction of truth predicates into first-order languages. In Guenthner & Schmidt, 1978, pp. 359–371.

Kripke, S. A., Outline of a theory of truth. *The Journal of Philosophy*, 1975, **72**, 690–716. (Also reprinted in Martin (1984).)

Maddy, P., Proper classes. *The Journal of Symbolic Logic*, 1983, **48**, 113–139.

Martin, R. L. (Ed.), *Recent Essays on Truth and The Liar Paradox*. Oxford: Oxford University Press, 1984 (forthcoming).

Martin, R. L. & Woodruff, P. W., On representing 'true-in-L' in L. *Philosophia*, 1975, **5**, 217–221. (Also reprinted in Kasher (1976) and Martin (1984).)

McGee, V., Technical notes on three systems of naive semantics (Ms.). University of California at Berkeley, 1983.

Parsons, C., The liar paradox. *Journal of Philosophical Logic*, 1974, **3**, 381–412. (Also reprinted in Martin (1984) and Parsons (1983a).)

Parsons, C., Postscript, 1983. In Parsons (1983a), pp. 251–267.

Parsons, C., *Mathematics in Philosophy*. Ithaca, NY: Cornell University Press 1983a.

Priest, G., The logic of paradox. *Journal of Philosophical Logic*, 1979, **8**, 219–241.

Priest, G., Logic of paradox revisited. *Journal of Philosophical Logic*, 1984, **13**, 153–179.

Skolem, T. A., Studies on the axiom of comprehension. *Notre Dame Journal of Formal Logic*, 1963, **4**, 162–170.

Skolem, T. A., Studies on the axiom of comprehension. *Notre Dame Journal of Formal Logic*, 1963, **4**, 162–170.

Tarski, A., The concept of truth in formalized languages. In *Logic, Semantics, Metamathematics*. Oxford: Clarendon Press, 1956, pp. 152–278.

Visser, A., Four valued semantics and the liar. *Journal of Philosophical Logic*, 1984, **13**, 181–212.

Woodruff, P. W., Paradox, truth and logic I. *Journal of Philosophical Logic*, 1984, **13**, 213–232.

Yablo, S., Grounding, dependence, and paradox. *Journal of Philosophical Logic*, 1982, **11**, 117–137.

Index